Worship Wars
in Early
Lutheranism

JOSEPH HERL

Worship Wars in Early Lutheranism

Choir, Congregation, and
Three Centuries of Conflict

OXFORD
UNIVERSITY PRESS

2004

OXFORD

UNIVERSITY PRESS

Oxford   New York

Auckland   Bangkok   Buenos Aires   Cape Town   Chennai
Dar es Salaam   Delhi   Hong Kong   Istanbul   Karachi   Kolkata
Kuala Lumpur   Madrid   Melbourne   Mexico City   Mumbai   Nairobi
São Paulo   Shanghai   Taipei   Tokyo   Toronto

Copyright © 2004 by Oxford University Press, Inc.

Published by Oxford University Press, Inc.

198 Madison Avenue, New York, New York, 10016

www.oup.com

Library of Congress Cataloging-in-Publication Data
Herl, Joseph.
Worship wars in early Lutheranism : choir, congregation, and three
centuries of conflict / Joseph Herl.
p.   cm.
Includes bibliographical references.
ISBN 0-19-515439-8
1. Church music—Lutheran Church. 2. Hymns,
German—History and criticism.   I. Title.
ML3168.H47 2004
264′04102–dc21   2003006771

1   3   5   7   9   8   6   4   2

Printed in the United States of America

on acid-free paper

PREFACE

✜

In the popular imagination, Martin Luther is the father of congregational singing in the modern western church. Before his time, so the legend goes, average church-goers were mute, denied the chance to express themselves in song or speech. But Luther opened the floodgates of song to the people, and suddenly churches were filled with eager singers belting out *A Mighty Fortress Is Our God* at the tops of their lungs. One can almost imagine Luther on his white horse, waving a banner reading "Here I stand" and riding off into the sunset as throngs of newly vocal Christians followed.

It is an inspiring picture, but even allowing for a bit of Hollywood excess, it isn't even close to reality. As this book shows, German congregations sang even before the Reformation, although a choral liturgy predominated. The choral liturgy con-tinued its dominance in Lutheran churches for many decades after Luther's death, and it took over two centuries for a service to develop that would be familiar to Lutherans today, with the congregation accompanied by organ and singing hymns from a hymnal. The process frequently placed choral and congregational music in competition with each other, resulting in the "worship wars" of this book's title. The following pages tell the story of these worship wars and the transition from a choral to a congregational liturgy.

The narrative begins with the publication of Martin Luther's first mass order in 1523 and ends about 1780, an era of some uniformity in the Lutheran liturgy. After 1780 the traditional liturgies were abandoned or greatly simplified in many places under the influence of the Enlightenment. My goal in writing has been to bring readers inside the story, as it were, to help them imagine what attending church would have been like in Germany several centuries ago. In telling the story, I have paid par-ticular attention to the role of the congregation in the church's song, which I believe is key to understanding the changes that occurred and the associated "worship wars."

I have limited the scope of this book to the liturgy at regular public services. These include masses, Matins, Vespers, sermons without communion, catechism instruction, weekly prayer services, and services on penitential days. Excluded are occasional services such as baptisms, weddings, ordinations, funerals, and special days of thanksgiving or prayer (in time of war or natural disaster, for instance); including these might be interesting to students of liturgical history, but it would add little to the topic under discussion. Also excluded are private services, such as the Daily Office, held in monasteries. In some monastic communities certain services were open to the public, and where these are known they have been included.

I should note that the primary research I have undertaken differs from prior scholarship in one significant way. Most previous writers on Lutheran liturgy and hymnody have relied almost exclusively on sources that are prescriptive in nature—that is, they specify how the liturgy was to be conducted. Chief among them are the several hundred church orders and private agendas in use during the period under study. I have also examined these, but have additionally sought out sources that describe what was actually happening in the liturgy, such as minutes of ecclesiastical visitations and memoranda by pastors describing how they conducted liturgies in the parish. These descriptive sources have served as a corrective to sources containing only liturgical prescriptions. Other primary sources of value were hymnals, hymn-based musical compositions, tutorials and method books for teaching music (especially church music), sermons on music, theoretical and polemical works by pastors and church musicians addressing the issues of the day, and, from the eighteenth century, journal articles and book reviews. Among the most useful secondary sources were histories of the musical life of individual cities, socioreligious histories of the Reformation, and the many excellent musicological studies on related subjects.[1]

This book may be divided into several parts. Chapters 1 through 6, comprising the first part, investigate the roles of the choir and congregation during the sixteenth century. Chapter 7 traces the "worship wars" over musical style from Luther's time to the end of the eighteenth century. Chapters 8 and 9 describe how hymns were sung during the seventeenth and eighteenth centuries. The concluding chapter relates this book to other scholarship in music and Reformation history and discusses why earlier scholars failed to reach similar conclusions.

❖

Acknowledgments

The number of people who have assisted me in this endeavor is quite large. Let me thank first of all the staffs of the various libraries where I have worked. The Herzog August Bibliothek in Wolfenbüttel, where I made my German home, is a scholar's paradise, and I would especially like to thank Dr. Sabine Solf, Dr. Gillian Bepler, and Christian Hogrefe for helping to make it so for me. I am also indebted to Günther Grünsteudel of the University of Augsburg; Rev. Martin Cressey, principal emeritus of Westminster College, Cambridge; Dr. Karl-Günther Hartmann and Dr. Hans-Otto Korth of the Edition des deutschen Kirchenlieds in Kassel; Reimer Eck of the Georg-August-Universität in Göttingen; Dr. Daniel Zager of the Sibley

Music Library of the University of Rochester; Eric Stancliff of Concordia Seminary; Andi Beckendorf of Luther College; and William McClellan and Leslie Troutman of the University of Illinois at Urbana-Champaign. Also particularly knowledgeable and helpful were the staffs of the Staatsbibliothek zu Berlin, the city library of Leipzig, and the British Library. Special thanks are due the librarians at my own institution, Concordia University in Seward, Nebraska; that is, to Buz Wehrman and Glenn Ohlmann, and especially to interlibrary loan clerk Lois Mannigel, who has processed with vigor every large stack of loan requests I have brought to her. I am also indebted to my colleagues in the music department at Concordia for their encouragement and support during the time this book was in preparation.

For scholarly help I am grateful to Prof. Dr. Martin Petzoldt, who was the first German scholar to take a real interest in my project and who led me to several important sources. Dr. Werner Greve assisted me during my first trip to Berlin and received me as a guest in his home. Dr. Daniela Wissemann-Garbe was completing her dissertation at the same time I was researching mine, and she proved to be a great sounding board for some of the ideas I have developed here; she also assisted me with housing during my stay in Göttingen. Rev. William Weedon is one of the few Americans intimately familiar with the old German liturgies, and his assistance has proven invaluable. Dr. Volker Schier caught several errors and inconsistencies in the manuscript that would otherwise have gone undetected. For assistance with the German language, I could not have wished for a finer scholar than Helga Beste, whose extensive knowledge of sixteenth- and seventeenth-century German has saved me from a number of errors in translation. Nicole Thesz has done a similarly outstanding job with eighteenth-century German. Thanks are also due to my colleagues on the Usenet newsgroups *alt.usage.german* and *de.etc.sprache.deutsch* for assistance with a few particularly difficult questions of historical usage. Dr. John Houlihan has contributed his substantial expertise in Latin, greatly improving the accuracy of my translations from that language; Dr. Stephen Trzaskoma provided additional assistance on a particularly challenging passage. Other scholars who have provided expertise on selected matters include Konrad Ameln, Bartlett Butler, Manfred Garzmann, Lowell Green, John Walter Hill, Roland Hutchinson, Joyce Irwin, Cleveland Johnson, Herbert Kellman, Robert Kolb, Robin Leaver, Inge Mager, Bodo Nischan, Lawrence Rast, Jr., Anthony Ruff, Thomas Schenk, Thomas Schmidt-Beste, George Stauffer, and Tom Ward.

I owe a special debt of gratitude to Dr. Nicholas Temperley of the University of Illinois, my advisor for the Ph.D. dissertation on which this book is based. He is the sort of advisor all graduate students wish for but few actually find—supportive, encouraging and generous with both criticism and praise, as needed. His own work is a model for how musicological research ought to be done. I also owe him thanks for his assistance with translations from Latin.

Financial assistance for this project was provided by a Fulbright dissertation research grant, which allowed me to spend eighteen months in Germany, and by the Elias Prize in Hymnology from Westminster College, Cambridge. Many people have assisted me with housing and other practical matters, including Matthias Bergmann, Wolfgang and Almuth Bretschneider, Nigel and Barbara Douglas, Günther and Angelika Holst, Joschi Kneihs, Gottfried Martens, Lothar and Katharina Niebuhr, Jorg and Marion Salzmann, Gerhard Schnell, Reinhard and Regina Schröter, Rüdiger and Claudia Singer, Ann Tasker, Wilhelm Torgerson, Mark and Susi White, and Hennig and Anneliese Zufall.

Words cannot express the debt I owe to my wife Jenny. Her support, love, and encouragement have been beyond measure; and when word came of my grant to conduct research in Germany for a year or more, she did not hesitate to make plans for a trip to a country whose language she did not (at the time) speak, even though it meant that her own Ph.D. work in computer-based science education might be out of date by the time we returned. This book is dedicated to her.

❖

Note on Translations and Spelling

Quoted matter is given in English translation. In most cases, the original text may be found in my dissertation *Congregational Singing in the German Lutheran Church 1523–1780* (University of Illinois, 2000), available from University Microfilms International (ProQuest). I have generally rendered technical terms in English; but where occasional German words occur, I have preferred modern spellings. Titles of hymns are given in modern standard German: the reader may use appendix 1 to locate them in German and English sources. Book titles are usually given in the original language if they are brief but in English if they are longer, especially if they might enlighten the reader or are simply interesting in themselves. The original titles can be found in the bibliography.

Personal names are a bit problematic. Musicological literature has generally preferred original-language forms of names (e.g., *Johann* Bugenhagen), but writers of religious history have often used English equivalents of given names (*John* Bugenhagen). I have compromised, using the original-language forms of personal names except where it would seem pedantic because the English form is so well known: *Johann* Bugenhagen, but *John* rather than *Jean* Calvin, and *Frederick the Wise* rather than *Friedrich der Weise*. With German names, I have used the form most commonly found in American library catalogs, which may differ from the form used in modern German writings, for example, *Johann* rather than *Johannes* Bugenhagen.

For place names, I have used the English name if it is commonly known, otherwise the German name. I have retained the original spelling of lesser-known places mentioned in visitation records in order to assist other scholars using these records; thus, Hül instead of the modern Hüll, Dennenlohe rather than Tennenlohe.

CONTENTS

ABBREVIATIONS

❖

Source abbreviations used in the appendixes are explained in the appendix introductions.

DKL   *Das deutsche Kirchenlied: Verzeichnis der Drucke von den Anfangen bis 1800,* edited by Konrad Ameln, Markus Jenny, and Walther Lipphardt, Répertoire international des sources musicales, series B, part 8, vols. 1–2 (Kassel: Bärenreiter, 1975–80). The abbreviation *DKL* is used when referring to the book as a whole; *RISM* is used when referring to individual items within the book in order to avoid confusion with the *DKL* siglum, which is different. For the use of this abbreviation in appendix 1, see the heading to that appendix.

Lesure   François Lesure, ed., *Écrits imprimés concernant la musique,* Répertoire international des sources musicales, series B, part 6, vols. 1–2 (Munich: G. Henle, 1971).

LW   *Luther's Works,* edited by Jaroslav Pelikan and Helmut T. Lehmann, 55 vols. (St. Louis: Concordia; and Philadelphia: Fortress, 1958–86).

Richter   A. L. Richter, ed., *Die evangelischen Kirchenordnungen des sechzehnten Jahrhunderts* (Weimar: Landes-Industriecomptoir, 1846).

RISM   The abbreviation used when referring to individual items within *Das deutsche Kirchenlied.* (See *DKL,* above.)

Sehling   Emil Sehling, ed., *Die evangelischen Kirchenordnungen des XVI. Jahrhunderts,* vols. 1–8, 11–15 in 15 physical volumes to date (Leipzig: O. R. Reisland, 1902–13; Tübingen: J. C. B. Mohr [Paul Siebeck], 1955–).

WA   *D. Martin Luthers Werke: kritische Gesamtausgabe,* 4 series (Weimar: Böhlau, 1883–). The abbreviation is for "Weimarer Ausgabe." Unless an additional designation follows, the reference is to series 1, Luther's printed writings.

WA Br   *D. Martin Luthers Werke* (as above), series 4, Briefwechsel.

Wackernagel Philipp Wackernagel, *Bibliographie zur Geschichte des deutschen Kirchenliedes im XVI. Jahrhundert* (Frankfurt/Main: Heyder & Zimmer, 1855; reprint, Hildesheim: Olms, 1961).

Worship Wars
in Early
Lutheranism

CHAPTER I

❖

Luther and the Liturgy in Wittenberg

M artin Luther was venerated by his followers even during his lifetime. In matters of faith, doctrine, and church life he was the court of final appeal among Lutherans throughout the German-speaking region. Cities and territories regularly sent him drafts of church ordinances for his approval, and it became common for territories to specify that any new priests be ordained in Wittenberg. The doctrine and practice of Wittenberg exerted an enormous influence over that of other evangelical areas, and so it is fitting to begin our investigation with the practice there and with Luther's writings on the subject.

❖

Luther's Writings Prior to 1526

The Abuse of the Mass

The earliest of Luther's writings with significance for the liturgy was *The Abuse of the Mass* of 1521.[1] In it he attacked the idea of the mass as a sacrifice made by a priest for the sins of the people. Especially objectionable to him was the canon of the mass, the long prayer forming its core, with its specific references to sacrifice and its invocation of saints. All mass orders later produced by Lutherans would omit the canon. In this writing Luther does not mention either the music of the mass or the participation of the people, except to say that there is no proper mass unless a congregation is present.

Invocavit Sermons

In 1521 Luther was condemned at the Diet of Worms, and in May he went into hiding at the Wartburg castle of his prince, the Elector of Saxony, where he remained until March 1522. During Luther's absence from Wittenberg, his university colleague and dean of the faculty Andreas Bodenstein von Karlstadt gradually wrested control of the Wittenberg reformation from Luther's own choice for leadership, Philipp Melanchthon. Karlstadt favored moving ahead with reforms more quickly than Luther or Melanchthon, and on Christmas Day he celebrated a German mass wearing street clothes and distributing the sacrament to the people in both kinds (that is, with both the Body and Blood of Christ being received), allowing them to take the consecrated host and the chalice into their own hands. All this was done against the Elector's express wishes, and the townspeople were divided in their opinions on the matter.

On January 24 the town council approved the changes to the mass and further directed that paintings and statues, which Karlstadt considered idolatrous and in violation of the First Commandment, be removed from the churches.[2] Sensing that the situation was getting out of hand, Luther ended his stay at the Wartburg and returned to Wittenberg on March 6. Two days later he preached the first of his Invocavit sermons, so called after the Introit for the day, the first Sunday in Lent.[3] These sermons demonstrate Luther's cautious approach to liturgical reform. Most of Karlstadt's changes were unobjectionable in themselves, Luther said, but they had been thrust on the people without warning. The changes were trampling the faith of those devout souls who held them to be unchristian. Much better, said Luther, would be to prepare the people through instruction and then to introduce any desired changes in love, when the people are ready for them. Luther proceeded to abrogate Karlstadt's reforms and introduced his own only gradually over the next several years.

Order of Divine Service in the Congregation

This order appeared around Easter 1523 in Wittenberg.[4] On January 29 Luther had promised the congregation at Leisnig an order "for singing, praying and reading." On March 23 the daily private masses in the Wittenberg city church, which had been discontinued under Karlstadt, were replaced with a service of readings and prayer. Neither of these events is specifically mentioned in the *Order of Divine Service,* and whether the daily services at Wittenberg followed the order exactly is a matter of conjecture. It is also unclear whether the order appeared before or after March 23, and whether it was intended to introduce the order to Wittenberg residents or to give guidance to churches in other cities on how to reform their services. Both may have been intended, and in any case the order quickly became widely known and was reprinted the same year in Wittenberg, Augsburg, Zwickau, and Strassburg.

According to the order, which is reprinted in full in appendix 2, there are three abuses in the divine service (*Gottesdienst*): (1) God's Word has been silenced;

(2) there are many unchristian fables and lies in the legends [of saints], songs, and sermons; and (3) the divine service is seen as a work to earn grace. In order to be rid of these abuses, the congregation should never assemble except to hear God's Word preached and to pray. It is still a good thing to assemble early in the morning and read the lessons in Matins, whether it be priests or schoolboys or whoever, either alone or with two people, or with two people alternating, or with two choirs alternating. The lesson should be from the Old Testament (or possibly the New Testament), reading a chapter or half a chapter, and so on through the entire Bible. When the lesson and sermon have lasted a half hour or longer the congregation should give thanks and pray with psalms, responsories, and antiphons, completing everything within an hour, or whatever time is desired, so that it is not tiring.

In the same way the community may assemble at 6:00 or 5:00 in the evening, with reading, explanation, songs of praise, and prayer as in the morning, lasting an hour. If desired, another assembly may be held after the meal. Everyone may not be able to come to these services every day, but at least the priests and schoolboys and those in training to be preachers should be there. On Sunday the entire congregation should be present, and mass and Vespers should be sung, with preaching on the Gospel in the morning and the Epistle in the evening, or the preacher may select a book of the Bible on which to preach. The daily mass should be abolished, since the Word is the important thing and not the mass. But if people desire the sacrament other than on a Sunday, then mass should be held as devotion and time permit; a law on this cannot be made.

The chants may remain in the Sunday mass and Vespers, for they are nearly all good and are taken from the Scripture, although their number may be decreased or enlarged. The pastor and preacher should select the chants and psalms for the daily morning and evening offices, with a psalm and responsory or antiphon with collect each morning; likewise in the evening with reading and singing after the lesson and explanation. But the antiphons, responsories and collects, and legends about the saints and the cross should be left alone for a time until they have been cleansed, since there is much filth in them. Festivals of saints should be abolished or, where they have good Christian stories, observed on Sunday with a reading after the Gospel.

Robin Leaver, who has written extensively on Lutheran liturgical history, considers this order to be of the greatest importance in the development of congregational hymnody. Describing it, he writes: "The implication is that there should be half-an-hour of psalm singing, with the psalms sung to the traditional psalm tones. What is somewhat revolutionary here is that Luther apparently intended that the whole congregation should sing the traditional psalm tones, something that only priests, monks, and nuns had done hitherto."[5] Leaver explains how the services described in this order established the foundation for traditional Lutheran vespers, which included both plainchant and congregational singing, creating a rich liturgy for the development of organ and choral music. But internal evidence suggests that this order was not a service for the entire congregation at all.

In fact, the people attending the daily services, as Luther twice noted, were primarily priests and schoolboys. Perhaps they were joined by a handful of devout

5

former schoolboys who had their mornings free and who could not imagine life without daily Matins. The language of the service was Latin: although not explicitly stated, this is clear from the fact that the Old Testament, which Luther had not yet translated into German, was read and that the traditional "psalms, antiphons and responsories" were sung.[6] Luther refused to allow German translations to be sung to the existing chants because the accents fell in the wrong places.[7] The daily service was therefore a form of the medieval secular (as opposed to monastic) office, a choral office of the same sort still sung in some Catholic, Lutheran, and Anglican cathedrals around the world. It served as the daily chapel service for schoolchildren, and lay adults, though welcome, were not expected. These services, which became common in Lutheran churches in larger towns and cities throughout Germany, tended to have very few adults present during the entire period under investigation, usually with only those required to attend—schoolboys and those conducting the service—actually present (see "Attendance at Services" in chapter 3 for a discussion). The idea that this was in any way a service for the entire community is therefore without foundation.

Formula Missae et Communionis

This Latin mass of 1523 for the church at Wittenberg was Luther's first attempt to describe an evangelical mass in its entirety.[8] It was entirely choral, with no provision for the participation of the people except as hearers of the sermon and recipients of the sacrament. The order is noteworthy for our purposes, though, because of a paragraph Luther added near the end, almost (so it seems) as an afterthought:

> I also wish for us to have as many vernacular songs as possible that the people could sing during the mass either along with the Gradual or along with the Sanctus and Agnus Dei. For who doubts that in times past all the people sang those things that now only the choir sings or answers in response to the blessing of the bishop?[9] Indeed, these songs could be appointed by the bishop to be sung either immediately after the Latin songs or on alternating days, being sung first in Latin, then in the vernacular, until the entire mass is done in the vernacular. But poets are lacking among us, or are not yet known, who could compose for us devout, spiritual songs (as Paul calls them) that are worthy of being used frequently in the church of God. In the meantime I think it best to have sung after the communion *Gott sey gelobet und gebenedeyet, der uns selber hatt gespeiset, etc.*, omitting the phrase, "Und das heilige sacramente, an unserm letzten ende, aus des geweyeten priesters hende" ["and (receiving) the holy sacrament at our final end from the hands of the consecrated priest"], which was added by someone from the cult of St. Barbara who, having had little regard for the sacrament his entire life, hoped in death to enter into life by this good work without faith. For both the meter and musical structure prove it to be superfluous. Another good hymn is *Nu bitten wyr den heyligen geyst*, likewise *Eyn Kindelin so lobelich*. For not many are found that exhibit a serious

character. I say this in order that, if there are any German poets, they might
be encouraged and might pound out spiritual poems for us.[10]

Here Luther clearly indicated his desire to have the people sing during the mass.
The reason is given in the second sentence; namely, that the choir has taken over
those parts of the mass that had originally belonged to the people. Ideally the entire mass would be sung in German, but this would have to wait until German
settings were available. Meanwhile, the anonymous hymn *Gott sei gelobet,* in Luther's
day attributed to Czech reformer Jan Hus (1369–1415), might be sung during the
communion distribution after the appointed communion chant.

Letter to Georg Spalatin, 1523

Toward the end of 1523 Luther wrote to his close friend Georg Spalatin, court
preacher and privy secretary to the Elector of Saxony, concerning his plans for de-
veloping a popular corpus of German hymns. The letter began as follows:

> Grace and peace. It is my plan, following the example of the prophets and
> ancient fathers of the church, to compose vernacular psalms for the
> masses; that is, spiritual songs, so that the Word of God might also remain
> in song among the people. To this end we are searching everywhere for
> poets. As you have truly been given both fluency and elegance in the Ger-
> man language, perfected through much practice, I ask that you work with
> us in this matter and try to transform some psalm or other into a song, as
> you have in my example here.[11]

The reason for such an undertaking was to benefit the singers, "that the Word of
God might also remain in song among the people." Because these were songs for
the people and not for learned scholars, Luther continued by asking Spalatin to
forgo fancy words of the kind used in official documents, using instead simple, direct words to convey the force of the original psalms.

Geystliche Gesangk Buchleyn

In 1524 Johann Walter, at the time a singer in the electoral chapel at Torgau, published this "spiritual songbook," for which Luther provided a preface. The book
is one of the earliest sources of Luther's hymns, which were arranged for choir in
four to five parts. The purpose of the book, according to the preface, was to wean
young boys away from love ballads and carnal songs and to teach them something
of value in their place.[12]

Subsequent prefaces Luther wrote for hymnals intended for general use and
published in 1533, 1542, and 1545 give no indication of how the hymns were to be
used. Chapter 6 discusses the contents of these books in more detail; it is sufficient
here to note that hymnal prefaces offered an ideal forum for encouraging congregational singing in church, and other reformers used them in this way (see chapter
6). Given the importance congregational singing is generally assumed to have had
for Luther, it is curious that he should have missed such a golden opportunity.

❖

The *German Mass* of 1526

The *Deutsche Messe und Ordnung Gottesdiensts* (*German Mass and Order of Divine Service*) appeared in 1526, after several mass orders in German had been published in other cities.[13] Not specifically intending it for Wittenberg, Luther wrote it "because of the widespread demand for German masses and services and the general dissatisfaction and offense that has been caused by the great variety of new masses, for everyone makes his own order of service."[14]

In publishing the *German Mass,* Luther followed the cautious, pastoral approach he had used after his return from the Wartburg. He began the preface with a plea:

> Above everything else, I would graciously and for God's sake request all those who see or intend to follow this our order of divine service to make no essential law of it nor ensnare or bind anyone's conscience with it; but rather out of Christian freedom according to your pleasure to use it how, where, when and for however long it is of use and benefit.[15]

He continued with a request that, for the sake of the laity, individual territories use a single order of service instead of each church having its own, which only produces confusion. But it need not be the rite used in Wittenberg, for others use or are capable of producing good orders of service. Luther was well aware that his words carried considerable weight. He was concerned that other people might argue for the adoption of his order of service simply because he wrote it, and so to avoid the impression that he was dictating a requirement he began the order with the above statement. Additionally, rather than giving liturgical prescriptions for the mass, he gave a narrative description, saying, in effect, "This is what we do in Wittenberg; you can take it or leave it."

The publication also included orders for Matins and Vespers. Latin was retained for them, but the mass itself was entirely in German except for the Greek *Kyrie*. Luther described the mass as follows: On Sundays, he wrote, a spiritual song or German psalm (such as Psalm 34) is sung, then the Kyrie. Then the priest chants a collect and the Epistle. *Nun bitten wir den Heiligen Geist* or another song is sung with the full choir, and the priest chants the Gospel. Then the entire church sings the Creed in German: *Wir gläuben all an einen Gott.* The sermon on the Gospel follows. Then the priest reads a paraphrase of the Lord's Prayer and an exhortation to the communicants. Then he chants the consecration. Ideally, the Lord's Body is distributed immediately after being consecrated, during which the German Sanctus *Jesaia dem Propheten, Gott sei gelobet,* or *Jesus Christus unser Heiland* is sung. Then the cup is consecrated and the Lord's Blood distributed, during which is sung the remainder of one of the above or the German Agnus Dei *Christe, du Lamm Gottes.*[16] The Elevation is retained. The rite is closed with the Thanksgiving collect "Wir danken dir" and the Aaronic benediction in German.[17]

There are five parts of the mass not assigned to the priest: the opening song or psalm, the Kyrie, the hymn after the Epistle (i.e., the Gradual hymn), the Creed, and the hymns during the communion distribution. In addition, it was common for a hymn to be sung before the sermon, and sometimes after it as well, even when the order did not specifically indicate it (more on this in chapter 2). Luther described the German Creed as being sung by the entire church. The Gradual hymn was sung by the choir. Who sang the other items: the entire congregation or just the choir?

The received tradition has been to see the *German Mass* as the paradigm of the congregational liturgy, with the people singing all the parts that had formerly been the province of the choir. Martin Brecht, who has written the most comprehensive and arguably the best biography of Luther, notes the important role of the congregation in the *German Mass:*

> The worship service began with a German hymn or the singing of a psalm. Congregational singing also had a secure place at other points in the worship service; e.g., Luther's hymnic version of the Creed was to be sung in unison. The congregation generally took part, with an entirely different intensity, in what was now a German worship service.[18]

Supporting this view is Luther's clear desire expressed in the *Formula missae* for the people to have something to sing along with the Gradual and during the communion. Against it is the fact that Luther did not explicitly state that the entire congregation sang anything but the Creed. Without such a clear indication, a contemporary reader would most readily assume that the pre-Reformation tradition would continue and that they would be sung by the choir.

The solution to this puzzle lies in the fact that the *German Mass* was describing (or at least claimed to describe) the actual services in Wittenberg at the time of its publication. The first copies likely came off the press around Christmas 1525 and certainly no later than the beginning of January 1526.[19] But the mass had been introduced on a trial basis only on October 29 and officially inaugurated only on Christmas Day, after its probable date of publication. The time between its very first use and the appearance of the order in print was less than two months, not nearly enough time for the people, who did not use hymnals, to have learned to sing much of it. To be sure, it is possible that a hymn or two had been sung in German even before the introduction of the *German Mass* (Luther had indicated in the *Formula missae* that he liked to have *Gott sei gelobet* sung during the communion); but it is clear from Luther's sermon for October 29, 1526, explaining the innovations to the congregation that the mass itself was quite new.[20] At the time of its publication, therefore, the *German Mass* was still for the most part a choral mass.

Having established the actual practice at the time of publication, the question remains as to whether it was actually Luther's intention that the people should eventually learn to sing the entire mass in German. This would seem to make sense given Luther's statements in the *Formula missae*. Supporting this conclusion, at least on the surface, is the comprehensive liturgical order for Wittenberg and surrounding villages drawn up as a result of the ecclesiastical visitations of 1528 and 1533.[21] Its author is unknown, but it certainly could not have been introduced without Luther's approval. Latin was still used extensively in the various liturgies, and the entire congregation was specifically directed to sing only a few items, at mass only the Creed and the Amens following the Lord's Prayer and the concluding benediction. But preceding the actual service orders is a paragraph of general instructions

9

concerning the singing, and there we find the interesting direction to the school-master that "the schoolboys shall not sing in German except when the people sing along."[22] In the mass order, the Introit could be sung in Latin or as a German psalm; a German song was sung in addition to or in place of the Gradual; in certain seasons a German hymn was inserted into the Latin Sequence; *Wir glauben all an einen Gott* was sung after or in place of the Latin Credo; after the sermon *Da pacem domine* was sung in Latin and German and optionally a German hymn was sung; and German hymns were sung during and after the communion. If German could not be used unless the people sang along, then it follows that the people were expected to sing whenever these parts of the mass were sung in German.[23]

What is interesting about this order, though, is that except for the Creed the items to be sung in German are not part of the ordinary of the mass. The Kyrie was to be sung in Greek, and the Gloria, Sanctus, and Agnus Dei in Latin. The Alleluia was also sung in Latin; the Introit, Gradual, and Creed were optionally sung in Latin; and the Sequence was sung as a Latin-German hybrid. Occasionally, especially on high feasts, the lessons and collects could also be sung in Latin. What was Luther's opinion of all this? In the preface to the *German Mass* Luther had written:

> I do not intend herewith to have this [the *Formula missae*] abolished or al-tered, but as we have thus far observed it among us its use shall still be permitted wherever and whenever it pleases us or circumstances demand. For by no means would I have the Latin language completely removed from the divine service, as my chief concern is with the youth.[24]

Luther's concern was that the youth would no longer learn Latin, the language zof both theological discourse and diplomacy, if it were removed from church services. This sentiment was to be echoed many times by various writers over the next two hundred years as Lutherans debated whether Latin services were still necessary or desirable. Luther had another reason for retaining Latin. In his *Exhortation to All Clergy* of 1530, he gave an extensive list of things that were not necessary for the Christian service, although some he considered useful. Among the very best, he said, were the "fine Latin songs, *de tempore,* although they have been almost drowned out by the new saint-songs . . . they truly please us from the heart."[25]

On March 14, 1528, Luther wrote to Wilhelm Pravest, pastor in Kiel, that he had not even favored the introduction of the mass in German:

> To be sure, I abolish no ceremonies except those that contradict the gospel; everything else I retain unaltered in our church. For the baptistry remains, and so does baptism if permitted in the vernacular; it has its rites, as for-merly. And indeed, I allow images in the church, except for the ones the enthusiasts destroyed before my return [from the Wartburg]. And so we also celebrate the mass with the usual vestments and rites, except that cer-tain vernacular songs are inserted and we speak the words of consecration in the vernacular in place of the canon. Finally, by no means do I wish to abolish the Latin mass, nor would I have allowed the vernacular if I had not been compelled.[26]

The compulsion Luther had felt undoubtedly refers to the pleas he had received from all quarters for a mass order in the vernacular.[27] Here we see a completely different Luther from the one who in 1523 had hoped that the entire mass would eventually be sung in German: in 1528 he was content simply to allow "certain vernacular songs" to be inserted into the traditional mass. That this was indeed the practice in Wittenberg is confirmed by a July 16, 1528, letter from Luther's colleague Philipp Melanchthon to Balthasar Thuring in Coburg:

> Therefore I wish that the ceremonies among you not be greatly unlike those of old. If the Latin mass has not been abolished, do not abolish it completely. It is enough to insert German songs somewhere, as we have done here; and you know that I had wanted this three years ago in your church as well.[28]

In 1536 Augsburg pastor Wolfgang Musculus visited Wittenberg and outlined in precise detail in his travel diary the services he attended there. The one mass he attended was on May 28, Exaudi Sunday, a nonfestival day. Four items were sung in German: the Gradual hymn *Gott der Vater wohn uns bei,* the Creed *Wir glauben all an einen Gott,* and the communion hymns *Jesus Christus unser Heiland* and *Gott sei gelobet* (see appendix 2 for his description of the mass).[29] The rest of the mass was in Latin. The situation was similar in the next decade. A surviving list of liturgical propers sung in Wittenberg in 1543 and 1544, two years before Luther's death, contains nearly all Latin titles. Adolf Boës has determined that around 90 percent of the items listed were to be found in the pre-Reformation liturgical books of the Archdiocese of Magdeburg, and most were still sung on the same days as before the Reformation.[30]

By the 1530s the Latin mass had returned to Wittenberg in full force, and if the above letters are trustworthy, then the experiment with the entire mass in German had already ended by 1528. In any case, one has to question just how much of the 1526 liturgy Luther had expected that the people would eventually sing. He certainly cannot have had ease of singing for the congregation in mind when he suggested that Psalm 34, a prose psalm set in plainchant to the first psalm tone, be sung in place of the Introit. The psalm occupies twelve pages in the original print. Its variations in flex and mediant from verse to verse would have presented formidable obstacles to a congregation without hymnals.[31] It is no surprise that the idea of using a prose psalm for the Introit never took hold among Lutherans, and later liturgies specified either the traditional Latin Introit or a German metrical psalm or hymn. In addition to the psalm's difficulty, there is also the question of whether much of a congregation was even present at the beginning of the service, as it was the custom in many places for a large part of the congregation to arrive just in time for the sermon (see chapter 3).

The only part of the *German Mass* that Luther explicitly directed the people to sing, the Creed, is not much easier. For its text, he rewrote a German paraphrase dating from around the fourteenth century.[32] The tune is also derived from a medieval model. There were several versions in circulation in the 1520s; the version

Example 1.1. *Wir glauben all an einen Gott* (*Geystliche Gsangbüchlin*, 1525, no. XXXVI)

found in today's hymnals, and indeed in most sixteenth-century sources, first appeared as a tenor part in Walter's *Geystliche gesangk Buchleyn* (1524; transcribed in Example 1.1 from an edition of 1525). Erik Routley, the indefatigable writer on hymnody, pointedly remarked that this hymn was a failure because its length, not to mention its melismatic passages, made it practically impossible to remember.[33] The judgment of "failure" is questionable, inasmuch as the hymn was sung weekly in Lutheran churches for over two hundred years; but one can easily imagine that congregations had difficulty learning it.[34] The congregation at Wittenberg may not have learned it for many years. Musculus noted in his diary in 1536 that the choir sang the Creed on the day he visited Wittenberg; the previous week in Eisenach it had been sung by the entire congregation.[35]

The hymns during the communion were not quite so difficult. Luther had indicated already in the *Formula missae* of 1523 that he liked to have *Gott sei gelobet und gebenedeiet* sung. But as with the Introit, one wonders whether there was anyone present outside of the choir to sing them. It was common at the time for those not receiving communion to leave the church after the sermon, and in the mass Musculus attended in 1536 most of the people did exactly that.[36] Luther surely did not expect many communicants: this is evident from the manner of communion distribution specified in the *German Mass*. It was the common practice of the time that when many communicants were expected the wine was consecrated immediately after the bread, and both were distributed at once. But if all communicants could fit at a single table (this would be known ahead of time because they would have come to confession the day before), then the usual practice throughout Germany was to consecrate the bread and distribute it, and then to consecrate the wine and distribute it. In the *German Mass,* Luther specified only the latter method, indicating that he expected the service to be used primarily when few communed (perhaps in smaller parishes). For his 1536 visit, Musculus did not record how many people received communion in Wittenberg, but the previous Sunday in Eisenach no men had communed and only a few women.[37]

Ironically, perhaps the most likely part of the *German Mass* after the Creed to have been sung by the whole congregation is the Gradual, which Luther directed should be sung by the choir. Luther's direction is curious, inasmuch as the Gradual is the very place he had indicated in the *Formula missae* that he wanted all the people to sing; and his choice for Gradual hymn, *Nun bitten wir den Heiligen Geist,* is one of two hymns Luther had given by name in the *Formula missae* as worthy of having them learn. Why would Luther now assign this hymn to the choir instead of to the people? A possible answer lies in the wording of this passage in the *German Mass:* "After the Epistle a German song is sung, *Nun bitten wir den Heiligen Geist* or another, and this with the full choir."[38] The more usual wording, had he intended the choir to sing alone, would have been "After the Epistle the choir sings a German song. . . ." But here he wrote simply that the song is sung, and that with the full choir. Why "full choir"? The most likely answer is that the traditional Latin Gradual was sung in part by a soloist and in part by the full choir; here Luther wanted to make it clear that this practice was not to be followed. In so doing, he was not necessarily excluding the rest of the congregation but in fact made it easier for them to participate by having the full choir sing the entire hymn.

In the case of the Gradual, even if Luther intended only the choir to sing it, we cannot rule out the possibility that individual members felt free to sing along with the choir whenever they knew the words and melody. The choir did not normally sing polyphonic settings of hymns. True, such settings did exist (the four- and five-part settings in Johann Walter's *Geystliche gesangk Buchleyn* of 1524, for example), but polyphonic performances by the choir were still rare in most churches. In 1542, Sixtus Dietrich wrote to Bonifacius Amerbach describing a visit to Wittenberg in 1540. Concerning the music, he wrote: "On all festivals a splendid rite is sung polyphonically [literally, "in figured notes"]: Introit, Kyrie, Et in terra [i.e., Gloria], Patrem [i.e., Credo], Alleluia, Sanctus, Agnus and Communion, as in ages past, so that hardly anything has been altered."[39] The words "on all festivals" imply that on ordinary days the rite was sung *choraliter*—that is, in unison chant. This is borne out by the practice in other major cities, where figural singing became a standard practice only in the second half of the century.[40]

Luther's goal in writing a new mass order was to create a German mass, but not especially a mass that all the people could sing throughout. In addition to the above evidence, we may add the fact that Luther's nine-page preface did not mention the singing of the people, which we would certainly expect it to have done if this had been important to its author. Luther did, however, desire that the people sing the Creed and perhaps one or two other items.[41]

❖

Reaction to the *German Mass*

Even after his enthusiasm for a complete mass order in German had waned, Luther still retained his desire to have the people sing "certain vernacular songs." The people, however, had other ideas. In his sermon for the First Sunday in Advent 1526, just over a year after the *German Mass* had been introduced, Luther admonished his flock:

> The gospel suffers great contempt. "The more wicked the Christian, the closer to Rome": so it is happening to us here. When we initiated the German mass, everyone wanted it; now it is all the same to you whether it is in German or Latin. You say "I have bought five yoke of oxen." The songs have been composed and are sung for your sake so that you can sing them here and at home, but you sit here like blocks of wood. Therefore I beg you, teach these songs to your children and sing them yourselves at the same time, as Paul teaches. From this you see who is a Christian and what is to be expected of him.[42]

Melanchthon had foreseen this outcome already in 1525. In a January 1 letter to the Nuremberg council, he wrote, "And even if everything were always sung in German they would not all sing along or understand the song [text]."[43]

On January 24, 1529, Luther chastised the people again over their failure to sing what they had been taught:

I see your idleness, how you fail to learn those sacred songs sung every day and how for nearly two years now you have had no interest whatsoever in those enduring songs of the schoolboys, but rather pay much more attention to popular ditties. Would that you fathers might strive to train those under your care! For such songs are a sort of Bible for the uncultivated, and even for the learned. See how the pious are set on fire through these songs! Observe the efficacy and power of *Ein Kindelein so löbelich!* That child has preserved the church: "Had this little child not been born for us, we would surely all have been lost"; likewise with *Nun bitten wir den Heiligen Geist.* And so we took care that a large number of the best spiritual songs might be composed for your use and edification. Therefore work hard that you might learn and cultivate them with greater diligence than you have up until now.[44]

One of the hymns here named, *Ein Kindelein so löbelich,* was a Christmas hymn and was to be designated in many later Lutheran liturgies for singing immediately before the sermon during the weeks after Christmas (usually until Purification on February 2). It makes sense that Luther would refer to it on January 24. *Nun bitten wir* had a dual use in later liturgies as both a Pentecost hymn and a hymn of invocation at the beginning of the service or sermon. It is quite a coincidence that Luther would mention the very same hymns that he had named in the *Formula missae* as being especially worthy of learning. Perhaps he had been trying since 1523 to persuade the people to learn them; but if so, then the reference to "nearly two years" is a mystery, as it would have been six years since the *Formula missae* had appeared.

This passage confirms the manner in which the songs were taught to the people; namely, by a choir of schoolboys who sang the liturgy from the choir area at the front of the church. This was to be the usual practice in Germany throughout the century. The Wittenberg liturgy of 1533 took the unusual step of having the boys leave the choir area and sit among the people each time the liturgy specified that something be sung by the people; namely, for the Creed at mass, the Magnificat at Saturday and Sunday Vespers, the Te Deum at Sunday Vespers (it was sung in Latin at Matins), and the Litany at the Wednesday morning sermon.[45] This did not disrupt the service because all of these were sung either immediately before or immediately after the sermon, and the boys listened to the sermon from the pew reserved for them in the nave (with the left balcony used for overflow). After the sermon they returned to the choir area.

The fact that the only items the people were specifically directed to sing were at a point in the service where the boys could sit among them suggests that they did not sing well without assistance, and the direction for Luther's Te Deum at Sunday Vespers confirms this. For the Te Deum, most of the boys were to remain in the choir stalls and sing the first half of each verse, but an older boy was to descend to the reserved pew and assist the singing of the people in the second half of the verse. If necessary, he was to take several boys from the choir with him until the people were accustomed to singing the Te Deum. Had the Te Deum just recently been introduced, or was this another case of the people being unwilling or unable to sing? If the latter, one wonders how many more years it would take before the people became accustomed to singing it. A similar concern was expressed in the order for Vespers in outlying villages. The preacher was to sing a German psalm with the farmers before and after the sermon so that the farmers and their children and helpers could learn to sing. Occasionally, the preacher was warned, he might need to exhort the people in this matter.[46]

❖

Later Liturgical Orders

Luther himself wrote no further liturgical orders after the *German Mass*, although he was closely connected with several, and they reflect Luther's conservative attitude toward congregational singing. We shall examine here the three with the closest connection to Luther.

Visitation Instructions for Electoral Saxony (1528)

By the mid-1520s it became evident that a coordinated effort would be required to introduce the Reformation into the territory of Luther's prince, the Elector of Saxony. Plans were made to visit every church in the territory, and to this end the *Instructions of the Visitors to the Pastors in the Electorate of Saxony* were published in 1528.[47] Written principally by Luther's colleague Philipp Melanchthon, they were proofread by Luther, who also added a preface. No mass order was included, but rather a directive was given that the many different ways of holding mass should, insofar as possible, be brought into conformity with each other. The instructions also included recommended orders for daily Matins and Vespers that were similar to those in the *Order of Divine Service in the Congregation* of 1523, except that German was allowed for certain parts of the office, and the option was given for the entire congregation to sing a single German song at the end.[48] The instructions were reprinted in 1539 with minor changes and a new preface by Luther in connection with the introduction of the Reformation into Albertine Saxony.

Bugenhagen's Church Order for Braunschweig (1528)

In 1528 the pastor of the Wittenberg city church, Johann Bugenhagen, traveled to the independent city of Braunschweig to assist in introducing the Reformation there. While there he drew up, with considerable input from the local clergy, the first of the several church orders he was to author.[49] It contained a complete liturgical agenda, with a mass order; Vesper orders for Saturdays, Sundays, and weekdays; and an order for weekday Matins. In the mass, the whole congregation was explicitly directed to sing the Amen after the collect preceding the Epistle, the German Creed *Wir glauben all an einen Gott,* the hymns *Jesus Christus unser Heiland* and *Gott sei gelobet* during the communion, and the German Agnus Dei *Christe, du Lamm Gottes* after the communion. During Vespers on holy days (which presum-

ably included Sundays) a German hymn could be sung by the laity before the sermon when they were present and wanted to sing along; otherwise, the schoolboys
sang a Latin hymn. Daily Matins and Vespers were sung entirely in Latin.

Luther had no direct influence on the Braunschweig order, but we see some
of his ideas in its provisions for congregational participation. The people were to
sing the Creed, a practice that was to become nearly universal among German
Lutherans, and Luther's vision of the people singing during the communion was
here fulfilled.

Duke Heinrich's Order for Albertine Saxony (1539)

In 1539 one of the Reformation's most entrenched opponents, Duke Georg of
Saxony, died. His brother and successor as ruling prince, Heinrich, was an adher-
ent of Luther, as were most of his subjects. Immediately upon his accession he
began to introduce the Reformation into his territory, and the same year saw the
publication of the church order that bears his name.[50] It proved to be the most
enduring Lutheran church order of all, being reprinted numerous times through
1748 with only minor changes. Although Luther did not participate directly in its
production, its preface was signed by some of his closest associates, including Justus
Jonas, Georg Spalatin, and Caspar Creutziger. It provided for the congregation to
sing the German Te Deum at Sunday Matins if desired, *Jesus Christus unser Heiland*
or *Gott sei gelobet* during the communion, and a German psalm or spiritual song
after the sermon on weekdays. It is likely that the people were also expected to sing
the German Creed during mass, but this is not explicitly stated. In villages where
the Latin mass ordinary and propers could not be performed, the whole congregation probably sang other items as well, such as the hymns substituting for the Introit
and Gradual. On the whole, the order was conservative, and the people had but a
minor role.

❖

Congregational Singing in Luther's Theology

The evidence presented thus far suggests that Luther valued both the traditional
choral mass (in either Latin or German) and also German hymns inserted into the
mass, sung preferably by the entire congregation. Some Lutheran writers, however,
have denied that Luther would allow a choral mass, considering it an important part
of his theology that the liturgy be sung by the people. Because an insistence on this
viewpoint would render the thesis of this book—that the early Lutheran liturgy was
mainly choral but gradually became congregational over the centuries—untenable,
it is necessary to address the issue here.

The writer most responsible for promulgating this interpretation among North
American Lutherans is Walter Buszin, whose 1940 *Doctrine of the Universal Priesthood
and Its Influence upon the Liturgies and Music of the Lutheran Church* has directly or in-
directly influenced the views of several generations of Lutheran scholars, pastors,

and musicians. Buszin's argument goes like this: One of the most important of Luther's doctrines, and one that Luther himself consistently emphasized, is that of the universal priesthood. Because all Christians are priests by virtue of their baptism, they all do what priests do—that is, offer sacrifices to God. The most proper sacrifice is that of thanksgiving and praise. This is the task of the entire congregation, and other churches (especially Roman Catholics and Anglicans) err when they allow choirs rather than all the people to sing the liturgy.[51] Buszin bemoans the fact that Lutheran writers of the late sixteenth and early seventeenth centuries, such as Martin Chemnitz and Johann Gerhard, all but ignored this important doctrine and credits the Pietists of the late seventeenth century with rediscovering Luther's teaching and restoring it to its rightful place.[52]

If Buszin's interpretation is correct, then it means that throughout Luther's lifetime the church in Wittenberg, not to mention other churches using liturgical orders written by Wittenberg theologians, contradicted one of Luther's chief teachings by assigning such a prominent role in the liturgy to the choir. Although this hardly seems likely, it could conceivably be explained by saying that even though Luther greatly desired a purely congregational liturgy, political considerations and the conservatism of the people made that impossible, so he did the best he could. A closer examination of the doctrine of the universal priesthood should reveal whether this possible explanation is in fact correct.

One of the most thorough recent treatments of Luther's teaching on the matter is contained in a 1992 thesis by Thomas Winger titled *The Priesthood of All the Baptized: An Exegetical and Theological Investigation.*[53] Winger first points out that Luther apparently never used the phrase "universal priesthood" or "priesthood of all believers." The usual terms were "spiritual" or "common" priesthood. Winger also notes that Luther, rather than presenting the idea in a systematic manner and making it a fundamental principle, instead used it in a piecemeal fashion to bolster his arguments in several different instances. Luther's first exposition of the teaching written for publication occurred in his treatise *To the Christian Nobility of the German Nation* (1520).[54] In this open letter, Luther argued that since the clergy had been unwilling to make necessary reforms in the church (in particular, to call a council to consider Luther's teachings), then princes and other secular authorities must do so. The clergy cannot legitimately claim that priests comprise a higher "spiritual estate" and are therefore not under the jurisdiction of the temporal authorities because all Christians are in fact priests and therefore members of the spiritual estate. Luther supported his argument with citations from 1 Peter 2, Revelation 5, and 1 Corinthians 12.

Later the same year, in the *Prelude on the Babylonian Captivity of the Church,* Luther used the idea of the spiritual priesthood to deny that the clergy could rule over the laity. In *The Freedom of a Christian* (1520), he stated that Christians are priests because Christ is a priest (using the parallel in law that the wife, here the Church as the bride of Christ, shares in ownership over her husband's possessions), and they are therefore entitled to appear before God, to pray for others, and to teach one another. This definition was repeated in *The Abuse of the Mass* (1522) and in several sermons from the early 1520s. In his *Answer to . . . the Goat Emser* (1521) Luther contrasted the spiritual priesthood with the office of an ordained priest,

denying that they were equivalent. On several occasions Luther, in denying that ordained priests possess an "indelible character" that allows them to perform sacraments and other priestly functions, stated that all Christians have the authority to
do these things, although he cautioned that no one should exercise such authority
without a proper call or mandate. In these early works there is no mention of the
liturgical role of the spiritual priesthood.

Winger notes that after 1523 the idea of the spiritual priesthood rarely appeared in Luther's works. One place it did appear is in his 1535 sermon on Psalm
110, where for the first time he associated it with worship, in this case the sacrificial worship of the Old Testament. Commenting on verse 3 of the psalm ("After
your victory your people will gladly offer sacrifice to you in holy vesture"), Luther
identified the priestly activity of Christian people as "praising and honoring God,
preaching and confessing the Gospel, and giving thanks to Him for His grace." A
few pages later he answered the question "Wherein does this priesthood of Christians consist, and what are their priestly works?" with the words "teaching, sacri-
ficing, and praying."[55]

Because the index to Luther's complete works is still being compiled, it is difficult to say with certainty that he did not mention the spiritual priesthood elsewhere, but the above references seem to be the principal ones. There were also a
few occasions when Luther referred to the role of the assembled congregation without specifically mentioning the spiritual priesthood. In a sermon for the dedication
of the palace church in Torgau in 1544, two years before his death, Luther exhorted
those assembled to take heed that "the purpose of this new house may be such that
nothing else may ever happen in it except that our dear Lord himself may speak to
us through his holy Word and we respond to him through prayer and praise."[56] Here
Luther referred to the sacramental and sacrificial aspects of the liturgy, something
he had also done fourteen years earlier in his *Admonition concerning the Sacrament*. In
that essay Luther, in opposing the teaching that the sacrifice of the mass consisted
of the offering of the body and blood of Christ for human sin, distinguished between the sacrament, in which the people received the gift of God's grace in
Christ's body and blood, and the remembrance, in which they offered their thanks
for that gift. The latter, wrote Luther, was the only part of the mass that could
properly be called a sacrifice:

> The remembrance should certainly be a sacrifice of thanks, but the sacra-
> ment itself should not be a sacrifice, but rather a gift of God, presented to
> us, which we should take and receive with thanks. . . .
>
> And from this I believe that much song in the mass was written and
> still remains that treats thanksgiving and praise in a fine and splendid man-
> ner, such as the Gloria in excelsis et in terra, the Alleluia, the Patrem [i.e.,
> Credo], the Preface, the Sanctus, the Benedictus, the Agnus Dei. In these
> parts you find nothing of sacrifice, but rather purely praise and thanks-
> giving. Therefore we also retain them in our masses. Particularly the
> Agnus Dei, above all songs, serves especially well for the sacrament, for it
> clearly sings about and praises Christ for having borne our sins, treating in
> beautiful, brief words the remembrance of Christ in a powerful and lovely

manner. In brief, whatever evil there is of sacrifice and works in the mass, God has miraculously arranged it so that the priest reads virtually all of it in secret, and this is called the "secret mass." But whatever is publicly sung by the choir and among the assembly is essentially a good thing and a song of praise.[57]

The sacrifice, therefore, was one of thanksgiving and praise sung by the choir and the people in response to the sacrament. It is worth noting that here Luther commended the use of the traditional Latin mass ordinary, which would have been sung only by the choir.[58]

A little later in the Torgau dedication sermon Luther posed the question "What does it mean to keep a day holy?" as the Third Commandment demands. First, he answered, it means that the Word of God is purely preached. This he understood to be the responsibility of the entire church, although the actual preaching was delegated to the individual called for that purpose. Second, it means that we receive the Word of God in order that it might bear fruit in our lives. Third, it means that in response to the Word we lift up our common supplications to God and thank and praise him for all his benefits.[59] Once again we see the sacramental aspect of liturgy in the preaching and reception of God's Word and the sacrificial aspect in the response to the Word.

One might consider the singing of the people to be purely sacrificial, but for Luther the songs had a sacramental function as well, something to which Luther alluded when he praised the text of the Agnus Dei in the *Admonition concerning the Sacrament*. Luther saw in the songs, and indeed in all liturgical ceremonies, the power to influence one's faith. He called ceremonies valuable exercises for piety (*WA* 5:39; *LW* 14:301–302). They inculcate the faith in young people so that they do not doubt it, forget it, or lose it (*WA* 36:604). They move the unrepentant to true repentance. If ceremonies are abolished, he asked, how will the youth be nurtured until they are able to take solid spiritual food (*WA* 5:403)? The songs had a similar nurturing function. He wrote that "St. Paul himself instituted this [psalm singing] in 1 Corinthians 14 and exhorted the Colossians to sing spiritual songs and Psalms heartily unto the Lord so that God's Word and Christian teaching might be instilled and implanted in many ways."[60] And so for Luther, singing in church drives the Word of God home to the singer and hearers, as it were, and fixes it in their hearts. This is in accord with the reason he gave in his 1523 letter to Spalatin (see subsection *Letter to Georg Spalatin, 1523* above) for writing German songs; namely, that the Word of God might remain in song among the people. It also follows from his 1529 sermon (see the subsection "Reaction to the *German Mass*" above), in which he waxed poetic about the efficacy and devotional power of *Ein Kindelein so löbelich*.

There is no doubt that Luther saw in congregational singing a valuable tool both for instilling the Word of God in people's hearts and for giving the people an opportunity to respond in thanksgiving. But nothing identified in his writings would indicate that he saw any conflict between these goals and a choral performance of the liturgy. If he had, it seems unlikely that he would have highly praised the traditional Latin liturgy. It is significant that although Luther wrote two mass orders, an order for daily prayer and prefaces to three hymnals and two collections of polyphonic hymn settings, the references to congregational singing can be counted on the fingers of one hand: once in the *Formula missae,* incidentally in the *Admonition Concerning the Sacrament,* obliquely in the Torgau dedication sermon, and in passing in the *German Mass* when he directed that the Creed be sung by the people. He apparently never mentioned it in connection with the spiritual priesthood, as Buszin and others have asserted. We must therefore conclude that the idea that Luther considered the only permissible liturgy to be one sung by the entire congregation cannot be substantiated.

❖

The Origins of Luther's Hymn Tunes

This topic is peripheral to the main point of this book, but it has been the subject of so much confusion that it seems worthwhile to consider it here. It is almost an axiom in the popular imagination that Luther, in order to further congregational singing and make his hymns more attractive to the people, used or adapted preexisting secular melodies, even drinking songs. The well-known question "Why should the devil have all the good tunes?"—attributed in Bartlett's *Familiar Quotations* to English preacher Rowland Hill (1744–1833)—is frequently attributed to Luther.[61] The origin of this attribution may have been Friedrich Blume's influential 1931 book *Die evangelische Kirchenmusik,* in which he stated "Luther believed 'the devil does not need to have all lovely tunes solely for himself'"[62] Unfortunately, Blume gave no citation for the quotation. The second edition of Blume's book, which appeared in 1965 with an English translation in 1974, continued to attribute the idea to Luther but omitted the quotation.[63]

Because Luther's works are so voluminous, comprising not only published writings and letters but also transcriptions of dinner table conversations, it is scarcely possible to state categorically that Luther never uttered or wrote these words. But other scholars have looked for them and failed to find them.[64] Recently, a new tool has appeared, with the 127-volume Weimar edition of Luther's works now available as a searchable online database. A search conducted on keywords in the foregoing quotation yielded nothing.[65] It therefore seems highly likely that such a statement is not to be found in Luther's works.

In truth, of all Luther's hymns, only one, *Vom Himmel hoch, da komm ich her,* is known to have had a secular origin.[66] He altered it from the popular song (*not* drinking song) *Ich kumm aus frembden landen her.* But he wrote it for the annual children's Christmas pageant, not for use in a church service. At first the original secular tune was used, but Luther apparently had second thoughts about this, as he wrote a new tune for the 1545 hymnal. It is Luther's new tune that appears in modern hymnals.

Most often, when Luther wrote a hymn using a preexisting melody, the melody was a Gregorian chant. But over 20 percent of his hymns are based on, or written in the form of, popular *religious* song (what would be akin to religious

Christmas carols today). *Gott der Vater wohn uns bei* is rewritten from *Sancta Maria ste uns bei* or the apparent older form of the text *Sanctus petrus won uns pey.* Nine hymns are in the form of the *Leise,* so called because of its characteristic last line Kyrie eleison or Kyrieleis:

> Christ ist erstanden
> Dies sind die heilgen zehn Gebot
> Gelobet seist du, Jesu Christ
> Gott sei gelobet und gebenedeiet
> Jesus Christus unser Heiland, der den Tod
> Mensch, willst du leben seliglich
> Mitten wir im Leben sind
> Nun bitten wir den Heiligen Geist
> Unser grosse Sünde und schwere Missetat[67]

Many of the models for these hymns had already been sung in churches before Luther's time. In making use of the models, Luther was continuing a tradition, not breaking new ground. There is in any case no justification for the argument that Luther attempted to promote congregational singing by catering to the tastes of the masses.

❖

Conclusion

Martin Luther regarded congregational singing as useful and desirable. He encouraged it in his own congregation, but not at the expense of the choral liturgy. In Luther's theology there is no conflict between a choral liturgy and his desire for the people to sing. The *German Mass* of 1526, widely regarded as a congregational service, actually describes what was at the time of its publication mostly a choral mass. It was not well received, and the congregation in Wittenberg continued to sing poorly for years. The choral mass in Latin remained the principal service in Wittenberg throughout Luther's lifetime.

❖

CHAPTER 2

Catholic Liturgy—Lutheran Liturgy

E ven though it seems that the people of Wittenberg sang very little in church, this was not necessarily true for other places in Germany. In evaluating the practice elsewhere, it would be helpful to establish a baseline for comparison; namely, the congregation's role in German churches in the years immediately preceding the Reformation. This will allow us to determine just how much of an innovator Luther was. It is also instructive to trace the development of Catholic and Lutheran liturgies in the years following. Accordingly, in this chapter I shall discuss first the characteristics of the pre-Reformation liturgy; second, Luther's changes to the liturgy; and third, parallels between Catholic and Lutheran liturgy in the course of the sixteenth century. My thesis is that in liturgical matters, and especially in hymn singing, Lutherans were not nearly so innovative as is often supposed.

❖

The Pre-Reformation Liturgy—An Overview

The pre-Reformation church was marked by liturgical diversity. It was not until the Tridentine missal appeared in 1570 that uniformity in liturgy was imposed on the Catholic Church. Before that time, each diocese or religious order had its own liturgical books with their own texts, music, and rubrics. Often there were variations from city to city within a diocese and even between different churches in a single city. Cathedrals, court chapels, and collegiate churches (such as the All Saints Foundation in Wittenberg) frequently had their own versions of the liturgy.

The pre-Reformation and post-Reformation Catholic liturgies from the German-speaking areas have gone largely uncollected and unstudied. There exists no source comparable to Emil Sehling's monumental collection of Protestant liturgies from the sixteenth century.[1] And so it is no easy task to compare the Lutheran liturgies with their pre-Reformation counterparts. The variations that existed among Lutheran liturgies may in many cases be due to differences in pre-Reformation practices, but this is difficult to prove.

There were, to be sure, many points of agreement among the pre-Reformation liturgies. All used the Roman Rite, the liturgy of nearly all western Europe. The overall shape of the mass and offices was the same. Sermons were widely held throughout the German-speaking region, and processions and pilgrimages were popular. The differences had to do mainly with the assignment of proper texts, the placement of certain variable elements (such as the sermon and congregational songs), the presence or absence of certain propers (such as the communion antiphon), the melodies used to carry liturgical texts, and the musical performance of the liturgy (for example, whether and in what way organs and choral polyphony were used).

❖

The Late Medieval Mass

The late medieval form of the Roman mass comprised the following elements: Introit, Kyrie, Gloria, Collect, Epistle, Gradual, Alleluia, Sequence, Gospel, Credo, Offertory, Secret, Sursum Corda, Preface, Sanctus and Benedictus with Elevation, Canon Major (conclusion), Pater Noster, Pax Domini, Agnus Dei, Communion antiphon, Postcommunion collect, and Dismissal.[2] This simple outline is useful as an overview, but the real picture is more complex, for not only were there variations in prescribed liturgical texts and rituals from place to place, but there is evidence that deviation from the locally prescribed liturgy was not uncommon.

One such form of deviation was the practice of truncating or omitting portions of the text of the public sung mass, substituting paraphrases or unrelated texts in the vernacular. The priest presumably still recited the full texts to himself, so technically nothing was omitted. Our evidence for this comes mainly from declarations of provincial synods and councils opposing the practice. According to Wilhelm Bäumker, the Basel Council of 1435 forbade the singing of German songs during the high mass and the truncation or omission of the Latin chants begun by the priest. The Synod of Eichstätt in 1466 forbade the truncation of the Latin Credo, Preface, and Pater Noster during the high mass and the interpolation of German songs. The Synod of Schwerin in 1492 required that when a priest sang the mass he must sing the Gloria, Credo, Offertory, Preface, and Pater Noster in their entirety and not allow the other clerics in the choir to substitute another responsory or a song in the vernacular for any of the above. The provincial council of 1536 in Cologne forbade the practice of shortening or omitting the Epistle, Creed, Preface, and Pater Noster.[3] To be sure, it is difficult to know how common these practices were, but the witness of several synods in different parts of the German-speaking region shows that they were not limited to a single area. In evaluating the foregoing evidence, Josef Gülden has concluded:

In the east as in the south, in the north as in the west of Germany around 1500 as well as before and after, in several churches German hymns and songs were indeed sung at high mass, both where there were no clerks and schoolboys (that is, in the country), but also even there where clergy were employed as singers in the choir, and in fact in various places: at the Gloria, during and after the Epistle, at the Sequence, before and after the sermon, at the Creed, at the Offertory, at the Preface, after the Elevation and at the Pater Noster.[4]

When an organ was used it alternated phrase by phrase with the choir in the performance of the liturgy. It was expected that the original chant form the basis for the organ music; but as with the choral music, the piece performed frequently did not fit the liturgy, and even secular music was common. The chief complaint about the organ music in Catholic churches during the sixteenth century was that it was "profane, worldly, farcical, exhibitionistic, theatrical, impure, frivolous, lascivious, shameless, obscene, etc."[5] A second complaint was that parts of the mass were truncated, with only the first few words sung and the rest played by the organ. This was documented not only for choral parts such as the Credo but also for parts sung by the priest, such as the Epistle, Gospel, Preface, and Pater Noster. Overlapping of liturgical sections was also common, with, for example, the priest beginning the Offertory while the choir sang the Credo (in 1558 the Jesuit General Francis of Borgia wanted to make this a requirement!). In 1512 the Council of Seville complained that in nearly every church in the archdiocese the usual practice was, when the sermon after the Gospel began, for the choir to sing the first words of the Credo and the organ to continue it during the sermon.[6] The Catholic Synod of Augsburg in 1527 prohibited the organist from covering up the reading of the Epistle and Gospel with his playing; the Trier Synod of 1549 took similar action.[7]

At this time only the largest churches and cathedrals owned organs, and only places with Latin schools or endowments could supply the choristers needed for a choir. If such deviations were the rule at these well-endowed institutions that could afford to do a proper Latin liturgy, how much more deviation would there have been in smaller parishes where the priest may barely have been able to say a proper Pater Noster?

It might seem surprising to us today that in the Middle Ages many church authorities apparently had no objection to the omission or truncation of texts in the public liturgies, the singing and playing of secular music during the mass, and the simultaneous performance of more than one part of the liturgy. But this is because today the mass is seen first of all as a public activity, one in which the entire assembly takes an active role; and private masses, though not forbidden in the Catholic Church, have been discouraged. This was not the case at the end of the Middle Ages. As long as the mass sacrifice was properly made, the mass was valid, whether or not anyone besides the priest was present. By far the most commonly performed mass during this period was the so-called low mass (*missa lecta*), in which the priest alone recited the parts formerly assigned not only to himself but also to the deacon, the choir, and the rest of the congregation. The idea of the low mass was carried over into the public mass, where the priest could recite the mass quietly while other activities occupied the choir and the rest of the congregation. Everyone but the celebrant was superfluous; according to Catholic liturgical scholar Hans Bernhard Meyer it was common for entire congregations, clerics and all, simply to leave the church after the Elevation, leaving only the celebrant to finish the mass.[8]

The Elevation, when the celebrant held Christ's body aloft for the people to adore, was the high point of the mass. Meyer reports that most people actually communed only at Easter (this was obligatory), although the very devout might have communed on the four chief feasts: Christmas, Easter, Pentecost, and Assumption or All Saints. The idea was that the priest offered the mass on behalf of the church; therefore, communion by all present was not necessary. Even in religious communities and orders communion more than once a month was rare. The great exception seems to have been Ulm, where around 1500 the sacrament was distributed to at least some people, mostly pregnant, sick, and devout women, every week. In general, even on festivals the distribution of communion was held separately from the mass, either before it or after it. This was possible because it was not considered necessary to distribute the host to the faithful in the same mass at which it was consecrated; rather, reserved hosts were used. At Easter especially the distribution took place outside the mass so as not to prolong the liturgy unreasonably.[9]

❖

The Liturgy of the Hours in the Late Middle Ages

The Liturgy of the Hours, also called the Daily Office, was essentially choral, not congregational, as can be seen in the German word for the Daily Office, *Chorgesang*. The entire series of offices was observed only in cloisters and in places where an endowment had been made especially for that purpose. The larger parishes generally held only Vespers in the evening and Matins in the morning. Compline was usually said immediately after Vespers and Lauds immediately after Matins. The Little Hours were not generally held in parishes.

It is unclear whether any hours were observed in smaller parishes and filials. If they were, they likely took the form of private devotions by the priest and perhaps an assistant.

❖

The Late Medieval Sermon and Its Annexes

According to Hans Bernhard Meyer, preaching was common in Germany before the Reformation. There was a sermon every Sunday and festival in court, city, and village churches. In Advent and Lent sermons were given three times per week in some places. Many preachers and writers of the time felt so strongly about the sermon that they would rather have omitted the communion. The sermons were usually dry, scholastic lectures, and the listeners not infrequently slept, talked, or even left and stood outside during them. More often than not the sermon was based, if loosely, on the Gospel for the day. Preaching outside of mass was common, and there was no fixed place for the sermon within it. It was held after the Gospel, after the Credo, at the Offertory, and after the Elevation. Preaching after the Elevation did not disrupt the mass, as it was customary to sing the mass only up through the Sanctus, then the sermon was held while the priest at the altar continued the mass by speaking it.

A favorite time for the sermon was between the early service and the main service on Sunday. Hymns were sung before and after the sermon, and these together with the sermon proper and the various annexes constituted the "pulpit service" (*Kanzeldienst*). The entire pulpit service was held in German and proceeded as follows: the preacher went to the pulpit, knelt and prayed briefly, then read a brief verse from the day's Gospel or from the liturgy or the Fathers. Then he exhorted the people to prayer, with the Ave Maria, the Our Father, or the Veni Sancte Spiritus said. A hymn could be substituted for the prayer. The explication of the text followed for about forty-five minutes, then another hymn was occasionally sung, especially when the sermon was held outside mass.

After the hymn came the various annexes to the sermon, namely the announcements; the common prayer; the recitation of the Lord's Prayer or Ave Maria, the Creed and the Ten Commandments; the public confession and absolution; and the remembrance for the dead. The common prayer, sometimes called the prayer for all classes(*für alle Stände*), consisted of exhortations to pray for the government, the church, spiritual welfare, peace, and various other urgent needs. The Lord's Prayer, Ave Maria, Creed, and Ten Commandments had been said for catechetical purposes since the thirteenth century, and a number of dioceses required that they be printed on boards in the church so they could be read by the people. The public confession and absolution had been practiced since the eleventh century, although preachers made it clear that it did not suffice for the remission of serious sins. A general penance was also assigned, which was almost always five Our Fathers and seven Hail Marys (sometimes three of each) to be said during the Elevation.[10]

❖

Congregational Singing before the Reformation

It is difficult to determine the extent of congregational singing before the Reformation because, although German hymns are known from a large number of manuscripts and books, in many cases we cannot be sure if they were sung by the entire congregation or only by the choir or, indeed, in church at all. There do exist throughout the German-speaking region books variously called *Agenda, Breviarum, Directorium, Ordo, Liber Oʳdinarius, Ordinarium, Consuetudo,* or *Ritus* from the twelfth century and later that contain references to German hymns, mostly incipits; these hymns, at least, we know were sung in church.[11] But only a very few sources unequivocally refer to singing by the assembly. Anthony Ruff cites instances from the eighth to the fifteenth centuries in which the people sang the Kyrie, *Christ ist erstanden,* and other songs.[12] Johannes Janota cites a reference from the thirty-first sermon of Berthold of Regensburg (d. 1272) to the people singing a creedal para-phrase in the vernacular: "For thereafter follows what is called the 'Credo in unum'; that is, the Creed. You begin thus and sing with common supplication: 'I believe in the Father, I believe in the Son of my lady Saint Mary and in the Holy Spirit; Lord, have mercy.'"[13] Beginning in the early thirteenth century there are many references to vernacular songs sung before and after the sermon.[14] The ver-nacular *Christ ist erstanden* was interpolated into the Easter sequence *Victimae paschali* and sung by the entire congregation, this practice being widespread.[15] Other vernacular hymns were later interpolated between the lines of the Christmas and Pentecost sequences as well, and the Lutherans retained what was to them an an-cient tradition of singing these sequences with their interpolations on the appro-priate days.

Even these few unequivocal references make it clear that congregational singing was practiced prior to Luther's time, but it is still uncertain how widespread congregational singing was across the German-speaking region and how frequently churches where it was in use actually employed it. The size of a typical congrega-tion's repertoire is also unclear, nor do we know how well the people sang. A situ-ation in which a different hymn was sung with enthusiasm each week before and after the sermon throughout Germany is a far cry from one in which a handful of former choir members in isolated churches sang *Christ ist erstanden* once a year on Easter. Unfortunately, while it is clear that neither extreme applied, we cannot tell from the currently available evidence which end of the continuum lies closer to the actual practice.

❖

Luther's Changes to the Mass

Luther's two masses, set against the late medieval Roman mass, are outlined in Table 2.1. The *Formula missae* of 1523, Luther's Latin mass, differs little from its precur-sor. Notable are the omission of the Offertory, Secret, and Canon Major; Luther objected to the idea of the mass as a sacrifice for sins by the priest, to which all of these refer. He suggested an alternate Postcommunion collect for the same reason. In making the Gloria optional he was only confirming in writing what seems to have been the prevailing practice; namely, that the Gloria was not always sung. It was traditionally omitted during Advent and from Septuagesima until Easter, and also on holy days with three or fewer lessons. An agenda from Hatzkerode in An-halt dating from around 1534 states that it was also omitted in winter in order to shorten the mass in the unheated church (Sehling 2:586). Several early Lutheran liturgical orders besides the *Formula missae* allow the Gloria to be omitted when-ever desired, including Thomas Müntzer's *Deutsch evangelisch messe* of 1524 (Sehling 1:498), Johannes Brenz's *Reformation der Kirchen in dem Hellischen* [i.e., Hallischen] *Land* of 1526 (Richter 1:43), and Johann Bugenhagen's 1529 church order for Hamburg (Sehling 5:528). The fact that the orders by Luther, Müntzer, and Brenz are historically unrelated to each other bespeaks a tradition of omitting the Gloria that is older than the Lutheran Reformation. This tradition is most likely the one described in the Wittenberg church order of 1533, which specifies that the Gloria is sung only after a ninefold Kyrie; for example, on festivals (Sehling 1:704). The Gloria is not even mentioned in the *German Mass* (which includes only a threefold Kyrie).

The *German Mass* deviates more from the textbook form of the Roman Mass. But when viewed in the light of the German songs and mass paraphrases that were apparently already sung in various places before the Reformation, it no longer seems so new. To be sure, there is no evidence that any mass parts had been sung in German in Wittenberg before 1525; but the practice is documented for other places, as shown above, and the Wittenbergers would likely have heard of it even if they had had no direct experience with it.[16]

Table 2.1. Luther's two mass orders compared with the medieval mass order

Roman mass	*Formula missae*	*German Mass*
Introit	Introit	German psalm or song
Kyrie	Kyrie	Kyrie
Gloria	Gloria (optional)	
Collect	Collect	Collect
Epistle	Epistle	Epistle
Gradual	Gradual and/or Alleluia	German song
Alleluia		
Sequence	Sequence[a]	
Gospel	Gospel	Gospel
Credo	Credo	Creed
Offertory	Sermon	Sermon
Secret		Paraphrase of Lord's Prayer and exhortation to communicants
Sursum Corda	Sursum Corda	
Preface	Preface	
Sanctus & Benedictus with Elevation	Consecration	Consecration with Elevation, then distribution, during which there is singing (optionally including the Sanctus and Agnus Dei)
	Sanctus & Benedictus with optional Elevation	
Canon major (conclusion)		
Pater Noster	Pater Noster	
Pax Domini	Pax Domini	
Agnus Dei	Agnus Dei	
Communion antiphon	Communion antiphon	
Postcommunion collect	Thanksgiving collect	Thanksgiving collect
Dismissal	Benedicamus & Benediction	Benediction

The order of the Roman Mass is from Harper 1991:115. Luther's *Formula missae* is found at Sehling 1: 4–9, *WA* 12:205–20 and *LW* 53:19–40. His *German Mass* is found at Sehling 1:10–16, *WA* 19:72–113 and *LW* 53:61–90.

[a]Luther does not explicitly mention the sequence, but he states that the gradual and/or alleluia may be sung and then names two "graduals" that in other sources are called sequences. He is evidently using the term *gradual* to include sequences.

❖

Luther's Changes to the Liturgy of the Hours

In the cities, the early Lutherans retained the forms of Vespers and Matins as they had been practiced. The sole change they made was to reduce the number of lessons to one and the number of psalms to one, two, or three, with a single antiphon for the entire set. This was evidently done so that these services did not become tiring to the participants, as Luther wrote:

> Now when the lesson and explanation have lasted a half hour or longer, the congregation shall then thank God, praise him and ask him for the fruit of the Word, etc. For this purpose the psalms and several good responsories and antiphons should be used. In brief, let everything be completed within an hour, or however long is desired, for one must not overwhelm the soul so that it becomes weary and bored, as until now in cloisters and chapters they have burdened themselves with the work of an ass.[17]

❖

The Sermon in the Lutheran Church

The Lutherans took over the pre-Reformation form of the pulpit service intact, except that the Ave Maria was not said and the remembrance of the dead was omitted. In addition, no penance was assigned at the absolution. But everything else was the same, including the length of the sermon (forty-five minutes, the entire pulpit service to last an hour), and this was true throughout Lutheran Germany. Only a few Lutheran liturgical orders specify the exact order of the pulpit service: a fair number say only that "the sermon (*Predigt*) follows," but in every case the entire pulpit service is meant, the German word *Predigt* being used for both the pulpit service and the sermon proper. In most Lutheran churches the placement of the sermon after the Creed became standard, but early in the Reformation a few churches kept the sermon at the beginning of the service, or between the early and late services.

❖

Luther and the Liturgical Song of the Congregation

It is clear that singing German hymns in church was not an innovation of Luther. But did not Luther, by encouraging the people to sing (whether or not they actually did so), give hymns a different function by making them a part of the actual liturgy rather than an extra item of little importance? Some Catholic scholars, apparently in an attempt to justify on a historical basis the continuation of the Latin mass as opposed to the introduction of the vernacular, have held the view that vernacular hymns in the mass have never been "liturgical," but were merely pious exercises done by the people without liturgical significance. This claim is worth examining, because if it is true, then it may be used as evidence that Lutherans, to the extent that they involved the congregation, made a conscious choice to alter existing practice.

The chief proponent of this view is Johannes Janota, whose book *Studien zu Funktion und Typus des deutschen geistlichen Liedes im Mittelalter* established the historical basis for this argument.[18] Janota took as his starting point the distinction made by the Congregation of Rites in its September 3, 1958, *Instruction* between liturgical actions and devotional exercises. Liturgical actions belong to the entire church and need to be approved by the pope; devotional exercises are overseen by the bishops (except for the Litany, which is a devotional exercise overseen by the pope). To account for the multiplicity of liturgical uses found in the Middle Ages, the author modified his definition for the medieval era to say that "liturgical acts are sacred acts which, on the basis of their institution by Jesus Christ or the Church in both names are performed according to the relevant liturgical books not contradicting the episcopal jurisdiction by persons lawfully appointed to show God, the saints and the blessed ones the honor befitting them; all other holy acts we call devotional exercises."[19] Specifically, Janota considered an act to be liturgical if it fit two conditions: (1) the possible inclusion of the liturgical act in a liturgical book ("possible" because sources such as parish books, mass explanations, and the like are not, strictly speaking, liturgical books; however, they do witness to acts considered liturgical); and (2) the lack of opposition to the act from the episcopal jurisdiction. The author concluded that German hymns were not a part of the liturgy because their texts did not appear in official liturgical books (although their incipits did) and because various diocesan synods condemned their use (see the references to the various councils and synods in the preceding section). According to this interpretation, liturgical song in the vernacular did not exist before the Reformation; therefore, Luther, although he was not the father of congregational singing, was, according to Janota, the father of *liturgical* congregational singing.[20]

This viewpoint has met with strong opposition. Walther Lipphardt and Philipp Harnoncourt argue independently of each other that Janota has misrepresented the nature of liturgical song. According to Lipphardt, Janota's principal mistake was that he attributed to the Middle Ages a centralization of "liturgy" of a kind that was not known until the nineteenth century. True, some dioceses did forbid vernacular songs in the liturgy, but others such as Passau, Salzburg, and Verden encouraged them. Janota made a false distinction between what was "pure" (officially recognized) and what was "impure" in the liturgy. In the Middle Ages, what was pure was what the cantors, under the supervision of the bishops, wrote in their liturgical books. Janota's second mistake is that he overvalued sources such as choral parts. In fact, the presence of many polyphonic hymn arrangements bespeaks the popularity of the monophonic forms.[21]

Lipphardt then reports on the contents of twenty-one prayer book manuscripts from the Cistercian nunnery at Medingen bey Lüneburg and two from the nunnery at Wienhausen. Unlike most prayer books, these contain such precise liturgical details that it is possible to reconstruct from them the liturgy used in the convents. The manuscripts cover the entire period from about 1290 to after 1540. There are sixty to seventy German hymns listed together with Latin hymns in the order of the liturgical year. The author concludes that in the cloister at Medingen and probably also in other cloisters in the Lüneburger Heide newly composed Latin and German hymns were used in the offices and mass on high feasts. After 1350 German hymns from the offices began to be transferred to the mass, where the laity could more easily participate. Congregational songs (actually *Leisen*) were sung during the Elevation and the Communion, and in individual instances there were Low German tropes of the Introit, the Gloria, and the Sequence. There is no mention in the sources of a sermon hymn. That the vernacular songs were truly to be sung by the whole congregation seems likely from an argument in the sources that no one should keep silent in the praise of God. The ordering of the German songs, even more than the Latin, is fairly fixed in the liturgy over a period of two hundred years. As in the liturgy, archaic word forms are preserved. The only possible conclusion to all this, writes Lipphardt, is that the German songs occupied a key role in the liturgy.[22]

Harnoncourt criticizes Janota on the grounds that (1) differentiation between "liturgical action" and "devotional exercise," first introduced by Pius XII in 1958, is not valid for the Middle Ages; (2) in the Middle Ages, "liturgical" actions cannot be limited to those appearing in liturgical books; and (3) the idea that only those persons specifically appointed or delegated may perform liturgical acts is often mentioned today, but it is theologically untenable and downright wrong. Harnoncourt cannot escape the conclusion that Janota had already decided on the answer to his question and was determined to interpret the evidence to fit it. His principal error was to take a definition of liturgy that many did not consider tenable even at the time of its appearance in 1958 (it was completely overhauled five years later by the Second Vatican Council) and use it for a period that had a completely different understanding of liturgy. In fact, the liturgy of the Middle Ages comprised all the forms that were used in the public service. It was regulated not only by books and constitutions but also by customs of relatively old or new origin.[23]

The refutations notwithstanding, Janota's argument that vernacular hymn singing was extraliturgical makes sense if one considers that all that was needed for the mass to be valid was for the priest to speak the proper texts and perform the sacrifice. But in this light, all other ceremony, including the singing of the choir, would be unnecessary and therefore extraliturgical. In any case, Janota has not proven that the Middle Ages knew a distinction between "liturgical acts" and "devotional exercises." Without such proof, we cannot conclude that if a synod disapproved of a practice taking part within the liturgy, that practice was therefore considered extraliturgical; we can only say that the twentieth-century Catholic Church would consider it extraliturgical. Using Janota's definition of a "liturgical act" can lead to the questionable assertion that a usage practiced in every church in a diocese, tacitly approved by decades of diocesan synods and bishops, became extraliturgical once it was condemned by a synod, whose reasons for the condemnation may not even be evident today. It appears to me, given the difficulty in constructing a definition for "liturgical act" suitable for the Middle Ages, that this term had no meaning at the time that is in any way comparable to the modern definition, and that it is useless to try to force a meaning onto it. The most we can say about a particular action or text is that it either had or did not have official sanction at a particular time or place. Just because it lacked official sanction does not necessarily mean that those performing the act considered it "extraliturgical."

Once Janota's contention is rejected and one acknowledges that vernacular song was a real part of the medieval liturgy, Luther's role as an innovator in German hymnody comes into question. Unquestionably, the strength of Luther's hymn texts did much to popularize the genre, but in assigning German song a part in the liturgy Luther was only introducing locally what was already the practice in a number of places. His close colleagues Justus Jonas and Philipp Melanchthon admitted as much when they said in the Apology of the Augsburg Confession (1531) that "This usage [congregational singing] has always been held in esteem in the churches. For although in some places more and in some places fewer German songs are sung, still in all churches the people have sung in German; and so it isn't all that new."[24]

❖

Congregational Singing in Catholic Churches after the Reformation

Lutherans had no monopoly on vernacular singing in the sixteenth century. To be sure, Lutheran hymnals printed in German during the century outnumbered Catholic hymnals by a wide margin,[25] but there is ample evidence that German singing continued in the Catholic churches. After 1535 it is clear that some of that singing, at least, was congregational.

The first Catholic hymnal that specifically called for the entire congregation to sing seems to have been *Ein new Gesangbüchlin geistlicher Lieder,* compiled by Michael Vehe, a Dominican and provost of the collegiate church in Halle, and printed in Leipzig in 1537.[26] It is not certain what motivated Vehe to publish his hymnal, but it might have been at least partly in response to the religious inclination of the people in Albertine Saxony, which leaned decidedly toward Lutheran teachings and which became officially Lutheran after the death of Georg, the last Catholic Duke of Saxony, in 1539. The hymnal's preface stated that the book was for use by the laity in singing before and after the sermon and at the time of the common pilgrimages (f. 2[b]). Eucharistic hymns were also included in the book, although the compiler did not mention how they were to be used. Gülden speculates that this may have been because that use was not officially sanctioned.[27]

Widespread interest in congregational singing did not arise in Catholic churches until after 1560, a date that corresponds roughly to increased Lutheran interest in the subject, as we shall see in the following chapters. In 1567 Johann Leisentrit published his *Geistliche Lieder vnd psalmen,* in which he stated that hymns may be sung "at mass, during the offertory and during holy communion." He also mentioned singing before and after the sermon.[28]

The preface to the Bamberg hymnal of 1576 contained the following notice:

> Whereas daily experience shows that German hymns and songs—many of which are not Catholic, but rather suspect—are sung in many places in the church before and after the sermon and also before, after and during the Holy Office of Mass [i.e., during the Elevation and communion]; it will be necessary to find herein the Christian means to abolish these and appoint good Catholic ones that can be trusted in their place.[29]

Other hymnals followed the Bamberg model, including Michael Peterle's *Christliche Gebet vnd Gesäng* (Prague, 1581), the Würzburg hymnal of 1591 and the Speyer hymnal of 1599, printed in Cologne.[30]

Similar hymnals continued to appear throughout the next century. In 1602 Nicolaus Beuttner published his *Catholisch Gesang-Buch* in Graz, which, according to Anthony Ruff "was reprinted at least ten times through 1718." Ruff adds that "the hymnal's foreword gives as a reason for the hymnal's compilation the fact that singers are not always available for Latin chant, especially in smaller parishes. No doubt many of the Latin Mass propers were often replaced by congregational vernacular song in Austrian parishes."[31] This situation is exactly parallel to what was happening in Lutheran churches at the time.

The Mainz *Catholisch Cantual* of 1605, which transmits the contemporary mass order in great detail, demonstrates how close Catholic and Lutheran liturgical practices were at the time. With just a few exceptions, this could be a Lutheran order. While admitting that the mass should ideally be sung in Latin throughout while the lay people contemplate the sufferings of Christ using their prayer books or rosary, the preface noted that in many places the priest and parish clerk were not capable of singing it. Therefore, it stated, the mass may be held in German as follows: (1) if sung at all, the Introit, Kyrie, Gloria, Et in terra, Collect, Epistle, and Alleluia are sung in Latin; (2) a German song may be sung before the Gradual, Tract, Sequence, or Alleluia (except on high feasts); (3) on great high feasts the Sequence incorporates the traditional German verses; (4) the Gospel is sung, and nothing else is sung during it; (5) the Creed is begun in Latin by the priest and continued in German by the parish clerk, then the sermon follows, then the clerk sings the Our Father and the Ave Maria and the pastor goes to the altar and reads the Offertory, during or before which the people may sing a German song, until the Preface; (6) the Preface and Sanctus are sung and never omitted; (7) German songs are not sung between the Sanctus and the Elevation; (8) after the Elevation a German song is always to be sung (titles are given); (9) on great feasts the Our Father and Agnus Dei are sung, otherwise a song on the holy Body of Christ; (10) if there are many communicants several verses from the *Ave vivens hostia* are sung in German and Latin; (11) the postcommunion collect and dismissal (or Benedicamus) are always sung; and (12) after the *Deo gratias* a brief song relating to the festival, our Dear Lady, or the patron of the place may be sung. If the mass is read rather than sung, the clerk may sing in German from the Introit to the Gospel, from the Offertory to shortly before the Elevation, from the Elevation until the blessing of the priest, and after the blessing, when the service may be closed with a song.[32]

❖

Conclusion

The paradigm of the medieval mass was the low mass, spoken by the priest. As long as the priest correctly performed the ritual, the mass was considered valid. This allowed sung portions to be truncated or omitted, and it also allowed vernacular texts to be substituted, as was done in some places. Congregational singing was not unknown before the Reformation, but it is difficult to know how widespread the practice was. Luther was therefore not so much an innovator as a popularizer of congregational singing. In the area of liturgy, Luther's changes to the mass, sermon, and Liturgy of the Hours were quite conservative; and even the changes in the *German Mass* were not so radical as is commonly believed. There is evidence that the late sixteenth-century Catholic mass as held in Germany was quite similar in outward appearance to the Lutheran mass.

All this shows us that the popular conception of congregational singing as a peculiarly Protestant phenomenon is mistaken. There was a tradition of such song even before the Reformation, and it continued long afterward in Catholic churches. The pieces would fit together well if we could demonstrate that congregational singing in Lutheran churches succeeded best where there had already been a strong tradition of it, but unfortunately there are too many holes in the evidence to support such a conclusion, logical as it seems. As will be shown in the following chapters, even in Lutheran churches the success of congregational singing was a patchwork: it succeeded in a few places, but in many others it did not, at least not for a long time.

CHAPTER 3

❖

The Church Orders: An Introduction

Official liturgies authorized by sixteenth-century Lutheran churches are the most complete source of information about choral and congregational singing during the period. Many of them contain detailed directions about what was to be sung, when, and by whom. But the practices described in these liturgies are far from uniform, and in this chapter and the next I shall attempt to sort out some of the complexities in the evidence.

❖

Nature and Function of Church Orders

As Catholic bishops lost their authority in the territories adopting the Reformation, a new system of church government was needed. The system that evolved placed the ruler of each duchy, county, independent city, or other territory at the head of the church for the territory, making the church consistory, a combination of governing council and judicial body, a department of state. Bishops were replaced by superintendents appointed by the consistory or directly by the territorial ruler. Regulations governing the churches appeared in documents called church orders (*Kirchenordnungen*).[1] Some of the more industrious territorial churches issued orders of up to several hundred printed pages covering every aspect of ecclesiastical life, ranging from an exposition of doctrine to the procedure for making distributions from the community chest. Other territories simply issued orders on particular topics, often only a few handwritten pages, whenever the need arose. And even the large printed orders were frequently revised or supplemented with additional regulations. To make things even more complex, individual parishes and cloisters sometimes issued their own liturgical orders to supplement or replace the territorial orders.

The term *agenda* (literally, "things to be done") is sometimes used to refer to church orders. In the sixteenth century the two terms were often synonymous, as in the Saxon *Agenda—das ist, Kyrchenordnung, wie sich die Pfarrherrn und Seelsorger in iren Ampten und diensten halten sollen* . . . (Leipzig, 1540). Modern scholars sometimes equate the two and sometimes distinguish between them. The most common distinction, which I have adopted, is that church orders refer to documents governing any and all aspects of church life, including the liturgy, while agendas cover only the liturgy. And so a comprehensive church order can contain an agenda.

The term church order has occasionally been broadened to include all documents relating to church life. Emil Sehling's collection of church orders contains not only regulations governing the church but also minutes of ecclesiastical visitations, decisions of occasional regional church councils (called "synods"), and various minutiae dealing with parish life, such as financial records.[2] I have adopted a strict definition, calling church orders or agendas only those documents containing regulations for church life and liturgy; that is, documents that are *prescriptive* in nature. I do not use the term for documents that are *descriptive*—that is, that describe what was actually happening in the churches. A distinction between these two types is useful because absent other evidence we cannot know to what extent the liturgical prescriptions in church orders reflected actual practice; but the descriptive documents provide that evidence, telling us (insofar as they are to be believed) exactly what took place in the churches. Chapters 3 and 4 cover only the church orders; the other documents will be discussed in chapter 5.

❖

The Schedule of Services

Although the details of the liturgies varied considerably among Lutheran churches, the schedule of services was remarkably similar throughout the German-speaking region. The weekend began with Vespers on Saturday afternoon, at which a sermon was preached. After Vespers, private confession was held for anyone planning to commune the next day.[3] Early on Sunday, Matins was held in the cities, generally in Latin with only the schoolboys present. In larger cities a shortened mass with sermon might be held prior to Matins for the sake of domestic servants who would not be able to attend the main service. Matins was not held in small villages. The main service, called *Messe* (mass) or *Tagamt,* was held after Matins (in cities) and lasted three hours in both city and village, with the sermon and its annexes occupying the middle hour. The sermon during mass was always on the day's Gospel. Communion was offered on all Sundays and holy days nearly everywhere as long as there were people desiring to commune, and larger cities held it on weekdays as well.[4] When there were no communicants, a truncated mass was held, skipping everything from the Preface through the Thanksgiving collect. After lunch either Vespers or a catechism service took place, or a combination of both. The high point of the catechism service was the examination, at which children from the parish stood up in front of the congregation and recited a part of Luther's *Small Catechism* with its explanation.[5] This was not a popular way to learn, and visitation records from the sixteenth and seventeenth centuries are full of complaints from pastors that few people, if any, attended the catechism service.[6] Churches that did not hold a catechism service on Sunday afternoons held it early on Sunday morning or on a weekday.

Services were also held during the week. In the largest cities masses took place daily at alternating churches. Most cities had sermons on several weekdays, generally in the morning; and village priests were encouraged to preach a sermon on at least one weekday. In places with Latin schools, Matins and Vespers were generally sung every day. A number of church orders specify that the Litany was to be sung once a week on Wednesday or Friday, but many places omitted the Litany except during times of war or other danger. The early seventeenth century saw the development of the weekday prayer service (*Betstunde*), which typically consisted of a hymn, the invocation, a reading from the Bible, various prayers, and the Blessing.[7] Some places had monthly or seasonal days of penitence.[8]

❖

Services on Holy Days

The list of holy days observed was fairly consistent among Lutheran churches. The three chief festivals (Christmas, Easter, and Pentecost) were generally observed for two and a half days; that is, with mass in the morning and Vespers with sermon in the afternoon on the first two days, and only mass in the morning on the third day. Single-day observances were Circumcision or New Year's (January 1), Epiphany (January 6), the Purification of Mary (February 2, also called the Presentation of Our Lord), the Annunciation (March 25, but moved to a different date if it fell during Holy Week), Ascension (the sixth Thursday after Easter), Trinity (the Sunday after Pentecost), St. John the Baptist (June 24), Visitation (July 2), and St. Michael (September 29). St. Stephen (December 26) was observed as a full-day festival because it fell on the second day of Christmas.

Days of the apostles (St. John the Evangelist, December 27; St. Matthias, February 25; SS. Philip and James the Younger, May 1; SS. Peter and Paul, June 29 [alternatively, St. Peter on August 1 and the Conversion of Paul on January 25]; St. James the Elder, July 25; St. Bartholomew, August 24; St. Matthew, September 21; SS. Simon and Jude, October 28; St. Andrew, November 30; and St. Thomas, December 21) were observed in many places with mass in the morning, as were the Conversion of Paul (January 25), Mary Magdalene (July 22), and the Beheading of John (August 29). In some places the observance of these days was moved to the nearest day with a regularly scheduled sermon.

Some Lutheran churches held half-day observances on other festivals as well, such as Holy Innocents (December 28), St. Lawrence (August 10), and All Saints (November 1). Other churches rejected All Saints because of its connection with prayer to the saints, a teaching the Lutherans opposed. The Catholic festivals of

Corpus Christi (the Thursday after Trinity) and the Assumption of Mary (August 15) were rarely observed in Lutheran churches,[9] although the Visitation was sometimes observed on August 15 rather than on its proper day, ostensibly to avoid keeping workers from the fields twice within a week when two holy days fell during the same week (the other being SS. Peter and Paul on June 29). The Holy Week observances of Maundy Thursday and Good Friday were mentioned in some orders but not in others. Maundy Thursday, where mentioned, was occasionally a full-day observance but more frequently a half-day one; in the 1552 order for the city of Buxtehude it was observed only if there were communicants.[10] Good Friday was nearly always a half-day observance.

Other holy days were occasionally mentioned in the church orders. In Oldenburg in 1573 and Hesse in 1574, monthly days of penitence were held. After 1650 these days were observed more widely and varied in frequency from once a month to four times per year. A few later orders mentioned a day of harvest thanksgiving to be held sometime after St. Michael. Special catechism sermons were held in some places at certain times of the year. Some orders specified the observance of days of local thanksgiving or remembrance. The 1569 order for Pomerania directed that a service be held on the anniversary of the Lutheran Reformation, which was commemorated on St. Martin's Day (November 11). This was apparently the only sixteenth-century order to note this anniversary. The 1626 order for Saxe-Coburg mentioned the annual "school festival" (*Schulfest*) or "Festum Gregorii," which included a procession through the churches, schools and streets, with singing. One of the boys was chosen bishop for the day (but he was not to ride on a horse, as things could get out of hand). Pretzels (*Bretzel*) and sweets (*Zuckerbäumen*) were carried in the procession and distributed to the children afterward in the school. Then the new pupils were greeted.[11]

Some orders mentioned ember days (*Vierzeittage*). These were not fast days in Lutheran churches, but rather the four days in the year on which the church tax was collected. They were typically Christmas, Easter, Pentecost (or John the Baptist), and St. Michael.

❖

City and Village

Many agendas had separate sections for city and village orders. The cities had a larger number of services, often with several weekday sermons divided among the various churches. Matins and Vespers were sung by pupils in the Latin schools. The services in the cities tended to be liturgically complex with a prominent place given to the choir. Because of this, city services had less participation by the rest of the congregation, and in some places the people seem to have been almost superfluous. Churches in larger villages with schools were expected to follow the city orders as closely as possible, but those in small villages and in the countryside did not have the resources needed to conduct choral services of any sort.

It is worth noting that the "cities" of which the church orders speak were hardly of the size familiar to us today. Most of the 2,800 places designated as cities in 1500 had populations of under a thousand, some well under that figure. About fifty cities in Germany had populations of 2,000 or more. According to historian Rhiman Rotz, Cologne was the largest, with 35,000 inhabitants. Lübeck and Nuremberg had around 25,000; and Augsburg, Strassburg, Ulm, and Danzig all had close to 20,000. Hamburg's population was about 12,000; and several cities had about 10,000 people, including Regensburg, Dortmund, Braunschweig, Breslau, Erfurt, Frankfurt am Main, and Magdeburg.[12] These population figures are estimates, and it is unclear how reliable any population statistics from the sixteenth century are. Nuremberg, for example, may have had as many as 40,000 people.

Latin was used in the city services in some territories, German in others, and in others a combination of both. Even where Latin was used, the sermon with its annexes, the Lord's Prayer, and the consecration were all done in German. The lessons were often read in German as well, or at least translated into German after they were read in Latin. Latin fell gradually out of use during the seventeenth and eighteenth centuries.[13] In villages where no one understood Latin, German was used exclusively, except that occasionally pastors were permitted to sing the traditional Latin introits and prefaces, especially on high feasts.

❖

Terminology

Before we can proceed to study the liturgical prescriptions in church orders in detail, it is first necessary to understand how certain terms were used in the sixteenth century.

Places of Worship

The first terms to consider are the names for the various kinds of places of worship discussed in the church orders: parish churches, filials, cathedrals, collegiate churches, monastery churches, court chapels, proprietary chapels, and hospital chapels. *Parish churches* (*Pfarrkirchen*) were churches that served a parish, generally a small city or large village, or part of a large city, or a group of small villages. A resident priest in charge of a parish was called a *Pfarrherr* (literally, "lord of the parish"); the contracted form *Pfarrer* was also used. *Filials* (*Filialen*) were churches within parish boundaries that were not parish churches, typically churches in outlying areas. They were not usually large enough to pay a pastor's salary, and so they were served by the local Pfarrherr. *Cathedrals* were the seats of bishops in pre-Reformation times. As Lutherans did not have bishops, there was no longer a qualitative distinction between cathedrals and parish churches, although cathedrals could support a larger number of resident clergy because they tended to have private sources of funding unavailable to most parish churches. Similarly well funded were many *collegiate churches* (*Stiftskirchen*), which were governed by a chapter of canons headed by a provost. The best-known collegiate church is the castle church of Wittenberg, officially called All Saints (*Allerheiligenstift*). *Monastery churches* were churches in men's and women's cloisters. Some were private, serving only the cloister; others, such as the one at the women's cloister at Isenhagen, doubled as the parish church.[14] Most accepted no new postulants after the Reformation and so were disbanded after the last remaining members of the order had died.

Court chapels (*Hofkapellen*) were private churches serving a territorial ruler; some, such as the palace church at Friedenstein in the Duchy of Gotha, doubled as the parish church.[15] *Proprietary chapels* (*Eigenkirchen*) were those funded by a private source of income or endowment; they were not technically a part of the surrounding diocese. *Hospital chapels* (*Spitale*) were those serving institutions for the old, sick, and poor. Occasionally those living near the hospital would attend services there, especially if the closest parish church was further away.

Clergy Titles

The most frequently used term in the church orders for an ordained clergyman throughout the period under study was *priest* (*Priester, Briester, Prester*). In every decade before 1570 it occurred more than all other terms combined. Thereafter other terms competed with it, notably [*Kirchen*]*diener* (servant) or its Latin form *Minister,* which were first popular in southern Germany and gradually made their way north. After 1600, *pastor* (*Pastor*), used infrequently in the sixteenth century, was found more frequently. I have used the English terms priest and pastor interchangeably. A *parson* (*Pfarrherr, Kerckhere*) was technically in charge of a parish church, but the term was also used (along with *Priester*) to refer to the priest presiding at a mass in which several priests took part. The term *Wochner* (from the German *Woche,* "week"), found in only a handful of orders, was used for churches with several priests on staff to designate the priest responsible for the services in a particular week.

An assisting priest in a parish was called a *deacon* (*Diakon, Diaconus*)[16] or *chaplain* (*Kapellan, Kaplan*).[17] The deacon had specific functions in a liturgical service, such as reading the Gospel and handling the chalice during communion. In a very few large churches with a great deal of ceremony, a *subdeacon* read the Epistle and carried the houseling cloth (a towel used to catch crumbs that might fall from the host while it was being distributed). Occasionally the term *Ministrant* was used to refer to a priest assisting during mass.

The word *preacher* (*Prediger, Predicant*) was used most often to designate the priest preaching the sermon on a given day. But some cities called priests specifically to preach in one or more churches and not to be in charge of a parish; in these cases the term refers to these people. Occasionally the word was used in a general sense as a synonym for priest.

The *superintendent* was a priest who oversaw the churches in a given region. Saxony had two kinds of superintendents, general and special, equivalent to bishops and rural deans.

Titles of Other Church Officials

Every parish had a lay assistant to the pastor called a *clerk* (*Küster, Custos, Opfermann*). This office derived from the same pre-Reformation office as the parish clerk in England and was similar to it, and so I have used this term in English. The standard translation today is "sexton," which is what the office in Germany has indeed become, but "clerk" better represents the nature of the office in the sixteenth through eighteenth centuries.

The duties of the clerk, according to the 1581 church order for Hoya, were (1) to ring the bell at the proper time; (2) to service the altar and the singing; (3) to attend with the pastor to baptisms, burials, and visiting the sick, to make certain that there is fresh water in the baptismal font, and to clean the font regularly; (4) if there is a clock tower, to attend to it each morning and evening; (5) to keep the church clean; (6) to drive from the church dogs that run around during services and bite each other; (7) to keep grazing animals away from the churchyard; (8) to know the catechism from memory, and be able to write, and sing the customary hymns in German and Latin; (9) when the pastor is ill and no substitute can be obtained, to read to the people the five chief parts of the catechism with Luther's explanation, and to examine the children in the catechism; (10) to assist the pastor in admitting and excluding people from the sacrament; (11) the clerk shall be dismissed if he does not attend the Lord's Supper after being warned; (12) to ring the prayer bell (*Betglocke*) each morning, noon, and evening; (13) to dress as befits a servant of the church; (14) not to sell beer or brandy, on threat of dismissal; and (15) not to set himself against the pastor. The somewhat cryptic requirement to "service the singing" refers to the task of leading the singing of the congregation.[18] The 1718 order for the Lutheran congregation in London additionally specified that the clerk select the hymns after the pastor has informed him of the text for the day, announce the hymns to the congregation, keep a register of those baptized and married, deliver to the pastor after the sermon a list of those to be prayed for, and report problems in the lives of the congregation's members.[19] In Braunschweig and other cities he also managed the church's books.[20]

In areas without schools, the clerk, as the most educated man in the village after the pastor, often took it upon himself to assist pupils who had a particular desire to learn to read and write. This not only produced an educated peasantry but also made the clerk's job of teaching the catechism easier. In areas with German schools, the schoolmaster (*Schulmeister*) undertook this task. The schoolmaster also led the unison singing of the boys' choir, and some orders assigned to him the clerk's task of leading congregational singing; others specified that this was to be done by either the schoolmaster or the clerk.[21] Generally, where there was a school choir to lead the congregation, the schoolmaster led the choir and the choir led the people. But where there was no choir, the clerk led the singing, thus substituting for the choir.

Occasionally the term *lead singer* or *precentor* (*Vorsinger*) was used to refer to the clerk or other person leading the singing in a particular service, although a document from Dinkelsbühl dated 1573 considered the precentor a position unto itself, to be filled by someone who (1) had the pastor's approval; (2) was a German schoolmaster, if possible; (3) if no German schoolmaster was available, was at least a good citizen; (4) was of good character and not critical of the church; (5) was willing to work for a low salary; and (6) was accomplished in the psalms and had a pleasing voice.[22]

Some cities had Latin schools, in which the instruction was done in that language. During the second half of the sixteenth century, all large and medium-sized cities in Saxony had Latin schools,[23] headed by a *rector* (*Rektor*). Where he was the only teacher, he taught all subjects, including music, and led the singing of the boys' choir in the church.

If the school was large enough, it had a second teacher, the *cantor* (*Kantor*). The title (from the Latin *cantus,* song) shows that the cantor was particularly responsible for the singing in the church and in the school, in which he taught the principles of music and singing and often other subjects as well. During the sixteenth century, schools had anywhere from two to six hours of music instruction per week, with most having four or five.[24] In most places from 1570 to 1730 cantors had no responsibility for composing music; Leipzig, at the time of J. S. Bach, and a few other large cities were exceptions.[25] Court chapels had cantors as well, and there the term was originally used to mean any singer, not necessarily the choir director, as when Paul Köler was installed in 1572 in Wolfenbüttel as "Kantor oder Sänger."[26] Prior to the middle of the sixteenth century the rector served the function of the cantor in all but the largest cities, but during the second half of the century cantorates developed in a number of smaller cities.[27] It was not unusual in the early decades for the cantorate to serve as a stepping stone to the pastorate, and in many places in Saxony and Thuringia during the sixteenth and seventeenth centuries more than half the cantors eventually became pastors.[28] In general the cantorate as an institution was more important in northern and middle Germany than in the south, where the influence of Calvin and Zwingli had a detrimental impact on the perceived importance of music.[29]

Some cities had an assistant cantor or *subcantor* (*succentor*). Occasionally in earlier documents one finds the terms cantor and succentor used interchangeably to refer to the same person.[30] During the sixteenth century the subcantor came to refer to a third schoolteacher who handled the simpler hymn and chant singing while the cantor directed the more complex figural music.[31] Zwickau had already adopted the two-cantor system by 1529, and the practice spread throughout middle Germany in the late sixteenth and seventeenth centuries. In 1583 Halle, with 620 pupils in the school, had four cantors.[32] Ulm had three cantors during the seventeenth century, called *Cantor, Succentor,* and *Vicesuccentor.*[33]

Churches with organs had an *organist* as well. Often the school rector or another teacher played the organ, otherwise the organist was a layman who was also employed outside the church. The social status of the organist who was not also a teacher was slightly lower than that of the cantor, for the cantor was educated, but the organist merely trained.

Choral Ensembles

The boys' choir from the school served as the church choir throughout Germany. There were actually two types of these choirs, one comprising all the boys in the school, or at least those in the upper grades,[34] and the other consisting of the musically most accomplished boys. This latter select group was sometimes called the *chorus musicus* or *chorus symphoniacus* to distinguish it from the larger group, especially after it began to sing polyphonic music; but the most commonly found terms for both choirs are simply *Chor* (choir) and *Schüler* (schoolboys). Cities with both Latin and German schools were served by choirs from both, with the Latin school choir being more prestigious. The Öhringen school order of circa 1582 assigned Saturday Vespers and the Friday sermon to the Latin school, and Monday and Wednesday sermons and the biweekly evening service in the hospital to the German school. Both were responsible for Sunday services.[35]

Both the *chorus musicus* and the larger group sang exclusively *choraliter*, that is, unison chant, in most places during the first half of the century. But in many places after about 1550 (earlier in some places) older boys and young men were added to the select choir to sing alto, tenor, and bass, and so music could then be performed *figuraliter*; that is, in parts with notes of differing rhythmic values.[36] Because boys' voices normally did not deepen until age 17 or 18, losing experienced singers who could navigate a more complicated soprano part was not a concern.[37] The older boys whose voices had changed were sometimes called *Adjuvanten* (helpers) or *Schulgesellen* (a term referring to schoolboys approximately in their mid to late teens; this latter term was also used for older boys who performed nonmusical tasks in the school).

As these boys became adults and joined the ranks of the townspeople, some continued to sing with the choir. At first this was done on an informal basis, but soon the Adjuvanten joined together into formal organizations called *Adjuvantengesellschaften* or, more commonly, *Kantoreien*. Rautenstrauch gives an excellent overview of the *Kantorei*, which is summarized as follows: The Kantoreien, directed by the cantor, comprised fifteen to forty members, depending on the size of the city. The members were from all professions: pastors, councillors, church leaders, doctors, pharmacists, rectors, cantors, teachers, and others. Membership fees were charged all members upon entrance to the Kantorei (in most cases). Nonsingers and nonmusicians were included among the ranks of the Kantorei; they paid an additional fee to be excused from musical service. This entitled them to festive funerals. Leading citizens, pastors from surrounding communities, and even nobility from the area took advantage of this. In Chemnitz in 1610 only fifteen of the forty-nine members were singers, and in 1617 only twenty-five of sixty-two. The usual term for those who sang was *Adjuvant,* indicating that the group was seen not as a second independent choir but as support for the schoolboys' choir. Occasionally a musical examination was required to be considered an Adjuvant. Each rehearsal of the Kantorei closed with a drink and a snack to which the wives of the members and the *Discantisten* (choirboys) were also invited; these were called *collationes.* In addition to their musical efforts, many Kantoreien provided a form of disability insurance for members unable to work. Kantoreien were especially popular in Saxony, and by 1600 even villages had them.[38]

The distinction between the Kantorei and the *Chorus musicus* was not always obvious. In mid-Germany in the second half of the sixteenth century the terms Chorus musicus, Chorus symphoniacus, and Kantorei seem to have been about equivalent, at least in terms of their repertoire and function.[39] But the Kantoreien were generally more formally organized, with bylaws and membership fees. In the seventeenth century the two groups differentiated themselves further as musical performance (as opposed to singing for devotional purposes) became more important in the church and instrumentalists accompanied the singing more frequently.

The citizen's Kantorei should not be confused with the court Kantorei (*Hofkantorei*), which comprised professional singers who performed both sacred and secular music. The court organist was also usually a member, and other instrumentalists were eventually accepted into membership as well.[40]

Many cities also had one other group of singers, called the *Kurrende*. The origin of the word is obscure; it may come from *curro* (to run) or from *corrado* (originally "to scrape together"; later also "to beg in the street").[41] The group's main function was to raise money for school tuition for its members; they did this by walking the streets and singing in front of houses in anticipation of a financial reward. This was done in various cities anywhere from several times a year to once each week. Schools made a special effort to ensure that the poorest scholars were able to sing with the Kurrende. Extra money was earned through singing for funeral processions; this was parallel to the extraliturgical function of the *chorus musicus*, who earned extra income by singing for weddings and official functions.[42] In some cities the *chorus musicus* also went on fundraising walks.[43]

Most sources indicate that the Kurrende sang primarily or exclusively choraliter in German, but in seventeenth-century Speyer the group sang both German psalms and Latin pieces, choraliter and figuraliter.[44] And already in 1588 the hymnal of Georg Weber of Weissenfels, published in Erfurt, was (according to the preface) intended specifically for *Kurrenden,* so that they might sing in four parts, as was already customary in other cities.[45] There is no question, though, that the repertoire was not so complex as that of the chorus musicus, nor was it as well rehearsed.[46] Apparently the Kurrende performed no liturgical function, except insofar as its members participated whenever the entire school sang in church.

Liturgical and Musical Terms

The usual term for a song or hymn sung in the church is *Gesang.* The term *Lied* means the same thing, although it is found less frequently. A *Psalm* is a metrical psalm, particularly a psalm or hymn of Luther; the term occasionally refers to metrical songs whose texts are not translations of a psalm. I generally use the English word *hymn* to translate all of the foregoing, although I occasionally use song or psalm in order to translate the German original more precisely. The German word Psalm can also, especially in connection with the Daily Office, refer to a prose psalm sung to a psalm tone. A *Choral* is a Gregorian chant, and a *Hymnus* is a Latin office hymn.

Chorgesang is not a choral hymn but, rather, the Liturgy of the Hours, also called the Divine Office. It is a generic term for the offices of Vespers, Compline, Matins, Lauds, Prime, Terce, Sext, and None. *Kirchenmusik* and *Musik* usually refer since the seventeenth century to music performed by choir with instruments, especially to what today is referred to as a sacred concerto or a cantata. The verb *mu-*

sicieren likewise implies the use of instruments. The *Gloria* refers to the phrase "Gloria in excelsis Deo" only; the remainder is called the *Et in terra*. Likewise, the *Credo* consists only of the phrase "Credo in unum Deum"; the remainder is called the *Patrem*. When the Creed is sung in German it is called the *Glaube;* in almost all cases Luther's version is meant. As pointed out in chapter 2, a sermon (*Predigt*) can refer either to the homily, to the homily with surrounding prayers, hymns, announcements, etc. (the *Kanzeldienst*), or to the entire service containing the sermon.

The verb *lesen* (to read), as in "The pastor reads a collect," includes both singing and speaking; a more specific verb is required in order to differentiate between the two meanings. Likewise, *sprechen* (to speak) does not exclude singing (except in phrases such as "The pastor sings or speaks a collect."). It was not unusual in some parts of Germany to sing the Epistle and Gospel, even as late as 1784.[47]

❖

Size of the Choir

The number of singers in the choirs varied from place to place. In Zwickau in 1566 there was a chorus musicus of 36 scholars, but in 1608 only 21. In Dresden there were 36 under Prince August. In 1581 there were 12 at the Thomasschule in Leipzig, and the same number in Annaberg and Coburg in 1605. In Nordhausen in 1583 there were 30 scholars in the chorus musicus; and in Erfurt in 1571 the number was not allowed to go over 60.[48] In Öhringen around 1582 only 15 boys at a time were to be used in weekday services, and a different set was to be used before and after the sermon, during which the boys were dismissed. This prevented any one group from missing too much instruction.[49] Martin Ruhnke, who provides summary tables of the vocal and instrumental composition of court chapels throughout Germany in the sixteenth century, reports choirs containing anywhere from two to two dozen boys, plus altos, tenors, and basses.[50]

In the Kurrende there were between 138 and 186 in Zittau in 1573–1574, 32 at the Thomasschule in Leipzig in 1581, 60 in Nordhausen in 1583, ca. 80 in Halberstadt in 1589, and 20 in Coburg in 1605.[51] In Erfurt in 1624 four choirs went through the city as Kurrenden, each with twelve singers, a prefect (an older boy who led the group), and his substitute. The choirs were the elite (*Elite*), the poor (*Armen*), the advanced (*Vorgeschrittenen*) and the beginners (*Anfänger*).[52]

❖

Location of the Choir

The location of the choir in the sixteenth century was the *Chor*. In modern German, Chor frequently refers to the west gallery or organ loft, but the church orders used the word in its older meaning of the portion of the chancel nearest the nave. It was often used to indicate where the communicants were to assemble after the sermon, and two agendas directed the schoolboys to stand to one side so that the communicants were not hindered.[53] Several orders noted that lessons at Matins and Vespers were read by boys who had assembled in the Chor.[54]

Confusion might arise because some orders referred to the people as being below the choir. This was the case in Harlingerland 1574, which stated that certain hymns were sung during the communion in alternation, in the "choir and down in the church."[55] The 1573 order for Hoya used exactly the same wording, but the 1581 order made it clear that the choir stood at the front of the church.[56] It seems unlikely that the choir would have moved from the gallery back to the chancel between 1573 and 1581, so one must conclude that "down" in the church meant down from the chancel. Danzig 1612 directed that those singing figural music go into the Chor to sing, then move "down" into the church to hear the sermon, moving back again after the sermon.[57] This makes sense only if the choir had been standing in the chancel, from where they could not see the preacher in the pulpit; if they had been in the west gallery there would have been no reason to move.

The 1576 order for Schweinfurt, which was written in both German and Latin, mentioned two possible places for the choir, one "above" and one "below."[58] A footnote in Sehling indicates that these refer to the west gallery and the chancel, adding that the Latin version makes it clear that the usual place for the choir was in the gallery with the organ. But this interpretation is inexplicable, inasmuch as the Latin clearly states that the choir assembled "in the choir below," omitting the choir "above" referred to in the German.[59] One can only conclude that the editors misread the Latin original. The choir "above" must in fact refer to the *Chorempore,* a raised platform between the chancel and nave. Such platforms were installed in a number of places during the sixteenth century to hold the choir, and Niemöller reports that one was erected in Schweinfurt in 1562.[60]

The choir was directed by the schoolmaster, cantor, succentor, or an older boy from the school. The sources show differing methods of leading the choir. In Sondershausen in 1574 the choir divided itself into two parts, each singing from one stand on which a large choir book stood. The cantor led the choir either through his own singing or by beating with hand movements.[61] A woodcut of a 1532 Catholic mass shows eight singers in front of a large choir book positioned at the top of the step leading up to the chancel; one singer is marking time with his left hand.[62] An illustration of a Lutheran service in or near Danzig at the end of the sixteenth century shows a choir of perhaps eight boys and young men dressed in peasant garb standing at the base of the steps leading into the chancel and facing the front. A cantor with a stick in his right hand is standing with them and pointing at the notes in a large choir book.[63] In 1619 Daniel Friderici implied that some cantors, at least, gave an audible beat when he instructed,

> Rule 14. In singing, the beat should by no means be heard, but only seen, or where possible only observed and felt. In this respect those *cantores* who beat with the choir stick so that pieces fly away from it and who think the singing is correctly conducted when they only beat down in a manly fashion, just as when they thresh straw, show that they know nothing about proper music.

Rule 15. In conducting, not just two or three boys should be directed, but the entire choir. Thus, *cantores* err when they have only one or two boys standing before them, and they beat time only to them and let the other *Concentores* follow along behind, just like a shepherd with his dogs.[64]

The choir moved from the chancel to the west gallery during the seventeenth and especially the eighteenth centuries as figural music accompanied by instruments became standard. In Leipzig, for example, Bach's choir sang from the west gallery.[65]

❖

The Organ and Other Instruments

The provisions in the church orders concerning the organ are so extensive that they will be discussed in a separate chapter. For now, it is enough to point out that very few churches had organs in the sixteenth century; and that in churches that did have them, its role consisted of (1) playing every other verse of certain parts of the liturgy, that is, alternating verses with the choir; (2) playing preludes to certain parts of the liturgy; and (3) rarely, substituting for the choir by playing certain parts of the liturgy by itself. Organ music before and after services was unknown at this time, as was the accompaniment of congregational singing. The latter developed gradually during the seventeenth and eighteenth centuries.

If the church orders are any indication, other instruments were rarely used in parish churches during the sixteenth century. The only reference I have found is to services at St. Michael's in Lüneburg, where in 1558 the city's official instrumentalists participated at Christmas by playing trumpets and zinks. The following year they played on at least five festivals, and in 1562 on about ten festivals. By 1584 at least one musician was playing every Sunday.[66]

❖

Attendance at Services

It has already been pointed out that poor attendance at the Sunday afternoon catechism service was a source of consternation to many pastors, with few people, if any, present.[67] Numerous reports testify that attendance at most other services was not much better; in fact, the only service at which attendance did not suffer was the principal sermon on Sunday morning. In places with schools, the boys sang for Vespers and Matins, and they were therefore required to attend; but Matins, even on Sundays, was considered a school exercise, and there was no expectation that the laity would attend.

Saturday Vespers was another matter: those communing the following day were supposed to attend the service and go afterward to confession, but this did not always happen. The visitation of Hohenlohe in 1582 discovered that only a small portion of the communicants were actually attending Vespers the previous evening.

Some of them appeared only afterward to register. The pastors were instructed to discourage this.[68] Pastors in the principality of Vohenstrauss were directed in 1586 to hold Vespers every week; in the event that no one came, they were still to ring the bell and read a chapter from the Bible.[69] Several church orders specified that a German lesson be read or a German hymn be sung at Vespers only if laity were present.[70]

In most places the Sunday morning sermon was apparently well attended, but there were exceptions. In Prussia and Kurland the populace was required to attend church services. This was enforced either by two men who counted those in attendance or by calling the roll after the sermon. These measures appear to have been largely ineffective. Visitor Paul Speratus reported to Duke Albrecht after the 1538 visitation that the people did not attend church. An order of 1543 reported that the people rarely attended church, and a large portion never attended. In 1562 there was a report that the people of Königsberg rarely attended church, and at weekday sermons in large churches barely twenty people were present. The visitation records from the 1570s and 1580s present a similar picture. Knights and village officials presented public announcements at the same time as the Sunday service, and the nobility went on hunts at that time. Public houses were popular as well. An order of 1543 had prohibited these things during services; dancing during the catechism service was also prohibited. Also in 1543 a system of fines was established for those who did not attend church. Those who were forced to attend services under these regulations often left early or fell asleep during the service. In several places ushers were employed to awaken sleepers.[71]

In the seventeenth century several places enacted laws requiring people to attend services. The 1602 visitation report for Uebigau in Saxony noted that attendance at church was generally quite good: the few that had been found reaping in the fields during the service had spent a week in jail.[72] In some places the sabbath rest was also enforced: in one town in Württemberg around 1670 only absolutely essential work was permitted on Sundays. No work was allowed that could be performed on another day. Baking or washing the goose was punishable. A woman who washed her windows on Sunday and then complained about the pastor was jailed. Games, dancing, and music were also forbidden on Sunday. Swearing was punishable at any time. In the public house, where swearing was common, a fine box was installed where the guilty party could immediately pay his fine. Since the money collected belonged to the proprieter, he had a vested interest in seeing the laws against swearing enforced![73]

I have been careful to note that it was the Sunday morning sermon, not the mass, that was well attended. This is because numerous sources complain that many people spent only the middle hour of the three-hour mass in church; that is, they arrived just before the sermon and left immediately afterward. Church orders from the sixteenth, seventeenth, and eighteenth centuries are full of instructions to preachers to admonish the people regularly that they are to remain in church until the service has ended, apparently to no avail whatsoever. The Steuerwald/Peine order of 1561 instructed the pastor that after he has read the exhortation to the communicants he should exhort those communing to remain in the church and not exit like cattle right after the sermon (an exception was made for pregnant women and those with small children).[74] Ulm 1747 contained a reminder that people should arrive on time, and Magdeburg 1685 and Holstein-Plön 1732 directed both that people not remain outside after the service has started and that they not leave before the communion.[75]

Other contemporary sources besides church orders bear witness to the problem. The general synod in Gotha in 1645 solved it by installing ushers to stop people from leaving until after the consecration was read.[76] A sermon published in 1632 by Cunrad Dieterich noted that most of the congregation did not enter the church in time for the singing but remained outside until a signal was given that the preacher was about to enter the pulpit.[77] In 1667 Theophilus Grossgebauer of Rostock decried the custom that "in large cities the people storm into the church as the bell strikes the hour for the preacher to mount the pulpit; then when the sermon ends they storm out again."[78] The orders from Saxony mention none of this, yet Johann Friedrich Leibniz noted in 1694 that the churches in Leipzig are "quite empty" at the beginning of the mass, and Christian Gerber confirmed this for Saxony in general in 1732.[79] It was still a problem in 1778, when the anonymous author of *Etwas von der Liturgie* reported that people tended to come too late even to sing the Creed and that many left immediately after the sermon, even during the prayers.[80] The ones who did arrive early often came to socialize, as Tanya Kevorkian reports for eighteenth-century Leipzig: "People observed one another and greeted their neighbours as they arrived. From their balcony pews, men, including students (who had their own balcony), could observe the women below. They also courted young unmarried women by visiting them at their pews."[81]

Weekday sermons seem to have been attended only by the very devout, and it is unclear whether there were many people in church even on holy days falling during the week. In the village of Bredelem in the Duchy of Braunschweig-Wolfenbüttel those conducting the ecclesiastical visitation of 1583 complained that the people did not cease their work on apostles' days, and very few came to the weekday sermon and litany.[82]

❖

Length of Services

A number of church orders indicated how long services were supposed to last, and in this there was virtual unanimity throughout Germany during the entire period under study. Mass on Sundays and holy days was to last three hours, the sermon with its annexes occupying the middle hour. Sunday early sermon (where it was held) lasted about an hour, as did Sunday Matins. The sermon at a Sunday afternoon catechism service was supposed to last about a half hour; the length of the rest of the service varied according to whether there was an actual Vespers, concerted music, or an examination of the youth in the catechism. Weekday sermons were to last forty-five minutes to an hour, with the sermon proper lasting thirty to forty-five minutes. Weekday Matins, Vespers, and prayer services without sermon lasted about a half hour. For some reason, the orders did not give the length of a typical

Saturday Vespers, but an hour or slightly more seems about right, with the sermon lasting a half hour or a little longer. A handful of orders gave slightly shorter times for some of the services.

The length of the principal service on Sunday could vary depending on the number of communicants. Where there were no communicants, it is reasonable to assume that the service would not last much longer than two and a quarter hours. But in the cities of Saxony, Christian Gerber reported in 1732, the starting time of 7:00 A.M. was retained in the winter for the mass (it would normally have been 8:00 A.M. in winter) because there were often very many communicants, and the service had to be out in time for the noon service to begin. Such a mass, lasting nearly five hours, appears to have been an unusual case, and in most places the masses appear to have stayed fairly close to the prescribed time of three hours.

It might appear, given the number of services and their length, that the ecclesiastical authorities had little concern for the stamina of the people. In fact, quite a few church orders had provisions such as "the following exhortation may be read if time permits" or "if time is short, the hymn may be omitted." This was of particular concern in winter, when the temperature in the unheated church became intolerable.

The part of the service most frequently omitted because of time constraints was the Preface together with the following Sanctus. In the church order prepared for Wittenberg as a result of the ecclesiastical visitation of 1533, the length of the Preface was specifically given as the reason for omitting it: "[the Preface] may generally be omitted in order to proceed more quickly to communion, which is the only thing necessary."[83] The Preface itself was not particularly long, but the succeeding Sanctus, which would have to have been sung before the Verba (instead of during the distribution), could have been, especially if it was sung polyphonically. Even when it was chanted it could have taken several minutes, depending on which setting was used. This would not have been so bad when the Consecration and Elevation had been performed during it, but when these ritual actions were moved to a later point in the mass the Sanctus could easily have seemed to drag on. The church orders for Prussia 1525 and Riga 1530 specified that a Sanctus "with few notes" be used.[84] Similar wording was used in several orders to specify that the Alleluia be performed without its long concluding *jubilus*. This is as likely to have been due to the lack of choirs able to sing it as it was to time constraints.

Luther himself frequently showed concern over the length of services. In *Concerning the Order of Public Worship* (1523) he wrote about the Liturgy of the Hours: "In brief, let everything be completed in one hour or whatever time seems desirable; for one must not overload souls or weary them, as was the case until now in monasteries and convents, where they burdened themselves like mules." Likewise, in the *Formula missae* (1523) he wrote: "If anything should be changed, the bishop may reduce the great length [of the services] according to his own judgment so that three Psalms may be sung for Matins and three for Vespers with one or two responsories." And in *On the Councils and the Church* (1539) he expressed the conviction that liturgical ceremonies must not become burdensome and that they must not be seen as a requirement for blessedness.[85]

51

❖

Demeanor at Services

I have already noted that sleeping during church was a concern to the ecclesiastical authorities. Talking was also an occasional concern, as Cunrad Dieterich noted in his 1632 sermon.[86] In the seventeenth century, the authorities became aware that many people would not understand the long liturgical singing by the choir (especially if it were in Latin) and the presentation of figural and organ music, so they encouraged the laity to purchase devotional materials and bring them to church so that they could read them during these moments.[87] Dieterich, however, discouraged the use of devotional books during what was supposed to be congregational singing, complaining that many, when they arrived for the singing, did not sing along but rather read a book instead.[88] These books were quite popular all over Germany into the eighteenth century: two, the *Leipziger Kirchen-Andachten* of Johann Friedrich Leibniz (Leipzig, 1694) and the *Leipziger Kirchen-Staat, das ist deutlicher Unterricht vom Gottes-Dienst in Leipzig* of Friedrich Groschuff (Leipzig, 1710), are especially useful to modern musicologists in that they provide extensive details of the Leipzig services shortly before Bach's arrival. These two books are unusual in this respect; most such books contain only devotional material without a description of the services. Bach himself made good use of the common practice by having the texts of his cantatas printed and sold so that churchgoers could follow along while the music was performed.

Another book that people brought with them to church was the hymnal. This, however, did not happen until the seventeenth and eighteenth centuries (the exact date varied from place to place, and frequently some churchgoers brought hymnals while others did not). During the sixteenth century hymnals were not in common use except in a few cities (see chapter 6).

It is difficult to determine whether the people were able to sit during services. Most places seem to have had pews by around 1600, at least for some of the members. The pastor at Gemünden complained in 1628 that he often preached to empty pews and chairs during the week.[89] An unidentified woodcut of the Penitents' Church in Herman Dechent's *Church History of Frankfurt am Main since the Reformation* shows the congregation listening to the sermon. There are closed pews on either side of the main floor with people sitting, but the center consists of a very wide aisle in which people are standing or sitting on chairs; some people are standing in the balconies as well. Fewer than half the available seats are taken. The date 1653 appears in the woodcut itself.[90]

Smaller churches might have lacked pews for some time. In 1608 the people in the Saxon villages of Grosskorga, Grosswick, Moschwitz, and Splauen complained that their women had no pews where they could sit in church.[91] In many places the pews were owned by the members who paid for them, and only they were entitled to use them. Martin Brecht reports that in Württemberg in the eighteenth century pews were regularly bought and sold.[92] The Saxe-Coburg order of 1626 reported that people had been complaining that pews (or chairs; the word is *Stühle*) had been erected in church where they blocked the view of the pulpit and altar, especially when they had been placed in the aisles. The order therefore directed that no one was to erect pews in church without the consent of the pastor and church leaders. These pews were to remain the property of the owner until he or she died, at which time they reverted to the church. The owner's heirs were then allowed to use the pew upon payment of a reasonable fee; if they did not so inform the church within thirty days the church could sell the pew to another person. These rules applied only to pews erected by private individuals; pews of nobility, city councillors, and others in public office were excluded.[93]

The Saxe-Lauenburg order of 1585 also contained the admonition that pews were not to be erected so as to block the vision or hearing of the people behind them. Here, the clerk was to unlock all locked and empty pews at the beginning of the sermon so that they could be occupied by others; unlocked pews might be occupied by others once the sermon had begun as well.[94] This was the sixteenth-century equivalent of opening the reserved seats at halftime. Tanya Kevorkian has indicated a similar practice for Leipzig churches in the eighteenth century.[95]

❖

Conclusion

The church orders present a complex tapestry of liturgical life among early Lutherans, including the Daily Office, mass, and catechism instruction, all interwoven into the fabric of the church year. But this does not necessarily indicate that society as a whole was particularly devout. Attendance at services was a problem in some places, and tardiness and leaving early were ubiquitous. One cannot help but gain from the church orders the impression that the typical service in many cities during the sixteenth through eighteenth centuries was something of a spectacle, with a fine show presented by the clergy and musicians, but one that only the participants and a few others could understand or appreciate. The rest of the people either read during the service out of boredom or avoided as much of the service as they could manage without being called to task. In fact, this very criticism was leveled by some Germans in the late seventeenth and eighteenth centuries, as we shall see in chapter 7.

CHAPTER 4

❖

Choral and Congregational Singing
in the Church Orders

As we have seen in chapter 1, the liturgy in Wittenberg during Luther's lifetime was sung mostly by the choir. Was this true of other parts of Germany as well? The church's printed and manuscript liturgies can help us answer that question, although they are not always as detailed as one might wish. Still, taken as a whole they shed quite a bit of light on our inquiry.

Over 250 church orders and private agendas appeared between 1523 and 1750 that contain enough liturgical details to draw conclusions regarding who sang what. Fully 172 contain instructions for the mass, including 134 orders from the sixteenth century alone.[1] The volume of material renders it impossible to discuss the contents of the orders in any great detail in this chapter, so I have placed most of the raw data in appendixes 3 and 4 and discussed it below. Appendix 3 summarizes the contents of appendix 4, which gives detailed information on the mass liturgy from each church order.

❖

Mass on Sundays and Holy Days

Table 4.1 gives for each part of the mass the percentages of choral versus congregational singing found in church orders appearing between 1523 and 1600. It is immediately apparent that relatively few orders (on average, about 33 percent) specified the mode of performance (choral or congregational). It is also apparent that which mode was specified depends greatly on the part of the liturgy. Of the tradi-

Table 4.1. Choral versus congregational singing in the Lutheran mass

Part of mass liturgy	Total orders[b]	Number of orders specifying mode of performance			Percentage of all orders in which mode of performance is certain[a]	
		Choral[c]	Congregational[d]	Either or both[e]	Choral[f]	Congregational[g]
Introit	163	38	8	17	35.6	5.5
Kyrie	138	24	0	6	44.6	0
Gloria (Et in terra)	137	25	2	14	31.0	3.3
Gradual	125	26	6	8	34.0	8.4
Sequence	67	14	0	1	71.6	0
Creed (Patrem)	157	8	26	32	15.9	24.8
Hymn before sermon	35	2	6	0	5.7	17.1
Hymn after sermon	73	4	9	2	7.5	13.0
Sanctus	98	20	2	5	41.8	3.1
Agnus Dei	104	19	11	5	33.7	12.5
Communion hymns	140	10	46	8	8.6	33.6
Dismissal hymn	43	4	8	0	9.3	18.6

The numbers in the table are derived from appendix 3, which contains similar information, but in more detail and for the entire period 1523–1780.

[a]The percentages do not total 100 because the mode of performance cannot be determined in many cases and because some orders specify both congregational and choral performance for certain items.

[b]This column gives the count of orders (out of 169 original editions and reprints) in which each part of the liturgy is present (whether it is to be sung every week or only occasionally). This count represents the sum of the first three rows of columns "L," "G," "L/G," "L-G," and "√" of each table in appendix 3. Only the first three rows of the tables in appendix 3 have been used in order to exclude church orders appearing after 1600.

[c]The number of orders explicitly specifying choral performance is the sum of the first three rows of column "Ch" of each table in appendix 3.

[d]The number of orders explicitly specifying congregational performance is the sum of the first three rows of column "Co" of each table in appendix 3.

[e]The number of orders in which either a choice of choral or congregational performance is given or which direct that both be done, either sequentially or in stanza-by-stanza alternation, is the sum of the first three rows of column "C/C" of each table in appendix 3.

[f]The percentage of orders in which it is certain the singing was intended to be choral was calculated by summing the first three rows of columns "Ch" and "Ch/L" of each table in appendix 3, then adding to this one-half the sum of the first three rows of column "L-G" and dividing the result by the "total orders" in the above table. Choral performance is assumed either if the order specifically mentions it or if the order specifies that a part of the liturgy be sung in Latin, necessitating performance by the choir.

[g]The percentage of orders in which it is certain the singing was intended to be congregational was calculated by summing the first three rows of column "Co" of each table in appendix 3, then adding to this one-half the sum of the first three rows of column "L-G" and dividing the result by the "total orders" in the above table.

tional parts of the liturgy, only the Creed was to be sung more frequently by the entire congregation than by the choir. All the additional hymns—before and after the sermon, during the communion and at the end of the service—were sung more frequently by the entire congregation.

It is no surprise that the hymns before and after the sermon were congregational, as this had been the practice even before the Reformation (see Chapter 2). The origin of congregational singing in the rest of the mass is less clear and will be discussed as we consider each part of the liturgy in turn.

Introit

In his Latin Mass Luther had already suggested replacing the Introit, which used a single psalm verse sandwiched between an antiphon and its repetition, with an entire psalm. He put the idea into practice in the *German Mass,* which used a full prose psalm in place of the Introit. From there it was a simple step to make use of metrical psalm paraphrases such as Psalm 51 (*Erbarm dich mein, o Herre Gott*) or Psalm 130 (*Aus tiefer Not schrei ich zu dir*), to name the two most popular.[2] Even more popular were the two German versions of the sequence *Veni sancte spiritus: Komm, Heiliger Geist, Herre Gott* and *Nun bitten wir den Heiligen Geist.* In some places they replaced the Introit; in others they preceded it. In the latter case, the Latin version was also occasionally used. Several orders directed that two or three of the above be used on alternating Sundays, or that a choice be made among them.

The language of the Introit was about equally divided between Latin and German in the sixteenth-century orders.[3] When it was in German, there was often no indication of whether the choir or the whole congregation was to sing it, although the numbers in the above table suggest that choral performance was more frequent. This is hardly surprising given the evidence for tardiness presented in chapter 3: the people could hardly sing if they had not yet arrived in church. Congregational singing was indicated, or a choice given between choral and congregational singing, a total of 25 times. Of these, 19 are in orders from the southernmost third of Germany, a disproportionate number considering that only one-third of all sixteenth-century orders (56 of 169) were from that region. This may have been due to the influence of the nearby Swiss Reformation, which championed congregational singing much more than did the Lutherans to the north.

In all parts of Germany, congregational singing was more frequently specified in connection with services in villages, where there was not likely to be a choir. This is true for other parts of the liturgy as well. Two orders, Brandenburg-Nuremberg 1533 and Palatinate-Neuberg 1543, directed that the people sing only when there is no choir, a reflection of the preeminence given to choral singing among some Lutherans. Veit Dietrich's handbook for rural churches (Nuremberg, 1543), the only private agenda to gain wide circulation, directed that the schoolboys sing the Introit, but where there were no schools and therefore no people that could sing in Latin, a German hymn was sung in its place. If the people could not even do that, then the pastor was exhorted to teach them.[4]

Kyrie

Only six orders specified even optional singing of the Kyrie by the people. Veit Dietrich's handbook (1543, 1556, 1563, 1569) directed the pastor to read the Kyrie and Et in terra in Latin; then the schoolboys or the people, whichever was customary, sang it in Latin or German.[5] Nördlingen 1544 assigned the two "Kyrie eleisons" to the choir and the "Christe eleison" to the people.[6] Rothenburg ob der Tauber 1559 repeated the text of Dietrich's handbook word for word.

Gloria

The Gloria and Et in terra were sung in German much more often than the Kyrie, but choral performance was still the rule. By far the most frequently used German Gloria was *Allein Gott in der Höh sei Ehr* by Nicolaus Decius, mentioned seventy-seven times in sixteenth-century orders. Originally in Low German, it was quickly translated into High German and became popular throughout Germany. By contrast, Luther's *All Ehr und Lob soll Gottes sein,* written in High German, is mentioned only seven times in sixteenth-century agendas.

Gradual, Alleluia, and Sequence

In light of the Council of Trent's decision to abolish all but four sequences, we are accustomed to considering the sequence the most expendable of the three liturgical items following the Epistle. But it was not so to the early Lutherans. Of the sixteenth-century Lutheran church orders (first editions only), 67 mentioned the sequence, 55 the Alleluia, and only 31 the Gradual. Only one order, Halberstadt 1591, specified that all three be performed; and even this case is tenuous, as the Gradual was replaced by an organ piece. The most typical formulation was Alleluia plus sequence, found in 25 orders (some specify the sequence only for festivals). The sequence alone was found in 22 orders (often with a German psalm sung either in addition to or optionally in place of the sequence). Ten orders specified the Gradual plus Alleluia, eight the Alleluia alone, and seven the Alleluia or Sequence. This distribution is borne out by Lutheran missals of the period. Johannes Keuchenthal's *KirchenGesenge Latinisch und Deudsch* (Wittenberg, 1573) contained Alleluias for every Sunday and holy day except Judica, Maundy Thursday, the Conversion of St. Paul, St. Matthias, and Mary Magdalene.[7] Sequences or hymns sung in place of the sequence were given for all but six days. But only two Graduals appeared: *Christus factus est pro nobis* to be sung on Judica and Maundy Thursday and *Haec est dies* to be sung on Easter.

Seventy-nine orders directed that a German psalm or hymn be sung for the Alleluia or Gradual, either in place of the Latin chants, in addition to them, or optionally in addition to them. Most orders did not mention specific hymns to be sung, but of those that did, the most popular was the German Litany (nine orders), followed closely by the Lord's Prayer, *Vater unser im Himmelreich* (seven orders). Fifteen orders explicitly directed the people to sing at this point, including eight in which congregational singing was an optional replacement for choral song.

Not every Sunday and holy day had its own proper sequence; that for Trinity, for example, was performed throughout the long post-Trinity season. Some orders directed that the sequence be performed on the chief feasts and their seasons (e.g., Easter and the seven weeks following); others specified its performance only on the feast itself. Particularly noteworthy are the sequences on the three chief feasts (Christmas, Easter, and Pentecost), which were sung in alternation with German paraphrases in the form of *Leisen*, religious folk songs in which each stanza ends with the word *Kyrieleis*, a contraction of *Kyrie eleison* (Lord, have mercy). The *Leise* for the Christmas sequence *Grates nunc omnes* was *Gelobet seist du, Jesus Christ*; for the Easter sequence *Victimae paschali*, either *Christ ist erstanden* or *Christ lag in Todesbanden*[8]; for the Pentecost sequence *Veni sancte spiritus*, always *Nun bitten wir den Heiligen Geist*. Many orders mentioning the sequences directed that the people sing the German verses (something not reflected in the data in the above table but mentioned in a note in appendix 4); according to Philipp Harnoncourt, this practice dates from the thirteenth century for the Easter sequence.[9] The 1572 order for Kurland referred to the alternation practice in the sequences as "an ancient custom."[10] It seems safe to assume that the entire congregation was expected to sing along even if this was not explicitly stated, inasmuch as the practice was both long established and widespread.

Two orders authored by Johann Bugenhagen, chief pastor at Wittenberg, gave directions as to exactly how the alternation was to proceed: at Christmas, one verse of the Latin was followed by two verses of the German, all this three times, then the final Latin verse was followed by the one remaining German verse; at Easter, one verse of the Latin was followed by one verse of the German all the way through; and at Pentecost, every two verses of the Latin were followed by one verse in German.[11]

Creed

According to the above table, whenever the church orders explicitly stated who was to perform the Creed, it was the congregation over 75 percent of the time (26 orders versus 8 for the choir).[12] A German paraphrase of the Creed, later reworked by Luther as *Wir glauben all' an einen Gott*, was already in existence in the late Middle Ages, but it is not known how it was used or whether congregations ever sang it. The first order to explicitly assign the Creed to the people was the Prussian order of 1525, and Luther's *German Mass* followed a year later. The Prussian order directed that the Creed was not to be intoned by the priest as previously but was to be sung in German by the choir and the people; and so at least in Prussia there was a conscious change in practice.[13] No reason was given in any source for the change, however, although once a decision had been made to sing the Creed in German, its performance by the people seems a natural consequence given the personal and confessional nature of its text.

The only German version of the Creed to achieve any wide currency was Luther's *Wir glauben* [occasionally *gläuben*] *all' an einen Gott*. Of the 121 orders that attached a name to the German Creed, 116 mentioned only this one. One, Kurland 1572, offered a choice between *Wir glauben all* and *Ich gleub an Gott Vater allmechtigen;* Rothenberg 1618 named only the latter. Braunschweig-Wolfenbüttel 1709 mentioned only *Ich glaub an einen Gott allein*. Hanau 1573 provided for a shorter one-stanza Creed, *Ich glaub in Gott Vater,* to be sung in winter when it was cold.[14] Luther's Creed was not always easy for congregations to learn: the 1534(?) order for Hatzkerode directed that the people sing *Wir glauben all* from Luther's hymnal, but until the people learned it, the Creed could be done "as usual."[15]

It was not uncommon for both the Latin and the German Creeds to be sung, one after the other. Twenty-four sixteenth-century orders so directed, although some allowed one or the other to be omitted if time was pressing. A further 33 orders offered a choice between the Latin *Patrem* and the German Creed.[16]

Hymns before and after the Sermon

The pulpit service (i.e., the sermon and its annexes) changed little during the entire period under discussion. Table 4.2 outlines three orders from different eras. Thirty-five sixteenth-century orders mentioned a hymn before the sermon, and 73 mentioned one after. It makes sense that fewer orders would specify a hymn before the sermon, as the congregation had just finished singing the Creed. Also, the hymn after the sermon had a specific purpose, which many orders stated: it was to be sung while those intending to commune assembled in the chancel, where they were to

Table 4.2. Order of the pulpit service in the Middle Ages, 1585 and 1710

Pre-Reformation	Saxe-Lauenburg 1585	Leipzig 1710
Preacher kneels to pray	Our Father or hymn (in certain seasons)	*Herr Jesu Christ, dich zu uns wend* sung
Verse read from Gospel, the Fathers, or the liturgy		Silent Our Father
Ave Maria, Our Father, Veni Sancte Spiritus, or hymn	Gospel read	Gospel read
Sermon	Sermon	Sermon
Hymn (optional)		
Announcements	[Announcements?]	Announcements
Common prayer	Common prayer	Common prayer
Our Father or Ave Maria	Our Father	Silent Our Father
Corporate confession	Psalm or hymn	Votum[a]

The pre-Reformation order is from Meyer 1965:99–102. The 1585 order is from the 1585 church order for Saxe-Lauenburg, ff. 2H3^b–2J4^b. The 1710 order is from Groschuff 1710:7.

[a]"The peace of God, which passes all understanding, keep your hearts and minds in Christ Jesus" [Phil. 4:7].

remain until after they had communed. These two hymns were unlike any others in the service, for they were the only two that were, according to a number of orders, intoned by the preacher. A typical formulation was that given in Amberg 1544: "Then the preacher mounts the pulpit and begins to sing *Komm, Heiliger Geist.*"[17] Interestingly, there was hardly ever an indication that the hymn was actually continued, only that it was begun. But the preacher's action here indicates that these hymns were intended for the entire congregation, not just for the choir, as several orders made explicit.

The hymn before the sermon was not mentioned in any great numbers until after about 1560. Before this date, only 10 out of 87 orders provided for one, and even afterward to 1600 fewer than half the orders mentioned it. Eight orders referred to a hymn before the sermon only on festivals: the traditional pre-Reformation hymns were *Ein Kindelein so löbelich* for Christmas (sung today beginning with the second stanza, *Der Tag, der ist so freudenreich*), *Christ ist erstanden* for Easter, and either *Nun bitten wir den Heiligen Geist* or *Komm, Heiliger Geist, Herre Gott* for Pentecost. The Easter and Pentecost hymns were the same as those sung in connection with the sequence, but they were not sung twice in the same service. The two Pentecost hymns were also occasionally sung on ordinary Sundays, as the text invoking the Holy Spirit would be a fitting prayer immediately before the sermon. Some orders offered a choice of hymns for the various festivals.[18]

The hymn sung while the communicants gathered in the chancel was generally a brief hymn or a single stanza, such as the closing stanza of *Nun bitten wir,* the rest of which had been sung before the sermon. Two popular hymns were *Erhalt uns, Herr, bei deinem Wort* and *Verleih uns Frieden gnädiglich,* the former a prayer for preservation in God's Word (especially fitting after the sermon) and the latter a German version of the Latin prayer for peace *Da pacem, domine.*[19] Both hymns are quite brief, and they were often sung together. *Verleih uns Frieden,* with its prayer to "send peace in our time," was especially popular in times of impending or actual war. Another popular hymn was *Es woll uns Gott genädig sein,* Martin Luther's setting of Psalm 67 with a decided missionary content.

It is worth noting that, except on festivals, the hymns surrounding the sermon were in no sense hymns relating to the day or to the sermon, at least not during the sixteenth century. This would not have been possible even if it had been desired, for there were many lectionary texts for which no German hymns yet existed. Most orders specified rather one particular hymn, or a choice among several hymns, to be sung each week before or after the sermon. Only three sixteenth-century orders—Naumburg [1538], Anhalt 1551, and Andorff 1567—contained *de tempore* lists of hymns to be sung before or after the sermon (see the further discussion of the hymn *de tempore* in chapter 9).

Sanctus

The Preface and Sanctus were frequently omitted from Lutheran orders or sung only on festivals (see "Length of Services" in chapter 3). When they were sung, a choral performance was usually indicated. But two orders, Braunschweig-Wolfenbüttel

1543 and a difficult-to-date order for villages surrounding Braunschweig (Braunschweig [ca. 1550]), assigned the German Sanctus to the whole congregation. Three others offered a choice between a Latin Sanctus sung by the choir and a German one sung by the people; and one (the Cologne *Reformation* of 1543) directed that the first three words ("Sanctus, sanctus, sanctus") be sung in alternation between choir and congregation, the German word *heilig* being sung after each sanctus, with the remainder sung in German by all.[20] In six orders the choir was explicitly assigned the Sanctus even when it was sung in German, showing how deeply rooted a choral performance of this part of the liturgy was.

The overwhelming choice for the Sanctus in German was Luther's *Jesaia dem Propheten, das geschah,* which first appeared in his *German Mass.* The text describes Isaiah's vision of heaven from Isaiah 6, and the melody is Luther's considerable reworking of the Sanctus for Advent and Lent from the *Graduale Romanum.*[21] A few orders instead used another version of the same Latin Sanctus beginning *Heilig ist Gott der Vater.*

Agnus Dei

The Agnus Dei did not have a fixed place in the Lutheran church orders but could be sung before, during, or after the communion. During the communion was the most popular, occurring in 64 orders in the sixteenth century, and after 1550 only 4 orders placed it in a different location. Fourteen orders placed it before communion, and 14 placed it after. Six offered a choice of during or after, 2 either before or after, and one specified that it be sung twice, once during and once after. In three orders the placement is uncertain. It was most likely to be sung by the people when placed during the communion. One order, Johann Bugenhagen's 1535 order for Pomerania, directed that "during the communion the church shall sing an Agnus Dei in Latin or German: O lam gades etc., Jesus Christus etc., Godt si gelavet etc., the psalm Confitebor, but not longer than the communion lasts. When the people have gone to the sacrament, another German Agnus Dei, Christe, du Lamm Gottes, should be sung."[22] This was the only church order in which the people were directed to sing anything at all in Latin, and it is possible that the wording was a mistake.

The most popular German version of the Agnus Dei was *O Lamm Gottes unschuldig* by Nicolaus Decius, who based it on the Agnus from Mass IX in the *Graduale Romanum.*[23] It was mentioned by name in 49 orders. Close behind was *Christe, du Lamm Gottes,* a setting using the first psalm tone that had first appeared in Johann Bugenhagen's 1528 order for Braunschweig. It was found in 39 orders. Some orders offered a choice between the two, and a number of orders specified only that "the German Agnus Dei" be sung, leaving us to guess which setting was meant.

Hymns during the Communion

Nearly five times as many orders specified congregational performance of these hymns as specified choral. As with the hymns surrounding the sermon, the choice of hymns was not large. Many orders gave a brief list from which to choose. The favorites by far were two pre-Reformation hymns reworked by Luther: *Jesus Christus unser Heiland,* found in 178 orders, and *Gott sei gelobet und gebenedeiet,* found in 154. Many orders listed both. Other popular hymns were *Jesaia dem Propheten* (when it had not been sung as the Sanctus); Luther's version of Psalm 111, *Ich dank dem Herrn vom ganzem Herzen,* set to a simplified form of the first psalm tone; and either of the two German versions of the Agnus Dei in common use: *O Lamm Gottes unschuldig* and *Christe, du Lamm Gottes.*

It was understood that the singing of these hymns continued only until the communion distribution was complete; a few orders stated this explicitly. On account of tradition, and because confession on the prior day was required in almost all Lutheran churches in the 1500s, the number of communicants on any given Sunday was relatively small. In most cases one hymn, or part of a hymn, would have sufficed. This was conveyed in the orders by such instructions as "*Jesus Christus unser Heiland* or *Gott sei gelobet* is sung, and if there is time, also Psalm 111 or the German Agnus Dei."

Dismissal Hymn

A hymn after the Benediction was something of a rarity in the first half of the sixteenth century, with only 10 orders (out of 65) appearing before 1550 providing for one. It was found slightly more often between 1550 and 1680, but it was only after 1680 that a majority of orders contained it. The three orders appearing before the mid-1530s to include it were all from southern Germany, pointing to a possible Swiss Reformed influence or perhaps to a pre-Reformation regional tradition. It spread to central and eastern Germany in the 1530s and was found for the first time in the north in the Schleswig-Holstein order of 1542.

The dismissal hymns most frequently found were *Gott sei gelobet* (33 orders), *Verleih uns, Frieden* (28 orders), and *Erhalt uns, Herr* (22 orders). The last two were especially popular in village orders.

❖

Vespers

Lutheran Vespers looked much like its medieval forerunner, the principal change being the reduction in many localities of the number of psalms from five to three or fewer. Different cities and territories had slightly different orders, as can be seen in three orders written by Johann Bugenhagen for the cities of Braunschweig (1528) and Lübeck (1531) and for Pomerania (1535). The following is a conflation of these three orders with detail filled in from Wittenberg 1533, Pomerania 1542, and Buxtehude 1552 (the items in square brackets were sometimes omitted, especially on weekdays):[24]

> ℣ : Deus in adiutorium meum intende. ℟ : Domine ad iuvandum me festina.[25]
> Antiphon—1–5 psalms—Gloria patri—antiphon

Lesson(s) or chapter (sometimes placed after hymn)
[Responsory] (some orders specify either a responsory or a hymn)
Hymn
[Sermon]
Magnificat with antiphon OR the Litany[26]
[Kyrie]
[Collect]
Benedicamus
[Closing hymn(s)][27]

The similarity of Lutheran Vespers to the pre-Reformation office was echoed by Transylvania 1547, which stated that "nothing at all is changed in Vespers," and by Brandenburg-Ansbach-Kulmbach 1548, which directed that "Vespers is held according to traditional usage," followed by an outline similar to the one above.[28]

A simpler order was used in places without choirs capable of singing in Latin. Here is the order from Veit Dietrich's agenda for rural pastors (Nuremberg 1543):[29]

German psalm
Chapter read from the Old Testament
Sermon on the catechism or catechism examination
(It would be good if the people could learn to sing the Magnificat and
    Nunc dimittis in German.)
Collect
Blessing

Saturday and Sunday Vespers were different from each other in character. Saturday was, in places that observed the traditional liturgy, a normal weekday Vespers with a sermon often added and perhaps German hymns for the congregation to sing before and after the sermon (although it seems doubtful that many parishioners attended). The service itself was apparently sung to plainchant or with German substitutions for the Latin chants. After Vespers, confession was held for those intending to commune the following day. The form for Saturday Vespers was also used on eves of festivals.

The German substitutions encountered in Saturday Vespers included the Magnificat, the office hymn and the *Da pacem domine* sung at the end of the Office.[30] Three German Magnificats were named in the church orders for Saturday and Sunday Vespers: *Mein Seel erhebt den Herren mein* (Symphorianus Pollio, 1524); *Mein Seel, o Herr, soll loben dich* (Hermann Bonnus, 1547); and a prose text sung to a Magnificat tone, generally the *tonus peregrinus*. The last was the most frequently found: it began "Meine Seele erhebt den Herren, und mein Geist freuet sich Gottes, meines Heilandes" and was preceded by the antiphon "Christum unser Heiland, ewigen Gott, Marien Sohn, preisen wir in Ewigkeit." Two office hymns were explicitly mentioned in the orders. The first was the German *Christe, qui lux es et dies,* for which both *Christ, der du bist der helle Tag* (Erasmus Alber, ca. 1556) and *Christe, der du bist Tag und Licht* (a fifteenth-century translation into High German that appeared in Wittenberg in 1526) were used; the second was the German *O lux beata trinitas,* sung as *Der du bist drei in Einigkeit* (Martin Luther, 1529). The *Da pacem domine* was sung as *Verleih uns Frieden gnädiglich,* a translation by Luther to which Johann Walter appended a prayer for good government beginning "Gib unserm Herrn und aller Obrigkeit Fried und gut Regiment." It was often preceded by Luther's *Erhalt uns, Herr, bei deinem Wort.*

Sunday Vespers was more festive in character, and in cities the Vespers canticle came to be sung in polyphony, especially on festivals. During the seventeenth and eighteenth centuries the performance of a cantata became popular in places with the necessary resources. The sermon text on Sundays was usually one of the six chief parts of Luther's catechism—the Ten Commandments, the Creed, the Lord's Prayer, Holy Baptism, Confession, and the sacrament of the altar—and Vespers was frequently followed by a recitation by the youth of the part of the catechism assigned for the day. Somewhere during the service, either at the beginning, after the sermon, or immediately before the catechism recitation, a hymn based on the chief part for the day was generally sung. Determining which hymns these were is problematic. Many orders explicitly named the hymn on baptism, *Christ unser Herr zum Jordan kam,* then mentioned the Ten Commandments and the Our Father but without naming the hymns to be used, followed by an "et cetera," leaving the uninformed reader guessing as to which hymns were meant. But some orders did name all the hymns, showing that while there was general agreement on several hymns, there was no set corpus of hymns for the entire catechism. Those named in at least one order include

> Ten Commandments
> > Dies sind die heiligen zehn Gebot (20 orders)
> > Mensch, willst du leben seliglich (3 orders)
> Creed
> > Wir glauben all an einen Gott (5 orders)[31]
> > Es ist das Heil uns kommen her (1 order)[32]
> Lord's Prayer
> > Vater unser im Himmelreich (15 orders)
> > Sei Lob und Ehr mit hohem Preis (1 order)
> Baptism
> > Christ unser Herr zum Jordan kam (25 orders)
> > Durch Adams Fall ist ganz verderbt (1 order)
> Confession
> > Erbarm dich mein, o Herre Gott (2 orders)[33]
> > Allein zu dir, Herr Jesu Christ (1 order)
> Holy Communion
> > Jesus Christus unser Heiland (6 orders)
> > Gott sei gelobet und gebenedeiet (2 orders)
> > Ich dank dem Herrn von ganzem Herzen (1 order)

Most orders did not state explicitly that the congregation sang the catechism hymns, but this seems likely given their pedagogical purpose.

As the office canticle, the Magnificat was found in German on Sundays a total of 73 times, compared with only 54 times on Saturdays. Of these 73, the congregation was specifically directed to sing eight times. In no order was the German

Magnificat reserved for the choir, and it seems likely that in most cases the congregation was expected to sing along.

Vespers on weekdays, where it was held, was generally an exercise for the schoolboys. Occasionally German hymns were sung at the beginning of the service, after the lesson, before the sermon, in place of the Magnificat or at the end; but there is little indication that parishioners were expected to sing or even attend.

❖

Matins

In the Lutheran churches, Matins was held only where there were schoolboys capable of singing in Latin. The office was simplified by reducing the number of psalms and lessons, and very few Lutheran orders contained an office hymn. The 1535 order for East Frisia looks like this:[34]

> 𝔙 : "Domine, labia mea aperies." 𝔥 : Et os meum annunciabit laudem tuam. OR
> 𝔙 : Deus in adiutorium meum intende. 𝔥 : Domine ad adiuvandum me festina.
> Invitatory and Psalm 95 (Venite, exultemus)
> 3–4 psalms with one or more antiphons
> 3 lessons with several responsories
> Sermon (optional)
> Benedictus with antiphon
> Benedicamus or German psalm

Some orders directed that both opening versicles be used, others one or the other, and still others omitted it altogether. Many did not require the singing of Psalm 95. The placement of the sermon in the middle of Matins is unusual: many orders omitted it or placed the entire office after the early sermon on Sundays. The canticle varied from order to order, by season and by day of the week. Besides the Benedictus (which was borrowed from Lauds), the Te Deum (the proper canticle for Matins) and the Athanasian Creed (*Quicunque vult*) were also sung. The Lord's Prayer and a collect were frequently placed before the Benedicamus.

The orders disclose that few, if any, adult lay members attended Matins; and there is no evidence of any congregational participation except occasionally on Sundays in places where Matins was combined with an early sermon or catechism instruction for servants and others who could not attend the later mass or catechism service. In these cases a sermon or catechism hymn could be sung. The only frequently found German hymns in Matins itself were those sung for the office canticle: normally the Te Deum or Benedictus. Luther's settings seem to have been used exclusively: *Herr Gott, dich loben wir* for the Te Deum and *Gelobet sei der Herr, der Gott Israel* for the Benedictus. Neither setting is in the form of a metrical hymn: the Benedictus is set to a psalm tone, and the Te Deum is a Gregorian melody revised to fit the German text.

❖

Other Services

Most orders specified that a sermon be held at least once during the week, and many directed that the Litany be sung weekly after the sermon. Luther composed both Latin and German settings of the Litany, and the latter was generally used on weekdays. *Erhalt uns, Herr* and *Verleih uns Frieden* were also frequently sung after the sermon.

The weekly prayer service developed in the late sixteenth and seventeenth centuries. There was no set order, but penitential hymns were sung during it. Such hymns were also sung on monthly or seasonal days of penitence, which developed during the same period as the prayer service.

❖

The Most Popular German Hymns

The most popular German hymns, ranked according to the total number of times they are mentioned in the church orders, are[35]

179	Wir glauben all an einen Gott OR the Creed in German
124	Gott sei gelobet und gebenedeiet
122	Jesus Christus unser Heiland, der von uns
116	the Litany in German
110	Erhalt uns, Herr, bei deinem Wort
97	Allein Gott in der Höh sei Ehr OR the *Et in terra* in German (this could also refer to another hymn)
	Nun bitten wir den Heiligen Geist
85	Verleih uns Frieden gnädiglich
81	the Magnificat in German
74	Vater unser im Himmelreich OR the Our Father in German
73	Komm, Heiliger Geist (including both texts with the identical incipit)
65	Herr Gott, dich loben wir OR the *Te deum laudamus* in German
51	Es woll uns Gott genädig sein
	Jesaia dem Propheten das geschah
41	Christ ist erstanden
38	O Lamm Gottes unschuldig
35	Gelobet sei der Herr, der Gott Israel OR the Benedictus in German
32	Ein Kindelein so löbelich
26	Christe, du Lamm Gottes
25	Gott der Vater wohn uns bei
	Ich dank dem Herrn von ganzem Herzen

Some hymns were used only in one liturgical context, while others were used in many different places in the various services. The hymns having the greatest number of different liturgical uses are[36]

27 Erhalt uns, Herr, bei deinem Wort
26 the Litany in German
22 Nun bitten wir den Heiligen Geist
20 Verleih uns Frieden gnädiglich
18 Herr Gott, dich loben wir OR the *Te deum laudamus* in German
    Vater unser im Himmelreich OR the Our Father in German
16 Es woll uns Gott genädig sein
15 Wir glauben all an einen Gott OR the Creed in German
14 Danksagen wir alle Gott
13 the Benedictus in German
    Gott der Vater wohn uns bei
    Komm, Heiliger Geist
11 Erbarm dich mein, o Herre Gott
    the Ten Commandments in German
 9 Aus tiefer Not schrei ich zu dir
    Ein feste Burg ist unser Gott
    Nimm von uns, Herr [Gott], all unser Sünd und Missetat

❖

The Quality of Congregational Singing

It is clear from the above that in most places the congregation was expected to participate in the services, whether merely by singing the German Creed or by singing a substantial part of the liturgy. Yet there are signs in the church orders that all was not well. The efforts of Luther to coax his flock into singing were discussed in chapter 1. Nördlingen 1579 directed the pastors to exhort the people to learn the assigned songs, not so that the liturgy might be accomplished but so that God's Word might be better internalized and bear fruit.[37] Saxe-Coburg 1626 (more than a hundred years after the Reformation!) instructed the preacher to exhort the listeners (*Zuhörer*) that they are to sing along on the German hymns.[38] Magdeburg 1685 likewise directed the preacher to exhort the people to join in the singing of the German hymns.[39] Mansfeld 1580 noted that many of the psalms of Luther and others had fallen into disuse. The reason was that they were rarely sung in church, or they were sung at the beginning of the service before people arrived. Another reason was that in the cities Latin hymns and figural music predominated. The order attempted to correct the situation by listing hymns from Luther's hymnal to be sung each week of the church year.[40]

The predominance in the cities of choral music and the resulting stifling of congregational singing will be discussed in more detail in chapter 6. But it is appropriate to point out here that at least in certain places the congregation was considered a mere substitute for the choir. Regensburg [1567?] stated that the Monday sermon in both hospitals was to be conducted simply, with German psalms before and after the sermon sung by the people, since there were no schoolboys.[41] And in Riga 1530 on weekdays the service was done as on Sundays through the sermon, but after the sermon the Our Father hymn was sung by the entire congregation so that the boys would not be kept from their studies.[42]

The foregoing examples notwithstanding, the subjection of the congregation was not universal. In Joachimsthal, for example, the people apparently sang well, at least outside of the actual services. According to Christopher Brown, during the mid-sixteenth century the laity would gather in the church for an hour before the Sunday service to sing German hymns. As the liturgy in Joachimsthal was still sung largely by the choir, this would have allowed the people to give voice to their own song. Such a practice seems to have been rare in German churches, but the musical and pastoral leadership in Joachimsthal made it one of the likelier places for it to occur. The city was blessed with both a famous cantor, Nicolaus Herman, who srved for around thirty years beginning in the 1520s, and an unusually capable senior pastor, Johann Mathesius, who served in various capacities from 1532 to 1565 (except for two years spent in Wittenberg) and who was also a hymn writer. Together, Brown reports, Herman and Mathesius were responsible for fully eight percent of sixteenth-century hymn publications in German, as tallied from *DKL*.[43]

❖

Conclusion

A wide variation existed within Germany as to whether the services were essentially choral or essentially congregational. Local variations also existed: in general, the smaller the parish (and the fewer the musical resources), the more congregational the liturgy. As a rule, the traditional parts of the mass tended to be sung by the choir, the exception being the Creed, which was usually sung by the people in a German paraphrase. German hymns inserted before and after the sermon, during the communion, and at the end of the mass tended to be sung by the whole congregation. Matins was a choral Office, and Vespers was usually sung by the choir if one was available, with the Office canticle often sung by the people. They also sang a catechism hymn at Sunday Vespers in places where catechism instruction was held at that time. In a few places, the singing of the people seems to have suffered because of the predominance of choral singing.

CHAPTER 5

❖

Ecclesiastical Visitations

The church orders for County Hohenlohe of 1553, 1558, 1571, and 1578 are full of directions that the entire church sing one part or other of the liturgy. Yet in 1582 the church hierarchy discovered that "in virtually all parishes only the schoolboys sing and no one from the congregation sings along."[1] This demonstrates that the liturgical prescriptions in the church orders cannot be taken at face value: they must be corroborated by other contemporary sources. Fortunately, we have an excellent tool for uncovering what actually took place in church: the ecclesiastical visitation.

It was the task of superintendents and other ecclesiastical authorities to ensure that the churches under their care were functioning properly, that pastors were teaching correctly, that church workers were living decent lives, that congregations were meeting their financial obligations, and so on. The principal tool in providing such supervision was the visitation, which was essentially an audit of local churches conducted by the authorities.

❖

Nature of the Visitation and Supporting Documents

The frequency of visitations varied from place to place. The Wittenberg visitation articles of 1542 required annual visitations, but it is unclear how often they were actually held.[2] Some territories held visitations only when circumstances warranted. In Saxony a distinction was made between the frequent ordinary visitations by local superintendents and the general visitations covering the entire territory that were conducted only occasionally.

In some places visitations were formal affairs, with a committee led by the superintendent spending several days in a town attending services, meeting with church workers and members of the congregation, auditing the church's books, reviewing records of sacramental acts, and hearing complaints from those in the community. In other places they were quite informal, apparently with only a written report being submitted by the pastor.

There are several kinds of documents connected with visitations. First are instructions to visitors on how to conduct a visitation, occasionally with a list of specific questions to be answered during the visitation. Occasionally, instructions for large territories appeared in print; for example, those for Albertine Saxony in 1539, 1557, and subsequent years. Second are reports written by pastors and submitted to the superintendent. Third are more or less detailed minutes (*Protokolle*) of visitations, which include rough notes, clean copies, and summaries. Fourth are edicts concerning church life and worship issued as a result of a visitation; that is, when the authorities discovered that local practices did not follow the church orders and tried to bring them into conformity. It is an edict of this sort that provides us with the information on Hohenlohe contained above in the first paragraph.

The first kind of document, the instructions for visitors, contains no useful information on liturgical practices and so is not considered further here. The other kinds are all valuable sources, in particular the visitation minutes, of which large numbers are extant and which are a gold mine of information about church, society, and the daily lives of clergy, peasants, and others. Unfortunately, the originals of all these documents exist only in manuscript, and they are scattered among various state, local, and parish archives. There is no comprehensive bibliography, and so they are difficult to find, let alone read.[3] A few, however, have been transcribed and published, and it is these that serve as sources for this chapter.

Visitation records are valuable liturgical sources because they are a corrective to information gleaned from church orders. Church orders are prescriptive in nature: they tell us what was supposed to happen in the churches, but visitation records describe what actually happened (or at least what informants *said* happened).[4] The two do not always agree in their depiction of the church's worship.

❖

Congregational Singing According to the Visitation Minutes and Pastors' Reports

Published visitation minutes and pastors' reports with information on congregational singing are available from eight areas of Germany. They will be considered in chronological order, with one publication covering a century and a half considered first.

Electoral Saxony 1529 to 1673

In the early part of the twentieth century Karl Pallas edited a seven-volume set of visitation minutes from Electoral Saxony (that is to say, the Electorate proper).[5]

General visitations were held in 1528–31, 1533–34, 1555, 1574–75, 1592, 1617–18, and 1671–73. Smaller visitations were held in 1598, 1602, and 1608. Regular local visitations by the superintendents were ordered by the Elector in 1577, and these were held from 1577 to 1586, mostly falling out of use after about 1583.[6] Pallas reprinted the instructions for these local visitations. Among the questions to be asked was whether the people sang along with the choir on the hymns, following the clerk or choir, and whether the pastor allowed the people so to sing; another was whether the schoolmaster sang familiar Lutheran hymns in church.[7] Answers to each question were not given for every church, but there was still plenty of information provided. Pallas summarized the original documents, and in some cases he presented together material from the visitation minutes themselves and from the instructions of the visitors in response to the visitation; accordingly, some of the material is descriptive and some prescriptive in nature.[8]

Schmiedeberg 1528—The schoolboys are to sing the hymns before and after the sermon "so that the people understand them and become accustomed to them." (1:300)

Altherzberg 1529—The clerk is assigned the task during the mass when there are communicants and otherwise when people assemble for sermons of singing the German hymns to the people (*dem volke fursinge*) and teaching the Our Father, the Ten Commandments and the songs to the children and youth. (3:492)

Falkenberg 1529—The clerk is to teach the youth the Ten Commandments, the Our Father and the Creed, especially after the sermons, and he is also to teach the hymns to the people. (4:168)

Langennaundorf 1529—The clerks are to sing the German hymns diligently to the people at mass before and after the sermon when there are communicants so that the people can learn them.[9] (5:84)

Schmerkendorf 1529—The clerk is to teach the youth the hymns, the Ten Commandments, the Creed and the Our Father and instruct the older people during the mass in the German hymns. (This visitation was performed by Luther's close associate Justus Jonas, who refers to himself in the minutes.) (5:104–5)

Uebigau 1529—The clerk is to instruct the youth according to the visitors' book and teach the Christian hymns to the people in the church.[10] (5:130)

Jessen (city) 1555—The boys are lax in attending school, so there are not enough boys to have figural singing in the church. It used to be that citizens who had formerly studied at the school would help out with the singing, but this no longer happens. The visitors request the Bürgermeister to ask those citizens who can sing to assist with the singing. (3:22–21)

Seyda 1574—Christian songs and psalms of Luther and other godly men are sung before and after the sermon, and the people sing along with the cantor. The cantor always accompanies the chaplain to the villages and leads the singing there. (1:569)

Zwethau 1575—After the catechism instruction the clerk is to sing a German psalm to the children and adults present so that they learn the songs and can sing along in the church. (3:382)

Clöden (with Schützberg and Dröben) 1577—The pastor uses Luther's hymnal, but the congregation remains mute and cannot be moved to sing even by the landowner's example. (3:140)

Züllsdorf 1577—The pastor reports that he is unable to say the words of distribution "Take the precious body . . ." to each communicant; because he has no clerk he has to sing instead. The visitors direct him to inquire whether some goodhearted people might be found to sing during the communion; otherwise, he should leave the hymns until after the communion. (3:670)

Belgern 1586—"The council tolerates it when the people, during the singing and the reading of the Epistle and Gospel, stand outside in front of the church and chatter loudly, and during the reading of the Gospel from the pulpit they troop out of the church and raise such a ruckus outside that nothing can be heard inside; furthermore, [the council] does not punish the irresponsible farm hands (particularly the younger boys) who play ball in front of the gate or stand around in groups in the marketplace during services, especially during the afternoon sermons." (4:399)

Ahlsdorf (with Schmilsdorf and Kunssdorf) 1598—The congregation does not sing very well, and they do not attend church regularly. (3:485)

Apollensdorf 1598—Communion is held every two weeks; normally it would be every four weeks, but the [Lutheran refugees from] Anhalt have made it necessary to hold it more frequently. Hymns are from Luther's hymnal, and the people sing along on those they know. There is no school, as not more than eight boys would attend. (1:97)

Elsnig 1598—Before and after the sermon the pastor sings Luther's hymns with the congregation. The people complain that the pastor has made additions to certain hymns, as *Gott der Vater wohn uns bei, Ein feste Burg ist unser Gott,* and *Nun freuet euch, lieben Christen gemein.* These additions are unfamiliar to the people: they cannot sing along, and they request their abolition. The visitors direct that the hymns be sung as they are printed. (4:164)

Herzberg 1598—Luther's hymns are used on Sundays, but the people barely sing along. They should be admonished to do so. (3:450)

Trossin (with Rötzsch) 1598—The people of Rötzsch complain that too little singing is done, and what is done is too fast, so that the congregation is confused and is not able to sing along. (4:283)

Wahrenbrück (city) 1598—The people sing very weakly in the service.[11] (5:180)

Axien (Amt Schweinitz) 1602—The congregation sings along very little. (3:82)

Apollensdorf 1602—The pastor complains that the people do not send their children to catechism and do not sing along on the hymns. (1:98)

Bergwitz 1602—The pastor complains about the lack of honor toward the pastorate, shameless dancing, poor church attendance (usually no men and barely seven women attend catechism) and nonparticipation of the congregation in singing. (1:217)

Elster 1602—The people do not sing along even on familiar hymns, such as the Ten Commandments, the Creed, and the Our Father. In the daughter church at Rulssdorf the pastor has to sing alone during the communion, and so he says the words of distribution "Take and eat, this is the body . . ." and "Take and drink, this is the blood . . ." only to the first and last communicants. The visitors find this unacceptable and direct that henceforth the pastor is to say the words to each communicant, and if the people refuse to sing then the communion should be held in silence. A request by the caretaker at Elster to accompany the pastor to Rulssdorf and handle the singing was turned down even though he wanted from each farmer only one peck (*Metze*) of grain per year (as salary). The people explained that they did not want to have anything new imposed on them, and with that they got up and walked out of the visitation meeting. (1:130)

Herzberg 1602—Hardly anyone attends the catechism sermon in the city, and even the adults are lax in their church attendance. The people do not sing along, even in the Litany. (3:453)

Hohenleipisch 1602—The pastor complains that the clerk does not pay proper attention to his book while singing, so that he often omits verses; once he even had to remain silent during the communion while the clerk paid no attention to the singing. The clerk admits that he is inattentive to the singing; during the communion this occurs because many people go to the sacrament, and because there is little room around the altar (where he stands), he is crowded and cannot see properly into the book.[12] (5:377)

Wildschütz 1602—The congregation complains that the pastor does not hold catechism examination and rarely sings the [German] Creed (*Glaube*). (4:323)

Ahlsdorf (with Schmilsdorf and Kunssdorf) 1608—The congregation in Ahlsdorf does not sing along; the congregation in Kunssdorf sings well. (3:487)

Hohenleipisch 1608—The congregation sings poorly during the service. (5:378)

Liebenwerda 1608—The deacon has, reportedly at the request of the congregation that the service not last too long, omitted the hymn before the sermon; in the future he will reinstate it, as the congregation has now requested. (5:47)

Schmiedeberg 1608—The council has complained that the pastor preaches too long and that he has the people sing unfamiliar hymns, such as *Ach Herr, mit deiner Hilf* and *Gelobet seistu Christe, da du am Kreuz hängest;* the visitors direct that he is not to do this any more. (1:336)

Wiederau (with Drasdo, Neideck and Banssdorff) 1608—in Drasdo the congregation barely sings along. (5:213)

Wildschütz 1608—The congregation does not sing along at all. (4:324)

Arzberg 1618—The people do not sing along well. In addition, absentees [from the service] are not punished. (3:434)

Blönsdorf, Danna and Melmessdorf 1618—The congregation sings along well in the services. (1:420)

Mügeln (Amt Seyda) with Lindwerder (Amt Schweinitz) 1618— All penitents are absolved privately, and the listeners (*Zuhörer*) sing along diligently. (1:519)

Schmerkendorf (with Falckenberg, Kiebitz, Lönnewitz, and Marxdorff) 1618—in Lönnewitz the people hardly sing along at all on the hymns. (5:123)

Wahrenbrück (city) 1618—The people complain that the deacon does not always sing the German Creed before the sermon; he will henceforth do so. (5:189)

Ortrand 1657 (excerpt from the school order for Ortrand)—The cantor is to intone the German hymns in the church himself, and he is to make certain that no one else begins the stanzas and verses and so confuses the congregation with one person starting before another. During the communion "not only the cantor but in addition to him the entire choir is to sing the German hymns so that the communicants hear well the beginning of each stanza and verse and also so that the boys can follow along in the singing." (5:543)

Arzberg 1671—Sundays in the principal church, when communion is held, five hymns are sung before the sermon and 2, 3, or 4 after it and during and after the communion, depending on the number of communicants. But because there are so few boys the schoolmaster has to sing practically alone. At funeral processions the pastor has to sing along with the schoolmaster, as there are usually few boys available, or none at all. (4:439, 443)

Beyern 1672—Hardly anyone sings, even though this is strongly advocated in the sermons. (3:541)

Hohenleipisch 1672—The pastor is to select the hymns, but only those on which the congregation can sing along. (5:384)

Langennaundorf 1672—The songs should accord with the Gospel and be familiar to the people so that they can help sing them. (5:101)

Schönewalde 1672—The pastor complains of low participation by the congregation in the singing: even though many can read, they nonetheless sit in the church without books and without moving their mouths, although their traps are evident enough on the streets and in the spinning rooms and beer halls. The people, especially the younger ones, bring no prayer books to Holy Communion and meanwhile spend the time pondering inappropriate thoughts. (3:644–45)

Treben 1672—The people are not sending their children to school, and so the children are not present to assist with the singing in the church, and the schoolmaster frequently has to sing by himself. (3:189)

The foregoing reports are from the birthplace of the Reformation, the area around Wittenberg. Those from the 1520s show a concern for teaching the people to sing the German hymns. Those from after 1570 show that the authorities expected the congregation to sing. Indeed, the Saxon church order of 1539, in use with very slight modifications through the eighteenth century, encouraged the use of German hymns to a greater extent than more conservative orders such as those of Brandenburg and Mecklenburg. Yet nearly two-thirds of the reports indicate that the people did not sing, or sang poorly. Why is this?

One possible explanation is that Pallas, when he edited the documents, simply omitted information he found less interesting, which might have included congregations singing well. But this seems unlikely given the exhaustive nature of his collection. Another possible reason is that the visitors commented only when they found the singing unacceptable. If this was the case, then we may expect that the congregation also sang acceptably in many places where no report on the singing is given. This explanation is rendered less likely by the fact that several reports note specifically that the singing was acceptable, but it cannot be completely ruled out. Another possibility is that the visitors did not inquire into the matter at all unless the pastor or congregation raised the issue; or it may be that some visitors were interested in the subject and so inquired about it, while others did not. Finally, it is possible that this is indeed a fair sample and that two-thirds of all parishes had little or no singing by the congregation. What is clear in any case is that congregational singing was poor to nonexistent in a number of places, and so it was not an unqualified success even seventy-five to a hundred years after the Reformation was introduced.

There are some curiosities in the above reports. In Apollendorf in 1592 the people sang along on the hymns they knew, but four years later the pastor complained that they did not sing (perhaps a new pastor chose unfamiliar hymns?). Likewise in Wildschütz in 1602 the people complained that the pastor rarely sang the German Creed—the implication is that the people would like to have sung along—but in 1608 it was reported that the people did not sing at all. Perhaps the most startling reports are from Züllsdorf in 1577 and Elster in 1602, where the pastors took it upon themselves to sing the hymns during the communion because no one else would, apparently not even the clerk whose duty it was to lead the singing. Because they were singing, they were unable to speak to each communicant as they distributed communion, a situation the visitors found unacceptable.[13]

Some of the phraseology in the reports is interesting. In Langennaundorf in 1672 the hymns were to be familiar to the people "so that they can help sing them" (*daß sie mit helfen können*), implying that the clerk or choir was primarily responsible for the hymns and that the people merely assisted. The use of the term "listeners" (*Zuhörer*) for the congregation in Mügeln in 1618 is another possible indication of their passivity, assuming that the term was actually in the original document and is not an interpolation by the editor. This word is frequently found in discussions of worship by Enlightenment authors after about 1760, but the usual terms before then are "congregation" (*Gemein[d]e*) and "church" (*Kirche*).

Regarding the actual performance of the hymns, we learn that in Rötszch in 1598 the singing was too fast; in Hohenleipisch in 1602 the clerk stood near the altar during the communion to lead the singing; in Ortrand in 1657 hymnals were not yet in use (or else the people would not have been confused about what stanzas were being sung); and in Schönewalde in 1672 most people did not bring hymnals to church. In 1671 in Arzberg, which was a large enough town to have more than one church, five hymns were sung before the sermon and two to four after it, depending on the number of communicants. According to the Saxon church order, these would have included a hymn in place of the Introit, possibly a Gloria such as *Allein Gott in der Höh,* a Gradual hymn, the Creed, hymns before and after the sermon, and one or more hymns during the communion.

Braunschweig-Wolfenbüttel and Calenberg-Göttingen 1542 and 1543

Karl Kayser, superintendent in Göttingen, has produced a well-edited collection of visitation minutes from the four territories into which the Duchy of Braunschweig-Lüneburg was divided during the Reformation.[14] The minutes from two of them, Braunschweig-Wolfenbüttel and Calenberg-Göttingen, contain information on congregational singing:

From Braunschweig-Wolfenbüttel
  Alfeld 1542—The psalms and songs are to be sung according to Luther's hymnal, with the choir and congregation singing verses in alternation. (p. 90)
  Gandersheim (city) 1542—The choir is to be open for all sermons and services, and the schoolmaster and schoolboys with the canons are to sing the psalms and songs from it in alternation with the congregation. (p. 77)
  Gandersheim (women's cloister and chapter) 1542—Whenever there is a sermon, the canons enter the choir and sing with the schoolmaster and schoolboys German psalms and other songs chosen by the preachers, alternating verses with the congregation below. The schoolboys are to sing from the choir whenever there is a sermon, and not down below among the people. (p. 40)
  Wolfenbüttel 1542—The schoolmaster, with the schoolboys and other capable people, is to teach the German psalms and other songs from Luther's hymnal in the congregation and church, and the schoolmaster and schoolboys are to sing verses in alternation with the congregation. (p. 105)

From Calenberg-Göttingen
  Eldagsen (women's cloister) 1543—The women are to be taught to sing the German psalms and Christian songs, not least so that they will not be embarrassed during the service. (p. 389)
  Reinhusen (cloister) 1543—The people are diligently to be taught to sing the German "hymns, psalms and songs" (*lieder, psalmen und gesenge*). (p. 298)

Wennigsen (women's cloister) 1543—The younger women are to learn the German psalms and hymns and sing them in the church with the congregation, and the provost is to purchase for them several *Enchiridia*.[15] (p. 378)

The foregoing directives were issued in conjunction with the introduction of the Reformation into these territories. The Braunschweig-Wolfenbüttel visitation was conducted by Johann Bugenhagen, Anton Corvinus, and others following the expulsion of the Catholic Duke Heinrich the Younger by the Protestant Smalcald League in 1542. Heinrich was to regain his duchy in 1547, but not before the land had had a taste of reform. Calenberg-Göttingen adopted the Reformation after the death of Erich I in 1540, and a general visitation was conducted by Anton Corvinus in 1542 and 1543.

In both territories the visitors desired the people to learn the German Lutheran hymns; in Braunschweig-Wolfenbüttel they further directed that the singing be done in alternation between choir and congregation. The schoolboys were to sing from the choir in the front of the church, not from among the people. It was the responsibility of the preachers to select hymns for services.

The Territory surrounding Nuremberg, 1560 to 1561

Gerhard Hirschmann has compiled visitation minutes from the territory surrounding Nuremberg.[16] Most of the reports are silent concerning congregational singing, which is mentioned in only a few places. In Velden in 1560 it was reported that the cantor had angered parents by teaching the children Latin against their parents' wishes. He had insisted on singing the Introit, Et in terra, and other liturgical items in Latin even though no one could understand them. Because there was no Latin school there, the visitors recommended that German songs be substituted for the Latin items in the liturgy. This recommendation was enacted by the council on July 31, 1561.[17] In Hiltpolstein in 1560, the two men hired to sing the canonical offices reported that they had been requested to allow a German song or two to be sung and a chapter or two read from the Bible for the sake of the people, using the same form as in Nuremberg. Otherwise, they said, there would be complaints that the church could not decide whether it should be evangelical or papist. In this case, the council decided that the offices should be held as at the Church of Our Lady.[18] The reports from both Velden and Hiltpoltstein attest to the difficulty of keeping proponents of both Latin and German liturgies satisfied.

From Velden and Hiltpoltstein we learn that Latin was still very much in use, sometimes even where it was not wanted. The report from Velden underscores the connection between the use of Latin in the church and the presence of a Latin school; where there was no such school, then there was no need for a Latin mass.

In Altdorf the visitors instructed in 1561 that if the pastor and chaplain desire to help the schoolmaster sing, they are not to improvise but rather sing according to the notated music so that the people can better follow and learn to sing.[19] This brief entry shows that (1) the performance of the liturgy was chiefly the responsibility of the schoolmaster (with the choir?); (2) the pastor and chaplain felt that the schoolmaster needed help in leading the singing; (3) the pastor and chaplain "improvised" (perhaps they embellished the tune, or simply sang a different version from that of the schoolmaster?); and (4) the people were expected to sing but were still learning the songs.

Did the visitors consider it unusual that the people were still learning what was sung weekly in church? If so, there is no indication of it, even though the Reformation had been introduced into the territory already in the 1520s. But we must remember that the Reformation did not automatically bring with it congregational singing. Bartlett Butler, in his dissertation *Liturgical Music in Sixteenth-Century Nürnberg,* notes that there was little, if any, congregational singing in the churches of the city of Nuremberg.[20] This observation is borne out by the agendas in use in Nuremberg, which provided for congregational singing mainly as a substitute when choral music was not possible. The first official Lutheran church order (in manuscript) had been promulgated in 1528, and it stated that "in villages where Latin singing is not possible . . . the congregation may sing a good German song or several, and the pastors should exhort the people to learn such songs."[21] According to the printed church order of 1533, in villages where people were not available to perform the Latin songs, German songs should be used instead. If the people could not sing at all, the pastor should learn.[22] The 1543 agenda of Veit Dietrich, which was probably in use when the visitation was conducted, provided for congregational singing particularly where there was no choir (see "Henneberg 1566" below).

The 1561 minutes for Hül directed the pastor to conduct the Litany even if it could not be sung, because it could be read instead. In addition, the sacristan was to check with the pastor concerning hymns, and no hymns were to be sung except those of Luther and others contained in the hymnal.[23]

Many church orders listed several possible hymns for use during communion, and some (such as *Jesus Christus unser Heiland*) were quite lengthy. One might wonder how many of these hymns small villages might require, especially given that confession was widely required before each communion, and so one might expect that few people would commune on any given Sunday. The 1561 entry for Dennenlohe and Eltersdorf gives us a clue. The pastor there complained that at times on Sundays the communicants wanted to register even after the bell had rung, and there was not enough time to hear and instruct them. Sometimes there were a hundred or more people and only one or two clergy to serve them.[24] With such large numbers of people and altars that fit only a small number at a table, communion could easily have taken twenty to thirty minutes, time enough to sing several hymns if the tempos were quick enough.

Guttenberg 1562

Two entries from the visitation minutes of the tiny Palatine territory of Guttenberg, where a Lutheran church order had been introduced in 1558, contain items of interest:[25]

> Minnfeldt—In order that the people may sing along better on the songs, the visitors directed that the pulpit be moved to the corner next to the

chancel on the right side against the wall, the font moved to the same side; in its place at the entrance to the chancel an altar is to be erected for the Lord's Supper, and immediately next to it on the right a lectern is to be placed for the singing (*Gesang*). (pp. 4–5)

Freckenfeldt—So that the people can better assist in the singing, the visitors directed the pastor to sing standing at the lectern in the front of the chancel. (p. 6)

It is difficult to picture exactly the renovations made in Minnfeldt without knowing how the church looked, but it is clear that the visitors believed that the people could be led more effectively in the singing if the choir or clerk stood at the new lectern. Apparently there was no clerk in Freckenfeldt, for the pastor was directed to stand at the lectern to lead the singing. As in Langennaundorf in Saxony (see the published visitation and pastors' reports above), the people were understood to be "assisting" in the singing.

Henneberg 1566

In 1566 Superintendent Christoffer Fischer conducted a visitation in the County of Henneberg, situated in Thuringia (in central Germany) with Saxony to the north and east and the Diocese of Würzburg to the south. Wilhelm IV, Count of Henneberg, who ruled for sixty-four years from 1495 to 1559, was well disposed toward Luther; but he kept his territory officially Catholic for political reasons. Even so, when his son and heir Georg Ernst became Lutheran upon his betrothal to a member of the ruling family of Braunschweig-Calenberg in 1544, the provost of the Lutheran church of St. Lorenz in Nuremberg, Johann Forster, was installed as preacher and superintendent at the Henneberg court in Schleusingen. From there he introduced the Reformation, using the agenda of Veit Dietrich, into the nominally Catholic territory between 1544 and 1546. And so at the time of Superintendent Fischer's visitation Lutheran services had been held for about twenty years, although the churches in Henneberg did not officially adopt the Lutheran faith until the accession of Georg Ernst in 1559.[26]

Veit Dietrich's agenda, first published in Nuremberg in 1543 and reprinted numerous times through 1755 (with revisions), called for the whole congregation to sing whenever no schoolboys were available. For example, the agenda directed that "the schoolboys sing the Introit, but where there are no schools and therefore no people that can sing the Latin, a German hymn is sung. If the people cannot even do that, the pastor should teach them." Either the schoolboys or the people, whichever was customary, sang the Gloria and Creed. The people also sang the responses to the Litany with the major part of the choir after two or three singers intoned the petitions. In small villages this was done after the Epistle. They also sang during the communion if there were no schoolboys to sing the Agnus Dei and perhaps a responsory.[27]

The minutes from Superintendent Fischer's visitation include reports from the pastors on the conduct of their services. For most items in the liturgy, the reports mention only what was sung, not who did the singing. But there are a few exceptions, noted as follows:[28]

Belrieth and daughter church at Einhausen—The clerk sings a German psalm or hymn after the Epistle with the schoolboys.

Goldlauter—There are no schoolboys at this church, but the common people do sing. Sung parts of the liturgy include *Komm, Heiliger Geist, Herre Gott; Allein Gott in der Höh;* the response to the salutation "And with your spirit"; a German psalm after the Epistle; the Creed, *Verleih uns Frieden* after the sermon; and one or more hymns during the communion.

Herpf—At Saturday Vespers, the pastor sings a brief psalm with the schoolmaster and schoolboys [followed by the rest of the office]. On Sunday morning, the choir sings the response "And with your spirit" and *Verleih uns Frieden* while the communion is prepared, but the people sing *Wir glauben all an einen Gott.*

Meiningen—On high feasts, the organist or schoolmaster introduces the hymn *de festo* figurally after the Epistle, and the people sing alternating stanzas. On ordinary Sundays the choir sings *Jesus Christus unser Heiland, Jesaia dem Propheten* or something similar during the communion distribution.

Niederlauer—No introit is sung with the clerk and schoolboys, but rather the *Veni sancte spiritus* in German, then a German Kyrie. Then the pastor sings "Glory to God in the highest," and the "clerk, schoolboys and others" sing *Allein Gott in der Höh.*

Obermassfeld—*Kyrie, Gott Vater,* and *Allein Gott in der Höh* are sung "with the schoolmaster and boys and the church." On Tuesday there is a sermon with catechism instruction in the hospital chapel, but nothing is sung before or after the sermon because there are not enough people.

Ritschenhausen—When there are communicants all sing the *Veni sancte* in German, then a German psalm that the people know. The people sing half the Creed after the Epistle.[29] During the communion the clerk sings *Jesus Christus unser Heiland* with the people.

Suhl (service order dated 1562)—During the communion the boys sing *de tempore,* usually concluding with *Christe, du Lamm Gottes.*

Sulzfeld and Klein-Bardorf—The schoolmaster sings the Benedictus with the boys in place of the Introit (high feasts have their own hymns). The choir and people sing *Allein Gott in der Höh.* The choir answers "And with your spirit." The schoolmaster begins a German psalm after the Epistle and *Wir glauben all;* before the sermon the schoolmaster sings *Nun bitten wir.* During the communion the choir sings *Jesus Christus unser Heiland, Gott sei gelobet,* and *Jesaia dem Propheten.* After communion the people speak the collect with the pastor [this is highly unusual!].

These reports show little consistency in village churches as to who sang what. In Goldlauter the people sang often and apparently well, but in Herpf and other places the schoolboys apparently sang much of the liturgy. In most places the people sang at least one or two items. The diversity in practice fits well with the options given in Dietrich's agenda.

Saxony 1569 to 1582

Sehling gives isolated visitation reports from several places in Saxony. The reports show that much of the liturgy was still done in Latin, but a few refer explicitly to singing by the people:[30]

> Kapellendorf 1569—The pastor gives a report of how he has been conducting the service for the past six years. On high feasts the liturgy is sung alternating verses between polyphony and unison singing so that both the schoolboys and the people can participate.
>
> Schandau 1577—The entire church sings the Nicene Creed in German during the mass. The Sunday afternoon sermon begins with the boys singing a Latin psalm with an antiphon from the Sunday Gospel, then a Latin responsory or hymn *de tempore,* then a German hymn "on which the people can assist" (*das das Volk helfen kan*). After a lesson is read, a catechism hymn or the Magnificat is sung "with the people."
>
> Weissenfels 1578—The congregation sings a German hymn after the Epistle.
>
> Oelsnitz 1582—The people sing two hymns, one before the Epistle and the other before the Gospel.

Grubenhagen 1617

The Reformation was introduced into this central German duchy gradually after 1532.[31] A general visitation was conducted in 1617, with the visitors finding that several different agendas were in use in the territory. In the district of Catelenburg Luther's psalms were sung well, likewise in the village of Saltz der Helden; but in Andreasberg the singing was "in disarray" because the people were "burdened with many Latin songs" so that they did not even arrive at church until the preacher mounted the pulpit. The visitors directed the superintendent to prescribe one of the commonly used agendas for use there.[32]

Hesse 1628 to 1632

One of the best historical studies of liturgical practice in German churches is Wilhelm Diehl's *Zur Geschichte des Gottesdienstes und der gottesdienstlichen Handlungen in Hessen* (Giessen, 1899). It is one of the few studies to compare what was specified in the church orders with actual practice as recorded in the visitation records.

The author notes first that fewer services were actually held than were supposedly required. But in fact, he continues, the church orders did not require four Sunday observances but merely indicated the possibilities. And so in nearly half the congregations in the Marburg district in 1634 only the principal service and catechism instruction without sermon were held. Similarly, in the Giessen district fewer than one-third of the congregations with extant visitation minutes reported that a Sunday afternoon service with sermon took place on a regular basis. The author concludes that in the majority of congregations in the territory only one Sunday service was held plus catechism instruction.[33]

The 1574 church order for Hesse directed that "the people are to be reminded and exhorted in the sermon as often as the opportunity arises to learn the common church songs and always, when there is singing in the common assemblies, to sing along, in particular each for himself, and therefore harmoniously praise God."[34] But in many places it seems that the exhortations, if delivered, were not taken to heart. Diehl notes the difference in congregational singing between churches in areas with established schools and those with newer schools or none at all. In the area of Hessen-Darmstadt, which had had schools for some time, most of the congregations reported good singing. Two such congregations complained when the schoolmaster sang hymns incorrectly or to a tune different from the one the people knew. In answer to a question in the 1628 visitation instructions as to whether the women sang, most parishes reported that they did. But in Oberhessen (with principal cities Marburg and Giessen), which had fewer and more recently founded schools, most congregations were apparently silent. There were comments in the visitation records about pastors singing alone and schoolmasters and clerks singing badly, and the pastor at Understen-Rosphe reported that there was not a single person left to sing the hymns during the communion distribution, not even the clerk whose duty it was to lead the singing. Some parishes reported that the women sang, but in one place only one woman sang, and in most places none did. In Wetter, one of the most important parishes in the territory, the pastor complained that the people simply would not accustom themselves to singing Luther's psalms: they said that if they wanted to sing they would go to a tavern![35]

Diehl concludes that the founding of schools, in the first years, had a negative effect on congregational singing as people who had previously sung under the leadership of the clerk now simply listened to the learned singing of the schoolboys. But eventually this improved the singing, as the schoolboys grew up and continued to sing.[36]

❖

Edicts Resulting from a Visitation

Most problems encountered by visitors were handled locally with the parish where the problem occurred. But occasionally such serious and widespread breaches of order were found that the church authorities felt it necessary to issue edicts to correct them. Three such edicts containing instructions on the singing were found for this study: Stettin 1573, Hohenlohe 1582, and Gotha 1645. The 1533 order for Wittenberg also resulted from a visitation, but because it contains a complete agenda, not just selected instructions, it was considered in chapter 4.

Stettin 1573

The visitation ordinance of May 10, 1573, directs that because the people do not sing fluently and together, the clerk at St. Jacob's is not to absent himself after the sermon, much less is he to fail to appear altogether, but rather he is to stand by the altar and sing along.[37]

Hohenlohe 1582

During the visitation it was discovered that in virtually all parishes only the school-boys sing and no one from the rest of the congregation sings along. Because hymns contain much good teaching and many useful things, and congregational singing is thus a worthy practice, the pastors are to exhort the people in their sermons how useful it can be. In each house the parents should send at least one child to school, and they should teach their children and servants not only the catechism but also to sing psalms. The people should pay attention to the schoolmaster and schoolboys when they sing and sing neither too loudly nor too high, nor in a disorderly fashion, as when they are shouting in the field. It is further ordered that in all parishes, especially in cities, Sunday catechism is to be rung a quarter or half hour earlier and the extra time used to practice psalm singing with the children. The pastors and schoolmasters are to use the common, well-known, and simple psalms and spiritual songs already known to the people until they become accustomed to the new. The young people are to learn to sing under threat of punishment (revoking permission for dances, etc.), and at social gatherings in the winter they are to sing only psalms and spiritual songs. A fine will be imposed on those violating this order.[38]

Gotha 1645

Latin hymns and collects during Vespers should be replaced with German ones where this has not already been done. A catechism hymn or the Magnificat (alternating weeks) is to be sung before the midday sermon on Sundays; on festivals, however, hymns relating to the festival should be sung so that they become more familiar to the people. *Wir glauben all* is not sung everywhere before the Sunday sermon; this is to be corrected. The Litany is sung too slowly in some places and too quickly in others, and in some places verses are added or omitted. The synod therefore orders that the Litany be printed with the division of the verses between the boys on one hand and the entire choir and congregation on the other correctly indicated.[39]

❖

The Reliability of Visitation Records

In 1978, a book appeared that challenged the accepted view that Luther's teachings quickly found their way into the hearts and minds of Germany's common folk. Its author was Gerald Strauss, a history professor at Indiana University, and the book was *Luther's House of Learning: Indoctrination of the Young in the German Reformation.* In it, Strauss used visitation records, among other sources, to argue that preaching and education failed to produce a lasting change in the spiritual lives of a large segment of Lutheran Germany.

Strauss recognized possible dangers in using these records, and to forestall criticism he mentioned six possible objections to their use, summarized here:

1. The types of questions varied from one visitation to another, making comparisons difficult.
2. In preparing summaries, visitors may have misrepresented the collected data in order to make a particular impression on their supervisors.
3. Visitors may not have transcribed answers accurately.
4. The visitors may have wished to find fault, therefore they found it.
5. It is uncertain whether respondents were telling the visitors the truth or how much information they were withholding.
6. Visitations were unpopular in urban areas, so there is a dearth of data from large cities.

Strauss addressed each objection and concluded that despite the potential for error the visitation records were generally reliable.[40]

Strauss's book has received widespread attention from social and religious historians, but not all have accepted its conclusions. In a 1982 article, James Kittelson argued that visitation records from the city of Strassburg and its environs in the late sixteenth century contradict Strauss's results for Germany as a whole, showing instead a populace largely familiar with Lutheran teachings, with only a handful of scattered dissenters, mostly Anabaptists.[41] In a subsequent article aimed directly at Strauss, Kittelson detailed how visitation records could be misunderstood by those who do not use them carefully. In particular, he sought to prove that the visitation records for Strassburg in the late sixteenth century are in fact reliable even though the summaries of them by the chief pastor are colored by the interests of the senate to which he reported (a problem Strauss had foreseen). The main problem with Strauss's work, Kittelson implied, was in using only a small sampling of visitation records from each region rather than surveying all records over a span of several years. A second problem was that Strauss's standard for religious change was too high: the popular social and religious deficiencies described in the visitation records were not nearly so serious as Strauss made them out to be. Kittelson's clear implication was that if Strauss had misinterpreted the visitation records for Strassburg, then he may have done so for other areas of Germany as well, casting his entire thesis into doubt.[42]

Stephen Ozment, in his 1992 book *Protestants: The Birth of a Revolution,* expressed doubt whether public records such as visitation accounts are even appropriate sources for the kind of task Strauss had undertaken; that is, learning about the personal thoughts and feelings of common people. Ozment noted that such records can describe group behavior; but preferred souces such as family chronicles, diaries, housebooks and especially letters for the task of determining the religious beliefs of ordinary people.[43]

The writings of Strauss, Kittelson, and Ozment are relevant here because a recent criticism of my use of visitation records (in Herl 2000) cites all three. Christopher Brown, in his 2001 dissertation from Harvard University titled *Singing the Gospel: Lutheran Hymns and the Success of the Reformation in Joachimsthal,* has stated that my conclusion, "that sixteenth-century congregations sang very little, unfortunately follows G. Strauss' lead in relying rather uncritically on the evidence of the visitation reports."[44]

This statement is problematic on three accounts. First, I do not argue, nor did I argue in 2000, that sixteenth-century congregations sang very little. I believe rather that evidence shows congregational singing to have been poor in many, but not all, churches. This is an important distinction. In some places the singing was evidently quite good, but the quality of singing varied considerably from place to place. A blanket statement about congregational singing over the course of the century must be nuanced to acknowledge exceptions and differences at various dates and places.

Second, Brown's reason for rejecting visitation records is not relevant to the use I have made of them. Echoing Ozment, and citing both Ozment and Kittelson, he writes:

> Ultimately, those scholars who depend on the visitations claim to overwhelm competing assessments by sheer numerical weight—no number of pious Lutherans discovered through pamphlets, letters, diaries, or other sources can outweigh the archives full of official reports and protocols which reveal the poor moral behavior and inadequate religious knowledge of laymen summoned to give an account of themselves and their faith before visitation committees. Yet the presumption that such souces provide an objective measure of popular religious devotion and identity has been called into serious question: the visitations may reveal more about about [sic] the clergy and magistrates who wrote the scripted questions and shaped their reports to serve their own interests than they do of ordinary Lutheran laymen."[45]

Whether this is a valid criticism of Strauss's methods, I am not qualified to judge. But my work and Strauss's are qualitatively different: he was interested in individual beliefs, while I am interested in group behavior; specifically, how well congregations sang. The answer to this can be known through direct observation by people present, and so this is the sort of question the visitation reports are well suited to answer. Therefore, Brown's criticism of Strauss's work—that he attempted to derive conclusions about the religious beliefs of ordinary people from sources unsuited to that purpose—simply does not apply to mine.

The third problem with Brown's statement is that he seems to reject my conclusions more on the basis of his experience with Joachimsthal sources than on their own lack of merit, not having investigated their claims in any detail. Brown asserts that in Joachimsthal the congregation sang well in church (see chapter 4 under the heading "The quality of congregational singing"). His work with local sources seems well done, so I have no cause to doubt this assertion. But he appears to believe that because people in Joachimsthal sang well in church, then my conclusion—

that German congregations "sang very little"—must be without foundation. The misunderstanding of my conclusions aside, it is sufficient to point again to the evidence that in some places congregational singing was good, and apparently Joachimsthal was one of these places.[46]

Although I find no grounds for accepting Brown's criticism of my methodology, I have attempted to address the various concerns that have been raised regarding visitation records by presenting as much raw data from primary sources as possible, using actual minutes of visitations whenever they have been available. All relevant references that I have found have been presented, whether or not they support my thesis. In this way readers will be able to examine my arguments carefully and draw their own conclusions.

My rejection of Brown's argument notwithstanding, there are nonetheless two concerns I do have in connection with my use of visitation records. The first is the paucity of records. As noted above, relatively few visitation records have been transcribed from manuscript and published, and of those only a few contain information on singing in church. It is helpful that the useful records come from various parts of Germany, but a larger sample would have been preferable. The second concern is one Strauss raised and for which he had no adequate solution; namely, the fact that larger cities are poorly represented in visitation records. It is partly in order to address this concern that the next chapter treats hymnal use and hymn singing in cities.

❖

Conclusion

The visitation records show us that around the end of the sixteenth century the choir or clerk was still responsible for singing large portions of the liturgy, although in most places the rest of the congregation was encouraged to "assist," especially where there was no choir. In Braunschweig-Wolfenbüttel the people took a more active role, alternating verses with the schoolboys.

Braunschweig-Wolfenbüttel and the area surrounding Nuremberg aside, for which information is scanty or unavailable, all the areas studied had parishes where the congregation sang well, and all had parishes where the singing was poor. In general, poor singing is reported more frequently than good singing, but this may simply reflect the desire to note what was wrong rather than what was right. Notoriously poor singing is found in many places in Electoral Saxony, in parts of Hesse and in Hohenlohe.

It is clear, however, that—despite the differences in detail and the incomplete and inconsistent evidence—there was not yet any conception among Lutherans that the liturgy properly belonged to the people; rather, the people were expected to sing because the practice, as the edict from Hohenlohe noted, was "useful" in teaching the faith and because the entire congregation was needed to take the choir's role when there was no choir. Braunschweig-Wolfenbüttel may have been an exception, for the people were expected to assume the role of a second choir.

CHAPTER 6

❖

Congregational Hymnals

This chapter is mostly about church life in the larger cities, where the populace was more educated and informed and took a greater interest in matters theological and ecclesiastical. Whereas in smaller towns and country churches the Reformation sometimes had to be imposed through visitations, in several cities the people compelled more or less unwilling city fathers to allow Lutheran teaching and practice. It was in the cities where the conflict between choral and congregational singing became most heated in the seventeenth and eighteenth centuries, and a closer look at sixteenth-century practice is helpful in understanding the events that were to occur.

The particular question I plan to address here is "To what extent were hymnals used by congregations (as opposed to choirs and clergy) in the sixteenth century?" This is worth asking because if the people had hymn texts in front of them, then there was less need of a choir or clerk to help them sing the right words, and congregations could assert themselves more readily in the liturgy. Several scholars have indicated, and many nonspecialists have simply assumed, that Lutheran congregations used hymnals (or printed broadsheets) already at the start of the Reformation. The city of Wittenberg is a case in point. Friedrich Blume, in his comprehensive *Protestant Church Music: A History,* calls the *Enchiridion* of 1526 the "first Wittenberg congregational songbook."[1] Johannes Rautenstrauch, in *Luther and the Cultivation of Church Music in Saxony,* writes that Luther's first congregational hymnal appeared in 1529.[2] Robin Leaver, one of the most influential of recent scholars, writes concerning the introduction of congregational singing in Wittenberg around 1524 that "at this stage the congregation used broadsheet copies of the hymns, but within a matter of months a congregational hymnal was issued in Wittenberg. . . ."[3] Occasionally a scholar has disagreed with this assessment. Daniela Garbe, in her article on congregational singing for the new edition of the encyclopedia *Die Musik in*

Geschichte und Gegenwart, states that "the visitors to the service [in Wittenberg] received no hymnals; the ability to sing the hymns from memory was presupposed."[4]

Obviously both opinions cannot be correct. This chapter, therefore, attempts to answer the question "When did German Lutheran congregations begin to use hymnals?" The answer is in fact more complicated than the question might indicate, for variations in practice in different parts of Germany need to be taken into account.

❖

Overview

The period following the Reformation saw a great renaissance of hymn writing. New texts and tunes appeared in abundance. Because of the need to disseminate both, nearly all sixteenth-century Lutheran hymnals contained at least some tunes as well as texts. Small pamphlets with only one or a few hymns often contained only texts, but they were exceptions (and will be discussed later in this chapter).[5]

In 1975 an exhaustive bibliography of German hymnals with music appeared under the title *Das deutsche Kirchenlied.*[6] Covering the years 1500 to 1800, it was intended as the first volume of a critical edition of German hymn melodies. One further volume, divided into six physical volumes and containing melodies printed through 1570, has appeared to date.[7] These two volumes provide us with the title and musical contents of every known German hymnal appearing through 1570. They show that between 1524 and 1570 approximately 288 German-language hymnals with music were published.[8] This number excludes broadsheets and pamphlets, hymn collections published in partbooks for choir, and agendas containing scattered hymns. Of these 288 hymnals, 209 were intended for Lutherans, 24 for the Bohemian Brethren, 13 for the Reformed, 7 for Catholics, and 35 for "Evangelicals"; that is, Protestants who do not fit neatly into one of the other categories.

Of the 209 Lutheran hymnals, 82 are either bibliographic variants or reprints with exactly the same tune content as earlier editions; approximately 48 are later editions of earlier books;[9] and 11 are no longer extant. This leaves 68 books to consider. But many of the later books drew heavily on the contents of the last hymnal for which Luther provided a preface, *Geystliche Lieder. Mit einer newen vorrhede, D. Mart. Luth.,* published in Leipzig by Valentin Babst in 1545. Even Luther's preface was often reprinted and, there being no indication in the books or from external evidence that these later books were used any differently from the earlier ones, the discussion below concentrates mainly on publications dating from before 1545, when the various Lutheran areas were still establishing their forms of worship.

❖

Broadsheets and Pamphlets

The first Lutheran hymn publications were broadsheets (also called broadsides), single sheets of paper printed on one side, and pamphlets, single gatherings of leaves usually containing only one, two, or three hymns. They were not a Lutheran innovation—the earliest surviving German hymn print with musical notation dates from 1496[10]—but the Reformation gave a new impetus to their production as tools for spreading Luther's teaching. In no case were they official publications of a church or government but were rather commercial endeavors by printers.

Das deutsche Kirchenlied lists 111 Lutheran and Evangelical broadsheets and pamphlets with music appearing before 1570. How great the output truly was is unknown, for it is likely that a large number have not survived.[11] Still, the number of prints with music is dwarfed by the number containing only hymn texts. As an illustration, the Palatine collection in the Vatican Library contains two sets consisting entirely of German hymn pamphlets, Pal. V.182 and Pal. V.444.[12] Pal. V.444 contains 83 pamphlets with a total of 148 hymns mostly from the presses of Valentin Newber and Friderich Gutknecht in Nuremberg, but only one hymn is printed with music. The others contain the name of a familiar hymn (or occasionally a secular song) to which the text is to be sung: for example, "Ein schön Geistlich Lied, Von der heiligen Dreyfaltigkeit . . . Jn dem Thon, Kompt her zu mir spricht Gottes Son" (A lovely spiritual song on the Holy Trinity . . . to the tune *Kommt her zu mir, spricht Gottes Sohn*). Pal. V.182, with prints mostly from the presses of Newber, Gutknecht, and Mattheus Francke in Augsburg, contains even more pamphlets, but only two have music.

Were these broadsheets and pamphlets used in church by congregations, as Leaver (above) states? One account from Magdeburg suggests that they were, where on May 6, 1524, an old cloth maker stood by the memorial to Emperor Otto and "sold the first spiritual songs, *Aus tieffer noth schrey ich zu dir* and *Es wolt uns Gott genedig sein* and sang them to the people." For this he was arrested and placed in jail but was released after two hundred citizens pleaded his cause. His accusers were jailed in his place and were eventually deported.[13] According to another account of the same incident:

> A poor beggar sold several of Martin's hymns at the market in Magdeburg and sang them openly here and about, wherever he came, and taught man and wife as well as girls and boys, so many that the German hymns and psalms became so commonplace that they were thereafter openly sung and are still sung by the common people themselves daily in all the churches before the sermons [or services] are begun.[14]

The account does not state explicitly that the people used the pamphlets they had purchased when they sang these hymns in church, but that seems probable. We should note, however, that the singing was not a part of the mass liturgy (the sermon was extraliturgical) and that the clergy may not even have approved of it, as the Reformation had not yet been introduced in Magdeburg (although it would be introduced within two months). The singing by the congregation had rather the character of a popular protest.

Similar protest singing occurred in other German cities as well. In 1527 a visiting preacher from Magdeburg, in his first and only sermon in Braunschweig, extolled the saving virtue of good works; whereupon: "a citizen by the name of Henning Rischau began and said in a loud voice: 'Father, you're lying!' He then just as loudly began to sing the twelfth psalm, which Dr. Luther had just recently set in thought-provoking German verse as *Ach Gott, vom Himmel sieh darein.*"[15] In Göttingen in 1529 a group of protesters disrupted the Corpus Christi procession by singing German psalms, beginning with Luther's *Aus tiefer Not schrei ich zu dir.* In 1529 in Lübeck and 1530 in Lüneburg congregations disrupted the sermons by singing, seemingly spontaneously, Luther's *Ach Gott, vom Himmel sieh darein.*[16] This hymn seems to have been so ubiquitous as a protest song that it, rather than the better-known *Ein feste Burg ist unser Gott,* deserves the epithet "battle hymn of the Reformation." The Lüneburg accounts also mention the people singing *Es woll uns Gott genädig sein* and *Gott der Vater wohn uns bei* while the preacher was attempting to preach.[17] Hymn pamphlets seem not to have played a direct role in any of these further cases; in three of them the people had learned the songs by attending Lutheran services in the vicinity.[18]

Were pamphlets and broadsheets used by the congregation in any official way? If so, then either the church would have purchased sufficient copies for those attending, or people would have brought them from home to use in church. The former certainly did not happen, as this would be the only known instance of a church providing worship aids for a congregation during the first three centuries after the Reformation. The latter is possible, even likely, with individual persons in some cities; but there is no contemporary record of any congregation using them in large numbers (or using them at all, for that matter). The scenario of a printer hawking his wares outside the door of the church much as programs are sold at sporting events today seems not to have taken place.

The titles of pamphlets bear this out. Hymnal titles occasionally bear witness to the use of their contents in church, but pamphlet titles hardly ever do. Many of those in the Palatine collection V.444, which seem to have been published after mid-century (only four are dated, and those between 1554 and 1571), contain adjectives such as "new" or "lovely," descriptions that would appeal to consumers looking for the latest songs but which would hardly indicate a use in church. Earlier titles (as given in *DKL*) also lack any indication of church use but usually give simply the title or biblical source of the text and occasionally the author's name and a descriptive adjective such as "new."

If pamphlets and broadsheets were used to any great extent in church, then many more copies of those hymns sung in church ought to have been sold than copies of other hymns not used in church. One might expect that more copies of these would have survived, but the library holdings information in *DKL* (which lists all known copies) does not bear this out. It is of course equally possible that publications carried to church would have worn out more quickly and thus did not survive, so this fact alone adds little to the argument. But it is interesting that of the 148 hymns in Pal. V.444, only seven are mentioned in any of the church orders included in the Bibliography, and so at least in midcentury Nuremberg there was little overlap between hymns published in pamphlets and those sung in the churches of German-speaking Lutheranism.[19]

The fact that so many hymn pamphlets appeared in Nuremberg supports the idea that the primary market was consumers purchasing them for use outside the church, for Nuremberg was notable in its continuation of the choral service at the expense of congregational singing, especially in its two principal churches,

St. Sebald and St. Lorenz. Bartlett Butler, in his dissertation *Liturgical Music in Six-teenth-Century Nürnberg,* writes ". . . except for the sermon service [in Nuremberg the sermon was held apart from the mass], the evidence for congregational singing in the churches of Nuremberg is by no means conclusive."[20] Nonetheless, song pamphlets appeared in impressive numbers, and not only with sacred texts but with secular and political ones as well.

In the absence of conclusive proof, all of this suggests that any use of broad-sheets and pamphlets in church was the decision of individual parishioners. Their use does not seem to have been particularly encouraged by church authorities, nor does it appear that printers intended them to be used in church. We shall now seek out the same evidence for hymnals, and this requires that we consider their use on a city-by-city basis.

❖

Nuremberg

The Achtliederbuch

The earliest printed hymn collection for Lutherans appeared in Nuremberg early in 1524. Hardly a hymnal, it comprised but twelve leaves and was constructed partly from preexisting broadsheets. It is generally known today as the *Achtlieder-buch* because of its eight hymns: four by Luther, three by the Königsberg reformer Paul Speratus, and one anonymous two-voice setting.[21] It sold well enough to be reprinted twice the same year in Nuremberg and once in Augsburg.

Its title reads: *Etlich Cristlich lider Lobgesang, vn[d] Psalm, dem rainen wort Gottes gemeß, auß der heylige[n] schrifft, durch mancherley hochgelerter gemacht, in der Kirchen zu singen, wie es dann um* [correct: *zum*] *tayl berayt zu Wittenberg in übung ist* (*Several Christian Songs, Hymns of Praise and Psalms, in Accordance with the Pure Word of God, from Holy Scripture, Produced by Various Highly Learned Individuals, for Singing in the Church, as in Part Is Already the Practice in Wittenberg*). This title, though quite clear, is not without its difficulties. To begin with, the place of publication given on the title page is Wittenberg, which is false: the printer was unquestionably Jobst Gutknecht, active in Nuremberg from 1509 to 1542.[22] The deception was likely due to the political situation in Nuremberg in 1524: the city had not yet officially adopted the Lutheran Reformation and printing was strictly controlled, with books confiscated that might cause difficulties for the city in Imperial circles. Second, the title does not actually say that the book itself was to be used in church but rather the songs contained in it. Third, the liturgy in Wittenberg was quite conservative (see chapter 1), and there is no evidence that these German hymns were in use there; the phrase "as in part is already the practice in Wittenberg" may well have been merely another attempt by the printer to deflect attention from his own press.

And so we cannot definitively conclude from the title page alone that the printer intended the collection to be used by a singing congregation. Still, it would have been in his economic interest to encourage that, for the greater sales resulting from regular use would have meant greater profits for him. The fact that the last item in the collection, a two-voice setting of *In Jesu Namen heben wir an*, could not have been sung by a congregation does not necessarily mean that the other hymns were not. The final setting could have been added at the last minute to fill leftover space; it may have been all the printer could get his hands on as he rushed the book into publication before some other printer produced something similar. In any case, we can be fairly certain that the book was intended for use primarily by individuals as opposed to a choir: the title page seems directed toward the average church-goer, and three of the hymns have commentary appended as to the biblical sources of the texts, something geared more toward the edification of the individual than to the needs of a choir. And so, as with the broadsheets discussed above, individuals may well have purchased the book with the intention of taking it to church with them. Whether they were actually able to use it there is another question altogether. Butler notes that pressure from the city council apparently discouraged further publications of this type, even if the clergy had been inclined to encourage their use in church, which is doubtful.[23]

The Enchiridion

In 1525 Nuremberg printer Hans Hergott published an edition of the *Enchiridion*, which had appeared in several editions in Erfurt beginning the previous year. According to Butler, the Erfurt edition used by Hergott stated in its title that the songs in it were "now sung in church," but Hergott omitted the phrase when he copied the publication. Hergott also retained a reference to educating the young that had been deleted from the later Erfurt print. Butler takes this as an indication that Hergott was trying to avoid the impression that his collection was intended for use in the Nuremberg churches.[24] In fact, all this can be explained more easily. Butler believed that Hergott used as his model an Erfurt edition of 1525, either *RISM* 1525[06] or *RISM* 1525[07], both of which have the altered wording in the title. But a comparison of the contents of Hergott's volume with the Erfurt prints shows that he could only have used *RISM* 1524[05], whose title wording is similar to Hergott's. So there is no mystery after all, and no need for an explanation.

The following year Hergott issued another print of the *Enchiridion* attached to the *Form and Order of the Office of the German Mass*. The new print's title notes that the songs were sung "on Sundays and holy days in the office of the mass as well as before and after the sermon in the new hospital in Nuremberg."[25] That same year Jobst Gutknecht issued his *Form and Order of Spiritual Songs and Psalms that Are Sung in the Assembly at Nuremberg in the New Hospital*.[26] The two publications are not identical, but they contain several of the same hymns.

How were these two publications used in the mass and sermon (which in Nuremberg were held separately from each other)? The hospital referred to on the title pages, the Heilig-Geist-Spital, was a significant institution in Nuremberg. Its main purpose was to care for the elderly, the poor, and the ill, although it also operated a school. Founded by Konrad Gross in the fourteenth century, by the time of the Reformation it had come under the control of the city council. The attached church housed the imperial regalia and relics (most notably the Holy Lance), and services such as commemorative masses for the emperor were held there, with the schoolboys serving as the choir. In 1525 the church's chaplain, Andreas Döber, introduced an evangelical mass.

It is somewhat surprising that such an experimental liturgy should have been possible in Nuremberg. To be sure, popular sentiment did lie with the Lutherans. But the city was important in the empire, and the emperor was a staunch defender of the traditional faith. Between 1522 and 1524 the imperial diet met three times in Nuremberg; and the Imperial Governing Council was located there under its viceroy, Archduke Ferdinand of Austria, brother of the emperor. The eyes of the emperor, the Catholic princes, and the pope were therefore fixed on the city. They were surely concerned when an evangelical preacher, Andreas Osiander, was appointed at St. Lorenz, one of the two principal churches, in 1522. But Osiander's reforms were conservative, and those of Dominicus Schleupner at St. Sebald even more so. The city was thus able to satisfy the desires of the people to adopt Lutheran teachings while outwardly adhering to Rome, a policy the city would maintain for several decades.[27]

The church of the Heilig-Geist-Spital could more easily tolerate liturgical experimentation because it was under the control of the city council rather than the bishop of Bamberg. Its reduced visibility in comparison with the parish churches made this an ideal institution for such a purpose, the significance of the imperial regalia and relics notwithstanding. The liturgical experimentation began gradually. In 1524 a mass in German was introduced in the infirmary chapel. It was apparently spoken in its entirety, with no sung parts.[28] The evangelical mass introduced in the church the following year was a Latin liturgy into which several German hymns were inserted: *Nun bitten wir den Heiligen Geist* in place of the Introit (replaced by *Aus tiefer Not* in the 1526 reprint), *Es ist das Heil* in place of the Alleluia (replaced by *Dies sind die heilgen zehn Gebot* in 1526), *Wir glauben all an einen Gott,* an unnamed psalm or other song in place of the communion chant, and *Es woll uns Gott genädig sein* after the concluding Benedicamus Domino.[29] All the sung parts, even the Creed, were assigned to the choir rather than to the entire congregation.

This presents us with an interesting question. If the liturgy at the Heilig-Geist-Spital was essentially choral in nature, then why were books published containing its liturgy, if not to allow a congregation to participate? Printers would not have wanted to publish such a book unless they could make a profit from its sale. Official agendas for large territories were often printed so all the churches in the territory could purchase them; but agendas for single churches were rarely printed, because there was no market for them. Luther's mass orders for Wittenberg were an exception, because everyone was interested in what was happening there, and Luther's books were automatic best sellers. But what could have been the reason to publish liturgies for, of all places, a hospital chapel?

One possibility is that the publication was intended for students at the attached school. Another takes into account the pathbreaking nature of the reforms in Nuremberg. Just as Wittenberg was a model for all of Germany, so was Nuremberg a model for southern Germany. According to Volker Schier, the councils of south German cities regularly sent letters to the Nuremberg city council inquiring about the liturgical revisions there and seeking advice. Printing the new practices of the Heilig-Geist-Spital would therefore have given the publisher a large market in southern Germany.[30]

Das Teutsch gesang

Between 1525 and 1528 five editions of *German Song as Sung in the Mass, Printed for the Use and Benefit of Young Children* appeared in Nuremberg.[31] The book was entirely in German and contained no music. The preface bade parents and teachers to rehearse the hymns with their children so that they could sing them in the church with the entire congregation as they attended the daily sermon.[32] The book itself was not meant for use in church, and Butler questions even whether it can be taken as a reliable witness for congregational singing:

> In itself, of course, this statement implies congregational singing in the Mass, which the editor, like most evangelical pastors, hoped to promote. But again the language is not unequivocal, for understanding is stressed more than actual singing (note also the emphasis on the sermon). The implications of the book for liturgical practice specifically in Nürnberg are also somewhat dubious, for the publisher and place of publication are missing from the prints themselves, in contrast to the explicitness of *FuO* [*Form und Ordnung des Ampts der Meß Teütsch*]. . . . the limited contents of the booklet and the absence of music further indicate that its purpose was not church use but religious education and training in worship.[33]

In fact, the statement does not refer to congregational singing in the mass at all but rather at the sermon, which was delivered apart from the mass. It is altogether believable that the people sang hymns before and after the sermon, as was customary in many other places. Butler is certainly correct, though, in pointing out that the book itself was meant to be used at home, where the hymns could be taught by rote to the children in the household.

Gantz newe geystliche teütsche Hymnus

In 1527 Jobst Gutknecht published his *Entirely New Spiritual German Hymns and Songs pertaining to each Festival throughout the Entire Year, also the Corresponding Histories and Prophecies, for Singing Devotionally, Conveniently and in a Superior Manner in the Church or Otherwise, and with Everything Based on Clear Divine Scripture.*[34] It was modeled on a similarly titled book published earlier that year in Königsberg.[35] The publisher omitted the place of publication from the imprint, which may have made it easier to export to other cities. There is no indication that the book was actually used in the churches in Nuremberg or that it was intended for use by the congregation.

Summary

There was no organized use of hymnals by the congregation in Nuremberg, and it is uncertain whether individuals carried them to church for use there. One must question how much opportunity the people had to sing in church outside of the sermons, as the liturgy in Nuremberg continued to be quite conservative through-

out the century, as can be seen in the relevant church orders and in the following
report of Sir Thomas Eliot, a Catholic visiting Nuremberg in 1532:

> The Preest in vestments after oure manner, singith everi thing in Latine,
> as we use, omitting suffrages. The Epistel he readith in Latin. In the meane
> time the sub Deacon goeth into the pulpite and readeth to the people the
> Epistel in their vulgare; after thei peruse other thinges as our prestes doo.
> Than the Preeste redith softly the Gospell in Latine. In the meane space
> the Deacon goeth into the pulpite and readith aloude the Gospell in the
> Almaigne tung. Mr Cranmere sayith it was shewid to him that in the
> Epistles and Gospels thei kept not the ordre that we doo, but doo peruse
> every daye one chapitre of the New Testament. Afterwards the prest and
> the quere doo sing the Credo as we doo; the secretes and preface they
> omitt, and the priest singith with a high voyce the wordes of the conse-
> cration; and after the Levation the Deacon torneth to the people, telling
> to them in Almaigne tung alonge process how thei shold prepare them
> selfes to the communion of the flessh and blode of Christ; and than may
> every man come that listeth, withoute going to any Confession. But I, lest
> I sholde be partner of their Communyon, departid than.[36]

❖

Erfurt

In 1524 two hymnals appeared in Erfurt, both entitled *Enchiridion,* a Greek word
meaning "handbook" that was a popular title of the period for theological and devotional works. They were the works of two competing publishers, who have been
identified as Johannes Loersfelt, in business "yn der Permenter gassen, zum Ferbe-
faß" (in Permenter Lane, at the dyer's vat), and Mathes Maler, with a shop "zcum
Schwartzen Hornn, bey der Kremer brucken" (at the Black Horn, near the grocer's
bridge).[37] Both books contained the same twenty-six hymn texts, but they differed
in the number of tunes: Loersfelt's had sixteen, Maler's only fifteen. The books'
titles differed only insignificantly; Loersfelt's read: *An Enchiridion or Little Handbook,
Quite Useful for a Contemporary Christian to Have with Him, for the Constant Practice
and Use of Spiritual Songs, Well Done and Artfully Rendered in German.*[38]

The title suggests that the book was intended for an individual's private use,
and the preface reinforces the idea, saying that the book was produced to make
Christian teaching accessible to the common people and to counteract heresy as
spread by those preaching and singing in Latin. For, according to the editor, choristers in chapels and cloisters stand around all day in the choir and, just as the priests
of Baal howled and shrieked so that no one could understand them, they too bray
like asses to a deaf God. For they often do not even understand the words they are
singing or speaking, and this harms not only them but the entire congregation. And
so this book is presented in German so that a Christian may carry it around with
him and practice the hymns contained in it. It is also useful in the upbringing of
children.[39]

95

A supplemental volume appeared the following year from Loersfelt's press entitled *Several Christian Songs and Psalms Not Previously Included in the Enchiridion, with Great Diligence Rendered in German and Printed, with a Preface by the Highly Learned Dr. Martin Luther.*[40] Luther's preface was simply copied from Johann Walter's *Geystliche gesangk Buchleyn* of 1524.

There is no internal evidence that either of these books was used in church, at least not initially. But the *Enchiridion* became quite popular and was reprinted and expanded numerous times throughout the century, not only in Erfurt but also in Breslau, Strassburg, Nuremberg, Zwickau, Wittenberg, Rostock, Leipzig, Magdeburg, Lübeck, Parchim, Hamburg, and Wesel.[41] Most of the editions simply reprinted Luther's preface, so no new information is to be gained there. But a new title was given in Loersfelt's Erfurt edition of 1525: *Enchiridion of Spiritual Songs as Are Now (Praise God) Sung in the Churches, Drawn from Holy Scripture, Enlarged, Improved and Diligently Corrected, with a Lovely Preface by Martin Luther.*[42] Maler, who had stolen Loersfelt's original edition of the previous year, also reprinted this one, with the title page reading ". . . enlarged, improved and diligently corrected by Doctor Martin's [!] Luther,"[43] which was patently false, not to mention grammatically incorrect.[44] All the subsequent Erfurt editions referred to the songs "now sung in the churches," and the Zwickau edition of 1525 had its own interesting variant: *A Little Hymn Book, Which a Person Is Used Now and in Churches:*[45] it seems as though the printer began to set the title in the active voice, was interrupted, and when he returned forgot what he had done and finished it in the passive! Editions of the book published after 1527 no longer have "as sung in the churches," but rather an indication that the book is published "for the laity" or simply that it is "newly edited."

Of course just because the songs were "sung in the churches" does not mean that the hymnal itself was necessarily used by the entire congregation; but if the people did sing hymns in the services, it seems only logical that at least some of them would have brought their copy of the book with them to church. Church use might possibly be indicated by the 1526 editions of the *Enchiridion*, which were organized in such a way that finding the hymns during the service would be easier, with hymns for mass and for Matins and Vespers placed together. But the books also included the biblical sources of the hymns for the edification of the reader, something that would have been more useful for private devotion (or perhaps for reading during soporific sermons!).[46] In brief, there simply is not enough evidence to determine the extent to which the hymnal might have been used by those attending church in Erfurt.

❖

Strassburg

It is a stretch to call Strassburg a Lutheran city, at least for the first few decades of the Reformation. The principal Strassburg reformer, Martin Bucer, took an independent theological position between that of Luther and those of the Swiss reformers Ulrich Zwingli and John Calvin, and indeed borrowed from all of them and influenced in particular Calvin, who spent 1538 to 1541 as pastor of the French congregation in Strassburg. In 1530 the Lutherans refused permission for Strassburg to sign the Augsburg Confession because it accepted a Calvinistic view of the Lord's Supper.[47] *Das deutsche Kirchenlied* accordingly classifies all Strassburg hymnals published prior to 1550 as generic "evangelical" rather than Lutheran. Still, after mid-century the city's theological position became recognizably Lutheran, and its church orders held great sway among Lutherans in southern and western Germany, and so we consider it here.

Bucer's principal treatise on the liturgy appeared in 1524: the *Foundation and Cause, from Divine Scripture, of the Innovations in the Lord's Supper (as the Mass is Called), Baptism, Holy Days, Images and Song in the Congregation of Christ, When It Assembles, Undertaken in Strassburg through and on the Basis of the Word of God.*[48] In it he discussed the theology of baptism and the Lord's Supper, including reasons why the latter should no longer be called the mass nor the table called the altar; ordered the elimination of the Elevation, mass vestments, images such as statues and paintings, and the observance of holy days (except Sundays); and gave an explanation of the changes in liturgical song and prayer. These changes included the elimination of the Latin language, the exclusive use of biblical texts, and the encouragement of congregational singing, particularly before and after the sermon. The declaration was signed by Bucer and the other leading clergy of the city.[49]

One might expect that we should find the same encouragement of congregational singing reflected in hymnals published in Strassburg, and in fact we find exactly that. The same year saw the publication of Strassburg's first service book and hymnal, the *German Church Order with Songs of Praise and Godly Psalms, as the Congregation at Strassburg Sings and Practices It, Entirely Christian.*[50] A second edition appeared later in the year and a third edition in 1525.[51] The exact circumstances surrounding their publication and the extent to which they represented the official position of the clergy are debated; the earliest edition at least appears to have been a private publication by the printer Wolff Köppfel done without consultation with the local clergy.[52] This edition contained hymns to be sung before and after the sermon (Luther's Ps. 130 *Aus tiefer Not schrei ich zu dir* and Ps. 67 *Es woll uns Gott genädig sein*) and three hymns to be sung at Vespers. It is significant that the title referred specifically to the congregation singing the service.

The year 1525 also saw a Nuremberg reprint of the Erfurt *Enchiridion* and the publication of the *Strassburg Church Order*, actually a hymnal containing an order for the liturgy.[53] It called for the congregation to sing psalms in place of the Introit, after the Epistle, before the exhortation to communicants and during the communion distribution; they also sang the Creed after the sermon.[54] According to the preface, Wolff Köpffel had printed the "usual songs of the congregation" in three volumes.[55] The reference is to a 1525 reprint of the *Teutsch kirchen ampt* bound with the *Straßburger kirchengesang* and the *Straßburger kirchen ampt* (*RISM* 1525[18]). As with the *German Church Order*, the *Strassburg Church Order* appears to have been a private undertaking by the printer; but there is no reason to suspect that its provisions do not accurately represent what was practiced in Strassburg at the time. Köppfel enlarged and republished the *Strassburg Church Order* in 1526 under the title *Psalms, Prayers and Church Practices as They Are Done at Strassburg.*[56] It was further revised in 1530, and this edition was reprinted unchanged in 1533.[57] It is once again clear from the 1530 preface that the psalms in the book were intended for the use of the congregation.[58]

In 1536 or 1537 Köpffel brought out the first edition of *Psalms and Spiritual Songs that Are Commonly Sung in Strassburg and Also in Other Churches.*[59] It contained not only psalms and hymns but also orders for marriage, baptism, the Lord's Supper, visitation of the sick, and burial of the dead. Its editor is not named, but it may be presumed that Martin Bucer, although he probably did not edit the book himself (inasmuch as the preface is signed by the printer), at least played a role in its preparation.[60] It was reprinted with the same contents in 1537, 1538, 1541, and 1543. The earliest edition in which the preface survives is that of 1541, which was reprinted from the *Psalter; that Is, All the Psalms of David, with Their Melodies,* first published in 1538.[61] Echoing the title, it gives the book's hymnic contents as "the psalms and spiritual songs that are sung in the Christian congregations here and elsewhere."[62]

Another agenda appeared in 1539 as the *Psalter with All Church Usages that Are Commonly Sung in the Christian Congregation at Strassburg and Elsewhere,*[63] and once again the congregation is prominent, singing hymns in essentially the same places as in the *Strassburg Church Order* of 1525.[64]

In 1541 the first hymnal with a preface written by Bucer was published. It bore the title *Hymnal, in Which Are Included the Most Distinguished and Best Psalms, Spiritual Songs and Chants from the Wittenberg, Strassburg and Other Churches' Hymnals, Brought Together and with Particular Diligence Corrected and Printed. For City and Village Schools, Latin and German Schools.*[65] Beautifully printed in black and red and in large format (33 × 48.5 cm), it was intended for choristers to read from a lectern. According to the preface, a number of churches had arranged to have such books for the young choristers copied by hand. But that was extremely expensive, so

> the honorable printer Jörg Waldmüller, called Messerschmid, for the benefit of our dear churches and to promote sacred song in the Christian assemblies, schools and teaching institutions, has at no little expense and labor offered and arranged to print a hymnal and to spare no effort, as the work itself shows, in assuring that the psalms and spiritual songs included herein are published in the most accurate way and corrected as carefully as possible. Because this work is intended for many churches that do not all use the same songs, many different psalms and spiritual songs are brought together here so that each church can find herein those that it is accustomed to using. And so you will find here first of all nearly all those that Dr. Martin Luther brought out in Wittenberg in his little book, then the best that are generally sung here in Strassburg and in several other churches known to us.[66]

Until this time, the hymns were available "only in small books which Christians, each for himself, use in the church assemblies and otherwise."[67] Here is an unmistakable reference to individual members of the congregation using hymnals in church. It is unclear from this statement, however, what percentage of the congregation actually used hymnals and whether their use made a difference in the quality of the singing.

Fortunately, we have two other witnesses to congregational singing in Strassburg. As early as December 1525 one Gérard Roussel, in a letter to friends, described the Strassburg psalmody in which "the singing of women together with the men was so wonderful that it was a delight to hear."[68] And in 1545 a young man from Antwerp wrote to his cousins at Lille:

> On Sundays . . . we sing a psalm of David or some other prayer taken from the New Testament. The psalm or prayer is sung by everyone together, men as well as women with a beautiful unanimity, which is something beautiful to behold. For you must understand that each one has a music book in his hand; that is why they cannot lose touch with one another. Never did I think that it could be as pleasing and delightful as it is.[69]

This does answer our questions: the singing was evidently quite good; and all, or nearly all, used hymnals.

Truly, the participation of the people in the liturgy at Strassburg was highly valued, much more so than in places more authentically Lutheran. The 1544 catechism published in Strassburg went so far as to make congregational singing a theological necessity:

> Q. What is the third general church practice?
> A. The church's song.
> Q. Give me a scriptural citation for this?
> A. "Let the Word of God dwell in you," etc. [Col. 3:16]
> Q. What do you learn from this?
> A. Three things.
> Q. The first?
> A. That one should sing in church, that such should always be taken from the divine Word and should be brought together and arranged with holy wisdom.
> Q. In what words do you find this?
> A. In these: "Let the word of God dwell in you richly, in all wisdom." [Col. 3:16]
> Q. The second?
> A. That all the church's song should be designed to teach and to admonish us and to thank God the Lord.
> Q. In what words do you find this?
> A. As the holy apostle says, "Teach and admonish yourselves," etc. [Col. 3:16]
> Q. The third?
> A. That we should perform such song with heartfelt devotion.
> Q. Where do you learn this?
> A. Where the apostle says, "Sing to the Lord in your hearts." [Col. 3:16]
> Q. Should everyone in church sing?
> A. Yes, for the blessed Paul writes the exhortation to song to all Christians. In this way everyone in the church does together that which one asks, teaches, exhorts or gives thanks for in sacred song.

Q. But did not the ancient churches also have specially appointed singers?

A. Yes, to stimulate and lead the entire people in Christian song; but not to perform the church's song all alone, as for a time the aforesaid clergy did, who should have attended not to the singing, but to the preaching of God's Word and the care of souls.[70]

❖

Rostock

Rostock Reformer Joachim Slüter produced two companion volumes in Low German in 1525. One, a catechism, was entitled *A Lovely and Very Useful Catechism;* the other, a hymnal, was called *A Quite Lovely and Very Useful Hymn Book.*[71] The hymnal contained fifty-four hymns in three sections: hymns by the Wittenbergers, mostly Luther; hymns for Matins; and hymns for Vespers. A new edition appeared in 1531 that influenced later books published in Magdeburg and Lübeck.[72]

Slüter's hymnal contained no tunes; this, together with its association with a catechism, suggests strongly that the book was directed at the laity. According to the preface to the 1531 edition, the hymns were intended for "each individual Christian . . . to sing joyfully at all times, especially in the presence of the assembly when God's Word is proclaimed."[73]

The Rostock hymnal, like the Strassburg hymnal of 1541, was issued by the chief pastor in the city; it was not merely a commercial undertaking by a printer (in this case, Ludwig Dietz). We do not have direct evidence that the book was actually used in church by the people, but it was certainly the intent that the people would sing the hymns contained in it at sermons; from there it is a short step to imagine that they carried their books to church with them. This assumes, of course, that they followed the directive to sing in church at all, a question whose answer is rarely self-evident and differs from place to place.

❖

Wittenberg

In chapter 1 we examined Luther's liturgical writings and other witnesses to liturgical practice in Wittenberg. Here we discuss the hymnals published there. Often cited as the first Wittenberg hymnal is the *Geystliche gesangk Buchleyn* of Johann Walter.[74] But this was not really a hymnal at all; rather, it was a collection for choir issued in five partbooks, with the tunes in the tenor voice. To be sure, Luther did write a preface for the book, but it does not contain any clues to the practice of congregational singing, saying only that the book's purpose is to wean young boys away from carnal songs and "to teach them something of value in their place."[75]

A Wittenberg edition of the *Enchiridion*, first published in Erfurt in 1524, appeared in 1526. Its full title was *Enchyridion of Spiritual Songs and Psalms for the Laity, Improved with Many More than Previously.*[76] The designation "for the laity" is reminiscient of the Nuremberg edition of 1525, which states that the book is "for the lay Christian, especially in training the youth"; the exact form as in Wittenberg is also found in the Zurich edition of 1528 and the Leipzig edition of 1530. This was certainly not the first edition of the book, as is clear from the phrase "improved with many more than previously." But any previous edition has been lost.[77]

The 1526 book contained the same hymns as Walter's choir hymnal of 1524, in the same order. Ten hymns were added as well: seven at the end and three interspersed among the original thirty-two. Two of the three were new texts set to the tune of the hymns immediately preceding them. Four texts from 1524 were set to new tunes in 1526. This seems to have been a matter of the popularity of the tunes or the preference of the compiler, as the new tunes are neither easier nor harder to sing than the ones they replaced. Another four texts had been set twice in 1524 but only once in 1526: in each case one tune was retained and the other discarded.[78] One suspects that the ten additions were the "many more than previously" referred to in the title; if so, then the earlier edition of the book paralleled the choir hymnal of 1524 exactly.

This begs the question of whether the *Enchyridion* was, so to speak, the congregational edition of the Wittenberg hymnal, while Walter's book was the choir edition. There are several difficulties with this conclusion. First, Luther's preface to the choir book makes no mention of any liturgical use, but only its pedagogical value. Second, there is no evidence that the choir book was used in Wittenberg as opposed to Torgau, where compiler Johann Walter was employed and which had an excellent polyphonic choir. Third, the liturgies in Wittenberg were still in Latin until near the end of 1525, and even thereafter the use of German was limited (see chapter 1). Fourth, as has been shown in chapter 1, the congregation in Wittenberg sang very poorly, if at all, which should not have been the case if they were using hymnals. Fifth, if the 1525/26 book had been intended for congregational singing, it seems likely that Luther would have wanted to write a new preface introducing the idea. As it was, the printer simply used the old preface from the choir hymnal. Sixth, Luther's comments introducing the *German Mass* to the congregation have been preserved, and there is no mention of a hymnal for the people.[79]

There is no question of the *Enchyridion* being any sort of official hymnal for the congregation. In addition to the arguments in the preceding paragraph, one may add that there is no mention whatsoever of congregational use of hymnals—which would have been a clear innovation—in any of the numerous writings and reports we have from Wittenberg. We know much more about the choral music there; this is in contrast to Strassburg, where we know next to nothing about any choral participation in the liturgy. Of course it is possible that individual parishioners took their hymnals to church with them and sang from them, as in other cities. But given Luther's disappointment in 1529 over the people's unwillingness to learn the new hymns, the report of Musculus in 1536 of the Wittenberg liturgy that mentions no congregational participation at all, and Sixtus Dietrich's description of the splendid choral liturgy in 1540, it seems likely that very few did so.[80]

The next Wittenberg hymnal appeared from the press of Joseph Klug in 1529.[81] This hymnal, whose first edition is no longer extant, was reprinted in Erfurt in 1531 and in Wittenberg in 1533.[82] Both reprints carry the same title, *Spiri-*

tual Songs Newly Improved in Wittenberg, although the later edition contains more hymns.[83] To the preface from 1524 a second preface by Luther was added begging printers not to reprint his hymns with altered texts. The hymns themselves were divided into five sections. Part 1 contained twenty-eight hymns of Luther, Psalm 111, and the Litany in German and Latin. They were arranged in order of the liturgical year, and there was a collect provided for each season, often with an introductory versicle. Part 2, "hymns by others of us" [in the Wittenberg circle] contained Psalm 134 of Justus Jonas and Psalm 117 of Johann Agricola. Part 3 contained five pre-Reformation "spiritual songs": *Dies est laetitiae* in Latin and German, *In dulci jubilo, Christe, der du bist Tag und Licht;* and *Christ ist erstanden.* Part 4 contained fifteen hymns by others. Part 5 contained psalms and canticles from the Bible set (with two exceptions) to four-part psalm tones arranged by Johann Walter. In the 1533 edition, many melodies from Walter's choir hymnal were replaced with others, and the rests from the polyphonic tenor, where other voices sang, were omitted. In the Erfurt edition of 1531 both Walter's melodies and the rests were in many cases retained.

Konrad Ameln has seen the substitution of new melodies for those in Walter's hymnal as a way to make the hymns more accessible for congregational singing.[84] More recently Daniela Wissemann-Garbe has noted that not all the substituted melodies are easier than the ones they replaced, and that some difficult melodies in the choir book remained in the Klug hymnal. Furthermore, she notes, difficult melodies that were reworked for the later book were not always simplified. She concludes that suitability for congregational singing was not the reason for the changes in melodies, suggesting instead that the new melodies were included because they were the work of a single author who influenced the publication.[85] Whether or not she is correct, it seems unlikely, for the same reasons as given for the *Enchyridion,* that the book was used in large numbers in church. It is even less likely when we consider that Luther made no mention whatsoever of any intended church use in the new preface he wrote for the book, suggesting rather that a principal reason for issuing the book was to provide an authorized edition of all his hymns to date.[86]

In 1542 Joseph Klug published a small collection of Latin and German hymns for Christian burials with an extensive new preface by Luther which, alas, sheds no light on our questions.[87] The burial hymns were reprinted in 1545 as Part 2 of the *Spiritual Songs* published by Valentin Babst in Leipzig.[88] This book proved to be the most influential German hymnal of the century: *DKL* lists 53 new editions and reprints before 1570 alone (although none appeared in Wittenberg).[89] Several church orders refer to it simply as "Luther's hymnal." It comprised three parts: Part 1 was essentially the Klug hymnal with alterations, arranged in order of the church year; Part 2 was the burial hymns; and Part 3 was a collection of additional hymns without any discernible order. Luther's preface once again provided no information concerning the intended use of the hymns, but it did note two errors in Part 1 that remained uncorrected in publication.[90] This suggests that Part 1 was made available to Luther only after the printing was complete, the preface being added once it was received. Luther therefore had no active role in the compilation of the book, and it is possible that he never even saw the new hymns in Part 3.

Most of the changes in Part 1 from the Klug hymnal are minor, but two stand out: the replacement of simple melodies in Klug with the original Latin chants for *Christum wir sollen loben schon* and *Christe, der du bist Tag und Licht*. This suggests once again that the Babst hymnal, like the others associated with Luther, was not directed specifically at a singing congregation. In fact it was, like the others, a printer's undertaking for profit. In its various editions, it became the principal source of Luther's hymns for choirs and parish clerks for the rest of the century.

❖

Königsberg

Two small books of hymns appeared from the press of H. Weinrich in 1527. The first, a collection for saints' days, bore the title *Several Songs through Which God Is Praised in the Blessed Mother of Christ and Offering of the Wise Men, Also in Simeon, All Saints and Angels, Entirely Based on Holy Scripture etc.*[91] Its preface describes it as an attempt to provide acceptable hymns for saints' days to replace the traditional but unscriptural ones. The second was titled *Several New Christian Hymns and Songs Rendered into German and Based on Holy Scripture.*[92] It contains translations of Latin hymns and German originals for various festivals of the church year. There is no indication in either book of any particular intended use.

❖

Riga

This Livonian city produced an official church order in 1530 with an appended hymnal: *Brief Order of the Church Service, with a Preface on Ceremonies, to the Esteemed Council of the Honorable City of Riga in Livonia. With a Number of Psalms and Godly Songs of Praise that Are Sung in the Christian Assembly in Riga.*[93] The order was revised in 1537 and printed in Low German in 1549, 1559, and 1567.[94] The 1537 edition prints the following poem on the reverse of the title page:[95]

Geistlich sanckbuechlein man mich nent,	I am called "spiritual songbook,"
Zu Riga jn Lyfflandt wol kent,	well known in Riga in Livonia,
Da selb byn ich Christlicher gemein,	where I am in service to the Christian
Zu dienst wan sy singen jn eynn	congregation when they sing in unity,
Vnd sunderlich der lieben Jugent,	and especially to the dear youth,
Sye sich vleyst Christlicher tugent,	as they practice Christian virtue;
Vill neyer Psalmen vnd geseng,	many new psalms and songs
Auch mit den Noten ich hie breng,	I bring here with the music as well,
Mit wortten vnd orsachen	with words and reasons
Worym man mich thet ney machen,	why I am produced anew,
Der halben geliebter leser sich,	for the benefit of the dear reader himself,
Vm eyn kleyn gelt kauffstu mich,	you can purchase me for a small amount,
Vnd ich dyr gros nutzenkan,	and I can be of great use to you
Wie du wierst lesende wol verstan.	as you will understand when you read.

The title, introductory poem, and preface all point to a hymnal intended for use in church by the people. The title clearly indicates that the hymns are "sung in the Christian assembly in Riga," whether by choir or the entire congregation it does not say. But the above poem says that the book is "in service to the Christian congregation when they sing in unity" (or "in unison"), which suggests that it was used by the people for singing in church. And according to the preface, the book has been produced "for the praise of God, the use of the congregation, and the instruction and betterment of youth."[96]

❖

The Later Sixteenth Century

The later sixteenth century has not been researched well enough for contemporary reports from manuscripts of hymnal use to have surfaced, and so the available evidence is from printed sources, principally hymnals. The *Gsangbüchlein Geistlicher Psalme[n]* (Bonn, 1550) was described in the title as being "for the practice and use of the Christian congregation."[97] Similarly, the *Psalmen, geistliche gesenge, Kirchen-Ordenung* (Frankfurt/Main, 1565) was "for the use of the Christian congregation."[98] Neither, however, can be properly called a Lutheran hymnal, as opposed to simply "evangelical." The Strassburg hymnals continued to indicate congregational use.[99]

The latter part of the century saw the publication of several large and important hymnals designed for liturgical use by the choir. The first, authored by Johann Spangenberg and published in 1545 in Magdeburg, was actually two books: *Cantiones ecclesiasticae* (with Latin texts) and *Kirchengesenge Deudsch* (with German texts).[100] It was followed in 1553 by the *Psalmodia, hoc est cantica sacra veteris ecclesiae selecta* of Lucas Lossius of Lüneburg, easily the most popular of such books, being mentioned by name in several church orders.[101] It was reprinted in 1561, 1569, 1579, and 1580. Johannes Keuchenthal published his *KirchenGesenge Latinisch vnd Deudsch* anonymously in 1573 and Nicolaus Selneccer his *Christliche Psalmen, Lieder und Kirchengesenge* in Leipzig in 1587.[102] Franz Eler brought out his *Cantica sacra* in Hamburg in 1588; and Matthäus Ludecus published two volumes in 1589, a *Vesperale et matutinale* for the Divine Office and a *Missale* for the mass.[103] These volumes were of immense importance to the Lutheran liturgy, but unfortunately no comprehensive study of them has yet appeared, and no modern edition of them is available.

❖

The Seventeenth and Eighteenth Centuries

In most places in Germany reports indicate that congregational hymnals were not introduced until the seventeenth or even the eighteenth century. Cities had them before villages and rural areas. In Ulm, they were in use by the early 1600s. Cunrad Dieterich, church superintendent of that city, preached a sermon on music in the Ulm cathedral sometime before 1629, the date of the preface to his collection of sermons. In it he exhorted the people: "We should be reminded that we are to present ourselves gladly for the singing in church and then, when the church bell is rung, not wait until the singing is finished, but appear right away, having our books there in front of us, opening the same, and singing along with mouth and heart."[104] He then answered possible objections by individuals to singing along:

(1) "I want to sing, but don't have a voice." Answer: If you are a human being, then you have a voice.
(2) "I don't know the psalms;" and
(3) "I don't have a hymnal." Answer: If you don't know the psalms and don't have a hymnal, buy one and learn them: it doesn't cost that much, and that is why we have hymnals, so people can bring them to church with them if they don't have the hymns memorized.
(4) "I don't know how to read." Answer: If you can't read, then have someone teach you, or learn the hymns from listening to them, the same way you learn secular songs.[105]

In Göppingen listening to hymns was exactly the way people learned them. A report from 1601 notes that the hymns were rehearsed with the congregation after the Sunday catechism sermon. First the text was read for as long as it took for the people to memorize it, then the melody was practiced.[106] Of course, most or all of the congregation at the catechism sermon likely consisted of children. Most of the other accounts we have date from several decades later. Arno Werner notes that in 1656 one evangelical pastor, Balthasar Schupp, bade the congregation to bring hymnals to church with them. Werner also cites several towns where hymnals were introduced in the late seventeenth and early eighteenth centuries: Nordhausen in 1687, Lengsfeld in 1717, Reibersdorf in 1726, Rudolstädt in 1734, and Remberg (one of the last to introduce hymnals) in 1746.[107] In Waldeck hymnals were introduced in the late seventeenth century; in Württemberg they were not yet in use in the 1600s.[108] In the foreword to the Breslau hymnal of 1703, Kaspar Neumann criticized the still common practice by the congregation of singing from memory.[109] Likewise, Caspar Ruetz, cantor at Lübeck, noted in 1753 that the people did not use their books for familiar hymns, suggesting that they might find their minds wandering less if they read even familiar hymns from the books.[110]

Christian Gerber, whose *Historie der Kirchen-Ceremonien in Sachsen* (*History of Church Ceremonies in Saxony, Leipzig, 1732*) is a gold mine of information about liturgical practices of the time, gave the following report concerning hymnal use in the territory:

And it is known that forty or fifty years ago a listener seldom brought a hymnal along to church. I have heard and experienced it that whenever someone brought a hymnal with him, it was said by those without understanding to be a pretense of holiness. A leading royal minister just a short time ago told me that a farmer on his lord's estate not far from Merseburg frequently traveled to Halle with his grain, and because he went to church there and saw that nearly all the people were singing devotionally from hymnals, he liked it so well that he purchased a hymnal in Halle for himself. This occurred sometime around 1697 or 1698. The farmer took his book with him to church and sang out of it, but he was the only one with a book. The pastor, an old man, noticed it and called the farmer to him and asked where he had obtained the book and why he was bringing it along to church. The man answered, he saw in Halle that all the people had hymnals with them; he considered that useful and edifying and so obtained one for himself so that he would not sing incorrectly. The quaint old pastor with great earnestness forbade him such a thing: he was not to introduce anything new; it was the schoolmaster's right to sing with a book, and not his and other people's. The farmer, however, did not pay attention to such an unreasonable prohibition, and in this was upheld by his magistrate.[111]

Gerber continued by noting that at the time he was writing (before 1731, the year of his death) most people brought hymnals to church and could sing many more hymns, and many fine hymns had been introduced in the previous thirty or forty years.[112]

Gerber's comment that people using hymnals could sing many more hymns is an important one. We shall examine the size of a congregational repertoire more closely in chapter 9; but we should note here at least that as congregations learned more hymns, choirs became less important for the conduct of the liturgy. During the seventeenth century the role of the choir began to shift, a development that did not please everyone, as we shall see in the next chapter.

❖

Conclusion

In the sixteenth century hymnals are best understood in commercial terms: they were books without official status compiled by printers in order to make a profit. If they were used by singing congregations, so much the better, for that would increase sales. But except in Strassburg, Rostock and Riga there does not seem to have been any real effort on the part of church leaders to establish hymnal use by congregations. In these three places hymnal use by the congregation established itself, especially in Strassburg; but in the rest of Germany this was evidently not the case. Hymnals were introduced gradually during the seventeenth and early eighteenth centuries, first in the cities and then in rural areas. They were not supplied by churches, but rather the people purchased their own and brought them to church services.

CHAPTER 7

❖

Choral Music versus Congregational Singing

The Mansfeld church order of 1580 lamented that many of the psalms of Luther and others had fallen into disuse. The reason given was that they were rarely sung in church, or they were sung at the beginning of the service before the people arrived. Another reason was that in the cities Latin hymns and figural music predominated.[1] The officials conducting the ecclesiastical visitation in Oschatz in Saxony directed in 1555 that the superintendent should occasionally have German hymns sung in the church in addition to the Latin singing, figural music and organ playing. Similar directions were given for Torgau in 1575, Meissen in 1589, and Merseburg in 1595.[2] Such complaints and ecclesiastical visitors' instructions, which became common toward the end of the sixteenth century, were but a harbinger of a much larger issue: the question of whether "artistic" music belonged in the service at all, and if so, to what extent. This question had arisen already at the beginning of the Reformation and continued to generate controversy for as long as choirs played a regular part in the liturgy.

❖

The Sources of the Debate

Already in the 1520s, some reformers objected to the use of polyphonic music in church, including Wittenberger Andreas Bodenstein von Karlstadt and the Swiss reformers John Calvin and Ulrich Zwingli. Karlstadt's influence proved to be short-lived, but the controversy with followers of the Swiss Reformation continued into the next century.

Karlstadt

In March 1522 Luther, who had been hiding from the emperor at the Wartburg Castle since the previous year, returned unexpectedly to Wittenberg to deal with the disruption in church life caused by those who tried to push reforms too quickly and too far. Chief among the offenders was fellow theology professor Andreas Bodenstein von Karlstadt (1477–1541), who had assumed the leadership of the Wittenberg reformation in Luther's absence. At the beginning of 1522 Karlstadt had issued a church order for Wittenberg that called for the removal of all images (i.e., paintings and statues) in the church and that provided for the distribution of the cup as well as the host, with the host being received in the hand rather than in the mouth, as had been customary.[3] Luther abrogated Karlstadt's order upon his return, and Karlstadt was soon deported from Electoral Saxony. In 1534 he became Professor of Theology in the Reformed city of Basel and remained there until his death.

Already in 1521 Karlstadt had written a "Disputation on Gregorian Chant" in which he called for the abolition of chant performed by trained singers because "if performance of the chant is to be of a high order, the singer must concentrate so intently on the music that by necessity he must first of all be a musician and only secondarily a human being at prayer."[4] For the same reason Karlstadt also called for the removal of instruments from worship, retaining only unaccompanied psalms sung by the congregation. Singing in parts was similarly disallowed, for just as there is only one God, one baptism and one faith, so should there be only one song.[5]

But Luther, in the preface to Johann Walter's choir hymnal of 1524, took direct aim against fanatics who would ban artistic music: "I am also not of the opinion that through the Gospel all arts should be dashed to the ground and pass away, as a number of anticlericalists assert."[6] So did Erasmus Alber, whose *Against the Accursed Teaching of the Followers of Karlstadt* appeared in 1556. When Alber had been a young man, Karlstadt's teaching had caused him to rip apart all his partbooks and hymnals; but now he saw Karlstadt's polemic against music as a sign that he had had an evil spirit. In answer to Karlstadt's argument that the unity of God requires unison singing, he replied that such a conclusion made as much sense as claiming that it was proper to have only "one eye, one ear, one hand, one foot, one knife, one garment, or one penny." For the diabolical sign of all antisacramentarians and anabaptists, wrote Alber, is that they abhor music and consider it frivolous that the organ is played in church and music sung in parts. They say that singing in Latin in church is papist.[7] Alber's arguments were to be repeated many times by orthodox Lutherans in the decades to come.

The Swiss Reformers

John Calvin's theology of music has been well documented by Charles Garside.[8] Calvin was strongly influenced by Martin Bucer (see the "Strassburg" subsection in chapter 6) and held that the only necessary music in church was the singing of biblical psalms in the vernacular. Like Karlstadt, he feared that more complex music might cause the singers to delight in the music for its own sake, lessening the effect of the text: "There must always be concern . . . that the song be neither light nor frivolous, but have gravity and majesty, as Saint Augustine says" so that "our ears be not more attentive to the melody than our minds to the spiritual meaning of the words." That is, "such songs as have been composed only for sweetness and delight of the ear . . . are unbecoming to the majesty of the church and cannot but displease God in the highest degree."[9]

Calvin's compatriot Ulrich Zwingli rejected the historic liturgy of the church because Christ had not explicitly commanded it. True worship is in spirit, he said, not in outward forms; and the paradigm for all worship is private prayer. Therefore no music at all, even unaccompanied singing, was to be permitted in the service.[10] Zwingli seems to have moderated this extreme position after about 1523, but his followers maintained it after Zwingli's death in 1531.[11] Interestingly, Zwingli was the most accomplished musician among all the reformers and remained active in private life as a musician until his death.

During the course of the century Calvin's more tolerant attitude toward music gradually won out over Zwingli's among churches following the Swiss Reformation, but it still could not be reconciled with Luther's. In 1586 a colloquium was held in the palace at Mömpelgard (that is, Montbéliard in northeastern France) between Jacob Andreae, provost of the Lutheran university at Tübingen, and Théodore Beza, professor in Reformed Geneva. One of the topics discussed was the place of instrumental and polyphonic music in church (see appendix 2 for a transcription and translation of the relevant portions of the discussion). Andreae argued that such music is a special gift of God with power to move the spirit, citing particularly the example of the young David soothing King Saul with the music of his harp; therefore, such music is appropriate for the divine service. Beza countered that the only music that can move the soul toward God is music in which the text can be clearly understood, which is not the case with either instrumental or polyphonic music. With such music the ear, with no text to occupy it, is led only to appreciate the artistry involved and so is directed to the music itself rather than to God.[12]

In a 1593 defense of Calvinist teaching and ceremonies, Simon Stein echoed Beza's objections to instrumental music and added one more: its secular association. In describing a typical Calvinist worship service, he noted that Calvinists objected to organs and instruments because they had been used more for entertainment in public houses than for edification in Christian congregations. And if people could hardly understand figural music in four or five parts, usually in Latin, how much more this was true of organ and instrumental music![13] A year earlier, Christoph Pezel had explained his rejection of organs and instrumental music by stating that the great costs expended on them can be better used to support churches and schools.[14]

Although the Reformed theologians brought these issues to the forefront of theological debate, they were not the only ones concerned. The famed humanist Desiderius Erasmus (1466?–1536), in a commentary on 1 Corinthians 14, had lamented:

We have introduced an artificial and theatrical music into the church, a bawling and agitation of various voices, such as I believe had never been heard in the theatres of the Greeks and Romans. Horns, trumpets, pipes vie and sound along constantly with the voices. Amorous and lascivious melodies are heard such as elsewhere accompany only the dances of courtesans and clowns. The people run into the churches as if they were theatres, for the sake of the sensuous charm of the ear.[15]

The Council of Trent (1545–1563), which seated only those churches remaining loyal to the pope, also dealt with the issue of the purity of liturgical music; and in 1562 the Council directed: "Let them keep away from the churches compositions in which there is an intermingling of the lascivious or impure, whether by instrument or voice."[16]

The Anhalt Controversy and Its Effects

During the 1580s and 1590s the debate between the Lutherans and the Reformed became even more polarized after the principality of Anhalt-Dessau, under Joachim Ernst and his son Johann Georg, began to introduce Reformed liturgical practices into its Lutheran realm. Wolfgang Amling, the leading theologian in Anhalt, wrote a defense of the removal of the baptismal exorcism in 1590,[17] and an anonymous *Memorial Publication* in 1596[18] defending further changes touched off a series of attacks and counterattacks from Lutheran and Reformed writers continuing into the next decade.[19] The topics involved in the controversy were exorcism in baptism, baptism in general, the person and work of Christ, the use of the Ten Commandments, altars, images, liturgical vestments, organs, Latin singing, the blessing of the bread and wine in communion, the bread used in communion, and the fraction of the bread. In the end, the ceremonial matters under dispute became points of resistance for Lutherans, a means of distinguishing themselves from the Reformed. And so thereafter any Lutheran pastor who, for example, preferred to wear a cassock and surplice at mass rather than an alb, chasuble, and stole was immediately suspected of Reformed tendencies by the Orthodox wing.

Similar polarization took place in the area of music. Polyphonic choral music, which might otherwise have played a lesser role, was emphasized by Lutherans once Reformed theologians had declared it unacceptable. In 1616 Philipp Arnoldi, Archpriest of Tilsit in Prussia, published his *Lutheran Ceremonies,* an exposition of Lutheran teaching and practice over against "the false teaching of the Calvinist fanatics." In the heading to the chapter on music he stated:

Before as well as after the sermon is delivered, and of course during the administration of the Holy Supper, it is praiseworthy not only to sing psalms and Christian songs, either chanted or performed figurally in 4, 5, 6, 8, 12 and more voices; but also to play the organ and praise and glorify God the Lord with other edifying stringed music.[20]

In the sixteenth century, the songs before and after the sermon and during the communion had typically belonged to the congregation. Now an influential writer was giving his unqualified blessing to the choral performance of these songs, removing from the service what little the congregation had hitherto been accustomed to singing. This would have been unnecessary had it not been for the Reformed threat.

The Reformed, for their part, continued to find large parts of Lutheran teaching and practice offensive. In 1616 Johann Georg, Margrave of the Silesian duchy of Jägerndorf, attempted to convert his strongly Lutheran territory to the Reformed confession and issued a decree containing the following points:

All images are to be removed from the church and sent to the court.

The stone altar is to be ripped from the ground and replaced with a wooden table covered with a black cloth.

When the Lord's Supper is held, a white cloth covers the table.

All altars, panels, crucifixes and paintings are to be completely abolished, as they are idolatrous and stem from the papacy.

Instead of the host, bread is to be used and baked into broad loaves, cut into strips and placed in a dish, from which the people receive it in their hands; likewise with the chalice.

The words of the supper are no longer to be sung, but rather spoken.

The golden goblets are to be replaced with wooden ones.

The prayer in place of the collect is to be spoken, not sung.

Mass vestments and other finery are no longer to be used.

No lamps or candles are to be placed on the altar.

The houseling cloth is not to be held in front of the communicants.[21]

The people are not to bow as if Christ were present.

The communicants shall no longer kneel.

The sign of the cross after the benediction is to be discontinued.

The priest is no longer to stand with his back to the people.

The collect and Epistle are no longer to be sung, but rather spoken.

Individuals are no longer to go to confession before communing, but rather register with the priest in writing.

The people are no longer to bow when the name of Jesus is mentioned, nor are they to remove their hats.

The Our Father is no longer to be prayed aloud before the sermon, but rather there is to be silent prayer.

Communion is not to be taken to the sick, as it is dangerous, especially in times of pestilence.

The stone baptismal font is to be removed and a basin substituted.

Epitaphs and crucifixes are no longer to be tolerated in the church.

The Holy Trinity is not to be depicted in any visual form.

The words of the sacrament are to be altered and considered symbolic.

The historic Epistles and Gospels are no longer to be used, but rather a section of the Bible [selected by the minister] read without commentary.[22]

The people resisted the changes, and a hundred fifty soldiers were sent for three months to enforce them. But the people prevailed, and Lutheran practices were reintroduced until 1623, when the territory was gradually recatholicized.

❖

The Rise of Polyphonic Choral Music

Choral polyphony was heard in only a few German churches before about 1550.[23] Torgau, for example, had a polyphonic choir at the time of the Reformation. As schools were established after the Reformation, the boys attending them doubled as choristers, and some of them were deemed talented enough to participate in figural choirs with older boys and men. In a typical choir, boys whose voices had not yet changed sang the treble part; there were generally two to four times as many trebles as any other part. The older boys and men sang alto, tenor, and bass (see "Choral Ensembles" in chapter 3 for a further description of the figural choir). This makeup of the choir continued in use for as long as Renaissance polyphony was sung. In recent years, Joshua Rifkin and Andrew Parrott have advanced the idea that an ensemble of soloists was used for the concerted *Kirchenmusik* of Bach and possibly for earlier music in a similar style. As of this writing, the jury is still out on the matter, but the idea is compelling.[24]

In the second half of the century polyphony was heard in an increasing number of German churches, especially in the north and east, which were less influenced by the Swiss Reformation. The type of music performed varied from place to place, but it included mass ordinaries, introits, graduals, Latin and German motets sung during the communion, hymn and psalm motets, and settings of the canticles in Vespers.[25] In many places instruments were eventually added to accompany the choral performances, especially on festivals. In Dresden, for example, a Kantorei was formed in 1548 to sing figural music, but it was not until 1577 that the cantor was directed to provide accompanied figural music once per month; in 1581 the frequency increased to every other week.[26]

As long as choirs sang choraliter—that is, monophonically—congregations could easily join in the singing of German hymns if they were so inclined. But once figural performance became the rule, this was impossible. Still, compromises were sought so that congregations would not be completely deprived of song. In some places, such as Zittau, the service was sung choraliter and figuraliter on alternating weeks.[27] In others, monophonic and polyphonic singing alternated within the same hymn. This was the case, for example, in the Saxon town of Kapellendorf in 1569, where the pastor reported that on high feasts stanzas were sung alternating choraliter and figuraliter so that both schoolboys and other people might participate.[28] In 1595 the cantors at Strehla determined that on Sundays when there was figural music a German hymn of Luther would be sung before the Gospel, with the first stanza sung in polyphony and the rest in unison with the whole congregation.[29] The Annaberg order of 1579 reports a particularly interesting use of such alternation:

> During Vespers on the first, second and third days of Christmas, on Circumcision and Epiphany and on Purification, with young and old around the altar, the Magnificat has been sung since the time of Dr. Pseudner alternating verses, so that after the organ plays, the choir figures a verse, after or before which it sings a little Christmas piece, and all the children in

the lower choir stand along with the entire church and sing a verse in German in the sixth Magnificat tone; then immediately a Christmas cradle song in honor of the Newborn is sung. This is done with each verse of the Magnificat.[30]

Alternation of stanzas between choir and the entire congregation was practiced in some places even when the choir itself sang in unison; this was a continuation of the ancient tradition of alternating between choirs in the singing of psalms, hymns, and various parts of the liturgy. Sometimes a part of the choir was directed to stand with the congregation to help them sing. Church orders mentioning such alternation, with the part of the service involved, include Braunschweig 1528 (hymn before sermon at catechism Matins), Hamburg 1529 (creed), Nordheim 1539 (Te Deum), Calenberg-Göttingen 1542 (Te Deum), Nördlingen 1544 (Et in terra), Stralsund 1555 ("at certain times when the congregation sings along"), Pomerania 1569 (communion hymns), Oldenburg 1573 (Te Deum), and Nördlingen 1579 (Introit hymn, hymns during communion, hymn before the sermon at Matins, and Magnificat at Vespers).[31] There is also the 1538 order for St. Wenceslaus in Naumburg (and the nearly identical language in Nördlingen 1555) that directs that all German hymns are to be sung in alternation between the school choir, the people, the organ, and the girls' choir (see "Women in Hymn Singing" in chapter 9 for information on girls' choirs).[32] Several records from the 1542 visitation in the Duchy of Braunschweig also bear witness to the practice of alternation (see chapter 5); likewise, service reports from Greifenberg (Pomerania) in 1540 and Meiningen (County of Henneberg in Saxony) in 1566.[33] And, as has been pointed out above (see "Gradual, Alleluia, and Sequence" in chapter 4), the people alternated with the choir nearly everywhere in the Sequence on high feasts.

Occasionally, confusion arose regarding the alternation practice. Matthäus Hertel, organist in Züllichau, reported how the first stanza of a hymn was sometimes performed by the choir and organ with the full congregation, with the second supposedly sung by the choir alone, played by the organ alone, or sung by a boy soloist with organ accompaniment. But, Hertel continued, a problem arose if the people failed to realize that they were supposed to remain silent every other stanza, and then the performance by the choir, organ or soloist went for naught.[34]

❖

The Cantional Style

With choral polyphony and congregational singing in unison competing for space in the liturgy, it was only a matter of time before someone thought of a way to combine the two. Württemberg court preacher Lucas Osiander wrote in the preface to his *Fifty Spiritual Songs and Psalms in Four Voices, Set in Contrapuntal Style for the Schools and Churches in the Honorable Principality of Württemberg, So that an Entire Christian Congregation Is Able to Sing Along Throughout* (Nuremberg, 1586):

Yet there are (the Almighty be thanked) many German spiritual songs with many voices set artistically, charmingly, and heartily. However, although one understands the melody and text, so an amateur can certainly not sing along but only listen since he is not acquainted with Figural music. . . . Therefore I have placed the chorale in the discant so that it is truly recognizable and every amateur can sing along.[35]

The type of setting in Osiander's book, with the hymn melodies in the top voice and simple counterpoint underneath, came to be known as the *cantional* style, possibly from the title of the well-known *Cantional oder Gesangbuch Augspurgischer Confession* of Johann Hermann Schein (1627); books containing settings of this type are called *cantionales*. Fifty cantionales intended for Lutheran use are listed in *Das deutsche Kirchenlied* for the period 1580–1620 and a further twenty-six for the remainder of the seventeenth century.[36]

The prefaces to these other books, like Osiander's, also occasionally provide clues to how the hymns were intended to be performed. Like Osiander, Bartholomäus Gesius compiled his book, *German Spiritual Songs* (Frankfurt an der Oder, 1601), especially to allow congregations to sing along:

> . . . such songs in the Christian congregation are without exception pleasing as well as charming and beneficial to listen to when they are used *alternatim* in chorus and organ; that is, when a boy with a lovely, pure voice sings a verse along with the organ, then the second verse is sung by the *chorus musicus* so that everyone can also hear, along with the harmony, the intelligible word in the common and usual tune and sing along, which is not accomplished without great and noteworthy benefits.[37]

Congregational singing was also unquestionably the intent of Johann Georg Schott as he wrote in his *Psalm and Hymn Book* (Frankfurt am Main, 1603):

> For the advantage of the beloved youth I have maintained the chorale in the discant in all psalms and hymns, to enable the schoolmasters to familiarize the boys with the execution of the divine psalms and hymns as soon as they begin to sing or begin to learn music at school. This strengthens the choir in the church and edifies the common people as well, who follow youth rather than pedagogues. Do not become confused when the octave [i.e., the melody] is sung underneath like a tenor part [i.e., an octave lower] by men, who already know how the psalms and hymns go. This procedure, although it may hinder the counterpoint, strengthens the choir to such an extent that the voices and manner are more easily heard and learned by many.[38]

The Hamburg hymnal of 1604, with arrangements by the four official organists of the city—Hieronymus Praetorius, Joachim Decker, Jacob Praetorius, and David Scheidemann—contained the following explanation by Gabriel Husduvius:

> In this little book you will find German hymns that are the very best and most commonly found in German churches arranged by the four appointed organists of this honorable city in four parts, so that any Christian, inexperienced in music and illiterate, may nonetheless, with the other

three distinct voices sounding in concord, make music just the same, and next to and with them sing the discant to God the Lord in a sweet and lovely tone and superbly thank and praise him with heart and voice. For the discant, which is always on top, has and sings the common tune, especially the one known in these localities, which is never made difficult and lengthened with ornaments and artistic passages, but rather kept quite simple, in the way that they [!] have come to us and are known to the common people in churches and homes, without even the slightest alteration having been retained.[39]

❖

The Writings of Michael Praetorius

The most comprehensive instructions for unifying choral and congregational singing were given in the several volumes of music by Michael Praetorius, court Kapellmeister at Wolfenbüttel. The preface to his *Urania* (1615) was unusually detailed. In it he gave a list of suggestions for performing the German Gloria, *Allein Gott in der Höh sei Ehr* (the following is a summary):

1. After an organ introduction, stanzas 1 and 3 may be sung in unison with the people; stanzas 2 and 4 are sung figurally by the choir in simple counterpoint with the people singing along; stanza 5 is sung *figuraliter* and *choraliter* at the same time. Or a more complex style of counterpoint may be used in the figural stanzas.
2. All stanzas may be sung figurally with the people singing along.
3. The first stanza may be sung *choraliter* and the rest *figuraliter*.
4. The first phrase may be sung in unison with the people and the remainder of the first stanza *figuraliter*. Subsequent stanzas may be sung the same way, only *figuraliter,* or alternating *figuraliter* and *choraliter* stanza by stanza.
5. The first phrase of stanza 1 may be sung by a tenor soloist, the second phrase by the full choir with instruments, and so on to the end of the hymn. Because the hymn has an odd number of phrases, the last phrase of each stanza is divided so that the soloist sings the first half phrase and the chorus the remainder. Praetorius warns that this method is appropriate for small rooms only and will not work in large churches.
6. Instead of a tenor soloist, a quartet of singers may be used to sing phrases alternating with the full chorus of instruments and singers.
7. After an organ introduction, the first stanza may be sung in complex counterpoint of two or more voices, the second stanza in unison with the people, the third in simple counterpoint, and so on.
8. The hymn may be performed by multiple choirs, alternating either full stanzas or phrases.[40]

In two of the foregoing methods an organ introduction was mentioned, and it can probably be inferred for the rest. Other instruments were mentioned in methods 5 and 6; and the word *municiren,* which often implied the use of instruments, was used in reference to the full chorus in methods 2 and 8. Praetorius continued with additional recommendations as to how to perform the music with two or more choirs. With two choirs (specifically, a vocal choir and an organ), he suggested performing one stanza polyphonically with four or more singers; another with the organ and one or two trebles or a tenor singing the tune, the whole congregation joining in; another with all the singers and the organ playing; and so on, again with the whole congregation joining in. With three choirs another vocal or instrumental group was added, and with four choirs he suggested a vocal choir and separate ensembles of brass instruments, stringed instruments, and flutes (the organ could replace an ensemble if necessary). Finally, he advised that if desired the choirs might alternate every phrase, or every two phrases, instead of every stanza.[41]

Praetorius noted that the first four methods in the above list were "already in use in many places." Just how many is not clear, but he admitted that he had previously heard simultaneous figural singing by the choir and unison singing by the people in the court chapel in Hesse.[42] He further stated that "in most places in Germany, when a spiritual psalm is sung choraliter in church with the entire congregation, it is quite customary (as described above) to sing along simultaneously figuraliter on alternating verses, or even every verse."[43] The large number of cantionales published suggests that this style was at least widely attempted. But there are many questions: How many of the books in this style were compiled with the intention of having the congregation sing along? Did cantors actually use the books in this manner? If so, how did congregations react? How many hymns in the service were sung in this way? Was this done every Sunday or only on high feasts? Was the practice limited to a few well-funded court and city churches? Most seventeenth-century references to figural singing treat it as something that was done *by* the choir *for* the rest of the congregation, but the evidence is not so overwhelming as to be conclusive. A comprehensive study of the cantionales would be valuable in answering these questions, but to date none has appeared.

❖

The New Italian Style

Around 1600 a new style of vocal music made its appearance in Italy. In the last decades of the sixteenth century, Italian composers such as Giovanni Gabrieli (ca. 1557–1612) and Carlo Gesualdo (ca. 1561–1613) experimented with new techniques of harmony, rhythm, and texture that resulted in music expressing emotion that was novel in its intensity. Voices and instruments combined to produce music that could be alternately wonderfully sweet or overwhelming in its effect. Early seventeenth-century composers developed the style further, among them Claudio Monteverdi (1567–1643), *maestro di cappella* at the court of the Duke of Mantua (1602–1612) and at St. Mark's in Venice (from 1613 to his death).

Characteristic of the new style were mixed homophonic and polyphonic textures, ornamented melodies, and an accompaniment consisting of a bass part over which chords were improvised (the *thoroughbass*). The concerted style, in which two separate vocal or instrumental choirs took turns predominating in the musical texture, was popular, as was *recitative,* declamatory solo song accompanied by thoroughbass. The more expressive devices used in secular music to highlight individual words of the text, such as sudden and extreme harmonic shifts, were mostly avoided in sacred music; but composers of the latter did not scorn the use of less intrusive devices, such as descending chromatic lines to express sadness, quick melismas to express joy, and so on.

The new style was brought into the German Lutheran churches in the hymn-based compositions of Michael Praetorius and furthered by such composers as Johann Hermann Schein (1586–1630) at Leipzig, Samuel Scheidt (1587–1654) at Halle, and Heinrich Schütz (1585–1672) at Dresden.[44] Schein and Scheidt also used Lutheran hymns as the basis for many compositions in the Italian style, but Schütz favored original melodies unrelated to preexisting tunes. But even when the music was based on familiar hymns, the manner in which the tune was presented, with brief motives from the melody divided among the voices and phrases rarely presented in their entirety, made it impossible for congregations to sing along, even if they were so inclined. The division between the music of the choir and that of the people thereby deepened; this is in marked contrast to the cantional style, which had attempted to combine the two.

❖

Opposition to the New Style

By the second quarter of the seventeenth century the laity had become accustomed to singing in church and began to oppose the encroachment of figural music on their territory. In Ulm parishioners complained that congregational singing was being suppressed by the learned singing of the choir. Ulm superintendent Cunrad Dieterich defended figural music in a sermon preached sometime before 1629, saying that (1) it ornaments the service and allows it to proceed more smoothly; (2) it is lovely (*lieblich*); (3) the average person is moved by it, even without understanding it, just as with organ music (which there are no demands to abolish); and (4) it is not sung nearly so often as hymns, so there is really no cause for complaint. In any case, he continued, most of the congregation does not enter the church in time for the singing, but remains outside until a signal is given that the preacher is about to enter the pulpit. Many, when they do arrive for the singing, do not sing along but read a book instead (presumably a devotional manual of the sort described in "Demeanor at Services" in chapter 3). Furthermore, many chat during the singing (although they are quiet during the prayers); and the higher classes tend not to sing at all, but only the poor and simple folk.[45] Dieterich's complaint about chatter and other disturbances during (in this case) the figural music was echoed by Laurence Schröder, organist of the Holy Ghost Church in Copenhagen, in a book published in 1639.[46]

To be sure, figural music in the new style with instruments could be performed only in places with well-funded music programs, which for practical purposes meant city churches and court chapels. According to Christoph Frick's manual on church music (2d ed., Lüneburg, 1631), such music was gladly heard in the cities, but was not possible in smaller places. In towns, he reported, at least organs could be heard in addition to the unison singing; and even in the smallest villages hymns were sung before and after the sermon.[47] After the Thirty Years' War ended in 1648, funds to support such music became more widely available, and the performance of figural music with instruments gained in popularity. In Hamburg in 1685 Cantor Gerstenbüttel complained to the Ministerium that two, three, four and even more pieces of music with choir and instruments were performed during the communion so that frequently there was not enough time for the congregation to sing even one hymn.[48] During Bach's tenure in Leipzig, cantatas were divided into halves, with the first half performed before the main sermon and the second half after it (or sometimes during the communion). By the middle of the eighteenth century Johann Adam Hiller was able to report that cantatas had been introduced in large, medium, and small cities and even in villages, although in the latter they were poorly done.[49]

Grossgebauer and Mithobius

Learned reaction against performances of *Kirchenmusik,* as it was called, arose in the second half of the seventeenth century. At issue was the question of whether music in the Italian style with soloists and chorus accompanied by orchestra was capable of directing the listener's attention to God rather than to the impressive music itself. A secondary issue was whether the performing musicians themselves were devout Christians.

In 1661 an enormously influential and controversial book appeared: Theophilus Grossgebauer's *Warning Cries from Ravaged Zion; That Is, a Frank and Necessary Disclosure of Why Evangelical Congregations Bear Little Fruit of Conversion and Blessedness, and Why Evangelical Congregations at Today's Sermons from the Holy Word of God Become More Unspiritual and Godless.*[50] The book treated all sorts of abuses in the church; chapter 11 concerned the divine service. In it the 33-year-old theologian from Rostock advanced the idea that the introduction of organs, instrumental music and choral polyphony into the church had been a deliberate plot by the papacy to silence the Word of God by distracting the people from it with music that sounded impressive but which had no spiritual effect. Then, showing this to have been a rhetorical exaggeration, he said that no matter who had really introduced these things, their effect had in fact been exactly as described. In a passage that was to be widely quoted, he depicted the result of importing the new style from Italy (see appendix 2 for a complete transcription of the relevant parts of chapter 11):

> Hence organists, cantors, trained brass players and [other] musicians,
> for the most part unspiritual people, unfortunately rule the city churches.
> They play, sing, fiddle and make sounds according to their own wishes.
> You hear the whistling, ringing and roaring but do not know what it is,

whether you should prepare yourself for battle or retreat; one is chasing the other with concerto-style playing and several of them are fighting each other over who plays most artistically and who can most subtly resemble the nightingale.

And just as the world is not now serious, but rather shallow, having lost the old, quiet devotion, so songs have been sent out of the south and west to us in Germany in which the biblical texts are torn apart and chopped up into little pieces through quick runs in the throat: these are "the improvisations" referred to in Amos 6:5 which, as with birds, can pull and break the voice. Then an ambitious collective howling commences to determine who can sing best and most like the birds. Now it's Latin, now it's German; very few can understand the words, and if they do understand it, it still doesn't stick. There sits the organist, playing and displaying his artistry—so that the artistry of one man might be displayed, the entire congregation of Jesus Christ is supposed to sit there and hear the sound of the pipes, on account of which the congregation becomes sleepy and lethargic. Many sleep, many chatter, many look about where they should not, many would like to read but cannot because they have not learned how, although they could be well instructed through the spiritual songs of the congregation, as Paul demands. Many would like to pray, but are so occupied with and bewildered by the howling and din that they cannot. Occasionally it goes right to the edge, so if an unbeliever were to come into our assembly would he not say we were putting on a spectacle and were to some extent crazy?[51]

In 1665, four years after Grossgebauer's book was published, a refutation appeared in the form of a collection of sermons edited by Hector Mithobius, pastor in Otterndorf, a village in Hadeln north of Bremen, and first cousin once removed of composer Heinrich Scheidemann's wife, as he proudly asserted. In the preface Mithobius told how his father, Dr. Hector Mithobius, pastor in Böblingen, would take special care to ensure that any figural music sung there was appropriate for the service. The elder Mithobius used to instruct the schoolboys himself in figural and instrumental music each day to prepare them to play in the church. And when he was at Ratzeburg, he would require a list from the cantors of all the music they desired to perform so that he might review it and request any changes that might better accommodate it to the ecclesiastical time and the sermon. Before the sermon, hymns were sung in four parts, but simply, so that the people could sing along with the discant. After the sermon a motet or concerto of five to eight or more voices was performed. In this way both old and new musical styles were heard.[52] Mithobius admitted that there were occasions when the divine gift of music was abused, but denied that the solution was to abolish the music. Rather, he said, figural and instrumental music were able to proclaim the death of Christ just as well as unison singing, and with even greater joy and distinction.[53]

In the decades after Grossgebauer and Mithobius the question of the "abuse of music," as it was called, was hotly debated. Johannes Muscovius, in a 1687 polemic against the use of Latin in the service, cited Grossgebauer frequently and added a few well-chosen and colorful words of his own concerning the music.[54] Johann Schiecke's dissertation at Leipzig weighed in supporting the use of organ and instruments.[55] Andreas Werckmeister provided a balanced view, favoring performed music in church but issuing warnings and practical advice to musicians concerning its use and abuse.[56] Gottfried Vockerodt, school rector in Gotha, touched off a controversy after three of his students read papers on August 10, 1696, on the Roman emperors Caligula, Claudius, and Nero (whom the students had recently studied) and how their early experiences with musical and theatrical entertainment had led them down the path of ruin. The following year Johann Beer, court Kapellmeister at Weissenfels, reprinted Vockerodt's public invitation to the presentation together with a point-by-point refutation, and in the next four years at least a dozen attacks and counterattacks by various authors appeared in print. The entire controversy has been well documented by Joyce Irwin and need not be covered in detail here.[57]

Gerber and Motz

The next player in the debate over the Kirchenmusik was Christian Gerber, pastor in Lockwitz, near Dresden. Toward the end of his life (he died in 1731) he wrote a reserved and sensible, if still opinionated, history of ecclesiastical ceremonies in Saxony;[58] but earlier in his career his writings possessed much more fire. The controversy began innocently enough: in 1690 the Saxon pastor published a little book titled *The Unrecognized Sins of the World,* which detailed seventeen sins that are widely ignored as such: sleeping in church, hypocrisy, parents complaining when they have more children than they would like, dealing unfairly with the poor in making purchases, complaining about unfavorable weather, slandering foreign or heathen governments, dwelling on sadness, disregarding God's love out of coldness of heart, remaining silent in the face of evil, speaking jokingly of shameful things, calling one another names, being superstitious, dressing up as Christ at Christmas for the sake of the children, being too curious about the mysteries of God and nature, youth reading romance novels and seeking to emulate them, a superior offending an inferior and refusing to apologize, and not taking sins of youth seriously.[59] The book was so popular that Gerber produced a sequel in 1699 listing eighty more unrecognized sins (two more volumes later appeared, bringing the total number of sins to 257). In the 1699 book he graphically described the current state of music in the larger churches, of which the following is a summary (see appendix 2 for a complete transcription of the chapter on church music):

1. Music is the gift of God, but it is commonly abused in church.
2. Italians often serve as musicians in Lutheran churches; and many musicians, whether Italian or German, are unspiritual people.
3. The music currently performed in churches entertains the ear but does not benefit the soul.
4. Current church music is just so much noise, and often the text cannot be understood clearly.
5. The music of the Old Testament and the early church was truly spiritual.

6. Theophilus Grossgebauer has also written about this (he is quoted at length).
7. Congregational hymns are to be preferred to performed music.
8. Some performed music is appropriate in the service, but large sums should not be spent on it.

Gerber's opinions on church music were answered point by point in 1703 by Georg Motz, cantor in the Prussian city of Tilsit (the following is a greatly abbreviated summary):

1. Purely vocal music is also subject to abuse, but God desires to be praised with music. Well-composed music reflecting the text does not constitute abuse.
2. Italians do not serve as soloists in Lutheran churches, for they are not satisfied with the low pay. It is not sinful to allow Italians to complete a choir lacking voices. And even if singers are evil and godless, their singing may still be good. Just as the office of a priest remains holy even if the man himself is unholy, so also is the singing and playing of an evil musician holy.
3. Artistic compositions are from the Holy Spirit, not from the spirit of this world, and so cannot fail to benefit the soul.
4. Church music is a God-pleasing noise. Just because the text may be difficult to understand does not mean that the music serves no purpose; even the sermon is often difficult to understand given the acoustics in many churches. It is not always necessary to understand what is being played or sung; it is sufficient to recognize that it is spiritual music.
5. It cannot be proven that our music is any different from that of the Old Testament. The early church used both vocal and instrumental music.
6. Grossgebauer claims that the music disturbs the people, but how can it be disturbing if it is well done? He also claims that the sound of the organ tends to lull people to sleep, but this is even more the case with the sermon! Neither the preacher nor the musician is to blame: almost more people are asleep than awake.
7. Praising God with instruments is commanded in Scripture and pleasing to the human soul. Both hymns and performed music are useful.
8. Music honors God and preserves order in the church. Concerning the cost of a music program: Solomon, the wisest of all men, spent a fortune on the temple. Cities can certainly afford to build both organs and orphanages.[60]

It is interesting that Motz did not deny that musicians were unspiritual people, but stated only that their music may nonetheless be acceptable. He may have had in mind situations such as that in Hamburg, where the choir order of 1644 directed that choir members may no longer visit wine and beer houses during the sermon, as the practice had been causing great anger among the people.[61] In response to

Motz's counterarguments, Gerber penned a 32-page open letter to Motz dated October 30, 1703, and published in 1704 that reiterated his previous arguments. He summarized his latest missive by saying that church music does not serve the praise of God when (1) godless people or those of another religion are used as musicians, or (2) more attention is paid to art than to devotion.[62] Motz published one further reply to Gerber in 1708, but it added nothing of substance to the discussion.

Other Writers

To modern readers, some of the most interesting arguments were made by writers who attempted to prove their opinions through an analysis of sacred scripture. Wolfgang Caspar Printz, writing in 1690, offered what seemed to him irrefutable evidence that the music at the time of Kings David and Solomon was figural. Drawing on biblical descriptions of large performing forces, he reasoned that since so many musicians were playing together, they must have been playing in harmony. They could not have all sung together in unison because people's voices have different ranges, he wrote. He considered it unbelievable that they could have played together in octaves, and because other intervals would produce an unpleasant sound, he concluded that the ancient music was like that of his own time, and therefore figural![63]

The Eighteenth Century

The debate over musical style in the church intensified in the eighteenth century. Opponents of the new music were quick to point out its resemblance to operatic music; and theologian and poet Erdmann Neumeister, one of its most vocal supporters, did not help matters when he boldly proclaimed "In a word, a cantata appears to be a piece from an opera."[64] The debate was at its fiercest from about 1700 to about 1740. After that polemical writings still appeared occasionally, but they lacked the immediacy of the earlier works. The authors and publications in the debate have been adequately covered by Joyce Irwin (see Irwin 1993, chapter 12: "The cantata debate"), so it is sufficient here to make a few observations.[65]

First, the principal players in the eighteenth-century debates were musicians, not pastors and theology professors, as in earlier times. Partly this was due to the fragmentation of Lutheran orthodoxy during the eighteenth century, but even more important were the increase in the status and influence of church musicians due to the increased demands placed on them by the new musical style and the growing prosperity of German society that allowed church musicians, who were now better paid, to publish their opinions in print.

Second, the attitude of the defenders of the new style became more militant. In the seventeenth century supporters of the new style defended it on the grounds that it was permissible in the church and a useful aid to devotion alongside hymns. Now some eighteenth-century writers argued that instrumental performances in church were not only permissible but were in fact commanded by God in Scripture. Christoph Raupach took this view, saying that God had commanded music, and that this is the most important reason for having it in church, but that it was also important because it was edifying. The Kirchenmusik in particular was joyful music, and Christians were commanded to make joyful music in the church.[66] Gottfried Ephraim Scheibel, in an attempt to prove the necessity of Kirchenmusik, traced the history of music from the creation of the world, through the Old and New Testaments and the history of the church.[67] Johann Sebastian Bach wrote in his personal Bible next to 1 Chronicles 25, which relates the extensive use of music in temple worship, that "This chapter is the true foundation of all God-pleasing *Kirchenmusik.*" Bach further cited 1 Chronicles 28:19–21, in which King David ascribes the plan of temple worship to God, as proof that God had instituted music.[68]

Third, the debate reflected a change toward a more anthropocentric view of church music. In the sixteenth century the effect of music on its hearers was a peripheral concern at best. Sixteenth-century Lutherans had no need for a theology of church music; they never addressed the question of the purpose of music in the church, as its purpose was obvious: it either conveyed a liturgical text or substituted for one. A more philosophical observer might have said that its purpose was to glorify God. But by the eighteenth century writers saw the purpose of music as being the arousing of emotion; and the more emotion the music produced in the listener, the better it was considered to be. Of course, the emotions produced had to be the right ones, ones that would direct the minds of the people to God.

Writer after writer espoused this view of church music. Scheibel argued in 1721 that performed music was superior even to hymns because it could better move the emotions; in fact, he believed that church music would be better if it were more theatrical.[69] Heinrich Bokemeyer, cantor at Wolfenbüttel, wrote around 1725 that the purpose of the performed music in church was to "instruct the audience in a genteel and agreeable manner."[70] Johann Mattheson, who by day was assistant to the English ambassador and by night was the most influential German writer on music of the century, took issue with Bokemeyer's opinion, saying that church music's purpose was not merely to instruct the listeners but to move them emotionally.[71] In 1728 Mattheson published *Der musicalische Patriot,* a defense of the theatrical style of church music. In it he stated outright that the purpose of church music was the same as that of theatrical music: to move the emotions of the listeners.[72] Johann Adolph Scheibe, Kappellmeister to the King of Denmark, wrote in 1745 that "the chief purpose of church music is mainly to edify the audience, to arouse them to devotion, in order to awaken in them a quiet and holy fear toward the Divine Essence."[73]

It is noteworthy that all the foregoing writers spoke of the "audience" or "listeners" (*Zuhörer*) rather than of the "congregation" (*Gemein[d]e*). They saw the assembly more as passive spectators to be moved than as active participants in the liturgy, at least insofar as the Kirchenmusik was concerned. Indeed, the criticism of Grossgebauer, Gerber and others that the Kirchenmusik served only to entertain struck perilously close to the truth. For Scheibe, the difference from operatic music was only one of degree, with the joy and delight (*Freude und Lust*) of the Kirchenmusik somewhat moderated from what one heard in the theater.[74]

❖

The Influence of Pietism

The arguments of Grossgebauer, Gerber, and others against performed music in church hardly sounded new, as similar criticisms had been made a century earlier by Reformed writers such as Beza, Stein, and Pezel. But while earlier Lutherans had cast aside such opinions, in the late seventeenth century more attention was being paid to them, both by traditional "Orthodox" Lutherans and especially by those of the Pietist persuasion.

The word Pietist dates from about 1690 and refers to German Lutherans of the period from about 1675 to about 1730 who placed an emphasis on living a pure Christian life and who employed certain practices to assist them in that endeavor.[75] Among those practices were six proposed in what is widely regarded as the Pietist manifesto, Philipp Jakob Spener's *Pia desideria* of 1666 (republished in 1675); namely, greater opportunities for Bible reading and small-group Bible studies, an increased emphasis on the priesthood of all believers, spiritual life counseling by a confessor or trusted friend, a reduced emphasis on dogmatic disputations among those holding differing beliefs, careful attention to the personal and devotional life of students studying to be pastors, and required practical fieldwork in ministry of those students.[76] Pietists became known for their fervent spirituality, their concern for the poor, their zeal for evangelism and foreign missions, and their ecumenical attitude toward other Christians.

Reaction against the Pietists began slowly but increased in momentum during the early eighteenth century. Johann Friedrich Mayer, professor in Greifswald (later in Hamburg), wrote a *Brief Report on Pietists* under the persona of "a Swedish theologian." Mayer's report was partly in response to a 1702 dissertation by Conrad Ludwig Wagner, delivered in Halle (a center of Pietism) under license from his advisor, Samuel Stryk, in which the author advanced the opinion that liturgical ceremonies were superstitious.[77] In his book, Mayer answered the question "What are Pietists?":

> Answer: They are the fanatics who under the pretext of piety persecute the pure, true Lutheran religion, casting aside its most holy foundation and the doctrine derived from it as well as praiseworthy, most needed ordinances that are in agreement with the Word of God, opening the door to all heretics in the church, taking them under their care and defending them, allowing each person to believe whatever he will; but bewitching poor souls with their hypocrisy so that they, like the idols of the heathen, which have eyes but do not see and ears but do not hear, follow their obvious lies and deceptions quite closely, thereby rushing along with them toward eternal damnation.[78]

Lest anyone doubt the danger in following the Pietist fanatics, Mayer continued with an exposition detailing a number of errors of Pietists: they accused the Lutheran confessional documents of having grievous faults, they did not accept the Bible as God's Word, they denied the possibility of heresy, they believed that one could be saved without Christ, they denied the doctrine of the Trinity, and so on. Some, said Mayer, even believed that Christ became human again and had been born in Guthenberg, one mile from Kulmbach.[79] In the area of liturgical practice, Mayer accused them of wanting to abolish the singing of the hymns *Jesu, meine Freude* and *Meinen Jesum lass ich nicht.* In addition, they demanded that the Benediction not be spoken over the entire congregation, and they wanted to abolish prescribed prayers, altars, candles, the sign of the cross at the Benediction, the use of the crucifix, church towers, bells, organs, Kirchenmusik, and so on. For communion, said Mayer, they wanted to use bread instead of the host and ordinary beer or wine glasses instead of the chalice.[80]

It should have been obvious to any neutral observer that Mayer's diatribe was grossly exaggerated, and four Pietist responses to his accusations appeared within a few months.[81] One was an official response by the theology faculty at Halle written by Joachim Justus Breithaupt. His answers to Mayer claimed either that Mayer had misrepresented the Pietist position (for example, regarding the last things), that he had quoted writings of people that are not Pietists (for example, on the sufficiency of Christ, the author denied that Democritus Christianus represented the Pietist viewpoint), or that something a Pietist had written did not truly represent the Pietist view (for example, Dippel's writing denying the orthodox doctrine of Holy Communion). In no case did the author defend the viewpoint Mayer had attacked. Regarding the hymns mentioned, the Benediction, altars, candles, the host, the chalice, the sign of the cross, towers, bells, organs, Kirchenmusik, etc.: all of these were approved, although profane abuses of them were not.[82]

It is not possible to evaluate here all the claims and counterclaims made by the two parties, nor can we investigate Pietist teachings in any depth. What is significant for our topic is that the Pietists were, almost from the start of the movement, accused of destroying the liturgical traditions of Lutheranism; and they continue to be thus castigated up to the present day. Paul Graff, author of the most influential book of the twentieth century on Lutheran liturgical history, took this view.[83] Friedrich Kalb, whose seminal work on seventeenth-century Lutheran liturgy was translated into English as *Theology of Worship in 17th-Century Lutheranism,* believed that the Pietists had been the source of a substantial decay in the seventeenth-century Lutheran liturgy.[84] Luther Reed, whose book *The Lutheran Liturgy* is still the most thorough work available in English, had equally unappreciative things to say about Pietism.[85] Yet the argument that Breithaupt and other Pietists were making, that the various ornaments to a liturgical service were acceptable in theory but subject to abuse, was exactly the argument made by Grossgebauer and by later writers such as Göttingen professor Joachim Meyer, neither of whom were connected with Pietism. Erich Beyreuther, in an essay critical of Kalb, has pointed out that neither Halle Pietist leader August Hermann Francke nor his son nor the more radical Gottfried Arnold changed a single part of the service.[86] Pietism has therefore unfairly taken the blame for causing the downfall of the Lutheran liturgy. As Joyce Irwin has noted, "it is nearly impossible to distinguish nonseparatist Pietists from late Orthodox theologians solely on the basis of liturgical theory or attitude toward music in worship."[87]

That said, Pietist influence was much greater on hymnody and hymn singing. The most popular hymnal of the eighteenth century, Johann Anastasius Freyling-hausen's *Geistreiches Gesangbuch* of 1704, was a Pietist hymnal. Freylinghausen was a leader of the Pietist movement in Halle and prepared his hymnal for the large private school there (originally a school for underprivileged children, it was called the *Waisenhaus,* literally "orphanage"). It became popular throughout Germany and was reprinted nineteen times through 1759. The second edition of 1705, which served as a basis for all subsequent editions, contained 785 hymn texts. Melodies, which were printed only if they were unfamiliar, were included with 194 hymns, 100 of which were appearing for the first time in print.[88]

Freylinghausen's book had an enormous impact on subsequent hymnals, and several tunes appearing there for the first time are still in use among Lutherans today.[89] Christian Gerber, crediting the new hymns of the Pietists with a contemporary renaissance in hymn singing, wrote:

> But now our merciful God has caused a great light to shine among teachers and listeners, that not only do most listeners bring books with them, but also that in addition to the old hymns many new and edifying spiritual ones are being introduced and used . . . the old hymns are also being sung and have not been replaced; the new ones are usually sung out of the book, and the mind does not wander, and the eyes do not look about hither and thither, and the devotion is unquestionably better in this respect than when one is able to sing the hymns from memory without a book.[90]

But it was not merely that congregations found the new songs attractive. The Pietists' emphasis on active participation by all Christians in the work of ministry extended to the service as well, and congregations thus empowered began to sing with enthusiasm.

❖

The Lutheran Service of the Mid-Eighteenth Century

By midcentury church music was decidedly compartmentalized, with distinct parts for the people (the hymns) and the choir (the Kirchenmusik). The service was now seen as the activity principally of the people, and the choir's main function was no longer one of singing the liturgy but of performing sacred music for an audience. Christian Gottlieb Steinberg described in 1766 how the service was conducted "in the majority of our evangelical Lutheran churches" in Saxony:

> The opening of the service, in the so-called High Mass, is done with a *hymnus* or a morning hymn. Then follows the *Kyrie eleison* set to music [i.e., polyphonically], which is abused by many composers and set rather gaily. Then in front of the altar the angelic song is sung by the deacon: "Gloria in excelsis Deo" is intoned, upon which the congregation sings *Allein Gott in der Höh sei Ehr.* This is followed by the *Kirchenmusik. [Footnote in original:* I do not approve at all when in a number of churches the

Musik is not done until after the completion of the service. The end goal cannot thereby be reached at all, and it really ought to be.] Then follows the collect with the reading of the Epistle text in front of the altar, upon which the hymn pertaining to the sermon is sung by the congregation. Then another collect along with the Gospel text is sung by the deacon in front of the altar. Immediately after this reading the congregation sings the Apostles' Creed or the Creed ["Glaube"; i.e., *Wir glauben all an einen Gott*]. After this comes the sermon, after whose conclusion the usages regarding the prayers, the hymns, the collects before the communion, etc. are observed as well as we find them prescribed in the liturgies or agenda of the early Christian church.[91]

The end goal of the Kirchenmusik, as mentioned in the passage, was given by Steinberg earlier in the book (1) to beautify and enrich the service and (2) to encourage devotion.[92]

Not everyone appreciated the predominance of the Kirchenmusik in the liturgy. Music critic and composer Johann Friedrich Reichardt wrote in 1774 concerning his visit to Herrnhut, where Count Nicolaus Ludwig von Zindendorf had led a renewal of the Moravian Church earlier in the century, that he had been impressed with the simplicity of the building, the silence and the "simplest music and a pure, unadorned song," which he had not previously experienced in other churches. But demonstrating the everything is relative, Reichardt noted that after the service his host had criticized the organist for showing off too much and disturbing his devotion.[93]

❖

The Influence of Rationalism

All was not well in the German Lutheran church of the early eighteenth century. While many were distracted by disputes over Pietism, the idea of "natural religion" with its claim that divine relevation must be evaluated by the dictates of reason was being promoted by writers such as John Locke (1632–1704) in England and Christian Wolff (1679–1754) in Germany. By the second half of the century the whole idea of revealed religion was rejected by some, while others sought to preserve what they could of Christianity through compromise: the essential history and basic moral truths could stay, but any hint of the miraculous or supernatural would have to go. Both these views, as well as those of Locke and Wolff, may be considered Rationalist; but it was understandably those theologians that did not reject Christianity entirely who still cared about the church's worship and who took it upon themselves to adapt it to Rationalist principles.

Calls for liturgical reform written from a Rationalist perspective began to appear in the 1780s. They called for drastic modifications to the traditional liturgy or even wholesale abandonment of it. Wilhelm Crichton wrote in 1782 that as the earliest Christianity was the purest, the church of his own day should be compared with that one. Since the early days various people (such as those in Rome, Dordrecht, and Wittenberg) had introduced so many additions to doctrine that unity was no longer possible. But each Christian must be allowed his own beliefs. "The divine service, or public devotions, is a fitting means . . . to keep, continue and enlarge religion in thought and deed. . . . If it is established for any other purpose, a correction is necessary." A formal liturgy was not necessary for the efficacy of the sacraments, and it should be revised or eliminated.[94]

Johann Wilhelm Rau argued in 1786 that the old formulas were no longer usable because the expressions in them were in part no longer understandable and in part objectionable. Fixed forms in general were not good, and even the Lord's Prayer was meant only as an example to follow and not as a prayer to be repeated. Some said that liturgical formulas served to ease the task of the pastor and preserve order in the service. But the advantages were specious: very few pastors had so little time left over from other duties that they could not prepare a service, and in Dortmund (for example) no liturgical formulas were prescribed, without disruption to the service. Each pastor used his own self-written order or spoke extemporaneously. According to Rau, the most important abuses to curb were the too-frequent use of the Lord's Prayer, the making of the sign of the cross, the Aaronic benediction, chanting by the pastor, the use of candles on the altar, private confession, the use of the appointed lectionary texts for sermons, and various superstitious practices surrounding communion, such as carrying the houseling cloth to catch crumbs that might fall and referring to the "true" body and blood of Christ.[95]

Peter Burdorf, writing in 1795, argued that repetition in the liturgy weakened the attention of the listener and the impact of the form. The current liturgy did not hold people's attention, nor did the sermon. The sermon (now called the "Vortrag," or lecture) would be more tolerable if hymn stanzas were interspersed during it. The author would prefer to return to the communion observance as Jesus celebrated it, without ceremony, consecration, or singing of the Words of Institution. The formula "This is the true Body; this is the true Blood" led inevitably to the superstition that the communicants were actually receiving the body and blood of Christ! The teaching that the communion imparts the forgiveness of sins was especially harmful to public morality. Some liturgy was necessary for public services to be held, but it should be as simple as possible in order to meet the needs of contemporary Christians.[96]

Rationalist writers backed up their words with deeds and produced a number of new liturgies written with the above concerns in mind. Luther Reed reprinted excerpts from two of them and offered the opinion that these liturgies "ranged in character from empty sentimentality to moralizing soliloquy and verbosity."[97] Still, they answered many theological concerns of the time; and many territorial churches adopted revised agendas with Rationalistic liturgies. Hymns were rewritten as well with a view to removing "superstition" and outdated theology. One of the most notorious hymnals in this regard was the Prussian hymnal of 1780, titled *Gesangbuch zum gottesdienstlichen Gebrauch in den Königlich-Preußischen Landen.* Its Christmas hymns, according to one anonymous contemporary commentator, contained no mention of the deity of Christ; and the idea of eating and drinking the body and blood of Christ was completely absent from the communion hymns. References to hell and the devil had been carefully pruned. Many traditional

Lutheran hymns had been omitted, their place taken by a large crop of moralistic hymns, especially those of Christian Furchtegott Gellert. Interestingly, the author of these criticisms declared himself to be in favor of alterations to hymns, even major changes; but in this case he felt they had been taken too far.[98]

This, then, was the situation around the turn of the nineteenth century. In 1817, the three hundredth anniversary of the Lutheran Reformation, Claus Harms published his anti-Rationalistic *Ninety-Five Theses,* which marked the beginning of a revival of Lutheran theology and liturgy that was to continue for more than a century.

❖

Conclusion

The style of music appropriate for the church service was a topic of debate during the entire period under investigation. The sixteenth century saw Lutherans pitted against followers of the Swiss Reformation. Later in the century an increase in polyphonic choral music competed with congregational singing for supremacy. Attempts were made to use both by alternating services at which they were used, alternating stanzas within hymns, or having the people sing a hymn melody while the choir sang in parts (the cantional style). In the seventeenth century the new Italian style was imported into Germany and caused considerable controversy, which continued into the eighteenth century. This was coupled with a change in the understanding of the choir from a group whose role was to sing the liturgy to one whose purpose was to awaken devotion in the people by performing sacred music. Opposition to the new style, which has sometimes been linked with Pietism, was actually found among both Pietist and Orthodox writers. Pietism did, however, provide a new emphasis on congregational singing. The result was that by 1750 the liturgy was truly congregational in virtually all of Germany.

CHAPTER 8

❖

The Organ and Hymn Singing

Thus far we have identified three causes of the transformation of the liturgy from one that was essentially choral to one that was essentially congregational. One was the introduction of hymnals for use by the people. A second was the change in the style of choral music and the perception of the choir's function from a liturgical ensemble to a performing ensemble. A third was the increased emphasis by Pietists on the universal priesthood. In this chapter we shall explore a fourth cause, and quite a significant one: the use of the organ to accompany congregational singing.

❖

Traditional Functions of the Organ

The organ was by no means a fixture in German churches before the nineteenth century. Relatively few churches possessed one already in the sixteenth, and this number increased only gradually over the next two centuries. Where organs existed, they performed the same functions in the sixteenth century as they had before the Reformation: substituting for the choir and giving the choir the pitch. Substituting for the choir took two forms: playing alternating verses of a liturgical chant and playing *intabulations,* polyphonic motets transcribed into tablature for the organ. Giving the pitch was done with a *praeambulum* (also called *praeludium*), which was a brief piece, typically improvised, in the same plainchant mode as the following choral piece.[1] These traditional functions were still practiced well into the seventeenth century.[2]

130

By the second half of the seventeenth century, organists in most places were no longer required to play motets, but two new functions were added to their duties: continuo playing from figured bass and (in some places) hymn accompaniments. In 1673 Danzig organist Johann Jacob Hamischer was hired as organist of St. James in Stockholm. One of the questions asked of applicants for the position was "What should a good organist be able to do upon the organ?" Hamischer answered that a good organist should be able to

1. improvise a prelude with pedals in each musical mode;
2. improvise a hymn setting in fugal style;
3. improvise a fugue in four parts on a given subject;
4. play figured bass—this is of equal importance to all the other points put together—and be able to direct an ensemble if the director is absent;
5. play in the current Italian manner according to the mood of the liturgical season; and
6. maintain the organ in good repair.[3]

Improvisation had always been a requirement for organists at major churches, but the fourth and fifth items were new in the seventeenth century. Hymn accompanying was not mentioned here, but it was in the job description of Johann Heinrich Buttstedt, organist of the Predigerkirche in Erfurt. His duties in 1693 were to

1. play the organ mornings and afternoons on Sundays and holy days and for the usual Vespers; also for the daily sermons at which Kirchenmusik is performed, staying until the end of the service and playing the hymns as is usually done, preluding on them thematically (*thematicè;* i.e., using the hymn melody) and accompanying them throughout (*durchgehends mitspielen*); similarly playing the regal [a small portable reed organ] at the two school examinations;
2. keep the organ in good tune and repair;
3. provide an acceptable substitute when absent;
4. lead a devout life; and
5. play a half-hour recital annually following the afternoon service on St. John the Baptist [June 24].[4]

❖

The Introduction of Organ Accompaniment

According to Christoph Hartknoch's *Preussische Kirchen-Historia* (1686), the Reformed faction gained control of several churches in the city of Danzig (now Gdańsk in Poland) in 1589–90, eliminating paintings, private confession, the reading of the Latin epistles and gospels, Latin singing, candles on the altar, the host (replacing it with bread), the chanting of the Words of Institution, and the fraction. In 1591 the pastor of Holy Trinity Church abolished the five- to eight-part Latin motets sung in the church, replacing them with the metrical psalms typically sung in Reformed churches. In order to please those who enjoyed music, the psalms were sung "in four parts in the choir, and the organ was played with them."[5] This is the earliest documented evidence for organ accompaniment of hymn singing that has surfaced to date.

The next citation occurs in a 1601 "Order for Singing in the Choir and in the Church" for St. Katharine's Church, also in Danzig.[6] It states:

> Since during the distribution of the Lord's Supper or during the communion on holy days and Sundays after the sermon the German psalms of praise on the Lord's Supper have previously been sung, as desired by the council, the same shall henceforth once again be sung during the communion in the choir; on the first Sunday the first psalm, *Gott sei gelobet und gebedeiet,* and on the following Sunday the second, *Jesus Christus, unser Heiland,* in their entirety shall be sung and simultaneously played on the organ. Thereby the common man inexperienced in reading may be awakened to thanksgiving.[7]

The singing of these two psalms during the communion was nothing new, according to the directive. The innovation was that they be accompanied on the organ. The direction in both Danzig citations that the psalms be sung "in the choir" (*zu Chore*) refers to the place where the singing was done; that is, in the chancel. It does not necessarily restrict the singing to the choir alone. The choir stood in the chancel, to be sure, but it was common throughout Germany for the communicants to assemble there as well, or as many as would fit. For hymns sung during the communion (as at St. Katherine's), those not immediately communing would be able to sing along, and so would the people down below in the church who were not receiving communion. The direction that the hymns be sung "in the choir" would not, therefore, have excluded the rest of the congregation from participating, and the use of the organ would have encouraged it.

Three years later, in 1604, we find an unambiguous indication that the organ was to accompany the singing of the congregation. In that year the *Melodeyen Gesangbuch* was published in Hamburg, with hymn tunes arranged in four parts by the organists of the four leading churches of the city: Hieronymus Praetorius, Joachim Decker, Jacob Praetorius, and David Scheidemann. The settings were simple, with the unornamented tune in the top voice. According to the preface by Gabriel Husduvius,

> For when either the dear youth in the choir sweetly sing such Christian songs, or when the organist artfully plays them on the organ, or both of them produce one choir and the boys sing to the organ [in die Orgeln singen] and the organ once again plays to the song [die Orgel hinwiederumb in den Gesang spielet] (as at present is common in this city, just as not only the heathen Orpheus and Pindar have been accustomed to singing to the lyre, but also David and the prophets to the cithara, yes, to the trumpet, psaltery, cymbals and organ; indeed it is quite pleasant, sounds delightful

and calms a Christian heart, and aids not inconsiderably in devotion to the Word, provided that each gives due regard to the other), then each individual Christian may also raise his simple lay voice with just enough confidence and volume, and now thereby not as the fifth but rather as the fourth and quite fitting wheel powerfully join in pulling the music carriage of the praise and glory of the divine name and help to drive and bring it up to the Most High.[8]

Here we learn that it was already the practice in Hamburg for the organ to accompany the singing of the boys. It was the intention of the hymnal editors that the entire congregation also sing along. Whether they were already accustomed to doing so is not certain, for one might interpret the words of the preface as an indication that the people needed encouragement to sing. The metaphor of the wheel and the vehicle is interesting, for it shows that the editors saw the participation of the whole congregation not as an additional fifth wheel that could be taken or left as desired, but rather as the essential fourth wheel.

We do not know how well the congregation actually sang in Hamburg in 1604, but in Danzig in 1614 the people certainly made a good attempt to sing while the organ played hymns. According to the minutes of St. Bartholomew's Church, the organist was dismissed in that year because "hardly any psalm or motet . . . is played by him in such a way that the congregation can thus sing along."[9] But apparently the organ did not accompany the congregation in all the Danzig churches at this early stage, for in 1633 the organist of St. Mary's, Paul Siefert, complained about the "new and not insignificant work" demanded of him; namely, that he "play the spiritual songs before and after the sermon on the organ, joining in with the congregation."[10]

In 1617 the city of Rostock celebrated the one hundredth anniversary of the Reformation in festive style. According to a contemporary report, on October 31 (which was a Friday under the Julian calendar then in use) a service was held, and the organ accompanied certain parts of the liturgy. In some cases, an indication is given that the entire congregation sang along (*die ganze Gemeine hat mitsingen können*). The parts thus described are:

> *Allein Gott in der Höh sei Ehr* sung figurally after the Latin Gloria with organ accompaniment;
> *O Herre Gott, dein göttlich Wort* sung figurally after the Epistle with the organ and the entire congregation;
> A figural piece sung with organ after the final benediction;
> *Nun lobe, meine Seele, den Herrn* and other German psalms sung at unspecified places with the organ and the entire congregation;
> The Magnificat at Vespers sung figurally with organ, with the entire congregation joining in the German Te Deum of Luther; and
> *Nun lobe, meine Seele, den Herrn* sung figurally after the Vespers sermon with the organ and the entire congregation.[11]

These early examples notwithstanding, organ accompaniment of congregational singing became much more popular during the century from 1650 to 1750, although even in the late 1700s there were still many places, especially in smaller parishes, where it was not practiced.[12] In general, as with the introduction of congregational hymnals, the larger cities were the first to have the congregation accompanied by the organ, and the practice gradually spread to smaller places. Even where the practice had been introduced, not all singing by the people was necessarily accompanied: in Dahlen in 1738 some singing was accompanied and some not, and in Frankfurt am Main organ accompaniment was not used at funerals until 1828 even though it had been introduced in the principal service as early as 1711.[13] In Leipzig it was 1788 before the organ was used for every hymn.[14] And even in 1858 it was reported that in Prussia the brief hymn concluding the service was sung unaccompanied in many places.[15]

In Lüneburg hymn accompaniments were apparently not the favorite duty of organists, for in September 1767 the city organist recommended upon the introduction of a new hymnal that the organist in each church accompany the hymn singing; but a year later the organists still had to be remonstrated to accompany the hymns during the communion throughout and to play only brief introductions to them.[16]

❖

The Purpose of Organ Accompaniment

Every writer addressing the question of why the organ should accompany congregational singing mentioned the need to hold the congregation together and on pitch. For nearly all this was either the first or the only reason. In 1637 Siegmund Theophilus Stade wrote in the preface to a new edition of Hans Leo Hassler's *Psalmen und geistliche Lieder*[17] that he had dedicated the work in part to his "dear and faithful colleagues, who by means of the organ hold the congregation together on the right pitches."[18] Several eighteenth-century writers echoed Stade; Georg Preus, writing in 1729, was quite confident about the matter: "It is well known that the church organ in the service was in part introduced with the goal of keeping the congregation together and on pitch."[19] Christian Gerber, as usual, had an entertaining anecdote to tell; namely, that organs are useful

> because they serve the purpose of starting the hymns in the correct key
> and also of continuing them and concluding them in a single key. Other-
> wise it can easily happen that the precentor, cantor or schoolmaster allows
> the pitch to slip, and the hymn can hardly be finished. And even if the pre-
> centor holds the pitch pure and constant, the congregation, singing along,
> will pull down the pitch anyway. The first time I attempted to go into the
> pulpit and preach, there was a schoolmaster in that place who started the
> first hymn, *Aus meines Herzens Grunde,* too low and was unable to finish
> the stanza. So then he started it differently, but it was too high, and once
> again he couldn't continue. The patron, a noble lord, called toward the
> choir from his raised seat, saying to the schoolmaster, "Now what's the
> matter with you?" Then he started the hymn a third time. If there had

been an organ in that church, the good schoolmaster could have given the
pitch and would not have been allowed such a mistake.[20]

And Caspar Ruetz wrote in 1753:

An organ must be strong enough to outshout the entire congregation and
maintain it in the correct key. If it is too weak, so that it is covered by the
congregation, it cannot be heard well. Then the organ, to be sure, remains
at the pitch in which it began, but the congregation lets the pitch of its
chorale sink. And when the organ reverberates [at the end of] each phrase,
it sounds a half or whole tone, or even more, too high.[21]

Gottfried Ephraim Scheibel noted that organ accompaniment was useful for
more than just keeping singers on pitch; it could actually make hymn singing more
musical. In a 1721 essay discussing the merits of performances of figural music in
church, he wrote:

Spiritual songs or chorales are therefore not to be discarded; in fact, with
them one pays more attention to the words than to the melody. To this end
we use for the most part the organ so that the congregation might remain
on pitch, and an accomplished organist can additionally give to them a
pleasant charm. . . .[22]

In a 1726 sermon dedicating a new organ, Hamburg preacher Nicolaus Lütkens listed the functions of the organ as enhancing devotion, informing the congregation of the melody about to be sung, and keeping the singing in good order.[23] The
printed version of the sermon itself, by the way, is of more than average ostentation,
with footnotes often occupying more space on a page than the text. J. F. W. Sonnenkalb, concentrating more on the organ as a performing instrument, wrote in
1756 that the principal reason organs were used in church was

so that through the power of harmony the souls of the listeners might be
freed from all wild and destructive affects; and in the place of these wild and
destructive affects, as it were, the beginning stages toward certain noble
affects and holy feelings might be aroused.[24]

Here Sonnenkalb referred to the widely held belief in the eighteenth century that
the purpose of music, whether sacred or not, was to arouse targeted passions or af-
fections; in this case, perhaps awe, joy, or a feeling of reverence. In a footnote the
author added that a second purpose of the organ was to keep the congregation on
pitch and prevent disorder in the singing. Lütkens and Sonnenkalb were unusual in
not giving this purpose first place.

There is one further reason for the organ to accompany congregational singing
that none of the writers mentioned. It was perhaps better left unstated, lest its hon-
est admission incur the ire of the Pietists. But the simple truth is that many churches
owned no organ and so lacked the prestige of those with such glorious instruments.
If an organ were now needed to accompany singing, then—praise God!—who
could resist the call to glorify the Lord with the sound of mighty pipes, especially

if the donor's name or image were placed on the instrument? And of course it would be even more compelling if the new organ happened to be bigger and better than the one at St. Wigbert's in the next town!

❖

How Did Organists Harmonize Hymns?

If the purpose of accompaniment was to help the congregation stay together and on pitch, then the easiest way of doing this would have been to have the organ or another instrument play the melody alone, without harmonization. But there is no indication that this was ever done. Nor is this surprising, for the organ had always been an instrument of polyphony. By the time it took over the task of accompanying the congregation (in many places not until the eighteenth century), it had additionally become known as a continuo instrument; that is, as an instrument that provided a bass line and harmony.

Georg Rietschel has theorized that organ accompaniment came about because congregations were unable to follow the choir's figural hymns and sing in the right places, and so the organ took over the choir parts, perhaps playing the accompanying voices on a softer registration and the melody, which the congregation sang, on a stronger one.[25] The idea of soloing out the melody is purely speculation on Rietschel's part based on later practice; in fact, there is no evidence whatsoever that this was even thought of before the late eighteenth century. The first part of his thesis is at least plausible, but it was not so simple as an organist reading out of a modern hymnal. To begin with, the cantionales of the time were typically published in *cantus lateralis* format, with each voice part appearing on its own staff in its own corner of the opened page. This would have been impossible for an organist to read. In addition, Cleveland Johnson shows in his *Vocal Compositions in German Organ Tablatures 1550–1650* that most organists of the time did not read staff notation well. The traditional notation for organ music was tablature, and the German organ tablature of the period was purely a letter notation with no notes used at all. Organists who needed to accompany choral singing generally transcribed the choral parts from staff notation into tablature, and sometimes even printed continuo parts were intabulated. Often organists did not even transcribe all the parts but only the outer voices, either improvising the harmonies in the inner parts or omitting them altogether.[26]

Johnson reports that German archives contain perhaps thousands of manuscript hymn harmonizations in three and four parts. Many of these appear in tablature books with the pieces arranged in liturgical order, sometimes even with the place in the service mentioned, suggesting that they are organists' working copies. What is undetermined is whether the arrangements are actually copies of cantionale settings or original harmonizations.[27] Unfortunately, no one to date has studied the manuscripts, and there is not even a good list of them.[28] But even assuming that the organ settings are transcriptions of vocal settings, we cannot be certain that they were used to accompany the congregation. They might have been used instead to accompany the choir as it sang figural stanzas in alternation with the people. They could also have been used as hymn preludes, but this is unlikely, as it appears that organists of the period rarely played straight through hymns in order to introduce them; in fact, there are many complaints that the hymn tunes could not even be recognized from the preludes.

In summary, it seems possible that in the early decades of organ accompaniment of congregational singing organists read from their own manuscript intabulations of choral settings, or perhaps from their own harmonizations that they then notated on paper. But it is also possible that organists improvised harmonizations. The number of hymn tunes in use is unlikely to have been so great that an organist would not have been able to work out harmonizations for most of the tunes he would have been called upon to play. Of course, this would have been more difficult than simply reading someone else's arrangement, but organ accompaniment of the congregation was extremely rare before 1650 and seems to have been practiced mostly in the larger cities, which tended to have the more accomplished organists. The comment by the Danzig organist Paul Siefert in 1633 that such accompaniment was a "not insignificant work" (see above, under "The Introduction of Organ Accompaniment") attests that some organists, at least, did find the task daunting.

For organists trained in the new Italian method of figured bass, Johann Hermann Schein's *Cantional oder Gesangbuch Augspurgischer Confession* of 1627 provided a source of hymn settings.[29] The title page indicated that the settings were used in both churches in Leipzig (by the choirs, that is), and the preface noted that figured bass had been added for the use of "organists, instrumentalists and lutenists"; i.e., anyone planning to play the hymns at church or in the home.[30] In 1650 another resource appeared: Samuel Scheidt's *Tablature Book: A Hundred Spiritual Songs and Psalms of Doctor Martin Luther and Other Blessed Men, for the Organists to Play and to Sing with the Christian Churches and Congregation[s] on the Organ, Likewise at Home, for All Festivals and Sundays Throughout the Entire Year, Composed in Four Voices.*[31] The preface pointed out that this was the first collection to include all the usual hymns for Sundays and holy days, and absolutely the first to appear in print.[32]

Soon figured bass, which organists were increasingly able to read, became the principal method of setting hymn tunes in print. Several seventeenth-century hymnals included it; the earliest such book specifically intended as an accompaniment book for organists was Johann Georg Brandaw's *Psalmodia Davidis* (Kassel, 1665, RISM 1665[02]; reprinted in 1675, RISM 1675[03]). Published for use by Reformed churches in the principality of Hesse, it contained French psalm and Lutheran hymn tunes set to figured bass for use by organists accompanying congregational singing. Alto and tenor parts did not appear in this book, nor in most later chorale books, as they were called, although a few included them. The only known copy of the earliest chorale book for Lutheran use, the *Musicalisch Hand-Buch der Geistlichen Melodien à Cant. et Bass* (Hamburg, 1690, RISM 1690[08]), was lost in the Second World War. The earliest extant Lutheran chorale book is Daniel Speer's *Choral Gesang-Buch, auff das Clavir oder Orgel* (Stuttgart, 1692, RISM 1692[12]). These were the only chorale books published in the seventeenth century. Table 8.1 is a census of chorale books published after 1700.

Table 8.1. Census of chorale books published after 1700

Publication Date	Catholic	Bohemian Brethren	Evangelical	Lutheran	Reformed
1701–1710	0	0	0	3	1
1711–1720	0	0	2	8	0
1721–1730	0	0	0	6	0
1731–1740	0	0	4	3	2
1741–1750	0	0	1	3	4
1751–1760	0	0	1	5	1
1761–1770	0	0	1	9	1
1771–1780	1	0	0	3	1
1781–1790	2	1	0	15	4
1791–1800	2	2	0	16	1

The numbers in the table are derived from the bibliographic information in *Das deutsche Kirchenlied*. "Chorale book" is defined as a "musical hymn source containing melodies with the figured bass necessary for the accompaniment (less often containing four-part passages) and mostly only one verse of text or even just the outline of a text." (*Das deutsche Kirchenlied,* p. 21★) The count includes new editions and reprints (which were, in fact, rare); "evangelical" books are those not specifically identifiable as either Lutheran or Reformed.

There was no uniformity in the melodies and rhythms used in the various books, and by the second half of the eighteenth century this became an often insurmountable problem for travelers. Jacob Adlung wrote concerning the situation in Erfurt:

> Concerning the disunity in the tunes there would also be much to recall. No village in the present territory is identical to another in all pieces of music: in fact no church in this city sings the tunes in the same way as another. Either they use completely different ones, or they are so greatly altered, that no player is capable of playing a hymn on other organs outside his own church if someone does not set in front of him a tune book that has been introduced in that place. And when an honest citizen attends another church, he must quite often remain a mere listener.[33]

Occasionally, Adlung continued, a church will use music by a composer from another place who has set a hymn tune according to the way he knows it. If the congregation then tries to sing along, a horrible sound results.[34]

❖

Interludes

In 1733 Georg Friedrich Kauffmann published a set of hymn preludes with accompaniments entitled *Harmonische Seelen Lust*. Example 8.1 is a setting of *Ein feste Burg ist unser Gott* intended for accompanying a congregation. One notes immediately that the phrases of the hymn tune have ornaments added; this was standard practice in eighteenth-century hymn accompaniments. Between the phrases the composer has inserted running passages (*passagi*). These appear, he explains, because something is needed to fill up the space at the ends of phrases.[35] These *passagi* came to be called interludes (*Zwischenspiele*), and in the following decades they were to become widely heard throughout Germany, continuing in use well into the nineteenth century.

Interludes between phrases of hymns originated around the beginning of the eighteenth century or slightly earlier. They first appeared in print in England in *The Psalms by D'* [John] *Blow Set Full for the Organ or Harpsicord as They Are Play'd in Churches or Chapels*. The earliest extant copy dates from 1718, but earlier editions had appeared in 1703 and 1705.[36] The book contains settings of metrical psalms with interludes between phrases varying in length from one-half measure to one full measure of mostly sixteenth notes. Also in 1718 appeared *The Psalms Set Full for the Organ or Harpsicord as They Are Plaid in Churches and Chappels in the Maner Given Out; As Also with Their Interludes of Great Variety by M'': Dan'': Purcell*. Its interludes are in the same style but slightly longer, about one to one and one-half measures. The earliest German printed source was Kauffmann's *Harmonische Seelen Lust* (Leipzig, 1733), but interludes of some sort were already known much earlier in Germany, for they are mentioned in a sermon by Hector Mithobius delivered in 1661 and published in 1665:

> Therefore it is also a sin when organists, with their ill-timed playing and runs, hinder and impede devotion much more than they further it, such as with the unison psalms, when the congregation is supposed to sing along, they impede the congregation and cause devotion to go awry through their running interludes, odd preluding before every verse, cutting apart, piecing together, holding out for a long time after every line, splitting apart, and ornamenting, when they could readily play along quite pleasantly and harmoniously in a truly unobtrusive manner.[37]

Unfortunately, it is not clear whether Mithobius was referring here to interludes between lines or between stanzas, but the style of accompaniment is nonetheless unmistakable. The earliest surviving German interludes between phrases occur in some of the early hymn settings of J. S. Bach, probably composed during his time in Arnstadt between 1703 and 1708.[38] It appears to have been some time before they came into general use: J. A. Scheibe, in a 1739 article on the responsibilities of the organist, did not mention them.[39]

One of the most thorough explanations of interludes was provided by Johann Carl Angerstein, whose 248-page manual on hymn playing appeared in 1800. He wrote that their purpose was (1) to indicate to the singers the starting note for the following phrase, and (2) to draw out the emotions (*Empfindung*) present in the preceding and following lines. He added that interludes should generally all be about the same length so that the congregation might become accustomed to when it should enter; in addition, they should lead the congregation easily into the following line by making the last note of the interlude a second below or above the note on which the congregation enters (especially if the hymn is not well known). If this

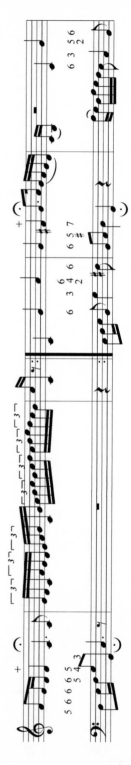

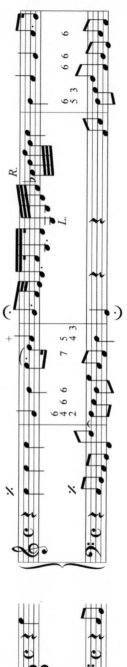

Example 8.1. G. F. Kauffmann, *Ein feste Burg ist unser Gott* (Kauffmann 1733:3)

141

last note is held slightly, or is longer than the preceding notes, then the congregation should have no difficulty. The pedal should not be played in an interlude, as that is a sign to the congregation that the next phrase is beginning (although outstanding organists know how to use the pedal to good effect in interludes). In general, the shorter the interlude and the slower it is played, the more easily it will achieve its goal. In any case, memorized pieces and pieces from operas, dances, and so on detract from the sacredness of the hymn and are not appropriate.[40]

Not everyone was in favor of organ interludes. After J. S. Bach's return from visiting Dietrich Buxtehude in Lübeck in 1705–6 the consistory at Arnstadt criticized him for the "many peculiar *variationes*" and "many strange notes" in his hymn playing that confused the congregation.[41] The "many strange notes" could refer to something as simple as raised leading tones at cadences when the congregation was not accustomed to them;[42] but the "peculiar variations" could also refer to overly complex accompaniments with interludes, especially as the only hymn settings of Bach that use interludes date from approximately this time. Another possibility is that they might refer to melodic embellishments of the sort described by Angerstein (Example 8.1). This is all speculation, however, as the consistory minutes are not clear enough to support a definitive interpretation. But there is evidence of further opposition to interludes. Music pedagogue Jacob Adlung wrote in 1758 that some organists (such as [Johann Nicolaus] Bach in Jena) did not play interludes because they considered them unnecessary; others were forbidden to play them, and still others made so much of an effort at them that devotion was hindered. In any case, Adlung continued, they should not be used with sorrowful or penitential hymns or with hymns about death.[43] In 1767 an anonymous contributor to a periodical wrote concerning interludes that "there is gaiety and occasionally nonsense: there is breaking up, chopping, jumping, tumbling, now unison, now duet, now trio, now duple, now triple meter, and all sorts of further distortions."[44] And in 1785 an anonymous author (possibly Johann Gottfried Hingelberg) criticized the church music in Danzig:

> Among the Lutherans the chorales are mostly over-refined, and it will just become more so for as long as it is considered a great thing to be able to play them through with variations, as is commonly heard *ad nauseam* from our organists every Sunday. The chorale must be performed with all voices, without chromatic modulations, interludes and the like, so that it can keep the congregation together, inspire it to devotion, and so that an individual who, for example, sings by nature bass or tenor can comprehend it right away, and in this way it can be sung in four parts by the assembly. But alas, how I have seen the hymns in a number of churches disfigured by the organists! I heard on a festival in one church the playing of the Creed and thought I was at a carnival, so similar the interludes were to a dance known around here.[45]

The criticism notwithstanding, it is clear from comments by Daniel Gottlob Türk that interludes were in use in all parts of Germany by the 1780s.[46] In 1787 Georg Friedrich Seiler reported that in Augsburg, the organists play the chorale as it has been prescribed to them, with brief interludes, without strange cadences and leading away into distant keys, without a profusion in the song of all kinds of running passages and embellishments, which perhaps glorify the accomplishment of the player, but hardly ever his own devotion and good taste in the presentation of the chorale.[47]

Interludes continued to be used well into the nineteenth century, and Arno Werner has assembled a list of reasons given in nineteenth-century sources for playing them: (1) without interludes, the choir sitting in the back has not yet finished with one line before the precentor begins the next; (2) the congregation needs time to breathe and read the next line; (3) the congregation needs time to find the right note to start the next line; (4) without interludes the playing of the hymn is too boring; (5) interludes give the congregation time to meditate on the text of the hymn; and (6) without interludes the organist may be thought unnecessary.[48] In 1858 one writer reported that interludes were played nearly everywhere. But because they could be disturbing, some places had abolished them entirely, and others had limited them to the break between stanzas. The same writer also mentioned the curious practice of vocal interludes:

> And remembering the precentor at least with a word: it was formerly the custom that he would repeat the last syllables of each line of verse by singing them; and he, when the singing was without organ, would lead the congregation to the following melody note through a kind of interlude, which was rarely done without excessive embellishments. Now with a competent cantor one is accustomed to only a modest lengthening of the last note of a line of verse and an accurate start to the note at the beginning of a new line of verse.[49]

This practice had also been known in 1834, when another writer, speculating that the organ interlude had originated from a practice of vocal interludes, not *vice versa,* noted that it was still customary for precentors leading hymns without an organ to fill in the break between phrases with a few notes.[50]

❖

Preludes

The practice of preluding on the organ is much better known than that of constructing interludes. It originated prior to the Reformation as organists improvised *praeludia* to parts of the liturgy sung in alternation between choir and organ. It reached its peak in the late seventeenth and eighteenth centuries with the works of Dietrich Buxtehude, J. S. Bach, Johann Pachelbel, and Johann Ludwig Krebs, to name only a few of the most accomplished. Johann Adolph Scheibe, music director at the court of Copenhagen, listed the ability to improvise preludes as a necessary qualification of an organist, along with knowledge of figured bass, familiarity with hymns and the ability to evaluate an organ.[51]

Hymn preludes, or introductions, were not a simple playing through of the hymn melody, but could be as complex as the organist was capable of playing. Türk (1787) listed four types of preludes, which in modern terms would be the cantus firmus chorale with preceding imitation (*Vorimitation*) in the accompanying voices, the fugue, the organ trio, and the chorale fantasia. In the cantus firmus chorale the melody could be in any voice, including the pedal. Normally the hymn melody was to be played in its entirety, but Türk allowed exceptions if the tune was very long. In any case, the prelude should not be so long that it fatigues the listeners, especially during the winter: a quarter hour (!) is much too long, he wrote, as even music lovers would become bored. The prelude preceding the Kirchenmusik may be longer than one preceding a hymn, though.[52]

The purposes of the prelude were, according to Jacob Adlung, (1) to give the members of the congregation the starting pitch for a hymn; (2) to inform them of the melody; and (3) to satisfy them with "well-flowing thoughts."[53] Johann Mattheson saw the prelude functioning (1) to prepare the listeners for the following piece or hymn; (2) to organize the time of the service properly, with a short hymn having a long prelude and vice versa, so that the total time taken up by the singing would be the same each week; and (3) to modulate between pieces. He added that it should contain the *affect* of the piece that follows and not be too long.[54] Mattheson's contemporary Lorenz Christoph Mizler agreed with the last point, mentioning also that the organist must not play about in various keys, and he should include the hymn melody in the prelude so that the congregation would know what to sing. According to Mizler, there were many organists who set the melody properly as a fugue or who figured it so that its form could still be discerned, but recent organists just out of school played an "unorganized fantasy or *capriccio*" in which the melody was unrecognizable. Mizler saw nothing wrong with this new theatrical style in itself, but thought it did not belong in church.[55]

J. A. Scheibe also recommended that the organist should base the prelude on the hymn melody, in either a fugal style (following the rules of counterpoint) or a free style (such as a trio, or with the melody in the pedal). But one could also play a melody that had some similarities to the tune but which was not the same, although it should be related in mood.[56] J. F. W. Sonnenkalb, in a 28-page book titled *Brief Answer to the Question "How Should the Preludes of an Organist in the Service Be Devised?" or "What Are the Marks of a Sensible Organist in the Execution of His Office?"* noted with disapproval that some organists memorized their preludes, one for each major and minor key, and played them once or even twice every Sunday. Others played whatever first came into their minds, whether or not it had anything to do with the hymn. Some played a minuet, polonaise, or aria, which pleased the people but did not glorify God. But good organists played preludes that created the same mood in the listeners that the following hymn expressed. There were seven kinds of *affects* useful in forming such moods: (1) *adagio*, which awakens sad and sorrowful feelings in the listeners; (2) *lamento*, which expresses grief; (3) *lento*, which calms and quiets; (4) *affectuoso*, which expresses a noble love, yearning, and desire; (5) *andante*, which awakens even-temperedness and hope; (6) *allegretto*, which creates a fearless and faithful heart; and (7) *allegro*, which expresses or awakens feelings of joy and happiness.[57]

The most detailed possibilities for preluding were given by Christoph Rau-pach in *Der vollkommene Kapellmeister* of Johann Mattheson (1739) and were re-garded highly enough that they were reprinted in two other publications:

With sad hymns [the organist] plays:
   a) a slow fugue;
   b) the chorale in the pedal, 4-voiced;
   c) the chorale in the left hand, the right playing on the same manual or on another one two additional voices, thus making a trio;
   d) the left hand taking the chorale in the tenor, the pedal the bass, and the right hand something else, thus also making a trio;
   e) the chorale with weak stops, like a lament;
   f) the chorale in the left hand, the right playing a 2-voice variation;
   g) ditto but reversed, with the left hand playing the variation. . .

With joyful hymns:
   a) a symphonia, sonatina or large sonata is played with and without a fugue, with strong stops, on which the simple unison chorale is at-tached;
   b) fughettas are produced from the beginning of a tune, and so forth;
   c) a *cantus firmus* (the slow tune itself) is done with the right hand on one manual, and with the left on another manual a 2-voice variation is done in the bass;
   d) the cantus firmus is played with the left hand as a foundation on one manual, the right hand effecting a 2-voice variation on another manual;
   e) the cantus firmus is done as a bass in the pedal, to which both hands play variations, so that it becomes 3-voiced;
   f) the cantus firmus is taken on one manual with the right hand, to which the pedal plays a bass, and the left hand plays a variation on an-other manual—this is also a trio;
   g) the left hand plays the cantus firmus on one manual as a middle voice in the tenor, the right plays a variation on another manual, and the pedal produces its own bass;
   h) one plays alternating *forte* and *piano* on two keyboards, so that the simple chorale performs something artistic, the pedal not entering until the entire verse is ended;
   i) 3-voiced, with the left hand having the simple chorale in the tenor, the right hand and the pedal playing variations;
   j) reversed, with the right hand playing the cantus firmus and the left hand and pedal playing variations.[58]

If the highly ornamented chorale preludes of Buxtehude, Bach, and other composers are any indication, it was not considered essential that the congregation be able to identify the hymn tune from the prelude. In Lübeck, number boards were hung in 1701 because the hymns could no longer be recognized from the organ

145

prelude.[59] Sonnenkalb admitted in 1758 that the congregation might not know which hymn the organist was introducing.[60] It is possible, though, that Sonnenkalb meant that the congregation could recognize the tune but did not know which text to sing to it. This problem had already been identified by Werckmeister in 1707, who noted that several texts were often sung to the same tune, so that if a congregation was not paying attention when the cantor began a hymn they could find themselves singing the wrong text, even if the organist had already played a prelude based on the hymn tune.[61]

Hymn preludes were only one kind of prelude. Mizler listed three: preludes to hymns, preludes to the Kirchenmusik, and preludes during communion. The preludes during communion alternated with hymns and gave the congregation a chance to rest from singing hymns; today they would be called voluntaries. These preludes were to be "majestic, magnificent, noble and solemn."[62] Preludes to the Kirchenmusik allowed members of the orchestra a chance to tune their instruments. Türk recommended that an organist begin in a key in which the strings could tune easily, such as (in ordinary choir pitch) C, G, or F major, or C or G minor; if the organ was tuned to a high pitch, one should use B, F-sharp, or E major (or B or F-sharp minor). He should stay in the first key until the strings finish tuning; if there are horns, trumpets, or trombones he should then modulate to the key in which they first play (which is not necessarily that in which the music began, since they might not play in the first movement); then he may modulate to the key of the music.[63]

❖

Accompaniment of Hymn Singing

Adlung (1758) provided a few suggestions for registering the organ for hymn accompaniment. For congregational singing during funerals, he recommended only the 8-foot Gedackt for small churches and two quiet stops with an 8-foot Principal and one or two stops in the pedal for larger churches. In introducing a hymn, he wrote, the melody should be played on a distinctive stop either on a second manual or in the pedal. He did not consider it necessary to change registration for every verse of a hymn. He recommend that if the organist hears that the congregation is singing the melody incorrectly, he should solo out the melody on a separate manual; a clear prelude is also helpful in this regard. When a hymn is sung every Sunday, the organist, if he is able, might vary the keys in which he plays it. For example, *Allein Gott in der Höh sei Ehr* can be played in E, F, F-sharp, G, G-sharp, A, and B-flat; other keys are not comfortable for singing. *Wir glauben all an einen Gott* can be played in C, C-sharp, D, D-sharp, E, and F. With old hymns in one of the church modes (such as *Erbarm dich mein, o Herre Gott, Ach, Herr, mich armen Sünder* and *Mensch, willst du leben seliglich*) one may according to Telemann's custom play them in modern style; that is, in the Ionian mode, changing the minor third to a major third (that is, harmonizing these Phrygian melodies so that the final on E is set as the third of a C major chord).[64] Adlung recommended that when an organist plays in an unfamiliar church he should inquire as to the custom in the church regarding the melodies.[65]

Pröhle (1858) informed us that "according to old practice" the last stanza of the hymn preceding the sermon was accompanied with a stronger registration, or even with full organ.[66] Voigt had recommended in 1742 that the organist play the final stanza with full organ so that the priest would know when to go to the pulpit or altar to preach or to continue the service.[67]

Several writers mentioned that organists in some places often accompanied only every other stanza of hymns. This was apparently a remnant of the older alternation practice. Adlung recommended against the practice, saying that it could be devastating if the congregation sank in pitch while it was not being accompanied.[68] F. W. Marpurg (1759) agreed, asking that even if the organist had to warm up his fingers in the winter, couldn't he at least play the bass with his feet and thus prevent the congregation from going flat? Of course, Marpurg noted wryly, the organists did the same thing in the summer, perhaps because the heat stiffened the fingers! Marpurg, by the way, limited the playing of alternate verses to his native Brandenburg, saying that he had heard it nowhere else.[69] Türk likewise lamented the practice, complaining that congregations tend to fall a quarter or eighth step below pitch.[70]

Voigt and Adlung both mentioned the problem of the organ covering up the clerk at the beginning of hymn stanzas so that the congregation could not hear what text he was singing. Voigt believed it would be better if the organ were to remain silent for the opening words of each verse except the last and allow the cantor to sing them unaccompanied. Thereby, those people singing from memory (but who often did not have the order of verses memorized), or who were singing from a different hymnal, could better hear which verse the cantor was singing. The organ would begin at the first cadence. While the cantor was singing, the organist could determine whether the text of the stanza was sad or joyful and register the organ accordingly.[71] Adlung agreed in principle but preferred the organ to remain silent (or, alternatively, to play in unison) at the beginning of the first stanza only.[72]

❖

Organ Use during Lent

In some places the organ was not used during Lent, either for hymns or for figural music. Other places allowed it to be used for hymns, but no figural music was performed. J. L. Albrecht considered it ridiculous that the organ could not be used at all during Lent in Mühlhausen in 1762, either in the city or in any of the surrounding territory. The exception was the festival of the Annunciation, if it fell during Lent.[73] The city church at Jena did not use the organ in afternoon services during Lent. Adlung disagreed with the practice, saying that it would be better to accompany hymns softly (lest the devotion be disturbed) so that the singing was not pulled under pitch and the congregation growled more than it sang.[74]

❖

Postludes

Perhaps the earliest mention of an organ postlude to a service is from Marburg, where "a lively piece or canzona" was played in 1628 at the end of the service.[75] One finds occasional references to postludes in the succeeding decades. In 1643 a motet was played on the organ in Dransfeld after the Benediction. In Bremen and Verden postludes were apparently popular toward the end of the century, for the church authorities found it necessary to include a provision in the church order that directed churches with organs to follow the Benediction with the singing of a hymn, not with organ playing.[76] They were still not common all over Germany, though. In 1687 the church council in Quedlinburg asked Andreas Werckmeister to play the organ at the end of services. Werckmeister replied that this had never been the custom, but he would gladly do it in the future.[77]

In 1710 F. E. Niedt complained that certain younger organists in Hamburg were in the habit of playing postludes of such a kind as to make people want to dance in the church, something of which a staid Lutheran would never approve.[78] Niedt was not the only writer to express himself in this way. In 1742 Johann Carl Voigt related an incident that had occurred to him a number of years before. He had visited a public house in a certain city and overheard the barmaid tell the serving boy "Today the schoolmaster played the hoppity." Upon inquiry, he learned that the schoolmaster could play three different postludes, which the barmaid called the hoppity, the skippity, and the jumpity. Voigt was sorry to report that at the time he had laughed, for he had not realized how often what was played in church could please those attending but could not possibly please God.[79]

By midcentury organ postludes were well established, and F. W. Marpurg noted in 1749 that they were customary among both Protestants and Catholics.[80] Adlung took them for granted in his 1752 music method book, indicating that they were usually (but not always) played with full organ.[81]

❖

The Use of Other Instruments

The use of instruments besides the organ to accompany hymn singing seems to have been limited to city and court churches with the means to hire professional musicians, and often only on festivals. There seems to have been no equivalent to the volunteer church bands found in England. To be sure, instruments played regularly in figural music such as cantatas, but they did not normally accompany hymn singing except when the hymns were sung figurally, as in the settings of Praetorius or the closing hymns in the cantatas of Bach. The Halle church orders of 1641 and 1660 directed that when the hymns *de tempore* were performed figurally "the organ and perhaps other musical instruments as well go into the songs, and the people join in."[82]

This is not to say that the practice was otherwise unknown, but one has to look hard to find examples. In Meissen in 1618 the cantor came into conflict with the pastor, who did not want the schoolboys to play violin during the German hymns.[83] (This might refer to figural music instead.) In 1787, Türk mentioned that in some places hymns were accompanied by brass on festivals and other occasions.[84]

❖

The Abuse of the Organ

Organists did not always play as the clergy or congregation wished. The most frequently encountered directive to organists during the entire period under study was that they play only sacred motets, responsories, and hymns on the organ and not frivolous secular songs and dances, suggesting of course that the latter kind of music was exactly what was being played. In the January 20, 1767, issue of J. A. Hiller's periodical *Wöchentliche Nachrichten und Anmerkungen die Musik betreffend* there appeared an anonymous caricature of various types of organists, including Lucilius, who played a polonaise as a prelude to the funeral hymn *Mitten wir im Leben sind;* Schwanzstern, who played long preludes even to recitatives and long conclusions at the end of hymns that ran through several major and minor keys; Fuselius, who could play quite well if he were not always so drunk; and Starkschall, who played so loudly that the choir and other instruments could not be heard.[85]

The February issue of the same periodical contained an anonymous commentary on the foregoing piece. The author sympathized with the story and added examples from his own experience, remarking that he had heard far too many dances as hymn preludes. He related the story of one organist who continued to play long after the congregation had finished singing, and the pastor had to wait a long time before he could continue the service. He found equally offensive the common practice by organists of pulling out all the stops for the last stanza of hymns, which merely sounded like the hacking of woodcutters or the falling of rocks.[86]

There were other sorts of offenses as well, some minor, some major, and some quite astonishing.

Length of Prelude

The length of preludes before hymns and figural music was another widely heard complaint. As noted above, it was customary for the orchestra to tune during the prelude to the figural music, and F. E. Niedt directed that the prelude be played on full organ (or close to it) and that organists play for as long as they like, or until a signal is given to them that the orchestra has finished tuning.[87] According to Christian Gerber, many organists simply wanted to allow their artistry to be heard, and so they played very long preludes. For a long time, Gerber wrote, cantors and even village schoolmasters had been allowed to perform music at their own volition for as long as they desired without being required to obtain any approval from the pastor ahead of time. The musicians had taken advantage of this privilege, and it should be stopped.[88] In another book published more than thirty years earlier, Gerber asked whether it could conceivably please God when the organist at times preluded for as much as a quarter hour and created as many flashy improvisations as might occur to him.[89] Fifteen minutes for a prelude seems as though it must have been an exaggeration, but Georg Motz, in his point-by-point refutation of Gerber's book, was quick to note even minor misstatements of fact by Gerber; and on this point he did not dispute the time but said merely that organ preludes served to enliven the listeners' joy in the Lord and that God was every bit as much pleased with the preludes of the organist as he was with the playing of King David on the harp.[90] Türk also mentioned preludes of fifteen minutes' length, saying that they were much too long and wearied even lovers of music, although he noted that preludes to the Kirchenmusik had to be longer than hymn preludes in order to give the orchestra sufficient time to tune.[91]

Mizler also complained about organists who cared only about displaying their skill. He recounted visiting one church where the organist began a prelude with full organ, playing quick passages and evoking lightning, thunder, and hail; then the sun came out with quiet and pleasant sounds, only to be followed by all sorts of confused passages that sounded like cats jumping on the keys. After prancing about through all twenty-four keys the organist finally landed in the key of the hymn to be sung, which was the penitential hymn *Erbarm dich mein, o Herre Gott*. Mizler noted wryly the words of King Solomon, "To everything there is a season" [Eccl. 3:1].[92]

Registration

F. E. Niedt complained of organists using inappropriate stops in accompanying hymns. He himself had heard organists accompanying *Herr Gott, dich loben wir* and *Nun bitten wir den Heiligen Geist* with such extra stops as the drum, the cuckoo, the cymbalstern, and the birdsong.[93]

Melodic Ornamentation

It was the custom in the eighteenth century to add trills and other ornaments to the melody when accompanying hymns, as can be seen in Example 8.1 above. The practice seems to have been widely accepted, and no complaints about it are on record (unless the complaint against J. S. Bach in Arnstadt, cited above, is relevant). But in the seventeenth century such ornaments were more of an innovation, and not everyone was happy with the idea. And so a 1653 Catholic hymnal from Würzburg implored organists and singers not to ornament hymn tunes:

> The songs, which have been set to particular tunes, have such a quality and nature that they, when their own notes and cadences are left honest and unchanged as they were composed by learned musicians with regard to the numbers of rhymes, sound much nicer and are remembered all the more easily by the congregation as well, even by people unaccustomed to singing. In order now to achieve such a goal in current Gospels and songs, the organists and cantors (or singers) are hereby duly requested and reminded that they are not to deprive these same tunes of their natural, established charm through unnecessary fugues, coloraturas, runs and rambling about,

or by running all over in a rushing, dancing or jumping manner; but rather play and sing devotionally according to the prescribed musical notes, figures and signs (which have been deliberately set down for this purpose in the thoroughbass to make it that much easier for all organists) in a natural manner, slowly, solemnly, and as befits such a holy text, teaching the youth so that the common people might comprehend the notes and tune all the more easily, so that these things might be learned and sung by all in the same way, without any differentiation.[94]

Adlung (1758) also spoke against organists who ornamented tunes too heavily, saying that it was very annoying when organists played variations during the accompaniment as if they were preluding: "one hears 2-voiced variations and diminutions, now the bass, now the upper voice making merry, then the organist fidgets with his feet, adding ornaments, breaking, chopping, and adding all sorts of other stuff so that one doesn't know what to think."[95] Adlung's comments are reminiscent of Grossgebauer's opinion of artistic singing (see "Grossgebauer and Mithobius" in chapter 7).

Text Expression

The best organists, according to eighteenth-century instructional manuals, expressed the mood or affect of hymns through their playing. But sometimes they got carried away, as Türk relates:

> A certain organist read the words "fear" and "terror" and immediately pulled on the tremulant. Then he laid both arms on the coupled *Hauptwerk* while setting both feet upon the pedals, thereby causing such a ghastly howl that the entire congregation, not least of all the poor organ blower, was quite alarmed. Another, at the words "died on the cross," played with his hands crossed over and thought he had discovered a very fitting means of expression. . . . I once heard a certain organist who, at the words "let not the light of my faith be extinguished," played at first with the full organ, then gradually softer and softer, then with just one finger, finally stopping altogether.[96]

❖

Conclusion

Between the sixteenth and eighteenth centuries, the role of the organ changed from performing the liturgy in alternation with the choir to accompanying a singing congregation or choir. The accompaniment of hymns gave support to the people and encouraged them to sing, putting the final nail into the coffin of the choral liturgy among Lutherans.

CHAPTER 9

❖

Performance Practice

Previous chapters have traced the development of the congregational service through the eighteenth century. This chapter completes the picture by discussing a few matters concerning the hymn corpus and how hymns were actually performed.

❖

Repertoire

Of the large number of hymns published between the sixteenth and eighteenth centuries, only a relatively small number were sung in church. Most popular were those written during the early years of the Reformation.

Size of the Repertoire

There are few indications in the sources of how many hymns a typical congregation knew. Before the second half of the seventeenth century (the eighteenth century in some places) hymnals for the congregation were not yet popular, so most people were able to sing only those hymns they had memorized. Churches were not limited to using memorized hymns, though, for the choir or clerk used hymnals, and they could sing even if no one else did. In one Waldeck parish in 1565 Pastor Bernhard Wahl counted thirty-three German hymns that were sung at least by pastor and clerk, and the entire congregation was said to have learned and sung several verses.[1] The 1573 church order for Hanau gave three "rules for singing": (1) what is sung in church should pertain to the liturgical season; (2) in villages one should not use many and various hymns but few, and particularly the metrical settings of the parts of the catechism; and (3) the sermon always closes with a hymn related to it.[2] If there were five or six catechism hymns in use in Hanau (one for each of the five, or six, chief parts of the catechism), then even doubling that number with other hymns would yield a repertoire of scarcely a dozen hymns.

After hymnals became common and the congregations were able to read the texts while singing, their repertoire grew. Christian Gerber (1660–1731) recalled that during his youth, when hymnals were not used, he had heard a total of only eight hymns sung in church.[3] This was apparently in addition to the half dozen or so hymns that would have been part of the liturgy or sung during the communion. When Gerber himself became a pastor, and after hymnals were introduced, he undertook each week to explain one hymn to the congregation, beginning on the first Sunday in Advent in 1718. It took two years to cover all the hymns the congregation knew, so his parish would have been familiar with about a hundred hymns.[4] Some of these would have been sung to the same tunes, so fewer hymn tunes than texts would have been familiar. A Nuremberg hymnal of 1731 noted that around eighty hymns were familiar to the people.[5]

Other sources placed the number of familiar hymns much lower. In 1720 Johann Andreas Edler published a dissertation in Rostock, titled *Theological Dissertation on the Prophetic Kantorei in the Church of God,* to which he appended a specimen checklist of questions about church music that he wanted superintendents to ask during official ecclesiastical visitations. One of the questions asked whether the pastor took it upon himself to introduce more hymns to the congregation, noting that many congregations knew barely twenty hymns.[6] It is possible that congregational hymnals were not yet commonly found in the churches with which Edler was familiar. This was apparently the case in 1726 in Silesia, when pastor Christian Marbach of Mertschütz published an essay saying that one reason mistakes were made when hymns were sung is that people preferred to sing from memory, implying that people owned hymnals but did not use them.[7]

Selection of Hymns

Where church orders specified that certain hymns be sung, parishes seem generally to have done so. But not all hymns in the services were specified, and pastors had ample opportunity to select hymns themselves. Sometimes this task was delegated to or assumed by the cantor or clerk, but this varied from place to place. The Braunschweig order of 1528 directed the schoolmaster (not the pastor) to make certain that the hymns were appropriate to the liturgical time; and the 1567 order for Andorff stated that the congregation might sing hymns with the clerk before the sermon, provided that no new hymns were introduced without the preacher's prior approval, to safeguard the doctrine. In the German Lutheran congregation in London in 1718 one of the duties of the clerk was to select the hymns after the pastor had informed him what sort of hymns would complement the sermon text. But visitation records for the Gandersheim cloister in 1542 and Hohenleipisch in 1672 noted that the preachers themselves chose the hymns. In Dinkelsbühl in 1573 the precentor did not select the hymns himself but was instructed to go to the sacristy before the service and inquire what was to be sung, then return to his seat and pass that information on to the boys so that they could find the psalms in their books. Service orders from late seventeenth-century Dahlen describe hymns as chosen variously by the pastor, the deacon, or the cantor.[8]

Number of Stanzas Sung

The church orders occasionally mention the truncation of hymns. Sometimes the hymn preceding the sermon was divided so that the last stanza was sung afterwards, and the hymn at the dismissal (if present) was frequently a single stanza. In some places only the first stanza of a hymn such as *Vater unser im Himmelreich* or *Nun bitten wir den Heiligen Geist* was sung before the sermon. Arno Werner reports that around 1760 several hymnals marked appropriate stopping places in the hymns. There were voices on both sides of this, including a delegation of farmers in Niemegk who petitioned the superintendent in Bitterfeld to have their pastor shorten the hymns so that the service would not last so long.

During the communion only as many hymns were sung as were needed to fill the time while the people communed. It is unknown whether the final hymn was sung in its entirety or stopped as soon as the last communicant had finished, or even whether there was a uniform practice in this regard. We do know that in 1770 the organist in Altenburg complained about the cantor, who led the congregation through seventeen stanzas at the close of communion. The cantor replied that he had begun the hymn through oversight, but he did not feel it was proper to stop in the middle, as that was not customary.[9] It is impossible, though, to generalize from this one report about the practice elsewhere and in earlier times.

Hymns de Tempore

Frequently an agenda specified that a hymn be sung *de tempore*; that is, "according to the time" of the church year. Usually this meant that the pastor chose an appropriate hymn from the repertoire of the choir or congregation, but several agendas contained lists of hymns to be used for each Sunday and holy day throughout the year. The earliest that has been identified is a manuscript order for St. Wenceslaus in Naumburg dating from 1538.[10] It contains an extensive list of Latin psalms, hymns, responsories, and sequences, together with German hymns and other propers. Other church orders containing *de tempore* lists include:

> Naumburg [1538]—hymns sung for the introit and gradual and
> following the sermon at mass, and hymns sung before and after the
> sermon at Vespers
> Anhalt 1551—hymns sung before the sermon at mass, Vespers, and
> weekday services
> Andorff 1567—hymns sung before the sermon at mass
> Pirna [before 1569]—Gradual hymns
> Annaberg 1579—hymns sung before the Epistle and before the Gospel

Nördlingen 1579–Gradual hymns

Mansfeld 1580—hymns sung at catechism and hymns sung in place of
the sequence at mass

Colberg 1586—Office hymns

Mecklenburg 1602—recommended psalms for the year

Magdeburg, Halberstadt 1632 (reprinted as Magdeburg 1663)—
Gradual hymns

Schwarzburg 1675—hymns sung before the main sermon on Sundays

Nördlingen 1676—hymns sung before and after the readings at the
weekly prayer services, hymns sung for the Gradual and before the
sermon at mass, and hymns sung at the beginning and end of
Tagamt and Vespers

Leipzig 1694—Gradual hymns

East Frisia 1716—hymns after the sermon

The hymnals of Spangenberg (1545), Keuchenthal (1573), and Selneccer (1587),
which are arranged according to the liturgical year, note the liturgical position of
the German hymns they contain.

Rochus von Liliencron has compiled a comparative list of hymns *de tempore*
from fifteen agendas and hymnals of the sixteenth and seventeenth centuries.[11] His
list and those in the above sources show that (1) the hymn *de tempore* was frequently
either a German substitute for the Latin Gradual or a hymn to be sung before
the sermon; (2) many hymns *de tempore* were sung on more than one Sunday during the year, either within a given season or in different seasons; (3) a choice of
hymns *de tempore* was frequently given, either for a single day or for a season; and
(4) there is quite a bit of variation from list to list as to which hymns are assigned
on which days.

Most agendas did not contain *de tempore* lists, at least not complete lists for
every week in the year. It is impossible to know how closely the hymn prescriptions that did exist were followed. It is also impossible to know, absent other evidence, whether these hymns were sung by choir or congregation.

In current Lutheran liturgies the hymn *de tempore* is called variously the gradual hymn, the hymn of the day or the chief hymn (*Hauptlied*). It is "the name given
to the chief hymn in the service on every Sunday and festival, so called because it
fits the specific day and season in the church year. It is the hymn that responds most
intimately to the dominant theme of the day, which is usually contained in the
Gospel for the day."[12] In the early Lutheran church, because of items (1), (2), and
(3) above, the hymn's connection with the Gospel was often tenuous and was usually evident only on festivals (with hymns related to the festival called hymns *de
festo*). It is more accurate to say that the hymn *de tempore* was related to the theme
of the season rather than to the theme of the day. Of course, during the half of the
church year when there was no seasonal theme; namely, the long season after Trinity, even this connection was lacking.

The *de tempore* principle was a mainstay of Lutheran liturgical life. David Gre-
gor Corner, in his 1631 hymnal intended for use in Catholic churches, related a
story about a Calvinist minister preaching in a Lutheran church:

I am not unaware that there are precocious heretics who would like to mix up all the differences among the festivals as well as the singing [pertaining to each festival], as I myself once heard in a Lutheran church where a se- cretly Calvinist preacher began to sing from the pulpit *Christ ist erstanden* [an Easter hymn] on the third Sunday of Advent; but his audience, who were at the time still Lutherans (who consider themselves quite a bit closer to Catholic devotion than are the Calvinists) laughed at him, and very few of them were inclined to sing along after the preacher. But when after the sermon the schoolmaster began to sing *Nun komm, der Heiden Heiland*, all the people sang along enthusiastically, for this was [a hymn] *de tempore*; the other was not.[13]

The hymn *de tempore* fell out of use in the eighteenth century as interest in the liturgical year waned and hymnals began to abandon their internal arrangement ac- cording to the *de tempore* principle.[14] It was replaced by a topical hymn related to the sermon.

New Hymns

In the early days, hymns were either taught to the boys in the school or learned in- formally through printed hymnals and broadsheets. In only a few places (Göppin- gen and a few villages in Saxony) is there any record of congregational rehearsals having been held.[15] When new hymns were introduced, it was sufficient to teach them first to the boys, who sang them in church or, as in Freiberg, on the streets during the fundraising efforts of the Kurrenden.[16] In one place, the county of Baden-Durlach in 1603, the pastors were directed "as much as possible to sing [psalms and hymns] in advance" (*soviel als möglich vorzusingen*); that is, the pastor had the hymnal in his hand and the congregation sang after him. Whether this was done by stanza or by phrase (as with the later English practice of "lining out") is un- known.[17]

The 1545 hymnal published by Valentin Babst and its later editions provided the basic hymn repertory for Lutherans throughout the entire period under study. For nearly two hundred years Lutherans sang little else: Eberhard Schmidt's analy- sis of the hymns sung in Dresden shows that only six hymns were added to the local repertoire in the entire seventeenth century even as the number of hymns in the Dresden hymnal increased from 276 in 1622 to 440 in 1694.[18] Although there was a flowering of new hymns in that century, very few found their way into common use. The greatest impediment was the fear that new hymns might introduce new and impure doctrine. This was the concern in Danzig during the 1640s, when or- ganist Paul Siefert tried to introduce his choral motets based on French psalm tunes. He was unsuccessful, as the authorities did not allow them to be performed in the liturgy because of their Reformed origin.[19]

The concern for pure doctrine was also the chief issue in the controversy that followed the introduction of Ambrosius Lobwasser's psalter in the Prussian city of Elbing (now Elbląg in Poland) in 1655. The psalter, which had originally appeared in 1573, was a translation of the French psalter of Clément Marot and Theodore Beza. Lobwasser, a Lutheran and professor of law at Königsberg, stated in his preface that he had undertaken his translation because he was disappointed that metrical psalms, which were being sung enthusiastically by the Reformed, had never taken hold among the Lutherans, a few paraphrases by Luther excepted.[20] Indications that he sympathized with Calvinist teachings may also have played a part.[21] His psalter was enthusiastically received in the German-speaking Reformed churches (with over a hundred editions appearing in the next two centuries) but was ignored by Lutherans. Shortly after its introduction in Lutheran Elbing a protest writing appeared anonymously titled *Project of Several Well-Founded Motifs against the Introduction of Lobwasser's Songs into a Congregation of Christ Adhering to the Unaltered Augsburg Confession*; its author was later revealed to be Johann Botsack.[22] Botsack asked the question "whether certain persons may introduce, without knowledge or consent of the church members, the erring psalms of Lobwasser into a church of the Unaltered Augsburg Confession." His answer was, of course, "no." Botsack supported his conclusion with twenty-three numbered points. His arguments occupy fifty pages and are somewhat repetitive, but they give such an insight into the theological thinking of many Lutherans of the period that I have summarized them here:

1. The psalms originate with people holding to false doctrine, namely Beza and Marot. The psalms themselves contain false, Calvinist doctrine. Lobwasser himself stated that he preferred Luther's hymns, and his purpose was not to introduce his psalms into the service. The first church to accept those psalms was the French.
2. Lobwasser's psalms are actually being preferred to Luther's hymns, which was against Lobwasser's intention.
3. The Lutherans and Calvinists differ in doctrine and should therefore also differ in ceremonies and hymns.
4. Lobwasser's psalms cannot be easily sung by a congregation on account of their manner of poetry, high tessitura, and forced rhymes.
5. The tunes are not simple, as are the Lutheran tunes, but are quite ornate and, to German ears, frivolous and designed simply to amuse the ear.
6. The psalms are difficult to understand because of the style of writing, are unedifying, and are not in accordance with the intentions of the Holy Spirit. The Holy Spirit speaks of Christ in the psalms, but Beza omits all references to Christ.
7. Lobwasser's psalms contain heretical (Arian, Photinian) doctrines. The psalms are not interpreted in the light of the New Testament; for example, the author fails to see Psalm 2 as referring to the divinity of Christ, and he also fails to see Christ in Psalm 8.[23]
8. It is not right to force new hymns into a church where established hymns already exist, especially hymns from a different church.
9. Hymns by devout Lutherans are much to be preferred.

10. If Lobwasser's psalms are introduced into a Lutheran congregation, people will soon start spreading rumors that the people there do not really believe Lutheran doctrine.

11. Luther's hymns are simple, understandable, expressive and contain the sum of divine teaching; they should therefore be retained.

12. Those who would introduce Lobwasser's psalms, which were unknown thirty years ago, have itchy ears, which St. Paul would punish (2 Tim. 4:3).

13. Those who sing Reformed psalms show that they share Reformed doctrine.

14. The name of Jesus does not appear in Lobwasser's psalms; therefore, they are not proper Christian hymns.

15. Introducing Lobwasser's psalms hinders ministers in their office, for they must explain the psalms according to the Holy Spirit's teaching, which Lobwasser contradicts.

16. Introducing Lobwasser's psalms forces teachers and preachers to go against their vows to maintain true doctrine. Lobwasser's psalms are not approved in any ordination rite or in any agenda based on the Augsburg Confession.

17. St. Paul commands that new inventions not be allowed into the church (2 Tim. 4:3).

18. Those who force Lobwasser's psalms onto those who do not want them violate the law of love.

19. Those introducing Lobwasser's psalms have also removed the old Lutheran hymns, causing dissension in the church.

20. Those who want to sing Calvinist psalms should first seek unity in doctrine.

21. The introduction of Lobwasser's psalms places the evangelical religion in danger.

22. Lobwasser's psalms are poorly translated and are of poor poetic construction, with impure rhymes.

23. No church of the Unaltered Augsburg Confession has yet accepted Lobwasser's psalms.

Within a space of several months a number of responses and counter-responses to Botsack's *Project* were published, bearing such interesting titles as *Rejectum projectum*; *Projectum protectum*; *Rejectus protector*, *Antworte dem Narren* (*Answer the Fool*) and *Antworte dem Narren nicht* (*Don't Answer the Fool*).[24] The first response to appear was the anonymous *Rejectum projectum, or Refutation of the Project of Several Unfounded Motifs which an Unnamed Writer Recently Proclaimed as the Lord's Command against Lobwasser, and Issued for the Protection of Those in Elbing Who Undertook to Abolish Lobwasser's Songs in Their Town.* The book's true author was one Reinhold Curike.[25] Curike asserted that Lobwasser's psalms had been in use in Elbing for several years without any difficulties. The author of the protest, said Curike, lived in a different city; he was spurred on not by the Elbing authories nor by church members there but by a few preachers seeking to cause controversy. Curike began with a response to Botsack's principal question, saying that the question was really whether the psalms, which had been sung for a number of years in Elbing already, should be removed from the services without the consent of the congregation. He then answered Botsack's twenty-three points in turn:

1. Lobwasser did not translate the erring opinions of Marot and Beza, and no one has ever shown that their erring religion has influenced the doctrinal content of their psalms. The fact that Frenchmen had a part in writing the psalms and the tunes is beside the point. And simply because Lobwasser preferred Luther's hymns and his purpose was not to introduce his own psalms into the service, it does not follow that they may not be so introduced. Just because the French church uses the psalms does not mean that we cannot: they also use the Bible, the Apostles' Creed, the Lord's Prayer, etc. In any case, the psalms did not originate with Beza and Marot but with King David.

2. It is not true that the psalms are replacing Lutheran hymns, and the author has not proven his claim.

3. It is not necessary that churches with differing doctrines have different ceremonies: the Lutheran church has retained a number of papist ceremonies.

4. New hymns by Lutherans have been introduced into the church. A difficult style is not necessarily bad (citing 2 Peter 3:16). And no one else has charged that the intention of the Holy Spirit has been subverted in Lobwasser's psalms.

5. The tunes are not so difficult as some hymns (*Mag ich Unglück nicht widerstahn, Christ unser Herr zum Jordan kam, Wie schön leuchtet der Morgenstern*). They are certainly not "frivolous and designed simply to amuse the ear" or such a large number of composers [names them] would not have used the tunes.

6. The author is criticising King David rather than Lobwasser. Although some things may be difficult to understand, that is not cause for abolishing the psalms. How can David's psalms be unedifying? In any case, the name of Jesus is not to be found in the original psalms.

7. If the author had his way, the entire Old Testament, which does not refer to Christ by name, would have to be abolished.

8. The question is really whether Lobwasser's psalms, which are over seventy years old and have been sung for some time in the church in question, may be abolished at the insistence of a few.

9. [Cites examples where Luther and his followers approved of hymns by those erring in doctrine.]

10. Such gossip is not to be approved, but this does not mean that the psalms may not be sung.

11. If Luther's hymns make such an impression, then so much more do David's psalms.

12. As Martin Opitz has written in the introduction to his psalter: ". . . the young people, who flee from the psalms on account of their style

and tunes, perhaps imagine that there is heresy in the parts and notes and will have nothing to do with them, because they live deprived of a lovely part of the external senses, namely, a good ear."

13. Once again, we are speaking of David's psalms, not merely a creation of Lobwasser's.

14. Other hymns are also difficult to understand in places. Regarding the place of Christ, see item 6.

15. The author has not proven his point: the psalms do not contain the false doctrine of which the author accuses them.

16. Of course Lobwasser's psalms are not mentioned in the Augsburg Confession, as they had not yet been written when it appeared. But the confession does allow (in Article 15) differences in ceremonies as long as good order is maintained. Regarding the doctrinal issue, if one says that the French psalms must be Calvinist because Beza and Marot were Calvinist, then it follows that the German psalms must be Lutheran because Lobwasser was Lutheran.

17. David's psalms are not a new invention; what is new is that people want to abolish them from the church.

18. It is more loving not to force out psalms that have been sung for some time. Singing these psalms has not forced out Luther's hymns.

19. If any argument is to be made whether certain hymns should be allowed in the church, it should be made against Luther's hymns, since they are human creations, not like the divine psalms of David. But in fact, Luther's hymns have not been forced out by Lobwasser's psalms: even the Reformed Germans still sing them heartily.

20. The patrons of Lobwasser's psalms do not allow all sorts of [doctrinal] changes into the church.

21. This is not confirmed by experience, and the author has not proven his point.

22. The author has not cited examples, but there are a number of such instances in Luther's hymns [they are cited].

23. Each city has its own customs in worship. For example, we in Elbing have the practice during the Creed of singing the words of institution of Holy Baptism, which is done nowhere else.[26]

Whether Botsack and his colleagues were successful in the end in having the Lobwasser psalter removed from use in Elbing is unknown, but by 1720 the congregation was singing German prose psalms at Sunday Vespers to the tune of *Meine Seele erhebt den Herren* (i.e., the *tonus peregrinus*).[27] A similar controversy erupted following the publication in 1704 of the *Geistreiches Gesangbuch* of Johann Anatasius Freylinghausen. In 1714 the County of Waldeck considered adopting it for use in its churches, and the nobility requested the theology faculty at Wittenberg to prepare an official review of the hymnal. The resulting 28-page document criticized the book at length, with most of the objections doctrinal in nature, although there were also complaints that some of the tunes were, in essence, too secular in style.[28]

Other reviews critical of the hymnal appeared in subsequent years, but they had little success in dampening the public's enthusiasm for the book.[29]

Occasionally one finds in contemporary sources instructions given to churches and organists concerning new hymns, and they almost invariably reflect an extremely conservative attitude:

> Grevenberg 1561—Only hymns in the hymnal may be sung.
>
> Steuerwald/Peine 1561—Above all, the German hymns of Luther, which contain nearly the entire catechism within them, should be used in the church.
>
> Andorff 1567—The clerk may not introduce new hymns without the preacher's approval.
>
> Halle 1573—The good old hymns from Luther's hymnal are to be used.
>
> Hoya 1581—Other Christian songs may be used as long as the old hymns are not neglected. (This is one of the few instances of such toleration!)
>
> Hohenlohe 1589—To prevent disorder, only the single authorized hymn (*Wo Gott der Herr nicht bei uns hält*) is to be used in the weekly prayer service.
>
> Baden-Durlach 1603—Pastors are not to introduce hymns not contained in the hymnal.
>
> Danzig 1614—The organist is to play the old hymns and not introduce new ones.
>
> Württemberg 1657—No hymn may be sung that does not have the prior approval of the superintendent.
>
> Danzig 1679—According to the organist's installation documents, he is not to play any new hymns.
>
> Bremen and Verden, late 17th century—Visitation records show that in all but one village (Dorum) only hymns from the hymnal were sung.
>
> Oettingen 1707—Only the old hymns are to be used.[30]

By the eighteenth century the situation was beginning to change. Hymns by seventeenth-century writers such as Johann Rist and especially Paul Gerhardt were finding wide acceptance; *Praxis pietatis melica,* the hymnal published in 1647 by the cantor of Gerhardt's parish, Johann Crüger, was well on its way to becoming the most popular hymnal of the century, appearing in forty-four editions by 1736. The Pietists, discussed in chapter 7, added greatly to the hymn repertory; and in 1756 J. F. W. Sonnenkalb reported that "very many unfamiliar hymns" were sung with which no one, not even the organist and cantor, was familiar. But, he added, this should not be a problem if the cantor is given enough time to find a suitable tune and the organist enough time to learn it.[31] By 1787 several of the old Lutheran hymns were no longer familiar, and Türk cautioned that special care must be taken with them, naming as examples *Christ lag in Todesbanden; Also heilig ist der Tag; Christ ist erstanden; Jesus Christus unser Heiland; Komm, Heiliger Geist, erfüll die Herzen;* and *Hilf Gott, dass mirs gelinge.*[32]

❖

Leadership

In the sixteenth century hymns were sung by the choir. In places where the people sang, they were led by the choir or clerk, who stood at the front of the church. Before the advent of organ accompaniment, the clerk simply began singing each hymn without any introduction. Except for an indication in the 1718 church order for London that the clerk was to announce the hymns prior to singing them so that the people could look them up, there is no indication that hymns were ever announced verbally.[33] As far as is known, the clerk's leadership was entirely vocal; he did not direct the singing with his hands. An exception was Hanau in 1659, where the precentor or schoolmaster was instructed to conduct the congregation with his hand, showing the beat on each syllable of the hymns.[34]

Occasionally one finds a directive for part of the choir to assist the people by singing in the nave. This was the case in Wittenberg 1533, Oldenburg 1573, and Hoya 1581.[35] The 1542 order for Calenburg-Göttingen instructed the clerk to leave the choir and lead the people during the singing of the Te Deum, which was sung in alternation verse by verse.[36] Johann Eccard, in the preface to his 1597 choir hymnal, wrote that the choir should "in singing the hymns strive for and maintain quite a slow beat, so that thereby it will allow the common man to hear the usual tune all the more accurately, and he will be able with his Kantorei to succeed all the more easily and better."[37] The Kantorei in this instance was evidently a part of the choir assigned to assist the people in singing the hymn melody while the rest of the choir sang in five-part harmony.

Today it is assumed that the organist serves to lead the congregation in singing, but several accounts reveal that even by the eighteenth century the organist was not seen everywhere as a leader but often merely as an accompanist who was to follow the leadership of the cantor or clerk. The report cited above of the organist in 1770 who objected to the cantor leading the congregation through seventeen stanzas shows that it was the cantor, not the organist, who was in control of the singing.[38] Sonnenkalb recommended that each text in the hymnal have its own proper tune, saying that it would avoid the problem arising when the organist introduced the hymn with one tune and the cantor, not liking the tune, sang another; once again, this shows how the cantor was able to overrule the organist.[39] Mattheson recommended that organists make use of a precentor who would let the organist know whether the singing congregation was staying with him, as the organist often could not hear the singing over the sound of the instrument.[40] It was not the congregation that followed the organist, but the organist who needed to be certain that he was staying with the congregation.

This was a problem, though, if the congregation did not stay together itself. Werckmeister lamented the current state of singing in the church, where in one corner people were singing two, three, or even four syllables ahead or behind those in another corner, with some singing a second too high and others singing a second too low. Werckmeister blamed the crisis on inadequate music instruction in the schools.[41]

❖

Hymn Boards

Boards listing the hymns to be sung were installed in some churches beginning in the sixteenth century. They were erected in the Reformed city of Geneva already in 1550;[42] and in 1579 the church order for the Lutheran town of Annaberg in Saxony directed that German hymns be sung before the Epistle and before the Gospel, and each Sunday the cantor was to post these hymns on a board so that the entire congregation might sing along.[43] Annaberg seems to have been unusual among Lutheran churches in having hymn boards, as the next references are not found until the late seventeenth and early eighteenth centuries: Frankfurt introduced them in 1687;[44] Nordhausen already had them by that date;[45] Lübeck introduced them in 1701,[46] Rostock in 1702;[47] in Weimar chalkboards were purchased for this purpose in 1714.[48] The Holstein-Plön church order of 1732 directed that the organist or clerk write the hymns on the hymn board a half hour before the service begins.[49] Boards were not used in Nuremberg in the early eighteenth century because so many different hymnals were in use as to make it unfeasible.[50]

According to Werner, in earlier times it was customary to write the first lines of the hymns on the board, but between 1720 and 1740 numbers were introduced as standardized hymnals became popular.[51] Apparently not all hymns were indicated on the hymn boards. Adlung (1758) gave this reason for recommending that the organ remain silent during the first phrase of the first stanza to allow the congregation to determine which hymn was being sung (see "Accompaniment of Hymn Singing" in chapter 8). As a second reason he noted that several hymns had similar text incipits, for example, *Jesu, meine Freude* and *Jesus, meine Freude* (a Christmas hymn), or the four hymns beginning *Meinen Jesus lass ich nicht*.[52] The second reason suggests that in Adlung's Erfurt hymn boards still used text incipits in 1758, because if numbers had been used it would have been a simple matter to differentiate among hymns with similar incipits. One reason for this may have been to eliminate the need to indicate several sets of numbers for different hymnals.

Voigt (1742) recounted an occasion when there were a large number of communicants at one service, and the hymn listed on the hymn board was not sufficient, so the cantor began to sing *Jesu, meine Liebe*. The congregation, however, thought that he was starting *Jesu, meine Freude* and sang that instead, or at least half of them did![53]

❖

Women and Hymn Singing

The question of whether women sang in church has been briefly touched upon in the chapter on ecclesiastical visitations, where in Hessen-Darmstadt the visitors wanted to ascertain whether the women did indeed sing as a part of the congregation and, if not, to encourage them to do so (see "Hesse 1628 to 1632" in chapter 5). This was the policy of Lutheran churches throughout the entire period under discussion: women as a part of the congregation were treated the same as men and were expected to sing. It was not even an issue in most places, although the 1581 church order for Hoya insisted that for sermons and catechism instruction the girls take their psalmbooks with them into the church and join in the singing when the people sang. If any parents did not allow this, the superintendent and inspectors were to expel the girl from school, after due warning.[54]

With few exceptions, there is no indication that girls participated vocally in the services except as members of the congregation. Three exceptions are found in church orders for individual cities: Zwickau 1529, Naumburg 1538, and Nördlingen 1555. The Zwickau order simply noted that the girls' choir was to be discontinued, as it was not necessary to saddle them with this task.[55] The Naumburg order was for St. Wenzel's Church; it directed that the German singing be done in alternation between the choir and the rest of the congregation. If the organ played, then it served as a choir, and so there were three choirs alternating. And when the girls also sang, there were four choirs.[56] The Nördlingen order contained the same provisions for alternation as in Naumburg but called a girls' choir something "we would like to institute eventually."[57] Two more exceptions are Hof, where it is reported that a girls' choir sang in German in alternation with the choir from the Latin school, and Joachimsthal, where a sixteenth-century pastor mentions a girls' choir, although its exact function is not noted. A final exception is conveyed by Rautenstrauch, who reports that in one Saxon village in the late seventeenth century the cantor's daughters sang in the figural choir for a festival service.[58]

No evidence has surfaced that adult women ever sang in choirs before the eighteenth century. The reason for this is not easily found in the sources, but the prevailing opinion that a woman's place was in the home doubtless played a part, as did the fact that the soprano part was already sung by young boys. There was also the belief that a woman should not occupy a leadership role in the church. By the eighteenth century, though, the choir was beginning to be seen more as a performing group than as a leader of the liturgy; and so Gottfried Ephraim Scheibel, writing in 1721, was in favor of allowing women to sing, "although it would cause consternation at first."[59] In 1739 Johann Mattheson wrote that it had been difficult for him to introduce women into the Hamburg cathedral choir: at first they had to be placed where they could not be seen, but eventually they could not be seen and heard enough! But in the city's parish choirs, he noted, women were still not allowed.[60]

As far as can be determined, women never served as cantors, clerks, or organists.

❖

Quality of Singing

Ample evidence has been presented in previous chapters to show that in many places during the sixteenth and early seventeenth centuries congregations sang only reluctantly, if at all. In some places, such as Strassburg, the singing seems to have been quite good; but in many cities choral music predominated and in rural areas the people often refused to participate. Matters improved during the seventeenth century. Cunrad Dieterich, in the church dedication sermon he preached sometime before 1629, spoke in glowing terms about the singing in Ulm, where he was superintendent:

> Oh, when someone sits there in the middle of our congregation and hears
> how many thousand Christian hearts are lifting their voice and giving
> honor, glory and praise with one mouth, one voice and one heart to God
> in psalms and hymns of praise, would his eyes not, as with Augustine, fill
> with tears? I must confess, and so must many of you, that again and again
> my heart fills with joy when I hear how our congregation, young and old,
> man and woman, performs its song in such a Christian manner and in one
> accord.[61]

By the eighteenth century the entire congregation was simply expected to sing, and there are very few reports of churches where congregations did not sing (although in Stettin in 1703 the organist had to play alone whenever the clerk had to be absent, because the people would not sing without his leadership).[62] In some places the problem was not so much that people would not sing but rather that they did, and badly. Such was the case in Bautzen in 1637, where "a great dissonance" was reported during the singing of the German hymns, especially during the communion.[63] In 1703, Georg Motz, defending choral music performed with instruments against the attacks of Christian Gerber, claimed that hymn singing was not much better, with hymns often sung by the people without devotion or understanding:

> Frequently it is in utter disarray: some sing quickly, some slowly; some pull
> the pitch upwards, some downwards. Some sing at the second, others at
> the fourth, this one at the fifth, that one at the octave, each according to
> his own pleasure. There is no order, no rhythm, no harmony, no grace,
> but for the most part pure confusion.[64]

Eighty-one years later C. G. Göz, in language unusually rough for this author, opined concerning the singing in country churches:

> It is lamentable how the singing is neglected in many country parishes.
> The wrong notes, the frequently indistinct shrieking like a Cyclops that
> one is forced to listen to, so that one's ears ring and sensitive auditory
> nerves suffer greatly under it! What revolting dullness! In the midst of this
> powerful yelling the precentor, in the rare places where for some reason
> there is no organ, must exert all his effort to scream over the congrega-
> tion; many schoolmasters and assistant masters develop an indistinct voice
> so that not a word of theirs can be understood during the singing: they
> manage as it were with just a few vowels. [It sounds as though] he often
> begins every hymn with the same letter, depending on whether his mouth
> and throat have been taught by simple teachers.[65]

But such reports are rare, and in general eighteenth-century congregations appear to have sung well. Indeed, Georg Motz later excused his own harsh comments by saying that he was writing not of the entire congregation but only of people who disturb those sitting near them with their poor singing.[66] Those few congregations where singing was less than adequate might have benefited from Daniel Speer's observation that congregational singing was better in places where beer and mead were drunk than where sour wine and hard water were drunk. He theorized that this was because the harder drinks contributed to sore throats and hoarseness. Lest anyone forget this, he offered a bit of doggerel to implant it in the memory:[67]

Harte[s] Wasser, sauren Wein	Hard water, sour wine—
Trincket diß die gröste Gmein,	if most of the parish drinks these,
Singt man schwer und sehr unrein.	The singing is harsh and quite out of tune.
Aber	But
Gutes Wasser, Meth und Bier,	Good water, mead and beer,
Alter Wein und Malvasier,	old wine and malmsey
Bringet gut Gesang herfür.	Bring forth good singing.

❖

Singing in Parts

Except for choirs singing the occasional polyphonic hymn settings, there are only scattered references to part singing of hymns, most of them quite late. One is a 1671 complaint by Matthäus Hertel, organist in Züllichau, that cantors would begin hymns by singing the melody but would then switch to a bass part. The boys in the choir would then become confused and lose their place. Hertel advised that cantors always sing the melody.[68]

In at least some places where hymns were accompanied by instruments the choir sang them in parts. In 1665 Hector Mithobius criticized cantors who did not have their choirs sing in parts:

> Therefore it is just laziness and obstinacy when on high feasts and holy days they [i.e., cantors] do not have alto, tenor and bass sung figurally to the familiar chorale in the discant; for in many well-appointed churches the hymns are sung figurally in four parts every Sunday morning, and the congregation diligently sings along *choraliter* with the discant, just as the congregation is able to sing the psalms with the organ even though more than four voices are played. . . .[69]

In the eighteenth century, Adlung complained about organists who occasionally altered the harmony when accompanying hymns. This was not a problem as long as the entire congregation sang in unison or octaves, but in many churches by 1758 a number of people, he noted, were accustomed to singing a bass under the melody, and so disorder would result.[70] Because the people did not have hymnals with tunes, the bass part was apparently learned from hearing the organ play it for each stanza. True four-part harmony was another question. Perhaps a few musical people in the congregation would have been able to manage it, but it seems unlikely that it was done to any great extent. According to Rietschel, the organist Buttstedt of Rothenburg ob der Tauber mentioned in a 1770 letter that his congregation divided itself into four parts, but if true, this must have been extremely rare.[71] And

J. G. Hingelberg suggested that Danzig organists refrain from ornamenting hymn accompaniments and playing interludes so that the congregation might sing in four parts; there is, however, no proof that the congregation actually did so.[72]

❖

Tempo

Indications of the tempo at which hymns were sung during the sixteenth and seventeenth centuries are difficult to find. Regarding Johann Eccard's directive in 1597 that the choir sing the hymns "quite slowly" (*fein langsam*), quoted above on page 236, Daniela Garbe has suggested that this implies that the congregation was in the habit of singing the hymns too quickly.[73] This might have been the case, or it could have been that Eccard simply wanted to be certain that the congregation could follow the melody and that his cautionary comment was not based on actual experience. In any case, it does not give us any sort of definite tempo indication.

For that Michael Praetorius provides some clues in Part 3 of his *Syntagma musicum:*

> I also want to remind [the reader] of this: that in the thoroughbasses I have always indicated at the end of each one how many *tempora* each piece or each part of a piece comprises. For as a matter of necessity I must observe how many *tempora,* when a fairly moderate beat is kept, can be performed in a quarter hour, namely: 80 *tempora* in half a quarter hour; 160 *tempora* in an entire quarter hour; 320 *tempora* in a half hour; 640 *tempora* in an entire hour. Thus one can all the better act according to how long the aforementioned singing or concerto will last; thereby the sermon is not pushed back, but will start at the proper time, and the other ecclesiastical ceremonies can also be performed accordingly.[74]

One *tempus* (pl. *tempora*), as Praetorius used the term, refers to what modern editions transcribe as one measure of common or cut time, or a breve in the original notation. Therefore, 160 measures containing four beats each, or a total of 640 beats, could have been performed in a quarter hour. This works out to a tempo of approximately 43 minima per minute, with the minim commonly transcribed as a half note.

Now the foregoing discussion refers not to hymns but to choral music, in particular the *Polyhymnia caduceatrix et panegyrica* of 1619. The *Puericinium* of 1621 also carried a count of *tempora* at the end of each piece. The pieces in these collections did in fact use hymn texts and melodies, but they were not designed for the congregation to sing along, as was the case with some of Praetorius's earlier works. But there does not seem to be any reason why we cannot apply the same idea to those works; namely, that the basic pulse, on average, should be about 43 half notes per minute.

This was the normal base tempo, represented by the common time signature (𝄴). In the preface to the *Puericinium* Praetorius also mentioned a quicker tempo, repre-

Example 9.1. M. Praetorius, *Vom Himmel hoch da komm ich her*, 1613

sented by the cut time signature (¢).[75] In the *Urania* of 1613, whose preface called for the congregation to sing along with the choral settings, most (but not all) of the hymn settings used the cut time signature, for example, *Vom Himmel hoch, da komm ich her* (Example 9.1). Now the question is, how much quicker should the tempo be with the cut time signature? Praetorius did not say. But it seems reasonable to allow a quicker tempo of about 150 percent of the base tempo, or about one half note per second. Singing *Vom Himmel hoch* at this tempo would be slow by modern standards, but not unreasonably so.

We must be careful not to read too much into this analysis. It tells us what hymn tempos were *probably* like in one court chapel with a full cadre of instrumentalists and singers to lead the congregation and sing individual stanzas in polyphonic settings. It tells us little of the tempo in the vast majority of churches where there was no accompaniment and where all the singing was in unison.

Eighteenth-century sources were witness to a relatively quick singing tempo in many places, and there are frequent reminders that hymns should be sung more slowly:

> Heinrich Georg Neuss, preface to the hymnal for Wernigerode, 1712—". . . in many a place the hymns are so rushed that one syllable is not finished before the next one starts, by which the emotions are set in disarray and devotion is disturbed; therefore it is advised that the preacher and singers, together with the congregation, strive earnestly to the end that the singing be orderly, slow and devotional and that each verse be held a little longer, and also that each word be allowed its time for devotion."[76]

> Hymnal for Vorpommern and Rügen, 1724—"Unfortunately the disgraceful bad habit has spread of singing the hymns much too quickly, as if one were on the hunt or on a fast postal car. One person is already finished with the phrase while another has barely started it. One screams

ahead of the other, to the annoyance of the person who wants to sing slowly and deliberately."[77]

Bitterfeld hymnal, 1734—"In addition, the spiritual songs must not be sung as if they were *en route* in the mail [i.e., quickly]; but rather the slower they are sung, the more edifying and enlivening they are."[78]

Dresden hymnal, 1766—"In this way one sings and plays to the Lord in his heart. But this cannot possibly happen when the hymns are sung so quickly and hurriedly."[79]

Johann Carl Voigt, 1742—"I have noticed that in a number of places the hymns have been sung in quite a frivolous manner, not only in the churches, but also in front of the houses and during funeral processions; it is unquestionably offensive to our dear God when the spiritual songs are sung so quickly, as if they should be danced to."[80]

Caspar Ruetz, 1752—"If there be any means to teach the congregation to sing slowly, I doubt it very much. The great organ at St. Mary's [Lübeck], even if all the stops were pulled, is not powerful enough to hold the congregation in check." And again, complaining about the length of services—"Should there be among so many hymns that are sung not even a few that are dispatched without proper devotion and lifting of the heart to God? Why do people like to sing the spiritual odes so quickly? Is it not because we want to be done with it? For if they were all sung with proper slowness, one could be stuck in church for four hours."[81]

Daniel Gottlob Türk, 1787—"In many places, particularly in the country, the singing is so fast that it requires effort for an inexperienced reader to keep pace. . . .If the organist or country schoolmaster introduced this nonsense in order to be finished a half hour earlier, or at least furthered it through his playing, it is disgraceful."[82]

One eighteenth-century source, Georg Friedrich Seiler's 1786 report on the services in his own church in Augsburg, contained a precise indication of hymn tempos. According to Seiler, the hymns were sung "neither too slowly nor too quickly. We sing approximately fifty phrases (*Zeilen*) in a quarter hour."[83] Given a hymn such as *Freu dich sehr, o meine Seele* (Example 9.2), which has phrases of average length, and allowing four beats at phrase endings to accommodate the brief interludes Seiler reported were done in Augsburg, in a quarter hour 537 quarter-note

Example 9.2. *Freu dich sehr* in the melodic form used by J. S. Bach, with phrase endings lengthened to accommodate interludes

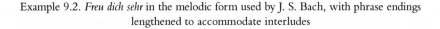

beats (representing 50 phrases) could have been sung. This works out to about 36 beats per minute, or about one beat every second and a half. This tempo, which is akin to the normal base tempo of Praetorius, seems quite slow to modern ears; but it explains how organists were able to play accompaniments with trills and other ornaments in the melody, and it also suits well the rich choral harmonizations in J. S. Bach's cantatas.

It also sheds light on another question. It has long been known that over the course of the seventeenth century hymns originally sung in rhythmic forms gradually took on isometric forms, as with *Ein feste Burg* (Example 9.3). Konrad Ameln has traced the melodic development of this hymn and several others through various hymnals as they gradually assumed isometric forms.[84] But Ameln did not address the question of *why* this happened. It certainly stands to reason, though, that if hymn tempos were slowing down during the seventeenth century, then congregations would have had a difficult time maintaining the underlying pulse necessary for singing the rhythmic forms of hymns, and hymn tunes would naturally have degenerated into a mass of equal notes, with longer notes at phrase endings.

Nicholas Temperley has documented this phenomenon for England during the seventeenth through nineteenth centuries, where psalm tunes ranged in tempo from two to four seconds for each note. He explains it thus:

> For us today the excessively slow manner of singing hymns is almost unimaginable. Yet it is not difficult to see how it came about. When singers depend on other singers for the pitch of the note they will sing next, they naturally tend to wait until they hear the note before they venture to sing

Example 9.3a. *Ein feste Burg* from *Geystliche Lieder*, 1545 (transposed from F)

Example 9.3b. *Ein feste Burg* from J. S. Bach, Cantata 80 (ca. 1732)

it. The result is a "drag." It is corrected by instrumental accompaniment, or by dancing or even foot-tapping such as often accompanies secular folk song. In church there was nothing to keep the rhythm going, and in addition there was often an echoing building to prolong each sound still more. Over many years the effect was cumulative. Each generation would aim to sing only as fast as it had learned to sing, but would insensibly slow down the "norm" that it passed on to its successors. A similar process took place in the singing of plainsong over the centuries. By the early nineteenth century, before the reforms of Regensburg and Solesmes, it had become a ponderous recitation in long, slow notes of equal duration, parodied in the "Dies irae" of Berlioz's *Symphonie fantastique*.[85]

In England, as in Germany, the tunes lost any complexities of rhythm over time, with each phrase assuming a similar shape: all notes equal in length except the first and last notes, which were longer. For Germany, we might add to Temperley's reasons for the slowing of tempo the fact that most people during this period learned hymn tunes by rote, providing an excellent opportunity for rhythmic subtleties to be lost.

Ameln's work, cited above, shows that the rhythmic versions of hymns were not lost, at least in print, until the seventeenth century. If such loss of rhythmic precision is, over a period of decades, a natural consequence of large groups singing unaccompanied hymns, then we might expect the rhythmic changes to have taken place earlier, in the sixteenth century, if whole congregations were in fact singing the hymns. The fact that this did not occur supports the evidence presented throughout this study that congregations did not sing well until after 1600 and that before then hymns were sung primarily by choirs whose directors could more easily manage the tempo.

The conclusion that the "straightening out" of hymn tunes was the result of natural processes at work in the congregation rather than, say, a deliberate effort by musicians to simplify the tunes is bolstered by Daniel Speer's instruction in 1692 that organists should note in their chorale books that hymns set in triple meter should actually be played in duple meter. The reason given was that many congregations would no longer sing hymns in triple meter.[86] The irony is that musicians, once given a taste of the slower tempos, began to insist upon them; and congregations, who might have preferred to sing more quickly, came to suffer under the tyranny of organists.

The tempo appears to have slowed down even more in the nineteenth century. In 1847, a church administrator named Bähr from Baden wrote in the *Evangelische Zeitung*: "Each syllable without distinction is held for the length of about four pulse beats; on the last syllable of each line of verse a fermata of eight to twelve pulse beats is observed, whose last part takes up a more or less confused interlude on the organ."[87] This is similar to the definition in several eighteenth-century English psalm books of the "slowest mood of common time" [notated by a semibreve] . . . as four beats of a large pendulum clock," which some books give specifically as four seconds.[88] Pröhle, in his 1858 book on church customs, confirmed that the tempo had slowed in the nineteenth century:

In earlier times, when the people had more stamina in church, not to mention a greater desire to sing, even the longest hymns were sung straight through from the first through the last verse. It is not to be denied that the quicker tempo in which the hymns were sung, and also in many churches the lack of an organ, shortened the time for singing.[89]

Quite inexplicable, though, is the description by inveterate traveler Charles Burney of a hymn he heard sung while in Bremen in 1772. It seems impossible that a single hymn could last so long, unless it had been divided by the sermon, or was even sung in two separate services, both of which Burney unknowingly managed to visit:

> However, I visited the Thumkirche or cathedral, belonging to the Lutherans, where I found the congregation singing a dismal melody, without the organ. When this was ended, the organist gave out a hymn tune, in the true dragging style of Sternhold and Hopkins [the English psalter of 1562]. The instrument is large, and has a noble and well-toned chorus, but the playing was more old-fashioned, I believe, than any thing that could have been heard in our country towns, during the last century. [Burney describes the interludes between phrases.]
>
> After hearing this tune, and these interludes, repeated ten or twelve times, I went to see the town, and returning to the cathedral, two hours later, I still found the people singing all in unison, and as loud as they could, the same tune, to the same accompaniment. I went to the post-office, to make dispositions for my departure; and, rather from curiosity than the love of such music, I returned once more to this church, and, to my great astonishment, still found them, vocally and organically performing the same ditty, the duration of which seems to have exceeded that of a Scots Hymn, in the time of Charles I.[90]

The explanation could simply be the one given by Johann Friedrich Reichardt: "I would put it quite frankly that Mr. Burney is a terrible musical observer."[91]

Eventually a reaction set in against the ponderous tempos, and in 1839 Friedrich Layriz published his *CXVII geistliche Melodien, meist aus dem 16. und 17. Jahrh[undert], in ihren ursprünglichen Rhythmen,* which reintroduced original rhythms of Lutheran hymns to German musicians. Occasionally individual parishes and territorial churches used these original versions, but it was not until the 1950s, after the introduction of the *Evangelisches Kirchengesangbuch,* that all of Lutheran Germany returned to the original rhythmic versions of hymns. H. A. Pröhle recounted in 1858 how he had tried ten years previously to introduce the rhythmic form of *Allein Gott in der Höh sei Ehr* in his congregation. First the schoolchildren learned it, then he sang it for the congregation before the service, then he announced the change again immediately before the hymn, the organist introduced it and the children sang the first stanza. Then the rest of the congregation entered and sang lustily exactly as they had been accustomed. The pastor was later told by a member that the people did not want to sing the hymn any differently from the way their fathers had done. A similar experience a few years later went much better.[92]

❖

The Abuse of Hymns

We have seen in previous chapters how, according to contemporary writers, the Kirchenmusik and the organ were abused. It is only to be expected that hymns could be abused as well. One of the most common complaints was that people sang the words incorrectly. Christian Marbach, writing in 1726, attributed this to several reasons: (1) the singer not paying attention; (2) the hymn being taught incorrectly either in the church or at home; (3) people preferring singing from memory to singing from the hymnal (the author implies that most people have hymnals but do not use them); and (4) hymnals having the words incorrectly printed.[93] This last reason was a common problem before official hymnals became widely used during the course of the century.

Hymns could powerfully affect an individual's faith and life, and so one would expect the devil to make every effort to counteract their influence. Ways in which he did so, according to Marbach, included:

(1) when hymn singing is forbidden (as by the Brownists in England or the Zwinglians in Switzerland);

(2) when people quote hymn texts in a joking manner, as when Olearius reported the case in Strassburg in 1588 when three people went swimming in the lake on day, and one cried out *Christ ist erstanden* as he jumped in and promptly drowned before the others could reach him;

(3) when foolish stories concerning hymns are told so that people can no longer sing them without laughing;

(4) when people make worldly parodies of hymns, such as the example, told in several sources, of the wedding of the rector of the school in Grimma in October 1637 where the hymn *Nun lasst uns den Leib begraben* (Now let us bury the body) was turned by a student attending the wedding into *Nun lasst uns die Braut begraben* (Now let us bury the bride), and God's judgment was such that the bride and two of her brothers died shortly thereafter;

(5) when so many changes are made to hymns that the congregation is confused;

(6) when scandalous nicknames are given to hymns, such as the whore's hymn ("Hurenlied") to *Erbarm dich mein, o Herre Gott,* because it was often sung when bands of prostitutes came to confession;

(7) when foolish or evil people misunderstand hymn texts, such as the incident in Lübeck in 1660 reported by Thomas Schmid in which a sermon was preached on the destruction of Jerusalem and the hymn *An Wasserflüssen Babylon* was sung, which contains the words "Wohl dem, der deine Kinderlein ergreifft und schläg sie an ein'n Stein" ("Blessed is he who takes your little children and smashes them against a rock," the concluding verse of Psalm 137, on which this hymn is based), whereupon a man went out, grabbed a little child and threw it against a rock (the child did, however, survive);

(8) when people provoke laughter by their choice of hymns at funerals, such as when the hymn *Einen gute Kampff hab ich auf der Welt gekämpffet* (I have fought a good fight in this world) is chosen for someone whose only battle on earth was a constant one with his neighbors;

(9) when people chatter while a hymn is being sung;

(10) when worldly songs are sung, since their only purpose is to distract people from spiritual songs;

(11) when Satan, appearing as an apparition, orders a hymn to be sung for his own devious purposes;

(12) when people attempt to spread false doctrine through hymns;

(13) when people take an aversion to old hymns and are too greatly attracted to the new.[94]

Conclusion

The hallmark of Lutheran liturgical development from the sixteenth to the eighteenth centuries was the change from a liturgy that was essentially choral to one that was essentially congregational. Choral music thus became a performance for an audience and was set against the music of the congregation, hence the "worship wars" of the seventeenth and eighteenth centuries. This change did not happen all at once but occurred over a period of about two hundred fifty years. Coupled with it was a change in the perceived purpose of liturgical music. Sixteenth-century writers did not attempt to define the purpose of music in church. Its purpose was obvious: it carried the liturgical text. By the eighteenth century the stakes were higher, and church music was expected to awaken devotion in the listeners and point them to God, as writer after writer declared. The irony is that, as church music became more complex, it simultaneously lost its impact on ordinary churchgoers, many of whom failed to understand the dazzling array of new sounds reaching their ears.

Where was the congregation in all this? In the sixteenth century, they were mostly spectators as the liturgy was conducted around them. They participated by hearing the Word and receiving the Lord's body and blood. Even when they were supposed to sing, in many cases they did not. This mattered little, for the liturgy was sung for its own sake and for God's, not for theirs. This was not unprecedented in church history. Jeffrey Dean, in a 1997 article that challenged all assumptions about the role of music in the late medieval church, concluded that the polyphonic music of the papal court in Rome around 1500 was not appreciated but merely tolerated, and in fact rarely heard:

> Most of the time the sacred polyphony of the papal chapel was being listened to by the singers alone. When they did sing in public at the papal

services we have scarcely any evidence for a positive response to their music before the middle of the 16th century. I conclude that sacred polyphony was composed and performed to be listened to by the singers themselves.[1]

The same could be said concerning the Lutheran liturgy in most of sixteenth-century Germany.

The seventeenth century saw a strengthening of both choral music and congregational singing. For a while, the two seemed to coexist peacefully in the cantionale style. But after the end of the Thirty Years' War in 1648, the new compositional techniques imported from Italy brought a more sophisticated choral style. The introduction of organ accompaniment, the growing use of congregational hymnals, the shift in the choir's focus from the liturgy to the performance of sacred music and the emphasis by Pietists on the participation of every believer in the religious life of the community all contributed to a marked increase in both the quantity and quality of congregational singing, which continued into the eighteenth century. By 1750 or slightly later, hymns were sung in a manner that would be familiar to modern churchgoers, except for the slow tempos and organ interludes between phrases. By 1780 the choir's chief role had shifted from singing the liturgy to performing a cantata, and the rest of the congregation was left to take up the slack. The liturgy had become the liturgy of the people, and the church's song was now truly the people's song.

Because my conclusions on this topic differ from both received tradition and popular understanding, it is useful to pause a moment to consider how scholars came to assume that congregational singing was the norm right from the beginning of the Reformation. The story unfolds with the efforts of liturgical scholars at the beginning of the nineteenth century.

By the nineteenth century, church life in German Lutheranism had reached a crisis point. Theologians were struggling to find answers to questions posed by Enlightenment writers, who had challenged doctrines that were at the very core of the traditional faith. Attendance at services was down, and the liturgy had in many places been purified of its last vestiges of ceremony and formality. Hymn singing was rhythmically lifeless, tempos were ponderous, and the organ imposed itself after every phrase with running passages while the singers caught a much needed breath. For certain influential churchmen, the solution was a simple one—a return to authentic Lutheran doctrine, liturgy and hymnody; that is, to the Lutheranism of the sixteenth century. But first it was necessary to establish exactly what constituted authentic Lutheranism, for much of it had been obscured in the preceding century. Efforts in this regard gave rise to the academic study of German liturgy and hymnody.

From the very beginning of these efforts, scholars assumed that hymns had the same function in early Lutheranism as in their own time; that is, as songs intended for and sung by congregations. Sometimes a researcher would notice that the liturgy in a particular locality was sung almost entirely by the choir, but this would be regarded as an exception. Until recently, no one questioned the received notion that the early Lutheran liturgy was essentially congregational in nature and that hymns sung by the people were an outstanding feature of that liturgy.

Yet the evidence presented above shows that the break with the past was not nearly so complete. The transition from a choral to a congregational service was a gradual one, occurring over a period of about two hundred fifty years, with bumps and starts in the process as churches tried at various times to accommodate proponents of both choral and congregational liturgies. Sometimes the transition was acrimonious, giving rise to various so-called worship wars; more frequently there was simply an undercurrent of tension, sometimes recognized by the participants, sometimes not. Occasionally a church would rise to the occasion and develop a liturgy in which both choral and congregational music flourished, each enhancing the other, as with Praetorius in Wolfenbüttel or Kuhnau and Bach in Leipzig.

The change from a choral to a congregational liturgy took place more slowly than most modern scholars have recognized. The emphasis on congregational singing as an essential part of the liturgy, frequently ascribed to Luther, was actually more representative of the reformers in Switzerland and southern Germany and of the Pietists of the seventeenth and eighteenth centuries than of sixteenth-century Lutherans. In many places Lutheran congregations, far from enthusiastically supporting Luther's reforms with their singing voices, chose instead to remain silent in church, or mostly so, for many decades after the Reformation was introduced. It was only in the eighteenth century, with the introduction of organ accompaniment and official congregational hymnals, that the song of the people came to resemble what is familiar to us today.

In retrospect, it seems obvious that the sixteenth-century Lutheran liturgy is yet another example of the maxim that a scholar should, lacking compelling evidence to the contrary, apply the concept of inertia to historical conditions; that is, one should expect that a historical condition, such as how the liturgy was sung, probably did not change much unless one finds evidence that indicates otherwise. This begs the question of how several generations of scholars from the nineteenth to the late twentieth century missed this conclusion. The answer lies partly in the questions they asked and partly in their purpose in conducting the research. The fact that early scholars in liturgy and hymnody failed to discern the continuance of liturgical tradition does not mean that their research was flawed. In fact, much of it was exceptional and still stands today, but it was concerned mostly with establishing original forms and not with understanding how these forms had been used.[2] It is not surprising that these scholars failed to reach the same conclusions that are evident today, for they were asking different questions.

We should also keep in mind that nineteenth-century scholars, almost without exception, had a particular goal in mind; namely, to reconstitute early Lutheran liturgy and hymnody in the modern service. This goal is nowhere more evident than in the twentieth century's most influential book on Lutheran liturgical history, Paul Graff's two-volume *Geschichte der Auflösung der alten gottesdienstlichen Formen in der evangelischen Kirche Deutschlands* (1937–39). The author, a parish pastor in Hannover, consulted a prodigious number of Lutheran church orders to produce a comprehensive work that treated in minute detail the liturgical provisions of the sixteenth through eighteenth centuries. The profusion of detail in Graff's book was dedicated to proving a simple thesis: that the history of the Lutheran service is the history of its decline. The author saw the sixteenth century as a golden age for

Lutheran liturgy, but thereafter the Lutherans steadily chipped away at the liturgy until its very foundation was lost with the advent of Rationalism in the late eighteenth century. Graff's viewpoint was transmitted to America in the major work on the subject in English, Luther Reed's *The Lutheran Liturgy* (1947, revised 1960), which relied heavily on Graff.

Graff's thesis makes sense if one reads only the liturgical prescriptions of the church orders, but it is less defensible if the actual conduct of the liturgy as described in visitation records, local histories, and other documents is considered. It is questionable, for example, whether the reduction in the use of Latin, the increase in congregational participation and the vast improvement in congregational singing documented in the two centuries following the Reformation constituted a liturgical decline.

Graff's interpretation relied on his perception that the early Lutheran service was essentially a congregational activity. By taking this viewpoint he was attempting to counter the opinions of other writers (whom he did not name) who had claimed that the Lutheran reformers had considered the service to have primarily a pedagogical purpose. On the contrary, wrote Graff, the reformers had regarded the service as principally an offering of thanks and praise with the Holy Communion as its high point. The sermon was not an opportunity for catechetical instruction, as some had claimed, but rather a sermon for the *cultus,* a self-witness of the celebrating congregation, done as much by the congregation as by the pastor, and so the service was a true congregational service. This, wrote Graff, was precisely Luther's view of the service.[3]

By viewing the sixteenth-century service as essentially congregational and noting that in the seventeenth and eighteenth centuries the people seemed alienated from the liturgy, Graff concluded that the liturgy had declined under the influence of Lutheran Orthodoxy, Pietism, and especially Rationalism. During the period of Orthodoxy, he wrote, the success of the service depended on the proper preaching of pure doctrine. During the Pietistic era the service was seen as a time for conversion and "building up" of the individual through the sermon, the individual having become more important than the assembly. Rationalism, whose influence was being felt as early as 1700, saw the pastor as religion instructor.[4]

To be sure, Luther spoke of both the sacramental and sacrificial roles of the liturgy, but this did not necessarily mean that the people sang the entire liturgy, or even most of it. In fact, as we have seen, in the sixteenth century the liturgy was essentially a function of the priest and choir, not of the congregation. In many places a large part of the congregation was not even present for much of the service, arriving only in time for the sermon and leaving immediately afterward. It was during the seventeenth and eighteenth centuries that the congregation began to assert itself, a development resisted by certain musicians who felt that it somehow cheapened the liturgy and that music performed for the people was superior to that performed by the people. Eventually, though, the congregational conception of the service won out.

Recent scholars have begun to recognize this development. Friedrich Blume's highly regarded *Geschichte der evangelischen Kirchenmusik* (1964) supplied a profusion of detail on choral and congregational music, including some information on how hymns were sung. Even so, the author was forced to admit that "how the congregation actually carried out the assignment intended for it [hymn singing] is even today not completely clear."[5] More recently, Hans-Otto Korth, Daniela Garbe, and Bartlett Butler, in excellent articles in two separate encyclopedias, have questioned some of the traditional assumptions about early Lutheran singing; but they have not been able to give more than a summary of their findings in the limited space allotted to them.[6] In this study I have attempted to fill in the details and present enough evidence to provide a balanced view; namely, that although the people sang to some extent in sixteenth-century Lutheran churches, it was nonetheless a long time before they took ownership of the liturgy and the Lutheran Church became truly "the singing church."

APPENDIX I

Sources of German Hymns

Below is a list of the hymns named in the church orders found in the bibliography and their locations in the following scholarly sources and hymnals. Excluded for reasons of space and significance are hymns found in the *de tempore* lists identified in chapter 9, section "Hymns *de Tempore*."

B (1)   *Geystliche Lieder.* Leipzig: Valentin Babst, 1545. Reprinted as *Das Babstsche Gesangbuch von 1545,* ed. Konrad Ameln. Documenta musicologica, series 1, no. 38. Kassel: Bärenreiter, 1988.

B (2)   *Psalmen vnd geistliche Lieder, welche von fromen Christen gemacht vnd zu samen gelesen sind.* Leipzig: Valentin Babst, 1545. Reprint bound with B (1).

CW   *Christian Worship: A Lutheran Hymnal.* Authorized by the Wisconsin Evangelical Lutheran Synod. Milwaukee: Northwestern, 1993.

DKL   *Das deutsche Kirchenlied.* Abteilung III, Band 1. Vorgelegt von Joachim Stalmann; bearbeitet von Karl-Günther Hartmann (Teil 1), Hans-Otto Korth (Teile 1–3) und Daniela Wissemann-Garbe (Teile 2–3). 1 vol. in 6 physical vols. Kassel: Bärenreiter, 1993–98. To date DKL covers hymns appearing in printed sources only through 1570; future volumes will cover publications through 1680. Numbers in italics denote tunes originally published with a different text.

EG   *Evangelisches Gesangbuch.* Ausgabe für die Evangelisch-Lutherischen Kirchen in Niedersachsen und für die Bremische Evangelische Kirche. Hannover: Lutherisches Verlagshaus; Hannover: Schlütersche Verlagsanstalt und Druckerei; and Göttingen: Vandenhoeck & Ruprecht, 1994. Numbers 1–535 may be found in any regional edition of this hymnal.

ELH   *Evangelical Lutheran Hymnary.* Prepared by the Worship Committee of the Evangelical Lutheran Synod, Mankato, Minnesota. St. Louis: MorningStar Music Publishers, 1996.

ELKG   *Evangelisch-Lutherisches Kirchengesangbuch.* [Hannover]: Verlag der Selbständigen Evangelisch-Lutherischen Kirche, 1987. Numbers 1–394 may also be found in any edition of the *Evangelisches Kirchengesangbuch* of 1950ff.

FT   Fischer, Albert. *Das deutsche evangelische Kirchenlied des 17. Jahrhunderts.* Completed after the author's death by Wilhelm Tümpel. 6 vols. Gütersloh, 1904–16.

J   Jenny, Markus, ed. *Luthers geistliche Lieder und Kirchengesänge.* Cologne: Böhlau, 1985.

LBW   *Lutheran Book of Worship.* Prepared by the churches participating in the Inter-Lutheran Commission on Worship. Minneapolis: Augsburg and Philadelphia: Board of Publication, Lutheran Church in America, 1978.

LW   *Lutheran Worship.* Prepared by the Commission on Worship of the Lutheran Church—Missouri Synod. St. Louis: Concordia, 1982.

S   Schoeberlein, Ludwig. *Schatz des liturgischen Chor- und Gemeindegesangs nebst den Altarweisen in der deutschen evangelischen Kirche.* 3 vols. Göttingen: Vandenhoeck & Ruprecht, 1865–70. This source is cited only for hymns not found in the more scholarly W or FT.

TLH   *The Lutheran Hymnal.* Authorized by the synods constituting the Evangelical Lutheran Synodical Conference of North America. St. Louis: Concordia, 1941.

W   Wackernagel, Philip. *Das deutsche Kirchenlied von der ältesten Zeit bis zu Anfang des XVII. Jahrhunderts.* 5 vols. Leipzig, 1864–77.

Z   Zahn, Johannes. *Die Melodien der deutschen evangelischen Kirchenlieder.* 6 vols. Gütersloh, 1889–93. Only tunes published through 1780 are cited. Numbers in italics denote tunes originally published with a different text.

Of these, FT and W are compendia of texts, DKL and Z are critical editions of tunes (with at least one stanza of text given for each hymn), J and S give both full text and tune, and the rest are hymnals. Several hymns have variant forms in W and FT. These variants are given below if they are essentially the same hymn. They are excluded if they are new hymns based on the listed hymn or are variants of a common ancestor but with widely diverging texts. Translations of Latin texts in the English-language hymnals are listed only where there is evidence that the translator either made use of the German text or (in the case of prose texts) fit the English text to the tune used with the German text.

If a biblical or liturgical source is known for the German text, it is given in parentheses following the text incipit, and cross-references are given at the appropriate place. Occasionally a church order will name only such a source, the reader being expected to know the corresponding German hymn. The cross-references are helpful in this regard, but they are not complete: the "German Te Deum," for example, usually (perhaps always) refers to Luther's *Herr Gott, dich loben wir,* as this is the only German Te Deum given a title in any church order. But it is conceivable that a particular locality might have had its own German Te Deum which was used nowhere else and that the local church order refers to this version and not Luther's.

Spelling and dialectical variants in the original sources are subsumed under the modern standard German form without comment. But in a few cases where the spelling differs so much that identification would be hindered, or the first word of the text is different, the original form is indexed, and the reader is referred from it to the modern form.

Psalms are numbered according to the Hebrew (as in traditional Lutheran usage), and headings from the Latin Vulgate are also given for the convenience of those familiar with them. All numbers in sources refer to hymns, not pages, except that items from the liturgical section in the front of modern hymnals are given page numbers (indicated by a "p." preceding the number).

If no hymn with a given incipit could be found in any of the sources listed above, "not found" is indicated. If more than one hymn with the same incipit was found and it is uncertain which hymn is meant, "unidentified" is indicated. An explanation follows in either case.

First lines of German hymns are in roman type; Latin and English titles, and German titles that are not first lines, are in italic. English translations are noted in parentheses following the first listed source in which they appear. Translations by different authors are listed separately even if their first lines are identical. If an English source has no translation indicated, it uses one previously listed (possibly with alterations).

A solis ortus cardine → Christum wir sollen loben schon

Ach bleib bei uns, Herr Jesu Christ (from stanza 3 based on Ps. 122 : Laetatus sum)—W 4:392; Z 613; ELKG 207; EG 246; TLH 292 (Lord Jesus Christ, with us abide); LW 344 (Lord Jesus Christ, will you not stay); CW 541; ELH 511

Ach Gnad über alle Gnaden—FT 5:235

Ach Gott, laß dir befohlen sein—W 4:731, 5:1267

Ach Gott und Herr, wie groß und schwer—FT 1:52; Z 2049–53, 8212; ELKG 168; EG 233; LW 232 (Alas, my God, my sins are great)

Ach Gott vom Himmel sieh darein (Ps. 12 : Salvum me fac)—W 3:3; J 8; B (1) 22; Z 4431–32; DKL *Ea2*, Ea5, Ebr, Eb6A, Ec3, Ee9; ELKG 177; EG 273; TLH 260 (O Lord, look down from heaven, behold); CW 205

Ach Jesu Christ, dich zu uns wend → Herr Jesu Christ, dich zu uns wend

Ach Vader alder högeste Godt → Kyrie, ach Vater allerhöchster Gott

Ach wir armen Sünder → O wir armen Sünder

Agnus dei → Christe, du Lamm Gottes; O du Lamm Gottes, das du trägst die Sünde der Welt; O Lamm Gottes unschuldig

All Ehr und Lob soll Gottes sein (Gloria in excelsis)—W 3:252; B (1) 61; Z 8618; DKL A51, *Ei2;* ELKG 503; TLH 238 (All glory be to God alone); LW 210; CW 262; ELH 36

Alleeniste gud y himmerick → Allein Gott in der Höh sei Ehr

Allein Gott in der Höh sei Ehr (Gloria in excelsis)—W 615–17; Z 4457; DKL Ei2; ELKG 131; EG 179; TLH 237 (All glory be to God on high); LBW 166 (All glory be to God on high); LW 215; CW 263; ELH 35

Allein zu dir, Herr Jesu Christ—W 3:201–4; B (2) 11; Z 7292–94; DKL B47, B47A, Eb49; ELKG 166; EG 232; TLH 319 (In thee alone, O Christ, my Lord); LBW 395 (I trust, O Christ, in you alone); LW 357; CW 437; ELH 415

Als Jesus Christus unser Herr—W 3:606; Z *8303;* DKL *Eb14*

Also heilig ist der Tag (Salve, festa dies)—W 2:968–70; Z 7149; DKL *D12*, D12A–D

Apostles' Creed → Ich glaub in Gott Vater, den Allmächtigen; *possibly others as well*

Athanasian Creed—not found; Liegnitz and Brieg 1592 indicates that this may be found in the "Triller Gesangbuch" (RISM 1555[07], 1559[07]).

Auf meinen lieben Gott—W 5:660; Z 2162–66; ELKG 289; EG 345; TLH 526 (In God, my faithful God); LW 421; CW 438; ELH 467

Aufer a nobis → Nimm von uns, Herr [Gott]

Aus meines Herzens Grunde—W 5:248; Z 5269; ELKG 341; EG 443; TLH 548 (My inmost heart now raises); ELH 79

Aus tiefer Not schrei ich zu dir (Ps. 130 : De profundis)—W 3:5–6; J 11; B (1) 28; Z 4437–38; DKL Ea6, Eb2, Eb2A; ELKG 195; EG 299; TLH 329 (From depths of woe I cry to thee); LBW 295 (Out of the depths I cry to you); LW 230 (From depths of woe I cry to you); CW 305; ELH 452

Baptism, German hymn on → Christ unser Herr zum Jordan kam

Behalt uns, Herr → Erhalt uns, Herr, bei deinem Wort

Benedicite omnia opera → Gelobet seist du, Herr, der Gott unsrer Väter
Benedictus → Gelobet sei der Herr, der Gott Israel

Christ, der du bist der helle Tag → Christe, du bist der helle Tag
Christ fuhr gen Himmel—W 2:976–80, 3:1143–45, 1358–59; B (1) 62; Z 8586–87; DKL
   C11D–E, Ek2; ELKG 90; EG 120
Christ ist erstanden—W 2:39, 935–40, 942–50; J 32; B (1) 59; Z 8584–85; DKL C11,
   C11B–C, C18; ELKG 75; EG 99; TLH 187 (Christ is arisen); LBW 136 (Christ is
   arisen); LW 124 (Christ the Lord is risen again); CW 144; ELH 344
Christ lag in Todesbanden—W 3:15; J 12; B (1) 8; Z 7012; DKL Ea8, Ea8A; ELKG 76; EG
   101; TLH 195 (Christ Jesus lay in death's strong bands); LBW 134; LW 123; CW 161;
   ELH 343
Christ unser Herr zum Jordan kam—W 3:43; B (1) 18; Z *7246;* DKL *Ec4;* ELKG 146; EG
   202; LBW 79 (To Jordan came the Christ, our Lord); LW 223; CW 88; ELH 247 (To
   Jordan came our Lord, the Christ)
Christe, der du bist Tag und Licht (Christe, qui lux es et dies)—W 3:161; B (1) 58; Z 343;
   DKL B12, B12B–D, Eh13; ELKG 353
Christe, du bist der helle Tag (Christe, qui lux es et dies)—W 3:1037; Z 383–84; DKL
   A324, Eg59A; ELKG 354; EG 469
Christe, du Lamm Gottes (Agnus dei)—J 27; Z 58; DKL D20, D20A; ELKG 136; EG 190.2;
   TLH 147 (O Christ, thou Lamb of God); LBW 103; LW 7; CW p. 23; ELH p. 55
Christe, qui lux es et dies → Christ, der du bist der helle Tag; Christe, der du bist Tag und Licht
Christo unserem Herrn—*not found; sung at Sunday Vespers in place of the Salve Regina in Cologne*
   1543
Christum wir sollen loben schon (A solis ortus cardine)—W 3:17–18; J 16; B (1) 2; Z 297;
   DKL *C50, D4,* D4A–C, *D4D;* ELKG 411; TLH 104 (Now praise we Christ, the holy
   one); CW 39
Christus, der uns selig macht (Patris sapientia, veritas divina)—W 3:289; Z 6283; DKL B7;
   ELKG 56; EG 77
Communion, German hymn on → Gott sei gelobet und gebenedeiet; Jesus Christus unser Hei-
   land, der von uns den Zorn Gottes wandt
Confession, German hymn on → Erbarm dich mein, o Herre Gott
Confitebor tibi, domine → Ich dank dem Herrn von ganzem Herzen
Creed → Ich glaub . . .; Wir glauben all an einen Gott

Da Israel aus Ägypten zog (Ps. 114 : In exitu Israel)—W 3:124; B (1) 79; Z 8466a; DKL
   B27, A170
Da Jesus an dem Kreuze stund—W 2:1327–28, 5:1394; Z *1706;* DKL Ek7A–B; ELKG 425
Da pacem domine → Verleih uns Frieden gnädiglich
Danket dem Herrn, denn er ist freundlich—*usually a versicle following communion, but in the*
   1538 order for St. Wenceslaus in Naumburg it is a psalm listed with the other communion hymns.
   See DKL A38, A40, A174.
Danksagen wir alle Gott (Grates nunc omnes)—W 3:599; Z 8619b–e; DKL D15B
Danksagen wir nun alle → Danksagen wir alle Gott
Dat heyl de ys vns ghekamen → Es ist das Heil uns kommen her
Der du bist drei in Einigkeit (O lux beata trinitas)—W 3:50; J 41; B (1) 63; Z 335b, e; DKL
   Eg40, Eg40A–B; ELKG 352; EG 470
Der Herr ist mein getreuer Hirt (Ps. 23 : Dominus regit me)—W 3:162; B (2) 7; Z *4432a,*
   4507, 4511; DKL *Ec3;* ELKG 178; EG 274

Der Name des Herrn sei gelobet—*not found; sung after sermons in Braunschweig-Wolfenbüttel 1709*

Der Tag der ist so freudenreich (Dies est laetitiae)—W 2:689–95, 697–99, 3:573–74; B (1) 53; Z 7870; DKL Eg17B; ELKG 18; TLH 78 (Hail the day so rich in cheer); ELH 131 (Now hail the day so rich in cheer)

Dies est laetitiae → Der Tag der ist so freudenreich

Dies sind die heilgen zehn Gebot (Ten Commandments)—W 3:22; J 1; B (1) 14; Z *586, 1951–54;* DKL *A309,* Ea1, Eb9, Eb48, *Ec14;* ELKG 240; EG 231; TLH 287 (That man a godly life might live); LW 331 (Here is the tenfold sure command); CW 285 (The ten commandments are the law); ELH 488 (I am, alone, your God and Lord), 490

Domine deus Abraham—*German version not found; office canticle for weekday Vespers in Danzig 1567*

Du hast uns Leib und Seel gespeiset—W 3:667; EG 216

Du Lebensbrot, Herr Jesu Christ—FT 2:253; Z 4680–81, 5755; ELKG 473; TLH 312 (Lord Jesus Christ, thou living bread); LW 248; ELH 322

Durch Adams Fall ist ganz verderbt—W 3:71; B (1) 43; Z 7547–49, *7583;* DKL Ec7–8, *Ec13,* Ee13; ELKG 243; TLH 369 (All mankind fell in Adam's fall); LW 363; CW 378; ELH 430 (By Adam's fall is all forlorn), 491

Ehr sei dem Vater [und dem Sohn]—*probably a Gloria patri, of which there are several at W 3:1147; see also EG 177.1*

Ehr sei Gott in der Höh [Gloria in excelsis]—*possibly Z 5160*

Ehre sei dem Vater und dem Sohn → Ehr sei dem Vater [und dem Sohn]

Ein feste Burg ist unser Gott (Ps. 46 : Deus noster refugium)—W 3:32–34; J 28; B (1) 24; Z 7377–79; DKL B31; ELKG 201; EG 362; TLH 262 (A mighty fortress is our God); LBW 228–29 (A mighty fortress is our God); LW 297–98; CW 200–201; ELH 250, 251 (A mighty fortress is our God)

Ein Kind geboren zu Bethlehem—W 2:904–9, 3:1109, 4:37, 5:1226, 1393; B (1) 47; Z 192; DKL *A46, A210,* Eb43, Eb43A–B

Ein Kindelein so löbelich (*stanza 2 of Der Tag der ist so freudenreich*)—DKL *Eg17B*

Erbarm dich mein, o Herre Gott (Ps. 51 : Miserere mei deus)—W 3:70; B (1) 42; Z 5851–52; DKL Ea7, Ec5

Erhalt uns, Herr, bei deinem Wort—W 3:44, 46–48; B (1) 30; Z 350; DKL Ee21; ELKG 142; EG 193; TLH 261 (Lord, keep us steadfast in thy Word); LBW 230; LW 334; CW 203; ELH 589

Es ist das Heil uns kommen her—W 3:55; B (1) 44; Z 4430; DKL *B15;* ELKG 242; EG 342; TLH 377 (Salvation unto us has come); LBW 297; LW 355; CW 390; ELH 227

Es spricht der unweisen Mund wohl (Ps. 14 : Dixit insipiens)—W 3:4; J 9; B (1) 23; Z *4433, 4436;* DKL *Eb6,* Ec15

Es wollt uns Gott genädig sein (Ps. 67 : Deus misereatur nostri)—W 3:7; J 10; B (1) 25; Z 7246–47; DKL B17, Ec4; ELKG 182; EG 280; TLH 500 (May God bestow on us his grace); LBW 335; LW 288 (May God embrace us with his grace); CW 574; ELH 591

Et in terra → All Ehr und Lob soll Gottes sein; Allein Gott in der Höh sei Ehr; Ehr sei Gott in der Höh

Fröhlich wollen wir halleluja singen (Ps. 117 : Laudate dominum omnes gentes)—W 3:74; B (2) 3; Z 1625a, 1626–27; DKL Ec11, Ec11A

Gebenedeiet bist du, Herr—*not found; gradual for Sunday in Lippe 1533*

Gelauet systu Jesu Christ → Gelobet seist du, Jesu Christ

Gelobet sei der Herr, [der] Gott Israel (Benedictus)—W 3:1044, 4:273; J 45, B (1) 76; Z 5854; DKL Eg125; ELKG p. 267; EG 783.6

Gelobet sei der Herr von Israel—*presumably a variant of* Gelobet sei der Herr, der Gott Israel

Gelobet seist du, Herr, der Gott unsrer Väter (Benedicite omnia opera)—*not found; office canticle for weekday Matins in Mecklenburg 1572*

Gelobet seist du, Jesu Christ—W 2:910, 3:9, 5:1168–71; J 5; B (1) 3; Z 1947; DKL Ec10; ELKG 15; EG 23; TLH 80 (All praise to thee, eternal God); LBW 48; LW 35 (We praise, O Christ, your holy name); CW 33; ELH 136 (O Jesus Christ, all praise to thee)

Gepreiset seist du, Jesu Christ—Z 4655, *or possibly a variant of* Gelobet seist du, Jesu Christ

Gib unseren Fürsten—*presumably a variant of* Gib unserm Herrn und aller Obrigkeit

Gib unserer christlichen Obrigkeit—*presumably a variant of* Gib unserm Herrn und aller Obrigkeit

Gib unserm Herrn und aller Obrigkeit—Z 1945b; *see also* Verleih uns Frieden gnädiglich, *to which this text was often appended*

Glaube → Creed

Glori sei Gott in der Höhe—*not found; possibly not a hymn at all but a German translation of the celebrant's chant "Gloria in excelsis deo" (cited in Schwäbisch Hall 1543)*

Gloria in excelsis → All Ehr und Lob soll Gottes sein; Allein Gott in der Höh sei Ehr; Ehr sei Gott in der Höh

Gott der Vater wohn uns bei—W 3:24; J 23; B (1) 13; Z 8507; DKL Ec17, Ec17B; ELKG 109; EG 138; TLH 247 (God the Father, be our stay); LBW 308; LW 170; CW 192; ELH 18

Gott gib unserm Fürsten—*presumably a variant of* Gib unserm Herrn und aller Obrigkeit

Gott sei gelobet und gebenedeiet—W 2:989, 3:11; J 4; B (1) 21; Z 8078; DKL Eb1, Eb1 ; ELKG 163; EG 214; TLH 313 (O Lord, we praise thee); LBW 215; LW 238; CW 317; ELH 327

Gott sei uns gnädig und barmherzig—*not found; sung at the end of services in several late 17th- and early 18th-century Saxon orders*

Gott Vater, Gott Sohn, Gott Heiliger Geist—S 2:485

Gott Vater in dem Himmelreich (Litany)—W 3:230; Z *2561,* 2567–69; DKL Eb35A, Ek12

Grates nunc omnes → Danksagen wir alle Gott; Lasst uns nun alle danksagen

Heilig, heilig, heilig ist der Herr Zebaoth (Sanctus)—*not found; the entire text is given in Cologne 1543*

Heilig ist Gott (Sanctus)—*unidentified; sung as Sanctus in Annaberg 1579*

Heilig ist Gott der Herre Zebaoth (Sanctus)—*not found; possibly the end of* Jesaia dem Propheten das geschah

Heilig ist Gott der Vater (Sanctus)—W 3:618; Z 8630b–c; DKL A44, D22, D22A

Heilig ist unser Gott, heilig ist unser Gott, der Herre Zebaoth (Sanctus)—*not found; sung as Sanctus in East Frisia 1593*

Heiliger . . .—*not found; according to Brandenburg-Ansbach-Kulmbach 1548, this Sanctus hymn appeared in Andreas Döber's 1525 order for Nuremberg*

Herr Christ, der einig Gotts Sohn—W 3:67–69; B (1) 47; Z 4297a; DKL Ea4; ELKG 46; EG 67; LBW 86 (The only Son from heaven); LW 72; CW 86; ELH 224

Herr Gott, dein Treu mit Gnaden leist—Z *8304,* 8311; DKL *Ea11, Eb14–15*

Herr Gott, dich loben wir (Te deum laudamus)—W 3:31; J 31; B (1) 36; Z 8652; DKL *D7,* D7B; ELKG 137; EG 191; ELH 45 (We sing thy praise, O God)

Herr Gott und Schöpfer aller Ding—W 4:324; Z 514–15

Herr Gott Vater, allerhöchster Gott → Kyrie, ach Vater allerhöchster Gott

Herr Gott Vater, erbarm dich unser—*possibly* S 1:56; *sung as Kyrie in Ritzebüttel 1570*

Herr Gott Vater, wohn uns bei → Gott der Vater wohn uns bei

Herr Gott, wir loben dich → Herr Gott, dich loben wir

Herr Jesu Christ, dich zu uns wend—FT 2:73; Z 624; ELKG 126; EG 155; TLH 3 (Lord Jesus Christ, be present now); LBW 253; LW 201; CW 230; ELH 23

Herr Jesu Christ, du höchstes Gut—W 4:1523; Z *4525*, 4542–50; ELKG 167; EG 219

Herr Jesu Christ, wahr Mensch und Gott—W 4:2, 5:1593; Z 422–23, 424a, 425–30, *2570*, 8711; DKL *Eb35, Eg97A;* ELKG 314; ELH 238 (Lord Jesus Christ, true man and God)

Herr, nun lässt du deinen Diener (Nunc dimittis)—B (1) 77; ELKG p. 30, 291; EG 786.10; TLH p. 29 (Lord, now lettest thou thy servant); CW p. 24; ELH p. 81

Herr, sieh nicht an die Sünde mein—*not found; sung after the sermon at Saturday Vespers in Altenburg 1705*

Heut triumphieret Gottes Sohn—W 5:629; Z *2440c,* 2585; ELKG 83; EG 109; LW 136 (Today in triumph Christ arose); CW 164; ELH 358

Hilf, Gott, dass mir gelinge—W 3:112; B (2) 14; Z 4329–31; DKL Ek8, Ek8A–B

Holy Spirit, hymn on the—*probably* Nun bitten wir den heiligen Geist

Ich dank dem Herrn von ganzem Herzen (Ps. 111 : Confitebor tibi, domine)—J 43; B (1) 19

Ich dank dir, lieber Herre—W 3:114; B (2) 18; Z *5352,* 5354b; DKL B41, *B41A;* ELKG 335

Ich danke dir, Herr, das du sehr zörnig—B (1) 68

Ich glaub an einen Gott allein (Creed)—FT 2:377

Ich gläub an[in] Gott Vater allmächtigen (Creed)—W 5:1273; DKL A12, Ef15

Ich glaub in Gott Vater (Creed)—*presumably a variant of* Ich gläub an[in] Gott Vater allmächtigen

Ich glaub in Gott Vater, den Allmächtigen (Apostles' Creed)—Z 8625

Ich ruf zu dir, Herr Jesu Christ—W 3:78–79; B (2) 16; Z 7400; DKL B21, Ee17; ELKG 244; EG 343; ELH 255 (Lord, hear the voice of my complaint)

Ich will den Herrn loben allezeit—*a prose psalm set to tone 1 in Wittenberg 1526*

In dulci jubilo—B (1) 56; Z 4947; DKL Ee12; ELKG 26; TLH 92 (Now sing we, now rejoice); LBW 55 (Good Christian Friends, Rejoice); LW 47 (Now sing we, now rejoice); CW 34; ELH 135

Jam lucis orto sidere → *German version not found; sung after the Benedicamus at Matins in Pomerania 1542*

Jesaia dem Propheten das geschah (Sanctus)—W 3:30; J 26; B (1) 29; Z 8534; ELKG 135; TLH 249 (Isaiah, mighty seer, in days of old); LBW 528 (Isaiah in a vision did of old); LW 214 (Isaiah, mighty seer, in spirit soared); CW 267; ELH 40

Jesu, du mein liebstes Leben—S 2:305; Z *7887,* 7891–93

Jesu, meine Freude—FT 4:103; Z 8032–35, *8052;* ELKG 293; EG 396; TLH 347 (Jesus, priceless treasure); LBW 457–58; LW 270; CW 349; ELH 263–64

Jesus Christus unser Heiland → Jesus Christus unser Heiland, der den Tod überwand (an Easter hymn); Jesus Christus unser Heiland, der von uns den Zorn Gottes wandt (a communion hymn)

Jesus Christus unser Heiland, der den Tod überwand—W 3:13–14; J 13; B (1) 9; Z 1976–78, 1979c; DKL Ea9, Ec16, Ee6, Ee6A–B; ELKG 77; EG 102

Jesus Christus unser Heiland, der von uns den Zorn Gottes wandt—W 3:10; J 6; B (1) 20; Z 1576–79; DKL B14, B14A, B14C, Ee8, Ee8A; ELKG 154; EG 215; LW 236–37 (Jesus Christ, our blessed Savior); CW 313

Jetzund so bitten wir dich, Herr—W 3:675; Z 2541

Komm, du herzlicher Tröster—W 3:723; Z *8594;* DKL D18B

Komm, Gott Schöpfer, Heiliger Geist (Veni creator spiritus)—W 3:20–21; J 17; B (1) 10;

Z 294–95; DKL *D14,* D14A–C, *D14D;* ELKG 97; EG 126; LBW 284 (Creator Spirit, heavenly dove); LW 156

Komm, Heiliger Geist → Komm, Heiliger Geist, erfüll die Herzen; Komm, Heiliger Geist, Herre Gott

Komm, Heiliger Geist, erfüll die Herzen (Veni sancte spiritus, reple tuorum)—Z 8594, 8596; DKL D18, D18E; EG 156

Komm, Heiliger Geist, Herre Gott (Veni sancte spiritus, reple tuorum)—W 2:986–88, 3:19; J 15; B (1) 11; Z 7445; DKL Ea11, Ea11A, Ea11C–D; ELKG 98; EG 125; TLH 224 (Come, Holy Ghost, God and Lord); LBW 163; LW 154; CW 176; ELH 2

Komm, Heiliger Geist, mit deiner Gnad—Z 2016a

Kyrie → Kyrie, ach Vater allerhöchster Gott; Kyrie, Gott Vater in Ewigkeit; [Kyrie, milde Vater, wir bitten dich alle?]; O Herr Gott, Vater in Ewigkeit; O Vater, allmächtiger Gott; *possibly also the brief Kyrie from Luther's German Mass*

Kyrie, ach Vater allerhöchster Gott (Kyrie fons bonitatis, called the "Kyrie summum" because of its use on the highest festivals)—W 3:1114; Z 8600a, 8601; DKL Eg7B–C

Kyrie cunctipotens → O ewiger, barmherziger Gott, wir danken dir der Wohltat

Kyrie fons bonitatis → Kyrie, ach Vater allerhöchster Gott; Kyrie, Gott Vater in Ewigkeit

Kyrie, Gott aller Welt Schöpfer und Vater (Kyrie paschale)–W3:1115; Z 8607b

Kyrie, Gott Vater in Ewigkeit (Kyrie fons bonitatis, also called the "Kyrie summum")—W 3:250; Z 8600c–d; DKL Eg7A; ELKG 130; EG 178.4; LBW 168 (Kyrie! God, Father in heaven above); LW 209; CW 266; ELH 34

Kyrie, o Herre Gott → O Herr Gott, Vater in Ewigkeit

Kyrie magne deus → O Vater, allmächtiger Gott, zu dir schreien wir in der Not

Kyrie, milde Vater, wir bitten dich alle, Vater, erbarm dich unser [Kyrie?]—*not found (but not W 3:1092, which has the same text incipit); sung as Kyrie in Ritzebüttel 1570*

"Kyrie minus summum" → O Vater, allmächtiger Gott, zu dir schreien wir in der Not

"Kyrie paschale" → Kyrie, Gott aller Welt Schöpfer und Vater; O allmächtiger, ewiger Vater, erbarm dich unser; O Herr Gott, Vater in Ewigkeit

"Kyrie summum" → Kyrie, ach Vater allerhöchster Gott; Kyrie, Gott Vater in Ewigkeit

Lam Gads unschuldich → O Lamm Gottes unschuldig

Lasst uns Christen alle singen (Victimae paschali laudes)—DKL *D16*

Lasst uns doch Christo dankbar sein—*not found; sung on Good Friday in Braunschweig-Wolfenbüttel 1709*

Lasst uns nun alle danksagen (Grates nunc omnes)—S 2:84; Z 8619a; DKL D15D

Liebster Jesu, wir sind hier—FT 5:250; Z 3498b, 3499–3501; ELKG 127; EG 161; TLH 16 (Blessed Jesus, at thy word); LBW 248; LW 202; CW 221; ELH 1

Litany, the lesser → Nimm von uns, lieber Herr

Litany → Litany (Luther's version); Gott Vater in dem Himmelreich; Nimm von uns, lieber Herr

Litany (Luther's version)—J 29; B (1) 37; Z 8651; ELKG 138; EG 198

Lobet den Herren, alle Heiden (Ps. 117 : Laudate dominum omnes gentes)—FT 1:208, J 44; Z 2026

Lobet den Herrn—*unidentified; sung as the sequence in Braunschweig-Lüneburg 1564*

Lobt Gott, ihr Christen alle gleich [allzugleich]—W 3:1365; Z *198,* 199–200; DKL B60

Lord's Prayer → O Vater aller Frommen; Vater unser im Himmelreich

Magnificat → Magnificat (prose text); Mein Seel erhebt den Herren mein; Mein Seel, o Herr, soll loben dich

Magnificat (prose text)—B (1) 75; ELKG p. 276; EG 785.6

Media vita → Mitten wir im Leben sind

Mein Seel erhebt den Herren mein (Magnificat)—W 3:561; DKL Eb5

Mein Seel, o Gott, muss loben dich → Mein Seel, o Herr, muss [soll] loben dich

Mein Seel, o Herr, muss [soll] loben dich (Magnificat)—W 3:1282; Z 467, 1747b, *5855*; ELKG 200; EG 308

Meine Seele erhebt den Herrn (Magnificat)—DKL Eg123

Mensch, willst du leben seliglich (Ten Commandments)—W 3:26; J 20; B (1) 15; Z 1956; DKL Ec9

Mit Fried und Freud ich fahr dahin (Nunc dimittis)—W 3:25; J 21; B (1) 7; Z 3986; DKL Ec13, Ec13A–B; ELKG 310; EG 519; TLH 137 (In peace and joy I now depart); LW 185 (In peace and joy I now depart); CW 269; ELH 48

Mitten wir im Leben sind (Media vita)—W 2:991–99, 3:12; J 3; B (1) 35; Z 8502; DKL Ec1; ELKG 309; EG 518; TLH 590 (In the midst of earthly life); LBW 350 (Even as we live each day); LW 265 (In the very midst of life); CW 534; ELH 527

Nicene Creed—*usually* Wir glauben all an einen Gott

Nimm von uns, Herr, all unser Sünd und Missetat → Nimm von uns, Herr [Gott]

Nimm von uns, Herr, du [ge]treuer Gott—W 5:73; Z 447–48; *2570*, 2607–8; ELKG 119; EG 146

Nimm von uns, Herr [Gott] (Aufer a nobis)—Z 8599

Nimm von uns, lieber Herr—*not found; called the "lesser litany" in Kurland 1572*

Nu frowet jw → Nun freut euch, lieben Christen gmein

Nun bitten wir den Heiligen Geist—W 2:43–44, 3:28–29; B (1) 12; Z 2029; DKL Eb8, Eb8A–C; ELKG 99; EG 124; TLH 231 (We now implore God the Holy Ghost); LBW 317 (To God the Holy Spirit let us pray); LW 155; CW 190; ELH 33

Nun danket alle Gott—FT 1:526; Z 5142; ELKG 228; EG 321; TLH 36 (Now thank we all our God); LBW 533–34; LW 443; CW 610; ELH 63

Nun freut euch, lieben Christen gmein—W 3:2; J 2; B (1) 32–33; Z 4427–29; DKL B15, *Ea2*, Ec6–7; ELKG 239; EG 341; TLH 387 (Dear Christians, one and all, rejoice); LBW 299; LW 353; CW 377; ELH 378

Nun Gott lob, es ist vollbracht—FT 4:323; Z 3504–6; ELKG 141; TLH 45 (Now, the hour of worship o'er); CW 330

Nun hilf uns, Herr, den Dienern dein—*not found; sung on penitential days in Braunschweig-Wolfenbüttel 1709*

Nun ich danke dir von Herzen—*not found; sung on Good Friday in Braunschweig-Wolfenbüttel 1709*

Nun komm, der Heiden Heiland (Veni redemptor gentium)—W 3:16; J 14; B (1) 1; Z 1174–75; DKL A219, D1B–C, Ea10; ELKG 1; EG 4; TLH 95 (Savior of the nations, come); LBW 28 (Savior of the nations, come); LW 13 (Savior of the nations, come); CW 2; ELH 90

Nun lasst uns Christen fröhlich sein—W 3:853, 1466; Z 4478; DKL E15

Nun lasst uns Gott dem Herren—W 4:932; Z 156–59; ELKG 227; EG 320

Nun lob, mein Seel, den Herren (Ps. 103 : Benedic anima mea . . . et omnia)—W 3:968–70; Z 8244–45; DKL A409, Ef16, Ef16A–B; ELKG 188; EG 289; TLH 34 (My soul, now bless thy maker); LBW 519; LW 453; CW 257; ELH 456

Nunc dimittis → Herr, nun lässt du deinen Diener; Mit Fried und Freud ich fahr dahin

O allmächtiger, ewiger Vater, erbarm dich unser (Kyrie paschale)–W 3:427; Z 8607a

O Christ, wir danken deiner Güt—W 3:1059–61; Z *4493b*; DKL En2A–B

O du Gottes Lamm—*not found; sung at the beginning of Saturday Vespers in Altenburg 1705*

O du Lamm Gottes, das du trägst die Sünde der Welt (Agnus dei)—*not found; probably a variant of* Christe, du Lamm Gottes

O ewiger, barmherziger Gott, wie danken dir der Wohltat (Kyrie cunctipotens)—— W 3:345; Z 8609

O Gott, du höchster Gnadenhort—W 3:1134; Z 359–60; DKL Eb4A; ELKG 143; EG 194

O Gott und Herr, wie groß und schwer → Ach Gott und Herr, wie groß und schwer

O Gott Vater, du hast Gewalt—W 3:87; B (1) 48; Z 8283; DKL Ee16, Ee16A

O godt, wi loven di—*sung at the beginning of mass (i.e., at the end of Matins immediately preceding) in Ritzebüttel [after 1570]. This is probably the fairly literal translation of the Te deum laudamus found in Lossius 1561, pp. 348b–351a* [ff. 354b–3T3].a

O Gott, wir danken deiner Güte → O Christ, wir danken deiner Güt

O Herr Gott, gib uns deinen Fried[en]—S 1:293; Z 8641

O Herr Gott, Vater in Ewigkeit ("Kyrie paschale")—W 3:251; Z 8607c–f

O Herr, nun lastu deynen diener → Herr, nun lässt du deinen Diener

O Herre Gott, begnade mich (Ps. 51 : Miserere mei deus)—W 3:120; B (2) 20; Z 8451; DKL Eb11

O Herre Gott, dein göttlich[s] Wort—W 3:163; Z 5690–91; DKL Ee3; ELKG 117; TLH 266 (O God, our Lord, thy holy word); LW 341; CW 204; ELH 549

O Herre Gott, erbarme dich—W 3:950; Z 8452; DKL Eb24

O lamb gottes, wilchs du weg nimpst die sunder der welt *(no standard German form known)*— *with musical notation in Allstedt 1524b*

O Lamm Gottes unschuldig (Agnus dei)—W 3:619–21; Z 4360–61; DKL D21, D21A–B; ELKG 55; EG 190.1; TLH 146 (Lamb of God, pure and holy); LBW 111 (Lamb of God, pure and sinless); LW 208; CW 268; ELH 41

O lux beata trinitas → Der du bist drei in Einigkeit

O Mensch, bewein dein Sünde groß (the Passion history)—W 3:603; Z *8305a*; DKL *Eb14*; ELKG 54; EG 76; ELH 272

O Traurigkeit, o Herzeleid—FT 2: 186; Z 1915–16; ELKG 73; EG 80; TLH 167 (O darkest woe); LW 122 (O darkest woe); CW 137; ELH 332

O Vater aller Frommen (Our Father)—W 4:294, 5:16; DKL *Ea14*

O Vater, allmächtiger Gott, zu dir schreien wir in der Not (Kyrie magne deus; called the "Kyrie minus summum" because of its use on lesser festivals)—W 3:1116; Z 8603b; DKL Eg51

O Vater, deine Sonne scheint—FT 2:390

O Vater der Barmherzigkeit—*possibly either* W 3:262, 3:346 or 4:695; Z 4698; DKL Eg51 *or* Eg7

O Vater unser, gnädiger Gott—W 4:1186

O wir armen Sünder! Unsre Missetat—W 3:849–50; Z *8187*, 8188; DKL Ef7E; ELKG 57

Our Father → O Vater aller Frommen; Vater unser im Himmelreich

Pange lingua—*German version not found; mentioned in Palatinate 1546. There are two well-known Latin hymns with this incipit, but its use during communion identifies it as a German setting of the* Pange lingua gloriosi, corporis mysterium *of Aquinas*

Passion history → O Mensch, bewein dein Sünde groß

Pater noster → O Vater aller Frommen; Vater unser im Himmelreich

Patris sapientia, veritas divina → Christus, der uns selig macht

Psalm 2 (Quare fremuerunt gentes) → Hilf, Gott, wie gehet das immer zu

Psalm 12 (Salvum me fac) → Ach Gott vom Himmel sieh darein

Psalm 14 (Dixit insipiens) → Es spricht der unweisen Mund wohl

Psalm 23 (Dominus regit me) → Der Herr ist mein getreuer Hirt; Was kann uns kommen an für Not

Psalm 46 (Deus noster refugium) → Ein feste Burg ist unser Gott

Psalm 51 (Miserere mei deus) → Erbarm dich mein, o Herre Gott; O Herre Gott, begnade mich

Psalm 67 (Deus misereatur) → Es wollt uns Gott genädig sein

Psalm 103 (Benedic anima mea . . . et anima) → Nun lob, mein Seel, den Herren

Psalm 111 (Confitebor tibi, domine) → Ich dank dem Herrn von ganzem Herzen

Psalm 114 (In exitu Israel) → Da Israel aus Egypten zog

Psalm 117 (Laudate dominum omnes gentes) → Fröhlich wollen wir halleluja singen; Lobet den Herren, alle Heiden

Psalm 122 (Laetatus sum) → Ach bleib bei uns, Herr Jesu Christ

Psalm 124 (Nisi quia dominus) → Wär Gott nicht mit uns diese Zeit; Wo Gott der Herr nicht bei uns hält

Psalm 127 (Nisi dominus aedificaverit) → Wo Gott zum Haus nicht gibt sein Gunst

Psalm 128 (Beati omnes) → Wohl dem, der den Herrn fürchtet; Wohl dem, der in Gottes Furcht steht

Psalm 130 (De profundis) → Aus tiefer Not schrei ich zu dir

Sanctus → Heilig . . .; Jesaia dem Propheten das geschah

Schaffe in mir, Gott—Z 8628; *see also* ELKG p. 27; EG 230; TLH p. 12 (Create in me a clean heart, O God)

Schmücke dich, o liebe Seele—FT 4:96; Z 6923–25; ELKG 157; EG 218; TLH 305 (Soul, adorn thyself with gladness); LBW 224 (Soul, adorn yourself with gladness); LW 239; CW 311; ELH 328

Sei Lob und Dank mit hohem Preis—*not found; sung after the Elevation in Brandenburg 1540 and 1572 and at the end of mass in Ritzebüttel 1570*

Sei Lob und Ehr mit hohem Preis—DKL Ea2

Sei Lob und Preis mit Ehren—*not found; sung at the end of Saturday Vespers in Braunschweig-Wolfenbüttel 1709*

Sein Zorn auf Erden hat ein End—*not found; sung as the Gloria in excelsis in Schwarzburg 1675*

Sieh nicht an unsre Sünde groß—*not found; sung on penitential days in Braunschweig-Wolfenbüttel 1657 and 1709*

So pitten wir den Heiligen Gaist → Nun bitten wir den Heiligen Geist

Te deum laudamus → Herr Gott, dich loben wir

Ten Commandments → Dies sind die heilgen zehn Gebot; Mensch, willst du leben seliglich

Uth deper nodt → Aus tiefer Not schrei ich zu dir

Vater unser im Himmelreich (Our Father)—W 3:41; B (1) 17; Z 2561–64; DKL C28–29, Eb35; ELKG 241; EG 344; TLH 458 (Our Father, thou in heaven above); LW 431 (Our Father, who from heaven above); CW 410; ELH 383

Vater unser, wir bitten dich (Our Father)—Z 7747; DKL Eb12

Veni creator spiritus → Komm, Gott Schöpfer, Heiliger Geist

Veni redemptor gentium → Nun komm, der Heiden Heiland

Veni sancte spiritus, reple tuorum corda fidelium (antiphon) → Komm, Heiliger Geist, erfüll die Herzen; Komm, Heiliger Geist, Herre Gott

Verleih uns Frieden gnädiglich (Da pacem domine)—W 3:35–38; J 30; B (1) 31; Z 1945; DKL D1A, D1A ; ELKG 139; EG 421; LBW 471 (Grant peace, we pray, in mercy, Lord); LW 219; CW 522; ELH 584

Vexilla regis—German version not found; sung at the weekly prayer service in Aschersleben 1575

Victimae paschali laudes → Lasst uns Christen alle singen

Vom Himmel hoch da komm ich her—W 3:39; J 33; B (1) 4; Z *192a, 297d,* 344, 346; DKL Ec30, Ee18, Ee18A, Ei1; ELKG 16; EG 24; TLH 85 (From heaven above to earth I come); LBW 51; LW 37–38; CW 38; ELH 123–24

Vom Himmel kam der Engel Schar—W 3:49; J 39; B (1) 5; Z *192a,* 297d, 449a; DKL *Ei1;* ELKG 17; EG 25; TLH 103 (To shepherds as they watched by night); LW 52 (From heaven came the angels bright); CW 53; ELH 154

Vorlene uns frede → Verleih uns Frieden gnädiglich

Wär Gott nicht mit uns diese Zeit (Ps. 124 : Nisi quia dominus)—W 3:27; J 22; B (1) 26; Z 4434–35, *4440;* DKL Ec14, Ec22, *Ee18;* ELKG 192; TLH 267 (If God had not been on our side); CW 202; ELH 396

Was kann uns kommen an für Not (Ps. 23 : Dominus regit me)—W 3:147

Wenn wir in höchsten Nöten sein—W 4:6; DKL B81; ELKG 282; EG 366; TLH 522 (When in the hour of utmost need); LBW 303; LW 428; CW 413; ELH 257

Wi [ge]löven → Wir glauben all an einen Gott

Wir glauben all an einen Gott (Creed)—W 3:23; J 24; B (1) 16; Z 7971–72; DKL Ec18, Ec18A; ELKG 132; EG 183; TLH 251 (We all believe in one true God); LBW 374; LW 213 (We All believe in one true God); CW 271; ELH 38

Wir glauben [all] und bekennen frei—W 3:414; Z 7971–72; DKL Eg79; ELKG 468

Wir Menschen sind zu dem, o Gott—FT 2:450

Wo Gott der Herr nicht bei uns hält (Ps. 124 : Nisi quia dominus)—W 3:62; B (1) 40–41; Z 4440–43; DKL Ea18, *Ec14,* Ee4, Ee11, Ek23; ELKG 193; EG 297

Wo Gott zum Haus nicht gibt sein Gunst (Ps. 127 : Nisi dominus aedificaverit)—W 3:113; B (1) 52; Z 304–5; DKL *Ee10,* Ea19; ELKG 194

Wo soll ich fliehen hin—FT 1:322; Z 2177, 8701

Wohl dem, der den Herrn fürchtet (Ps. 128 : Beati omnes)—W 3:602

Wohl dem, der in Gottes Furcht steht (Ps. 128 : Beati omnes)—W 3:8; J 7; B (1) 27; Z 298–303; DKL *B14, Ea2,* Eb10, Ec12, Ec21, Ee10

Wohl mir!—*probably* Wohl mir, Jesus, meine Freude: FT 5:300; Z 3722a, 3723, 3724a, 3725–27

APPENDIX 2

✦

Translations of Selected Writings

1. Martin Luther, *Von ordenung gottis diensts ynn der gemeyne* (1523, translated from *WA* 12:35–37).

The service of God, as it is now conducted everywhere, has a fine Christian origin, just like the preaching office. But just as the preaching office has been corrupted by the ecclesiastical tyrants, so also has the service of God been corrupted by the hypocrites. Just as we do not now abolish the preaching office, but rather desire to reestablish it in its proper condition, so it is likewise not our intent to remove the service of God but rather to restore it to its proper use.

Three great abuses have occurred in the service of God. The first—that the Word of God has been silenced and there is only reading and singing in the churches—is the worst abuse. The second, since God's Word had been silenced, so many unchristian fables and lies were brought in, in legends, songs, and preaching, it is dreadful to see. The third, that people have performed this service of God as a work promising God's grace and salvation, so that faith has been lost and everyone has wanted to build churches, endow them, and become priests, monks, and nuns.

Now in order to do away with these abuses, it is first necessary to know that the Christian congregation should never assemble unless God's Word is being preached and prayed there, no matter how briefly. As in Psalm 101: "Whenever the kings and the people assemble to serve God, they shall extol the name and praise of God." And Paul says in 1 Corinthians 14 that there should be prophesy, teaching, and exhortation in the congregation. Therefore where God's Word is not preached, it would be better if one neither sang nor read nor even assembled.

It was the practice among Christians at the time of the apostles, and should still be the practice, for them to assemble daily for an hour at four or five o'clock in the morning and have a reading, whether it be schoolboys or priests, or whoever, just as the lesson is still read at Matins today. One or two persons should do this, or one after the other, or one choir after the other, however is preferred.

Then the preacher, or the one to whom it is assigned, should step up and expound on a part of the same lesson, so that the others all understand, learn, and are exhorted. The former activity Paul calls in 1 Corinthians 14 "speaking in tongues." The latter he calls "expounding" or "prophesying" or "speaking with meaning or understanding." Where this does not occur, the congregation is not made any better by the lesson, as has been the case until now in cloisters and monasteries, where they have only blabbered at the walls.

This lesson should be from the Old Testament; namely, that one should take a book and read a chapter or two, or one-half chapter, until the book is finished, then take up another, and so on until the entire Bible is read; and wherever it is not understood, pass over it and glorify God, so that Christians might become, through daily exercise in scripture, knowledgable, skilled and at ease. For in former times true Christians were made in this way, virgins and martyrs, and this should also be the case today.

Now when the lesson and explanation have lasted a half hour or longer, the congregation shall then thank God, praise him and ask him for the fruit of the Word, etc. For this purpose the psalms and several good responsories and antiphons should be used. In brief, let everything be completed within an hour, or however long is desired, for one must not overwhelm the soul so that it becomes weary and bored, as until now in cloisters and monasteries they have burdened themselves with the work of an ass.

In the same way, one should assemble again at six or five o'clock in the evening. Here books from the Old Testament should be taken in order, namely the prophets, just as in the morning Moses and the historical books are read. But because the New Testament is also a book, I have the Old Testament read in the morning and the New Testament in the evening, or vice versa, with reading, explanation, praising, singing, and praying just as in the morning, also an hour long. For everything is to be done according to God's Word, that it might have free course and ever uplift and enliven souls so that they do not become slothful.

If one desires to hold such an assembly one more time during the day after the meal, this is a matter of choice.

And if perhaps the entire congregation were unable to attend such a daily service of God, at least the priests and schoolboys and especially those whom one expects will become good preachers and caretakers of souls should do so. And one should exhort them to do it by choice, not by force or unwillingly, not for the sake of temporal or eternal reward, but solely to honor God and for the good of one's neighbor.

But on Sunday such an assembly should be held for the entire congregation, in addition to the daily assembling of the smaller group, and there mass and Vespers should be sung, as has been customary until now. At both times one should preach to the entire congregation: in the morning the usual Gospel and in the evening the Epistle, or the preacher should decide whether he will select one or two books, however it appears best to him.

If anyone then wishes to receive the sacrament, it should be given to him, as one can well arrange everything mutually according to the time and person.

The daily masses shall by all means be discontinued, for the Word is the important thing and not the masses. Of course if several people desire the sacrament other than on Sunday, then mass is held as devotion and time allow, for in this no law nor goal can be established.

The songs in the Sunday masses and Vespers may remain, for they are quite good and drawn from scripture, although one may decrease or increase their number. But selecting the songs and psalms daily in the morning and evening shall be the office of the pastor and preacher, so that they select for each morning a psalm, a good responsory or antiphon with a collect; likewise in the evening to be read and sung publicly after the lesson and explanation. But the antiphons, responsories, and collects, the legends of the saints and of the cross, should be laid to rest for a while until they are cleansed, for there is an awful lot of filth in them.

All saints' festivals should be discontinued or, if there is a good Christian legend, it may be inserted as an example on Sunday after the Gospel. Now I allow the festivals of Purification and Annunciation of Mary to remain; the Assumption and the Nativity of Mary must be allowed to remain for a while yet, even though the song in them is impure. The festival of John the Baptist is also pure. None of the legends of the apostles is pure except for St. Paul; therefore, one may move them to a Sunday or, if desired, celebrate them specially.

Other concerns will take care of themselves over time, as needed. But the sum of the matter is this: that everything be done so that the Word may have free course, not turning into harping and noise again, as has been the case until now. It would be better to let everything go besides the Word. And nothing is more productive than the Word. For the entire scripture testifies that it should have free course among Christians, and Christ himself also says in Luke 10 "One thing is needful"; namely, that Mary sit at the feet of Christ and hear his Word daily. That is the best part that may be chosen and shall never be taken away. It is an eternal Word; everything else must pass away, regardless of how much it might concern Martha. God help us in this regard! Amen.

2. Except from the travel diary of Augsburg pastor Wolfgang Musculus describing the mass he attended in Wittenberg on May 28, 1536. (Source: Theodor Kolde, ed., *Analecta Lutherana: Briefe und Actenstücke zur Geschichte Luthers* [Gotha, 1883], 216)

At the sixth hour a sermon was held in the castle.

At the seventh hour we returned to the city church and observed by which rite they celebrated the liturgy; namely thus: First, the Introit was played on the organ, accompanied by the choir in Latin, as in the mass offering. Indeed, the minister meanwhile proceeded from the sacristy dressed sacrificially and, kneeling before the altar, made his confession together with the assisting sacristan. After the confession he ascended to the altar to the book that was located on the right side, according to papist custom.

After the introit the organ was played and the *Kyrie eleison* sung in alternation by the boys. When it was done the minister sang *Gloria in excelsis,* which song was completed in alternation by the organ and choir. Thereafter the minister at the altar sang "Dominus vobiscum," the choir responding "Et cum spiritu tuo." The collect for that day followed in Latin, then he sang the Epistle in Latin, after which the organ was played, the choir following with *Herr Gott Vater, wohn uns bei.* When it was done the Gospel for that Sunday was sung by the minister in Latin on the left side of the altar, as is the custom of the adherents of the pope. After this the organ played, and the choir followed with *Wir glauben all an einen Gott.* After this song came the sermon, which Bucer delivered on the Gospel for that Sunday in the presence of Luther and Philipp [Melanchthon]. After the sermon the choir sang *Da pacem domine,* followed by the prayer for peace by the minister at the altar, this in Latin as well.

The communion. The communion followed, which the minister began with the Lord's Prayer sung in German. Then he sang the words of the supper, and these in German with his back turned toward the people, first those of the bread, which, when the words had been offered, he then elevated to the sounding of bells; likewise with the chalice, which he also elevated to the sounding of bells.

Immediately communion was held. Pomeranus [Johann Bugenhagen] went first, then Fabricius Capito, and after him Bucer. During the communion the Agnus Dei was sung in Latin. The minister served the bread in common dress but the chalice dressed sacrificially [i.e., in mass vestments].

They followed the singing of the Agnus Dei with a German song: *Jesus Christus* [*unser Heiland*] and *Gott sei gelobet*.

After the sermon the majority of the people departed.

Even Luther himself, because he felt dizzy during the communion, had to leave attended by Philipp.

The minister ended the communion with a certain thanksgiving sung in German. He followed this, facing the people, with the benediction, singing "The Lord make his face to shine on you, etc." And thus was the mass ended.

3. Excerpt (pp. 703–704, 730–34) from the minutes of the colloquium between Jacob Andreae and Theodore Beza, held at Mömpelgard in 1586.

Andreae (opening statement): Music, when sung with many voices or played on instruments, is a special gift of God and should chiefly be used in the divine service, as the example of the blessed kings attests.

Beza (opening statement): And as far as the instruments of music are concerned, we do not condemn music; but when one sings in four or more voices, so that it cannot be understood, the work itself proves the result, namely, that gradually over time a large part of the service is transformed into song, and the spirit is not nourished with the Word of God, but rather the ears are stroked and entertained with a charming voice.

Beza (discussion): As far as the organ and other instruments of music are concerned, we know that they have a special power to move human emotions. And we do not see how music can better be used than for the praise of God and his divine name, so that the hearts of people might be awakened to the true service of God and devotion, and encouraged.

But we see, as has happened under the papacy, that the organ does not communicate, and all that is heard is how lovely the voices sound together, without any understanding, through which not the heart and spirit but only the ears are entertained—to this end the singers are appointed. But what is played on the organ or sung with many voices the common people do not understand; rather, the spirit is centered only in the attractiveness of the song, which alone strikes the ears and entertains the same.

But the music used in the church ought to be such that everyone understands, and the soul comprehends what sounds in the ears, so that everything that is sung is understood: the singing itself should fit the text that is sung. And that is just the style of singing to which the psalms are sung, as is now common in the churches, which music we by no means reprove or discard.

But when the organ or other instruments of music are played in the church, or there is singing with many and various kinds of voices, and the people do not understand what is being sung or played, then the sound or echo stays in the ears, so that it lingers more than the text that is sung.

Therefore we banish only this kind of music from church, for we cannot see how it might be useful there.

In other assemblies, particularly when the people come together in homes, we do not reject such music. But in church the mind should be entirely directed to those things that lead us to God and to the true service of God.

And it is no secret at all that organists frequently play bawdy, disgraceful songs on the organ, which likewise should not occur in church.

Therefore we also confess and do not deny that such instruments of music (*adiaphora*) are neither forbidden or commanded by God. And so we do not anger God by either using or not using them.

I shall now continue and also read the following article.

Andreae (discussion): I'd just like to mention something briefly first and thereby demonstrate our agreement in this as well. For as much as I understand of what you said, you believe that organs in churches (an *adiaphoron*) are something that one may either have or not, because they are neither commanded nor forbidden by God. In this matter we agree with you.

But you add that in music (*musica figurali*), either when many sing together in various voices or when one plays the organ or another instrument of music, the listeners pay attention only to the sound and not to what is sung; therefore, such music is not considered beneficial in church as long as only the ears are tickled by it and the soul is not awakened to devotion. To that I give this answer: that which is sung with many and various voices in church is not unfamiliar to everyone, but is well known to the learned who have studied the Latin language or music; indeed with them such song goes to the heart, and the sound does not just echo in their ears.

And I can truthfully say for myself, as I have a special appreciation for such music and the organ, that I do not simply receive the sound with my ears, but my spirit and soul are also awakened through such charming voices, so that I pray all the more fervantly and eagerly, or I deliver sermons with a more burning spirit, or I listen when a hymn is either sung with many and various pleasant voices or played on the organ before the preacher mounts the pulpit, as is the custom in our churches. It is then that I feel within me this secret power hidden in such music, of which you have spoken above, that singing must move a person's heart. I have also heard from many devout, godly people who have not been educated and are not learned in music that they find this to be true for themselves in the same way as well.

In addition, the story of David is well known, who before King Saul, when the latter was plagued by the evil spirit, played on his harp and through such pleasant sound drove away the evil spirit from him; this sound did not merely reach the ears of King Saul but also touched and moved his heart so that, temporarily relieved of the evil spirit, he found rest. For one does not read that David sang, but rather, as the text clearly indicates, played on his instrument, regardless of what instrument he used.

Therefore the power is not to be rejected that God, in a hidden manner, has implanted in song and in the instruments of this music, power which drove away the evil spirit from Saul, which also penetrates the heart regardless of whether what is sung or played on such instruments is understood by all people. This power is much stronger and mightier in those who also understand the text and the words that are sung with such pleasant voices.

As far as the abuse of organs in churches is concerned, if at times worldly and indecent songs are played on them (which I judge to be a misunderstanding) this is not the fault of the organ but is to be attributed to the organists who abuse such an organ, which was not intended to serve such purposes in church. But it does not follow that because of such abuse the good, right, and beneficial use of the organ should also be abolished and organs removed from the church; otherwise one would have to deny wine to everyone because many abuse it to excess and drunkenness.

Therefore, when organists want to play shameful worldly songs on the organ, one should forbid them to do so and earnestly urge them not to do it in the future but rather diligently strive to ensure that the temple might no longer be defiled, so that God might be praised and extolled and everything might proceed and be carried out in good order and form.

4. Excerpt from Theophilus Großgebauer, *Wächterstimme aus dem verwüstetem Zion* (Frankfurt/Main, 1661), chapter 11.

If through psalms and spiritual songs the word of Christ can be richly planted among us and dwell, but it is quite hurtful to the realm of the pope that the word of Christ is read, sung, and acted upon by the people; for this reason the psalms and spiritual songs have necessarily been taken away from the congregation and entrusted solely to the canons, monks, and other religious.

And so that the people would meanwhile have something to look at and listen to in the assembly, the pope has in place of the psalms hung for them wooden, tin, and lead pipes that produce a great din, having persuaded the people that God is thereby praised. But are not such organ pipes nothing more than living images of a dead Christianity, which to be sure bawl and howl mightily but have neither heart nor spirit nor soul? By this means he has made the people deaf and mute, so that they can neither praise God nor comprehend his Word, but—deafened through the sound of the organ and the brilliant, peculiar performance of music—are rather stunned in amazement and tickled in the ears. The world-reknowned monk Thomas Aquinas, writing around the year 1270, testified (in 2.2.q.91.a.2) that the sound of the organ had during his time not yet been introduced into the church; the church, he said, employed no musical frivolity such as harp and psalter in the praise of God so that it would not appear as if the church had become Jewish . . . for in the Old Testament such stringed music was used in part because the people were more carnal and harder of spirit and had to be moved through such instruments, just as through earthly promises, and in part because such earthly instruments by their image signified something else. Aquinas finds in Aristotle's *Politics* (8, chapter 6) the reason why the church needs no string and organ playing in the service, for (the Philosopher says) it is not pipes, harps, and shawms that are necessary for the acquisition of proper arts and virtues, but rather that which makes the listener devout and virtuous. For musical performances entertain the spirit rather than instill within the heart the things of God. (The same Aristotle says that musical instruments serve to deafen and shout down the pensiveness of the soul rather than to give it aid. He reproves the Lydians because they used sweet-sounding music in their fasts and praises the Dorians because they used a sad, sharp music that would be very conducive to the acquisition of virtues.) Therefore Augustine writes in the tenth book of his *Confessions:* "When it happens that the song entertains me more than the things that are sung move me, then I am culpable and would much rather never have heard the song at all. . . . Where someone sings for the sake of devotion, he considers much more closely what is said, for he remains with and adheres to a text longer than otherwise." Thus far Thomas [i.e., Augustine].

Now no matter who first introduced organs and musical performance in the church, it is certain that the Roman clergy have made a concerted effort, along with the Latin psalms, to place a bit into the church's mouth and render it mute, so that only the pope may speak, and say whatever he wants, and the church is virtually enraptured by the din, astonished by the power and splendor of the Beast [i.e., the pope]. Against this Erasmus holds that such piping, fiddling, drumming, warbling, and artificial movements in the throat were heard neither among the Greeks nor among the Romans in their dramas as among us in our churches.

This is how it has been up until now: at the beginning of the Reformation it happened that the *adiaphora* were used in love and for the edification of the weak; but what was then an indifferent matter done in the good hope that those who had such ceremonies would join us is now a requirement, having become nearly an article of faith, so that we change nothing even when we clearly grasp that it is necessary and useful. We fail to see that Luther ordained these things on account of the particular requirements of his time.

Certainly superstition is not faith. The church and her shepherds must be alert to the fact that, depending on how the times are, on how the congregations increase in godless, unspiritual ways, the church usages must be adjusted accordingly. "Be alert on all sides," Paul exhorts. The evangelical church, after she had withdrawn from Babel, has forgotten the words that the heavenly voice cried out to her: "The righteous one will become yet more righteous, and the holy one will become yet holier" (Rev. 22:11). Rather, she has much more acquired the arrogant pride of the Laodicean congregation, saying: "I am rich and quite satisfied, and I need nothing." But she will be answered: "You do not know that you are destitute and pitiable, blind and naked" (Rev. 3:17).

Oh, such a wretched state! What is happening? To be sure, after the Reformation the congregation of Christ did indeed attain its freedom from the Babylonian Captivity insofar as it was permitted to hear a number of German psalms and to hear the prophecies and psalms in its mother tongue. But just because the pope once upon a time gave only the clergy the authority to sing and to play music, it strikes us as difficult to discard such human silliness with the command of God. Hence organists, cantors, trained brass players, and other musicians, for the most part unspiritual people, unfortunately rule the city churches. They play, sing, fiddle, and make sounds according to their own wishes. You hear the whistling, ringing, and roaring but do not know what it is, whether you should prepare yourself for battle or retreat; one is chasing the other with concerto-style playing, and several of them are fighting each other over who plays most artistically and who can most subtly resemble the nightingale.

And just as the world is not now serious but rather shallow, having lost the old, quiet devotion, so songs have been sent out of the south and west to us in Germany in which the biblical texts are torn apart and chopped up into little pieces through quick runs in the throat: these are "the improvisations" referred to in Amos 6:5 which, as with birds, can pull and break the voice. Then an ambitious collective howling commences to determine who can sing best and most like the birds. Now it's Latin, now it's German; very few can understand the words, and if they do understand it, it still doesn't stick. There sits the organist, playing and displaying his artistry—so that the artistry of one man might be displayed, the entire congregation of Jesus Christ is supposed to sit there and hear the sound of the pipes, on account of which the congregation becomes sleepy and lethargic. Many sleep, some chatter, others look about where they should not, many would like to read but cannot because they have not learned how, although they could be well instructed through the spiritual songs of the congregation, as Paul demands. Many would like to pray, but are so occupied with and bewildered by the howling and din that they cannot. Occasionally it goes right to the edge, so if an unbeliever were to come into our assembly would he not say we were putting on a spectacle and were to some extent crazy?

During the Holy Communion the death of the Lord is extolled and proclaimed only rarely and for the shortest amount of time; instead, the body of the Lord, broken on the cross, and his shed blood are distributed during the sounding of the organ and during charming string music and artificial, indistinct singing, just as if Satan with all his power wanted to impede and obstruct matters so that the death of the Lord would be torn from the mind, heart, and memory of the communicants and the death of the Lord would by no means be proclaimed and extolled by the entire congregation.

5. Christian Gerber, *Die unerkanten Sünden der Welt,* vol. 1, chapter 81.

Concerning the Abuse of the Performed Music in Church
    1. Just as human nature has been so completely corrupted through the fall of Adam that it does not allow any of the creatures and gifts of God, whether physical or spiritual, to remain in proper order and use; in the same way, we see that music is in various ways also abused and subjugated to the service of sin. Nebuchadnezzar abused it for purposes of idolatry when he consecrated his great and lovely image (Daniel 3:5). The godless abuse it for drunkenness, carousing, lewdness, and so on. Therefore Job says, "They exult with drums and harps and are joyful with pipes" (chapter 21, verse 12). But even in the divine service the music is used in such a way that not only abuse results from it, but also great scandal. Such singers and such amazingly peculiar compositions are used that the church has greater cause to be ashamed than to rejoice.
    2. We want first of all to say a bit about the singers used in many large cities and their principal churches, not to mention princely and royal court chapels: occasionally these include people of various religions and nationalities. Among these one finds idolatrous servants of Baal, papist standard-bearers of Mary, unchaste Italians and *castrati,* which Luther, in his little book on marriage (vol. 2, f. 210a) calls a wretched people. For he says, "Although they are certainly unfit for marriage, they are nevertheless not free of evil desire and become more addicted to women than before, and quite feminine; and they are as the proverb says: 'Whoever is unable to sing always wants to sing.' And so they are also troubled in that they want all the more to be with women but cannot." The use of such people, who hold to an errant and idolatrous religion, is not avoided in the divine service these days. Such an Italian comes into our assembly for the sake of money and profit and squawks something as ridiculously as he wants. Otherwise, our service is an abomination to him; he scorns it in his heart and takes care lest he be made unclean by it; and so he runs out of the service as soon as he has finished singing and the sermon has begun, exercising his wantonness during it with drinking or with fornicating and carrying on with a mistress, then he comes back. Or even if in many places no Italians are used, but rather Germans, experience shows that they are at times whoremongers, adulterers, drunkards, and otherwise depraved individuals who lead an immoral, unchristian life; but if they just happen to be perfect musicians who sound impressive in vocal and instrumental music, then all is well. I knew a cantor in a leading city who placed more stock in drunkenness than in prayer; he was often in the habit of saying he could compose best when he drank a glass of wine with friends and had a smoke. The bassist with whom the cantor generally performed on Sundays lived in fornication and prostitution and was also much addicted to drunkenness. I have seen in common cities where the citizens, even the workers, that were members of the *chorus musicus* assisted in making music in the churches on Sunday, singing something from Hammerschmidt; but in the afternoon these same individuals would sit in the beer hall drinking and carousing, singing the bawdiest drinking songs and love songs, and in festival seasons they would go right back into the choir the next morning, even though they were not quite sober and stunk of brandy, like pigs.

3. Such people, and others like them, are now used in many places for the music in churches, so a sensible Christian must judge how our dear God is pleased by such praise as is brought to him by people who are unholy and impure in both body and spirit. What is more, many masters and great artists compose such things from a spirit of worldliness and foolish imagination as would be better suited to war to rouse soldiers to battle or to a dance floor than to devotion in church. Often so many things are mixed together that not a single person in the assembly knows what it is supposed to be: now it's German, now Latin, now even Italian—it doesn't matter whether the congregation of God understands it or not; it is sufficient if it sounds pleasant and fills the ears, even if the heart is not improved by it. And so most of today's composers and singing masters generally mind only that the music entertain the ear; the spiritual element they leave out of consideration, often knowing nothing about it themselves. Now certainly singing and praising should be done in spirit and truth, just as with worship. But let us hear what God the Lord might say concerning such singing that consists solely in the external consonance of voices, filling the ears: "Take away from me the bawling of your songs, for I do not wish to hear the sound of your psaltery" (Amos 5:23). Why? Because it was done without devotion, say all the Christian teachers. A well-known commentator recalls in these prophetic words quite thoughtfully: "Let Christian choristers and singers take care," he says, "not to invest all their musical energy in a sonorous voice, subtlety of modulation, nimbleness in diminishing tones, etc., while they twitter like birds so as to titillate the ears of the curious, drawing attention to themselves and distracting them from prayer, so that they are not heard by God: I will not hear the songs of your lyre, to which the Arab whirls; do not create embellishment (variety, twists, and turns) for me in the sounds of your hymns" (Cornelius a Lapide [van Steen]). That is, all Christians should keep watch in their singing lest they make their entire devotion depend on a bright voice, artistic style, accomplished modulation of the tone, and so on; lest the singers twitter like birds so that the ears of the listeners are tickled and drawn away from devotion.

4. The excellent Augustine has shown in his *Distich* that through singing not only should the ears be entertained, but much more the heart: "Not the voice, but the prayer; not stringed music, but the heart; not by singing, but by loving does one sing in the ear of God." Just as Jerome has also written: "One must sing to God not with the voice but with the heart." ("One must sing to the glory of God not only with the mouth, but also with the heart.") And the already cited Augustine says again in the explanation to the 18th psalm quite thoughtfully: "Let us sing as rational people, not as with the voice of birds. For the blackbirds, parrots, ravens, magpies, and birds of this kind are frequently taught by humans to make sounds, which they do not understand. But to sing intelligently has not been granted in the divine will to birds but to humans." That is: "We should sing as rational people, not as birds. For the blackbirds, parrots, ravens, etc. learn to some extent to whistle and make sounds, which of course they do not understand. But intelligent singing is something God has given only to humans." But look at the present-day manner of making music in our church, God help us, what a clamor and din that is! One hears organs, violins, trumpets, trombones, zinks, and kettledrums, often all together, and at the same time several voices yelling now and then, and one chases the other, trying to outdo the other, striving to be heard with all diligence, artistry, and loveliness; but the listeners seldom understand a word of it, and the text is generally so chopped up and mutilated that one cannot make any sense out of it, even if one can catch several words. Such music is considered quite splendid and is highly praised, but if a stranger were to attend who had not previously heard anything like it, he would think that people had lost their senses or that they wanted to prepare for battle.

5. To be sure, I do not deny that in the Old Testament stringed instruments performed music in the divine service and that there was singing in the upper choir; but no one would claim, much less be able to prove, that everything proceeded in such a haphazard way or that the text was so broken and chopped up. In addition, the Old Testament had much that was temporal and all kinds of ceremonies that the church of the New Testament never accepted, in which more emphasis was always placed on the spiritual than physical, more on the internal than external. The blessed [Johann] Arndt says in the second book of *True Christianity* (chapter 43, section 3, part 331): "The various kinds of marvelous, lovely musical instruments in the Old Testament which David commemorates in the 150th Psalm refer to nothing other than the various gifts of the Holy Spirit, through which God's name, praise, recognition, work, blessings and miracles are made known: Therefore they have also passed away, so that the spiritual harps and psalter of the praise of God might take their place." Accordingly we also find reported in the ecclesiastical histories and writing of the Fathers that the saints have always set greater store by the living human voice than by the sound of pipes and brass instruments. And so Augustine wrote in the tenth book of his *Confessions:* "When it happens that the singing entertains me more than what is sung moves me, then I am culpable and would much rather never have heard the song." The world-famous monk Thomas Aquinas, writing around the year 1270, testified that the sound of the organ had during his time not yet been introduced into the church; the church, he says, employed no music such as harp and psalter in the praise of God so that it would not appear as if the church had become Jewish, for in the Old Testament such stringed music was used in part because the people were more carnal and harder of spirit and had to be moved through such instruments, just as through earthly promises, and in part because such earthly instruments signified by their image something else. For musical performances entertain the spirit more than they focus the heart within on divine concerns. Thus far Thomas. Only after this time the popes brought organs, kettledrums, schalmeis, and trumpets into the church so that the people would have something to see and hear, while the congregation was little by little in large manner drawn away from the Word of God and the spiritual songs; and out of the divine service a worldly amusement was created, certainly through the hidden craft of the devil. Nonetheless we take great pleasure in this style; and the more such music is performed in a church, the greater the crowd is there, and many come purely on account of the jolly music in the church and leave perhaps more godless than when they came. Erasmus of Rotterdam, even though he was a papist, nevertheless wrote in one place that he did not believe such fiddling, piping, drumming, warbling, and artificial turning or moving of the throat were heard of either among the Greeks or among the Romans in their dramas as among us in our churches. The blessed Enoch Zobel, zealous and well-deserving preacher in St. Annaberg, writes in the preface to his *Christmas Vespers* (section 2, page 2): "We might of course consider here figural music in the divine service, which has at least lesser, if not greater, defects connected with it than does the singing of chants and hymns, inasmuch as now and then their Christian purpose is forgotten and a profane and at times absurd worldly performance is made from it."

6. Once again I must introduce the testimony of that zealous servant of God, Theophilus Grossgebauer, who in his *Wächterstimme* (chapter 2, page 207) states: "Oh, such a wretched state! What is happening? To be sure, after the Reformation the congregation of Christ did indeed attain its freedom from the Babylonian Captivity insofar as it was permitted to hear a number of German psalms and to hear the prophecies and psalms in its mother tongue. But just because the pope once gave only the clergy the authority to sing and to play music, it strikes us as difficult to discard such

human silliness with the command of God. Hence organists, cantors, trained brass players, and other musicians, for the most part unspiritual people, unfortunately rule the city churches. They play, sing, fiddle, and make sounds according to their own wishes and imagination. You hear the whistling, ringing, and roaring but do not know where it comes from nor where it is going nor what it is, whether you should prepare yourself for battle or retreat; one is chasing the other with concerto-style playing and several of them are fighting each other over who plays most artistically and who can most subtly resemble the nightingale. And just as the world is no longer serious, but rather shallow, having lost the old, quiet devotion, so songs have been sent out of the south and west to us in Germany in which the biblical texts are torn apart and chopped up into little pieces through quick runs in the throat: these are 'the improvisations' referred to in Amos 6:5 which, like birds, can pull and break the voice. Then an ambitious collective howling commences to determine who can sing best and most like the birds. Now it's Latin, now it's German; very few can understand the words, and if they do understand it, it still doesn't stick. There sits the organist, playing and displaying his artistry—so that the artistry of one man might be displayed, the entire congregation of Jesus Christ is supposed to remain silent and hear the sound of the pipes, on account of which the congregation becomes sleepy and lazy. Many sleep, some chatter, others look where they should not be looking, many would like to read but cannot because they have not learned how, although they could be well instructed through the spiritual songs of the congregation, as Paul demands. Many would like to pray, but are so occupied with and bewildered by the howling and din that they cannot. Occasionally it goes right to the edge, so if an unbeliever were to come into our assembly would he not say we were putting on a spectacle and were to some extent crazy?" 1 Corinthians 14. Thus far Grossgebauer.

7. Now all this is the plain truth. Nonetheless many of our people are so accustomed to the music making and din that they esteem it as the most important part of the service, and they are ill-pleased with anyone who would not consider the music making in the church to be praiseworthy and beneficial. But I ask you, in what way do you better yourself from the music? Do you have any use for it at all? Certainly none insofar as your ears are filled and tickled. You say, "I also hear the text." Answer: But just in pieces and mutilated; it would be better if a spiritual hymn were sung in its place so that you could hear the entire text and be edified by it. Perhaps someone would further say, "I read a book during the music." Right, then the music making is of no use if you don't want to listen to it. In addition, it must be quite a devotional reading that occurs amidst such a din, and you may say what you want, but I don't believe that you can read with devotion, for your thoughts must necessarily be scattered all about by so many instruments and voices. Perhaps someone would say, "The music is performed to glorify God, so I can't disregard it, can I?" First of all, God has never required anything like this, but self-chosen divine services never please him. Second, the first Christian church never did any such thing. Third, God looks not at the external but at the internal; and where the internal is deficient the external is an abomination to him. Do you imagine that our dear God enjoys it when the organist at times preludes for as much as a quarter hour and creates as many flashy improvisations as might occur to him? I have frequently observed in many places where more than a hundred communicants received the holy supper that the organist raved about on the organ for so long that the communion was nearly finished and there were only twenty or thirty persons remaining to be fed, then the cantor finally began "Gott sei gelobet und gebenedeiet." Or during the communion an entertaining musical performance with all kinds of string playing was done. Would it not be better, though, because during the supper the Lord's death is to be pro-

claimed, if one would sing *O Lamm Gottes unschuldig* and other Passion and communion hymns in place of the considerable music making and organ playing? Then the communicants would truly receive, especially the simpler souls, good thoughts in their hearts from their Savior; since it is to be desired in any case that our conduct of the holy supper have a little more to it, whereby the comfort the communicants seek might be conveyed to them and the opportunity given them to proclaim the death of the Lord more emphatically.

8. No one should think, however, that all music is to be discarded. No! That the organ is played to accompany Christian hymns is to a certain extent useful. Also, if an excellent scriptural text or spiritual song were sung with modest and unpretentious instruments, without the mixing in of artificial improvisations, so that the congregation could clearly understand it, that could well be tolerated: as with this also the people ought to be adorned with faith and true godliness and be devoted to good behavior. Then I would believe that such music is useful to the congregation and pleasing to God. Besides this, I am very concerned about the generally large sums wasted in many places on the singers and instrumentalists, string and brass players, organs and trumpets; and God says: "Who requires such a thing from your hands?" In many places large amounts are spent on organs; in particular, many cost several hundred, even several thousand, *Reichsthaler.* And I have heard that an organ is to be built now in one well-known city that will cost nearly ten thousand *Reichsthaler* just so it can have the honor of saying that an instrument of such size and cost is nowhere else to be found. Oh, how much better it would be if such a city were to erect an orphanage for the same amount of money or, if there were already one there, it could be repaired and improved; with this they would bring God's blessing upon their city. For God has so very often and earnestly commanded us to care for the poor, but nowhere has he said anything about organ building; indeed I don't believe that one should expect any reward at all from God for building such an organ. When God one day inquires about your good works, and you answer, "Lord, haven't I built, or helped to build, an organ for you?" do you really think that God is going to be pleased with you? But if you really want to build an organ, then do it, but consider the words of Sirach: "Be moderate in all things." One hundred Thaler is certainly better than two, three, or four hundred; just do not forget the living organ pipes, by which I mean the poor and the orphans. For one day when all organ pipes will have been burned up, these will just begin to sound splendidly and render an account before the judge of all the world that your faith was evident in good deeds.

In conclusion I want to cite a quite remarkable place from Luther's sermon on good works (vol. 1, f. 426b). Luther speaks of the general prayer and desires that in the service there should be more, and more earnest, prayer than is the case. Thereafter he says: "For truly the Christian church on earth has no greater power or works than such common prayer against all that would repel it. The evil Spirit knows that well, therefore he does everything in his power to hinder this prayer: he has us build lovely churches, with many endowments, pipes, much reading and singing, holding many masses, and employing pageantry beyond measure; for that reason he is not sorry, indeed he even assists us to esteem such ways most highly and think that we have done well with them. But where he would perceive that we desire to properly employ true Christian prayer, even though it be under a straw roof or in a pigsty, he would surely not allow it to happen, but rather would fear the pigsty far more than any tall, large, lovely church, tower, bells, or organ that might be found anywhere, as long as such prayer were not present there. Truly it does not depend on the cities and buildings, nor on singing and playing where we assemble, but only on this inconquerable prayer, that we pray it together rightly and let it come before God."

APPENDIX 3

❖

Choral versus Congregational
Singing in the Mass

The tables below summarize the frequency of Latin versus German singing and choral versus congregational singing in the mass, as indicated in the church orders. The data on which the tables are based are contained in appendix 4.

The dates in the far left column are the dates the orders were published (for printed orders) or written (for manuscript orders). The numbers within the table are a count of church orders; totals are given as both sums and percentages. Percentages for the Latin vs. German data are calculated from the first four columns only. The fifth column (the number of orders in which the language cannot be determined) is useful in determining the completeness of the data in the first four columns, and it is used in the calculations of the choral vs. congregational percentages, but it is irrelevant to the ratio of Latin to German parts of the liturgy. Percentages may not total one hundred because of rounding.

Proportions for choral vs. congregational singing are given in two ways. The upper row gives the percentage of total orders containing the part of the liturgy under consideration in which we know the singing was by the choir (either because it is so specified in the order or because the singing was in Latin), followed by the percentage of total orders in which we know the singing was by the congregation (because it is so specified in the order; the use of German is not necessarily an indication of congregational performance). These percentages are calculated by first adding either the total of column "Co" (for the congregational percentage) or the sum of the totals of columns "Ch" and "Ch/L" (for the choral percentage) to one-half the total of column "L-G" (thus including in the calculation parts sung twice, once by choir and once by all), then dividing the result by the sum of the totals in the five Latin vs. German columns. The percentage for column "C/C" is calculated by dividing the total in that column by the sum of the totals in the five Latin vs. German columns.

The lower row gives the ratio of orders that expressly call for choral performance to those that expressly call for congregational performance. Each ratio is calculated by dividing the total of each column ("Ch" and "Co") by the sum of the totals of these columns.

These two rows tell us different things about whether the singing was choral or congregational. The upper row indicates a minimum percentage of total orders in which we can be certain that the singing was by either the choir or the congregation. The actual percentages (if the church orders are to be taken at face value) cannot be less than these figures. The lower row, which is based on explicit directions in the church orders, puts the figures for choral vs. congregational performance on an equal footing. These numbers are much less precise than those in the upper row, but they are the best estimates we can produce as to actual practice.

For simplicity's sake, the fact that the choir would sing on congregational parts and the possibility that at least some members of the congregation would sing along on choral parts are ignored in the calculations. The sequence, where performed in Latin, is counted as a choral performance even though congregational verses in German were commonly interspersed on the three chief feasts.

It is important that the conclusions drawn from the data not be overly broad. Territories that frequently revised or reprinted their agendas will be represented to a greater degree than those that continued to use existing copies of agendas throughout decades or centuries. Territories also varied considerably in size, and accurate population estimates are rarely available for the sixteenth century, so there is no means of assessing how many people used each agenda.

Later Editions of Church Orders with Substantially the Same Liturgical Content

Appendix 4, the source of data for the tables below, saves space by excluding editions of church orders whose liturgical content is substantially the same as that of an earlier edition (see part 1 of the bibliography for an explanation of "substantially the same"). But in order to present a more accurate picture, most of these later editions are represented here. Not represented are new editions that appeared within five years of an earlier one. They are excluded in order to avoid allowing territories that produced church orders in several formats (quarto and octavo, with music and without, in both Low and High German, etc.) to exercise undue influence on the results. Five years is an arbitrary choice, but it accomplishes its purpose and avoids the need to conduct an enormous amount of bibliographical research for relatively little gain.

Following is a list of later editions of church orders containing mass liturgies, arranged by date of the original edition. Those excluded under the five-year rule are struck through with a line. Those remaining are represented in the tables. The total number of orders providing the data for the tables is shown following the list.

Wittenberg (Luther) 1523—~~1524~~

Braunschweig 1528—~~1531,~~ 1563

Brandenburg-Nuremberg 1533—~~1534, 1536,~~ 1556, 1564, 1592

Augsburg 1537—1545

Saxony (A) 1539/40, city—1548, 1555, ~~1558,~~ 1563, ~~1564,~~ 1580, ~~1582, 1584,~~ 1600, 1618, 1647, 1658, 1681, 1712, 1748

Saxony (A) 1539/40, village—1548, 1555, ~~1558,~~ 1563, ~~1564,~~ 1580, ~~1582, 1584,~~ 1600, 1618, 1647, 1658, 1681, 1712, 1748

Calenberg-Göttingen 1542—~~1544~~

Nuremberg (Dietrich) 1543/45, villages with schools—~~1546,~~ 1556, ~~1560,~~ 1563, ~~1565,~~ 1569

Nuremberg (Dietrich) 1543/45, villages without schools—~~1546,~~ 1556, ~~1560,~~ 1563, ~~1565,~~ 1569

Mecklenburg 1552, city—~~1554,~~ 1562

Mecklenburg 1552, village—~~1554,~~ 1562
Württemberg 1553—~~1555,~~ 1559, 1582, 1615
Palatinate 1554—~~1556~~
Waldeck 1557—1640
Wittenberg 1559, city—1565, ~~1566~~
Wittenberg 1559, village—1565, ~~1566~~
Palatinate-Zweibrücken 1563, city—1570
Palatinate-Zweibrücken 1563, village—1570
Braunschweig-Lüneburg 1564, city—1598, 1619, 1643
Braunschweig-Lüneburg 1564, village—1598, 1619, 1643
Prussia 1568, city—1598
Prussia 1568, village—1598
Pomerania 1569, city—1591, 1661, 1690, ~~1691,~~ 1731
Pomerania 1569, village—1591, 1661, 1690, ~~1691,~~ 1731
Hesse 1574—1662, 1724
Saxe-Lauenburg 1585, city—1651
Saxe-Lauenburg 1585, village—1651
Strassburg 1598—~~1601, 1603,~~ 1605, ~~1606,~~ 1633
Mecklenburg 1602, city—1650, 1708
Mecklenburg 1602, village—1650, 1708
Braunschweig-Wolfenbüttel 1615, city—1649, ~~1651~~
Braunschweig-Wolfenbüttel 1615, village—1649, ~~1651~~
Magdeburg (Han) 1615—1647, 1692
Magdeburg (Schrader) 1621—1636, 1649, 1660, 1670
Saxe-Coburg 1626, city—1713
East Frisia 1631—1716
Württemberg 1657—~~1660,~~ 1743
Magdeburg 1663—1727, 1740
Braunschweig-Wolfenbüttel 1709—1769

Date of Publication	Count of Orders from Appendix 4	Count of Later Editions of Orders	Total Orders Represented in Appendix 3
1523–1540	35	0	35
1541–1560	52	9	61
1561–1600	47	26	73
1601–1650	17	19	36
1651–1780	21	29	50
TOTAL	172	83	255

Explanation of Abbreviations in the Column Headings

L—performed in Latin. Represents the designations L, (L) or L/(G?) in appendix 4.

G—performed in German. Represents G, (G) or (L?)/G in appendix 4.

L/G—performed in either Latin or German, whichever was possible or desirable in a locality. Represents L/G or G/L in appendix 4.

L-G—performed in Latin by the choir and also in German by the congregation or choir. Represents L-G or G-L in appendix 4.

√—an indication is given in the order for the part to be done, but it is unclear whether the performance is in Latin or German. Represents √ or (L?) or (G?) in appendix 4.

Ch—indicated in the order as performed by the choir. Represents °L, °G, °L/G, °L-G or °L/°G in appendix 4.

Ch/L—not specifically indicated as performed by the choir, but so presumed because it is in Latin. Represents L, (L) or L/(G?) in appendix 4.

Co—indicated in the order as performed by the congregation. Represents G° in appendix 4.

C/C—indicated in the order as performed by either the choir or the congregation, or once each by choir and congregation. Represents °L/G°, °L-G°, L/G°, (L)/G° or °G° in appendix 4. Also includes instances in which choir and congregation are directed to alternate stanza by stanza (indicated by a footnote in appendix 4).

Introit

Date	Latin vs. German					Choral vs. Congregational			
	L	G	L/G	L-G	✓	Ch	Ch/L	Co	C/C
1523–1540	7	10	13	0	5	4	4	1	3
1541–1560	14	19	21	1	4	14	7	4	8
1561–1600	19	24	21	1	4	20	8	3	6
1601–1650	13	11	9	0	2	7	7	0	0
1651–1780	15	20	8	0	1	12	8	2	0
TOTAL	68	84	72	2	16	57	34	10	17
Percent	30.1	37.2	31.9	0.9		38.0		4.5	7.0
Ratio						85.1		14.9	

Kyrie

Date	Latin vs. German					Choral vs. Congregational			
	L	G	L/G	L-G	✓	Ch	Ch/L	Co	C/C
1523–1540	10	5	5	1	9	1	9	0	0
1541–1560	23	8	6	0	11	12	13	0	4
1561–1600	15	20	14	0	11	11	15	0	2
1601–1650	12	8	3	0	3	7	9	0	0
1651–1780	14	13	6	0	5	11	7	0	0
TOTAL	74	54	34	1	39	42	53	0	6
Percent	45.4	33.1	20.9	0.6		47.3		0.2	3.0
Ratio						100.0		0.0	

Gloria and Et in terra

Date	Latin vs. German					Choral vs. Congregational			
	L	G	L/G	L-G	✓	Ch	Ch/L	Co	C/C
1523–1540	6	4	11	1	8	2	5	0	2
1541–1560	14	13	12	4	4	12	6	1	7
1561–1600	8	23	27	0	2	11	4	1	5
1601–1650	6	8	12	0	0	10	2	1	0
1651–1780	6	16	14	1	2	12	1	5	1
TOTAL	40	64	76	6	16	47	18	8	15
Percent	21.5	34.4	40.9	3.2			33.7	5.4	7.4
Ratio						85.5		14.5	

Alleluia or Gradual

Date	Latin vs. German					Choral vs. Congregational			
	L	G	L/G	L-G	✓	Ch	Ch/L	Co	C/C
1523–1540	6	11	5	4	4	6	5	2	2
1541–1560	12	19	13	4	0	11	5	2	4
1561–1600	6	27	13	1	0	9	2	2	2
1601–1650	2	21	3	0	0	2	0	1	2
1651–1780	2	34	4	1	0	5	0	2	1
TOTAL	28	112	38	10	4	33	12	9	11
Percent	14.9	59.6	20.2	5.3			26.0	7.3	5.7
Ratio						78.6		21.4	

Sequence

Date	Latin vs. German					Choral vs. Congregational			
	L	G	L/G	L-G	✓	Ch	Ch/L	Co	C/C
1523–1540	11	1	1	0	1	1	9	0	0
1541–1560	24	0	7	0	0	7	18	0	0
1561–1600	13	2	7	0	0	6	7	0	1
1601–1650	5	4	0	0	2	2	2	0	0
1651–1780	9	6	3	0	1	4	5	1	1
TOTAL	62	13	18	0	4	20	41	1	2
Percent	66.7	14.0	19.4	0.0		62.9		1.0	2.1
Ratio						95.2		4.8	

Credo and Patrem

Date	Latin vs. German					Choral vs. Congregational			
	L	G	L/G	L-G	✓	Ch	Ch/L	Co	C/C
1523–1540	2	21	3	5	2	1	2	7	4
1541–1560	2	24	18	10	0	4	1	8	15
1561–1600	1	31	27	11	0	3	1	11	13
1601–1650	0	15	11	5	0	4	0	6	4
1651–1780	0	25	11	7	1	2	0	6	3
TOTAL	5	116	70	38	3	14	4	38	39
Percent	2.2	50.7	30.6	16.6		15.9		24.6	16.8
Ratio						26.9		73.1	

Psalm or Hymn before Sermon

Date	Latin vs. German					Choral vs. Congregational			
	L	G	L/G	L-G	✓	Ch	Ch/L	Co	C/C
1523–1540	0	3	0	0	1	0	0	0	0
1541–1560	0	5	0	0	0	0	0	3	0
1561–1600	0	26	0	0	0	2	0	3	0
1601–1650	0	3	0	0	0	0	0	0	0
1651–1780	0	18	0	0	0	0	0	3	0
TOTAL	0	55	0	0	1	2	0	9	0
Percent	0.0	100.0	0.0	0.0		3.6		16.1	0.0
Ratio						18.2		81.8	

Psalm or Hymn after Sermon

Date	Latin vs. German					Choral vs. Congregational			
	L	G	L/G	L-G	✓	Ch	Ch/L	Co	C/C
1523–1540	0	10	2	1	0	0	0	2	2
1541–1560	1	21	1	0	0	3	1	3	0
1561–1600	0	36	1	0	0	1	0	4	0
1601–1650	0	20	0	0	0	0	0	0	0
1651–1780	0	34	0	0	0	2	0	2	0
TOTAL	1	121	4	1	0	6	1	11	2
Percent	0.8	95.3	3.2	0.8		5.9		9.1	1.6
Ratio						35.3		64.7	

Sanctus

	Latin vs. German					Choral vs. Congregational			
Date	L	G	L/G	L-G	✓	Ch	Ch/L	Co	C/C
1523–1540	13	5	3	0	3	7	7	0	0
1541–1560	13	5	20	1	1	8	7	2	3
1561–1600	6	6	17	1	4	5	6	0	2
1601–1650	6	1	9	0	0	2	4	0	2
1651–1780	7	10	6	1	1	1	6	2	0
TOTAL	45	27	55	3	9	23	30	4	7
Percent	34.6	20.8	42.3	2.3		39.2		4.0	5.0
Ratio						85.2		14.8	

Agnus Dei

	Latin vs. German					Choral vs. Congregational			
Date	L	G	L/G	L-G	✓	Ch	Ch/L	Co	C/C
1523–1540	6	11	14	1	1	6	4	3	1
1541–1560	19	10	6	1	6	9	6	2	2
1561–1600	5	14	7	2	1	4	4	6	2
1601–1650	1	10	9	0	0	0	1	1	0
1651–1780	5	9	6	0	0	1	5	5	0
TOTAL	36	54	42	4	8	20	20	17	5
Percent	26.5	39.7	30.9	2.9		29.2		13.2	3.5
Ratio						54.1		45.9	

Psalm(s) or Hymns during Communion

Date	Latin vs. German					Choral vs. Congregational			
	L	G	L/G	L-G	✓	Ch	Ch/L	Co	C/C
1523–1540	3	22	2	2	0	5	1	11	1
1541–1560	0	43	9	0	0	4	0	17	3
1561–1600	0	53	6	0	0	1	0	18	4
1601–1650	0	31	1	0	0	0	0	5	0
1651–1780	0	37	0	0	0	1	0	8	0
TOTAL	3	186	18	2	0	11	1	59	8
Percent	1.4	89.0	8.6	1.0		6.2		28.7	3.8
Ratio						15.7		84.3	

Psalm or Hymn after the Benediction

Date	Latin vs. German					Choral vs. Congregational			
	L	G	L/G	L-G	✓	Ch	Ch/L	Co	C/C
1523–1540	0	4	1	0	1	1	0	2	0
1541–1560	0	11	2	0	0	2	0	2	0
1561–1600	0	22	0	0	2	1	0	4	0
1601–1650	0	16	0	0	0	2	0	0	0
1651–1780	0	25	0	0	0	1	0	2	0
TOTAL	0	78	3	0	3	7	0	10	0
Percent	0.0	96.3	3.7	0.0		8.3		11.9	0.0
Ratio						41.2		58.8	

APPENDIX 4

❖

The Mass According to the Church Orders

The summary tables below contain information from Lutheran church orders on the presence or absence of the various parts of the mass. Indicated for each part present are its language (Latin or German) and whether it was performed by the priest, the choir, or the entire congregation. All orders listed in the bibliography that are prescriptive in nature and contain an order for mass are represented, for a total of 172 orders. This number includes 61 printed and 32 manuscript orders for territories larger than a city and 39 printed and 40 manuscript orders for cities, villages, and individual parishes. Two orders have been included that are not, strictly speaking, church orders: the Leipzig orders of 1694 and 1710 are actually devotional books intended for the people to read privately during services, but the running commentary on the mass is so detailed that it seems best to include them. Some church orders listed in the bibliography do not contain mass orders and so are not represented in this appendix.

There are substantially more orders from the sixteenth century than from the seventeenth and eighteenth. This is partly because many territories simply reprinted the older orders; but also because manuscript orders from the later centuries are difficult to locate, as the originals are likely to be locked away in archives, and only occasionally has one been printed as part of a historical study. In a few cases a later order has been changed only slightly from an earlier one; in the tables the changes are given in endnotes, and the column heading includes both dates. To save space, later editions of orders with substantially the same liturgical content are not represented here but are identified in appendix 3 and in the bibliography (see part 1 of the bibliography for an explanation of "substantially the same").

Only masses for Sundays and holy days are represented below. A few church orders have liturgies (usually simplified ones) for weekday masses that are not represented in the tables. For simplicity's sake, the tables do not report how the service is to be truncated when there are no communicants. If the mass order for villages is in a separate section in the agenda from the order for cities, it is given in a separate column (and counted separately in the total number of orders).

Below the name of each territory or city is given the type of order (PT—printed territorial; PC—printed city, village, or parish; MT—manuscript territorial; MC—manuscript city, village, or parish) and its approximate location within sixteenth-century Germany, abbreviated with standard compass directions plus "C" for "central." The distinction between territorial and city orders is somewhat academic, for some territories were hardly any larger than cities, and some cities had surrounding villages included in their territory. The distinction between printed and manuscript orders is significant only because the printed orders received much greater circulation and to that extent may be deemed more important in history.

The total number of editions represented in the tables in appendix 3 is also given. This figure may be less than the number of editions actually published on account of the "five-year rule" (see the introduction to appendix 3). For the number of editions actually published (and seen by this author), see the bibliography. Orders for which editions appeared in both the sixteenth and subsequent centuries have a number in parentheses following the total number of editions. This represents the number of editions published during the sixteenth century alone and is used in the calculations for the table at the beginning of chapter 4.

Explanation of Abbreviations and Symbols

+ indicates a part of the service sung or spoken by the priest or deacon.

L indicates a part of the service done in Latin; G indicates a part done in German; if the language is not explicitly specified in the church order but is evident with a high degree of probability from context or other evidence, the language indication is placed in parentheses. If the language to be used is less certain, the letter is followed by a question mark (L?).

L/G indicates a part of the service that may be done in either Latin or German; the order (L/G or G/L) is that given in the source.

L-G indicates a part of the service that is done in Latin, then done again in German.

A check mark (√) indicates a part of the service that either is untexted (e.g., Elevation) or whose language cannot be determined from the source, and Latin or German both seem equally likely.

A cross (×) indicates a part of the service whose omission is explicitly directed in the source.

A blank space indicates a part of the service not mentioned in the source.

A letter in square brackets indicates a part of the service virtually certain to have been done but which is not explicitly indicated in the order.

A raised circle to the left of a letter (°L) indicates a part of the service explicitly assigned to the choir; a raised circle to the right (G°) indicates a part of the service explicitly assigned to the congregation.

Lowered circles are used only in connection with the Agnus Dei. A lowered circle to the left of a letter (∘L) indicates that the Agnus is sung before the distribution of communion; a lowered circle to the right (G∘) indicates that it is sung after communion; and a lowered circle directly below (G̥) indicates that it is sung during communion. If nothing is indicated in this position, the place of the Agnus Dei cannot be determined.

Italics indicate a part of the service that may be omitted if desired or that is sung only on certain festivals.

Raised numbers refer to notes at the end of the appendix.

References to the Salutation are omitted; it may be sung before any collect and at the beginning of the Preface.

Minor deviations from the usual mass order, such as when the Verba precede the Sanctus, are not noted.

Extraliturgical figural and organ music mentioned in the sources is not noted.

	Wittenberg 1523	Allstedt 1524	Coburg 1524	Nuremberg 1524	Straßburg 1524	Nuremberg 1525	Nuremberg 1525	Prussia 1525
TYPE:	PC	PC	MC	MC	MC	PC	MC	MT
LOCATION:	C	C	C	S	SW	S	S	NE
TOTAL EDITIONS:	1	1	1	1	1	1	1	1
Confiteor or other preparatory prayers +						G[1]	✓	
Latin Introit or German psalm	L	G[2]	(L)	✓	✓	G	G	L/G
Kyrie[3]	(L)	G	(L)	✓	✓	G	✓	L/G
Gloria and Et in terra[4]	*(L)*	G	(L)	✓	✓	G	✓	G/L
Collect de tempore +	(L?)	G	(L)	✓	G	G	✓	G
Epistle +	(L?)	G	G	G	(G)	G	(G?)	(G)
Gradual, Alleluia or psalm	L	G	(L)	(L?)	(L?)	(G?)	G	G[5]
Sequence[6]		G						
Gospel[7] +	(L?)	G	G	G	(G)	G	(G?)	(G)
Credo and Patrem	*L*	G	(L)	✓	✓	G	°G	G°
Psalm or hymn				✓				
Sermon with prayers and other annexes[8] +	(G)	G		(G)[9]				
Psalm or hymn		G						
Exhortation to the communicants +		G		(G)	(G)	G	(G)	
Preface +	L	G	L	(L)	G	G		G
Sanctus[10]	L	G	°(L)	(L)	✓	G	°(L)	
Our Father[11] +	L	G	L	L	✓	G	L	G
Words of Institution (Verba) +	L	G	L	L	✓	G	(L)	G
Elevation	✓[12]		✓	✓	✓	✓	✓	✓
Agnus Dei	(L̪)	˳G°	°˳(L)	°(L̪)	˳G	˳G	°(L̪)	°G/°L
Psalms(s) or hymn(s) during communion	L			°L	G		°G	G°
Thanksgiving collect +	L	G	(L?)	✓	G	G[13]	✓[14]	G
Benediction +	(L?)[15]	G	(L?)		(G?)	G[16]		G
Psalm or hymn					✓[17]		G	

	Schwäbisch Hall 1526	Wittenberg 1526	Naumburg 1527	Brandenburg-Nürnberg 1528	Braunschweig 1528	Hamburg 1529	Frankfurt/Main 1530	Riga 1530
TYPE:	MC	PC	MC	MT	PC	PC	MC	MC
LOCATION:	S	C	C	S	N	N	W	NE
TOTAL EDITIONS:	1	1	1	1	2	1	1	1
Confiteor or other preparatory prayers +								
Latin Introit or German psalm	˙L	G	L[18]	L/G˙[19]	G	G/L	G[20]	L/G
Kyrie	(L)	G	L	L	L/G	(L/G)		L-G[21]
Gloria and Et in terra	(L)/G˙		L	L	L/G	(L/G)		L/G
Collect de tempore +	[22]	G	L	G/L	G	G		G
Epistle +		G	L	G	(G)	(G)		G
Gradual, Alleluia or psalm		˙G	L	L	˙(L)-G[23]	˙L-G		G[24]
Sequence	L		L		L			
Gospel +	L-G	G	L	G	(G)	(G)	L-G[25]	G
Credo and Patrem	˙L-G˙	G˙	G˙	G	G˙	G		G˙
Psalm or hymn								
Sermon with prayers and other annexes +		(G)	(G)	(G)	(G)	(G)	(G)	(G)
Psalm or hymn			G˙		G	˙G˙[26]		
Exhortation to the communicants +	(G)	G			G	G	G	
Preface +				L	L	(L)		G
Sanctus			˙L	L	L[27]	˙L		˙G/˙L
Our Father +		[28]	L	L	G	G		G
Words of Institution (Verba) +	G	G	L	✓	G	G	G	G
Elevation		✓						
Agnus Dei		G̨		.L/.G	G˙.	G.		:G/˙L
Psalms(s) or hymn(s) during communion	˙L	G		G[29]	G˙	G˙	G˙	G˙
Thanksgiving collect +		G	L	G	G	G	G	G
Benediction +	(G)	G		G	G	G	G	G
Psalm or hymn	G˙							

	Straßburg 1530	Lübeck 1531	Lippe [before 1533?]	Brandenburg-Nürnberg 1533	Saxony (E) 1533	Wittenberg 1533	Hatzkerode [1534?]	East Frisia 1535
TYPE:	PC	PC	MT	PT	MT	MC	MC	MT
LOCATION:	SW	N	NW	S	C	C	C	NW
TOTAL EDITIONS:	1	1	1	4	1	1	1	1
Confiteor or other preparatory prayers +	G[30]		L	(L?)				
Latin Introit or German psalm	G•	G/L	•L/•G•[31]	L/G•[32]	L/G	L/G[33]	•L[34]	G/L
Kyrie	G	(L/G)	L	L		(L?)	(L)	G/L
Gloria and Et in terra	G	(L/G)	G	•L/G•	L/•G	(L?)	(L)-G[35]	G/L
Collect de tempore +	G	G	G	G	(L/G?)	G	G	G/L
Epistle +	(G)	(G)	(G)	G	G	(G)	G	(G)
Gradual, Alleluia or psalm	G•	•L-G	G	•L	(L/G)	•L-G	L/G	G
Sequence						L	L	L
Gospel +	(G)	(G)	(G)	(G)	G	(G)	G	(G)
Credo and Patrem	G•	G	G	•L/G•	(L?)/G	•L-G•	•L-G•	G
Psalm or hymn							G	
Sermon with prayers and other annexes +	(G)	(G)		(G)[36]	(G)	(G)	(G)	(G)
Psalm or hymn		•G•[37]	G[38]			L-G	G	(G)
Exhortation to the communicants +	G	G		G	G		G	G
Preface +		(L)	G			L	L	
Sanctus		•L	G	L/G	G	(L?)	L	L
Our Father +		G	G	L/G	G	G	G	G
Words of Institution (Verba) +	G	G	G	G[39]	G	G	G	G
Elevation						✓		
Agnus Dei		G.	•G	•L/•G•	(G?)	(L)-G.[40]	L	L
Psalms(s) or hymn(s) during communion	G•	G•	G	•(L/G)•	G	G-L	G-L	•G
Thanksgiving collect +	G	G	G	G	G	G	G	G
Benediction +	G	G	G	G[41]	G	G	G	G
Psalm or hymn							G•	

219

	Liegnitz and Brieg 1535	Pomerania 1535	Württemberg 1536	Augsburg 1537, 1545	Naumburg 1538	Gnandstein 1539	Lippe 1539	Northeim 1539
TYPE:	MT	PT	MT	PC[42]	MC	MC	MT	PC
LOCATION:	E	NE	S	S	C	C	NW	C
TOTAL EDITIONS:	1	1	1	2	1	1	1	1
Confiteor or other preparatory prayers +								
Latin Introit or German psalm	✓	L/G [43]	G	G	G/L	°L/°G	✓	(L?)
Kyrie	✓	(L?)			G[44]	✓	✓	(L?)
Gloria and Et in terra	✓	L/G			G/L	✓	✓	(L?)
Collect de tempore +	G	G			(G)		✓	G
Epistle +	G	(G)			(G)	G	(G)	G
Gradual, Alleluia or psalm	(L)	G°/L			G/L		(L?)	G°
Sequence	*(L)*	*L*				(L/G)	(L?)	°L
Gospel +	G	(G)		(G)	(G)	G	(G)	G/L
Credo and Patrem	G	L-G	G		G	G°	(G)[45]	L/G
Psalm or hymn	G				G			
Sermon with prayers and other annexes +	(G)	(G)	(G)	(G)	(G)	(G)		(G)
Psalm or hymn		L/G			G			G°
Exhortation to the communicants +	G	*G*	G[46]	G[47]	G	G		G
Preface +	✓	L						
Sanctus	✓	L/G			G			
Our Father +		G	G°	G	G	G		G[48]
Words of Institution (Verba) +	(G)	G	G	G	G	G		G
Elevation								
Agnus Dei		L°/G°			°G			✓.
Psalms(s) or hymn(s) during communion	G	G°	G°	G°	°G			G
Thanksgiving collect +	G	G	G	G	G	G		G
Benediction +		(G)	G	G	G	G		G
Psalm or hymn	G							°L/°G

	Saxony (A) 1539/1540 (city)	Saxony (A) 1539/1540 (village)	Brandenburg 1540	Calenberg-Göttingen 1542	Hadeln [ca. 1542]	Pomerania 1542	Regensburg 1542	Schleswig-Holstein 1542
TYPE:	PT	PT	PT[49]	PT	MT	PT	PC	PT
LOCATION:	C	C	NE	C	N	NE	S	N
TOTAL EDITIONS:	12 (6)	12 (6)	1	1	1	1	1	1
Confiteor or other preparatory prayers +			L				(L?)[50]	(L)
Latin Introit or German psalm	*(L)	(G)	L	*(G?)[51]	(G)	*L/*G[52]	*(L?)[53]	(L)/G
Kyrie	*L		L	(L)	L/G	*L	*(L?)	(L)
Gloria and Et in terra	*L		L	L/G	G	*L-G*[54]	*(L?)	(G)*
Collect de tempore +	G/L	G	L	✓	(G)	✓	(G?)	G
Epistle +	G	G	L-G[55]	G	(G)	G	G	G
Gradual, Alleluia or psalm	G	G	L/G*[56]	*L/G*	G[57]	*L		*L-G
Sequence	L[58]		L	L	L	*L/*G[59]	*L	(L)
Gospel +	G	G	L-G	(G)	(G)	G	G	G
Credo and Patrem	L-G	G	L/G	G*	*G	L/G	*L	G
Psalm or hymn								
Sermon with prayers and other annexes +	(G)	(G)	(G)	(G)	(G)	(G)		(G)
Psalm or hymn			L/G[60]	G	(G)			
Exhortation to the communicants +	G[61]	G	G[62]		G	G	G[63]	G
Preface +	L		L	(L?)	L/G	L/G		L
Sanctus	L		L	G	(L/G?)	L/G	*(L)	L
Our Father +	G		G[64]	G	G	G	(L?)	G
Words of Institution (Verba) +	G	G	G	G	G	(G)	G	G
Elevation			✓[65]				✓	
Agnus Dei	L/G.		.L	G.	G		*(L)	G
Psalms(s) or hymn(s) during communion	G*	G*	L/G		G	G		G
Thanksgiving collect +	G	G	G?	G	G	G	(G?)	G
Benediction +	(G)	G		(G)	G	(G)	G	G
Psalm or hymn								G

	Schönburg 1542 (city)	Schönburg 1542 (village)	Wurzen 1542	Braunschweig-Wolfenbüttel 1543	Cologne 1543	Nuremberg 1543, 1545 (villages with schools)	Nuremberg 1543 (villages without schools)	Osnabrück 1543 (city)
TYPE:	MT	MT	MC	PT	PT	PC	PC	PC
LOCATION:	C	C	C	N	W	S	S	NW
TOTAL EDITIONS:	1	1	1	1	1	4	4	1
Confiteor or other preparatory prayers +				L		*L*		
Latin Introit or German psalm	L/G	G	°L/°G	L/G[66]	G°-°L[67]	°L/G°	G°	L/G
Kyrie	✓	G	(L)	(L)	°L[68]	°L/G°		(L)
Gloria and Et in terra	✓		(L)	°L-G°[69]	°L	°L/G°		G-L
Collect de tempore +	G/L	G		G	G	G		L/G
Epistle +	(G)	(G)	G	G	G	(G)	[70]	G
Gradual, Alleluia or psalm	°L-G°	G	(L/G)	°L-G°	°L	°L[71]		L
Sequence	°L			(L)				L/G
Gospel +	(G)	(G)	G	G	G	(G)	(G)	(G)
Credo and Patrem	L-G°	G	G°	L-G		°L/G°		G/L
Psalm or hymn								
Sermon with prayers and other annexes +	(G)	(G)	(G)	(G)			(G)	(G)	(G)
Psalm or hymn	G°							G
Exhortation to the communicants +		G	(G)	*G*		G	G	G
Preface +	*(L)*			L	G			L
Sanctus	G/L[72]			G°	°L-G°[73]	L/G		L
Our Father +	G	*G*	(G)	G	G	G	G	G
Words of Institution (Verba) +	G	G	(G)	G	(G)	G	G	G
Elevation								
Agnus Dei	*ƚ*			G°.	L̦-G[74]	°ƚ		L/G.[75]
Psalms(s) or hymn(s) during communion	G/L	G°		G°	G	*G°*	G	G/L
Thanksgiving collect +	G		(G)	G	G	G	G	
Benediction +	G	G	(G)	G	G	G	G	
Psalm or hymn	G	*G*						

222

	Osnabrück 1543 (village)	Palatinate-Neuburg 1543	Schwäbisch Hall 1543 (city)	Schwäbisch Hall 1543 (village)	Schweinfurt 1543	Amberg 1544	Bergedorf 1544	Hildesheim 1544
TYPE:	PT	PT	PC	PC	PC	PC	MC	PC
LOCATION:	NW	SE	S	S	C	S	N	N
TOTAL EDITIONS:	1	1	1	1	1	1	1	1
Confiteor or other preparatory prayers +		(L)					✓	L
Latin Introit or German psalm	L/G	(L)/G[76]	L	G	(L)	°L[77]	G/L	*G*
Kyrie	(L?)	(°L?)	L		(L)	°L	✓	L
Gloria and Et in terra	G	(°L?)	L		L	°L	G	°L-G°
Collect de tempore +	L/G	G	L	G[78]	L/G	(G?)	G	G
Epistle +	G	(G)	L[79]	G	(G)	G	G	G
Gradual, Alleluia or psalm	L	°L/G°	L	G	*G*	°L°G	G	°L-*G*
Sequence	*L/G*	°L			*L*	°L	*L*	*L*
Gospel +	(G)	(G)	L		(G)	G	(G)	G
Credo and Patrem	G	°L/G°	*L*		L-G	°L-G°	G°	°L-G°
Psalm or hymn			G°[80]			G		
Sermon with prayers and other annexes +	(G)	(G)	(G)[81]	(G)[82]	(G)	(G)	(G)	(G)
Psalm or hymn	G		G	*G*	G	°G[83]		
Exhortation to the communicants +	G	(G)	G	G	G	G	G	G
Preface +							L/G	
Sanctus		°L/G°	°L		(L?)	°(L)	L/G	
Our Father +	G	G	G	G	G	G	G	G
Words of Institution (Verba) +	G	G[84]	G	G	G	G	G	G
Elevation		✓[85]						
Agnus Dei	G°/L°	°L			✓°	L°	*G*°	°L/G°
Psalms(s) or hymn(s) during communion	G	°L/G°[86]		G	G	G°	G°	G
Thanksgiving collect +	G	G-L[87]			G	G	G	G
Benediction +	G	G[88]	G	G	G	G	G	G
Psalm or hymn							G°	G

	Nördlingen 1544	Mecklenburg 1545	Saxony (A) 1545	Palatinate 1546	Transylvania 1547	Anhalt 1548	Brandenburg-Ansbach-Kulmbach 1548	Schwarzburg 1549
TYPE:	MC	PT	MT	MT	MT	MT	MT[89]	MT
LOCATION:	S	N	C	SW	SE	C	S	C
TOTAL EDITIONS:	1	1	1	1	1	1	1	1
Confiteor or other preparatory prayers +	(L)			L[90]		(L)	L	
Latin Introit or German psalm	˙G˙[91]	˙L/G[92]		˙L	L/G	(L)	L	L
Kyrie	˙G˙[93]	˙L/G[94]		˙L	✓	(L)	L	L
Gloria and Et in terra	G[95]	G		˙L	✓	(L)	L	L
Collect de tempore +	G	G		G	(G)	(L)	L/G	G
Epistle +	(G)	G	(G)[96]	G	G	L/G[97]	L-G	L-G
Gradual, Alleluia or psalm	G[98]	˙L/G		˙L	L/G	L/G	L/G	L/G
Sequence		L	L/G[99]	˙L	L	L	L	
Gospel +	(G)	(G)	(G)	G	(G)	L/G	L-G	L[100]
Credo and Patrem	G˙	G/L-G˙	G	˙L-G˙	G˙/L	L-G	L/G	L-G
Psalm or hymn	G˙							
Sermon with prayers and other annexes +	(G)	(G)	(G)	(G)	[101]	(G)	(G)	(G)
Psalm or hymn	˙G		L			G	L/G[102]	G
Exhortation to the communicants +	G			G		G	(G)	G
Preface +		L/G	(L)	L	(L?)	L	(L)	L/G
Sanctus	˙G	L/G	L	˙L	(L)	˙L	L/G	˙L/G˙
Our Father +	G	G	G	G	G	G	L/G	G
Words of Institution (Verba) +	G	G	G	G	G	G	L/G	G
Elevation		✓		✗			✓	✓
Agnus Dei			˙L.	˙(L).	.(L)	↳	L	
Psalms(s) or hymn(s) during communion	G˙	G		G˙/˙L	G	G	L/G	G˙
Thanksgiving collect +	G		G	G	G	G	L/G	G
Benediction +	G		(G)	G	G	G	✓	G
Psalm or hymn								

	Braunschweig [ca. 1550]	Buxtehude 1552	Mecklenburg 1552 (city)	Mecklenburg 1552 (village)	Plauen 1552	Hohenlohe 1553	Regensburg 1553	Württemberg 1553
TYPE:	MC	MC	PT	PT	MC	MT	MC	PT
LOCATION:	N	N	N	N	C	S	S	S
TOTAL EDITIONS:	1	1	2	2	1	1	1	4 (3)
Confiteor or other preparatory prayers +		✓			L	L	(L)	
Latin Introit or German psalm	G°	L/G	°(L?)[103]	G[104]	°L	°L	°L	G
Kyrie	G	*L/G*	✓	G	°L	°L	°L	
Gloria and Et in terra	G	L/G	L/G	G	°G/L	°L	°L	
Collect de tempore +	(G)	(G?)	G	G	(G?)	L/G	G	
Epistle +	(G)	G	(G)	G	G	L/G	(G)	
Gradual, Alleluia or psalm	G°	L		G	G°	°L/°G[105]	G/L	
Sequence		L/G	L/(G)[106]				L	
Gospel +		(G)	(G)	G	(G)	L/G	(G)	
Credo and Patrem	G°	G°	°L-G°	G	G	°L/G°	°G	G
Psalm or hymn	G°							
Sermon with prayers and other annexes +	(G)	(G)	(G)	G	(G)	(G)	*(G)*	(G)
Psalm or hymn				G	G	°G		
Exhortation to the communicants +	G	G	*(G)*		G	G	G	G[107]
Preface +		L	G/L		G	(L?)		
Sanctus	G°	L/G	L/G			L/G	°L	
Our Father +	G	G	G	G	*G*	(L?)	G	G°[108]
Words of Institution (Verba) +	G	G	G	G	G	G	G	G
Elevation			✗				✗	
Agnus Dei		L°/G°	✓	Ģ	(L̦)	∴✓	°(L̦)	
Psalms(s) or hymn(s) during communion	G°	G	G	G	L/G[109]	°G/L	°G	G°
Thanksgiving collect +	G	G	G	G		G	G	G
Benediction +	G	G	G	G	G	G	G	G
Psalm or hymn	G°	°L/°G	G	G				

	Eisfeld 1554	Palatinate 1554	Braunschweig-Lüneburg [1555]	Nördlingen 1555	Stralsund 1555	Amberg 1555–57	Hamburg 1556	Waldeck 1557, 1640
TYPE:	MC	PT	MC	MC	MC	MC	MC	PT
LOCATION:	C	SW	N	S	N	S	N	W
TOTAL EDITIONS:	1	1	1	1	1	1	1	2 (1)
Confiteor or other preparatory prayers +								
Latin Introit or German psalm	G	G[110]	(L)	L/G[111]	L/G	°L/G°	°L/G°	L/G
Kyrie			(L?)	G	✓	(L)	(L)	G
Gloria and Et in terra			L/G	G	G	L/G	L/G	G
Collect de tempore +			✓	G	G	G	G	G
Epistle +	(G)		G	G	G	G	G	G
Gradual, Alleluia or psalm	G			G	G	L/G	L/G	(G)
Sequence			L		L		L	(L)
Gospel +	(G)		G	G	G	(G)	G	G
Credo and Patrem	G	G	L/G	L/G	G/L	°L/°G[112]	G°	L-G/G°
Psalm or hymn				G				
Sermon with prayers and other annexes +	(G)	(G)	(G)	(G)	(G)	(G)	(G)	(G)
Psalm or hymn	G			G			G°	G[113]
Exhortation to the communicants +	G	G[114]	G	G		G	G	G
Preface +			L		(L)	G/L[115]	L	(L)
Sanctus				G	L/G	L/G	L/G	L/G
Our Father +	G	G°[116]	G	G	G	G	G	G
Words of Institution (Verba) +	G	G	G	G	G	G	G	G
Elevation						×		
Agnus Dei	Ç		(Ĺ?)			Ç/Ļ	Ļ/Ç	
Psalms(s) or hymn(s) during communion	G	G°	L/G	°G	G	G	°G	°G°[117]
Thanksgiving collect +	G	G	G	G	G	G	G	G
Benediction +	G	G	G	G	G	G	G	G
Psalm or hymn							°L/°G	G

	Prussia 1558 (city)	Prussia 1558 (village)	Rothenburg ob der Tauber 1559 (city)	Rothenburg ob der Tauber 1559 (village)	Wittenberg 1559 (city)	Wittenberg 1559 (village)	Steuerwald/Peine 1561	Feuchtwangen 1563
TYPE:	PT	PT	MC[118]	MC	PC	PC	MT	MC
LOCATION:	NE	NE	S	S	C	C	N	S
TOTAL EDITIONS:	1	1	1	1	2	2	1	1
Confiteor or other preparatory prayers +			*L*					
Latin Introit or German psalm	L	G	°L/G°	G°	°(L?)[119]	G[120]	G	°L
Kyrie	✓	G	°L/G°		✓	G		L
Gloria and Et in terra	°L	°G	°L/G°		L/G	G	G	L
Collect de tempore +	G	G	G		G	G	G	G
Epistle +	G	(G)	(G)	[121]	(G)	G	(G)	G
Gradual, Alleluia or psalm	°L	G	°*L*[122]			G	G°	G/L
Sequence	°*L*				L/(G)[123]			
Gospel +	(G)	(G)	(G)	(G)	(G)	G	(G)	G
Credo and Patrem	G°	G	°L/G°		°L-G°	G	G°	L/G
Psalm or hymn							G°	G
Sermon with prayers and other annexes +	(G)	(G)	(G)	(G)	(G)	G	(G)	(G)
Psalm or hymn		G°				G		
Exhortation to the communicants +	(G)	G	G	G	*(G)*		G	G[124]
Preface +	×				*G/L*			
Sanctus	°L/°G		L/G		L/G			
Our Father +			G	G	G	G	G	
Words of Institution (Verba) +	(G)	(G)	G	G	G	G	G	
Elevation	×				×			
Agnus Dei	Ļ		°Ļ		✓	Ģ		
Psalms(s) or hymn(s) during communion	G	G°	G°	G	G	G	G°	
Thanksgiving collect +	G	(G)	G	G	G	G	G	
Benediction +	(G?)[125]	(G)	G	G	G	G	G	
Psalm or hymn					G	G	G°	

	Palatinate-Zweibrücken 1563 (city)	Palatinate-Zweibrücken 1563 (village)	Braunschweig-Lüneburg 1564 (city)	Braunschweig-Lüneburg 1564 (village)	Thüngen 1564	Württemberg 1565 (city)	Württemberg 1565 (village)	Hesse 1566
TYPE:	PT	PT	PT	PT	MT	PT	PT	PT
LOCATION:	SW	SW	N	N	C	S	S	C
TOTAL EDITIONS:	2	2	4 (2)	4 (2)	1	1	1	1
Confiteor or other preparatory prayers +								
Latin Introit or German psalm	•(L)/G[126]	G[127]	(L)	L/G		•(L)[128]	G[129]	G[130]
Kyrie	G	G	L/G	G	G	(L?)	G	G
Gloria and Et in terra	G	G	L/G	G	G	L/G	G	G
Collect de tempore +	G	(G)	(G?)	G	G	G	G	G
Epistle +	G	(G)	G	G	G	G	G	G
Gradual, Alleluia or psalm	G	G		G	G	L/G	G	G
Sequence			G[131]					
Gospel +	G	(G)	(G)	G		G	G	G
Credo and Patrem	•L/G•	G	L/G	G•	G	•L-G•	G•	G•
Psalm or hymn			G		G			
Sermon with prayers and other annexes +	(G)	(G)	(G)	(G)	(G)	(G)	(G)	(G)
Psalm or hymn		G		G			G	(G)
Exhortation to the communicants +	(G)		(G)	G	G	G		
Preface +			(L)			(L)		
Sanctus	L/G		•L/G•		G	L/G		
Our Father +	G[132]	G	G	G	G	G	G	G
Words of Institution (Verba) +	G	G	G	G	G	G	G	G
Elevation	×				×	×		
Agnus Dei	Ģ•	Ģ	(L)/Ģ	Ģ		(L)/Ģ	Ģ	
Psalms(s) or hymn(s) during communion	G•	G	G	G	G•	G	G	G•
Thanksgiving collect +	G	G	G	G	G	G	G	G
Benediction +	G	G	G	G	G	G	G	G
Psalm or hymn		G		G		G	G	

	Andorff 1567	Regensburg [1567?]	Anhalt 1568	Prussia 1568 (city)	Prussia 1568 (village)	Rostock [ca. 1560–76]	Braunschweig-Wolfenbüttel 1569 (city)	Braunschweig-Wolfenbüttel 1569 (village)
TYPE:	PC	MC	MT	PT	PT	MC	PT	PT
LOCATION:	C	S	C	NE	NE	N	N	N
TOTAL EDITIONS:	1	1	1	2	2	1	1	1
Confiteor or other preparatory prayers +								
Latin Introit or German psalm	G•[133]	•L/•G	✓	L/G	G[134]	L/G	L/G	L/G
Kyrie		•G/L	✓	(L?)	(G)	✓	L/G	G
Gloria and Et in terra		•G/L[135]	(L?)/G	•L/•G	G	•G/•L	L/G	G
Collect de tempore +		(G?)	(G?)	G		(G)	(G)	G
Epistle +		(G)	(G)	G	(G)[136]	(G)	G	G
Gradual, Alleluia or psalm							•L/G•	G
Sequence		•L/•G[137]	L/G[138]	L		L/G	•L	
Gospel +		(G)	(G)	(G)	(G)	(G)	G	G
Credo and Patrem	G	•L/•G	L-G	L/G	G[139]	G/L-G	L/G	G•
Psalm or hymn	G				G		G	
Sermon with prayers and other annexes +	(G)		(G)	(G)	(G)	(G)	(G)	(G)
Psalm or hymn	G		(L?)/G	G•		G		G
Exhortation to the communicants +	G	G	G	G	G	G	G	G
Preface +						(L?)	(L)	G
Sanctus		•L/•G				•G/•L		
Our Father +	G	G	G			G	G	G
Words of Institution (Verba) +	G	G	G	G	G[140]	G	G	G
Elevation		✗						
Agnus Dei	G•						(L)/G	G•
Psalms(s) or hymn(s) during communion	G•	•G		G[141]		G•	(G)[142]	G
Thanksgiving collect +	G		G	G		G	G	G
Benediction +	G	G	G	G		G	G	G
Psalm or hymn						G•		

	Pomerania 1569 (city)	Pomerania 1569 (village)	Ritzebüttel [after 1570]	Hohenlohe 1571	Kurland 1572	Hanau 1573	Oldenburg 1573 (city)	Oldenburg 1573 (village)
TYPE:	PT	PT	MC	MT	MT	PT	PT	PT
LOCATION:	NE	NE	NW	S	NE	C	NW	NW
TOTAL EDITIONS:	5 (2)	5 (2)	1	1	1	1	1	1
Confiteor or other preparatory prayers +	L	(L?)						
Latin Introit or German psalm	˙L/˙G	G	G	G	L/G	˙L/G	(˙L)	
Kyrie	L/G	G	G		(L)	G	(˙L?)	G/L[143]
Gloria and Et in terra	L/G	G	G˙		L/G	G[144]	˙L/G˙	G
Collect de tempore +	G	G	G		(G)		(G)	G
Epistle +	(G)	G	G	(G)[145]	(G)	(G)	G	G
Gradual, Alleluia or psalm	˙L/˙G	G	G		L/G[146]		˙L/G˙[147]	G
Sequence	˙L[148]							
Gospel +	(G)	G	G	(G)	(G)		G	G
Credo and Patrem	G/L	G[149]	G˙	G	L/G	G	˙L-G˙	G
Psalm or hymn	G		G		G			
Sermon with prayers and other annexes +	(G)	(G)	(G)		(G)	(G)	(G)	(G)
Psalm or hymn	G	(G)	G				G	G
Exhortation to the communicants +	G[150]	G	G			G[151]	G	G
Preface +	G/L	(G?)		(G)	G		L	G
Sanctus	L/G	G			˙G		L	
Our Father +	G	G	G	G	G	G	G	G
Words of Institution (Verba) +	G	G	G	G	G	G	G	G
Elevation	×							
Agnus Dei	Ļ		G˙		˙L/˙G		G/Ļ-G.	
Psalms(s) or hymn(s) during communion	G/L[152]	(G)	G˙			G	G	G
Thanksgiving collect +	G	G	G	G			G	G
Benediction +	G	G	G	G		G	G	G
Psalm or hymn	G	G	G˙				G	G

	Dresden 1574	Hesse 1574	Schwarzburg 1574	Wolfstein 1574	Aschersleben 1575	Lüneburg 1575	Thorn 1575	Amberg 1576
TYPE:	MC	PT	MT	MT	MC	MC	MC	PC
LOCATION:	C	C	C	SE	C	N	NE	S
TOTAL EDITIONS:	1	3 (1)	1	1	1	1	1	1
Confiteor or other preparatory prayers +				*(L)*				
Latin Introit or German psalm	(L)[153]	L[154]	°(L)[155]	L/G	°G-(L?)[156]	(L)	[157]	°L/G°
Kyrie	(L)	(L?)	°L/°G	L/G	✓	(L?)		(L)
Gloria and Et in terra	(L)	(L?)	°L/°G	L/G		L/G	✓	L/G
Collect de tempore +	(L?)		(G)	G	(G)	G	✓	G
Epistle +	L-G	(G)	(G)	(G)	(G)	G	✓	G
Gradual, Alleluia or psalm	L/G		L/G[158]	L/G		L/G[159]		
Sequence	L	G/L						
Gospel +	L-G	(G)	(G)	(G)	(G)	G	✓	
Credo and Patrem	L-G	G	°L/G°	L/G	°G/L	G-*L*[160]		°L/°G[161]
Psalm or hymn		G°	*G*°	G		°G	G[162]	
Sermon with prayers and other annexes +	(G)	(G)	(G)	(G)	(G)	(G)	(G)	(G)
Psalm or hymn		G	G	*G*		G		
Exhortation to the communicants +		G		G	G	G	*G*	G
Preface +	(L?)		*L*			G/L	*(G/L?)*	
Sanctus				L/G[163]		✓	°L-°G	L/G
Our Father +	G	[G]	G	G	G	G	(G)	G
Words of Institution (Verba) +	G	[G][164]	G	G	G	G	(G)	G
Elevation							✕	✕
Agnus Dei	*(L)*		°*L*			*L/G*	°*L*-°*G*	*G/L*
Psalms(s) or hymn(s) during communion	L/G		°G°[165]	*G*°		G	°G	G
Thanksgiving collect +	G		G	G	G	G	G	G
Benediction +	G	(G)	G	G	G	G	G	G
Psalm or hymn		(G)			°(G?)			

	Schweinfurt 1576	Hohenlohe 1578	Annaberg 1579	Nördlingen 1579	Hoya 1581	Henneberg 1582	Teschen 1584	Saxe-Lauenburg 1585 (city)
TYPE:	MC	MT	MC	MC	PT	PT	MT	PT
LOCATION:	S	S	C	S	NW	C	SE	N
TOTAL EDITIONS:	1	1	1	1	1	1	1	2 (1)
Confiteor or other preparatory prayers +								
Latin Introit or German psalm	˙*L*	˙*G*	(L)	˙(L)[166]	(L?)[167]	L-G˙	(L)	(˙L)
Kyrie	˙L/˙G		(L)		˙L		(L)/G[168]	(˙L)
Gloria and Et in terra	˙L/˙G		(L)		G		G/L	˙L/G
Collect de tempore +	✓	(G)	L/G	(G)	G		G	G
Epistle +	✓	(G)	(G)[169]	(G)	G	(G)	G	G
Gradual, Alleluia or psalm	˙*G*		G˙	[170]	G		˙G/˙L	˙L
Sequence	˙*L*		L					˙L/˙*G*˙[171]
Gospel +	✓		(G)[172]		G		G	G
Credo and Patrem	˙L/˙G	G˙	˙L-G	˙G˙[173]	˙L-G	G˙	G/L	˙L/G˙
Psalm or hymn	˙*G*	*G*	(G)	G	*G*			*G*
Sermon with prayers and other annexes +	(G)	(G)	(G)	(G)	(G)	(G)	(G)	(G)
Psalm or hymn	˙*G*		*(G)*	G˙	G	G[174]	G/L	G
Exhortation to the communicants +	G	G		G		G	✓	G
Preface +			*L*				*L*	(L?)
Sanctus	✓[175]		*G*					(L?)
Our Father +		G	G	G	G	G	G[176]	G
Words of Institution (Verba) +		G	G	G	G	G	✓	G
Elevation								
Agnus Dei	✓˳				*G̦*			*G̦*
Psalms(s) or hymn(s) during communion	G	G˙	L/G	˙G˙[177]	G	G	G[178]	G
Thanksgiving collect +		G	G	G	G	G	G	G
Benediction +		G		G	G	G	G	G
Psalm or hymn			✓		G			G˙

232

	Saxe-Lauenburg 1585 (village)	Halberstadt 1591	Niederlausitz 1592	Liegnitz and Brieg 1592	East Frisia 1593	Straßburg 1598	Mecklenburg 1602, 1708 (city)	Mecklenburg 1602, 1708 (village)
TYPE:	PT	MC	MT	MT	MT	PC	PT	PT
LOCATION:	N	C	E	E	NW	SW	N	N
TOTAL EDITIONS:	2 (1)	1	1	1	1	3 (1)	3	3
Confiteor or other preparatory prayers +								
Latin Introit or German psalm	G/L[179]	˚(L)		(L)		(G)[180]	(˚L?)[181]	G
Kyrie	G	˚(L)	(L)	(L)	˚G[182]		(˚L?)	G
Gloria and Et in terra	G	˚(L)	L/G	(L)			˚L/˚G	G
Collect de tempore +	G	L/G	(L/G)	(L?)			(G)	G
Epistle +	(G)	L-G	(L?/G)	L			G	G
Gradual, Alleluia or psalm	G	˚L		(L)/G				G
Sequence		˚L					(L?)	
Gospel +	(G)	L-G	(L?/G)	L/G	(G)	(G)	G	G
Credo and Patrem	G˚	˚L-G	L/(G?)	L-G	G		˚L-G˚	G˚
Psalm or hymn				(G)	*G*			
Sermon with prayers and other annexes +	(G)	(G)	(G)	(G)	(G)	(G)	(G)	(G)
Psalm or hymn	G	G		G	G˚	G	G	G
Exhortation to the communicants +	G			*G*	[183]	G[184]	*G*	
Preface +		L	L	*L*			*G/L*	
Sanctus		˚(L?)	(L)			G	*L/G*	
Our Father +	G	G[185]	L/(G?)	(G)			G	G
Words of Institution (Verba) +	G		G	(G)	G	G	G	G
Elevation								
Agnus Dei	*G̦*		(L)		˚G˚		*L/G*	*G̦*
Psalms(s) or hymn(s) during communion	G		G[186]	G	G	G	G	G
Thanksgiving collect +	G				G	G	G	G
Benediction +	G			G	G	G	G	G
Psalm or hymn							G	G

	Verden 1606	Braunschweig-Wolfenbüttel 1615 (city)	Braunschweig-Wolfenbüttel 1615 (village)	Magdeburg 1615	Schwäbisch Hall 1615 (city)	Schwäbisch Hall 1615 (village)	Upper Austria 1617	Rothenberg 1618
TYPE:	MT	PT	PT	PC	PC	PC	PT	MT
LOCATION:	N	N	N	N	S	S	SE	S
TOTAL EDITIONS:	1	2	2	3	1	1	1	1
Confiteor or other preparatory prayers +								
Latin Introit or German psalm	L[187]	L/(G?)	L/G	°(L)	(L)	G		G
Kyrie	L	L/(G?)	G	°(L)	(L)			
Gloria and Et in terra	L	L/G	G	°(L)	L			
Collect de tempore +	L/G	G	(G)	G		(G)		
Epistle +	L/G	G	G	L-G		(G)		(G)
Gradual, Alleluia or psalm	L/G[188]	°L/G°	G	°L	G	*G*		G
Sequence				°L				
Gospel +	L/G	G	(G)	L-G		G		[189]
Credo and Patrem	°L/°G	L/G	G°	°L-G°		G[190]		G
Psalm or hymn	*G*							
Sermon with prayers and other annexes +	(G)	(G)	(G)	(G)	(G)	(G)	(G)[191]	(G)
Psalm or hymn	G	*G*	G		G		G	(G)
Exhortation to the communicants +	G	G	G				G	G
Preface +	*(L)*	*L*	G	L				
Sanctus	L/G	*L*		°L				
Our Father +	G	G	G	G	(G)[192]	(G)[193]	G	G
Words of Institution (Verba) +	G	G	G	G	(G)	(G)	G	G
Elevation		×						
Agnus Dei	*G/L*	*G*	*G*	*L/G*				.G
Psalms(s) or hymn(s) during communion	G	G	G	G	G		G	G
Thanksgiving collect +	G	G	G	G	(G)	(G)	G	G
Benediction +	G	G	G	G	(G)	G	G	G
Psalm or hymn	*G*			°G				

	Bischofswerda [ca. 1620]	Magdeburg 1621	Saxe-Coburg 1626 (city)	East Frisia 1631	Magdeburg, Halberstadt 1632	Nuremberg 1639 (city)	Nuremberg 1639 (village)	Osnabrück 1652
TYPE:	MC	PC	PT[194]	PT	PT	PC	PC	PC
LOCATION:	C	N	C	NW	N	S	S	NW
TOTAL EDITIONS:	1	5	2	2	1	1	1	1
Confiteor or other preparatory prayers +								
Latin Introit or German psalm	G/L	(L)[195]	°L/(G?)[196]	L/G	L/G	(G)	(G)	
Kyrie	(L?)	(L)	°L/(G?)	G	L			(L?)
Gloria and Et in terra	G/L	°L/°G	°L/G	G°	L/G			G
Collect de tempore +		G	G	G	G	(G)	G	G
Epistle +	(G)	(G)	G	(G)	G	(G)	(G)	(G)
Gradual, Alleluia or psalm	(L?)/G	G	G°		G	(L?)/G	(G)	G
Sequence				G				
Gospel +		(G)	G		G	(G)		
Credo and Patrem	G	°L/°G	G	G	L-G	L/G	G	(G?)
Psalm or hymn								
Sermon with prayers and other annexes +	(G)	(G)	(G)	(G)	(G)	(G)[197]	(G)[198]	(G)
Psalm or hymn	(L?)/G	(G)		G[199]				G
Exhortation to the communicants +		G	G		G	(G)	(G)	G
Preface +		L-G[200]			G			L
Sanctus		L/G			G			(L)
Our Father +	201	G	G		G[202]	G	G	G
Words of Institution (Verba) +		G	G		G	G	G	G
Elevation								
Agnus Dei			Ḻ		Ğ°			
Psalms(s) or hymn(s) during communion	L/G	G	G		G°	G	G	
Thanksgiving collect +		G	G		G	G	G	G
Benediction +	G	G	G		G	G	G	G
Psalm or hymn	G	G				G	G	

	Braunschweig-Wolfenbüttel 1657 (city)	Braunschweig-Wolfenbüttel 1657 (village)	Württemberg 1657	Hanau 1659	Magdeburg 1663	Nuremberg 1664	Saxe-Weimar 1664	Magdeburg 1667
TYPE:	PT	PT	PT	PT	PC[203]	PC	PT	PC
LOCATION:	N	N	S	C	N	S	C	N
TOTAL EDITIONS:	1	1	2	1	3	1	1	1
Confiteor or other preparatory prayers +								
Latin Introit or German psalm		˙G	G	G	L/G	(L)	G	(L)
Kyrie	˙G	G			L	(L)	(G)	(L)
Gloria and Et in terra	G˙	G˙			L/G	L	G	˙L-G˙
Collect de tempore +	G	G			G	(G)	(G)	G
Epistle +	(G)	(G)			G	(G)	(G)	L-G
Gradual, Alleluia or psalm	G	G			G	L/G˙	G	L-G
Sequence	G˙					*L*	G	
Gospel +	(G)	(G)			G	(G)	(G)	L-G
Credo and Patrem	G	G˙			L-G	L/G	G	G˙
Psalm or hymn					*G*	G		*G*
Sermon with prayers and other annexes +	(G)	(G)	(G)	(G)	(G)	(G)[204]	(G)	(G)
Psalm or hymn	G˙	˙G[205]	G[206]	G			G	G
Exhortation to the communicants +	G[207]	G	G	G	*G*	G	G	*G*
Preface +	G	G			*G*			*L*
Sanctus	G	G			*G*	L		*L-G*
Our Father +	G	G	G[208]		*G*[209]	G	G	G
Words of Institution (Verba) +	G	G	G	G	G	G	G	G
Elevation	×							
Agnus Dei	G˙	G			G˙	˙L[210]		
Psalms(s) or hymn(s) during communion	G	G	G		G˙	G˙	G	˙G
Thanksgiving collect +	G[211]	G[212]	G	G	G	(G?)	G	G
Benediction +	G	G	G	G	G	(G?)	G	G
Psalm or hymn	G	G						G˙

	Schwarzburg 1675	Nördlingen 1676	Saxony (E) 1685	Leipzig 1694	Altenburg 1705 (city)	Altenburg 1705 (village)	Braunschweig-Wolfenbüttel 1709	Leipzig 1710
TYPE:	PT	PC	PT	PC	PT	PT	PT	PC
LOCATION:	C	S	C	C	C	C	N	C
TOTAL EDITIONS:	1	1	1	1	1	1	2	1
Confiteor or other preparatory prayers +								
Latin Introit or German psalm	G	G•[213]	G	L[214]				L[215]
Kyrie	G		•L/•G	L/G	•(L?)	(G)	G	G/L
Gloria and Et in terra	L/G		•G	•L/G	G	(G)	G•	•G/L
Collect de tempore +	(G)	G	(G)	L/G	(G)	(G)	G	L
Epistle +	(G)	G	(G)	(G)	(G)	(G)	G	(G)
Gradual, Alleluia or psalm	G	G	G	G	(G)	*(G)*	G	G
Sequence	G		*G*[216]					
Gospel +	(G)	[217]	(G)[218]	(G)	(G)	*(G)*		(G)
Credo and Patrem	L-*G*	G•	G[219]	*L*-G[220]	G[221]	G	G	G
Psalm or hymn		G		G	G		*G*	G
Sermon with prayers and other annexes +	(G)	(G)	(G)	(G)	(G)	(G)	(G)	(G)
Psalm or hymn		G	*G*	G	G	(G)	G	G
Exhortation to the communicants +	G	G[222]		*G*	G	G		
Preface +				*L*			G	
Sanctus							G•[223]	
Our Father +	G	G	[G]	G	G	G	G	G
Words of Institution (Verba) +	G	G	[G][224]	G	G	G	G	G
Elevation								
Agnus Dei								
Psalms(s) or hymn(s) during communion			G	G[225]	✓[226]		(G)[227]	G[228]
Thanksgiving collect +	G	G	G	G	G	G	G	G
Benediction +	G	G	G	G	G	G	G	G
Psalm or hymn			G		G	G	G	G

	Henneberg 1713	London 1718	Holstein-Plön 1732	Ulm 1747
TYPE:	PT	PC	PT	PC
LOCATION:	C	NW	N	S
TOTAL EDITIONS:	1	1	1	1
Confiteor or other preparatory prayers +				
Latin Introit or German psalm	G°	G[229]	G	G
Kyrie				
Gloria and Et in terra			G	
Collect de tempore +			G	
Epistle +	(G)	(G)	G	(G)[230]
Gradual, Alleluia or psalm		G	G	G
Sequence				
Gospel +				
Credo and Patrem	G°		G°[231]	
Psalm or hymn			G°	
Sermon with prayers and other annexes +	(G)	(G)	(G)	(G)
Psalm or hymn	°G[232]	G		G°[233]
Exhortation to the communicants +	G			G
Preface +				
Sanctus				
Our Father +	G	G[234]	G[235]	
Words of Institution (Verba) +	G	G	G	G
Elevation				
Agnus Dei				G°[236]
Psalms(s) or hymn(s) during communion	G	G		G
Thanksgiving collect +	G	G	G	G
Benediction +	G	G	G	G
Psalm or hymn		G	G	

Notes

1. A confession and absolution are done with the people.
2. Preceded by a psalm and corporate confession.
3. The text of a "Latin" Kyrie is actually in Greek.
4. The Gloria and Et in terra are typically omitted during Lent (and sometimes Advent) even where this is not indicated.
5. The Alleluia is sung "with the melody rhymed according to the German psalm."
6. On high feasts and sometimes during their seasons, the Sequence is typically performed with a German version sung by the congregation placed between phrases of the Latin sung by the choir.
7. In some orders the Gospel is omitted because it is read from the pulpit before the sermon.
8. The pulpit service is rarely given in full in the sources, as it was done similarly all over Germany and was therefore well known. An outline is given in chapter 2.
9. The sermon follows the communion.
10. The Sanctus is indicated only when it is sung after the Preface or the Verba. When the German Sanctus is sung during the communion distribution, it is counted under "psalm(s) or hymn(s) during communion."
11. The Our Father is never omitted, but occasionally it may appear only as a paraphrase within the exhortation to communicants.
12. The Elevation may be omitted if the people have been instructed as to its true meaning.
13. After the communion and before the collect the priest speaks the Nunc dimittis in German.
14. Followed by the Benedicamus Domino and three verses of *Es woll uns Gott genädig sein.*
15. Preceded by the Benedicamus Domino.
16. Preceded by the Benedicamus Domino.
17. The Nunc dimittis is sung.
18. Preceded by the singing of *Alma redemptoris mater.*
19. In villages where Latin is not possible the people may sing a German Christian hymn to begin the mass. Where the Introit, etc., is already sung in German it may remain.
20. Followed by a prayer for grace and the Holy Spirit and a brief hymn.
21. Inasmuch as the Kyrie is sung three times, it would be good to sing it once in each of Greek, Latin, and German (presumbably the Greek and Latin would be the same!).
22. The common prayer for the needs of all Christendom and the emperor is said here.
23. If there are no scholars the Alleluia is not done.
24. Sung to the rhymed German version so that one may sing along.
25. "A lesson" is read here, not necessarily the Gospel.
26. The people and choir alternate verses on the Nicene Creed while the communicants assemble in the chancel.
27. The Preface and Sanctus may remain even if there are no scholars, for "one enjoys singing such a thing" ("me wolde denne susse gerne singen").
28. A silent Our Father is done at the end of the exhortation.
29. A German hymn is sung in places where there are insufficient resources for performing in Latin.
30. A confession and comfortable words ("Trostspruch") are done with the people.
31. The choir sings the Introit while the priest reads the Confiteor. Then the Introit *Aus tiefer Not* or another psalm is sung. At times the choir or people sing the antiphon *Veni sancte spiritus/Komm, heiliger Geist* in place of the Introit.
32. Sung if there is no choir to sing an introit.
33. Preceded by the Benedictus.
34. Preceded by the choir singing *Veni sancte spiritus* on high feasts or *Komm, heiliger Geist* on other days.
35. The Et in terra may be omitted in winter.
36. Sermon held on Fridays.
37. The people and choir alternate verses on the Nicene Creed while the communicants assemble in the chancel.
38. A German hymn is sung in place of the Offertory.
39. Sung immediately following the exhortation to communicants. Followed by the Pax Domini in Latin or German.

40. Sung in Latin during the communion distribution and in German when the communion is done.

41. Preceded by the Benedicamus Domino in Latin.

42. The printed order for 1537 is supplemented by a manuscript order of the same year that gives additional details concerning the service.

43. The German Benedictus is sung, then a Latin Introit may be sung where there are good scholars.

44. Preceded by a corporate confession and absolution.

45. Either the mass order ends here, or Richter does not reprint those portions dealing with communion.

46. Followed by a corporate confession and absolution.

47. Followed by a corporate confession and absolution and a Collect. In 1545 the absolution is replaced with the comfortable words.

48. The direction given is simply that the priest "holds the Lord's Supper in German," which presumably includes at least the Our Father and the Verba.

49. This order was slightly revised in 1572, but the differences are not significant and so are not reported here.

50. Preceded by the sermon and the singing of the Litany.

51. Apparently a German translation of the Latin introit is sung. In villages, the order should be kept as closely as possible, but a (German) psalm may be sung in place of the Introit, the Et in terra, the Alleluia and the Sequence.

52. In villages: first a Latin Introit or German psalm, then Kyrie, *Allein Gott* (both of which may be omitted), Collect, Epistle, German psalm, Gospel, sermon, exhortation to communicants, Our Father, Verba, (communion), collect, benediction.

53. The directions are for the schoolmaster to sing the Introit, Kyrie, etc.; but there is no question that what is meant is that the schoolmaster with the boys in the choir should sing.

54. The choir sings the Latin Gloria, then the congregation sings the German *Allein Gott in der Höh sei Ehr.* If this is too long, either the Latin or the German may be omitted, or the entire Gloria may be omitted if desired.

55. In villages where no one understands Latin the Epistle and Gospel are read only in German.

56. A German song is sung by the people, followed by a Latin Alleluia and Sequence or Tract.

57. The sequence or a German psalm is sung.

58. Either a Latin Sequence or a German psalm or other song is sung.

59. In certain seasons a German psalm is sung in place of the Sequence.

60. An offertory or a German psalm is sung.

61. The exhortation, which includes a paraphrase of the Our Father, may occasionally be replaced with a Latin preface, Latin Sanctus and German Our Father, with the Latin Agnus Dei sung during the communion.

62. Follows the Agnus Dei and a prayer in Latin. The Agnus Dei precedes the other songs during communion.

63. Follwed by a corporate confession and absolution.

64. Sung after the responsory or German song.

65. Followed by the Pax Domini in German.

66. Preceded by the German Benedictus sung by the people.

67. The sequence of events is: the people sing a German psalm, the pastor reads a lesson on Holy Communion, an exhortation and corporate confession are done, and where there are clerics and scholars they sing an Introit in Latin. Where there are no clerics, everything is sung and read in German, and the singing is shortened so as to be most edifying to the people.

68. The pastor should see to it that the people learn to sing the Kyrie and Gloria in German as well.

69. The German Gloria sung by the congregation is placed within the Latin Gloria sung by the choir.

70. The exhortation to prayer for all sorts and conditions is read in place of the Epistle, followed by a section of the catechism.

71. In small villages two or three scholars sing the Litany in German after the Epistle, and the rest of the choir and people answer; followed by the Da pacem with the Collect. In 1545 the direction is that the priest may read whatever is most serviceable to his office, or the scholars may sing an Alleluia and Gradual or a German psalm.

72. Sung during the communion.

73. The Latin of the choir alternates with the German of the congregation.
74. Sung in alternation.
75. The mass presumably concludes with the Collect and benediction, as in the village order for the same year.
76. The Introit, Kyrie and Gloria are sung by the choir. Where there is no choir, the priest may sing or speak them or the congregation may sing a German hymn.
77. Preceded by the singing of the *Veni, sancte* by the schoolmaster and the boys and the singing of a German collect for the Holy Spirit by the priest.
78. Followed by a brief hymn.
79. Lacking in the order but presumed to have been present.
80. The congregation sings the German Creed or another hymn at the beginning of the sermon.
81. The sermon follows the communion. The German creed is sung by the congregation immediately before the sermon.
82. The sermon follows the communion.
83. Another psalm is sung, or the choir sings the German Litany.
84. Before the Verba a brief eucharistic prayer is read, and the Verba precede the Sanctus and Our Father.
85. Followed by the Pax Domini in German.
86. The choir sings the Latin Communion and perhaps a responsory; where there is no choir the people sing a German hymn.
87. Two Collects are done, the second in Latin.
88. Preceded by the Benedicamus Domino in Latin.
89. This is an Interim order and so cannot be taken as representative of the Lutheran position. German is to be used only where the choir cannot sing in Latin.
90. During the Confiteor the choir sings the Veni Sancte is Latin, after which the priest sings a versicle and Collect in Latin or German.
91. Sung by the choir and people in alternation; followed by a corporate confession and absolution.
92. Preceded by a corporate confession and absolution.
93. Sung by the choir and people in alternation.
94. The choir or clerk sings the Kyrie to the people so that they might learn it, or the choir sings it in Latin.
95. Sung by the "two choirs" in alternation. It is unclear whether this refers to the two halves of the choir or to the choir and the people.
96. For all preceding the Epistle the reader is referred to the "agenda"; according to Sehling (1:101), no such agenda has been found.
97. The Epistle and Gospel are sung in Latin on high feasts.
98. Sung by the "two choirs" in alternation. It is unclear whether this refers to the two halves of the choir or to the choir and the people.
99. The German Litany is occasionally sung in place of the Sequence.
100. The Gospel is read in German immediately before the sermon.
101. In villages the sermon is held after the Creed.
102. The Offertory, a Latin responsory, or a German psalm or hymn is sung.
103. Preceded by a corporate confession and absolution.
104. Preceded by a corporate confession and absolution.
105. The choir sings an Alleluia, Gradual, Sequence, or German psalm.
106. A sequence or other spiritual song is sung.
107. Followed by a Collect.
108. Sung by the entire church.
109. Options for singing during the communion include the Latin or German Sanctus and the Agnus Dei.
110. Where there are schools a German or Latin Introit, Kyrie, and Et in terra are sung, then the Collect, the Epistle, and further as above.
111. Followed by a corporate confession and absolution.
112. In the 1557 revision, on festivals the choir sings the hymn *de festis* instead of the Creed.
113. Mentioned in 1640 but not in 1557.

114. Followed by a Collect.

115. The instruction to sing the Preface if time permits, especially on festivals, is present in 1555 but lacking in 1557.

116. Sung by the entire church.

117. In 1557, German hymns are sung by either the choir or the congregation; in 1640 they are sung by the choir and congregation together.

118. The Rothenburg orders are copied almost exactly from Veit Dietrich's order for Nuremberg (1543, 1545).

119. Preceded by a corporate confession and absolution.

120. Preceded by a corporate confession and absolution.

121. The exhortation to prayer for all sorts and conditions is read in place of the Epistle, followed by a section of the catechism.

122. In small villages two or three scholars sing the Litany in German after the Epistle, and the rest of the choir and people answer; followed by the Da pacem with the Collect. In 1545 the direction is that the priest may read whatever is most serviceable to his office, or the scholars may sing an Alleluia and Gradual or a German psalm.

123. A Sequence or other spiritual song is sung.

124. No instructions are given for communion, although it is noted that only very rarely are there no communicants.

125. Preceded by the Benedicamus Domino.

126. Preceded by a German psalm or hymn and a corporate confession and absolution.

127. Preceded by a corporate confession and absolution.

128. Preceded by a corporate confession and absolution.

129. Preceded by a corporate confession and absolution.

130. Several psalms are sung (in villages one or two psalms), followed by a corporate confession and absolution.

131. Either a Sequence or an Alleluia is sung in German, followed by "O allmächtiger Gott" or another Collect, then the confession *Nimm von uns, Herr* is sung, then the tract *Domine non secundum peccata nostra.*

132. Sung by either the priest or the congregation.

133. The only direction given for any part of the service preceding the sermon is that "the congregation may sing hymns with the clerk before the sermon. Before the sermon *Wir glauben all* is sung.

134. The children sit in the chancel, and the pastor exhorts them to sing along on the psalms.

135. Because the sermon is so long it is frequently shortened by omitting the Et in terra, the Patrem and the Sanctus, and the shortest hymns are chosen.

136. Followed by the singing of the Litany.

137. Either the sequence, *Erhalt uns, Herr* or something else in German is sung.

138. A Sequence, motet, or German hymn is sung, or it is omitted if time is limited.

139. Followed by *Nun bitten wir den heiligen Geist.*

140. The service directions end here, but it may be presumed that the mass is concluded as in the cities.

141. The Latin Sanctus may also be sung.

142. The Sanctus and Agnus Dei are included among the songs that may be sung during the communion.

143. On high feasts a hymn *de festo* is sung before the Introit.

144. Followed by a corporate confession, declaration of grace ("Trostspruch") and absolution.

145. A prayer and the catechism are read in place of the Epistle.

146. The sequence pro tempore is sung with an Alleluia, or on ordinary Sundays a psalm, or occasionally the Litany (long or short form).

147. A Sequence or Alleluia is sung by the choir, or a German psalm from Luther's hymnal by the congregation.

148. Before the Sequence the Latin or German Da pacem domine may occasionally be sung.

149. Before the Creed the clerk reads to the people a section of the catechism with (Luther's) explanation. Another German hymn may be sung in place of the Creed.

150. The exhortation should not be readily omitted, but rather the preceding hymn should be shortened or omitted if time is short.

151. Followed by a corporate confession and absolution. This instruction is given only in the (separate) order for communion, which is held six times per year; it is not clear whether this confession replaces the one earlier in the service or whether two confessions are held.

152. The Latin Agnus Dei is included among the songs that may be sung during the communion.

153. Preceded by *Gelobet sei der Herr Gott Israel* with its antiphon.

154. Preceded by *Komm, heiliger Geist* sung by the choir.

155. The choir sings *Veni sancte spiritus* or (in places without schools) *Komm, heiliger Geist* before the Introit.

156. The instruction here and throughout the order is for the "cantor" to sing, presumably with choir or congregation.

157. The order notes that the entire liturgy is not given but only those portions needing commentary. Presumably there was an Introit, Kyrie, Gradual, etc., even though they are not mentioned.

158. The Sequence or a German psalm is sung.

159. A Sequence, Alleluia or German psalm is sung.

160. Sung after the sermon, during (!) which the minister goes to the altar and reads the exhortation to the communicants.

161. On festivals the choir sings the hymn *de festo* instead of the Creed.

162. Preceded by the singing of the *Da pacem* in German, Polish, or Latin.

163. The reader is referred to Veit Dietrich's order (Nürnberg 1543, 1545) for the communion liturgy.

164. The order simply says that the communion is done, then the blessing and a hymn of praise. We may assume that the communion included at least the Our Father and Verba and probably the Thanksgiving Collect.

165. During the distribution the choir sings psalms or the congregation sings *Jesus Christus, unser Heiland*; *Gott sei gelobet*; and the like.

166. Followed by an exhortation to prayer and a corporate confession and absolution.

167. The Introit, which is sung by the pastor, is preceded by *Herr Gott, wir loben dich* played on the organ, or sung if there is no organ.

168. In villages a German or Bohemian psalm or hymn may be sung in place of the (Introit and?) Kyrie.

169. German hymns are sung by the entire congregation before the Epistle and Gospel, and the cantor is to post the hymn numbers on a board so that the people can sing along from Luther's hymnal

170. The organist plays a motet and the choir sings.

171. The choir sings a Latin sequence or *Nimm von uns, Herr Gott;* then if desired the people may sing a German psalm.

172. Preceded by an exhortation to confession and a form of prayer.

173. The first stanza is played by the organ, the second is sung by the choir, and the third is sung by the congregation.

174. The cantor sings *Verleih uns Frieden* or another verse.

175. Most of the communion order is omitted, but it probably included (in addition to the Sanctus and Agnus Dei) the Our Father, the Verba, the Thanksgiving Collect and the benediction.

176. In German or Bohemian.

177. German hymns are sung by the choir and congregation, alternating verses; if there are many communicants a figural piece may be sung.

178. In German or Bohemian.

179. The pastor sings a German psalm or Latin song with the clerk.

180. Followed by a versicle, corporate confession and absolution and another hymn.

181. In 1708 only German hymns are to be used.

182. Following the Kyrie the organist alternates with the choir and congregation in the Te Deum; this is followed by a psalm or hymn selected by the preacher.

183. The exhortation to the communicants is to be read the previous day.

184. Followed by a Collect.

185. The order directs that the mass proceed further as directed (where?).

186. German hymns are sung except when there is figural music.

187. Preceded by the choir singing *Veni sancte spiritus* and the Collect of the Holy Spirit.

188. A Sequence or Alleluia is sung, or a German psalm related to the Gospel.

189. A chapter from the Old Testament is read, or on high feasts the lesson *de festo*. Then two school-boys recite the six chief parts of the catechism. Confession and absolution follow before the Creed.

190. Either the Creed or *Nun bitten wir* is sung.

191. To begin the service there is figural music and chant ("Figural und Choral Gesang") related to the Gospel; then an exhortation, corporate confession, absolution, and prayer; then a part of the catechism is read; then there is another "Figural und Choral Gesang"; then the preacher reads the Gospel and preaches the sermon.

192. The order for communion is not specified, but it may be presumed to include at least the Our Father and the Verba, ending with a collect and benediction.

193. The order for communion is not specified, but it may be presumed to include at least the Our Father and the Verba, ending with a collect and benediction.

194. There is no corresponding mass order for villages.

195. Preceded by the *Veni sancte spiritus*.

196. The Introit is preceded by *Veni sancte spiritus* or *Komm heiliger Geist* sung by the choir.

197. The sermon follows the communion.

198. The sermon follows the communion.

199. The order of service ends here, but there are directions elsewhere to sing the Our Father and the Verba to the usual melody.

200. Either the full Latin preface may be used, or a half-Latin, half-German preface.

201. The communion order is incomplete, but it would certainly have included at least the Our Father and the Verba.

202. Either the Our Father is sung or the exhortation with the paraphrase of the Our Father is read, whichever is customary.

203. This order is a reprint of Magdeburg, Halberstadt 1632.

204. The sermon precedes the service.

205. The clerk sings a psalm.

206. The German Creed or another hymn is sung.

207. A prayer replaces the exhortation.

208. Sung by the congregation.

209. Either the Our Father is sung or the exhortation with the paraphrase of the Our Father is read, whichever is customary.

210. The Agnus Dei is sung at St. Lorenz but not at St. Sebald.

211. Following the communion and before the Thanksgiving the priest reads Psalm 23 to the congregation.

212. Following the communion and before the Thanksgiving the priest reads Psalm 23 to the congregation.

213. Followed by a corporate confession and absolution.

214. Preceded by an organ prelude and a motet, or in Lent by the Benedictus or Nunc dimittis and Vivo ergo. This order and the 1710 order are, strictly speaking, not church orders but rather devotional books intended to be read by the people during the service; the service directions serve as a commentary on the liturgy.

215. Preceded by an organ prelude and a motet.

216. On festivals figural music replaces the hymn.

217. The Gospel is replaced by a reading from Luther's catechism.

218. The direction is for "a chapter from the Bible with the summary" [of Veit Dietrich] to be read.

219. After the Creed a German hymn is sung, or figural music is performed on festivals, where possible.

220. The Credo is always intoned, but the Patrem is sung only during Advent and Lent when there is no instrumental music; in other seasons a piece of concerted music is performed. The German Creed is sung after the music.

221. After the Creed *Herr Jesu Christ, dich zu uns wend* is sung.

222. Followed by a Collect.

223. A Collect follows.

224. The liturgy immediately preceding the communion is not given, but it may be assumed to include at least the Our Father and the Verba.

225. Music or a motet precedes the German hymns.

226. Either figural music is performed or there is *choraliter* singing.
227. After the communion the priest or congregation reads Psalm 23.
228. Preceded by a Latin motet.
229. Preceded by the reading of one or two chapters from the Old Testament.
230. Followed by a corporate confession and a sentence from Scripture (replacing the absolution).
231. *Herr Jesu Christ, dich zu uns wend* or *Liebster Jesu, wir sind hier* is sung after the Creed.
232. *Verleih uns Frieden* or something similiar is sung by the cantor.
233. The Creed is sung here.
234. The exact order for communion is not given, but it may be presumed to include at least the Our Father and the Verba.
235. The liturgy preceding the communion is not given, but it would have included at least the Our Father and the Verba.
236. Sung as a dismissal hymn on days when communion is held.

NOTES

❖

Here, if a citation is to a source that has been reprinted or translated, the dates of both the original edition and the reprint or translation are given, separated by a slash; for example:

> Gerber 1706/1725 (the citation is to the 1725 edition of a book
> originally published in 1706);
> Blume 1965/1974 (the citation is to the 1974 English translation of a
> book originally published in German in 1965).

❖

Preface

1. For my purposes, the most useful histories of the musical life of individual cities have been Rauschning 1931 (Danzig), Stahl 1952 (Lübeck), Schmidt 1961 (Dresden), Daebeler 1966 (Rostock), Moser 1967 (Quedlinburg), Butler 1970 (Nuremberg), Stiller 1970/1984 (Leipzig), Greve 1985 (Braunschweig), Brandhorst 1991 (Minden), and Brown 2001 (Joachimsthal). Recent socioreligious histories of the Reformation that have provided context for my work include Brecht 1967, Strauss 1978, Karant-Nunn 1979, Nischan 1994, Tolley 1995, Dixon 1996, Lindberg 1996, Karant-Nunn 1997, Nischan 1999, and Strom 1999. Musicological studies, of which there are a great many, include Rietschel 1893, Diehl 1899, Rautenstrauch 1907, Schrems 1930, Werner 1932, Boës 1959–61, Krickeberg 1965, Niemöller 1969, and Irwin 1993, to name just a few of the most relevant.

❖

Chapter 1

1. *Vom Mißbrauch der Messe: WA* 8:482–563; *LW* 36:127–230.
2. Karlstadt's order is reprinted in Richter 2:484–85 and Sehling 1:697–98. In addition to the changes in the mass and the abolition of images, it also provides that any beg-

gars in the city are to be either required to work or banished and that foreign scholars are not allowed in the city unless they provide for their own support.

3. *WA* 10:3:1–13; *LW* 51:70–75

4. *Von Ordnung Gottesdiensts in der Gemeine.* Wittenberg, 1523. Reprinted in *WA* 12:35–37; *LW* 53:11–14; Richter 1:1–2; and Sehling 1:2–3.

5. Leaver 1990:145.

6. The "explanation" of the lesson, actually a sermon, would have been in German, as Luther was to state explicitly in the *Formula missae* of 1523.

7. Luther wrote in a letter of March 26, 1525, to his friend Nicolaus Hausmann: "It does not altogether please me to have Latin notes set above German words. I said to this bookseller, "What kind of singing in German is this, that I would want it to be introduced here?" (*WA Br* 3:462). In *Against the Heavenly Prophets* (1525), he wrote: "I would gladly have a German mass today. I am also occupied with it. But I would very much like it to have a true German character. For to translate the Latin text and retain the Latin tone or notes has my sanction, though it doesn't sound polished or well done. Both the text and notes, accent, melody, and manner of rendering ought to grow out of the true mother tongue and its inflection, otherwise all of it becomes an imitation in the manner of the apes" (*LW* 40:141). Luther's colleague, Wittenberg pastor Johann Bugenhagen, wrote similarly in the 1543 church order for Braunschweig-Wolfenbüttel: "And again one finds a number of preachers and schoolmasters who have no talent in music (which is not the fault of the schoolmasters when they have no good musicians available to sing) and who have no understanding of what sounds good or bad. These same people allow themselves to think it is a wonderful thing to sing all the fine Latin songs [*i.e.,* chants] in German with the Latin melodies, thus producing a caricature of song—whenever they sing a German Preface (which is not at all necessary) with the *Dominus vobiscum, sursum corda,* etc., in German. This may well work with some songs, such as when we sing the German Magnificat to the *tonus peregrinus,* with which the entire church can sing along. But mostly it sounds bad, for such incapable songleaders carry over the Latin word for word into German, setting it to the long Latin notes, creating a long, dreadful *ha, ha, ha, he, he, he,* etc.: it is disagreeable to listen to such howling. When schoolchildren and apprentices flock to books and no one can tell what they are singing, how then should the people sing along?" (Sehling 6:1:60).

8. Wittenberg (Luther) 1523a. Reprinted in *WA* 12:205–20; *LW* 53:19–40; Richter 1:2–7; and Sehling 1:4–9.

9. Luther sometimes used the Latin term "episcopus" (bishop) to refer to the pastor. The German translation of Speratus (see next note) reads "Bischofs oder Pfarrers" here and "Pastor" in the next sentence.

10. *WA* 12:218. My translation is informed by the 1523 translation into German by Luther's associate Paul Speratus (Luther 1740–53/1880–1910, vol. 10, col. 2252), which clarifies some terms; for another translation, see *LW* 53:36–37.

11. *WA Br* 3:220. Luther's example was evidently enclosed with the letter.

12. *LW* 53:316; original in *WA* 35:475.

13. Wittenberg (Luther) 1526. Reprinted in *WA* 19:72–113; *LW* 53:61–90; Richter 1:35–40; and Sehling 1:10–16.

14. *LW* 53:61; *WA* 19:72.

15. *WA* 19:72.

16. See appendix 1 for locations of German hymns in modern German and English sources.

17. Summarized from *WA* 19:80–102; an English version is at *LW* 53:69–84.

18. Brecht 1986/1990:256.

19. The dates of publication and introduction of the mass come from evidence in

Luther's sermons and correspondence; see *WA* 17:1:459 and 19:50–51. The date on all extant copies is 1526.

20. *WA* 19:50–51.

21. Wittenberg 1533.

22. "Deutsch sollen die schüler nicht singen, on allein, wenn das volk mitsinget" (Sehling 1:703).

23. One other liturgical order contained a similar instruction: the 1535 order for Pomerania directed that "Latin is used when the congregation is present but does not sing along; German otherwise" (Sehling 4:340). This order was one of several prepared by Pomeranian native Johann Bugenhagen, pastor of the city church in Wittenberg, professor of theology and Luther's father confessor. As with the Wittenberg order, the whole congregation was explicitly directed to sing only a couple of the parts of the mass, in this case the Gradual hymn and a hymn during communion. But, unlike Wittenberg, the options were structured so that the entire mass could be sung in German if desired.

24. *WA* 19:74; *LW* 53:62–63.

25. *LW* 34:59; *WA* 30:2:352. *De tempore* means "related to the time"—that is, related to a specific day or season of the church year.

26. *WA Br* 4:411–12.

27. See the background to the *German Mass* in *WA* 19:44ff.

28. *Corpus reformatorum* 1:991.

29. Herbst 1968:73.

30. Boës 1958–61, vol. 4, p. 35.

31. Luther did, of course, offer the option of singing another German hymn, which would have been much easier for the people to manage. His main reason for printing the psalm here was undoubtedly because the idea of singing a prose psalm in German was new, and he wanted to demonstrate how it could be done. It also gave him the chance to present an entire psalm as Introit, as he had suggested in the *Formula missae*.

Friedrich Blume makes an interesting suggestion: namely, that the priest may have performed the Introit in Luther's *German Mass* alone (Blume 1965/1974:60). This is, however, highly unlikely, for not a single Lutheran liturgical order from the sixteenth century gave this as a preferred option. Rather, the Introit was always assigned either to the choir or to the people (in the form of a metrical psalm), or occasionally to the schoolmaster or parish clerk if there was no choir and the people were not able to sing. Only a very few orders even mentioned the possibility of the pastor performing the Introit, and then only in exceptional circumstances, such as when there was no choir or clerk and the people could not sing at all (as in Brandenburg-Nuremberg 1528 [Sehling 11:137] and 1533 [original, f. M1ᵃ] and in Palatinate-Neuburg 1543 [Sehling 13:70]) or when the mass was held in a hospital chapel (as in Nuremberg 1525a [Sehling 11:52]). The only other case is the 1542 church order for Pomerania (Sehling 4:368), in which pastors in villages without choirs are given the option of singing a Latin Introit on high feasts.

32. Jenny 1985:89.

33. Routley [n.d.], tape 2.

34. A syllabic version of this Creed more amenable to congregational singing was published in Zwickau in 1525. Although it seems likely that Luther had the locally published version in mind when he wrote the *German Mass,* it is at least possible that the Zwickau version originated with Luther as a reworking of the medieval model. Markus Jenny, editor of the standard edition of Luther's hymns, points out that Luther had previously transformed three other melismatic medieval hymn melodies into syllabic forms (*Nun komm, der Heiden Heiland, Christum wir sollen loben schon,* and *Komm, Gott Schöpfer, Heiliger Geist*), and there is no reason to suppose that he would not have done so with the Creed. Jenny also cites the

use of bar form (repeating the first section of the hymn) in the Zwickau version and the placement of the caesura after the words "hut und wacht" as being characteristic of Luther's hymn editing style (Jenny 1985:90–95). But, as Jenny remarks, there is no external evidence for any of this, and we cannot be certain whether Luther himself edited the melody of either version.

35. Herbst 1968:72–73.

36. Herbst 1968:73. See chapter 3 for details on attendance, tardiness, and leaving early at services.

37. Herbst 1968:72.

38. "Auff die Epistel singet man eyn deudsch lied: 'Nu bitten wyr den heyligen geyst', odder sonst eyns, und das mit dem gantzen Chor" (*WA* 19:90).

39. Quoted in Jenny 1960:134–35.

40. In Dresden, figural masses were held once a month beginning in 1577 (Held 1894:12). In Hamburg and Lübeck, there was figural music during the sixteenth century only on high feasts (Edler 1982:149). In Frankfurt, the boys in the Latin school sang figural music for the first time in 1573 (Krickeberg 1965:160). In Breslau, regular figural music began earlier, in 1540 (Niemöller 1969:7).

41. The singing of the Creed by the people was to become the norm in Lutheran churches, probably because of its didactic value and its nature as a confessional statement, both of which were important in Luther's thought.

42. *WA* 20:546. The "five yoke of oxen" are a reference to Luke 14:19, where those invited to a feast make one excuse after another, including one who declines the invitation because "I have bought five yoke of oxen, and I am going to examine them." The reference to St. Paul is given above the original text as Ephesians 5 [verses 18–19]: ". . . be filled with the Spirit, speaking to one another in psalms and hymns and spiritual songs, singing and making melody in your heart to the Lord."

43. Boes 1958/59:14, citing *Corpus reformatorum* 1:719.

44. *WA* 29:44.

45. The people were also instructed to sing the Amens after the Lord's Prayer and final benediction at mass, but these would have been very simple.

46. Sehling 1:703–5.

47. *Unterricht der Visitatoren an die Pfarrherrn im Kurfürstenthum zu Sachsen*. Wittenberg, 1528. Reprinted in *WA* 26:195–240; Richter 1:77–101; Sehling 1:149–74.

48. Sehling 1:168–69.

49. Braunschweig 1528 (see the bibliography, part 1).

50. Albertine Saxony 1539.

51. Buszin [1940]: [1, 10, 13, 15]. Buszin also states that these churches err when they hold to a hierarchical form of church polity, for the doctrine of the universal priesthood demands that the church be a democratic institution, as is the Lutheran Church. A corollary to this is that Lutherans do not demand liturgical uniformity; rather, each congregation is free to makes its own choices in the matter (Buszin [1940]: [18–19, 25]. In a November 2003 conversation, Buszin's daughter, Connie Seddon, informed me that later in life her father moderated the fairly rigid stance he took in this early publication.

52. Buszin [1940]: [1–2].

53. The information in this and the following paragraph is from Winger 1992:131–72.

54. He had previously mentioned it in a letter to Spalatin dated December 18, 1519 (see *WA Br* 1:595).

55. *LW* 13:295, 332 (*WA* 41:210). It should be noted that Luther did not publish this sermon, but it was rather copied down as he delivered it by one of his colleagues, who later saw to its publication.

56. *LW* 51:333 (*WA* 49:588).

57. *WA* 30:2:614–15; *LW* 38:122–23.

58. The clue that Luther refers here specifically to the Latin liturgy and not to its German paraphrase is the use of the Latin term "Patrem" for the Creed rather than the German "Glaube."

59. *WA* 49:598–99; *LW* 51:342–43.

60. *LW* 53:316 (*WA* 35:475).

61. The citation is to Edward W. Broome, *The Rev. Rowland Hill, Preacher and Wit* (London, 1881), p. 93. Broome, in reporting the practice at Surrey Chapel of singing a text by Hill beginning "When Jesus first at heaven's command descended from his azure throne" to the tune of "Rule, Britannia," stated: "The singing of these words to the popular air of "Rule, Britannia," by the whole congregation, which was a regular custom at Surrey Chapel some years after Mr. Hill's death, had a grand effect. Mr. Hill once said he did not see any reason why the devil should have all the good tunes; hence some of them were frequently sung in his chapel." Broome continued by narrating the story of a young man without a religious background who, passing the chapel one evening and hearing the powerful singing of this hymn within, especially its chorus "Hail, Immanuel! Immanuel we'll adore and sound his fame from shore to shore," was so moved that he spent the rest of his life performing acts of Christian charity.

62. "Luther meinte, 'der Teufel brauche nicht alle schönen Melodien für sich allein zu besitzen'" (Blume 1931:12). Occasionally another scholar will attribute this remark to Luther, but without giving a citation. Such is the case in Charles Garside's informative study *The Origins of Calvin's Theology of Music,* which states "Luther had openly proclaimed his desire to use all available music, including the most obviously secular, for the worship of the church" (Garside 1979:19).

63. Blume 1965:18; Blume 1974:30.

64. Brauer 1997.

65. The online edition is available at <luther.chadwyck.co.uk>. The search was conducted in November 2003 on the keywords *Teufel, Teuffel, Teuffell, Teuffeel, Melodien, Melodeien, Melodeyen, Lieder, Music, diabolos, diabolus, canticum, cantica, cantus, melos,* and *meli.*

66. This is not to say that later Lutherans did not occasionally use the melodies of secular songs. Around 1555 the anonymous text *O Welt, ich muss dich lassen* was set to the tune of *Innsbruck, ich muss dich lassen,* which had become popular through a polyphonic setting by Heinrich Isaac (ca. 1515); and in 1613 Christoph Knoll's *Herzlich tut mich verlangen* was set to the love song *Mein G'müth ist mir verwirret,* a polyphonic arrangement of which by Hans Leo Hassler had appeared in 1601, to cite just two of the best known.

67. The information on the origins of Luther's hymns is from Jenny 1985, *passim.*

❖

Chapter 2

1. Emil Sehling, *Die evangelischen Kirchenordnungen des XVI. Jahrhunderts,* vols. 1–8, 11–15 in 15 physical volumes to date (Leipzig: O. R. Reisland, 1902–13; Tübingen: J. C. B. Mohr [Paul Siebeck], 1955–). The most recent volume appeared in 1980, and it is uncertain whether the series will be completed. Several orders missing from Sehling are included in whole or in part in Aemilius Ludwig Richter's *Die evangelischen Kirchenordnungen des sechzehnten Jahrhunderts,* 2 vols. in 1 (Weimar, 1846), namely, Halle 1526, Brandenburg-Ansbach 1526, Frankfurt am Main 1530, Goslar 1531, Württemberg 1536, Lippe 1538, Schleswig-Holstein 1542, Cologne 1543 (called the *Kölner Reformation*), Württemberg 1553, Frankfurt am Main 1554, Waldeck 1556, Württemberg 1559, Hanau 1573, and Hoya 1573.

2. Harper 1991:115.

3. Bäumker 1886–1911, vol. 2, pp. 8–10.

4. Gülden 1964:59.

5. Pacik 1978:126.

6. Pacik 1978:128.

7. Meyer 1965:64.

8. Meyer 1965:292.

9. The information in this paragraph is from Meyer 1965:304, 317–19.

10. The information in the preceding three paragraphs is taken largely from Meyer 1965:91–102, 113–24. Although sermons were widely held, the practice was not universal, as witnessed by the fact that the Synod of Eichstätt in 1447 and the Synod of Bamberg in 1491 had to remind the priests of their preaching obligation (Janota 1968:66).

11. Harnoncourt 1974:297–98.

12. Ruff, "A millenium," 1997:11–12.

13. Quoted in Janota 1968:43–44. Janota points out that this cannot take the place of the Latin Creed, for Berthold refers to the actual Credo when he instructs the people to kneel at the words "ex Maria virgine"; rather, this must be a paraphrase of the Creed sung as part of the brief catechesis found in the annexes to the sermon (pp. 44–45). A number of additional examples from the eighth to the eighteenth centuries are given in Ruff 1997:11–15.

14. Janota dicusses these on pp. 71–76.

15. Philipp Harnoncourt reports that *Christ ist erstanden* appeared in more than 160 sources between the thirteenth and seventeenth centuries (Harnoncourt 1974:301).

16. For a discussion of the reasons for the changes in the *German Mass,* see Herl 1997:16–24.

17. *WA* 12:36; also Sehling 1:2. See appendix 2 for the paragraph in context.

18. Janota 1968. The arguments summarized here are presented on pp. 10–12, 29–31, and 258. My thanks to Anthony Ruff, OSB, for directing me to the writings of Janota, Lipphardt, and Harnoncourt.

19. Janota 1968:29–30.

20. Janota 1968:258.

21. Lipphardt 1972:159–60.

22. Lipphardt 1972:161–64, 196–97.

23. Harnoncourt 1974:287–92.

24. *Die Bekenntnisschriften,* p. 350. This passage is lacking in Melanchthon's Latin original (and therefore in the standard English translation edited by Theodore Tappert, which was made from the Latin) but is found in the German version prepared by Jonas and corrected by Melanchthon. The most recent Latin version had been at the printer's when the translation was made, and so this passage may reflect an earlier state of the Apology.

25. Of the sources containing German hymns with music printed between 1521 and 1600, *DKL* identifies 499 as Lutheran, 74 as Reformed, 40 as Catholic, 32 as Bohemian Brethren, and 87 as other Protestant (most of them not identified with any particular group). Twenty-three Catholic sources were printed between 1501 and 1520.

26. Facsimile reprint edited by Walther Lipphardt as no. 11 of *Beiträge zur mittelrheinischen Musikgeschichte* (Mainz: B. Schott's Söhne, 1970).

27. Gülden 1964:60.

28. Gülden 1964:62.

29. Paul Hoffe, *Ein lobsame Catholische Frolockung von wegen des new gebornen Königs Jesu Christi vnsers Herren vnnd Heylandts* (Dillingen, 1576), quoted in Bäumker 1886–1911, vol. 1, p. 193.

30. Ruff, "A millenium," 1997:13; Hamacher 1985:14.

31. Ruff, "Unity," 1997:18.

32. Bäumker, vol. 1, pp. 198−200.

❖

Chapter 3

1. A better translation might be "church ordinance," but the term "church order" is universally used in English, and so I have retained it.

2. See "Sehling" in the bibliography.

3. The vast majority of Lutheran territories, especially in northern Germany, required private confession before each reception of communion. A private examination on the catechism was frequently included as a part of the confession. Over time the practice became in many places a perfunctory form, even (in large cities with few priests) a group act; but most Lutheran churches nevertheless retained this requirement until the end of the eighteenth century. Confession benefited the priest as well as the penitent, for he was paid a small amount (the so-called *Beichtpfennig*) for each confession. This pre-Reformation tradition was continued in most parts of Germany until almost 1800. See Herrliberger 1746:13; Diehl 1899:226; and Meyer 1965:354, note 23.

4. A few places in southern Germany had been influenced by the Swiss Reformation and offered communion less frequently.

5. The *Small Catechism* contains six "chief parts": three (the Ten Commandments, the Creed, and the Lord's Prayer) with their traditional texts followed by explanations written by Luther, and three (Baptism, Confession, and the Sacrament of the Altar) that have no traditional texts but only explanations. Some church orders named only five chief parts, omitting confession. The *Small Catechism* was used (nearly) universally among Lutherans; and according to one source, toward the end of the century even some Catholic priests used it in catechetical instruction (Veit and Lenhart 1956:13).

6. Adults as well as children were required to memorize the catechism. In Prussia, catechism examinations were to be held every six weeks, or at least once a quarter, in the 1540s to 1560s. Every parishioner was to answer catechism questions for the pastor, who kept a written record of the answers and passed it on to the superintendent. Needless to say, these examinations were not at all popular, and a 1538 visitation report by Paul Speratus noted that the farmers would deliberately avoid the pastor when he came to see them (Zieger 1967:50).

7. The earliest order with a prayer service is Aschersleben 1575, with a rather formal liturgy on Fridays sung by the boys. The *Befehl bei Einführung der Gesangsordnung* of Wolfgang, Count of Hohenlohe, issued on February 2, 1589, noted that there had been disorder in the singing on Sundays, holy days, and in the regular Betstunden (Sehling 15:596). A 1617 order from Albertine Saxony mentioned prayer services held on Sundays and Wednesdays (Schmidt 1957:128). Visitation records from Hesse in 1626 show that the prayer services were well established there (Diehl 1899:66, 68−69, 208). Hamburg in 1628 saw the publication of *Kirchen Ceremonien, das ist: Wie es by Anordnung der Bettstunden im Hamburg . . . ,* which contained texts and hymns for the prayer services. The services seem to have been well established by the second half of the seventeenth century. Other orders with weekly prayer services are Braunschweig-Wolfenbüttel 1657, Saxe-Weimar 1664, Nördlingen 1676, Altenburg 1705, Braunschweig-Wolfenbüttel 1709, and Ulm 1747.

8. These are first mentioned in Cologne 1543 and are later found in East Frisia 1593, Braunschweig-Wolfenbüttel 1657, Ernestine Saxony 1685, and Braunschweig-Wolfenbüttel 1709, among others.

9. The exceptions are: Assumption was observed in Weissenburg 1528, Dessau 1532, Nördlingen 1538, Brandenburg 1540, Palatinate-Neuburg 1543, Schwäbisch Hall 1543, Brandenburg-Ansbach-Kulmbach 1548, Hohenlohe 1553, and in Veit Dietrich's Nuremberg agenda of 1543 (where it is noted that it is observed not because it is scriptural but because the people do not want to give up the festival). Some of these places may have observed the Visitation on this day rather than the Assumption. Luther conceded in the *Formula missae* of 1523 that Assumption must be tolerated for a while yet, even though its liturgical texts were not pure (*i.e.,* doctrinally correct). Corpus Christi was observed in Dessau 1532, Brandenburg 1540, and Brandenburg-Ansbach-Kulmbach 1548. Many orders expressly stated that Assumption and Corpus Christi were idolatrous and not to be observed.

10. Sehling 7:1:79.

11. Saxe-Coburg 1626:40–41.

12. The population figures are from Rotz 1985:457–58. The correction for Nuremberg is from Volker Schier (e-mail of August 11, 2003).

13. Schrems 1930 gives dates for the elimination of Latin singing in various localities ranging from 1645 to 1708. But in other places, such as Leipzig, Dresden, Magdeburg, Lüneburg, and Hamburg, Latin remained in use for some time thereafter (pp. 104–106). In Schleswig-Holstein it was abolished in 1772 (Detlefsen 1961:170). The anonymous *Etwas von der Liturgie* noted in 1778 that Latin singing was prescribed in the Saxon church order but that there were very few places where it was still being practiced (*Etwas von der Liturgie* 1778:89). For a discussion of the use of Latin and German in the sixteenth-century Lutheran Vespers, see Heidrich 1998.

14. The order for this church is found at Sehling 6:1:609–18.

15. Brückner 1753–63:3.

16. There were one or two exceptions to this use of the term "Diakon." Philip Han's *Kirchen Buch* for Magdeburg (1615) used "Diakon" in the sense of "Pfarrer" and "Lector" in the sense of "Diakon." It is unclear whether Johann Gerhard's Saxe-Coburg order of 1626 used "Diakon" to refer to someone who was not yet ordained to the priesthood but who was fulfilling certain of its functions or simply to a priest who had not yet been assigned a parish of his own. The order directed that insofar as possible, students should not advance directly from school into the pastorate until they have spent time teaching or in the diaconate or otherwise in the preaching office so that they can learn the ceremonies of the church and gain experience. The deacon should be given a pastorate only after the Pfarrer has testified that the deacon has gained the necessary experience both in his preaching and in the discharge of his office in caring for the healthy and sick, and the prisoners. Cities may retain an older, senior deacon who instructs the younger ones. A person with the necessary qualifications who has not served as a deacon may be ordained into the pastorate (Saxe-Coburg 1626:131–32).

17. These are the modern spellings; sources from the sixteenth through eighteenth centuries spelled these words *Diacon* and *Capellan*. Similarly, *Küster* was spelled *Cüster; Kantor* and *Kantorei* were spelled *Cantor* and *Cantorei; Kapellan* was spelled *Capellan; Kurrende* (defined below under "Choral Ensembles") was spelled *Currende;* and *Musik* was spelled *Music.*

18. Sehling 6:2:1144. Similarly, according to the 1585 order for Saxe-Lauenburg, the clerk's office was to open and close the church at the proper times, keep it clean for services and funerals, ring the bells, take care of the belongings of the church, including items needed for mass, altar items, chalice, lamps, candles, etc. He also sang the psalms of Dr. Luther from the book, teaching them to the people. In the villages he taught arithmetic, reading, writing, and the catechism to boys and girls, and in the city he taught the same things to the girls, and his wife taught them sewing and other such things. On Sunday afternoons he instructed the young people in Luther's catechism. The clerk also had responsibilities at funerals, and

no one was allowed to bury his own dead to avoid paying the clerk his fee. He also assisted in visiting the sick and at baptisms of children (Sehling 5:422–23).

19. London 1718:39–40. See also the 1716 order for East Frisia, chapter 18, for a similar list of duties.

20. Stübner 1800:196–97.

21. Vollhardt 1899, page x. Girls also learned to sing, at least in places. The 1533 order for Meissen and Voitland and the 1533 Leiniger order both provide that there be one hour's practice of spiritual songs (*geistliche Lieder*) in the afternoon for the girls' school. (Rautenstrauch 1907:91)

22. Sehling 12:142.

23. Vollhardt 1899, page x.

24. Mertz 1902:544, 595; Biehle 1924:52; Rauschning 1931:58; Steinhäuser 1936:65; and Beinroth 1943:8. Sannemann 1904 (pp. 16–20) surveys the amount of music instruction in German schools during the sixteenth century; and Rautenstrauch 1907 (pp. 64–74) provides a list of schools in Saxony during the sixteenth century and the number of hours of music instruction in each.

25. Krickeberg 1965:128.

26. Ruhnke 1963:31.

27. Joachim Kremer, in his study of the north German cantorate, lists the cities of Jever, Buxtehude, Flensburg, Husum, Kiel, and Wismar as having founded cantorates during the second half of the century; several larger cities had already established them previously (Kremer 1995:24–25).

28. Werner 1932:122. Krickeberg, on the other hand, reports that in the seventeenth century few cantors in the smaller cities left the position once they occupied it (Krickeberg 1965:129).

29. Krickeberg 1965:178–79.

30. Niemöller 1969:628, citing the 1479 church order for Hof and the 1510 school order for Hiltpoltstain. The author traces the development of the cantorate from medieval times on pp. 629–37.

31. Krickeberg 1965:19.

32. Rautenstrauch 1907:63.

33. Blessinger 1913:25.

34. In Luther's day in Saxony the entire school participated in the service on Sundays, while smaller groups of schoolboys sang for weekday services on an alternating basis, so that no one group would have its studies disrupted too frequently (Rautenstrauch 1907:106). Likewise, we learn from the 1541 visitation of the city of Neuruppin in Brandenburg that the entire school sang for mass on high feasts and for Vespers the prior evening; on ordinary Sundays and holy days a smaller group was appointed (Zimmermann 1963:26).

35. Sehling 15:1:503–8.

36. The terms *choraliter* and *figuraliter,* adverbs corresponding to the adjectives *choralis* and *figuralis,* were used throughout the period under study. These and similar terms were defined in the many music tutors for young pupils. Martin Agricola's definition reads: "Music, an art of singing, is commonly divided into two types: *Choralis* and *Mensuralis. Choralis* refers to singing in a simple and common way, such as in church, so that the entire choir, that is, the entire congregation, everyone who is in church, sings along; it is called this because the notes used in this song are simple and elementary, that is, one like another, none is sung shorter or longer. *Mensuralis* or *Figuralis* is a well-mannered and artistic way of singing, when one note is sung longer, or occasionally shorter, than the next or the previous one, and when you sing together artistically in various ways and voices" (Agricola 1568:f. 4[b]). Most other tutors used a standard question-and-answer format to define these two terms: "What is

music? Music is the art of singing correctly and in a pleasing manner. How many kinds of music are there? Two: *musica choralis* and *musica figuralis*. What is *musica choralis*? In which one note is not of greater value than another. What is *musica figuralis*? In which one note is of greater value than another" (Demantius 1592, f. 4ᵃ).

37. See Parrott 2000:13 for evidence concerning voice change in boys in the eighteenth century.

38. Rautenstrauch 1907:121, 137, 140, 149–53, 159.

39. Niemöller 1969:55. According to Paul Graff, Adjuvanten choirs took the place of Kantoreien in villages. They were nearly the same thing, except that they did not have written bylaws. They existed even in villages with as few as three hundred people (Graff 1937–39, vol. 1, p. 260). In Joachimsthal, a *convivium musicum* was formed in 1558, which became a model for singing societies elsewhere in Germany (Brown 2001:106).

40. Rautenstrauch 1907:14; Ruhnke 1963:273–74.

41. Niemöller 1969:669; Greve 1985:62.

42. Niemöller 1969:672.

43. And in Ulm, large numbers of schoolboys went singing through the town at Christmas during the seventeenth century and were rewarded accordingly. At such occasions the cantor was often invited in for drinks at houses; not infrequently he became drunk and left his pupils by themselves. The older scholars then went and drank to excess themselves, and occasionally there would be fighting between the cantor and the pupils. The city council issued annual warnings about this (Blessinger 1913:26).

Street begging was not limited to schoolchildren. Christian Gerber reported in 1732 that when begging was still in full swing in Saxony, beggars would often bellow *O Lamm Gottes unschuldig* in front of houses at the tops of their voices. One beggar in Zeitz with a particularly unpleasant voice used to yell out that hymn at the door of Chancellor von Seckendorff, who finally asked him not to sing and he would still get his alms; but the beggar was much offended, and the townspeople thought badly of the chancellor for trying to deny the poor man his song (Gerber 1732:258).

44. Finkel 1973:227.

45. Finscher 1957:63.

46. Not that the *chorus musicus* was always well rehearsed, either. In 1558 Martin Tectander, pastor at the Johanniskirche in Zittau, wrote concerning the choir: "If an old skin were sewn together and filled with young dogs and cats and pigs, and someone beat on it with a big stick, they would yell, howl and drone just like those in the choir" (Rautenstrauch 1907:122).

47. Rolle 1784:42.

48. Rautenstrauch 1907:104–5.

49. Sehling 15:1:503.

50. Ruhnke 1963:292–99.

51. Rautenstrauch 1907:99.

52. Ziller 1935:30.

53. They are the 1543 order for the village of Lobenstein in Thuringia (Sehling 2:152) and the school order for Öhringen, circa 1582 (Sehling 15:1:508).

54. See Lübeck 1531 (Sehling 5:347), Pomerania 1535 (Sehling 4:340), Rostock [ca. 1560–76] (Sehling 5:289), Annaberg 1579 (Rautenstrauch 1907:166), Hoya 1581 (Sehling 6:2:1145), Saxe-Lauenburg 1585 (f. 2E4ᵇ), Mecklenburg 1602 (f. T6ᵇ), and Braunschweig-Wolfenbüttel 1709 (f. ²A2ᵃ). These are the orders in which the boys' place in the "Chor" is specifically mentioned; a number of other orders indicate that a boy reads the lessons without mentioning specifically where the choir is located, although it would have to be in the front of the church.

55. Sehling 7:1:739.

56. Richter 2:356; Sehling 6:2:1150.

57. Sehling 4:211.

58. "The boys shall assemble below or above in the choir, and the organist begins to play the Introit for that Sunday, which the choir then repeats, as usual" (Sehling 11:647–48).

59. "In inferiori choro chorus convenit et organum primum modulatur introitum de Trinitate [the Introit for Trinity was used in many places as the "ordinary" Introit], quem repetit chorus (Sehling 11:647–48).

60. Niemöller 1969:684.

61. Beinroth 1943:9.

62. Woodcut by an artist with initials F. I., reprinted in Salmen 1976:184.

63. Copper plate by Anton Möller (d. 1611) of Königsberg, reprinted in Salmen 1976:189.

64. Friderici 1619, chapter 7.

65. The choral and orchestral layout of the choir loft is diagrammed in Petzoldt and Petri 1990:95.

66. Walter 1967:40.

67. This was true in the area around Nuremberg in 1650–61, where pastors reported that the young people would rather go dancing on Sunday afternoon than attend catechism service, and several pastors discontinued the service altogether because of the attendance (Hirschmann 1994:109, 115, 124, 129, 137, 151, 180, 182, 211, 228, 267, 289). It was also true in the Duchy of Braunschweig-Wolfenbüttel during the period 1570–1600 (Wolters 1938–50, vol. 43:211, 223; vol. 46:128). The visitation of Grubenhagen in 1579 discovered that almost no one over eighteen attended the catechism service, and many children and young people danced, played, or took walks rather than attending (Spanuth 1954:115–16). The story was repeated in Gunzenhausen in Bavaria in the 1560s and 1570s (Clauß 1925:88). Bergwitz in Saxony seems to have fared better than most: the pastor reported in 1602 that seven women (but no men) attended catechism (Pallas 1906–18:2:1:217). The city of Braunschweig eliminated the Sunday afternoon service altogether in 1588 because of poor attendance (Sehling 6:1:344). The foregoing is only a sampling of many such reports too numerous to mention.

68. Sehling 15:1:449.

69. Lippert 1898:167.

70. In particular, see Braunschweig 1528 (Sehling 6:1:401), East Frisia 1535 (Sehling 7:380), Pomerania 1542 (Sehling 4:357), Mecklenburg 1545 (Sehling 5:150), Schwarzburg 1549 (Sehling 2:130), and Hesse 1574 (Sehling 8:230–31). Two orders had similar provisions for Matins: Cologne 1543 (Richter 2:50) and Palatinate 1546a (Sehling 14:91).

71. Zieger 1967:136–40. Sleeping in church seems to have been a common problem. A pastor named Ahasver Fritsch even published a sermon on the topic in 1675, called *The Sinful Church-Sleeper (Der sündliche Kirchen-Schläffer)*. In it he warned against sleeping in church, which he said was common everywhere. He suggested that people stand for the sermon rather than sit, noting that several places had introduced the laudable practice of having someone walk around and wake people up during the sermon (Fritsch 1675:42–43). The pastor at Niemegk in Saxony complained in 1598 that the people slept in church, inquiring whether a boy might carry a stick to awaken sleepers, as was common in other places. This had been done at Sandersdorff, he noted, but now the pastor there simply admonished the weary (Pallas 1906–18:2:2:176). In Derendingen (Württemberg) during the seventeenth century those falling asleep in church were fined (Brecht 1967:91). In 1735 sleeping during church services was prohibited in Oettingen. First, the clergyman was directed that he should issue a warning to the people. If this was not enough, someone was to be installed to

watch for sleepers and warn them. Repeat offenders would have their names read from the pulpit the week following the offense (Oettingen 1774:4).

72. Pallas 1906–18:2:4:147.

73. Brecht 1967:95–96.

74. Sehling 7:2:782. Other orders containing similar notices (but without reference to cattle, children, or pregnant women!) are: Pomerania 1535 (Sehling 4:341); Mecklenburg 1552 (Sehling 5:198); Palatinate-Zweibrücken 1563 (original, f. c3^b); Braunschweig-Lüneburg 1564 (Sehling 6:1:546); Württemberg 1565 (original, f. 88^b); Hesse 1566 (Sehling 8:319); Braunschweig-Wolfenbüttel 1569 (Sehling 6:1:146); Pomerania 1569 (Sehling 4:438); Wittenberg [1570] (original, f. B3^a); Hesse 1574 (Sehling 8:439); Lüneburg [1575] (Sehling 6:1:659); Henneberg 1582 (Sehling 2:311); Hohenlohe 1582 (Sehling 15:1:485)— notes that "the majority" of people leave after the sermon; Saxe-Lauenburg 1585 (original, f. 2K1^a); Mecklenburg 1602 (original, f. V2^b); Verden 1606 (Sehling 7:1:157); Braunschweig-Wolfenbüttel 1615 (original, pp. 19, 45); and Braunschweig-Wolfenbüttel 1657 (original, f. F3^a).

75. Ulm 1747 (original, pp. 146, 279); Magdeburg 1685 (original, p. 27); and Holstein Plön 1732 (original, p. 13).

76. *Synodal-Schluß* 1645:13.

77. Dieterich 1632:226.

78. Theophilus Großgebauer, *Drey geistreiche Schriften / 1. Wächterstimme aus dem verwüsteten Zion* (Frankfurt and Leipzig, 1710), p. 189, cited in Irwin 1993:80.

79. Leibniz 1694:11; Gerber 1732:241. One further anecdote, although it is from the later eighteenth century, is simply too good not to relate. It is told in Hermes, Fischer, and Salzmann's *Beytraege zur Verbesserung des oeffentlichen Gottesdienstes der Christen* [*Recommendations for the Improvement of the Public Service of Christians*] (1786) and concerns the traditional St. Michael's Day Vespers at the cathedral in Magdeburg. A piece of concerted music was performed after the sermon, during which (at a certain point in the music) a rooster was made to crow. This was repeated three times, to loud laughter from the congregation. After the third time the people left, without further regard for the music or the rest of the service. According to the book, an attempt had been made several years previously to leave out the rooster call, but the income from the service dropped so dramatically that it was quickly reinstated. After a few more years, the sermon was eliminated, as there obviously wasn't much use for it, and only the music and the rooster were left (Hermes/Fischer/Salzmann 1786:241–43).

80. *Etwas von der Liturgie* 1778:89–90.

81. Kevorkian 2002:31.

82. Wolters 1938–50, vol. 43, p. 227.

83. Sehling 1:704. Other church orders specifically allowing the Preface to be omitted if time was short include Hamburg 1529 (Sehling 5:528), Bergedorf 1544 (Sehling 5:387), Buxtehude 1552 (Sehling 7:1:75), Mecklenburg 1552 (Sehling 5:199), Amberg 1555 (13:291), Stralsund 1555 (4:551), Jever 1562 (Sehling 7:2:1:1241), Württemberg 1565 (original, f. 82^a), Pomerania 1569 (Sehling 4:438), Rostock [ca. 1560–76] (Sehling 5:288), Teschen 1584 (Sehling 3:462), Mecklenburg 1602 (original, f. V3^a), and Verden 1606 (Sehling 7:1:158). Hamburg 1556 provided that the Preface may occasionally be shortened if the priest and cantor are both aware of this ahead of time (Sehling 5:552). Other orders omitted the Preface altogether. Some orders indicated that either the exhortation to the communicants or the Preface be used, but not both, including Hatzkerode [1534?] (Sehling 2:587), Albertine Saxony 1540 (original, f. 23^a), Anhalt 1548 (Sehling 2:554), Prussia 1558 (Hubatsch 1968, vol. 3, p. 120), Prussia 1568 (Sehling 4:82), and Thorn 1575 (Sehling 4:237).

84. Sehling 4:32; Sehling 5:16. The Riga order also specified a Kyrie and an Agnus Dei "with few notes," except on high feasts.

85. *LW* 53:12, 53:38, 41:137.

86. Dieterich 1632:227. The 1564 order for Thüngen directed that "because in many places the simple farmers, especially the men and youths, go out in front of the church during the singing, sermon and communion and stand around and make a lot of useless noise, and they also leave the church before the entire service is done, and several even foolishly leave before the thanksgiving, the pastors are to earnestly punish such boors and by no means tolerate them, and diligently exhort the people to remain as quiet, restrained and respectable as possible during the entire service until its end" (Sehling 11:736).

87. The Gotha Synod of 1645 directed: "Because . . . it is common in a number of cities that those who can read do not, except when they go to Holy Communion, bring their prayer books to church and read them during the figural singing and organ playing, the pastors are to publicly and gently admonish the people from the pulpit that this should henceforth be done" (*Synodal-Schluß* 1645:12).

88. Dieterich 1632:227.

89. Diehl 1899:173.

90. Dechent 1913–21:1:189.

91. Pallas 1906–18:2:1:336.

92. Brecht 1967:92.

93. Saxe-Coburg 1626:324.

94. Saxe-Lauenburg 1585, f. L1[b].

95. Kevorkian 2002:28.

❖

Chapter 4

1. This is the number of original editions, excluding reprints, and includes only those orders I have actually consulted, as listed in the bibliography. The exact count is 272, plus 88 reprints and "later editions" (see the bibliography for a definition of this term). The number of extant orders is in reality somewhat larger, as I was limited to those orders available in major libraries. Sixteenth-century orders are well covered by the voluminous reprints of Richter and Sehling, and it is likely that I have seen close to 100 percent of extant orders from this period. Printed orders from the seventeenth and eighteenth centuries can be found in libraries, and a survey of several bibliographies of church orders (none complete) suggests that I have seen around two-thirds of those extant. Manuscript orders from this period have not been collected, however, and I have seen hardly any of these. This should not change the results given here, though, because such orders were apparently less numerous than in the sixteenth century; rarely circulated outside their place of origin; and, if the manuscript orders from the sixteenth century are any indication, were frequently based on printed orders and contained similar instructions.

2. Herl 2000, appendix 3 (pp. 221–38) contains a complete list of German hymns, arranged by liturgical use with frequency of occurrence indicated, from all the service orders consulted for this book. The information in this chapter regarding specific hymns used in the mass is taken from this source.

3. See appendix 3.

4. Nuremberg 1543, f. b4[a]. The part about the pastor teaching the people to sing was dropped in the 1545 edition (Sehling 11:495).

5. Nuremberg 1543, f. b4[b].

6. Sehling 12:312.

7. Herl 2000, appendix 6 (pp. 277–80), gives the entire list of graduals, alleluias and sequences from Keuchenthal's book.

8. In two orders, Nördlingen 1579 and Prussia 1558, the Leise "Jesus Christus, unser Heiland" was sung at Easter. Two different hymns begin with these words. One, a communion hymn, continues "der von uns den Gotteszorn wandt"; the other, an Easter Leise, continues "der den Tod überwand."

9. Harnoncourt 1974:302.

10. Sehling 5:88.

11. Braunschweig 1528, f. Q2ᵃ; Hamburg 1529 in Sehling 5:530.

12. This does not include the times when both choir and congregation were to sing the Creed or when a choice was given as to one or the other.

13. Sehling 4:32.

14. Sehling 5:88; Richter 2:4.

15. Sehling 2:586.

16. The orders refer to the Latin Creed as the *Patrem*, as this was the first word sung by the choir after the priest intoned "Credo in unum Deum."

17. Sehling 13:283.

18. See Herl 2000, appendix 3 for details.

19. The suitability of the second line of *Erhalt uns, Herr* for congregational singing was a source of debate among Lutherans for over two hundred years. In 1542, when the hymn first appeared, the Holy Roman Empire was in imminent danger of an invasion by the Turks, who had been repelled at Vienna in 1529. Rumors abounded that the Turkish Sultan had made an agreement with the pope and with France to conquer and divide the German territories. This accounts for the venom in the hymn's second line, "und steur des Papsts und Türken Mord" (and curb murder by the pope and Turks). This line was controversial almost as soon as it was written, and during the Nuremberg Interim in 1548 the authorities ordered that it be changed to "und wehr des Satans List und Mord" (and restrain the cunning and murder of Satan). The current wording, "und steure deiner Feinde Mord" (and curb the murder of your enemies), dates from the eighteenth century and is attributed to Count Ludwig von Zinzendorf (1700–1760) (Information from Weismann 1970:501–4).

20. Richter 2:44.

21. This is part of the mass ordinary no. XVII in the *Graduale Romanum*; it also appears in the *Liber usualis* of 1952, p. 61.

22. Sehling 4:341.

23. *Liber usualis* (1952), p. 42.

24. Braunschweig 1528, ff. J3ᵃ–J3ᵇ; Sehling 5:348; 4:340; 1:703; 4:354; 7:1:77–78. Edward T. Horn (1891) presents Matins and Vespers from sixteen early Lutheran church orders in list form (pp. 261ff.); these lists are reprinted in Senn 1997:338–41.

25. The opening versicle is not present in every order, but it is not certain whether it was omitted because it was not performed or because it was considered a minor part of the order not worth mentioning.

26. In Pomerania 1535 the Latin Litany replaced the Magnificat on nonfestival days; in the 1542 order it was sung after the Magnificat during Advent and Lent. Wittenberg 1533 placed the Latin Litany here on nonfestival days, the German Magnificat sung with the people on festivals, and the Da pacem in Latin and German (i.e., *Verleih uns Frieden*) when the part before the sermon was sung figurally. In Buxtehude 1552 the Nunc dimittis was sung after the Magnificat if time permitted, and the Pater Noster was sung after the Kyrie.

27. Braunschweig 1528 and Lübeck 1531 directed that the Nunc dimittis with the

Gloria patri be sung on a single tone, followed by *Jesu, redemptor seculi*; Pomerania 1542 placed the *Da pacem, domine* and *Verleih uns Frieden* here.

28. Teutsch 1862:68; Sehling 11:327. The Brandenburg-Ansbach-Kulmbach order was established by the Catholic Interim and is thus particularly reactionary.

29. Nuremberg 1543, f. h1[b].

30. The use of the *Da pacem* in this position in 1501 Rome is noted in Reynolds 1995:109. According to Tom Ward, this use was common in Italy in the second half of the fifteenth century [conversation with Tom R. Ward, April 2000].

31. *Ich glaub in Gott Vater, den Allmächtigen* is mentioned as an alternate choice following the sermon in Hohenlohe 1582 (Sehling 15:1:504), but it is not connected with the catechism examination.

32. This hymn and the others indicated as appearing in only one order are found in Magdeburg 1663, which includes two hymns for each part of the catechism even when the overwhelming historical precedent is for only one hymn, as with the Creed, the Lord's Prayer, and Baptism.

33. This hymn was originally written as a paraphrase of Psalm 130 and was mentioned only in Braunschweig-Wolfenbüttel 1657 and Magdeburg 1663, both fairly late orders, as a catechism hymn. Many orders did not include confession as one of the chief parts, and others apparently did not have a fixed catechism hymn for confession. J. S. Bach, for his settings of the catechism hymns in Part III of the *Clavierübung,* used another paraphrase of Psalm 130, *Aus tiefer Not schrei ich zu dir,* for this chief part. None of the catechism hymns listed is truly a catechetical hymn on confession, and it would not be surprising if some churches might have favored a hymn such as *So wahr ich leb, spricht Gott der Herr* by Luther's friend Nicolaus Herman, published in his popular *Sontags Euangelia vber das gantze Jar* (Wittenberg, 1560; *RISM* 1560[08]), although there is no evidence that this hymn was so used.

34. Sehling 7:1:380–81.

35. Hymns are counted once for each liturgical function they fulfill; for example, a hymn occurring in an order as both a gradual and a sermon hymn is counted twice. Reprints of church orders are not counted for the rankings.

36. See Herl 2000, appendix 3 for details.

37. Sehling 12:371.

38. Saxe-Coburg 1626, pp. 14–15.

39. Magdeburg 1685, p. 27.

40. Mansfeld 1580, f. c3[a].

41. Sehling 13:465.

42. Sehling 5:16.

43. Brown 2001:85, 178–81.

❖

Chapter 5

1. Sehling 15:1:443.

2. Pallas 1906–18, Abt. 1, p. 125.

3. The territories of Hesse and Baden-Württemberg are exceptions, for which there exists a comprehensive finding aid to visitation documents in archives. It is *Repertorium der Kirchenvisitationsakten aus dem 16. und 17. Jahrhundert in Archiven der Bundesrepublik Deutschland,* vols. 1 and 2, ed. Ernst Walter Zeeden (Stuttgart: Klett-Cotha, 1982–87). No further volumes have appeared.

4. For a more detailed description of the visitation procedures in parts of Germany, see Strauss 1978:249–67. The author discusses the reliability of the information in visitation minutes on pages 265–67.

5. Karl Pallas, ed., *Die Registraturen der Kirchenvisitationen im ehemals sächsischen Kurkreise,* 2 parts in 7 vols. (Halle, 1906–18). Between 1485 and 1918 Saxony was divided into two principal sections, called Ernestine Saxony and Albertine Saxony after the brothers who initially divided the territory, Ernst and Albrecht. There was also a third section known as the Electorate, so called because its ruler served as an Elector of the Holy Roman Emperor. It comprised Wittenberg and a small surrounding area. When Saxony was divided, the Electorate (which could not be divided) was given to the elder brother Ernst. Both Ernst and Albrecht were properly titled Duke of Saxony, but Ernst used the higher title Elector of Saxony. During Luther's lifetime the Electorate remained under the control of Ernst's son Frederick the Wise and his successors, and so Luther studies frequently use the term "Electoral Saxony" to refer to the Electorate and Ernestine Saxony together. But this is a misnomer inasmuch as Elector Johann Friedrich was forced in 1547 to cede the Electorate to his cousin Moritz, Duke of (Albertine) Saxony. I avoid ambiguity by specifying Ernestine Saxony, Albertine Saxony, or the Electorate whenever a distinction is necessary.

6. Pallas 1906–18, part 1, p. 131.

7. Pallas, part 1, pp. 143, 145, 147.

8. The citations are to volume and page from part 2 of Pallas; some earlier visitation reports are included if they are relevant. There was considerable work done on visitation and other parish records at the end of the nineteenth and beginning of the twentieth centuries, much of it by parish pastors. Many reports contain only summaries or paraphrases of the original records, as in this case. Pallas, however, seems to have taken unusual care to produce accurate summaries.

9. This parish fared less well in the visitation of 1592, during which the congregation asked the visitors to remove their pastor, charging him with false teaching (saying that the pope had put the exorcism into baptism and that Luther's Small Catechism will not be valid much longer) and with nine counts of administrative malfeasance. The visitors admitted that the pastor held to incorrect doctrine but found that the congregation was also at fault: they had thrown apples and carrots at him in the pulpit, they were now refusing communion from him, and one farmer, Balthasar Quick, had called the pastor "einen alten Schalk, Spitzbuben und Säuschneider (an old rascal, rogue and gelder of swine)!" The controversy had begun when the congregation tried to take the parish's pasture away, but the pastor refused permission. The visitors decided that the situation was irreconcilable and placed the pastor on leave with salary until St. Lucy's Day, allowing him time to find a new position (5:94).

10. Nothing was said concerning the singing in the visitation of 1602, but it was noted that most people attend church; the few that had been reaping in the fields during the services have now spent a week in jail (5:147).

11. Four years later the people complained that the pastor had many dogs that entered the church and bothered the communicants. The visitors told the pastor to leave his dogs at home (5:183).

12. This parish continued to have problems. In 1624 the clerk (perhaps the same one?) was sentenced to fourteen days in prison and fed only bread and water for having rebaptized a child with the name Conrad after the midwife had performed an emergency baptism without naming the child. The visitors directed that he was to be admonished upon threat of dismissal that he was not to ring the bell when the farmers wanted to drink beer or when runaway cattle needed to be driven home, and another method was to be found to inform the cowherds to hunt for the pastor's cattle and drive them home. Also, the person who,

upon being asked how many gods there were, answered "seven" was to be corrected and exhorted to the Lord's table (5:383).

13. The report from Elster includes a touching story about an old man who was permitted to commune even though he could neither hear nor speak more than a few words and knew from the catechism only the words "Our Father," "heavenly God," and "Christian Church." But he loved to go to church and sat or stood where he could look the preacher right in the mouth. When he saw the others remove their hats or bow or kneel, he did likewise. When others received the sacrament he refused to absent himself, and he was permitted to attend out of fear that if he were refused he would do something tragic or even jump into the river and drown himself (1:130).

14. *Die reformatorischen Kirchenvisitationen in den welfischen Landen 1542–1544: Instruktionen, Protocolle, Abschiede und Berichte der Reformatoren* (Göttingen: Vandenhoeck & Ruprecht, 1896).

15. The Bursfelde men's cloister visitation of 1542 directed that the brothers were to receive copies of the *Enchiridia geistlicher gesenge*. It seems likely that the same hymnal was meant here. *Eyn Enchiridion oder Handbüchlein* was originally published in Erfurt in 1524; it was reprinted in 1525 and subsequent years with the title *Enchiridion geystlicher Gesenge*.

16. *Die Kirchenvisitation im Landgebiet der Reichsstadt Nürnberg 1560 und 1561,* Einzelarbeiten aus der Kirchengeschichte Bayerns, vol. 68 (Neustadt a. d. Aisch: Degener, 1994).

17. Hirschmann 1994:57, 87.

18. Hirschmann 1994:70, 92, 109. In 1561, the caretaker at Hiltpoltstein also complained that the pastor kept people in church too long by singing all Ten Commandments at once (doubtless the twelve stanzas of Luther's hymn *Dies sind die heilgen Zehn Gebot* were meant).

19. Hirschmann 1994:197. The visitors also instructed at Altdorf that communicants were not to use a straw to drink from the chalice, as this was not customary in other places.

20. Butler 1970:188.

21. Sehling 11:137.

22. Brandenburg-Nuremberg 1533, f. M1^a.

23. Hirschmann 1994:144–45. The pastor was also directed to wear mass vestments whenever there were communicants.

24. Hirschmann 1994:246. Despite such large numbers the visitors directed that the clergy not try to cut corners in confession by hearing two, three, or four people at once, but rather each penitent must be heard individually.

25. Schneider 1878:1–52.

26. Thomas Klein, "Ernestinisches Sachsen, kleinere thüringische Gebiete," in Schindling and Ziegler 1989–97, vol. 4, pp. 30–31.

27. Nuremberg 1543, ff. b4^a–f1^a.

28. Sehling 2:330–57.

29. Perhaps the first stanza only of Luther's three-stanza "Wir glauben all an einen Gott" is meant.

30. Sehling 1:583, 621, 658, 693.

31. Walter Ziegler, "Braunschweig-Lüneburg, Hildesheim," in Schindling and Ziegler 1989–97, vol. 3, p. 21.

32. Spanuth 1955: 52, 60–61. The comments in quotation marks are Spanuth's paraphrase of the original source.

33. Diehl 1899:29–32.

34. Diehl 1899:72.

35. Diehl 1899:74–79.

36. Diehl 1899:72.

37. Sehling 4:533.

38. Sehling 15:1:444–45. It was also discovered in the visitation that only a small number of communicants actually attended Vespers on Saturdays and evenings before holy days. Some of them appeared only afterward to register. The pastors were to discourage this. In addition, the Friday sermons were poorly attended in both cities and villages; and on Sunday most people left church after the sermon. The pastors were to exhort the people to attend faithfully, and especially the civic leaders, that they might set a good example (Sehling 15:1:449, 451, 455).

39. *Synodal-Schluß* 1645:11–12.

40. Strauss 1978:262–67.

41. Kittelson 1982 (entire article).

42. Kittelson 1985:90–91.

43. Ozment 1992:170–72.

44. Brown 2001:16.

45. Brown 2001:4–5.

46. Brown 2001:60–62, 90. It is possible that Strassburg may be another special case in this regard. As I show in chapter 6, the ecclesiastical authorities in Strassburg went out of their way to encourage congregational participation in the liturgy, and the singing of the people there was reported to be excellent. Without intending to pass any judgment concerning Strauss's work (which I have not studied in detail), it may be that the extra effort to involve the people contributed to their relative willingness to accept Lutheran teaching.

❖

Chapter 6

1. Blume 1975:47; in the original German, "1526 erscheint als erstes Wittenberger Gemeindegesangbuch das *Enchiridion* des Hans Lufft . . ." (Blume 1965:29).

2. *Luther und die Pflege der kirchlichen Musik in Sachsen* (Leipzig, 1907), 13.

3. Leaver 1990:146.

4. Garbe 1995, col. 1165.

5. Other exceptions are Joachim Slüter's hymnal for Rostock, *Eyn gantz schone vnde seer nutte gesangk boek* (Rostock, 1525); *Das Teutsch gesang so in der Meß gesungen wirdt*, published in five editions in Nuremberg between 1525 and 1528; and the Strassburg *Psalter mit aller Kirchenübung* of 1539.

6. *Das deutsche Kirchenlied: kritische Gesamtausgabe der Melodien,* edited by Konrad Ameln, Markus Jenny, and Walther Lipphardt, 1 vol. in 2 physical volumes, Répertoire international des sources musicales (RISM), series B, vol. 8 (Kassel: Bärenreiter, 1975, 1980). Hymnals listed in this bibliography are given two sigla for identification: one a *DKL* siglum (e.g., ErfL 1524^a) from which knowledgeable readers can identify the book without consulting the bibliography; the other, a siglum of the type used for all volumes in the *RISM* series, consisting of a date with a sequential number superscripted (e.g., 1524^{03}). When further volumes appeared (see next footnote), a third siglum was assigned to each hymnal, the *EdK* siglum (e.g., ea1). *EdK* stands for *Edition des deutschen Kirchenlieds,* the new name for the project formerly called *Das deutsche Kirchenlied.* For a fuller explanation of the project and the various names and abbreviations, see the review by Robin A. Leaver in the June 1998 *Music Library Association Notes,* pp. 907–11. In references below, I have chosen to use the *RISM* siglum, because it is the only one that can be easily used with both the *RISM* bibliography volumes and the volumes of the new critical edition.

7. *Das deutsche Kirchenlied,* Abteilung III, Band 1, vorgelegt von Joachim Stalmann; bearbeitet von Karl-Günther Hartmann (Teil 1), Hans-Otto Korth (Teile 1–3), und Daniela Wissemann-Garbe (Teile 2–3), 1 vol. in 6 physical vols (Kassel: Bärenreiter, 1993–98).

8. The number is approximate because it is sometimes difficult to know whether an item should be classed as a hymnal or some other sort of publication.

9. The number is approximate because it is impossible to be certain without examining each book whether a later imprint with a slightly different title and contents is truly a later edition or another book altogether.

10. *RISM* 1496[01].

11. Rebecca Oettinger cites research estimating that the survival rate of seventeenth-century political broadsides is seven-tenths of one percent and that for fifteenth- and sixteenth-century broadside songs is one-half of one percent (Oettinger 2001:9).

12. The University of Illinois Rare Book Room holds photographic reprints of the collection.

13. Georg Butze's contemporary account, reprinted in *Die Chroniken der niedersächsischen Städte* (Leipzig, 1899) and quoted here from Brednich 1974–75, vol. 1, p. 87.

14. Account of Sebastian Langhans from the same *Chronik,* quoted in Brednich 1974:88.

15. Quoted in Mager 1986:30.

16. Mager 1986:32, 34.

17. Uhlhorn 1861:181.

18. Mager 1986:33–35. For Lüneburg, see also Uhlhorn 1861:176–82.

19. The seven hymns are *Allein zu dir, Herr Jesu Christ; Herr Gott, dich loben alle wir; Herr Jesu Christ, wahr Mensch und Gott; Hilf, Gott, daß mir gelinge; Ich ruf zu dir, Herr Jesu Christ; Ich dank dir, lieber Herre;* and *Nun lob, mein Seel, den Herren.*

20. Butler 1970:188.

21. A facsimile reprint is included as a supplement to vol. 2 (1956) of the *Jahrbuch für Liturgik und Hymnologie,* with an accompanying essay by Konrad Ameln on pp. 89–91 of vol. 2. The hymns are *Nun freut euch, lieben Christen gemein; Es ist das Heil uns kommen her; In Gott gelaub ich, dass er hat; Hilf, Gott, wie ist der Menschennot; Ach Gott, vom Himmel sieh darein; Es spricht der unweisen Mund wohl; Aus tiefer Not schrei ich zu dir;* and *In Jesu Namen heben wir an.*

22. See Ameln 1956:89.

23. Butler 1970:181.

24. Butler 1970:189–90.

25. *Form vnd Ordnung des ampts der Meß Teütsch. Auch dabey das handtbüchleyn Christlicher gesenge, die man am Suntag oder feyrtag im ampt der Meß, deßgleychen vor vñ nach der predig im newen Spital zu Nüremberg im brauch helt* (*RISM* 1526[05]).

26. *Form vñ Ordnung geystlicher gesenge vnd Psalmen, welche in der versamlung zu Nürnberg im Newen Spital gesungen werden. Gemert mit etlichen Psalmen* (*RISM* 1526[04]).

27. I am grateful to Bartlett Butler and Volker Schier for helping me to sort through the complicated political and ecclesiastical history of Nuremberg.

28. Nuremberg 1525a. See Simon 1959.

29. Nuremberg 1525b. See Butler 1970:183.

30. Volker Schier's comments are contained in an e-mail to the author dated August 11, 2003.

31. *Das Teutsch gesang so in der Meß gesungen wirdt, zu nutz und gut den iungern kindern Gedruckt* (not in *RISM*).

32. Butler 1970:195.

33. Butler 1970, p. 194, note 107; also p. 194, text.

34. *Gantz newe geystliche teütsche Hymnus vñ gesang, von eynem yeden Fest vber das gantz*

Jar, auch denselben geschichten vnnd Propheceyen, in der Kirchen oder sunsten, andechtlich, bequemlich vnd besserlich zusingen, vnnd alles inn klarer Götlicher schriefft gegründet (*RISM* 1527[07]).

35. *RISM* 1527[06].

36. Butler 1970:200–201, citing the letter of March 14, 1532, to the Duke of Norfolk printed in Henry Ellis, ed., *Original letters illustrative of English history*, 3rd series, II (London, 1846), 189ff.

37. *RISM* 1524[03] and 1524[06]. See Konrad Ameln, introduction to *Das Erfurter Enchiridion*, facsimile reprint, translated by Traute M. Marshall, Documenta musicologica, series 1, no. 36 (Kassel: Bärenreiter, 1983), 17.

38. *Eyn Enchiridion oder Handbüchlein. eynem ytzlichen Christen fast nutzlich bey sich zuhaben, zur stetter vbung vnd trachtung geystlicher gesenge vnd Psalmen, Rechtschaffen vnd kunstlich verteutscht.* There is a reprint available of this issue, edited by Konrad Ameln, in the series Documenta musicologica, series 1, no. 36 (Kassel: Bärenreiter, 1983).

39. Summarized here; the original is reprinted in Wackernagel 1855:542–43.

40. *ETliche Christliche Gesenge vnd Psalmen, wilche vor bey dem Enchiridion nicht gewest synd, mit hohem fleyss verdeutsche vnnd gedruckt, mit eyner vorrede des hochgelerten D. Marti. Luther* (*RISM* 1525[05]). The reprint of the *Enchiridion* mentioned in note 38 also includes this supplement.

41. See *DKL*, section 3, vol. 1, part 1, Textband, 26–28 for bibliographic details.

42. *Enchiridion Geystlicher gesenge vnd psalme[n] so man itzt (Got zu lob) yn[n] der kirchen singet, gezoge[n] auß d' heilige[n] schrift Gemehrt, gebessert vnd mit fleys corrigirt, mit eyner schönen vorrede Martini Luther* (*RISM* 1525[06]).

43. *Enchiridion Geystlicher Gesenge, So man ytzt (Got zu lob) in der kyrchen singt Gezogen auß der heyligen schryfft des waren vnd heyligen Euangelions, welchs ytzt von gottes gnaden wyder auffgangen ist, vnd mitt etzlichenn gesengen Gemehrtt, Gebessert, vnnd mitt fleyß Corrigyrt durch Doctor Martini Luther* (*RISM* 1525[07]). The use of the genitive "Martini" after the preposition "durch" could conceivably have been a local Erfurt usage, but was more likely a printer's error reflecting the haste in which the book was evidently prepared, as the use of "durch" with the accusative (and no other case) was established as early as the thirteenth century. Even in Old High German its cognate "duri" took the accusative (Grimm 1965– , vol. 6, cols. 1534–53).

44. See Ameln 1989:20.

45. *Eyn gesang Buchleyn, welche man[n] yetz und ynn Kirchen gebrauchen ist* (*RISM* 1525[11]). This edition has been reprinted in facsimile as *Das älteste Zwickauer Gesangbuch von 1525*, with an introduction by Otto Clemen (Berlin: Evangelische Verlagsanstalt, 1960). There is a another state of the book from the same printer with exactly the same title but with differing spelling (*RISM* 1525[12]), which causes even more puzzlement over the title.

46. Blindow 1966:165.

47. Brecht 1986/1990:409.

48. *Grund und ursach auß gotlicher schrifft der neüwerungen an dem nachtmal des herren, so man die Mess nennet, Tauff, Feyrtagen, bildern und gesang in der gemein Christi, wann die zusamenkompt, durch und auff das wort gottes zu Straßburg fürgenomen.* Reprinted in *Bucer* (ed. Stupperich), vol. 1, pp. 185–278.

49. For an extended discussion of Bucer and the liturgy, see Poll 1954. Regarding his influence on Calvin, see Garside 1979.

50. *Teütsch Kirchen ampt, mit lobgesengen, v\nn götlichen psalmen, wie es die gemein zu Straßburg singt v\nn halt, gantz Christlich* (*RISM* 1524[15]).

51. *RISM* 1524[16] and 1525[18].

52. See the discussion by Konrad Ameln in Ameln 1955:96–97 and Ameln 1967:140–48. The orders have been reprinted in Hubert 1900; see also Smend 1896. For a

concise discussion of hymnals published in Strassburg at the beginning of the Reformation, see Leaver 1991:22–33.

53. *Straßburger kirchenampt, nemlich von Jnsegung d' Eeleüt, vom Tauf vnd von des herren nachtmal, mit etlichen Psalmen, die am end des büchlins, ordenlich verzeychnet sein* (*RISM* 1525²¹).

54. Smend 1896:139–42.

55. "Der Straßburger kirchen handlung, mit gepreüchlichem gesäng der gemein, hab ich inn dreyen büchlin getruckt" (Wackernagel 1855:544).

56. *Psalme[n] gebett, vnd Kirchen übu[n]g wie sie zu Straßburg gehalten werden* (*RISM* 1526⁰⁸⁻¹⁰).

57. *RISM* 1530⁰⁶ and 1533⁰¹.

58. Wackernagel 1855:550.

59. *[Psalme[n] vnd geystliche Lieder, die man zu Straßburg, vnd auch die man inn anderen Kirchen pflegt zu singen]* (*RISM* 1537⁰³). The title is reconstructed and the date uncertain because the only known copy is missing the first section.

60. Poll 1954:32, note 7.

61. *Psalter. Das seindt alle Psalmen Dauids, mit jren Melodeie[n], sampt vil Schönen Christlichen liedern, vnnd Kyrche[n] übunge[n]* (*RISM* 1538⁰⁶).

62. Wackernagel 1855:565.

63. *Psalter mit aller Kirchenübung die man bey der Christlichen Gemein zu Straßburg vnd anders wa pflägt zu singen* (not in *DKL* as it contains no music; see Wackernagel 1855:155).

64. Leaver 1991:28–29.

65. *Gesangbuch, darinn begriffen sind, die aller fürnemisten vnd besten Psalmen, Geistliche Lieder, vnd Chorgeseng, aus dem Wittembergischen, Strasburgischen, vnd anderer Kirchen Gesangbüchlin zusamen bracht, vnd mit besonderem fleis corrigiert vnd gedrucket. Für Stett vnd Dorff Kirchen, Lateinische vnd Deudsche Schulen* (*RISM* 1541⁰⁶). A facsimile reprint is available from the Evangelisches Verlagswerk, Stuttgart, 1953.

66. F. A4ᵃ. For another translation of the entire preface, see Garside 1979:29–31.

67. F. A4ᵃ.

68. Quoted in Garside 1979:13.

69. Quoted in Garside 1979:18.

70. Quoted in Wackernagel 1855:580.

71. *Eyne schone vnnd ser nutte Christlike vnderwysynge* and *Eyn gantz schone vnde seer nutte gesangk boek.* Both are available in facsimile: *Ein gar schönes und sehr nützliches Gesangbuch, 1525,* edited by Gerhard Bosinski (Leipzig: Zentralantiquariat der Deutschen Demokratischen Republik, 1986). The hymnal contains no melodies, so it is not included in *DKL.*

72. See Leaver 1991:35 for details.

73. "... desuluigen leder ein yssliker Christen vor gudt wille annemen ... vnde ernstlick van herten, Gade tho laue, alle tidt, besondergen jn jegenwardicheit der vorsamlinge, Wenn Gades wordt wert verkündiget, fröliken singen. ..." (Wackernagel 1855:552).

74. *RISM* 1524¹⁸.

75. AE 53:316.

76. *Enchyridion geistlicher gesenge vnd psalmen fur die leyen, mit viel andern denn zuuor, gebessert* (*RISM* 1526¹¹).

77. Jenny has deduced from circumstantial evidence that at least one edition appeared in 1525 (Jenny 1985:25–30).

78. Information on the textual contents of the 1526 book is from "Das neu aufgefundene Wittenberger Gesangbüchlein vom Jahre 1526," in *Neuer deutscher Bücherschatz,* edited by Carl Biltz (Berlin, 1895; reprint Hildesheim: Olms, 1967), 249–52. Information on the tunes is from *Das deutsche Kirchenlied,* section 3, vol. 1, part 1, Textband, p. 34.

79. *WA* 17:1:459; 19:50–51.

80. See chapter 1 for a discussion of these events.

81. The American edition of *Luther's Works*, vol. 53, contains Luther's "preface to the Weiss hymnal, 1528." But the existence of this hymnal is speculative, and Jenny argues that if it existed at all it was probably a reprint of Walter's choir hymnal (Jenny 1985:31–35). The preface in *Luther's Works* (pp. 317–18) is actually from the 1531 Erfurt reprint of the Klug hymnal.

82. For an attempt at reconstructing the contents of the 1529 hymnal, see Konrad Ameln, "Das Klugsche Gesangbuch, Wittenberg 1529: Versuche einer Rekonstrucktion," *Jahrbuch für Liturgik und Hymnologie* 16 (1971): 159–62.

83. *Geistliche lieder auffs new gebessert zu Wittemberg* (*RISM* 1531^{03} and 1533^{02}). The book was further reprinted in 1535 (*RISM* 1535^{06}), and a new edition produced in 1543 (*RISM* 1543^{10}) with reprints in 1544 and 1545 (*RISM* 1544^{05}, 1544^{06}, 1544^{07}, and 1545^{06}). A facsimile of the 1533 edition is available as *Das Klug'sche Gesangbuch, 1533,* ed. Konrad Ameln, Documenta musicologica, 1st series, no. 35 (Kassel: Bärenreiter, 1983).

84. Ameln 1971:159.

85. Wissemann-Garbe 1998, *passim*.

86. The preface is reprinted in Wackernagel 1855:547 and in English in *Luther's Works*, vol. 53, pp. 317–18.

87. *Christliche Geseng Lateinisch vnd Deudsch, zum Begrebnis* (*RISM* 1542^{15}).

88. *Geystliche Lieder. Mit einer newen vorrhede, D. Mart. Luth* (*RISM* 1545^{01}). A facsimile reprint is available: *Das Babstsche Gesangbuch von 1545,* ed. Konrad Ameln, Documenta musicologica, series 1, no. 38 (Kassel: Bärenreiter, 1988).

89. *Das deutsche Kirchenlied,* section III, vol. 1, part 1, Textband, 40–44.

90. The preface is reprinted in Wackernagel 1855:583 and in English in *Luther's Works*, vol. 53, pp. 332–34.

91. *Etlich gesang dadurch Got ynn der gebenedeiten muter Christi vnd opfferu[n]g der weysen Heyden, Auch ym Symeone, allen heylgen vn[d] Engeln gelobt wirt, Alles auß grundt götlicher schrifft &c.* (*RISM* 1527^{05}).

92. *Etliche newe verdeütschte vnnd gemachte ynn göttlicher schrifft gegründte Christliche Hymnus vn [!] geseng, wie die am ennd derselben yn eynem sonderlichen Register gefunden werden* (*RISM* 1527^{06}). Both Königsberg hymnals are available in a facsimile reprint: *Zwei Königsberger Gesangbücher von 1527,* ed. Joseph Müller-Blattau (Kassel: Bärenreiter, 1933).

93. *Kurtz Ordnung des Kirchendiensts, Sampt eyner Vorrede von Ceremonien, An den Erbarn Rath der löblichenn Stadt Riga ynn Liefflandt. Mit etlichen Psalmen, vnd Götlichen lobgesengen, die yn Christlicher versamlung zu Riga ghesungen werden* (*RISM* 1530^{05}). A reprint is available: *Kirchendienstordnung und Gesangbuch der Stadt Riga nach den ältesten Ausgaben von 1530ff.,* ed. Johannes Geffcken (Hannover, 1862).

94. Three of these editions are in *DKL: RISM* 1537^{04}, 1559^{05}, and 1567^{16}. The only known copies of the 1537 and 1567 editions have been lost.

95. Wackernagel 1855:559.

96. We find the concern for youth expressed in several hymnals of the period, including Luther's preface to the 1524 choir hymnal; the Erfurt *Enchiridion* (1524); *Das Teutsch gesang so in der Mesz gesungen würdt* (Nuremberg, 1525); Katharina Zellin's *Von Christo Jesu vnserem säligmacher . . . etlich Christliche vnd trostliche Lobgsäng* (Strassburg, 1534).

97. *RISM* 1550^{05}.

98. *RISM* 1565^{03}.

99. *RISM* 1568^{10}.

100. *RISM* 1545^{14}–1545^{17}.

101. *RISM* 1553^{10}. Lossius's book is mentioned in Rostock [ca. 1560–76], Pomerania 1569, Oldenburg 1573, Lüneburg [1575], and Lohr 1588.

102. *RISM* 1573[11]; 1587[10].
103. *RISM* 1588[14]; 1589[17].
104. Dieterich 1632:227.
105. Dieterich 1632:230.
106. Graff, vol. 1, p. 265, citing Kolb 1913:59.
107. Werner 1932:103–104.
108. Baum 1969:33; Brecht 1967:92.
109. Blindow 1957, p. XI.
110. Ruetz 1753:19.
111. Gerber 1732:256–57.
112. Gerber 1732:257.

❖

Chapter 7

1. Mansfeld 1580, f. c3[a].
2. Rautenstrauch 1907:179–80. This was still a concern in 1645, when the Gotha synod complained that in many churches too much figural music in Latin was being sung and directed that one German hymn be sung for every piece of figural music (*Synodal-Schluß* 1645:12).
3. Sehling 1:697–98.
4. The quotation is a summary from Garside 1966:28. For Karlstadt's original text, see Hermann Barge, *Andreas Bodenstein von Karlstadt* (Leipzig, 1905), I, Exkurs V, 491–93.
5. Rietschel 1893:17.
6. *WA* 25:475, quoted in Honemeyer 1974:91; see also *LW* 53:316.
7. Alber 1556, ff. Y2[a–b].
8. Garside 1979.
9. Quoted in Garside 1979:20–21, citing *Institutes of the Christian Religion,* ed. John T. McNeill (Philadelphia: Westminster, 1960): 895–96, and *Ioannis Calvini opera quae supersunt omnia,* ed. W. Baum et al. (Braunschweig, 1863–1900), vol. 2, p. 659.
10. See Garside 1966, especially pp. 36–49.
11. Marcus 2001:729.
12. *Colloqvivm Mompelgartense,* pp. 703–704.
13. Stein 1593:28–29.
14. Pezel 1592:124.
15. Quoted in Reese 1959:448, citing Erasmus's *Opera omnia,* vol. 6 (1705), col. 731 (at F).
16. Translated in Monson 2002:11.
17. *Tauffbüchlein, für die Kirchen im Fürstenthumb Anhaldt* ([Zerbst], 1590). The baptismal exorcism consisted of the formula, directed to the individual about to be baptized, "Depart, thou unclean spirit, and give room to the Holy Spirit!" See Nischan 1987.
18. *Erinnerungs Schrifft etlicher vom Adel vnd Stedten* (Zerbst, 1596).
19. The writings in this controversy, in chronological order, were (+ pro-Anhalt; − anti-Anhalt): *Erinnerungs Schrifft* 1596 (+), *Notwendige Antwort* 1597 (−), *Anleytung* 1597 (+), *Abfertigung* 1597 (−), *Antwort auff die Wittenbergische Abfertigung* 1598 (+), *Endliche Ablehnung* 1598 (+), *Stattliches Schreiben* 1598 (−), *Endliche Antwort* 1600 (−), *Summarische Antwort* 1600 (+), *Augenscheinlicher Beweisz* 1600 (+), *Drey Schrifften* 1606 (+). The exact chronology is not certain for items marked with an asterisk.
20. Arnoldi 1616:164.

21. The *houseling cloth* is a towel used to catch any particles of the host that might accidentally fall while being distributed.

22. Bronisch 1897:385–86, quoting a manuscript from the Königliches Staatsarchiv in Breslau. The "commentary" was read in connection with the Epistle or Gospel. The *Summaria vber das alte Testament* (1541) and *Summaria vber das newe Testament* (1544) of Veit Dietrich were widely used commentaries. They were eventually combined to produce the *Summaria vber die gantze Bibel,* which was widely reprinted.

23. Only a brief overview is given here, as the subject has been adequately covered by Friedrich Blume and others. For more information, see Blume 1975:113ff.

24. See Parrott 2000.

25. Blankenburg 1967:49–50, 56–63.

26. Schmidt 1961:163; Held 1894:12.

27. Rautenstrauch 1907:177. The 1579 church order for Anhalt gives the same direction (Sehling 2:569).

28. Sehling 1:583.

29. Rautenstrauch 1907:181.

30. Rautenstrauch 1907:168. The identity of Dr. Pseudner is unknown.

31. Sehling 6:1:403, 5:528, 6:2:924, 6:2:792, 12:312, 4:550; Oldenburg 1573, f. 2B4b; Pomerania 1569, f. 75a; Sehling 12:370, 374.

32. Sehling 2:72, 12:320.

33. Kayser 1896:77, 90, 105; Heyden 1961–64, vol. 2, p. 54; Sehling 2:339.

34. Schünemann 1922:358, citing Hertel's *Verrostete Chorschlüssel* (1671).

35. Preface to *Fünfftzig geistliche Lieder vnd Psalmen. Mit vier Stimmen, auff Contrapuncts weise (für die Schulen vnd Kirchen im löblichen Fürstenthumb Würtenberg) also gesetzt, das ein gantze Christliche Gemein durchauß mit singen kan (RISM 1586[11]),* quoted and translated in Schuler 1986:67–68.

36. For a history of the cantional style, see Schuler 1986:41–56. For a description of the musical style of some important cantionales, see Finscher 1957:74–76. For musical excerpts from nine important books, see Blume 1974:136–37.

37. *Geistliche Deutsche Lieder. D. Mart. Lutheri: Vnd anderer frommen Christen (RISM 1601[03]),* quoted in Rietschel 1893:51 with modernized spelling.

38. *Psalmen vnd Gesang-Buch (RISM 1603[06]),* quoted in Liliencron 1893:95–96, translated in Riedel 1959:110 and corrected here.

39. Quoted in Rietschel 1893:52, with spelling modernized.

40. Praetorius, *Gesamtausgabe,* vol. 16, p. IX.

41. Praetorius, *Gesamtausgabe,* vol. 16, pp. IX–X.

42. Praetorius, *Gesamtausgabe,* vol. 16, p. VIII.

43. Praetorius, *Gesamtausgabe,* vol. 16, p. IX.

44. For a detailed account of the introduction of this style into the Lutheran church, see Blume 1974:192–219.

45. Dieterich 1632:226–27; the congregation's complaint about figural music is also noted in Blessinger 1913:19. Other writers confirm Dieterich's report of churchgoers attending only for the sermon. Johann Quistorp of Rostock wrote in 1659: "On Sundays before the preacher mounts the pulpit, few come to church to sing spiritual songs along with the cantor. Rather, when the singing is over they finally come, all dressed up as if they were going to a wedding." Theophilus Grossgebauer, also of Rostock, wrote in 1661: "That preaching is the worship service is doubted by no one. Thus I have seen how in large cities the people storm into the church as the bell strikes the hour for the preacher to mount the pulpit; then when the sermon ends they storm out again" (Both quotations from Irwin

1993:80). See also in chapter 3, "Attendance at Services," Dieterich's comments in 1632 sermon.

46. Schröder 1639:204.

47. Frick 1631, p. [140].

48. Röhlk 1899:39–40.

49. Hiller 1766–70:395. The report is from vol. 1, no. 51, dated 15 June 1767.

50. *Wächterstimme auß dem verwüsteten Zion* (Frankfurt/Main, 1661).

51. Großgebauer 1661:227–28.

52. Mithobius 1665: 46–47, 63.

53. Mithobius 1665:311–312. For a more in-depth look at Grossgebauer and Mithobius, see Irwin 1993, which devotes an entire chapter to each.

54. Muscovius 1687:5–9, 128–47.

55. Schiecke 1693.

56. Werckmeister 1691.

57. See Irwin 1993:118–26. This book on the Lutheran theology of music during the Baroque era has unfortunately not received nearly the attention it deserves. The author has read extensively writings of the period and has summarized and analyzed them with great insight.

58. Gerber 1732.

59. *Die unerkannten Sünden der Welt* (Dresden, 1690).

60. Motz 1703, passim. Another reply was written by one Christoph Lauterbach, *M. Christian Gerbers Pfarrers zu Lockwitz bey Dresden Unerkante Sünden, aus seinen von dieser Materie bißher unterschiedlich geschriebenen Büchern in einer vornehmen. . .Zusammenkunft Discursweise erwogen und gehandelt* (Leipzig, 1703), but the only known copy (at the Staatsbibliothek zu Berlin) has been lost. According to the preface to Gerber 1711, Lauterbach was not the author's real name; Gerber also states that the author, after receiving much criticism, later wished he had never written his response (Gerber 1711, vol. 2, part 1, p. [xxi]).

61. Röhlk 1899:31.

62. Gerber 1704/1709:29.

63. Printz 1690:36–43.

64. Neumeister 1722:284–85. Joyce Irwin provides a similar citation from a Neumeister publication of 1700 (Irwin 1993:127).

65. Interested readers are directed to the following sources for more information about the cantata debate (+ pro-cantata; − anti-cantata; ± balanced presentation): Fuhrmann 1706 (+); Preus [1706] (+); Raupach 1717 (+); Scheibel 1721 (+); Meyer 1726 (± but with cautions); Mattheson 1727 (+); Meyer 1728 (−); Fuhrmann:Strigel 1728 (+); Fuhrmann:Wag-Schal 1728 (+); Mattheson 1728 (+); Meyer 1729 (−) [the preceding six books are all responses to Meyer 1726]; Hoelling 1732 (−); Carpzov 1733 (±); Scheibel 1738 (+); Kästner 1740 (+); Mizler 1740 (−); Voigt 1742 (+); Martius 1762 (+); Albrecht 1764 (+); Steinberg 1766 (±); Reichardt 1774–76 (±); Fiedler 1790 (+).

66. Raupach 1717:11, 44. Raupach wrote under the pseudonym Veritophilus [lover of truth] and titled his essay *Clear Grounds of Proof on which the Proper Use of Music, Both in the Church and Outside of It, Is Based.*

67. Scheibel 1738.

68. See Leaver 1985:93–96.

69. Scheibel 1721:23, 39.

70. Bokemeyer 1725:297.

71. Bokemeyer 1725:298.

72. Mattheson 1728:105.

73. Scheibe 1745:161.

74. Scheibe 1745:161–62.

75. Joachim Justus Breithaupt wrote in 1707 that it had been seventeen years since the word "Pietist" had first been used (Breithaupt 1707:11).

76. Spener 1666/1964:88–89.

77. Wagner 1702.

78. Mayer 1706:5–6.

79. Mayer 1706:21–31. Other Pietist teachings reported by Mayer: some deny that Christ paid for our sins; they maintain that Christians are capable of fulfilling God's law; they do not believe that new birth and the Holy Spirit are given in baptism, but teach that no one should be baptized until one has faith; they believe that the Lord's Supper is nothing but a memorial of Christ's death and a communion of the faithful; they deny that the forgiveness of sins is imparted in communion; they do not believe that the pastor is given the authority to forgive sins—in fact, they believe that the pastoral office should be abolished; they teach that assemblies in homes are better than meetings in church buildings; they hold that sermons should not be prepared ahead of time but preached spontaneously and without the use of pericopes (scripture readings appointed for the day); they want to abolish the sabbath day and all holy days; they believe that Christians need no government; they teach that a clergyman's blessing is not needed for marriage and that adultery and prostitution are acceptable; they believe in the millenium and other unacceptable eschatalogical teachings; they believe that the devil and the damned will not be punished eternally; and they do not believe that the word "blessed" (*selig*) should be applied to the dead. (Mayer 1706:31–42)

80. Mayer 1706:38–39.

81. They are Dippel 1706 (written under the pseudonym Christianus Democritus); Francke 1706; Breithaupt 1707; and Stryk 1707.

82. Breithaupt 1707:133–34, 138–39.

83. Graff 1937–39, vol. 1, p. 16.

84. Kalb 1959/1965, p. xi.

85. Reed 1960:144–47.

86. Beyreuther 1960:394.

87. Irwin 1993:107. Lutheran Orthodoxy, referred to in the quotation, refers to the dominant theological perspective of the period from approximately 1580 to the first quarter of the eighteenth century that placed a high priority on unambiguous statements of correct doctrine.

88. McMullen 1987:32, 36.

89. Of the 100 tunes first printed in Freylinghausen's hymnal, eight appear in current Lutheran books: *Christe, wahres Seelenlicht* (p. 358); *Dir, dir, Jehova, will ich singen* (p. 379); *Eins ist not, ach Herr, dies eine* (p. 388); *Fahre fort, fahre fort* (p. 398); *Gott sei dank in aller Welt* (p. 408); *Macht hoch die Tür* (p. 467); *Morgenglanz der Ewigkeit* (p. 481); and *O Durchbrecher aller Bande* (p. 497). Page numbers refer to transcriptions of the tunes in McMullen 1987.

90. Gerber 1732:609.

91. Steinberg 1766:99–100.

92. Steinberg 1766:93. This author provides a fairly balanced presentation of the Kirchenmusik issue. He seems to go out of his way to avoid controversial statements and several places seems almost apologetic for his opinions. The tone is gentle and the arguments well reasoned but not scholarly when compared with other publications. For a discussion of the idea of "true" Kirchenmusik in late eighteenth-century writings, see the chapter "Was ist 'wahre' Kirchenmusik?" in Heidrich 2001:231–45.

93. Reichardt 1774–76, vol. 1, pp. 48–50.

94. Crichton 1782:8, 18, 21.

95. Rau 1786, in Seiler 1784–86, vol. 2, part 2, pp. 18–19, 25, 28, 45–69.

96. Burdorf 1795, part 1, pp. 21, 95; part 2, pp. 93, 100, 103.

97. Reed 1960:148–49.

98. *Anmerkungen bey neuen Gesangbüchern* (1786:8–9).

❖

Chapter 8

1. For more information on the functions of the organ in the sixteenth century, see Rietschel 1893:16; Pacik 1978 (entire); Bush 1982; and Edler 1982:149–51. For specifics of how chant alternation was done, see Rietschel 1893:15–16 (Introit, Kyrie, hymns); Leichsenring 1922:39 (Sanctus *Esaia dem Propheten*); Pacik 1978:123–25 (Vespers psalms, Magnificat, general rules). Church orders mentioning alternation practice with organ include Naumburg [1538] (Sehling 2:73); Schönburg 1542 (Sehling 2:171); Mecklenburg 1545 (Sehling 5:152–53); Nördlingen 1555 (Sehling 12:320); Regensburg 1553 (Sehling 13:419, 422); Feuchtwangen 1563 (Sehling 11:401, 404); Braunschweig-Lüneburg 1564 (f. E3ª); Prussia 1568 (f. B2ª); Braunschweig-Wolfenbüttel 1569 (Sehling 6:1:142); Schwarzburg 1574 (Sehling 2:133); Aschersleben 1575 (Sehling 2:477); Lüneburg [1575] (Sehling 6:1:658); Annaberg 1579 (Rautenstrauch 1907:168); East Frisia 1583 (Sehling 7:1:677); Halberstadt 1591 (Arndt 1913:241); East Frisia 1593 (Sehling 7:1:695); Braunschweig-Wolfenbüttel 1615 (p. 6); Magdeburg 1667 (f. F1ª); Braunschweig-Wolfenbüttel 1709 (f. ²A2ᵇ); East Frisia 1716 (chapter 18). Alternation between organ and congregation (rather than choir) is specifically mentioned in the East Frisian orders of 1583 and 1593.

2. Regarding the role of the organ in substituting for the choir, in 1641 the consistory at Stuttgart reported that a majority of the choir had died from the plague, and so the organ was needed to take the choir's part in the service (Blindow 1957:3).

3. Daebeler 1966:90–91, citing Tobias Norlind, "Was ein Organist im 17. Jahrhundert wissen mußte," Sammelbände der Internationalen Musikgesellschaft 7 (1905–6): 640–41.

4. Ziller 1935:126–27.

5. ". . . so sind diese Psalmen in vier Stimmen auff dem Chor gesungen, und dabey die Orgel geschlagen worden" (Hartknoch 1686:760, citing Jacob Schmidt, *Verantwortung*, part I, p. 60).

6. Arno Werner writes that he has seen manuscript accompaniments for congregational singing in Remberg bei Wittenberg dating from the sixteenth century, but inasmuch as he gives no further details it is impossible to evaluate his claim (Werner 1932:7).

7. "Weill bey der Ausspendung des Herren Abendtmahles oder vnter der Communion, des Fest undt Sontages nach der Predigt die deutschen Lobe-Psalme vom Abendtmahl des Herren vormals gesungen, alß wiel Ein Erb. Rahtt, das dieselben hinführo wiederumb vnter der Communion zu Chore, des einen Sontages der eine Psalm, nemblich Gott sey gelobet vndt gebenedeyet. Des anderen Sontags aber, der Andere nemblich, Jesus Christus, vnser Heillandt gantz sollen gesungen vndt zugleich auff der Orgel gespielet vnndt geschlagen werden. Damit der gemeine Man so im lesen vnerfahren, zuer Dancksagung erwecket werde" (Staatsarchiv Danzig 300, 35 (37B) 11, quoted in Rauschning 1931:79).

8. *Melodeyen Gesangbuch*, pp. 5–6.

9. Staatsarchiv Danzig 300, 37B, 18, quoted in Rauschning 1931:57.

10. Staatsarchiv Danzig 300, 42, 151, quoted in Rauschning 1931:151.

11. Report of Vicke Schorler (original source unidentified), quoted in *Neue wöchentliche Rostock'sche Nachrichten und Anzeigen*, no. 78 (September 30, 1841), reprinted in Daebeler 1966:131.

12. Arno Werner traces in minute detail the development of organ accompaniment during the period 1630–1800 (Werner 1932:88–95). Dietz-Rüdiger Moser provides a list of twelve cities and the dates (between 1647 and 1810) when organ accompaniment was introduced (Moser 1967:467). Horst Lindenberg identifies five cities where organ accompaniment was introduced during the eighteenth century (Lindenberg 1925:65).

13. Rautenstrauch 1907:398; Dienst 1963:149.

14. Blindow 1957:3.

15. Pröhle 1858:104.

16. Walter 1967:121.

17. *RISM* 1637[02].

18. Quoted in Rietschel 1893:49.

19. Preus 1729:1.

20. Gerber 1732:279. The "patron" (the original is *collator*) was the person owning the right to bestow a benefice; that is, to fill a pastoral vacancy in a particular place. There is a report from the Nicolaikirche in Leipzig from 1737 that the precentor began the hymn during the communion at so low a pitch that the congregation could not sing it (Williams 1980–84, vol. 3, p. 19).

21. Ruetz 1753:140–41.

22. Scheibel 1721:23.

23. Lütkens 1728:36.

24. Sonnenkalb 1756:9.

25. Rietschel 1893:55.

26. Johnson 1989:123, 131.

27. At least this is true in most cases. But Henrik Glahn has reported on an organ intabulation of the 1627 cantionale of J. H. Schein by Johannes Vockerodt of Mühlhausen in 1649 (see Glahn 1972).

28. The information in this paragraph is from conversations with Cleveland Johnson, November 1990 and August 1999. There is in fact much that is not known about the role of the organ during the seventeenth century. Friedrich Blume, whose *Protestant Church Music: A History* is the definitive study of the subject for Germany prior to 1800, admitted in 1965 that "there is still a need to clarify the duties of the organist during church services as well as the question of whether organ music had a liturgical or paraliturgical function between the times of Michael Praetorius and Dietrich Buxtehude" (Blume 1965:163; translated in Blume 1975:245). This is a very large uncertainty indeed, and unfortunately very little primary research has been done to fill in the gaps since this was written.

29. *RISM* 1627[10].

30. Johann Hermann Schein, *Neue Ausgabe sämtlicher Werke*, ed. Adam Adrio (Kassel: Bärenreiter, 1963–), vol. 2, pp. xi–xii.

31. *Tabulatur-Buch, Hundert geistlicher Lieder und Psalmen Herrn Doctoris Martini Lutheri und anderer gottseligen Männer, Für die Herren Organisten, mit der Christlichen Kirchen und Gemeine auff der Orgel, desgleichen auch zu Hause, zu spielen und zu singen, Auff alle Fest- und Sonntage, durchs gantze Jahr, mit 4. Stimmen componirt von Samuel Scheidt, C.*

32. Scheidt, *Werke*, vol. 1, p. x.

33. Adlung 1758:664.

34. Adlung 1758:665.

35. Kauffmann 1733, preface, last unnumbered page, item 2.

36. Temperley 1998, vol. 1, pp. 208–209.

37. Mithobius 1665:276.

38. Namely, *Allein Gott in der Höh sei Ehr* (BWV 715); *Gelobet seist du, Jesu Christ* (BWV 722, 722a); *Herr Jesu Christ, dich zu uns wend* (BWV 726); *In dulci jubilo* (BWV 729,

729a); *Lobt Gott, ihr Christen, allzugleich* (BWV 732, 732a); and *Vom Himmel hoch, da komm ich her* (BWV 738, 738a). E. E. Koch claimed in 1847 that Johann Pachelbel (1653–1706) of Nuremberg was the first to use organ interludes between stanzas, but he provides no documentation (Koch 1847, vol. 1, p. 457), and the comments of Mithobius show that interludes were in use before Pachelbel's time.

39. Scheibe 1745:413–31.

40. Angerstein 1800:221–38.

41. The entry in the consistory minutes reads: "We charge him with having played up to now many strange variations in the hymn melody and having mixed in many foreign notes, so that the congregation has been confused over it. In the future he will have to maintain a *tonus peregrinus* when he feels like introducing one and refrain from turning to something else too quickly, or, as has been the case up till now, even playing a contrary tone" (*Bach-Dokumente*, vol. 2 [1969], p. 20).

42. This is Martin Blindow's interpretation: see Blindow 1957:15.

43. Adlung 1758:683–84.

44. "Da passirt lustig, und auch tummes Zeug mit unter, da wird gebrochen, da wird gehackt, da wird gesprungen, da wird gepurzelt, bald unisono, bald duetto, bald trio, bald schlechter, bald Trippeltakt, und was der Fratzen mehr sind" (Hiller 1766–70, vol. 1, p. 263). The meaning of "schlechter Takt" is unclear: today it would refer to accenting the "wrong" beats of a measure, such as beats 2 and 4 instead of 1 and 3; but "duple" is possible (and makes more sense in this context) if "schlecht" is given its old meaning of "schlicht" (simple).

45. Hingelberg 1785:32–33.

46. Türk 1787:12.

47. Seiler 1784–86:180–81.

48. Werner 1932:115.

49. Pröhle 1858:103–4.

50. Häuser 1834:279. It is highly unlikely that Häuser was correct in his belief that vocal interludes preceded organ interludes, for Häuser was the first to mention the former, and evidence for the latter dates from much earlier.

51. Scheibe 1745:414.

52. Türk 1787:124–26. The concern with the length of the prelude was nothing new. Already in about 1630 a directive to the organist of the Petrikirche in Eisleben stated that "the preludes must be quite short. . . . The preludes must be constructed around those things that are about to be played and sung" (Haupt 1954:9). Such concerns were repeated throughout the later seventeenth and eighteenth centuries.

53. Adlung 1758:684.

54. Mattheson 1739:472.

55. Mizler 1740:58–59.

56. Scheibe 1745:424–26.

57. Sonnenkalb 1756:8–11.

58. Adlung 1758:685–87.

59. Lindenberg 1925:65.

60. Sonnenkalb 1756:21–22.

61. Werckmeister 1707:80–81.

62. Mizler 1740:61.

63. Türk 1787:136–37.

64. The three hymn tunes given as examples may be found in Zahn, nos. 5851, 5385a, and 1956.

65. Adlung 1758:487–90, 675–77.

66. Pröhle 1858:103.

67. Voigt 1742:95.

68. Adlung 1758:681.

69. Marpurg 1754–78, vol. 4 (1759), pp. 194–95.

70. Türk 1787:8.

71. Voigt 1742:94–95.

72. Adlung 1758:680–81.

73. Albrecht 1762:398. In Mühlhausen in 1732, though, the organist was asked to play a postlude to the service even during Lent (Werner 1932:113).

74. Adlung 1758:491.

75. Diehl 1899:164.

76. Wolters 1914–15:40.

77. Werner 1932:113. Werner provides other citations to the practice on pp. 113–14.

78. Williams 1980–84, vol. 3, p. 14, citing Niedt 1700/1710, § xiii.

79. The German reads "das huppigte . . . das tappigte . . . das springigte." Literally this would be "the hoppy, the clumsy, and the jumpy," but this does not have nearly the ring to it that "hoppity, skippity, jumpity" has! I therefore beg the reader's indulgence (Voigt 1742:41).

80. Marpurg 1750 (issue originally published November 11, 1749): 298.

81. Adlung 1758:491.

82. ". . . dass die Orgel und etwa auch andere musikalische Instrumente mit in die Gesänge gehen und das Volk sich damit conjugieren" (Quoted in Rietschel 1893:58).

83. Rautenstrauch 1907:180.

84. Türk 1787:11.

85. Hiller 1766–70, vol. 1, no. 30, pp. 229–32.

86. Hiller 1766–70, vol. 1, no. 34, pp. 261–64.

87. Niedt 1706, chapter 12 (glossary of terms), s.v. "Praeludium." The same is repeated in Niedt 1721, chapter 10, p. 102.

88. Gerber 1732:280–81.

89. Gerber 1699/1719:1072. See appendix 2, item 4, point 7 for a complete transcription of this statement and its context.

90. Motz 1703:220–21.

91. Türk 1787:124.

92. Mizler 1740:60.

93. Niedt 1717:46.

94. Bäumker 1886–1911, vol. 1, p. 231.

95. Adlung 1758:681–82.

96. Quoted in Werner 1932:116.

❖

Chapter 9

1. Baum 1969:33.

2. Hanau 1573, p. 9. The first two rules are repeated in Hohenlohe 1578 (Sehling 15:1:265–66).

3. They were *Vater unser im Himmelreich, O Herre Gott, dein göttlich Wort, Ach Gott vom Himmel, sieh darein, Wo Gott der Herr nicht bei uns hält, Es spricht der unweisen Mund wohl, Ich ruf zu dir, Herr Jesu Christ, Von Gott will ich nicht lassen,* and *Erhalt uns Herr bei deinem Wort* (Gerber 1732:256).

4. Gerber 1732:251–52.

5. Cunz 1855:277.

6. Edler 1720:45.

7. Marbach 1726:88. Other reasons given for mistakes in singing hymns were simply inattentiveness, hymns being taught incorrectly at home devotions, and mistakes in printed hymnals.

8. Braunschweig 1528, f. Q1^b; Andorff 1567, f. J2^a; London 1718:39–40; Kayser 1896:40; Pallas 1906–18, vol. 2, part 5, p. 384; Sehling 12:142–43; Rautenstrauch 1907:396.

9. Werner 1932:100–101.

10. Sehling 2:61–90.

11. *Liturgisch-musikalische Geschichte der evangelischen Gottesdienste von 1523 bis 1700* (Schleswig, 1893; reprint Hildesheim: Georg Olms, 1970), 61–77.

12. Edward Klammer, "De tempore hymn," in Schalk 1978:162–66.

13. *Groß Catholisch Gesangbuch,* 1631; reprinted in Bäumker 1886–1911, vol. 1, p. 228.

14. Horst Lindenberg wrote that the 1722 Augsburg hymnal was the earliest official congregational hymnal he had seen not arranged according to the liturgical year (Lindenberg 1925:32).

15. See pp. 102 and 148.

16. Wilisch 1735:34.

17. Erbacher 1984:34.

18. Schmidt 1961:86–87; the hymnal data is from Röbbelen 1957:18.

19. Rauschning 1931:167.

20. The preface is reprinted in Wackernagel 1855:646–47.

21. Nischan 1994:153.

22. *Project etlicher wolgegründeten Motiven, gegen die Einführung der Lobwassers-Lieder, in eine Ungeenderter Augßburgischer Confession zugethane Gemeine Christi.* The "Unaltered Augsburg Confession" was Philipp Melanchthon's original version of 1530, which he later revised to better accommodate the sacramental viewpoint of the Calvinists in the hope that they, too, might accept the Confession. Lutherans, especially those of the most orthodox wing, have since demonstrated their unwillingness to compromise on this doctrinal issue by making it clear that the version of the Augsburg Confession they accept is the original "unaltered" one. Many Lutheran churches in North America accordingly have the letters "UAC" inscribed on their cornerstones.

23. This point may have been an important one in the failure of Lobwasser's psalms to gain widespread acceptance among Lutherans. See Mager 1998.

24. The sequence of publication is Botsack, *Project* 1655; Curike, *Rejectum projectum* 1655; *Ein Reys-Gespräch* 1655; *Der ohnmächtige Fündling* 1655; *Antworte dem Narren* [1655]; *Antworte dem Narren nicht* [1655]; Botsack, *Protectum* 1655; Curike, *Reiectus protector* 1656. No copies of *Antworte dem Narren* and *Antworte dem Narren nicht* were accessible for this study.

25. *Rejectum Projectum, oder:Wiederlegung des Projects etlicher ungegründeter Motiven so ein ungenandter Scribent unlängst gegenst den Lobwasser für deß Herren Gebot außgegeben, und zum Schutz derer die in Elbing des Lobwassers Lieder abzuschaffen sich unterfangen außgefertiget.*

26. Unfortunately, the author does not specify exactly what was sung!

27. Edler 1720:50.

28. Dianne McMullen has reprinted the text of the Wittenberg review, together with an English translation, in her dissertation on Freylinghausen's hymnal (McMullen 1987:567–631). The original is the *Bedencken über das zu Glauche an Halle 1703. im Wäysen-Hause daselbst edirte Gesang-Buch.*

29. See McMullen 1987:232–79.

30. The sources for each item in this list are, in turn, Hirschmann 1994:104, 107; Sehling 7:2:1:780; Andorf 1567, f. J2^a; Sehling 2:438; Sehling 6:2:1151; Sehling 15:596–97;

Erbacher 1984:34; Rauschning 1931:82; Württemberg 1657:167; Rauschning 1931:279; Wolters 1914–15:140; Oettingen 1707:6.

31. Sonnenkalb 1756:18.

32. Türk 1787:16.

33. London 1718:39–40.

34. "Da der Choragus oder Vorsinger vnd Schulmeister in der Kirchen den Tact auff alle Syllaben (geschwind oder langsam, nach gestalt deß Chorals) in den Augen der gantzen Gemein geben solle, so wird eine schöne vnd bessere harmonia erfolgen" (Hanau 1659, p. 5).

35. Sehling 1:701, 7:2:1:1089, 6:2:1151.

36. Sehling 6:2:792.

37. Garbe 1995, column 1179.

38. Werner 1932:100–1.

39. Sonnenkalb 1756:22.

40. Mattheson 1739:431.

41. Werckmeister 1707:80.

42. Blankenburg 1961:609.

43. Rautenstrauch 1907:166.

44. Becker 1850:59.

45. Werner 1932:99.

46. Lindenberg 1925:66; Stahl 1952:93.

47. Lindenberg 1925:33.

48. Williams 1980–84, vol. 3, pp. 16–17.

49. Plön 1732:13.

50. Herold 1890:115.

51. Werner 1932:99.

52. Adlung 1758:680–81.

53. Voigt 1742:78.

54. Sehling 6:2:1180.

55. Sehling 1:722.

56. Köster 1898:73; Sehling 2:72.

57. Sehling 12:320.

58. Kätzel 1957:90; Brown 2001:109, 159; Rautenstrauch 1907:273.

59. Scheibel 1721:60.

60. Mattheson 1739:482.

61. Dieterich 1632, *Kirchweyh-oder Gesang-Predigt,* pp. 227–28.

62. Freytag 1936:13.

63. Biehle 1924:58.

64. Motz 1703:93.

65. Göz 1784, preface, pp. XCIII–XCIV.

66. Motz 1708:69–70.

67. Speer 1697:3.

68. Schünemann 1922:357, citing Hertel's *Verrostete Chorschlüssel* (1671).

69. Mithobius 1665:322.

70. Adlung 1758:679.

71. This information is given by Rietschel (p. 67), who received it from the "Hilfsprediger Fikenscher in Rotenburg a. d. T."

72. Hingelberg 1785:32. See the full quotation in chapter 8, "Interludes" section.

73. Garbe 1995, column 1179.

74. Praetorius 1619:87–88.

75. Praetorius, *Gesamtausgabe,* vol. 19, p. vii.

76. Quoted in Rietschel 1893:64.
77. Quoted in Werner 1932:97.
78. Quoted in Werner 1932:97.
79. Quoted in Werner 1932:97.
80. Voigt 1742:76.
81. Stahl 1952:92, quoting Ruetz 1753 [i.e., 1752]: 18. Also Ruetz 1752:155.
82. Türk 1787:84.
83. Seiler 1786:180.
84. Ameln 1980 and Ameln 1986.
85. Temperley 1979, vol. 1, pp. 92–93.
86. Blindow 1957:14.
87. Werner 1932:97. See the similar descriptions of nineteenth-century tempos in Blume 1965/1975:340.
88. Temperley 1979, vol. 1, p. 92.
89. Pröhle 1858:102.
90. Burney 1775, vol. 2, pp. 279–81.
91. ". . . ich sagte es doch unverholen—daß Herr Burney ein schlechter musikalischer Beobachter ist" (Reichardt 1774–76, vol. 1, p. 65).
92. Pröhle 1858:105–106.
93. Marbach 1726:87–88.
94. Marbach 1726:111–23.

❖

Conclusion

1. Dean 1997:620.
2. For example, in the area of liturgy, Ludwig Schoeberlein published a three-volume collection of Lutheran liturgical texts and music (Schoeberlein 1865–70); and A. L. Richter and Emil Sehling began separate efforts to assemble and publish the entire corpus of sixteenth-century Lutheran church orders, which eventually included several hundred documents related to the liturgy (Richter 1846; Sehling 1902–13, 1955–). Nineteenth-century writers Friedrich Armknecht and Rochus von Liliencron wrote careful academic studies of the Lutheran liturgy (Armknecht 1853, 1856; Liliencron 1893).

Nineteenth-century hymnological works concerned themselves mostly with establishing original forms of text and tune. For Lutheran hymnody, the multivolume sets by Philipp Wackernagel (for texts) and Johannes Zahn (for tunes) are notable (Wackernagel 1864–77; Zahn 1889–93). Most twentieth-century German works on hymnody have concentrated on hymns and hymnals rather than on the activity of singing. This is true of two major works: the two-volume historical companion to the hymns contained in the *Evangelisches Kirchengesangbuch* of 1950 and the exhaustive critical edition of German hymns in printed sources to 1680, intended to succeed the edition of Zahn, that has begun to appear under the title *Das deutsche Kirchenlied*.
3. Graff 1937–39, vol. 1, p. 5.
4. Graff 1937–39, vol. 1, pp. 15–16.
5. Blume 1965/1974:65.
6. Korth 1995; Garbe 1995; Butler 1996.

BIBLIOGRAPHY

❖

Part 1: Church Orders and Visitation Documents

Listed here are (1) agendas; that is, Lutheran church orders and private sources containing liturgical prescriptions; and (2) reports of ecclesiastical visitations containing descriptions of church services. They are arranged by the territory or city for which they were prepared, then chronologically by date. Agendas prepared for general use outside of a particular location are listed by the author's place of residence. Agendas for use within a single parish in a multiparish city have the name of the parish in parentheses after the city name. Private agendas without official sanction have the name of the author in parentheses. Agendas intended for use on a single occasion only (such as an anniversary observance in a certain year) are excluded. Visitation reports for small towns have the name of the territory in square brackets following the town name. Edicts resulting from visitations are prescriptive in nature and are therefore considered agendas. See chapter 5 for a full discussion of visitation records.

Titles are transcribed exactly as in the source used, whether an original or a secondary source, except that very long titles are truncated. The place of publication is given in its modern form. The author's name is given if known and easily available; no extra research has been done to discover or verify authors' names. If a document is available in a modern transcription or reprint, this information is then given, although no effort has been made to identify all modern editions. The following modern editions are identified only by the compiler's name: (1) J. J. Moser, *Corpus juris evangelicorum ecclesiastici, oder Sammlung evangelisch-lutherisch und reformirter Kirchen-Ordnungen,* 2 vols. (Züllichau, 1737–38); (2) K. Pallas, *Die Registraturen der Kirchenvisitationen im ehemals sächsischen Kurkreise,* 2 parts in 7 vols. (Halle, 1906–18); (3) A. L. Richter, *Die evangelischen Kirchenordnungen des sechzehnten Jahrhunderts,* 2 vols. in 1 (Weimar, 1846); and (4) E. Sehling, *Die evangelischen Kirchenordnungen des XVI. Jahrhunderts,* vols. 1–8, 11–15 in 15 physical volumes to date (Leipzig, 1902–13 and Tübingen, 1955–). Unfortunately, none include any musical notation present in the original sources; and Moser, Pallas, and Richter often provide only paraphrases instead of the actual text.

The dates of "later editions" of church orders are also given, by which is meant editions containing substantially the same liturgical prescriptions as in whose entry they appear. "Substantially the same" is an inexact term; but in general if the liturgical changes in a subsequent order do not affect any part of the liturgy sung by the choir or congregation (e.g., if the only changes are in the service times or in the texts of certain collects), then the order is considered a "later edition." But if the orders of service are different or different hymns are prescribed, then each edition is given its own bibliographic entry. Note that only the liturgical prescriptions are considered in determining whether a subsequent publication is a "later edition"; the other parts of a later edition may in fact be quite different, and the title may also have changed.

In angular brackets at the end of each entry a fingerprint is given for items for which I have seen the original (rather than a reprint). The fingerprint distinguishes among various printings of a book and is derived according to the rules of the *Short-Title Catalogue, Netherlands.* For a description, see P. C. A. Vriesema, "The STCN Fingerprint," *Studies in Bibliography* 39 (1986): 93–100. Also within the angular brackets are indications of

(1) the purpose of the document, whether prescriptive or descriptive:

  agenda: the document is prescriptive, containing instructions on how the liturgy is to be conducted (273 sources);

  service description: the document is descriptive, containing a report by an observer of how the service is conducted in one particular parish (127 sources) [Luther's mass orders of 1523 and 1526 are written in a style describing the practice at Wittenberg, but they were published with the intention of suggesting how evangelical masses might be conducted and so are considered prescriptive];

(2) whether the document is a *printed source* (129 sources) or a *manuscript* (271 sources);

(3) the kind of territory for which the document was intended (agendas only):

  city: the agenda was intended for use in more than one parish within a city (possibly including surrounding rural areas) (109 sources);

  cloister: the agenda was intended for use in a monastery or convent (15 sources);

  collegiate church: the agenda was intended for use in a church governed by a chapter of canons (4 sources);

  general: the agenda was not intended for use in any particular place (7 sources);

  hospital chapel: the agenda was intended for use in a chapel serving an institution for the ill or destitute (3 sources);

  parish: the agenda was intended for use within a single parish church (13 sources);

  territory: the order was intended for use throughout a kingdom, duchy, county, manor, diocese or other territory; orders for independent cities are designated city orders (122 sources);

(4) the degree to which the document represents an authoritative proclamation of the ecclesiastical government (agendas only):

  official: the agenda shows evidence of official adoption by the authority responsible for church government (237 sources);

  preliminary draft: the agenda is an early draft of an official order that is no longer extant (2 sources);

  private: the agenda was published by an individual and appeared without official sanction (11 sources);

  semiofficial: the agenda was widely used in a given area but does not seem to have been officially adopted; it is possible that many of these could, on closer investigation, be reclassified as either official or private (23 sources).

The list of documents in this part of the bibliography is not exhaustive but represents only those consulted for this study. All the liturgical documents in Moser, Richter, and Sehling were read, which together include nearly all sixteenth-century church orders (excluding reprints); but a number of seventeenth- and eighteenth-century orders were not available for consultation, including many that may (or may not) be reprints of earlier orders. Visitation reports were consulted only if they have been transcribed and published in modern editions, a distinct minority.

Ahlsdorf (with Schmilsdorf and Kunßdorf) [Saxony]
    1598 [Untitled visitation report]. Pallas 2:3:485. <service description, manuscript>
    1608 [Untitled visitation report]. Pallas 2:3:487. <service description, manuscript>

Alfeld [Braunschweig-Wolfenbüttel]
    1542 [Untitled visitation edict]. Kayser 1896:90–93. <agenda, manuscript, city, official>

Allersperg [bei Nürnberg]
    1560 [Untitled visitation report]. Hirschmann 1994:75. <service description, manuscript>

Allstedt
    1524a *Ordnung und berechnunge des teutschen ampts zu Alstadt durch Tomam Müntzer, seelwarters im vorgangen osteren aufgericht. 1523. Alstedt 1524. Ordnung und rechenschaft des teutschen ampts zu Alstet durch die diener gottis neulich aufgericht. 1523.* Eilenburg, 1524. By Thomas Müntzer. Sehling 1:504–7. <agenda, printed, city, semiofficial>
    1524b *Deutsch evangelisch messe, etwan durch die bepstischen pfaffen im latein zu grossem nachtheil des christen glaubens vor ein opfer gehandelt und itzt verordent in dieser ferlichen zeit zu entdecken den greuel aller abgötterei durch solche missbreuche der messen lange zeit getrieben. Thomas Münzer. Alstedt 1524.* Allstedt, 1524. By Thomas Müntzer. Sehling 1:497–504; *Thomas Müntzer: Deutsche evangelische Messe 1524*, edited by Siegfried Bräuer (Berlin: Evangelische Verlagsanstalt, 1988). <agenda, printed, city, semiofficial>

Altdorf [bei Nürnberg]
    1561 [Untitled visitation report]. Hirschmann 1994:197–99. <service description, manuscript>

Altenburg
    1705 *Agenda, oder Kirchen-Ordnung, Wie sich Die Pfarrherren und Seelsorger in ihren Aembtern und Verrichtungen, Jm Fürstenthum Altenburg, verhalten sollen.* Altenburg, 1705. <1705 04 - b1 A2 ele : b2 2D3 tliche—agenda, printed, territory, official>

Altherzberg [Saxony]
    1529 [Untitled visitation report]. Pallas 2:3:492. <service description, manuscript>

Amberg
    1544 *Ordnung der kirchen, wie man dieselben zu Amberg im spital pflegt zu halten.* Sehling 13:282–84. <agenda, manuscript, hospital chapel, semiofficial (?)>
    1555–57 *Kirchenordnung eins erbern rats zu Amberg der lehr und kirchenceremonien halb, wie diselben hinfüro in iren kirchen ze halten, Got dem almechtigen zu lob und verhuetung allerlai spaltung und ergernus furgenomen, darinne sie sich dann anderen christlichen*

evangelischen und sonderlich der meckhelburgischen kirchen und ordnung verglichen. Sehling 13:288–94. <agenda, manuscript, city, official>

1567 *Was der durchleuchtigist pfalzgraf Fridrich, churfürst etc., unser gnedigister herr, fur ergerliche ceremonien ab- und hergegen für verpesserung bei der kirchen und derselben dienern alhir angestellt haben will.* Sehling 13:303–4. <agenda, manuscript, city, official>

1576 *Warhaffter Bericht, Eines Erbarn Burgermeisters, innern und eussern Rahts, der Churfürstlichen Pfaltz Stadt Amberg. Das in jhrer angehörigen Kirchen vnnd Schule, die Christliche, reine Lehre, nach inhalt Gottes Worts, vnd der rechten waren Augspurgischen Confession gefüret, vnnd die hochwirdigen Sacramenta gereichet, auch alle andere actus Ecclesiastici verrichtet werden. Vnd Welcher gestalt sie bey gedachter Lehre vnd Kirchenordnung gelassen zu werden, jeder zeit vnd noch vnterthenigst gebeten vnd bitten, Sonsten aber alles schüldigen gehorsams sich verhalten haben, vnd noch erbieten. Wider die vngegründte beschüldigung DANIELIS TOSSANI, &c.* Leipzig, 1576. Not really a church order but a response to Daniel Tossanus's *Christliche erinnerung an einen Ersamen Rat vn[d] Gemeine der Churfürstlichen Pfaltz Stad Amberg* (1575), which criticizes Amberg's adherence to the 1556 order for the Palatinate. <1576 04 - b1 A2 te)aus : b2 F2 n en—agenda, printed, city, official>

Amberg (St. Mertein)

1550 *Kurzer und warhaftiger Bericht der kirchenordnung und ceremonien, wie si in S. Merteins kirchen alhie zu Amberg gehalten werden. 29. Nov. 1550.* Sehling 13:285–87. The purpose of this document is unclear. <service description, manuscript>

Andorff

1567 *Kirchenagend, oder Form vnd Gestalt, Wie es mit den Sacramenten vnd Ceremonien gehalten wird, in der Kirchen der Augspurgischen Confession zu Andorff. Durch die Ehrwirdigen Herrn vnd Predicanten daselbst gestelt, Welcher Namen am Ende gesetzt werden.* [N.p.], 1567. Prepared by a group consisting of Franciscus Alardus, Dythmarus Timannus, Christianus Vuernerus, Iohannes Veliger, Balthasar Houwart and Theodoricus Noteman; reviewed by several theologians, including Cyriacus Spangenberg and Flacius Illyricus. <1567 04 - b1 A2 d$erb : b2 J2 h$ne—agenda, printed, city, semiofficial>

Andreasberg [Grubenhagen]

1617 [Untitled visitation edict]. Spanuth 1955:52. <agenda, manuscript, city, official>

Anhalt

1548 [Untitled agenda]. Sehling 2:554–55. <agenda, manuscript, territory, official>

1551 *Ordnung der deutschen geistlichen gesenge, in dieser kirchen gebreuchlich und bequemlich, nach befehl unsern g. hern von Anhalt gericht.* Sehling 2:555–57. <agenda, manuscript, territory, official>

1568 [Untitled agenda]. Sehling 2:568–70. <agenda, manuscript, territory, official>

1645 *Ordnung, Wie es in den Kirchen, der Vngeenderten Augspurgischen Confession zugethan, des Fürstenthumbs Anhalt, im Zerbster Antheil, mit Christlichen Handelungen gehalten werden solle.* Zerbst, 1645. <1645 04 - b1 A2 n$wi : b2 H $E—agenda, printed, territory, official>

Annaberg

1579 [Untitled agenda]. Johannes Rautenstrauch, *Luther und die Pflege der kirchlichen Musik in Sachsen (14.–19. Jahrhundert)* (Leipzig: Breitkopf & Härtel, 1907;

reprint Hildesheim: Georg Olms, 1970), 165–76. Not in Richter or Sehling. <agenda, manuscript, city, official>

Apollensdorf [Saxony]
    1598   [Untitled visitation report]. Pallas 2:1:97. <service description, manuscript>
    1602   [Untitled visitation report]. Pallas 2:1:98. <service description, manuscript>

Arzberg [Saxony]
    1618   [Untitled visitation report]. Pallas 2:4:434. <service description, manuscript>
    1671   [Untitled visitation report]. Pallas 2:4:439–43. <service description, manuscript>

Aschersleben
    1575   *Kirchen-Agenda, derer sich der rath mit dem ministerio verclichen, anno 1575.* Sehling 2:477–83. <agenda, manuscript, city, official>

Augsburg
    1537a *Forma, wie von dem hailigen Tauff, vnd dem hailigen Sacrament des leibs vnd bluts Christi, vnd demnach vom Etlichen Stand bey dem Einsegen der Eeleüt, zureden sey, Gestellt in die Kirch vnd Gemaind Christi der Statt Augspurg.* Augsburg, 1537. By Martin Bucer. Sehling 12:72–92. Contains only orders for baptism, communion, and marriage. The communion order does not refer to the usual Sunday service. According to Sehling 12:26, the remainder of the order is handwritten, and that copy refers to the printed version at the appropriate points. <1537 04 - b1 a2 i t/d : b2 d5 u ts$/—agenda, printed, city, official>
    1537b [Untitled agenda]. By Martin Bucer. Sehling 12:50–64. Sehling 12:26 notes that this order omits the parts of the service printed in the same year. <agenda, manuscript, city, official>
  [1545] *FORMA, Wie vom hailigen Tauff vnnd dem H. Sacrament dess leibs vnnd bluts Christi Vnnd dem nach, vom Eelichen Stand, bey dem Einsegnen der Eeleüt zu reden sey. Gestellt in die Kirch vnd Gemaind Christi, der Statt Augspurg.* [N.p., n.d.]. Sehling 12:85–92. Later edition: [ca. 1550]. <0000 04 - b1 A2 es$be : b2 G3 /$noch—agenda, printed, city, official>
    1555   *FORMA, Wie vom hailigen Tauf, vnnd dem hailigen Sacrament des Leibs vnnd Bluts Christi, Deßgleichen wie auch von dem trost der Krancken, Vnd demnach vom Eelichen Stand bey dem Einsegen der Eeleüt, zureden sey, widerumb von newem getruckt. Gestellt in die Kirch vnd Gemaind Christi der Statt Augspurg.* Augsburg, 1555. Sehling 12:95–108. <1555 04 - b1 A2 and$v : b2 L3 ment$—agenda, printed, city, official>
    1718   *Agenda ECCLESIASTICA. Oder: Forma der Handlung der H. Sacramenten, Ehe-Einsegnung, und öffentlichen Gebet, Deren der Augspurgischen Confession zugethanen Kirchen, in der freyen Reichs-Stadt Augspurg. Revidiert und erneuert im Jahr Christi 1718.* [Augsburg, 1718]. <1718 04 - a1=a2)(2 t=$S - b1 A en : b2 M2 hat—agenda, printed, city, semiofficial>

Axien [Saxony]
    1602   [Untitled visitation report]. Pallas 2:3:82. <service description, manuscript>

Baden
    1556   *Kirchenordnung. Wie die inn der Marggraueschafft Baden, Pfortzheimer theils, auch andern Marggraff Carlins zu Baden vn[d] Hochberg, Marggraueschafft, Landtschafften vn[d] Herrschafften soll angericht vn[d] gehalten werden.* Tübingen, 1556. This

order was reprinted from Württemberg 1553. <1556 04 - b1 A2 derli : b2 S rg—agenda, printed, territory, official>

1775 *Kirchen-Agenda wie es in des Durchlauchtigsten Fürsten und Herrn, HERRN Carl Friedrichs, Marggrafen zu Baaden und Hochberg, Landgrafen zu Sausenberg, Grafen zu Sponheim und Eberstein, Herrn zu Röteln, Badenweiler, Lahr, Mahlberg und Kehl &c. &c. gesamten Fürstenthumen und Landen mit Verkündigung des göttlichen Worts, Administrirung und Austheilung der heiligen Sacramenten und andern Kirchen- Ceremonien gehalten werden solle.* Karlsruhe, 1775. <1775 04 - a1):(2 $Orte : a2):(3 Herk - b1 A il : b2 2U3 $Jahr—agenda, printed, territory, official>

Barum [Braunschweig-Wolfenbüttel]
1577 [Untitled visitation report]. Wolters 1938–50, vol. 43, pp. 210–11. <service description, manuscript>

Belgern [Saxony]
1586 [Untitled visitation report]. Pallas 2:4:399. <service description, manuscript>

Belrieth and Einhausen [County Henneberg]
1566 *Verzeichnis des pfarherrn zu Belerith, wie ers halte, in seiner heuptpfarr zu Belerith und in seinem filial zu Einhausen mit allen ceremonien, gesengen und predigten auf alle sontag und furnembste festa.* By Pancratius Treutel, pastor. Sehling 2:329–30. <service description, manuscript>

Belzig
1529 [Untitled agenda]. Sehling 1:527–28. <agenda, manuscript, city, official>

Bergedorf
1544 [Untitled agenda]. By Johann Aepin. Richter 2:76–78; Sehling 5:386–90. <agenda, manuscript, city, official>

Bergwitz [Saxony]
1602 [Untitled visitation report]. Pallas 2:1:217. <service description, manuscript>

Beyern [Saxony]
1672 [Untitled visitation report]. Pallas 2:3:541. <service description, manuscript>

Bischofswerda
[ca. 1620] [Untitled agenda]. Sehling 2:106. Sehling leaves this source undated but notes that the cantor referred to it in 1676 as very old (Sehling 2:104). The form of the service, the use of the organ, and especially the mention of the Betstunde, which in this order does not yet appear as a separate service, would place it around 1620. <agenda, manuscript, parish (?), official (?)>

Blönsdorf, Danna and Melmessdorf [Saxony]
1618 [Untitled visitation report]. Pallas 2:1:420. <service description, manuscript>

Brandenburg
1540 *Kirchen Ordnung im Churfurstenthum der Marcken zu Brandemburg, wie man sich beide mit der Leer und Ceremonien halten sol.* Berlin, 1540. Richter 1:323–34; Sehling 3:39–90. <[Part 1:] 1540 04 - b1 A2 fft$: b2 R3 zu$l || [Part 2:] 1540 04 - b1 a2 nd$: b2 2h3 nan || [Part 3:] 0000 04 - b1 A2 gt : b2 3A3 dem—agenda, printed, territory, official>

1572 *Die Augspurgische Confession, aus dem Rechten Original, welches Keyser Carolo dem V. auff dem Reichstage zu Augspurg Anno 1530. vbergeben, Der Kleine Catechismus.*

Erklerung vnd kurtzer Au$eszug aus den Postillen vnd Lehrschrifften des theuren Mans Gottes D. Lutheri, daraus zusehen, wie derselbe von fürnembsten Artickeln vnserer Christlichen Religion gelehret, Aus verordnunge des Durchlauchtigsten, Hochgebornen Fürsten vnd Herrn, Herrn Johansen Georgen, Marggraffen zu Brandenburg, des Heiligen Römischen Reichs ErtzCämmerers vnd Churfürsten, in Preussen, zu Stettin, Pommern, der Cassuben, Wenden, Auch in Schlesien zu Crossen Hertzogen, Burggraffen zu Nürnbergk, vnd Fürsten zu Rügen, Vor die Kirchen in seiner Churfürst. G. Landen, Neben einer allgemeinen Agenden oder Ordnung, nach welcher sich die Pfarherr vnd Kirchendiener zuuorhalten, zusamen gedruckt. Frankfurt/Oder, 1572. Moser 2:1301–1364; Richter 2:347–48; Sehling 3:94–104 (reprinted from Moser). <1572 02 - b1 A $: b2 2M4 eylands/$—agenda, printed, territory, official>

Brandenburg (Goltz)

1614 *Agenda Das ist Außerlesene Kirchen-Ceremonien Welche in den Kirchen Augspurgischer Confeßion in vblichem Brauche sein, vnnd hin vnd wieder gleich vnd vngleich Bey Dem Sacrament der H. Tauffe, Administration des HERRN CHRisti Nachtmahl, Copulation Breutigams vnnd Braut, Einsegnung der Sechswöchnerinnen, vnnd Christlichen Begrebnussen gehalten werden, Colligiret vnd zusammen getragen, Durch M. Joachimum Goltzium Seniorem Dienern Göttliches Wortts zu Franckfurth an der Oder, Mit Churfürstlichen Sächßischen vnd Brandenburgischen Befreyungen auff zehen Jahr.* Frankfurt/Oder, 1614. By Joachim Goltz. According to Graff (1937–39), this order was originally only for Frankfurt/Oder but was reprinted many times to 1697 and found widespread use. Later editions: 1679, 1697. <1614 04 - b1 A2 ck : b2 N3 r$tre—agenda, printed, general, private>

Brandenburg-Ansbach

1526 *Abschied vnnd maynung wes sich der Durchleüchtig Hochgeborn Fürst vnnd herr, Herr Casimir Marggraue zu Brandennburg. &c. von sein vnd seiner Fürstlichen gnaden mitregirenden bruders, Marggrauen Jörgen zu sampt jrer F. G. Lanndtschafft, auff negstgehaltem Landtag zu Onoltzbach biß auff ein zu künfftig Concilium, Nacional versamlung, oder seiner Fürstlichen Gnaden, weyttern beschayd, des abschieds halben, Jüngstgehaltens Reichstags zu Speyer, Jnn jrer Fürstlichenn Gnaden Land vnnd Fürstenthumb, zu halten vereynigt haben.* Richter 1:50–55. <agenda, printed, territory, official>

Brandenburg-Ansbach-Kulmbach

1533 [Untitled agenda]. Sehling 11:311–16. <agenda, manuscript, cloister, official>

1538 *Figural und coral zu ziemlicher zeit in der kirchen zu singen und in den schulen anzurichten 1538.* Sehling 11:397–98. <agenda, manuscript, territory, official>

1548 *Mehrung der vorigen kirchenordnung, aufgerichtet in unseres gn. herrn margg. Georg Friederichs Fürstentum. 1548.* Sehling 11:325–31. <agenda, manuscript, territory, official>

Brandenburg-Nuremberg

1528 [Untitled agenda]. Sehling 11:135–39. <agenda, manuscript, territory, official>

1533 *Kirchen Ordnung. Jn meiner gnedigen herrn der Marggrauen zu Brandenburg Vnd eins Erbern Rats der Stat Nürnberg Oberkeyt vnd gepieten, Wie man sich bayde mit der leer vnd Ceremonien halten solle.* 1533. Moser 2:665–760; Richter 1:176–211; Sehling 11:140–283. Later editions: 1534, 1536, 1556, 1564, 1592. <1533 04 - b1 A2 $gebe : b2 O4 d$den$—agenda, printed, territory, official>

Brandis

1574 [Untitled agenda]. Sehling 1:534. <agenda, manuscript, city, official>

Braunschweig

1528 *Der Erbarn Stadt Brunswig Christlike ordeninge, to denste dem hilgen Euangelio, Christliker lèue, tucht, frede vn[d] de eynicheit. Ock dar vnder vele Christlike lere vor de borgere. Dorch Joannem Bugenhagen Pomern bescreuen.* Wittenberg, [1528]. By Johann Bugenhagen. edited by Ludwig Hänselmann; Richter 1:106– 120; Sehling 6:1:348–455. Later editions: 1531 (High German), 1563 (High German). <1528 08 - b1 A2 inge$: b2 S3 de—agenda, printed, city, official>

[ca. 1550] *Ordnung der ceremonien auf den dorfern der stadt Braunschweigk.* Sehling 6:1:473– 75. A letter dated 17 November 1995 from Archivdirektor Dr. Manfred Garz- mann of the Stadtarchiv Braunschweig states that this source cannot be dated exactly, but the style of writing and watermark indicate that it was written be- fore 1580, possibly in the first half of the sixteenth century; therefore, I have assigned it a date of [ca. 1550]. The large amount of congregational singing and the mention of *Christ unser Herr zum Jordan kam* as a catechism hymn (which is not otherwise mentioned until Braunschweig-Lüneburg 1564) suggest that it might have been written later, but the evidence is not conclusive. <agenda, manuscript, city, official>

Braunschweig-Lüneburg

[1555] *Reformatio coenobiorum ducatus Luneburgensis.* Sehling 6:1:609–18. According to Sehling, a number of copies of this order exist, each one individualized for a different cloister. This version, found in the Staatsarchiv Hannover, is for the cloister at Isenhagen. <agenda, manuscript, cloister/parish, official>

1564 *Kirchenordnung: Wie es mit Christlicher Lere, reichung der Sacrament, Ordination der Diener des Euangelij, Ordentlichen Ceremonien, Visitation, Consistorio vnd Schulen, Jm Hertzogthumb Lünenburg gehalten wird.* Wittenberg, 1564. Richter 2:285–87; Sehling 6:1:533–75. Later editions: 1598, 1619, 1643. <1564 04 - b1 A2 en$g : b2 2A2 deita—agenda, printed, territory, official>

1574 [Untitled agenda]. Sehling 6:1:619–23. <agenda, manuscript, cloister, official>

Braunschweig-Wolfenbüttel

1543 *Christlike Kerken-Ordeninge, im lande Brunschwig, Wulffenbüttels deles.* Wittenberg, 1543. By Anton Corvinus. Richter 2:56–64; Sehling 6:1:22–80. <1543 04 - b1 A2 bro : b2 Y4 edel$M—agenda, printed, territory, official>

1569 *Kirchenordnung unser, von Gottes genaden Julii, herzogen zu Braunschweig und Lüneburg etc. Wie es mit lehr und ceremonien unsers fürstenthumbs Braunschweig, Wulffenbütlischen theils, auch derselben kirchen anhangenden sachen und verrichtungen hinfurt (vermittelst göttlicher gnaden) gehalten werden sol.* Wolfenbüttel, 1569. By Martin Chemnitz and Jacob Andreae. Richter 2:318–24; Sehling 6:1:83–335. <agenda, printed, territory, official>

1615 *KirchenOrdnung, Vnnser, von Gottes Genaden, Julij, Hertzogen zu Braunschweig vnd Lüneburg, etc. Wie es mit Lehr vnd Ceremonien vnsers Fürstenthumbs Braunschweig, Wolffenbütlischen Theils, Auch derselben Kirchen angangenden Sachen vnd Verrichtun- gen, hinfort (vermittelst Göttlicher Gnaden) gehalten werden soll.* Helmstedt, 1615. Hannover: Carl Rümpler, 1853. Later editions: 1649 (not seen), 1651. <1615 04 - a1 a2 /$D : a2 b3 rder - b1 A me : b2 3S en/$v—agenda, printed, terri- tory, official>

1657 *Agenda Oder: Erster Teyl der Kirchen-Ordnung, Unser von Gottes Gnaden AU- GUSTI, Herzogen zu Bruns-Wyk und Lunä-Burg. Wy es mit deñ Ceremonien, auch andern nootwendigen Sachen und Verrichtungen in deñ Kirchen Unserer Fürstentume Graf-Herrschaften und Landen zu halten.* Wolfenbüttel, 1657. <1657 04 - b1 A2 hoc : b2 2L3 kranke—agenda, printed, territory, official>

1709 *Erneuerte Kirchen-Ordnung Unser Von GOttes Gnaden Anthon Ulrichs Hertzogen zu Braunschweig und Lüneburg.* Braunschweig, 1709. Later edition: 1769. <1709 04 - 1b1 A2 $ric : 1b2 U3 ;$ - 2b1 A2 n$: 2b2 Z ol - 2c1)(ebe : 2c2 2)(2 be etze - 3b1 a Oe : 3b2 2e3 e$n—agenda, printed, territory, official>

Brehna [Saxony]
    1583 [Untitled visitation report]. Pallas 2:2:336. <service description, manuscript>

Brehna (cloister) [Saxony]
    1531 [Untitled visitation report]. Pallas 2:2:310. <service description, manuscript>

Breslau
    1557 [Untitled agenda]. Sehling 3:404–5. <agenda, manuscript, city, official>

Brugk [Brandenburg]
    1530 [Untitled agenda]. Müller 1904:133. <agenda, manuscript, city, official>

Bursfelde [Calenberg-Göttingen]
    1542 [Untitled visitation edict]. Kayser 1896:293. <agenda, manuscript, cloister, official>

Buxtehude
    1552 *Angenamen kerkenordeninge eynes erbarn rades der statt Buxtehude, gestellet dorch den erwerdigen, hochgelarten Doctorem Johannem Epinum, superintendenten der statt Hamborch.* By Johann Aepin. Sehling 7:1:68–91. <agenda, manuscript, city, official>
    1565 [Untitled agenda]. Sehling 7:1:92–129. <agenda, manuscript, city, official>

Calenberg-Göttingen
    1542 *Christliche Kirchen Ordnung, Ceremonien vnd Gesenge, Fur arme vngeschickte Pfarrherrn gestelt vnd in den Druck gegeben.* Erfurt, 1542. By Anton Corvinus. Richter 1:362–67; Sehling 6:2:708–843. Later edition: 1544. <1542 04 - b1 A2 ? $W : b2 t3 h$me—agenda, printed, territory, official>
    [1542] *Ordenungh vor die klosterleuth, in welcher sonderlich angezeigt wirth, was solche orden vor einen grunth in der heiligen schrift und fornembsten vetern haben, desgleichen, wie sich hinfuro solche leuthe in dem loblichen furstenthumb herzogen Erichs des jungern halten sollen.* By Anton Corvinus. Sehling 6:2:844–54. Later edition: 1544 (Low German). <agenda, manuscript, cloister, official>

Clöden (with Schützberg and Dröben) [Saxony]
    1577 [Untitled visitation report]. Pallas 2:3:140. <service description, manuscript>

Coburg
    1524 [Untitled agenda]. Sehling 1:542–43. <agenda, manuscript, city, official>

Cochstedt [Diocese of Halberstadt]
    1556 *Kirchenordnung, wie sie ist bis daher seit 1556 gehalten worden.* Sehling 2:483–84. <service description, manuscript>

Colberg
    1586 [Untitled agenda]. 1586. Sehling 4:500–506. <agenda, manuscript, cloister, official>

Cologne

1543 *Von Gottes genaden, vnser Hermans Ertzbischoffs zu Cöln, vnnd Churfürsten &c.*
einfaltigs bedencken, warauff ein Christliche, in dem wort Gottes gegrünte Reformation
an Lehr, brauch der Heyligen Sacramenten vnd Ceremonien, Seelsorge, vnd anderem
Kirchendienst, biß vff eines freyen, Christlichen, Gemeinen oder Nationals Concilij, oder
des Reichs Teutscher Nation Stende, im Heyligen Geyst versamlet, verbesserung, bey
denen so vnserer Seelsorge befolhen, anzurichten seye. By Martin Bucer and Philipp
Melanchthon. Richter 2:30–54. <agenda, printed, territory, official>

Croppenstedt [Diocese of Halberstadt]

1589 *Christliche kirchenordnung der ceremonien und gesenge, die hie zu Croppenstedt gehal-*
ten werden. Sehling 2:484–85. <service description, manuscript>

Danzig

1557 [Untitled agenda]. Sehling 4:181. <agenda, manuscript, city, official>
1570 [Untitled agenda]. Sehling 4:188–90. <agenda, manuscript, city, official>
1618 *Formul Der Christlichen Ceremonien, Welche in den Euangelischen Kirchen zu*
Dantzigk, Bey verhandlung des Hochwürdigen Abendmals, etc. gebreuchlich sein. Sampt
einer Vorrede an den Christlichen Leser, Darinnen ein kurtze vnterweisung zur
Gottseligkeit angezeiget, vnd auff etliche Streitpunct kürtzlich geantwort wird. Allen
Einfeltigen vnnd Jungen Leuten zum vnterricht gestellet, Wie sie sich selbst prüfen, vnd
zum würdigen gebrauch des heiligen Abendmals bereiten sollen. Danzig, 1618. <1618
08 - b1 A2 utu : b2 O5 ens—agenda, printed, city, semiofficial>
1708 *Verordnung E. E. Rahts Die Einrichtung Der geistlichen Ampts-Geschäffte und*
Kirchen-Gebethe Bey der Evangelisch-Lutherischen Gemeine der Stadt Dantzig be-
langend, publicirt Mense Mart. 1708. Danzig, [1708]. <1708 04 - b1 A2 nd$b :
b2 O3 gege—agenda, printed, city, official>

Danzig (Marienkirche)

1567 *Verzeichniss und ordnung, wie es mit predigt und anderem in der pfarrkirche zu St.*
Marien zu halten. Sehling 4:186–87. <agenda, manuscript, parish, official>
1612 *Alte kirchenordnung der kirchen Sanct Marien, in der rechten stadt Dantzig, nach itzi-*
gen zustande, und wie es mit allen derselben kirchenofficianten, nach dem gefallenen babst-
thumb biss dahero gehalten worden und noch gehalten wird. Item schulordnung der
schulen daselbst, wie sie die itzige kirchenväter vor sich gefunden, und in etzlichen
puncten verbessert. Durch die dahie bestellten kirchenväter oder vorsteher aufs neue revi-
diret und artickelweise in eine gewisse ordnung gebracht. Im jahre 1612. Sehling
4:197–218. <agenda, manuscript, parish, official>

Dennenlohe and Eltersdorf [bei Nürnberg]

1561 [Untitled visitation report]. Hirschmann 1994:244–60. <service description,
manuscript>

Dessau

1532 [Untitled agenda]. By Nicolaus Hausmann. Sehling 2:540–43. <agenda, manuscript, city, official>

Dingleben [County Henneberg]

1566 [Untitled visitation report]. By Georg Planck, pastor. Sehling 2:331–32. <ser-
vice description, manuscript>

Dohna [Saxony]

1578 [Untitled visitation report]. Sehling 1:550–51. <service description, manu-
script>

Dommitzsch [Saxony]
    1598   [Untitled visitation report]. Pallas 2:4:138. <service description, manuscript>

Dresden (Kreuzkirche)
    1574   [Untitled agenda]. By Daniel Greyser. Sehling 1:555–56. <agenda, manuscript, parish, official>

East Frisia
    1535   *Karckenordenynge vor dem pastoren unde kerckendenern. Wo men doepen schal. Van dem aventmall des Heren und andern kerckengebruyken.* Sehling 7:1:373–97. <agenda, manuscript, territory, official>

Eibach [bei Nürnberg]
    1561   [Untitled visitation report]. Hirschmann 1994:284–85. <service description, manuscript>
    1583   *Liturgia Engerhovana oder gewöhnliche formulen des gottesdienstes bey bedienung I. der heiligen taufe, II. des heil[igen] abendmahls, III. der copulation, trauung und einsegnung der angehenden eheleuten, IV. der kranken in der kirchen und gemeine Jesu Christi, der Augsburgischen Confession zugetan, zu Engerhove.* By Johannes Ligarius. Sehling 7:1:671–82. <agenda, manuscript, city, semiofficial>
    1593   [Untitled agenda]. Sehling 7:1:683–724. <agenda, manuscript, territory, official>
    1631   *Kirchen Ordnung, WJe es in Religions vnd Glaubens sachen mit der seligmachenden Lehr vnd Predigt des heiligen göttlichen Worts, Christlicher administration der hochwirdigen Sacramenten, bestellung der Kirchendieners gewöhnlichem Gebet vnd löblichen Ceremonien in der Graffschafft Ostfrießland, Augspurgischer Confession zugethan, vnd in den beyden Herrschafften Essens vnd Wittmund hinfüro einmütiglich gehalten werden sol.* Lüneburg, 1631. Later edition: 1716. <1631 04 - b1 A2 n/$a : b2 2D Cu—agenda, printed, territory, official>

Eilenburg
    1529   [Untitled agenda]. Sehling 1:560. <agenda, manuscript, city, official>

Eisfeld
    1554   *Ordenung der kirchen ceremonien vor die pfarher auf den dorfern.* Sehling 1:562–63. <agenda, manuscript, city, official>

Eldagsen [Calenberg-Göttingen]
    1543   [Untitled visitation edict]. Kayser 1896:389. <agenda, manuscript, cloister, official>

Elsnig [Saxony]
    1586   [Untitled visitation report]. Pallas 2:4:163. <service description, manuscript>
    1598   [Untitled visitation report]. Pallas 2:4:164. <service description, manuscript>

Elster [Saxony]
    1602   [Untitled visitation report]. Pallas 2:1:130. <service description, manuscript>

Ermsleben [Diocese of Halberstadt]
    1564   [Untitled visitation report]. Sehling 2:485–86. <service description, manuscript>

Eschenaw [bei Nürnberg]
    1561   [Untitled visitation report]. Hirschmann 1994:151. <service description, manuscript>

Falkenberg [Saxony]
1529 [Untitled visitation report]. Pallas 2:4:168. <service description, manuscript>

Felden [bei Nürnberg]
1560 [Untitled visitation report]. Hirschmann 1994:87. This is a directive by the town council. <agenda, manuscript, city, official>

Feuchtwangen
1563 *Verzeichnüs, wie es in beden kirchen alhie zue Feuchtwang gehalten würd.* Sehling 11:399–404. <agenda, manuscript, city, official>

Frankendorf, Holstet and Kötzschau [Saxony]
1569 [Untitled visitation report]. By Johannes Siebensohn, deacon. Sehling 1:583. <service description, manuscript>

Frankfurt/Main
1530 [Untitled agenda]. Richter 1:140–42. <agenda, manuscript, city, official>
1565 *Agend Büchlein, Der Christlichen Euangelischen Kirchen zu Franckfurt am Mayn, darinn die Gebet, vnd andere Ceremonien, so bey der Predig Gottes Worts, vnd den heiligen Sacramenten daselbst gebreuchlich sind, kürtzlich angezeigt werden, (begriffen sind.)* Frankfurt/Main, 1565. <1565 04 - b1 A2 en$ ei : b2 E2 nr#uffe—agenda, printed, city, semiofficial (?)>

Freckenfeldt [Guttenberg]
1562 [Untitled visitation report]. Schneider 1878:5–6. <service description, manuscript>

Gandersheim (city) [Braunschweig-Wolfenbüttel]
1542 [Untitled visitation edict]. Kayser 1896:77. <agenda, manuscript, city, official>

Gandersheim (cloister) [Braunschweig-Wolfenbüttel]
1542 [Untitled visitation edict]. Kayser 1896:40–41. <agenda, manuscript, cloister, official>

Gernrode (cloister) [Anhalt]
1541 *Ordnung wie es mit dem gottesdinst in der kirchen gehalten wird zu Gernrode.* Sehling 2:595. <service description, manuscript>

Gnandstein
1539 [Untitled agenda]. Sehling 1:564. <agenda, manuscript, city, official>

Goldlauter [County Henneberg]
1566 *Kirchenordnung wie ichs Cunradus Eberhardt dieser zeit pfarherr in der Goldlauter die funt jahr lange, so ich alda gewesen, gehalten habe und noch halte.* By Cunrad Eberhardt, pastor. Sehling 2:332–33. <service description, manuscript>

Goslar
1531/1651 [Untitled agenda]. Richter 1:154–56. <agenda, manuscript, city, official>

Gotha
1645 *Synodal-Schluß, welcher nach der in dem Fürstenthumb Gotha gehaltenen General-Kirchen- und Landes-Visitation . . . ratificirt worden.* Gotha, 1645. <agenda, printed, territory, official>

Gottleuba [Saxony]
1577 *Verzeichnus der kirchenordnung zur Gotleuben, welche von Jahr 1567 bis uf das 1577,*

gehalten ist worden, von Nicolao Andreae Pirnensi, pfarhern doselbst. Sehling 1:567–68. <service description, manuscript>

Grebern [bei Nürnberg]
    1561 [Untitled visitation report]. Hirschmann 1994:115. <service description, manuscript>

Greifenberg [Pomerania]
    1540 [Untitled visitation report]. Heyden 1961–64:2:53–54. <service description, manuscript>

Grevenberg [bei Nürnberg]
    1561 [Untitled visitation report]. Hirschmann 1994:104–107. <service description, manuscript>

Grubenhagen
    1538 [Untitled agenda]. Sehling 6:2:1028–30. <agenda, manuscript, territory, official>
    1544 *Reformatio, das ist fürstliche braunschweigische kirchenordenung des durchleuchtigen hochgebornen fürsten und hern, hern Philips, herzogen zu Braunschweig und Lüneburgk etc., Grubenhagischen theils, publicirt 1544.* Sehling 6:2:1031–39. <agenda, manuscript, territory, official>
    1581 *DEs Durchlauchtigen, Hochgebornen Fürsten vnd Herren, Herrn Wolffgangen, Hertzogen zu Braunschweig vnd Lüneburgk etc. Christliche Ordnung vnd Befehl. Wes sich Prediger vnd Zuhörer in Seiner F. G. Lande, auff jüngstgeschehene Visitation hinfüro verhalten sollen.* [Eisleben], 1581. Sehling 6:2:1041–1102. <1581 04 - 1b1 A2 ort/$: 1b2 Z3 i$e - 2b1 a2 üm : 2b2 g4 e u—agenda, printed, territory, official>

Hadeln
    [ca. 1542] [Untitled agenda]. Sehling 5:465–76. The date 1542 is approximate, as determined by Sehling. The order is based on a prior one of 1526 or 1529, no longer extant. <agenda, manuscript, territory, official>

Hadmersleben [Archdiocese of Magdeburg]
    1562–63 [Untitled visitation report]. Danneil 1867:1:34; Sehling 2:428–29. <service description, manuscript>

Halberstadt
    1591 [Untitled agenda]. In G. Arndt, "Die Entwicklung der evangelischen Gottesdienstordnung im Bistum Halberstadt während des 16. Jahrhunderts," *Monatschrift für Gottesdienst und kirchliche Kunst* 18/7 (July 1913): 235–43. This order was for the cathedral foundation, or collegiate church. <agenda, manuscript, collegiate church, official>

Haldensleben [Archdiocese of Magdeburg]
    1564 [Untitled visitation report]. Danneil 1867:1:53–54. <service description, manuscript>

Halle
    1543 *Kirchen-Ordnung der christlichen Gemein zu Halle.* Richter 2:14–21; Sehling 2:434–36. <agenda, manuscript, city, official>
    1573 *Kirchen-Ordnung der christlichen Gemein zu Hall in Sachsen.* Richter 1:339–42; Sehling 2:436–43. <agenda, manuscript, city, official>

Hamburg

    1529   *Der Erbaren Stadt Hamborg Christliche Ordeninge, tho denste dem Evangelio Christi, Christliker Leve, Tucht, Frede und Einicheit.* By Johann Bugenhagen. edited and translated by C. Mönckeberg (Hamburg, 1861); edited by Carl Bertheau (Hamburg, 1885); Richter 1:127–34; Sehling 5:488–540. <agenda, printed, city, official>

    1556   [Untitled agenda]. By Johann Aepin. Richter 1:315–20; Sehling 5:543–56. <agenda, manuscript, city, official>

Hanau

    1573   *Kirchenordnung, Wie es mit der Lehr vnd Ceremonien, in der Graffschafft Hanaw, vnd Herrschafft Lichtenberg, sol gehalten werden.* Strassburg, 1573. Richter 2:506–508. <1573 04 - a1$eqa2)(2 chgeb - b1 A : b2 L e—agenda, printed, territory, official>

    1659   *Hanauische vermehrte Kirchen unndt Schul-Ordnung.* Strassburg, 1659. <1659 04 - a1 a2 ir$ei : a2 d3 &$cu - 1b1 A e : 1b2 3Z3 ch$HEr - 2b1 4A /$die$: 2b2 4F3 .$III.98.$ e—agenda, printed, territory, official>

Harlingerland

    1574   *Deß wollgebornen und edlen herrn, herrn Erichs, graffen zur Hoya, Ritperch und Bruch-hausen, herrn zue Esenß, Stedeßdorff und Wittmundt, vorklerter und publicirter kirchen-und disciplinordnung kurzer summarischer extract, in aller maße, alß in den graff-und heerschaften Hoya, Rittpergk, Bruchhusen, Esenß, Stedeßdorff und Wittmundt mit ratt der theologen und rechtßgelehrten beschloßen und in gemelten Seiner Gnaden graff-und herrschaften durchauß von den predigstühlen, rattheusern nach gelegenheit eineß jeden ohrtß publiciret, auch in kumpstigen visitationen eindrechtig und einhelling gehal-ten und derselben gestrackß gehorsamet werden solle, 1574 etc.* Sehling 7:1:725–50. <agenda, manuscript, territory, official>

Hatzkerode

    [1534?]   [Untitled agenda]. Sehling 2:586–88. <agenda, manuscript, city, official>

Henneberg

    1582   *Des durchlauchtigen hochgebornen fürsten und herrn, herrn Georg Ernsten, graven und herrn zu Henneberg, etc. kirchen ordnung, wie es in s. f. g. fürstlicher graf- und herrschaft, beide mit lehr und ceremonien, christlich, und gottes wort ebenmessig, gehalten werden sol. 1582.* Schmalkalden, 1582. Sehling 2:298–324. <agenda, printed, terri-tory, official>

    1713   *Des Durchlauchtigen, Hochgebohrnen Fürsten und Herrn, HERRN Georg Ernsten, Grafen und Herrn zu Hennenberg, &c. Kirchen-Ordnung, Wie es in S. F. G. Fürstlicher Graf und Herrschafft, beyde mit Lehr und Ceremonien, Christlich, und GOttes Wort ebenmäßig, gehalten werden soll.* Schleusingen, 1713. <1713 04 - b1 A2 hen : b2 3B ugte#—agenda, printed, territory, official>

Herpf [County Henneberg]

    1566   [Untitled visitation report]. Sehling 2:334–36. <service description, manu-script>

Herzberg [Saxony]

    1579   [Untitled visitation report]. Pallas 2:3:437. <service description, manuscript>

    1598   [Untitled visitation report]. Pallas 2:3:450. <service description, manuscript>

    1602   [Untitled visitation report]. Pallas 2:3:453. <service description, manuscript>

Hesse

1526 *[Reformatio ecclesiarum Hassiae].* ed. by Heinrich Hermelink after the translation of Karl August Credner (Marburg, 1926); Richter 1:56–69; Sehling 8:43–65. Luther was asked to review this draft of the church order and declined to approve it; it was therefore never printed or authorized. <agenda, manuscript, territory, preliminary draft>

1532 *Ordenung der Christlichen kirchen in furstenthumb zu Hessen.* Richter 1:162–65; Sehling 8:75–79. <agenda, manuscript, territory, official>

1566 *Kirchen Ordnung: Wie sich die Pfarherrn vnd Seelsorger in jrem beruff mit leren vnd predigen, allerley Ceremonien vnd guter Christlicher Disciplin vnnd Kirchenzucht halten sollen: Für die Kirchen inn dem Fürstenthumb Hessen: Aus der Aposteln, jrer Nachfolger vnd anderen alten Christlicher reiner Lehrer schrifften gestellet.* Marburg, 1566. Richter 2:289–97; Sehling 8:178–337. <1566 04 - a1 AA3 tturfft$: a2 CC3 nd$auf - b1 a m : b2 2F2 ner$o—agenda, printed, territory, official>

1574 *Agenda Das ist: Kirchenordnung wie es im Fürstenthumb Hessen mit verkündigung Göttliches worts, reichung der heiligen Sacramenten vnd andern Christlichen handlungen vnd Ceremonien gehalten werden soll.* Marburg, 1574. Richter 2:393–95; Sehling 8:408–69. Later editions: 1662, 1724. <1574 04 - 1b1 A2 euor$e : 1b2 s2 n/$da - 2b1 2A2 zeitdas : 2b2 2R3 ge chlo e—agenda, printed, territory, official>

Hildesheim

1544 *Christlike kerckenordeninge der löffliken stadt Hildenssem.* Hannover, 1544. By Johann Bugenhagen. Richter 2:79–80; Sehling 7:2:1:829–84. <agenda, printed, city, official>

Hiltpoltstain [bei Nürnberg]

1560 [Untitled visitation report]. Hirschmann 1994:70. <service description, manuscript>

1561 [Untitled visitation report]. Hirschmann 1994:109. <service description, manuscript>

Hof (Michaeliskirche)

1592 *Ordo eorum, quae in omnibus sacris actibus ad S. Michaelis, quae Curiae parochialis ecclesia est, diebus tam festis quam profestis ad laudem Dei opt[imi] max[imi] et ad animos piorum in vero Dei cultu exuscitandos et retinendos religiose observantur* By Enoch Widmann. Sehling 11:405–77. <agenda, manuscript, parish, official>

Hohenleipisch [Saxony]

1602 [Untitled visitation report]. Pallas 2:5:377. <service description, manuscript>

1608 [Untitled visitation report]. Pallas 2:5:378. <service description, manuscript>

1624 [Untitled visitation report]. Pallas 2:5:383. <service description, manuscript>

1672 [Untitled visitation report]. Pallas 2:5:384. <service description, manuscript>

Hohenlohe

1553 *Christliche kirchenordnung der graveschaft Hohennloe etc.* Sehling 15:1:53–81. <agenda, manuscript, territory, official>

1558 *Bedencken, Wie man in vnsers gnedigen hern, Graue Eberharden von Hoenloe landt visitirn möcht.* Sehling 15:1:120–32. <agenda, manuscript, territory, official>

1571 *Ordnung, welche allen pfarherrn ubergeben worden, damit allenthalben in der herschaft der ceremonien halb nach der Oringer kirchenordnung gleicheit gehalten werde.* Sehling 15:1:167–69. <agenda, manuscript, territory, official>

1578 *Kirchenordnung Wie es mit der Lehre vnd Ceremonien, in der löblichen Grafschafft Hohenloe &c. soll gehalten werden.* Nürnberg, 1578. Richter 2::400–401; Sehling 15:1:254–353. <agenda, manuscript, territory, official>

1582 *[Verbesserung der kirchenordnung,] generalarticul, consistori-, synodi-, visitations-, examinations-, ordinations-, stipendiaten,- lateinische und deutsche schuel-, ehe- und andere dergleichen nutzliche und nottwendige ordnungen.* Sehling 15:1:437–508. <agenda, manuscript, territory, official>

1589 [Untitled edicts concerning singing in the service]. Sehling 15:596–97. <agenda, manuscript, territory, official>

Holstein-Plön

1732 *Fürstl. Holstein-Plönische Kirchen-Ordnung, Zum Nutzen Der in dem Hertzogthum Holstein Plönischen Antheils belegenen Kirchen und der dazugehörigen Kirch-Gemeinden sorgfältig verfasset, auch Unter Hoch-Fürstl. ernstlichen Befehl, daß solcher von allen, die derselben Amt-Ordnung- und Gewissenshalber zu folgen schuldig, a dato publicationis soll nachgelebet werden, ans Licht gestellt.* Plön, 1732. *System. Sammlung d. f. Schlesw.-Holst. geltenden Verordnungen,* vol. 3. <1732 04 - b1 A re : b2 N ten— agenda, printed, territory, official>

Hoya

1573 *Kirchen Ordnung der Graff- und Herrschafften Hoya, Rittpergh, Bruchausen, Esentz, Steddeßdorff und Wittmundt.* Richter 2:353–57. <agenda, manuscript, territory, official>

1581 *Kirchenordnung, wie es in religionssachen mit der seligmachenden lehr des heiligen göttlichen worts, christlicher administration der hochwirdigen sacramenten und allerley denselben anhengenden, auch sonst zu dem heiligen predigampt gehörigen, löblichen und heilsamen ceremonien in den graffschaften Hoya und Bruichausen einmütiglich gehalten werden sol. Darinne auch zu ende und sonst allerhand, eine gute disciplin betreffende, hochnötige artickel kürzlich verleibet befunden werden.* Leipzig, 1581. Richter 2:456–58; Sehling 6:2:1128–1203. <agenda, printed, territory, official>

Hül beim Petzenstein [bei Nürnberg]

1561 [Untitled visitation report]. Hirschmann 1994:144–46. <service description, manuscript>

Igensdorf [bei Nürnberg]

1561 [Untitled visitation report]. Hirschmann 1994:129. <service description, manuscript>

Imeldorf [bei Nürnberg]

1561 [Untitled visitation report]. Hirschmann 1994:226. <service description, manuscript>

Jessen [Saxony]

1555 [Untitled visitation report]. Pallas 2:3:220–21. <service description, manuscript>

Jever

1562 *Kerckenordeninge, wo ydt mit Christliker Lere, rekinge der Sacrament, Ordination der Dener des hilligen Evangelii, ordentliken Ceremonien yn den Kercken, Visitation unnde Scholen van der eddelen unde wolgebarn Maria, gebaren Dochter unde Frewchen tho Jheuer, Rustringen, Ostringen unnde Wangerlande etc. Underdanen schal geholden werden. Upt nye corrigert unde aversehen dorch M. Petrum Rodtbart.* Wittenberg, 1562.

Richter 2:225; Sehling 7:2:1:1225–45. There is also a 1927 reprint without place of publication indicated in the catalog of the Staatsbibliothek zu Berlin, shelfmark Dr 14012. <agenda, printed, territory, official>

Kalckreut [bei Nürnberg]
  1561 [Untitled visitation report]. Hirschmann 1994:211. <service description, manuscript>

Kapellendorf [Saxony]
  1569 [Untitled visitation report]. Sehling 1:582–83. <service description, manuscript>

Kassel
  1539 *Ordenung der Kirchenübung, Für die Kirchen zu Cassel.* Erfurt, 1539. Richter 1:295–306; Sehling 8:113–30. <agenda, printed, city, official>

Kempten
  1553 *Herrn Primus Trubers pastors und kuerchendieners zu Kempten einem ersamen rat daselbsten übergebene kuerchenordnung, weliche in den hauptpunkten und articuln lautet, wie hernach folget.* By Primus Truber. Sehling 12:175–77. <agenda, manuscript, city, semiofficial>

Königsberg [Brandenburg]
  1586 [Untitled visitation edict]. Sehling 3:236–37. <agenda, manuscript, city, official>

Kurland
  1572 *Kirchenordnung, wie es mit der lehre göttliches worts, austheilung der heiligen hochwirdigen sacrament, christlichen ceremonien, ordentlicher ubung des waren gottesdiensts, in den kirchen des herzogthums Churland und Semigallien in Liefland, sol stetes vermittelst göttlicher hülf gehalten werden. Anno salutis 1570.* Rostock, 1572. Sehling 5:66–110. <agenda, manuscript, territory, official>

Langennaundorf [Saxony]
  1529 [Untitled visitation report]. Pallas 2:5:84. <service description, manuscript>
  1592 [Untitled visitation report]. Pallas 2:5:94. <service description, manuscript>
  1618 [Untitled visitation report]. Pallas 2:5:97. <service description, manuscript>
  1672 [Untitled visitation report]. Pallas 2:5:101. <service description, manuscript>

Langenreichenbach [Saxony]
  1586 [Untitled visitation report]. Pallas 2:4:218. <service description, manuscript>

Leipzig
  1694 See "Leibniz, Johann Friedrich" in part 2 below.
  1710 See "Groschuff, Friedrich" in part 2 below.

Lenzen [Brandenburg]
  1558 [Untitled visitation edict]. Sehling 3:239–40. <agenda, manuscript, city, official>

Liebenhall [Braunschweig-Wolfenbüttel]
  1572 [Untitled visitation report]. Wolters 1938–50, vol. 46, p. 101. <service description, manuscript>
  1576 [Untitled visitation report]. Wolters 1938–50, vol. 46, p. 128. <service description, manuscript>
  1590 [Untitled visitation report]. Wolters 1938–50, vol. 48, p. 81–82. <service description, manuscript>

Liebenwerda [Saxony]

    1578   [Untitled visitation report]. Pallas 2:5:35. <service description, manuscript>

    1608   [Untitled visitation report]. Pallas 2:5:47. <service description, manuscript>

Liegnitz and Brieg

    1535   *Vergleichung des ausschusses und folgend aller diener des hl. evangelii dero Liegnitz- und Brigischen fürstentümer und derselben zugethanen weichbilder ob der spaltigen leher und brauch der hochwürdigen sacramente A% 1535.* Sehling 3:436–39. <agenda, manuscript, territory, official>

    1592   [Untitled agenda]. Sehling 3:444–48. <agenda, manuscript, territory, official>

Lindau

    1573   *Agenda, Das ist, Ordnunge wie es mit den Ceremonien vnnd anderm, in der Pfarrkirchen zu Lindaw am Bodensee gehalten wird. 1573.* Richter 2:353, Sehling 12:203–17. <agenda, printed, city, official>

Lippe

[before 1533?]   *De dudesche misse.* Irmlind Capelle, "Eine bislang unbekannte niederdeutsche Messe," *Lippische Mitteilungen aus Geschichte und Landeskunde* 56 (1987): 153–98. <agenda, manuscript, territory (?), official (?)>

    1539   *Ghestalthe Artickel Reformation der kirchen Jn der Graveschup Lyppe &c. dorch de Vorordenten der Landtschup avergegeven Anno 1538. Nu myt flythe revisert und bewaghen tho Wyttenberg dorch Justum Jonas: Martinum Luther: Johanen Bugenhagen: und Philippum Melanchton: als ohre eghen handt under gheschreven vormeldet Jm Jare 1539.* By Johann Ambsterdam and Hadrian Buxschoten. Richter 2:489–503. <agenda, manuscript, territory, official>

    1614   *Kirchen Ordnung Vnser Von Gottes gnade[n] Ernsts Graffen zu Holstein, Schcare[n]burg [!] und Sternburg, rud [!] Sternberg Hernn zu Gehmen Wie es mit lehr vnd Ceremonien in vnsern Graffschafften vnd Landen Hinführo mitt Gottlicher Hilff gehalten werden soll.* Stadthagen, 1614. <1614 04 - b1 A2 Evang : b2 2L3 /$auc—agenda, printed, territory, official>

Lobenstein

    1543   [Untitled agenda]. Sehling 2:152–53. <agenda, manuscript, city, official>

Lohr

    1588   [Untitled agenda]. Sehling 11:699. <agenda, manuscript, city, official>

London (St. Mary's, Savoy)

    1718   *Kirchen-Ordnung, Der Christlichen und der ungeänderten Augspurgischen Confession Zugethanen Gemeinde in LONDON, Welche, Durch Göttliche Verleyhung, Jm 1694. Jahre, Am 19. Sonntage nach dem Fest der Heiligen Dreyfaltigkeit, Solenniter eingeweyhet und eingesegnet worden, Jn St. Mary's Savoy.* [London], 1718. <1718 08 - b1 A2 nd$: b2 G5 en/$—agenda, printed, parish, official>

Löwenstein

    1756   *Kirchen-Ordnung und Agenda für die Hochfürstl. Löwenstein-Wertheimische Kirchen Augspurgischer Confession.* Wertheim, 1756. <1756 04 - b1 A o : b2 M kei—agenda, printed, territory, official>

Lübeck

    1531   *Der keiserliken Stadt Lübeck christlike Ordeninge tho denste dem hilgen Evangelio. Christliker leve, tucht, frede unde enicheit vor de jöget in einer guden Scholen tho lerene.*

Unde de Kerken denere und rechten armen Christlick tho vorsorgende. Dorch Jo. Bugen. Pom. beschreven. 1531. [Lübeck], 1531. By Johann Bugenhagen. Richter 1:145–49; Sehling 5:334–68; *Lübecker Kirchenordnung von Johann Bugenhagen 1531*, edited and translated by Wolf-Dieter Hauschild (Lübeck: Max Schmidt-Römhild, 1981). <agenda, printed, city, official>

Lüneburg
    [1575] [Untitled agenda]. Sehling 6:1:650–90. <agenda, manuscript, city, official>

Lychen [Brandenburg]
    1541 [Untitled visitation edict]. Sehling 3:240. <agenda, manuscript, city, official>

Magdeburg
    1663 *ErtzStifftische Magdeburgische Kirchen Agenda Auff gnädigste Anordnung Des Hochwürdigsten, Durchlauchtigsten Hochgebornen Fürsten und Herrn Herrn AUGUSTI, Postulirten Administratoris des Primat- und ErtzStiffts Magdeburg, Hertzogens zu Sachsen, Jülich, Cleve und Berg, Landgraffens in Düringen, Marggraffens zu Meissen, Ober und Nieder Lausitz, Graffens zu der Marck, Ravensberg und Barby, Herrn zum Ravenstein, &c.* Halle, 1663. Moser 1:820–884. Later editions: 1727, 1740. <1663 04 - b1 A2 iede : b2 P3 $alle - c1$eqc2 Q or—agenda, printed, city, official>

    1667 *Agenda So, Zu behueff der Primat-Ertzbischöfflichen Kirchen zu Magdeburg, Vff Verordnung Eines Hoch Ehrwürdigen DomCapituls hochgedachter Kirchen in Druck gegeben worden.* Magdeburg, 1667. <1667 04 - b1 A2 enw : b2 T2 ch$da—agenda, printed, city, official>

    1685 *ChurFürstliche Brandenburgische Jm Hertzothum [!] Magdeburg Publicirte Kirchen Ordnung.* Halle, 1685. Later editions: 1708, 1739. <1685 04 - a1)(2 $zuw : a2) (3 fart - b1 A r$: b2 Z2 ohl—agenda, printed, territory, official>

Magdeburg (Han)
    1615 *KirchenBuch D. Philip. Hanen, DomPredigers zu Magdeburgk, Darinnen die gewöhnliche Ceremonien, neben etlichen kurtzen Sermonen auß Gottes Wort, heilsamen Consilijs, Bedencken vnd Erinnerungen Herrn D. Lutheri, vnd anderer fürnemer, reinen Theologen, auch gemeine Gebet vnd Collecten verfasset sind: Welche bey Christlichen Kindtäuffen, Einsegnung der Sechswöchnerin, Ehelicher Copulation Braut vnd Breutigam, Vocation, Ordination vnd Introduction newer Prediger, Beicht, Absolution vnd Communion gesunder vnd Krancken, auch handlungen mit Gefangenen, Besessenen, vnd endlich der verstorbenen Begrebnissen; Jn den Kirchen deß Ertzstiffts Magdeburgk, vnd andern Christlichen versamlungen üblichen sein, vnd von Predigern, in allerhand fällen, nützlich zu gebrauchen. Jn Neun vnterschiedliche Tractätlein abgetheilet, deren Register, oder Summa vnd inhalt, zu ende deß Buchs zu finden. Jtzo vffs new in Truck verordnet.* Magdeburg, 1615. By Philip Han. The claim on the title page "Jtzo vffs new in Truck verordnet" notwithstanding, there is no evidence that this book had appeared previously, and the author dates his preface 1615; in addition, there is a reference on f. 3M3ᵃ to the cathedral choir book published in 1613. Later editions: 1647, 1692. <1615 04 - 1a1):(2 tige : 1a2 2)(3 .$Hoch - 2a1 a nd : 2a2 k3 $vnn - b1 A n$: b2 5H2 nvon tum—agenda, printed, general, private>

Magdeburg (Schrader)
    1621 *FORMULAR- Buch, Allerhand Christlicher Wort, vnd Ceremonien, deren ein Prediger in Verrichtung seines Ampts, vnd der Seelsorge kan gebrauchen. Mit sonderlichem*

Fleiß, also, das nicht das geringste Ministerij requisitum fast fürfallen mag, welches nicht darinne begriffen were, gestellet vnd colligiret, Durch Johannem Schraderum, AEgelensem, Pfarrern zu Alvensleben, im ErtzStifft Magdeburg, vnd Poëtam Coronatum. Magdeburg, 1621. By Johann Schrader. Later editions: 1636, 1649, 1660, 1670. <[Vol. 1:] 1621 04 - a1)(2 /$vn : a2 (?)3 im - b1 A Ot : b2 2B nge | | [Vol. 2:] 1621 04 - b1 A2 /$v : b2 2A3 $ inge | | [Vol. 3:] 1621 04 - b1 A2 rü : b2 3A3 burt/$hil—agenda, printed, general, private>

Magdeburg, Halberstadt

1632 *Magdeburg: vnd Halberstadische KIRCHEN-Agenda, Auff sonderbaren gnädigsten Befehl Des Durchlauchtigsten, Großmächtigsten Fürsten vnd Herrn, Herrn GVstav-ADolphs, der Schweden, Gothen vnd Wenden Königs, GroßFürsten zu Finland, Hertzogen zu Ehesten vnd Carelen, Herrn über JngermanLand, &c.* Halle, 1632. *Die Kirchenordnung des Schwedenkönigs Gustav Adolf für die Stifter Magdeburg u. Halberstadt vom Jahre 1632 veröffentlicht . . . v. Georg Arndt* (Tübingen and Leipzig, [1904?]). <1632 04 - a1)(2 t$sol : *a2)(3 me - b1 A am : b2 S f—agenda, printed, territory, official>

Mansfeld

1580 *Kirchen Agenda, Darinnen Tauff, einsegen, vnd Trawbüchlein, Communion, sampt den teglichen Collecten, welche in der Kirchen gebraucht werden. Für die Prediger in der Graff, vnd Herrschafft Mansfeld. Jtzunder auffs newe vbersehen, vnd mit vielen nützlichen, vnd nötigen Tractaten, für junge vnd vngeübete Kirchendiener, vermehret. Welche also bey einander nicht zu finden.* Eisleben, 1580. Sehling 2:215–48. <1580 04 - b1 A2 di c : b2 z2 er$—agenda, printed, territory, semiofficial>

Marisfeld [County Henneberg]

1566 *Ordnung wie die in der kirchen Marisfeld jeder zeit bei mir Johan Cöln zur vesper der hohenfest, sonabent, sontag und andern beweglichen feiertagen gehalten wurden.* By Johan Cöln, pastor. Sehling 2:337–38. <service description, manuscript>

Mecklenburg

1545 *ORdeninge der Misse, wo de vann denn Kerckheren vnnde Seelsorgern ym lande tho Meckelnborch, jm Fürstendom Menden, Swerin Rostock vnnd Stargharde schal geholden werden.* [N.p., 1540]. Sehling 5:150–61. The date 1545 is from the colophon; the title page gives the date 1540. Sehling surmises that the difference is due to the printing being interrupted during the visitation of 1541–42 (Sehling 5:131). <1540 04 - b1 A2 a : b2 S2 gen—agenda, printed, territory, official>

1552 *Kirchenordnung, so in unsern, Johan Albrechts, von gottes gnaden herzogen zu Meckelnburg, fürsten zu Wenden, graven zu Swerin, der lande Rostock und Stargard herrn, fürstenthumen und landen sol gehalten werden.* Wittenberg, 1552. Richter 2:115–28; Sehling 5:161–219. Later editions: 1554, 1562 (Latin). The title page is missing from the copy at Wolfenbüttel. A new title page is pasted in, but it is evidently incorrect, so the title is here supplied from Sehling. <1552 04 - b1 A2 fur$: b2 l3 eibl—agenda, printed, territory, official>

1572 *Der durchleuchtigen hochgebornen fürsten und herren, herren Johannes Albrechten und herren Ulrichen, gebrüder, herzogen zu Mecklenburg, fürsten zu Wenden, graven zu Schwerin, der lande Rostock und Stargard herren reformation und ordnung der jungfrau clöster, wie es darin mit christlicher lehr, gebrauch des hochwürdigen sacraments, teglich gesungen und an andern christlichen ubungen soll gehalten werden. 1572.* Sehling 5:250–62. <agenda, manuscript, cloister, official>

1602 *REVIDIRTE KJrchenordnung: Wie es mit Christlicher Lehre, reichung der Sacrament,*

Ordination der Diener des Euangelij, ordentlichen Ceremonien in der Kirchen, Visitation, Consistorio vnd Schulen: Jm Hertzogthumb Meckelnburg, etc. gehalten wirdt. Rostock, 1602. Later edition: 1650. <1602 04 - a1 (:)2 liche$: a2 (:)5 sion - b1 A i : b2 2N1 atu—agenda, printed, territory, official>

1708   *Erläuterung, Der Fürstl. Mecklenburgschen Kirchen-Ordnung, Wie derselben, Jnsonderheit in nachgesetzten Capitibus, als: I. Von der Lehre und Catechißmus-Ubung. II. Von den öffentlichen Kirch-Zeiten und Gottesdienst. III. Von Specialer Verwaltung der Priesterlichen Kirchen-Verrichtungen. IV. Von Kirchen, Pfarren, Schulen, Armen-Häusern und Kirchen-Gütern, und V. Von Beforderung Christlicher Devotion, und thätigen Christenthums. Jn dem gantzen Lande Mecklenburg, und allen darinn befindlichen Kirchen und Schulen, in geziemender Gleichförmigkeit, â dato Publicationis, von Jedermänniglich strictè nachgelebet werden soll.* Schwerin, 1708. <1708 04 - 1b1 A M : 1b2 L $ - 2b1 a e : 2b2 e3 e—agenda, printed, territory, official>

Meiningen [County Henneberg]

1566   *Verzeichnis wie es in der stat Meiningen mit der predigt gehalten wird.* By Mauricius Carolus. Sehling 2:339–40. <service description, manuscript>

Minnfeldt [Guttenberg]

1562   [Untitled visitation report]. Schneider 1878:4–5 <service description, manuscript>

Mügeln (Amt Seyda) with Lindwerder (Amt Schweinitz) [Saxony]

1618   [Untitled visitation report]. Pallas 2:1:519. <service description, manuscript>

Münsterberg [Silesia]

1560   [Untitled instruction for the organist]. Sehling 3:466. <agenda, manuscript, city, official>

Nassau

1713   *Kirchen-Ordnung, Wie es Mit der Christlichen Lehre, Und CEREMONIEN, &c. Jn Vnsern, Ludewigs, Grafens zu Nassau, zu Sarbrücken, und zu Sarwerden: Herrn zu Lahr, Wießbaden und Jetzstein, &c. Grafe- und Herrschaffien gehalten wird. Anfänglich gedruckt zu Franckfurt am Mäyn, Bey Johann Nicolao Stoltzenbergern, Anno M. DC. XVIII. und nun zum vierdten mal neu auffgelegt. Sammt angefügter Fürstl. Nassau-Jtzsteinischer SYNODAL-Verordnung.* Itzstein, 1713. <1713 04 - b1 A2 ALm : b2 2E2 ng$de—agenda, printed, territory, official>

Naumburg (cathedral church)

1543 [1541?] *Kurzer bericht wie es mit predigen, singen und lesen in der thumstifskirchen zur Naumburg teglichen gehalten wird.* Sehling 2:596. <service description, manuscript>

Naumburg (Wenzelkirche)

1527   [Untitled agenda]. Sehling 2:59–60. <agenda, manuscript, parish, official>

[1538]   [Untitled agenda]. By Nicolaus Medler. Dr. Köster, "Die Naumburger Kirchen- und Schulordnung von D. Nicolaus Medler aus dem Jahre 1537," *Neue Mitteilungen aus dem Gebiet historisch-antiquarischer Forschungen* 19 (1898): 497–569, also appendix pp. 1–32; Sehling 2:61–90. The manuscript is dated 1 May 1537, but Sehling corrects this to 1538 (Sehling 2:55). <agenda, manuscript, parish, official>

Niederlauer [County Henneberg]

1566   [Untitled service description]. By Wolfgang Prasius, pastor. Sehling 2:341–42. <service description, manuscript>

Niederlausitz
   1592   [Untitled agenda]. Sehling 3:363–64. <agenda, manuscript, territory, official>

Niemegk [Saxony]
   1529   [Untitled agenda]. Sehling 1:615–16. <agenda, manuscript, city, official>
   1598   [Untitled visitation report]. Pallas 2:2:176. <service description, manuscript>

Nimbschen
   1529   [Untitled agenda]. Sehling 1:616–18. <agenda, manuscript, cloister, official>

Nordheim
   1539   *Kirchenordnung der löblichen stadt Northeim, durch den erbaren radt, gilden und gemein daselbs angenomen und gestellet durch D. Anto. Corvinum.* Wittenberg, 1539. By Anton Corvinus. Richter 1:287–89; Sehling 6:2:922–39; see also the *Zeitschrift für niedersächsische Kirchengeschichte* (1900). <agenda, printed, city, official>

Nördlingen
   1522   *Von der Evangelischen Meß. Mit schönen Christlichen Gebetten vor und nach der empfahung des Sacraments. Durch Caspar Kantz von Nördlingen.* By Caspar Kantz. Smend (1896): 73–78; Sehling 12:285–88. <agenda, printed, city, semi-official>
   1538   *Der statt Nordling neu fürgenommne reformation und kirchenordnung auf den fünfzehenden tag Maii anno 1538.* By Caspar Kantz. Richter 1:286–87; Sehling 12:307–309. <agenda, manuscript, city, official>
   1544   [Untitled agenda]. By Caspar Löner. Sehling 12:310–16. <agenda, manuscript, city, official>
   1579   [Untitled agenda]. Sehling 12:335–93. <agenda, manuscript, city, official>
   1676   *Kirchen-Ordnung, Wie es mit der Lehr und Ceremonien bey dem offentlichen Gottes-Dienst, Jn deß H. Reichs Statt Nördlingen, Bißhero gehalten worden, und hinfüro, mit verleihung Göttlicher Gnade, gehalten werden solle.* [N.p.], 1676. <1676 04 - b1 A2 mö : b2 2C3 ten/$—agenda, printed, city, official>

Nördlingen (Georgenkirche)
   1555   *Ordnung der ceremonien in der pfarkirchen zu Sant Georgen der statt Nördlingen, gestelt durch M. Caspar Löhner, daselbst superintendens, im 1544. und jetzo wider ubersehen und mit der württembergischen kirchen und anderer, so von diser herkomen, zum bequemsten verglichen durch Melchior Runtzler, magister, der orts superintendens. Anno 1555.* By Melchior Runtzler. Sehling 12:317–29. <agenda, manuscript, parish, official>

Nuremberg
   1524a [Untitled agenda]. By Wolfgang Volprecht. Sehling 11:39–43. <agenda, manuscript, cloister, official>
   1524b [Untitled agenda]. Sehling 11:46–50. <agenda, manuscript, parish, official>
   1525a *Uon der evangelischen meß, wie sie zu Nürnberg im Newen Spital, durch Andream Döber, gehalten würdt, caplan doselbst.* Nürnberg, 1525. By Andreas Döber. Smend (1896): 163–70; Sehling 11:51–55. <agenda, printed, hospital chapel, semiofficial>
   1525b *Form vnd ordnung, eyner Christlichen Meß, so zu Nürmberg im Newen Spital, im brauch ist.* [1525]. Sehling 11:56–57. <agenda, manuscript, hospital chapel, semiofficial>
   1639   *AGEND-Büchlein, Für die Nürnbergische Kirchendiener, in der Stadt vnd auff dem Land.* Nürnberg, 1639. <1639 04 - b1 A2 ten$: b2 Bb2 fdensi—agenda, printed, city, semiofficial>

1755   *AGEND-Büchlein, für die Nürnbergische Kirchendiener in der Stadt und auf dem Lande.* Nürnberg, 1755. <1755 04 - b1 A2 end : b2 R3 s$—agenda, printed, city, semiofficial>

Nuremberg (Dietrich)

1543   *Agend Büchlein für die Pfar-Herren auff dem Land.* Nürnberg, 1543. By Veit Dietrich. <1543 04 - b1 a2 n. : b2 y3 llet/$a—agenda, printed, general, private>

1545   *Agend Büchlein für die Pfarrherrn auff dem Land. Durch Vitum Dietrich.* Nürnberg, 1545. By Veit Dietrich. Sehling 11:487–553. Later editions: 1546, 1556, 1560 (not seen), 1563 (not seen), 1565 (not seen), 1569. <1545 04 - a1 B2 ic : a2 ^BA3 er$werd - b1 a m : b2 F2 züchtig—agenda, printed, general, private>

1586   *Agend Büchlein, für die Pfarrherren auff dem Land.* Nürnberg, 1586. By Veit Dietrich. <1586 04 - b1 a2 ran : b2 y3 tellet—agenda, printed, general, private>

Nuremberg (St. Sebald)

1664   *OFFICIUM SACRUM, quod in AEde D. Sebaldi Norimbergensium primariâ, singulis anni diebus exhiberi solet: cum Introitibus, Tractibus, Responsoriis & Antiphonis. Accessit ORDO OFFICII SACRI, S. AEdi Laurentian consuetus; cum HYMNIS ECCLESIASTICIS.* Nürnberg, 1664. <1664 08 - a1 a2 ,$e : a2 a7 $l\|AE - b1 A le : b2 N7 $ple—agenda, printed, parish, official>

Oberlausitz

1696   *Die Evangelische Kirchen-Agenda, Auff sonderbahre Verordnung Der gesambten Stände des Marggraffthumbs Ober-Lausitz, von Land und Städten, in Die Wendische Sprache übersetzet, und nunmehr zum gemeinen Gebrauch Der Evangelischen Ober-Lausitzischen Kirchen in offentlichen Druck gegeben.* Bautzen, 1696. ed. Jules C. E. Riotte as *Die Obersorbische Agenda von 1696: Text und Untersuchungen,* Deutsche Akademie der Wissenschaften zu Berlin, Veröffentlichungen des Instituts für Slawistik, no. 20 (Berlin: Akademie-Verlag, 1959). Parallel texts in Wendish and German, with Wendish on odd pages and German on even. <1696 04 - b1 A3 en/ : b2 S2 twoje—agenda, printed, territory, official>

Obermassfeld [County Henneberg]

1566   [Untitled visitation (?) report]. By Nikolaus Heyden, pastor. Sehling 2:342–44. <service description, manuscript>

Oels

1664a   *Agenda, Oder ORDNUNG Derer Evangelischen Kirchen im Oelßnischen Fürstenthum und zugehörigen Weichbildern, Auff gnädigen Befehl J. F. G. Hertzog Carls zu Münsterberg, dieses Nahmens des Anderen, erstlich gestellt und zusammenbracht, und der Ehrwürdigen Priesterschafft übergeben Ao. 1593: Numehro aber auff gnädige Verordnung J. F. G. Hertzog SYLVII zu Würtenberg und Teck, auch in Schlesien zur Oelssen, &c. revidiret und zum Druck befödert Ao. 1664.* Oels, 1664. <1664 04 - b1 A2 ch t : b2 L t$—agenda, printed, territory, official>

1664b   *Nothwendige Kirchen-Constitution, welche für die sämtlichen Evangelischen Gemeinden Oelßnischen Furstenthumß, auf die in selbigem Anno 1662 und 63 gehaltene und glücklich verbrachte Visitation, Der Durchlauchtige, Hochgebohrne Fürst und Herr, Herr SYLVIUS, Hertzog zu Würtemberg und Teck, auch in Schlesien zur Oelßen, Graf zu Montbelgart, Herr zu Heidenheim, Sternberg und Medzibor, Durch gewisse darzu deputirte und beschriebene S. Fürstl. Sn. Consistorial- und Land- Räthe, auch Pfarrer und Seniores, in unterschiedenen Puncten und Articuln verfassen lassen, Anno 1664.* Oels, 1664. <1664 04 - b1 A u : b2 F3 men—agenda, printed, territory, official>

Oelsnitz [Saxony]

    1582   [Untitled visitation edict]. Sehling 1:620–21. <agenda, manuscript, city, official>

Oettingen

    1707   *Kirchen-Ordnung, Wie es bißhero mit der Lehr und CEREMONIEN Jn denen Fürstl. Oettingischen Kirchen gehalten worden ist, Und ins künfftige noch gehalten werden soll.* Oettingen, 1707. Later edition: 1773. <1707 04 - a1)(2 chri : a2 2)(2 eitlich - b1 A2 $Er : b2 3Y2 d$Fa t$eq—agenda, printed, territory, official>

    1774   *Der Oettingischen Kyrchen-Ordnung anderer Theil, welcher die Herrschaftlichen Edikte, Jnhäsive und Konsistorialverordnungen enthält.* Oettingen, 1774. Not a complete church order, but rather a summary of changes made by the consistory to the official church order. <1774 08 - a1)(2 $ied : a2)(3 icht - b1 A2 im$: b2 2B3 ichten—agenda, printed, territory, official>

Ogkeln [Saxony]

    1575   [Untitled visitation report]. Pallas 2:1:330–31. <service description, manuscript>

Öhringen

    1556   *Verzeichnus, wie es in den stiftskirchen mit singen und lesen soll gehalten werden etc.* Sehling 15:1:103–104. <agenda, manuscript, collegiate church, official>

Oldenburg

    1573   *Kirchenordnung, Wie es mit der Reinen Lere Göttliches Worts, vnd austeilung der Hochwirdigen Sacrament, auch allerley Christlichen Ceremonien, Vnd zum Heiligen Predigambt notwendigen Sachen, auch in Schulen, in der Löblichen Graffschafft Oldenburg etc. Sol eintrechtiglich gehalten werden.* Jena, 1573. Sehling 7:2:1:986–1162. <1573 04 - b1 A2 n/$v : b2 3B1 cht$au—agenda, printed, territory, official>

Ortrand [Saxony]

    1657   [Untitled visitation report]. Pallas 2:5:543. <service description, manuscript>

Oschatz

    1539   [Untitled agenda]. Sehling 1:622–25. <agenda, manuscript, city, official>

Osnabrück

    1543a   *Christliche kerkenordenunge der stadt Oßenbrugk.* [N.p.], 1543. By Hermann Bonn. Richter 2:23–26; Sehling 7:1:247–64. <agenda, printed, city, official>

    1543b   *Kerckenordnunge vor de landkercken des stifts Osenbrugge, uffgerichtet und verordnet a r[everendissi]mo et ill[ustrissi]mo d[omino], d[omino] Francisco, episcopo Monast[eriensi], Osnab[rugensi] et Paderbor[nensi], comite a Waldeck, durch M. Herm. Bonnum, superint[endentem] Lubec[ensem].* By Hermann Bonn. Sehling 7:1:222–26. <agenda, manuscript, territory, official>

    1618   *Agenda, das ist: Kirchenordnung, wie es in den evangelischen kirchen der statt Oßnabrück mit verkündigunge göttliches worts, reichung der h. sacramenten und anderen christlichen handelungen und ceremonien sol gehalten werden.* Osnabrück, 1618. Sehling 7:1:265–89. <agenda, printed, city, official>

    1652   *Agenda Das ist: Kirchen-Ordnung, Wie es in den Evangelischen Kirchen der Stadt Oßnabrück, mit Verkündigunge Göttliches Worts, Reichung der Heiligen Sacramenten vnd anderen Christlichen Handelungen vnd Ceremonien, sol gehalten werden.* Rinteln, 1652. <1652 04 - b1 A2 r a : b2 2A3 g/ode—agenda, printed, city, official>

Palatinate

   1546a *Bedencken des durchleuchtigsten pfaltzgraven Friederichs, churfursten und meins gnedig-*
      sten herren, auf trefflich gehalten rathe seyner churfürstlichen gnaden rethe und theolo-
      gen, wie der stift zum heyligen geist, daraus dan alle andere stieftkirchen, in der Pfaltz
      gelegen, solten reformirt werden, in christlich ordenug zu veriechten sey. Sehling 14:90–
      94. <agenda, manuscript, cloister, official>

   1546b *Gemaine maß, die kirchen- und gottesdinst anzurichten, bis das hierin durch kunftige*
      visitatores und superattendenten weiter bericht gegeben würde. Sehling 14:94–102.
      <agenda, manuscript, territory, official>

   1547 *Kirchenordnung, Wie es mit der Christlichen Lehre, heiligen Sacramenten, und allerley*
      andern Ceremonien, in meiner gnedigen herrn Otthainrichen, Pfaltzgraven bey Rhein
      Fürstenthumb gehalten wirt. Zum andern mal gedruckt Anno 47. Frankfurt, 1547.
      Sehling 14:109–111. <agenda, printed, territory, official>

   1554 *Kirchenordnung, wie es mit der Christlichen lehre, heiligen Sacramenten, und Cere-*
      monien, in meines Gnedigen Herrn, Herrn Otthainrichs, Pfaltzgraven bey Rhein, Hert-
      zogen in Nider und Obern Bayrn etc. Fürstenthumb gehalten wirdt. Nürnberg, 1554.
      Richter 2:146–47; Sehling 13:104–105. Later edition: 1556. <agenda,
      printed, territory, official>

Palatinate-Neuburg

   1543 *Kirchen ordnung, Wie es mit der Christlichen Lehre, heiligen Sacramenten, vnd allerley*
      andern Ceremonien, in meines gnedigen Herrn, Herrn Otthainrichen, Pfaltzgrauen bey
      Rhein, Hertzogen inn Nidern vnd Obern Bairn &c. Fürstenthumb gehalten wirt.
      [N.p.], 1543. Richter 2:26–30; Sehling 13:41–99. <1543 02 - a1 B2 S : a2 B3
      on - 1b1 a r : 1b2 i2 $Me - 2b1 A3 des : 2b2 N4 en$befe - 3b1 2a2 n$zu$ler
      : 3b2 2x4 thalben$f—agenda, printed, territory, official>

Palatinate-Zweibrücken

   1563 *Kirchenordnung Wie es mit der Christlichen Lere, Reichung der heiligen Sacramenten,*
      Ordination der Diener des Euangelij, vnd ordenlichen Ceremonien, Erhaltung Christ-
      licher Schulen vnd Studien, auch anderer der Kirchen notwendigen Stücken etc. Jn vnser
      Wolffgangs von Gottes Gnaden, Pfaltzgrauens bey Rhein, Hertzogens in Baiern, vnd
      Grauens zu Veldentz Fürstenthumb gehalten werden sol. Oberursel, 1563. Later
      edition: 1570. <1563 02 - b1 A2 on$: b2 r3 ei—agenda, printed, territory,
      official>

Penig [Saxony]

   1575 [Untitled visitation report]. Sehling 1:634. <service description, manuscript>

Perleberg [Brandenburg]

   1558 *Ordnung, so der stadt Perleberg in gehaltener visitation des 58. jahrs ist zugestalt wor-*
      den. Sehling 3:249–53. <agenda, manuscript, city, official>

Pezenstein and Stierberg [bei Nürnberg]

   1561 [Untitled visitation report]. Hirschmann 1994:136–37. <service description,
      manuscript>

Pirna

[before 1569][Untitled agenda]. By Anton Lauterbach. Sehling 1:641–45. <agenda, manu-
      script, city, official>

Plauen

   1529 [Untitled visitation report]. Sehling 2:111. <service description, manuscript>
   1552 [Untitled agenda]. Sehling 2:153–58. <agenda, manuscript, city, official>

Plossig [Saxony]
    1577 [Untitled visitation report]. Pallas 2:3:288. <service description, manuscript>

Pomerania
    1535a *Kercken-ordeninge des gantzen Pamerlandes dorch de hochgebaren försten und heren,*
           heren Barnym unde Philips, beyde geveddeten, up dem landdage to Treptow, to eeren dem
           hilligen evangelio bestaten. Dorch Doc. Joannem Bugenhagen. Wittenberg, 1535. By
           Johann Bugenhagen. Richter 1:248–60; Sehling 4:328–44; *Die pommersche*
           Kirchenordnung von 1535, edited by Hellmuth Heyden as *Blätter für Kirchen-*
           geschichte Pommerns, no. 15/16 (Stettin, 1937). <agenda, printed, territory,
           official>
    1535b *Pia et vere catholica et consentiens veteri ecclesiae ordinatio caeremoniarum in ecclesiis*
           Pomeraniae. Wittenberg, 1535. By Johann Bugenhagen. Sehling 4:344–53.
           <agenda, printed, cloister, official>
    1542   *Karcken Ordening,Wo sick die Parner vnnd Selensorger inn vorreikinge der Sacrament vnd*
           ouinge der Cerimonien holden scholen im Land to Pammern. [N.p.], 1542. Richter
           2:1–14; Sehling 4:354–70. <1542 04 - b1 A2 ande : b2 R3 ten/$J—agenda,
           printed, territory, official>
    1569   *Agenda Dat is, Ordninge der hilligen Kerckenempter vnde Ceremonien, wo sick de*
           Parrherren, Seelsorgere vnde Kerckendenere in erem Ampte holden schölen, Gestellet
           vor de Kercken in Pamern, vp beuel der Dorchlüchtigen, hochgebarnen Försten vnde
           Herren, Herrn Barnim des öldern, Herrn Johann Friderichen, Herrn Bugslaffen, Herrn
           ErnstLudwigen, Herrn Barnim des yüngern, vnde Herrn Casimiren, Geueddern vnde
           Gebröder, Hertogen tho Stettin Pamern, der Cassuben vnde Wenden, Försten tho
           Rügen, vnde Grauen tho Gutzkow, etc. Anno M. D. LXVIII. [N.p.], 1569. Sehling
           4:419–80. Later editions: 1591, 1661, 1690, 1691, 1731. <1569 04 - a1 #+3
           al$vp : a2 #+5 vnd - b2 A n$: b2 3N2 nen$Gr—agenda, printed, territory,
           official>

Poppenreut [bei Nürnberg]
    1561   [Untitled visitation report]. Hirschmann 1994:260–67. <service description,
           manuscript>

Prussia
    1525   *Artikel der ceremonien und anderer kirchen ordnung.* Königsberg: Hans Weinreich,
           1526. Richter 1:28–35, Sehling 4:30–38. Issued December 10, 1525. <agenda,
           printed, territory, official>
    1544   *Ordenung vom eusserlichen Gotsdienst und artickel der Ceremonien, wie es jnn den*
           Kirchen des Hertzogthumbs zu Preussen gehalten wirt 1544. Richter 2:64–72;
           Sehling 4:61–72. <1544 04 - b1 b / : b2 g3 chen—agenda, printed, territory,
           official>
    1552   *Kirchenordnung, wie es inn des durchleuchtigen . . . Fursten . . . Herrn Albrechts des*
           Jungern Marggrauen zu Brandenburgs . . . Fürstenthumb, Landt . . . mit der lehr und
           Ceremonien bis auff vernere Christliche vergleichung gehalten werden sol Leipzig,
           1552. <1552 02 - 1b1 A2 ri te : 1b2 L3 l$mü - 2b1 a2 ge : 2b2 o3 d$zu—
           agenda, printed, territory, official>
    1558   *Kirchen Ordnung Wie es im Hertzogthumb Preussen, beydes mit Lehr vnd Ceremonien,*
           sampt andern, so zu Fürderung vnd Erhaltung des Predigampts, Christlicher Zucht,
           vnd guter Ordnung, von nötens gehalten wird. Anderweit vbersehen, gemehret, vnd Pub-
           licieret. ANNO CHRISTI M. D. LVIII 25. Nouembris. Königsberg, 1558. In Wal-
           ther Hubatsch, *Geschichte der evangelischen Kirche Ostpreussens,* 3 vols. (Göttingen,

1968), vol. 3, pp. 34–134. <1558 02 - a1 *2 illich : a2 *5 Chri - 1b1 A di : 1b2 K4 aters. - 2b1 a2 ffen\$: 2b2 k4 hrlich\$—agenda, printed, territory, official>

1568 *Kirchen Ordnung vnd Ceremonien. Wie es in vbung Gottes Worts, vnd reichung der Hochwirdigen Sacrament, in den Kirchen des Hertzogthumbs Preussen soll gehalten werden. ANNO DOMINI M. D. LXVIII.* Königsberg, 1568. Sehling 4:72–106; *Altpreussisches Kirchenbuch, enthaltend . . . 3. die Kirchenordnung vom Jahre 1568 u. 4. die Preussische Kirchenagende vom Jahre 1780 . . .* (Königsberg, 1861). Later edition: 1598. <1568 02 - b1 A2 \$die\$: b2 M5 E—agenda, printed, territory, official>

Queienfeld [County Henneberg]

1566 *Kirche ordenung Oswaldi Wismans, wie ers helt in der kirchen zu Queienfelt.* By Oswald Wisman, pastor. Sehling 2:344–45. <service description, manuscript>

Rade [Saxony]

1577 [Untitled visitation report]. Pallas 2:3:305. <service description, manuscript>

Rasch [bei Nürnberg]

1561 [Untitled visitation report]. Hirschmann 1994:182. <service description, manuscript>

Rechtenbach [Guttenberg]

1562 [Untitled visitation report]. Schneider 1878:6–7. <service description, manuscript>

Regensburg

1542 *Wrahafftiger [!] Bericht eines Erbarn Camerers vnd Rats der Stat Regenspurg, Warumb vnd aus was vrsachen sie des Hern Abentmal, nach der einsatzung Christi, bey ihnen fürgenomen vnd auffgericht, auch mit was form, weyse vnd ordnung das selbig gehalten wirdet.* Sehling 13:389–93. <agenda, printed, city, official>

1543 [Untitled agenda]. By Hieronymus Nopp. Sehling 13:406–411. <agenda, manuscript, city, semiofficial>

[ca. 1543] *Ordnung des herrenabendmals und der vesper, bei doctor Noppe gehalten.* Sehling 13:412–13. <service description, manuscript>

1553 *Kirchenordnung, wie man alle ding zu Regenspurg in der christen kirchen mit singen, lesen, predigen und andern ceremonien an den feiertägen und werktägen zu halten pflegt.* By Justus Jonas. Sehling 13:419–27. <agenda, manuscript, city, official>

Regensburg (Neue Kirche)

[1567?] *Kirchenordnung der neuen pfarre zu Regenspurg.* By Nicolaus Gallus. Sehling 13:452–89. <agenda, manuscript, parish, official>

Reinhardtshoven [County Ortenburg]

1565 *Warhafter und grundlicher bericht, wie und welchermaßen die communicanten in der grafschaft Ortenburg examinirt, unterrichtet, geleret und getröst worden, bis doch beide, prediger und zuhörer, zum höchsten hierüber verfolget sind, beschrieben.* By Thomas Rorarius [pastor in Reinhardtshoven]. Sehling 13:531–32. <service description, printed>

Reinhusen [Calenberg-Göttingen]

1543 [Untitled visitation edict]. Kayser 1896:298. <agenda, manuscript, cloister, official>

Reutin and Eschach

    1573 *Agenda, wie es auf dem land in der pfarrkirchen zu Rüte und Eschach gehalten wird.* Sehling 12:218–20. Printed as an appendix to Lindau 1573. <agenda, printed, territory, official>

Riga

    1530 *Kurze Ordnung des Kirchendiensts, samt einer Vorrede von Ceremonien, an den Erbarn Rath der löblichen Stadt Riga in Liefland, dorch D. Joannem Brieszman. M.D.XXX.* [Rostock, 1530]. Richter 2:487–89; Sehling 5:11–17. <agenda, manuscript, city, official>

Risstelbach [bei Nürnberg]

    1561 [Untitled visitation report]. Hirschmann 1994:124. <service description, manuscript>

Ritschenhausen [County Henneberg]

    1562 [Untitled visitation report]. By Georg Linke, pastor. Sehling 2:345. <service description, manuscript>

    1566 [Untitled visitation report]. By Georg Linke, pastor. Sehling 2:346–47. <service description, manuscript>

Ritzebüttel

[after 1570] *Ordeninge der christlicken ceremonien, welckere bi dem gades dienste in den kercken, so in dem ampte Ritzebüttel belegen, gebruket werden.* Richter 2:78–79; Sehling 5:556–62. The date is from Sehling; Graff (1937–39) dates this source [ca. 1544]. <agenda, manuscript, territory, official>

Rostock

[ca. 1560–76]   *Conformitas ceremoniarum, in singulis templis ecclesiae Rostochiensis.* Sehling 5:288–91. <agenda, manuscript, city, semiofficial>

Rötenbach [bei Nürnberg]

    1561 [Untitled visitation report]. Hirschmann 1994:171–72. <service description, manuscript>

Rothenberg

    1618 *Christliche vereinigung, derer diener göttliches worts in der löblichen herrschaft Rotenberg, wie es forthin mit den kirchen- und anderen actibus, die ihnen ampts halber zu verrichten obligen, soll gehalten werden.* Sehling 13:547–57. <agenda, manuscript, territory, official>

Rothenburg/Tauber

    1559 *Ordnung der Kirchen in eines Erbarn Raths der Stat Rothenburg uf der Tauber Oberkeit und gebiet gelegen.* Rotenburg uf der Tauber: Albrecht Gros, 1559. Sehling 11:566–97. <agenda, manuscript, city, official>

Sachsen [bei Nürnberg]

    1561 [Untitled visitation report]. Hirschmann 1994:228. <service description, manuscript>

Salzwedel [Brandenburg]

    1579 [Untitled visitation edict]. Sehling 3:272–86. <agenda, manuscript, city, official>

St. Lienhard [bei Nürnberg]

    1561 [Untitled visitation report]. Hirschmann 1994:289. <service description, manuscript>

Saxe-Coburg

1626 *Ordnung Wie es in deß Durchleuchtige[n] Hochgebornen Fürsten vnd Herrn Herrn JO-HANN CASIMIRI Herzogen zu Sachsen, Gulich, Cleve vnd Berg, Landgraven in Thuringen, Marggraven zu Meissen, Graven zu der Marck vnd Ravenßburgk, Herrn zu Ravenstein &c. Fürstenthumb vnd Landen, Orts- Francken vnd Thüringen, in den Kirchen, mit Lehr, Ceremonien, Visitationen vnd was solchen mehr anhängig, Dann im Fürstlichen Consistorio, mit denen verbotenen gradibus in Ehesachen vnd sonsten, auch im Fürstlichen Gymnasio, so wol Land: vnd Particular Schulen, gehalten werden solle.* Coburg, 1626. Later edition: 1713. <1626 02 - a1 a t : a2 b4 gten$ge - b1 A d : b2 2M men$—agenda, printed, territory, official>

Saxe-Gotha

1647 *Kirchen-Agenda: Das ist, Ordnung, Wie es von Pfarrern und Seel-Sorgern, beym öffentlichen Gottes-Dienst, und sonsten, gehalten werden sol. Für die Kirchen im Fürstenthumb Gotha.* [N.p.], 1647. Later editions: 1682, 1689, 1753. <1647 04 - a1$eqa2 (:)2 ven p - b1 A r$: b2 2K2 uarij/$—agenda, printed, territory, official>

Saxe-Lauenburg

1585 *Kirchen Ordnung, Vnser von Gottes gnaden, Frantzen Hertzogen zu Sachsen, Engern vnd Westphalen. Wie es (vormittels Göttlicher gnaden) in vnsern landen mit Christlicher Lehr, außspendung der heiligen Hochwirdigen Sacramenten, Vocation, Ordination vnd verhaltung der Kirchen vnd Schulen Diener, auch Visitation, Consistorio, vnd andern hiezu gehörigen Sachen, vormüge heiliger Göttlicher Schrifft, hinfüro gehalten soll werden.* Lübeck, 1585. Sehling 5:397–460 (omits all orders of service except the confirmation order due to the length of the agenda). Later edition: 1651. <1585 04 - a1)(2 ht/$j : a2):(2 tliche$ - b1 A t : b2 4A3 r tocket$bleib—agenda, printed, territory, official>

Saxe-Weimar

1664 *Derer Durchleuchtigsten, Hochgebornen Fürsten und Herren, Herrn Johann Ernsts, Herrn Adolph Wilhelms, Herrn Johann Georgens und Herrn Bernhards Gebrüderer, Hertzogen zu Sachsen, Jülich, Cleve und Bergen, Land-Grafen in Thüringen, Marck- Grafen zu Meissen, gefürsteter Grafen zu Henneberg, Grafen zu der Mark und Ravens-Berg, Herren zu Ravenstein, Verbesserte Kirchen-Ordnung, Vff Jhrer Fürstl. Durchleuchtigkeiten gesambte Fürstenthume und Lande gerichtet.* Weimar, 1664. <1664 04 - a1 a2 eve : a2 a3 e - b1 A t : b2 4F3 nde$bega—agenda, printed, territory, official>

Saxony, Albertine

1539a *Kirchen-ordnunge zum anfang, fur die Pfarher in Hertzog Heinrichs zu Sachsen v. g. h. Fürstenthumb.* Wittenberg, 1539. Richter 1:307–315; Sehling 1:264–81. <1539 04 - b1 A2 ertzli : b2 F3 /$vn—agenda, printed, territory, official>

1539b *Vnterricht der Visitatorn, an die Pfarhern in Hertzog Heinrichs zu Sachsen Fürstenthum.* Wittenberg, 1539. A new edition of Ernestine Saxony 1528. Principally by Philipp Melanchthon, but Luther wrote the preface, and he refers to himself by name on f. E3.[a] <1539 04 - b1 A2 lten$: b2 K5 $dadu—agenda, printed, territory, official>

1540 *Agenda- Das ist, Kyrchenordnung, wie sich die Pfarrherrn vnd Seelsorger in jren Ampten vn[d] diensten halten sollen, Fur die Diener der Kyrchen in Hertzog Heinrichen zu Sachssen V. G. H. Fürstenthumb gestellet.* Leipzig, 1540. Later editions: 1548, 1555, 1558, 1563 (not seen), 1564, 1580, 1582 (not seen), 1584 (not seen), 1600, 1618, 1647, 1658, 1681 (not seen), 1712, 1748 (not seen). <agenda, printed, territory, official>

1545 [Untitled agenda]. Sehling 1:291–304. <1540 04 - b1 A2 ur$: b2 S2 egrebni—agenda, manuscript, territory, official>

1580 *DEs Durchlauchtigsten, Hochgebornen Fürsten vnd Herrn, Herrn Augusten, Hertzogen zu Sachsen, des heiligen Römischen Reichs Ertzmarschalln, vnd Churfürsten, Landgraffen in Düringen, Marggraffen zu Meissen, vnd Burggraffen zu Magdeburg, etc. Ordnung, Wie es in seiner Churf. S. Landen, bey den Kirchen, mit der lehr vnd ceremonien, deßgleichen in derselben beyden Vniuersiteten, Consistorien, Fürsten vnd Particular Schulen, Visitation, Synodis, vnd was solchem allem mehr anhanget, gehalten werden sol.* Leipzig, 1580. Moser 1:1047–1451; Richter 2:401–51; Sehling 1:359–457. From 1580 on, this order was printed at both Jena and Leipzig. The 1580 Jena printing copied the 1540 edition exactly, while the 1580 Leipzig printing consolidated the city and village orders and made other very slight changes. <1580 02 - a1)(3 /$jäm : a2 [symbol] ion/$k - b1 A $: b2 2O3 vndzu$— agenda, printed, territory, official>

Saxony, Ernestine

1528 *Unterricht der visitatoren an die pfarrherrn im kurfürstenthum zu Sachsen.* Principally by Philipp Melanchthon, with a preface by Luther. Wittenberg, 1528. Richter 1:77–101; Sehling 1:149–74. <agenda, printed, territory, official>

1533 *Gemeine verordnung und artikel der visitation in Meissen und der Voitlandt den herrschaften, haupt- und amptleüten, schossern, steten und dorfschaften zugestellt.* Richter 1:226–30; Sehling 1:187–95. <agenda, manuscript, territory, official>

1685 *Des weyland Durchlauchtigsten Fürsten und HERRN, Herrn ERNSTEN, Hertzogen zu Sachsen, Jülich, Cleve und Berg, Landgrafen in Thüringen, Marggrafen zu Meissen, Gefürsteten Grafen zu Henneberg, Grafen zu der Marck und Ravensberg, Herrn zu Ravenstein, &c. Hochseeligsten Andenckens, Ordnungen, Das Kirchen- und Schulwesen betreffende; Auf Befehl Seiner Fürstl. Durchl. Hern. Sohns, Des auch Durchlauchtigsten Fürsten und HERRN, Herrn ERNSTEN, Hertzogen zu Sachsen, Jülich, Cleve und Berg, Landgrafen in Thüringen, Marggrafen zu Meissen, Gefürsteten Grafen zu Henneberg, Grafen zu der Marck und Ravensberg, Herrn zu Ravenstein, &c. Zusammen getragen und erneuert herauß gegeben, Jn Zweyen Theilen, Vor die Kirchen und Schulen in Seiner Fürstl. Durchl. Antheil Landes.* Hildburghausen, 1685. <1685 04 - a1 a3 n : a2 b3 u$ t - 1b1 A d : 1b2 4C3 Confe i - 2b1 A e : 2b2 3E3 en/$d—agenda, printed, territory, official>

Schandau [Saxony]

1577 *Wie es in der kirchen zu Schandau mit predigen und singen gehalten wird.* Sehling 1:658–59. <service description, manuscript>

Schildau [Saxony]

1581 [Untitled visitation report]. Pallas 2:4:470. <service description, manuscript>

Schillingsfürst [County Hohenlohe]

1578 *Kirchenordnung, wie sie im ambt Schillingsfürst gehalten.* Report enclosed with a letter of 18 February 1578 from Amtmann Möt to Graf Wolfgang. Sehling 15:226–27. <service description, manuscript>

Schleswig-Holstein

1542 *Christlyke Kercken Ordeninge, De yn[n] den Fürstendömen, Schleßwig, Holsten etc. schal geholden werdenn.* Magdeburg, 1542. By Johann Bugenhagen. Richter 1:353–60; *Die Schleswig-Holsteinische Kirchenordnung von 1542,* edited by Ernst Michelsen as *Schriften des Vereins für Schleswig-Holsteinische Kirchengeschichte,* series 1, no. 5 (Kiel: Cordes, 1909; 2d ed., 1920); *Die Schleswig-Holsteinische*

Kirchenordnung von 1542, edited and translated by Walter Göbell as *Schriften des Vereins für Schleswig-Holsteinische Kirchengeschichte,* series 1, no. 34 (Neumünster: Karl Wachholtz, 1986). <1542 04 - b1 A2nyn : b2 Z3 borch—agenda, printed, territory, official>

Schmerkendorf [Saxony]

    1618 [Untitled visitation report]. Pallas 2:5:123. <service description, manuscript>

    1529 [Untitled visitation report]. Pallas 2:5:104–5. <service description, manuscript>

    1602 [Untitled visitation report]. Pallas 2:5:120. <service description, manuscript>

Schmiedeberg [Saxony]

    1528 [Untitled visitation report]. Pallas 2:1:300. <service description, manuscript>

    1608 [Untitled visitation report]. Pallas 2:1:336. <service description, manuscript>

Schönburg

    1542 *Kirchen-Ordnung in der edlen wohlgeb. herrn, Hans Ernsten von Schönburg und sr. gnaden gebrüdern herrschaft und gebieten auf derselben ihr. gn. verbesserung durch Johann Pfeffinger gestellet. Anno 1542 den 18. October.* Sehling 2:167–76. <agenda, manuscript, territory, official>

Schönewalde [Saxony]

    1672 [Untitled visitation report]. Pallas 2:3:644–45. <service description, manuscript>

Schwäbisch Hall

    1526 *Reformation der Kirchen in dem Hellischen Land Herr Jo: Brentz.* By Johannes Brenz. Richter 1:40–49. <agenda, manuscript, city, official>

    1543 *Ordnung der Kirchen, inn eins Erbarn Raths zu Schwäbischen Hall, Oberkeit vnd gepiet gelegen.* Schwäbisch Hall, 1543. By Johannes Brenz. Richter 2:14. <1543 04 - a1$eqa2 ★2 rdnu - b1 A ür : b2 2B2 $nic—agenda, printed, city, official>

    1615 *Christliche Agenda oder Kirchen Ordnu[n]g, Wie es mit der Lehr Göttliches Worts, vnd den Ceremonien, auch mit andern darzu nothwendigen Sachen, Jn den Kirchen, so in eines Erbarn Raths, Deß Heiligen Römischen Reichsstatt Schwäbischen Hall, Obrigkeit vnd Gebieth gelegen, soll gehalten werden.* Ulm, 1615. <1615 08 - b1 A2 or : b2 T5 abe—agenda, printed, city, official>

Schwarzburg

    1549 *Ordenunge der religion, wie es in grafschaften Schwarzpurg und Stalberg sall gehalten werden. 1549.* Sehling 2:129–30. <agenda, manuscript, territory, official>

    1574 *Kirchenordnung wie dieselbe in Ober-Schwarzburgischer herrschaft mit ceremoniis in stedten und dorfern eintrechtig gehalten werden.* Sehling 2:132–36. <agenda, manuscript, territory, official>

    1587 *Ordnung der fest und feiertage durchs jahr wie dieselben eintrechtig gehalten werden sollen.* Sehling 2:137. <agenda, manuscript, territory, official>

    1675 *J. N. J. Agenda SCHVVARTZBURGICA, Das ist: Verzeichniß der Ceremonien, Wie solche Die ietzo regierende Gräfliche Schwartzburgisch und Honsteinische sämptliche Herrschaft Beyder, Sondershäusisch- und Rudolstätischer Linien, in ihren Kirchen wollen gehalten haben.* Rudolstadt, 1675. <1675 02 - a1$eqa2 b di - b1 A h : b2 3D ffen$—agenda, printed, territory, official>

Schweinfurt

    1543 *Kirchenordnung Eines Erbarn Raths, des heiligen Reichs Stat Schweinfurt in Francken, Wie man sich beide mit der Lehre vnd Ceremonien halten solle.* [Nürnberg], 1543.

By Johann Sutel. Richter 2:21–23; Sehling 11:624–44. The catalog of the Staatsbibliothek zu Berlin also lists a 1963 reprint printed in Schweinfurt (shelfmark: 18 A 1311). The author's name is from Graff (1937–39). <1543 04 - b1 a2 l$vnd : b2 h4 leich$w—agenda, printed, city, official>

1576 *Ordnung, wie es an den sontagen und festtagen alhie zu Schweinfurt unterscheidlich mit orgelschlagen, deutsch und lateinisch singen in unserer kirchen sol gehalten und volendet werden. Zusammengericht anno 76.* Sehling 11:645–48. <agenda, manuscript, city, official>

Seyda [Saxony]

1574 [Untitled visitation report]. Pallas 2:1:569. <service description, manuscript>

Stade

[ca. 1620–22] *[Untitled agenda].* Sehling 7:1:50–61. <agenda, manuscript, city, official>

Stendal [Brandenburg]

1578 [Untitled visitation edict]. Sehling 3:317–32. <agenda, manuscript, city, official>

Stettin

1573 [Untitled agenda]. Sehling 4:531–34. <agenda, manuscript, city, official>

Steuerwald/Peine

1561 *Kirchenordnunge in baiden gerichten, Steurwoldt unde Peine.* Hamburg, 1561. Sehling 7:2:1:769–86. <agenda, manuscript, territory, official>

Stolzenhain [Saxony]

1577 [Untitled visitation report]. Pallas 2:3:363. <service description, manuscript>

Stralsund

1555 [Untitled agenda]. Richter 2:167–69; Sehling 4:550–52. According to Graff (1937–39), this is a preliminary draft. <agenda, manuscript, city, preliminary draft>

Strassburg

1524 *Ordenung und inhalt, Teutscher Mess, so yetzund im gebrauch haben Ewangelisten und Christlichen Pfarrherren zu Straszburg.* 1524. Smend (1896): 125–38; also in Friedrich Hubert, *Die Straßburger liturgischen Ordnungen im Zeitalter der Reformation* (Göttingen, 1900), pp. 57–77. <agenda, manuscript, city, semiofficial>

1525a *Strassburger kirchenampt, nemlich von Insegnung der Eeleut von Tauf vnd des herren nachtmal, mit etlichen Psalmen, die am end des büchlins, ordentlich verzeychnet sein.* By Wolf Köpfel. <agenda, manuscript, city, private (?)>

1525b *Teutsch Kirche[n] ampt mit Lobgsengen, un[d] gotlichen psalmen, wie es die gemein zu Straßburg singt.* Strassburg, 1525. In Friedrich Hubert, *Die Straßburger liturgischen Ordnungen im Zeitalter der Reformation* (Göttingen, 1900), pp. 77–82. The catalog of the Staatsbibliothek zu Berlin also lists an 1848 reprint printed in Erfurt (shelfmark: an Eh 516). On the question of dating, see Konrad Ameln, "Zur Frage der Datierung des "Teutsch Kirchen ampt,"" *Jahrbuch für Liturgik und Hymnologie* 12 (1967): 140–48. <agenda, manuscript, city, official>

1530 *Psalmen, gebett und kirchenübung, wie sie zu Strassburg gehalten werden.* [N.p.], 1530. By Wolf Köpfel. Smend (1896): 138–42. <agenda, printed, city, private>

1598 *KirchenOrdnung, Wie es mit der Lehre Göttliches Worts, vnd den Ceremonien, Auch mit anderen dazu nothwendigen Sachen, Jn der Kirchen zu Straßburg, biß hieher gehalten worden, Vnd fürohin, mit verleihung Göttlicher Gnade, gehalten werden soll.* 1598.

Richter 2:479–83. Later editions: 1601, 1603, 1605, 1606, 1633. <1598 04 - b1 A2 fftß$: b2 3B3 159.$Fo—agenda, printed, city, official>

1670 *REVIDIRTE Kirchen-Ordnung, Wie es mit der Lehre Göttliches Worts, und den Ce- remonien, auch mit andern darzu nothwendigen Sachen, Jn der Kirchen zu Straßburg, biß hieher gehalten worden, und führohin, mit verleyhung Göttlicher Gnade, gehalten werden soll.* Strassburg, 1670. Apparently the only changes from the 1598 order are in the service times. <1670 04 - a1):(2 $ elb t : a2):(3 d$Chri - b1 A $: b2 3H3 farr$eqSc—agenda, printed, city, official>

Suhl [County Henneberg]
1562 *Gemeiner bericht von tagen und zeiten, daran predigte und lectiones in der kirchen gehal- ten werden.* Sehling 2:350–52. <service description, manuscript>

Sulzfeld and Klein-Bardorf [County Henneberg]
1566 *Verzeichnus, wie es mit allen ceremonien, gesengen und predigten in der kirchen zu Sulzfeld am Hassberg gehalten wird.* By Caspar Engelhaubt, pastor. Sehling 2:352– 53. <service description, manuscript>

Teschen
1584 [Untitled agenda]. Sehling 3:458–63. <agenda, manuscript, territory, official>

Thorn
1575/1712 *Kirchenordnung, wie es zu Thorn in Preussen beide in der alten als neuen stadt mit lehr und ceremonien, samt andern ding, so zu förderung und erhaltung des lehr- und predigt- ambts christlicher zucht und guter ordnung von neuen gehalten wird, aus der wittenber- gischen, nürnbergischen, breslauischen, mecklenburgischen, preussischen und andern guten kirchenordnungen treu und fleissig zusammengetragen. Anno 1575.* Sehling 4:233–44. <agenda, manuscript, city, official>

Thüngen
1564 *Thüngenische Kirchenordnung 1564. Gründlicher bericht, was sich [die von den] gestrengen, edlen und ernvesten brüdern und vettern von Thüngen verordnete pastores und kirchendiener in einrichtung einer gleichförmigen christlichen kirchenordnung ver- glichen haben zu Grefendorf den 19. Septembris dises 1564. jars.* Sehling 11:731– 42. <agenda, manuscript, territory, official>

Torgau [Saxony]
1580 [Untitled visitation report]. Pallas 2:4:49. <service description, manuscript>

Transylvania
1547 *[Latin:] Reformatio ecclesiarvm Saxonicarvm in Transylvania; [German:] Kirchenord- nung aller Deutschen in Sybenbürgen.* [Latin:] Coronae, 1547 [German:] Cron, 1547. By Johannes Honterus. In G. D. Teutsch, *Urkundenbuch der Evangelischen Landeskirche A. B. in Siebenbürgen,* erster Theil (Hermannstadt, 1862), 6–36 (Latin); 36–71 (German). <agenda, manuscript, territory, official>

Treben [Saxony]
1672 [Untitled visitation report]. Pallas 2:3:189. <service description, manuscript>

Trossin (with Rötzsch) [Saxony]
1598 [Untitled visitation report]. Pallas 2:4:283. <service description, manuscript>

Uebigau [Saxony]
1529 [Untitled visitation report]. Pallas 2:5:130. <service description, manuscript>
1602 [Untitled visitation report]. Pallas 2:5:147. <service description, manuscript>

Ulm

    1747   *Kirchen-Ordnung Wie es Mit der Lehre Göttlichen Worts, Ausspendung der Heil. Sacramenten, Ceremonien, auch mit anderen nöthigen Verrichtungen Jn der Stadt Ulm und deroselben Gebiet bißhero gehalten worden, und mit Verleihung Göttlicher Gnade fürohin solle gehalten werden.* Ulm, 1747. <1747 04 - a1)(2 en$eq : a2)(3 ta,$d - b1 A te : b2 4A2 $Beichtstu—agenda, printed, city, official>

Upper Austria

    1617   *Christliche Kirchen Agenda So Bey Offentlichem Gottesdienst der Gemeinden Augspürgischer Confession nutzlich gebraucht werden kan.* Tübingen, 1617. The Wolfenbüttel catalog classifies this as a Tübingen order, but Graff (1937–39) says it is from Österreich ober der Enns. <1617 04 - b1 A2 eliti c : b2 2X3 .$Vm—agenda, printed, territory, semiofficial>

Velden [bei Nürnberg]

    1560   [Untitled visitation report]. Hirschmann 1994:57. <service description, manuscript>

Verden

    1606   *Kirchenordnung, wie es mit christlicher lehr und ceremonien, verreichung der h[eiligen], hoch[wirdigen] sacramenten und andern kirchensachen im stift Verden hinfort durch Gottes gnad und beystand ordentlich gehalten werden soll.* Lemgo, 1606. Sehling 7:1:145–208. <agenda, manuscript, territory, official>

Wahrenbrück [Saxony]

    1598   [Untitled visitation report]. Pallas 2:5:180. <service description, manuscript>
    1602   [Untitled visitation report]. Pallas 2:5:183. <service description, manuscript>
    1618   [Untitled visitation report]. Pallas 2:5:189. <service description, manuscript>

Waldeck

    1557   *Kirchen Ordnung Wie es mit der Raynen Lehr des Euangelij, Administration der heyligen Sacrament, Annehmung, verhörung, vnd bestetigung der Priester, Ordentlichen Ceremonien in den Kirchen, Visitation vnd Synodis, in der Herrschafft Waldeck gehalten werden soll.* [Marburg, 1557]. Richter 2:169–77. <1567 04 - b1 A2 ewa : b2 R3 einer—agenda, printed, territory, official>

    1640   *Kirchen Ordnung, Wie es mit der reinen Lehr des Evangelij, Administration der heiligen Sacrament, Annehmung, Verhörung vnd Bestettigung der Prediger, Ordentlichen Ceremonien in den Kirchen, Visitation vnd Synodis, in der Graffschafft Waldeck einhelliglich gehalten werden soll.* [N.p.], 1640. <1640 04 - b1 A2 $wi : b2 X3 nom—agenda, printed, territory, official>

    1731   *Fürstlich Waldeckische Kirchen Ordnung Wie es Mit der reinen Lehre des Evangelii, ADMINISTRATION der Heiligen Sacramenten, Annehm- Verhör- und Bestättigung der Prediger, ordentlichen Ceremonien in den Kirchen, Visitation und Synodis gehalten werden soll. Anjetzo revidiret und zum Dritten mal aufgelegt.* Mengeringhausen, 1731. <1731 04 - a1)(2 $La : a2)(3 dig - b1 A e : b2 Z3 em—agenda, printed, territory, official>

Wasungen [County Henneberg]

    1566   *Bericht auf des ehrwirdigen hern m. Christoffori Fischeri hennenbergischen superintendenten begern, wie es mit predigen, sacramenten und ceremonien in der pfarre Wasungen gehalten wirt.* By Martin Keiser, pastor. Sehling 2:355–57. <service description, manuscript>

Weissenburg

1528   *Ein kurtzer auszug und summari der ordnung in dem gottesdienst bei der christlichen gemain zu Weißenburg, durch die diener der kirchen doselben aufzurichten furgenommen. Anno 1528.* Sehling 11:657–64. <agenda, manuscript, city, official>

Weissenfels [Saxony]

1578   *Ordnung der geseng, so zu Weissenfels in der kirchen das jahr uber gehalten wird.* Sehling 1:693–94. <service description, manuscript>

Wennigsen [Calenberg-Göttingen]

1543   [Untitled visitation edict]. Kayser 1896:378. <agenda, manuscript, cloister, official>

Wertheim

[ca. 1555]   [Untitled agenda]. Sehling 11:708–25. <agenda, manuscript, territory, official>

Wiederau (with Drasdo, Neideck and Banßdorff) [Saxony]

1608   [Untitled visitation report]. Pallas 2:5:213. <service description, manuscript>

Wildschütz [Saxony]

1602   [Untitled visitation report]. Pallas 2:4:323. <service description, manuscript>
1608   [Untitled visitation report]. Pallas 2:4:324. <service description, manuscript>

Wittenberg

1522   *Ain lobliche Ordnung der furstlichen stat Wittemberg. Im tausent funfhundert vnd zway vnd zwaintzigen jar auffgericht.* [N.p., n.d.]. By Andreas Bodenstein von Carlstadt. Richter 2:484–85; Sehling 1:697–98. <agenda, printed, city, semiofficial>

1525a   *Wie es einer zeit mit den ceremonien der kirchen gehalten wirt zu Wittemberg am tag Galli ubergeben 1525.* By Johann Bugenhagen and Justus Jonas. Sehling 1:698–700. <agenda, manuscript, collegiate church, semiofficial>

1525b   *Vertzeichnus wie die Ceremonien im Stifft zu Wittenberg sollen geordent werden. .1.5.2.5.* By Georg Spalatin. Theodor Muther, "Drei Urkunden zur Reformationsgeschichte," *Zeitschrift für die historische Theologie* 30 (1860): 456–61. <agenda, manuscript, collegiate church, semiofficial>

1533   *Registration der stat Wittemberg, durch die verordenten visitatores beder visitacion gemacht und aufgericht.* Richter 1:220–25; Sehling 1:700–710; Pallas (1906–18):2:1:2–16 (for musical notation, see part 1, pp. 238–40 and tables 1–4). <agenda, manuscript, city, official>

1559   *Kirchenordnung: Wie es mit Christlicher Lere, reichung der Sacrament, Ordination der Diener des Euangelij, ordenlichen Ceremonien, in den Kirchen, Visitation, Consistorio vnd Schulen, zu Witteberg vnd in etlichen Chur vnd Fürstenthum, Herrschafften vnd Stedte der Augsburgischen Confession verwand, gehalten wird.* Wittenberg, 1559. Later editions: 1565, 1566. <1559 04 - b1 A2 dfur : b2 n3 an—agenda, printed, city, official>

[1570?]   *Christlike Kerckengesenge unde ordeninge uth der Augßburgeschen Confeßion und Wittenbergeschen Kerckenordeninge thosamen gebracht.* [N.p., 1570?]. <0000 08 - b1 A2 ikew : b2 L4 ft$verl—agenda, printed, city, semiofficial>

Wittenberg (Luther)

1523a   *FORMVLA MISSAE ET COMMVNIONIS pro Ecclesia vuittembergensi. MARTINI LVTHER.* Wittenberg, 1523. By Martin Luther. Richter 1:2–7; Sehling 1:4–9; WA 12:205–220; AE 53:19–40. This book appeared in three separate issues in 1523; the original printing (according to the Wolfenbüttel catalog) has a fingerprint of 1523 04 - b1 a2 e$E : b2 b3 bom.[2] Later edition: 1524 (German). <1523 04 - b1 a2 e$E : b2 b3 bom—agenda, printed, city, private>

1523b *Von Ordnung Gottesdienstes in der Gemeine.* Wittenberg, 1523. By Martin Luther. Richter 1:1–2; Sehling 1:2–3; WA 12:35–37; AE 53:11–14. <agenda, printed, general (?), private>

1526 *Deudsche Messe vnd ordnung Gottis diensts.* Wittenberg, 1526. By Martin Luther. Richter 1:35–40; Sehling 1:10–16; WA 19:72–113; AE 53:61–90. <1526 04 - b1 A2 $noc : b2 F3 ynac—agenda, printed, city, private>

Woldenberg [Braunschweig-Wolfenbüttel]

1586 [Untitled visitation report]. Wolters 1938–50, vol. 43, p. 233. <service description, manuscript>

Wolfenbüttel

1542 [Untitled visitation edict]. Kayser 1896:105. <agenda, manuscript, city, official>

Wolfstein

1574 *Christliche Instructio, wie die getrückte brandenburgische und nürnbergische kürchenordnung mit andern nötigen angehengten artikeln in unsers genedigen herrn, hern Hans Endresen vom Wolffstain, freihern zur Obernsulzbürg, land und herrschaft in seinem rechten, christlichen gebrauch fortgesetzt und erhalten werden soll, gestelt durch M. Thomam Stibarum, pfarhern zum Sulzberg und der löblichen freien herrschaft Obernsulzbürg superintendenten, anno verbi incarnati 1574.* By Thomas Stieber. Sehling 13:566–92. <agenda, manuscript, territory, official>

Wollin [Pomerania]

1535 [Untitled visitation report]. Heyden 1961–64:1:18. <service description, manuscript>

Württemberg

1536 *Gemein kirchen ordnung, wie die diser Zeit allenthalb im Fürstenthumb Wirtemberg gehalten soll werden. Anno. MDXXXVI.* By Schnepf; approved by Johannes Brenz. Richter 1:265–73. <agenda, manuscript, territory, official>

1553 *Kirchenordnung, wie es mit der Leere vnd Ceremonien, im Fürstenthumb Wirtemberg angericht vnd gehalten werden soll.* Tübingen, 1553. By Johannes Brenz. Richter 2:128–41. Later editions: 1555, 1559, 1582, 1615. <1553 08 - b1 A2 eilige : b2 M3 ch$men—agenda, printed, territory, official>

1565 *Kirchenordnung, das ist, Form vnd weise, nach welcher die reyne Christliche Lere, Sacramenten, vnd allerley nötige Ceremonien, in etlichen fürnemen der Augspurgischen Confession verwandten Kirchen, deren Namen hernach in jrer ordnung gefunden werden, bißher verrichtet vnd im brauch gewesen vnd noch seind. Jetzt mit sonderlichem fleiß vbersehen, vnd auffs newe getruckt.* Frankfurt/Main, 1565. The catalog of the Staatsbibliothek zu Berlin identifies this as a Württemberg order, but there is no indication of this in the title or preface, which is undated and unsigned. <1565 04 - a1)(2 egebe : a2)(3 öttlic - b1 A $: b2 2K rzey—agenda, printed, territory, official (?)>

1657 *Kirchen-Ordnung, Wie es mit der Lehr vnd Ceremonien im Hertzogthumb Würtemberg angerichtet vnd gehalten werden soll.* Stuttgart, 1657. Later editions: 1660, 1743. <1657 08 - b1 A2 Lehr : b2 O3 en$H—agenda, printed, territory, official>

Wurzen

1542 *Wes sich die pfarrer, kirchner, gemein mann und pauern zu Wurzen und in demselben ampt halten sollen.* Sehling 2:95–98. <agenda, manuscript, territory, official>

Züllsdorf [Saxony]
    1577   [Untitled visitation report]. Pallas 2:3:670. <service description, manuscript>

Zwethau [Saxony]
    1575   [Untitled visitation report]. Pallas 2:3:382. <service description, manuscript>

Zwickau
    1529   [Untitled agenda]. Sehling 1:721–22. <agenda, manuscript, city, official>

❖

Part 2: Other Sources

Primary and secondary sources are intermixed in this section. Ellipses (. . .) indicate that part of a title has been omitted; if they appear at the beginning of a title the omitted words are not part of the title itself but rather appear on the title page before the actual title. They typically consist of the name and academic titles of the author or an introductory phrase such as "In nomine Jesu." These introductory words are omitted unless they affect the grammatical case of the first few words of the actual title, in which case the beginning of the title is given in full.

The number of pages or leaves is given for most monographs published before 1800. The name of the publisher is given only for books published after 1950 and for earlier books that might still be in print. Fuller citations for books about music published before 1800, with library locations, may be found in François Lesure, ed., *Écrits imprimés concernant la musique*, 2 vols., Répertoire international des sources musicales, series B, part 6, vols. 1–2 (Munich: G. Henle, 1971); these are indicated in this bibliography by "Lesure" and a page number. Hymnals printed before 1800 may be found in *Das deutsche Kirchenlied: Verzeichnis der Drucke von den Anfängen bis 1800*, Répertoire international des sources musicales, series B, part 8, vols. 1–2 (Kassel: Bärenreiter, 1975–80), referred to as *RISM*. Some eighteenth-century books were reviewed in contemporary music periodicals, and citations to these reviews are given if known.

Abfertigung der zu Amberg ohnlangst ausgesprengten Anleytung etlicher Caluinischen Blindenleyter, in welcher sie sich vnterstanden, der Wittenbergischen Theologen Notwendige Antwort, auff die im Fürstenthumb Anhalt ausgegangene hefftige Schrifft, etc. mit greifflichen Teuschereyen zuverkehren. Wittenberg, 1597.

Adlung, Jacob. . . . *Anleitung zu der musikalischen Gelahrtheit*. Erfurt, 1758. Reprint: edited by Hans Joachim Moser, Documenta musicologica, series 1, no. 4 (Kassel: Bärenreiter, 1953). Lesure: 67.

Aepin, Johann. See "Bergedorf," "Buxtehude," and "Hamburg" in part 1 above.

Agricola, Martin. *Deutsche Musica vnd Gesangbüchlein, der Sontags Euangelien, artig zu singen, für die Schulkinder, kneblein vnd megdlein, etwa in deutsche Reim verfasset.* Nürnberg, 1568. 112 f. Lesure: 69.

Alberus, Erasmus. *Widder die verfluchte Lere der Carlstader, vnd alle fürnemste Heubter der Sacramentirer, Rottengeyster, Widderteuffer, Sacramentlesterer, Eheschender, Musicaverechter, Bildstürmer, Feiertagfeinde, vnd Verwüster aller guten Ordnung.* Neubrandenburg, 1556. 184 f.

Albrecht, Johann Lorenz. . . . *Abhandlung über die Frage: ob die Musik bey dem Gottesdienste der Christen zu dulden, oder nicht?* Berlin, 1764. 32 pp. Lesure: 75; reviewed in Hiller (1766–70): 148–50.

———. "Hrn. M. Johann Lorenz Albrechts kurze und unpartheyische Nachricht von dem Zustande und der Beschaffenheit der Kirchenmusik in der oberstädtischen Hauptkirche

Beat\ | ae Mari\ | ae Virginis zu Mühlhausen." In *Historisch-kritische Beyträge zur Aufnahme der Musik*, edited by Friedrich Wilhelm Marpurg, vol. 5, part 5 (Berlin, 1762): 381–409.

Ambsterdam, Johann. See "Lippe" in part 1 above.

Ameln, Konrad. "Das Achtliederbuch vom Jahre 1523/24." *Jahrbuch für Liturgik und Hymnologie* 2 (1956): 89–91.

———. "'Herzlich tut mich erfreuen': Wandlungen einer Melodie." In *Ars musica musica scientia: Festschrift Heinrich Hüschen*, edited by Detlef Altenburg. Beiträge zur rheinischen Musikgeschichte, vol. 126, 10–16. [N.p.]: Verlag der Arbeitsgemeinschaft für rheinische Musikgeschichte, 1980.

———. "Kirchenliedmelodien der Reformation im Gemeindegesang des 16. und 17. Jahrhunderts." In *Das protestantische Kirchenlied im 16. und 17. Jahrhundert: Text-, musik- und theologiegeschichtliche Probleme*, edited by Alfred Dürr and Walther Killy, 61–71. Wiesbaden: Otto Harrassowitz, 1986.

———. "Das Klugsche Gesangbuch, Wittenberg 1529." *Jahrbuch für Liturgik und Hymnologie* 16 (1971): 159–62.

———. "Luthers Kirchenlied und Gesangbuch: offene Fragen." *Jahrbuch für Liturgik und Hymnologie* 32 (1989): 19–28.

———. "Teutsch kirchen ampt Straßburg 1524 oder 1525?" *Jahrbuch für Liturgik und Hymnologie* 1 (1955): 96–97.

———. "Zur Frage der Datierung des 'Teutsch Kirchen ampt.'" *Jahrbuch für Liturgik und Hymnologie* 12 (1967): 140–48.

[Amling, Wolfgang]. *Tauffbüchlein, für die Kirchen im Fürstenthumb Anhaldt, mit Erzelung etlicher hochwichtigen Vrsachen, warumb der Exorcismus abgeschafft.* [Zerbst], 1590. 135 p. The author is named in the title of Johann Limator's *An M. Wolffgangum Amling Superintendent zu Zerbst, von abschaffung des Exorcismi, vnd andern nachfolgenden enderungen* ([N.p.], 1590).

Andreae, Jacob. See "Braunschweig-Wolfenbüttel" in part 1 above.

Angerstein, Johann Carl. . . . *Theoretisch-practische Anweisung, Choralgesänge nicht nur richtig, sondern auch schön spielen zu lernen.* Stendal, 1800. XVI, 248, [13], 86 pp. Lesure: 88.

. . .*Anleytung, wie man das Wittembergische Buch, hievon geschrieben, mit Frucht vnd Nutz lesen möge.* Amberg, 1597. [84], 40, [1] pp. Attached to the 1597 reprint of the *Erinnerungs Schrifft*. Reprinted in *Drey Schrifften* (1606).

Anmerkungen bey neuen Gesangbüchern und Gesängen, vornehmlich in Absicht der Weglassung oder Veränderung alter Lieder. Gotha, 1786. 142 pp.

Antwort auff die Wittenbergische Abfertigung der Ambergischen Anleytung: belangend die Anhaltische Reformation. Amberg, 1598. [12], 343 pp. Reprinted in *Drey Schrifften* (1606).

Anwander, Georg. *Christliche Predigt, von der vocal und instrumentalischen Music.* Tübingen, 1606. 37 pp. Lesure: 91.

Armknecht, Friedrich. *Die alte Matutin- und Vesper-Ordnung in der evangelisch-lutherischen Kirche nach ihrem Ursprung, ihrer Einrichtung, ihrem Verfall und ihrer Wiederherstellung dargestellt.* Göttingen: Vandenhoeck und Ruprecht, 1856.

Arndt, G. "Die Entwicklung der evangelischen Gottesdienstordnung im Bistum Halberstadt." *Monatschrift für Gottesdienst und kirchliche Kunst* (1913): 235–43.

Arnoldi, Philipp. *Caeremoniae Lutheranae, das ist, ein christlicher, gründlicher Unterricht von allen fürnembsten C\ | aeremonien, so in den lutherischen preussischen Kirchen, in Verrichtung des Gottesdienstes, adhibirt werden, alß, von Hostien, Brodtbrechen, consecriren Easein, Altharen, Bildern, brennenden Lichten, Kniebeugen, Hut abnehmen, Musicâ Orgeln, Exorcismo, Festagen, vnd andern Kirchensachen mehr.* Königsberg, 1616. [18], 189 [i.e., 187], [1] pp.

Augenscheinlicher Beweisz, dasz die Wittenberger jhr vngegründ Lästern wider die Anhaltische Reformation nicht behaupten, vnd auff die Ambergische Beantwortung jhrer Abfertigung fast nichts haben antworten können, wiewol sie sich zwey gantzer Jahr darauff besonnen. Amberg, 1600. [8], 71, [1] pp. Reprinted in *Drey Schrifften* (1606).

Bach-Dokumente. Edited by the Bach-Archive Leipzig. 3 vols. Supplement to *Johann Sebastian Bach: Neue Ausgabe sämtlicher Werke.* Kassel: Bärenreiter, 1963–72.

Baum, Herbert. "Kirchengesang, Gesang- und Choralbücher in Waldeck." In *Beiträge zur Geschichte der evangelischen Kirchenmusik und Hymnologie in Kurhessen und Waldeck,* edited by the Landesverband der evangelischen Kirchenchöre, 32–43. Kassel: Bärenreiter, 1969.

Bäumker, Wilhelm. *Das katholische deutsche Kirchenlied in seinen Singweisen.* 4 vols. Freiburg i. B., 1886–1911. Reprint: Hildesheim: Georg Olms, 1962.

Beck, Dorothea. *Krise und Verfall der protestantischen Kirchenmusik im 18. Jahrhundert.* Dissertation, Martin-Luther-Universität, Halle-Wittenberg, 1951 [i.e., 1952]. The date on the title page is corrected in pencil to [1952], with a notation on the verso "Tag der mündlichen Prüfung: 5.6.1952. Referent: Prof. Dr. Max Schneider. Koreferent: Prof. D. Kurt Aland."

Becker, Carl Ferdinand. *Systematisch-chronologische Darstellung der musikalischen Literatur von der frühesten bis auf die neueste Zeit.* Leipzig, 1836.

Becker, Karl Christian. *Die Kirchenagenden der evangelisch lutherischen Gemeinde zu Frankfurt am Main.* 2d ed. Frankfurt/Main, 1850. 72 pp.

. . . *Bedencken über das zu Glauche an Halle 1703. im Wäysen-Hause daselbst edirte Gesang-Buch.* Frankfurt and Leipzig, 1716. 28 pp. Reprinted and translated into English in McMullen 1987.

Beinroth, Friedrich Wilhelm. *Musikgeschichte der Stadt Sondershausen von ihren Anfängen bis zum Ende des 19. Jahrhunderts.* Innsbruck: Universitäts-Verlag Wagner, 1943.

Die Bekenntnisschriften der evangelisch-lutherischen Kirche. 2d ed. Göttingen: Vandenhoeck & Ruprecht, 1952.

Beyreuther, Erich. "Die Auflösung des reformatorischen Gottesdienstes in der reformatorischen Orthodoxie des 17. Jahrhunderts." *Evangelische Theologie* 20 (1960): 380–97.

Biehle, Herbert. *Musikgeschichte vom Bautzen bis zum Anfang des 19. Jahrhunderts.* Veröffentlichungen des Fürstlichen Institutes für musikwissenschaftliche Forschung zu Bückeburg, 4th series, vol. 3. Leipzig, 1924.

Blankenburg, Walter. "Die Geschichte der evangelischen Kirchenmusik." In *Die Evangelische Kirchenmusik,* edited by Erich Valentin and Friedrich Hofmann, 38–106. Regensburg: Gustav Bosse, [1967].

———. "Der gottesdienstliche Liedgesang der Gemeinde." In *Leiturgia: Handbuch des evangelischen Gottesdienstes,* edited by Karl Ferdinand Müller and Walter Blankenburg, vol. 4:559–660. Kassel: Johannes Stauda-Verlag, 1961.

Blessinger, Karl. *Studien zur Ulmer Musikgeschichte im 17. Jahrhundert insbesondere über Leben und Werke Sebastian Anton Scherers.* Dissertation, Munich, 1913. Ulm a. D., 1913.

Blindow, Martin. *Die Choralbegleitung des 18. Jahrhunderts in der evangelischen Kirche Deutschlands.* Kölner Beiträge zur Musikforschung, vol. 13. Regensburg: Gustav Bosse, 1957.

———. "Die Erfurter Enchiridien von 1526 als liturgische Quellen." *Jahrbuch für Liturgik und Hymnologie* 11 (1966): 165–67.

Blume, Friedrich. *Die evangelische Kirchenmusik.* Potsdam, 1931.

———. *Geschichte der evangelischen Kirchenmusik.* Kassel: Bärenreiter, 1965.

———. *Protestant Church Music: A History.* New York: Norton, 1974. A translation of Blume 1965, with additions.

Boës, Adolf. "Die reformatorischen Gottesdienste in der Wittenberger Pfarrkirche von 1523 an und die 'Ordenung der gesenge der Wittembergischen Kirchen' von 1543/44." *Jahrbuch für Liturgik und Hymnologie* 4 (1958/59): 1–40; 6 (1961): 49–61.

Bokemeyer, Heinrich. "Melodischer Vorhof." *Critica musica* (edited by Johann Mattheson) 2

(1725): 291–334, 345–79. Most of the essays in *Critica musica* had been previously published and were reprinted here with Mattheson's comments. This essay follows the same format (i.e., printed with Mattheson's comments), but there is no evidence that it had been printed previously.

Bonn, Hermann. See "Osnabrück" in part 1 above.

Boor, Friedrich de. "Der Nordhauser Gesangbuchstreit 1735–1738: Orthodoxie, Pietismus und Frühaufklärung im Kampf um das rechte Gesangbuch." In *Pietismus und Neuzeit: Ein Jahrbuch zur Geschichte der neueren Protestantismus,* edited by Andreas Lindt und Klaus Deppermann. Jahrbücher zur Geschichte des Pietismus, vol. 1, pp. 100–13. Bielefeld: Luther-Verlag, 1974.

[Botsack, Johann]. *Project etlicher wolgegründeten Motiven, gegen die Einführung des Lobwassers-Lieder, in eine ungeenderter Augßburgischer Confession zugethane Gemeine Christi.* [N.p.], 1655. [6], 57, [1] pp. The author's last name is from section 4 of the preface to Gerber 1732; the first name is from the catalog of the Herzog August Bibliothek, Wolfenbüttel.

———. *Projectum protectum: das ist, Gründliche Vertheidigung, der XXIII. Gründe, im Project 1654. eingeführet wider die Einführung und Vbung der Lieder, D. Lobwassers, jn einer der ungeänderten A. Confession zugethanen und derselben, durch Hand und Siegel befestigten Kirchen und Gemeine: und wieder ein Tractätlein, Rejectum projectum, genant, 1655. außgegangen, sampt einem Register der Fähler und Sophisterey.* [N.p.], 1655. [8], 92 pp. The author's name is mentioned in Curike 1656 and Gerber 1732 and is written on the title page of the Göttingen copy.

Brandhorst, Jürgen. *Musikgeschichte der Stadt Minden.* Schriften zur Musikwissenschaft aus Münster, vol. 3. Hamburg: Karl Dieter Wagner, 1991.

Brauer, James. "The Devil's Tunes," *Concordia Journal* 23/1 (January 1997):2–3.

Brecht, Martin. *Kirchenordnung und Kirchenzucht in Württemberg vom 16. bis zum 18. Jahrhundert.* Quellen und Forschungen zur württembergischen Kirchengeschichte, no. 1. Stuttgart: Calwer, 1967.

———. *Martin Luther: shaping and defining the Reformation 1521–1532.* Translated by James L. Schaaf. Minneapolis: Fortress Press, 1990. A translation of *Martin Luther: Zweiter Band: Ordnung und Abgrenzung der Reformation, 1521–1532* (Stuttgart: Calwer, 1986).

Brednich, Rolf Wilhelm. *Die Liedpublizistik im Flugblatt des 15. bis 17. Jahrhunderts.* 2 vols. Baden-Baden: Koerner, 1974–75.

[Breithaupt, Joachim Justus]. *Verantwortung gegen Hn. D. Joh. Fried. Mayers . . . so genannten kurtzen Bericht von Pietisten.* Halle, 1707. 166 pp. The author's name is written in pencil in the Wolfenbüttel copy. The preface is dated "Novemb. ao. 1706."

Brenz, Johannes. See "Schwäbisch Hall" and "Wurttemberg" in part 1 above.

Bronisch, P. "Versuch einer Verdrängung lutherischer Kirchengebräuche durch calvinische." *Monatschrift für Gottesdienst und kirchliche Kunst* 1/12 (1897): 385–87.

Brown, Christopher Boyd. *Singing the Gospel: Lutheran Hymns and the Success of the Reformation in Joachimsthal.* Ph.D. thesis, Harvard University, 2001.

[Brückner, Johann Georg, ed.]. *Sammlung verschiedener Nachrichten zu einer Beschreibung des Kirchen- und Schulenstaats im Herzogthum Gotha.* 3 vols. Gotha, 1753–63. The editor's name is from the Wolfenbüttel library catalog.

Bucer, Martin. *Martin Bucers deutsche Schriften.* Vol. 1, edited by Robert Stupperich. Gütersloh: Gerd Mohn, 1960. See also "Augsburg" and "Cologne" in part 1 above.

Bugenhagen, Johann. See "Braunschweig," "Hamburg," "Hildesheim," "Lübeck," "Pomerania," "Schleswig-Holstein," and "Wittenberg" in part 1 above.

Burdorf, P[eter]. *Winke zur Beförderung der Feyerlichkeit des öffentlichen Gottesdienstes.* 2 vols. in 1. Schleswig and Leipzig, 1795. XII, 148, [IV], 172, [1] pp.

Burney, Charles. *The Present State of Music in Germany, the Netherlands and United Provinces.* 2d ed., 2 vols. London, 1775.

Bush, Douglas Earl. *The Liturgical Use of the Organ in German Regions prior to the Protestant Reformation: Contracts, Consuetudinaries, and Musical Repertories.* Ph.D. thesis, University of Texas at Austin, 1982.

Buszin, Walter E. *The Doctrine of the Universal Priesthood and Its Influence upon the Liturgies and Music of the Lutheran Church.* St. Louis: Concordia, [1940].

Butler, Bartlett R. "Hymns." In *The Oxford Encyclopedia of the Reformation,* vol. 2, 290–99. New York: Oxford University Press, 1996.

Butler, Bartlett Russell. *Liturgical Music in Sixteenth-Century Nürnberg: A Socio-Musical Study.* Ph.D. thesis, University of Illinois at Urbana-Champaign, 1970.

Buxschoten, Hadrian. See "Lippe" in part 1 above.

Carlstadt, Andreas Bodenstein von. See "Wittenberg" in part 1 above.

Carolus, Mauricius. See "Meiningen" in part 1 above.

Carpzov, Johann Gottlob. . . . *Unterricht vom unverletzten Gewissen beyde gegen Gott und Menschen, in vier und achtzig Predigten, vormahls der Gemeine Gottes zu St.Thomas in Leipzig vorgetragen.* Leipzig, 1733. [32], 1656, [87] pp.

Chemnitz, Martin. See "Braunschweig-Wolfenbüttel" in part 1 above.

Christian Worship: A Lutheran Hymnal. Authorized by the Wisconsin Evangelical Lutheran Synod. Milwaukee: Northwestern, 1993.

Churmärckische Visitations- und Consistorial- Ordnung von Anno 1573 samt einem kurtzen jedoch vollständigen Auszug der nachher emanirten Königl. Preuss. und Chur-Brandenburgischen Edicten und Verordnungen, welche den Inspectoribus, Predigern, Schulleuten und Candidaten vornehmlich zu wissen nöthig sind. Berlin, 1761. [4], 284 pp.

Clauß. "Aus Gunzenhäuser Visitationsakten des 16. Jahrhunderts." *Beiträge zur bayerischen Kirchengeschichte* 31 (1925): 101–10; 32 (1925): 32–39, 87–96.

Colloqvivm Mompelgartense. Gespräch . . . zwischen den Hochgelehrten, D. Iacobo Andreae, Propst vnnd Cantzler der Hohen Schul zu Tübingen, vnd D. Theodoro Beza, Professorn vnd Pfarrern zu Genff. Tübingen, 1587. [28], 988 pp.

Cöln, Johan. See "Marisfeld" in part 1 above.

Corpus reformatorum. 87 vols. Halle, 1834–1900.

Corvinus, Anton. See "Braunschweig-Wolfenbüttel," "Calenberg-Göttingen," and "Nordheim" in part 1 above.

Crichton, Wilhelm. *Ueber die Unverbesserlichkeit der Religion, des Gottesdienstes und der Liturgie freyer Christen.* Halle, 1782. [6], 129 pp.

Crist, Stephen A. See *Enchiridion geistliker Leder vnde Psalmen.*

Cunz, F. A. *Geschichte des deutschen Kirchenliedes vom 16. Jahrhundert bis auf unsere Zeit.* Leipzig, 1855. Reprint ed., 2 vols. in 1. Wiesbaden: Martin Sändig, 1969.

Curike, Reinhold. See also the anonymous *Der ohnmächtige Fündling* and *Ein Reys-Gespräch.*

[Curike, Reinhold]. *Reiectus protector, oder Wiederlegung des Proiecti protecti, der vermeinten 23 gründen, so ein engenanter scribent, kegenst den Lobwasser heraus gegeben, und zu vertheydigen sich vergebens unterstanden.* [N.p.], 1656. [12], 395 pp. The attribution is from a manuscript entry in the copy at the Georg-August-Universität, Göttingen..

———. *Rejectum projectum, oder: Wiederlegung des Projects etlicher ungegründeter Motiven so ein ungenandter Scribent unlängst gegenst den Lobwasser für des Herren Gebot außgegeben, und zum Schutz derer die in Elbing des Lobwassers Lieder abzuschaffen sich unterfangen außgefertiget.* 1655. 110, [3] pp. The author's name is from a manuscript entry on the title page of the copy at the Georg-August-Universität, Göttingen.

Daebeler, Hans Jürgen. *Musiker und Musikpflege in Rostock von der Stadtgründung bis 1700.* Dissertation, Rostock, 1966.

Dannhauer, Johann Conrad. *Catechismus-Milch oder der Erklärung deß Christlichen Catechismi.* 10 vols. in 4, plus an index volume. Straßburg, [1642–78].

Dean, Jeffrey. "Listening to Sacred Polyphony c. 1500." *Early Music* 25/4 (November 1997): 611–38.

Dechent, Hermann. *Kirchengeschichte von Frankfurt am Main seit der Reformation.* 2 vols. Leipzig and Frankfurt, 1913–21.

Demantius, Johann Christoph. *Forma musices. Gründtlicher und kurtzer Bericht der Singekunst fur [!] die allererst anfahende Knaben, wie die können gelehret und auffs kürtzeste underwiesen werden, damit die ohne grosse Arbeit und Mühe, in kurtzer Zeit singen lernen.* Bautzen, [1592]. 16 f. Lesure: 257.

Democritus, Christianus. See "Dippel, Johann Conrad."

Detlefsen, Hans Peter. *Musikgeschichte der Stadt Flensburg bis zum Jahre 1850.* Schriften des Landesinstituts für Musikforschung, Kiel, vol. 11. Kassel: Bärenreiter, 1961.

Das deutsche Kirchenlied. Abteilung III, Band 1. Vorgelegt von Joachim Stalmann; bearbeitet von Karl-Günther Hartmann (Teil 1), Hans-Otto Korth (Teile 1–3) und Daniela Wissemann-Garbe (Teile 2–3). 1 vol. in 6 physical vols. Kassel: Bärenreiter, 1993–98.

Das deutsche Kirchenlied: Verzeichnis der Drucke von den Anfangen bis 1800. Edited by Konrad Ameln, Markus Jenny and Walther Lipphardt. 1 vol. in 2. Répertoire international des sources musicales, series B, part 8, vols. 1–2. Kassel: Bärenreiter, 1975–80.

Diehl, Wilhelm. *Zur Geschichte des Gottesdienstes und der gottesdienstlichen Handlungen in Hessen.* Giessen, 1899.

Dienst, Karl. "Das Frankfurter Gesangbüchlein von 1599." *Frankfurter kirchliches Jahrbuch* 1963: 35ff. Reprint: Christoph Führ and Jürgen Telschow, eds., *Die evangelische Kirche von Frankfurt am Main in Geschichte und Gegenwart,* 2d ed. (Frankfurt/Main: Evangelischer Regionalverband, 1980), pp. 145–56.

Dieterich, Cunrad. "Kirchweyh- oder Gesang-Predigt, darinn vom ersten Ursprung vnd Brauch des Gesangs in der Christlichen Kirchen, Summarischer weise discurriret vnd gehandelt wird." In . . . *Sonderbarer Predigten von vnterschiedenen Materien, hiebevor zu Vlm im Münster gehalten,* by Cunrad Dieterich, vol. 1, pp. 208–236. Leipzig, 1632. The sermon was probably originally published separately, but the date is unknown. The book's dedication is dated "den 1. Aprilis vorgehenden 1629. Jahrs."

———. "Kirchweyh- oder Orgel-Predigt, darinn von dem ersten Ursprung der Instrumental-Music ins gemein, sonderlich aber von dero Orgeln Erfindung vnd Gebrauch, in der Kirchen Gottes, von Anfang der Welt biß hieher, kürtzlich discurriret, zugleich auch die schöne herrliche Ulmer Orgel beschrieben wird." In . . . *Sonderbarer Predigten von vnterschiedenen Materien, hiebevor zu Vlm im Münster gehalten,* by Cunrad Dieterich, vol. 1, pp. 236–63. Leipzig, 1632. Lesure: 266. The sermon was originally published separately in 1624 (*see* "Lesure").

Dietrich, Veit. See also "Nuremberg (Dietrich)" in part 1 above.

———. *Summaria vber das alte Testament.* Wittenberg, 1541.

———. *Summaria vber das newe Testament.* Wittenberg, 1544.

[Dippel, Johann Conrad]. *Unpartheyische Gedancken, uber eines so genannten schwedischen Theologi kurtzen Bericht von Pietisten &c.* 1706. 185 pp. The author uses the pseudonym Christianus Democritus; his real name is from the Wolfenbüttel library catalog.

Dixon, C. Scott. *The Reformation and Rural Society: The Parishes of Brandenburg-Ansbach-Kulmbach, 1528–1603.* Cambridge University Press, 1996.

Döber, Andreas. See "Nuremberg" in part 1 above.

Drey Schrifften von der Anhaltischen Reformation, das ist, von der Frage: obs recht sey, dasz man die Götzen Bilder, vnd andere vom Papsthumb bißdaher in etlichen evangelischen Kirchen vberbliebenen Mißbräuche vollendts abschaffe. Jtem, daß man das Brotbrechen beym H. Nachtmal gebrauche: vnd das Volck Gottes anweise, daß sie die zehen Gebott Gottes gantz, vnd also wie sie in der Bibel stehen, lehrnen sollen. Neustadt, 1606. [40], 248 pp. Reprints *Anleytung,*

Antwort auff die Wittenbergische Abfertigung and *Augenscheinlicher Beweisz,* with a new preface dealing mostly with Communion.

Eberhardt, Cunrad. See "Goldlauter" in part 1 above.

Edler, Arnfried. *Der nordelbische Organist: Studien zu Sozialstatus, Funktion und kompositorischer Produktion eines Musikerberufes von der Reformation bis zum 20. Jahrhundert.* Kieler Schriften zur Musikwissenschaft, no. 23. Kassel: Bärenreiter, 1982.

Edler, Johann Andreas. *Dissertatio theologica de choris prophetarum symphonicis, in ecclesia Dei.* Rostock, 1720. 50 pp. Lesure: 289.

Eyn Enchiridion oder Handbüchlein. Eynem ytzlichen Christen fast nutzlich bey sich zuhaben, zur stetter vbung vnd trachtung geystlicher gesenge vnd Psalmen, Rechtschaffen vnd kunstlich verteutscht. Erfurt, 1524. Reprint: edited by Konrad Ameln, Documenta musicologica, 1st series, no. 36 (Kassel: Bärenreiter, 1983).

Enchiridion geistliker Leder vnde Psalmen, Magdeburg 1536. Introductory study and facsimile edition by Stephen A. Crist. Emory Texts and Studies in Ecclesial Life, no. 2. [Atlanta]: Scholars Press, 1994.

Endliche Ablehnung der Theologischen Facultet zu Witenberg Einrede, wider die Fürstliche Anhältische Christliche Kirchen Reformation. Zerbst, 1598. [4], 383 pp.

Endliche Antwort auff der Anhaltischen Prediger, anno 1598. publicierte endliche abfertigung, betreffend die im Fürstenthumb Anhalt angestelte Calvinische Reformation. Wittenberg, 1600. [8], 286, [1] pp.

Endriß, Julius. *Die Ulmer Synoden und Visitationen der Jahre 1531–47.* Ulm: Karl Höhn, 1935.

Engelhaubt, Caspar. See "Sulzfeld and Klein-Bardorf" in part 1 above.

Erbacher, Hermann. *Die Gesang- und Choralbücher der lutherischen Markgrafschaft Baden-Durlach 1556–1821.* Veröffentlichungen des Vereins für Kirchengeschichte in der evangelischen Landeskirche in Baden, vol. 35. Karlsruhe: Verlag Evangelischer Presseverband für Baden, 1984.

Erinnerungs Schrifft etlicher vom Adel vnd Stedten, an den Durchleuchtigen Hochgebornen Fürsten vnd Herrn, Herrn Johann Georgen. Zerbst, 1596. 152 pp.

Etwas von der Liturgie, besonders der Chursächsisch-Evangelischen. Halle, 1778. [4], 210 pp.

Evangelical Lutheran Hymnary. Prepared by the Worship Committee of the Evangelical Lutheran Synod, Mankato, Minnesota. St. Louis: MorningStar Music Publishers, 1996.

Evangelisch-Lutherisches Kirchengesangbuch. [Hannover]: Verlag der Selbständigen Evangelisch-Lutherischen Kirche, 1987.

Evangelisches Gesangbuch. Ausgabe für die Evangelisch-Lutherischen Kirchen in Niedersachsen und für die Bremische Evangelische Kirche. Hannover: Lutherisches Verlagshaus; Hannover: Schlütersche Verlagsanstalt und Druckerei; and Göttingen: Vandenhoeck & Ruprecht, 1994.

Fiedler, Samuel Christlieb. *Zufällige Gedanken über den wahren Werth und moralischen Nuzzen einer harmonischen und zweckmässigen Kirchenmusik.* Friedrichstadt, [1790]. 16 pp. Lesure: 316.

Finkel, Klaus. *Musikerziehung und Musikpflege an den gelehrten Schulen in Speyer vom Mittelalter bis zum Ende der freien Reichsstadt.* Mainzer Studien zur Musikwissenschaft, vol. 5. Tutzing: Hans Schneider, 1973.

Finscher, Ludwig. "Das Kantional des Georg Weber aus Weissenfels (Erfurt 1588)." *Jahrbuch für Liturgik und Hymnologie* 3 (1957): 62–78.

Fischer, Albert. *Das deutsche evangelische Kirchenlied des 17. Jahrhunderts.* Completed after the author's death by Wilhelm Tümpel. 6 vols. Gütersloh, 1904–16.

Fortgesetzte Sammlung von alten und neuen theologischen Sachen, Büchern, Uhrkunden, Controversien, Veränderungen, Anmerckungen, Vorschlägen, u.d.g. Leipzig, 1720–50. Continues: *Unschuldige Nachrichten von alten und neuen theologischen Sachen* (Leipzig, 1702–19). Continued by: *Neue Beyträge von alten und neuen theologischen Sachen* (Leipzig, 1751–61). With supplements *Theologische Annales* (1721/30–1731/40) and *Frühaufgelesene Früchte der theologischen Sammlung von Alten und Neuen* (1735–42).

Francke, August Hermann. . . . *Aufrichtige und gründliche Beantwortung eines an ihn abgelassenen und hiebey abgedruckten Send-Schreibens eines Christl. Theologi.* Halle, 1706. 96 pp.

Frandsen, Mary E. *The Sacred Concerto in Dresden, ca. 1660–1680.* Ph.D. thesis, University of Rochester, 1996.

Freylinghausen, Johann Anastasius, ed. *Geist-reiches Gesang-Buch.* Halle, 1704. [38], 1062, [74] pp. *RISM* 1704.[04]

Freytag, Werner. *Musikgeschichte der Stadt Stettin im 18. Jahrhundert.* Dissertation, Greifswald, 1936. Köslin (Pommern): C. G. Hendeß, 1936.

Frick, Christoph. *Music-Büchlein oder nützlicher Bericht von dem Uhrsprunge, Gebrauche vnd Erhaltung christlicher Music vnd also von dem Lobe Gottes, welches die Christe[n] theils in dem niedern Chor dieses elenden berrübten Jammer- vnd Thränen-thals verrichten sollen.* [1631]. [22], 347, [13] pp. Reprint: 2 vols. in 1 (Leipzig: Zentralantiquariat der Deutschen Demokratischen Republik, 1976). Lesure: 331.

Friderici, Daniel. *Musica figuralis, oder newe klärliche richtige, und vorstentliche Unterweisung der Singe Kunst.* Rostock, 1619. 44 f. Lesure: 332. Originally published in 1618 (*see* "Lesure").

Fritsch, Ahasver. . . . *Der sündliche Kirchen-Schläffer.* Jena, 1675. 45 pp.

[Fuhrmann, Martin Heinrich]. *Gerechte Wag-Schal, darin Tit. Herrn Joachim Meyers, J. U. Doctoris &c. so genannter Anmaßlich Hamburgischer criticus sine crisi, und dessen Suffragatoris, Tit. Herrn Heinr. Philipp. Guden, S. Theol. Doctoris &c. superlativ suffragium, und Tit. Herrn Joh. Matthesons, &c. Hoch-Fürstl. Schleswig-Hollstein. Capellmeisters Göttingischer Ephorus, richtig aufgezogen, genau abgewogen, und darauf der Calculus gezogen: daß der Capell-Meister die 2. Doctores überwogen, und diese beyde in die Lufft geflogen, und weniger denn nichts gewogen. Und daß dis nicht erlogen, haben erwiesen in diesen 3. Bogen die 2. Colloquenten Laurentius und Innocentius.* Altona, [1728?]. 48 pp. Lesure: 338. The preface is signed "Innocentius Franckenberg, Cantor an der St. Jacobs-Kirche. (Gen. 30, 32)" and dated "Brandenburg, Auf Laurentii Tag, 1728." The author is identified in Voigt (1742).

———. *Musicalischer-Trichter, dadurch ein geschickter Informator seinen Informandis die edle Singe-Kunst nach heutiger Manier bald und leicht einbringen kan.* Frankfurt/Spree, 1706. 96 pp. Lesure: 338. The preface is signed "Meines Hertzens Freude"; i.e., Martin Heinrich Fuhrmann, as he is so identified in his *Musica vocalis in nuce* (1715).

Gallus, Nicolaus. See "Regensburg (Neue Kirche)" in part 1 above.

Garbe, Daniela. "Gemeindegesang. B. Der deutsche evangelische Gemeindegesang. III. Die Entwicklung in den lutherischen Gebieten etwa von 1550 bis 1750." In *Die Musik in Geschichte und Gegenwart,* 2d ed., Sachteil, vol. 3 (1995), cols. 1174–81. Kassel: Bärenreiter and Stuttgart: Metzler, 1994–. See also *Das deutsche Kirchenlied* and "Wissemann-Garbe, Daniela."

Garside, Charles. *The Origins of Calvin's Theology of Music: 1536–1543.* Transactions of the American Philosophical Society, no. 69, part 4. Philadelphia: American Philosophical Society, 1979. 36 pp.

Garside, Charles Jr. *Zwingli and the Arts.* New Haven: Yale University Press, 1966.

Gerber, Christian. *Historie der Kirchen-Ceremonien in Sachsen.* Dresden and Leipzig, 1732. [20], 779, [23] pp. The preface by the author's son Christian Gottlob Gerber, dated "20. Augusti, 1731," indicates that Gerber had died on May 25, 1731. The work was unfinished at the time of his death.

———. *Die unerkannten Sünden der Welt, aus Gottes Wort, zu Beförderung des wahren Christenthums, der Welt vor Augen gestellt, und in achtzehen Capitel deutlich abgefasset.* Dresden, 1690. [24], 200, [1] pp.

———. *M. Christian Gerbers, Pastoris in Lockwitz bey Dreßden Unerkante Sünden der Welt, samt einem Bericht, von dem Sünden der Menschen nach ihrem Tode*. Dresden and Leipzig, 1719. [44], 1456, [62] pp. The preface is dated "25. April. 1699." The copy used is the eighth printing. The first eighteen chapters appeared as Gerber 1690.

―――. *Fortsetzung der unerkannten Sünden der Welt*. Frankfurt, 1725. [42], 856, 552, [44] pp. The preface is dated "1 April 1703."

―――. *M. Christiani Gerbers, der unerkannten Sünden der Welt dritter Theil*. Dresden, 1725. [46], 1546, [21] pp. The preface is dated "2. Mart. 1706."

―――. *Die unerkannten Wolthaten Gottes*. Dresden, 1709. [22], 760, [16] pp. Originally published in 1704; the date is given in section 11 of the preface to volume 2 of Gerber 1711.

―――. *Der unerkannten Wolthaten Gottes anderer Theil*. Dresden, 1711.

Gesangbuch darinn begriffen sind, die aller fürnemisten vnd besten Psalmen, geistliche Lieder, vnd Chorgesang, aus dem Wittembergischen, Strasburgischen, vnd anderer Kirchen Gesangbüchlin zusamen bracht, vnd mit besonderem fleis corrigiert vnd gedrucket. Straßburg, 1541. [36], 158 pp. Reprint: Stuttgart: Evangelisches Verlagswerk, 1953. *RISM* 1541[06].

Gesius, Bartholomaeus. *Geistliche Deutsche Lieder D. Mart. Lutheri: und anderer from[m]en Christen, welche durchs gantze Jar in der christlichen Kirchen zu singen gebräuchlich*. Frankfurt/Oder, 1607. *RISM* 1607[03].

Geystliche Gsangbüchlin [tenor partbook]. [Worms], 1525. *RISM* 1525[22].

Geystliche Lieder. Leipzig: Valentin Babst, 1545. Reprinted as *Das Babstsche Gesangbuch von 1545*, ed. Konrad Ameln. Documenta musicologica, series 1, no. 38. Kassel: Bärenreiter, 1988.

Glahn, Henrik. "J. H. Scheins Kantional 'in die Tabulatur transponiert von J. Vockerodt, Mühlhausen 1649.'" In *Festskrift Jens Peter Larsen*. Copenhagen: Wilhelm Hansen, 1972.

Goltz, Joachim. See "Brandenburg (Goltz)" in part 1 above.

Graduale triplex seu Graduale Romanum. Solesmes: Abbaye Saint-Pierre, 1979.

Graff, Paul. *Geschichte der Auflösung der alten gottesdienstlichen Formen in der evangelischen Kirche Deutschlands*. 2d ed., 2 vols. Göttingen: Vandenhoeck & Ruprecht, 1937–39.

Greve, Werner. *'Musicam habe ich allezeit lieb gehabt . . .': Leben und Wirken Braunschweiger Organisten, Spielleute und Kantoren an der Altstadt-Kirche St. Martini in Braunschweig 1500–1800*. Braunschweig: Gesellschaft zur Förderung der Musik an St. Martini, 1985.

Greyser, Daniel. See "Dresden (Kreuzkirche)" in part 1 above.

Grimm, Jacob and Wilhelm Grimm. *Deutsches Wörterbuch*. 16 vols. in 32 physical vols. Leipzig: S. Hirzel, 1854–1954.

―――. *Deutsches Wörterbuch*. New edition, 8 vols. to date. Leipzig: S. Hirzel, 1965–.

[Groschuff, Friedrich]. *Leipziger Kirchen-Staat, das ist deutlicher Unterricht vom Gottes-Dienst in Leipzig, wie es bey solchem so wohl an hohen und andern Festen, als auch an denen Sonntagen ingleichen die gantze Woche über gehalten wird*. Leipzig, 1710. [13], 288, [4] pp. According to Beck (1952), citing Schering, *Musikgeschichte Leipzigs*, vol. 2, the author's name in the book (at the end of the dedication "An eine GOtt- und Tugend-liebende Dame Hohes Standes in Leipzig") is given as "F.G.A.M." and means "Friedr. Groschuff Artium Magister."

Großgebauer, Theophilus. *Wächterstimme auß dem verwüsteten Zion. Das ist, treühertzige und nothwendige Entdeckung. Auß waß evangelischen Gemeinen wenig zur Bekehrung und Gottseligkeit fruchte, und warumb evangelische Gemeinen bey den häutigen Predigten des H. Worts Gottes ungeistlicher und ungöttlicher werden*. Frankfurt/Main, 1661. [24], 444, 210 [i.e., 108] pp.

Gülden, Josef. *Johann Leisentrits Bautzener Meßritus und Meßgesänge*. Katholisches Leben und Kämpfen im Zeitalter der Glaubensspaltung, no. 22. Münster: Aschendorff, 1964. 68 pp.

Hamacher, Theo. *Beiträge zur Geschichte des katholischen deutschen Kirchenliedes*. Paderborn: the author, 1985.

Han, Philip. See "Magdeburg (Han)" in part 1 above.

Harnoncourt, Philipp. *Gesamtkirchliche und teilkirchliche Liturgie: Studien zum liturgischen Heiligenkalender und zum Gesang im Gottesdienst unter besonderer Berücksichtigung des deutschen Sprachgebiets.* Untersuchungen zur praktischen Theologie, vol. 3. Freiburg i.B.: Herder, 1974.

Harper, John. *The Forms and Orders of Western Liturgy from the Tenth to the Eighteenth Century.* Oxford: Clarendon Press, 1991.

Hartknoch, Christoph. *Preussische Kirchen-Historia.* Frankfurt am Main and Leipzig, 1686. [1], [28], 1098, 12, [149] pp.

Haupt, Rudolf. *Die Orgel im evangelischen Kultraum in Geschichte und Gegenwart.* Rundbrief der Orgelwissenschaftlichen Arbeits- und Musikgemeinschaft, no. 2. [N.p., 1954].

Häuser, Johann Ernst. *Geschichte des christlichen, insbesondere des evangelischen Kirchengesanges und der Kirchenmusik.* Quedlinburg and Leipzig, 1834.

Hausmann, Nicolaus. See "Dessau" in part 1 above.

Heidrich, Jürgen. "'deütsch oder lateinisch nach bequemigkeit'? Zur Bedeutung der Volkssprache für die protestantische Vesperpraxis im 16. Jahrhundert." *Kirchenmusikalisches Jahrbuch* 82 (1998): 7–20.

———. *Protestantische Kirchenmusikanschauung in der zweiten Hälfte des 18. Jahrhunderts: Studien zur Ideengeschichte "wahrer" Kirchenmusik.* Abhandlungen zur Musikgeschichte, vol. 7. Göttingen: Vandenhoeck & Ruprecht, 2001.

Held, Karl. *Das Kreuzkantorat zu Dresden nach archivalischen Quellen.* Leipzig: Breitkopf & Härtel, 1894. Reprint: Wiesbaden: Dr. Martin Sändig oHG, 1972.

Herbst, Wolfgang, ed. *Quellen zur Geschichte des evangelischen Gottesdienstes von der Reformation bis zur Gegenwart.* Göttingen: Vandenhoeck & Ruprecht, 1968.

Herl, Joseph. "Luther's German Mass: A Congregational Hymn Sing?" *Doctrine and Practice* 4/1 (February 1997): 13–31.

———. *Congregational Singing in the German Lutheran Church 1523–1780.* Ph.D. thesis, University of Illinois at Urbana-Champaign, 2000.

Hermes, Fischer and Salzmann. *Beytraege zur Verbesserung des oeffentlichen Gottesdienstes der Christen.* Leipzig, 1785–88. [14], 244, [6], 248, [6], 264, [4], 252 pp. Four volumes appeared (one per year); they are bound in two physical volumes.

Herold, Max. *Alt-Nürnberg in seinen Gottesdiensten: Ein Beitrag zur Geschichte der Sitte und des Kultus.* Gütersloh, 1890.

Herrliberger, David. *Gottesdienstliche Ceremonien, oder H. Kirchen-Gebräuche und Religions-Pflichten der Christen.* Basel, 1746.

Heyden, Hellmuth. *Protokolle der Pommerschen Kirchenvisitationen.* 3 vols. Cologne: Bohlau, 1961–64.

Heyden, Nikolaus. See "Obermassfeld" in part 1 above.

Hiller, Johann Adam. *Wöchentliche Nachrichten und Anmerkungen die Musik betreffend.* Leipzig, 1766–70. Lesure: 415. From 1770 entitled *Musikalische Nachrichtungen und Anmerkungen.*

[Hingelberg, Johann Gottfried?]. *Über Danziger Musik und Musiker.* Elbing, 1785. 92 pp. Lesure: 415. The author's name is from the Leipzig library catalog and from Lesure.

Hirschmann, Gerhard. *Die Kirchenvisitation im Landgebiet der Reichsstadt Nürnberg 1560 und 1561.* Einzelarbeiten aus der Kirchengeschichte Bayerns, vol. 68. Neustadt a. d. Aisch: Degener, 1994.

Hoelling, Johann Conrad Stephan. *Oratio de musica ecclesiastica, qvvm novvs templi et scholae Alfeldensis cantor constitveretvr.* Hildesheim, 1732. 20 pp. Lesure: 417.

Honemeyer, Karl. *Thomas Müntzer und Martin Luther: ihr Ringen um die Musik des Gottesdienstes. Untersuchungen zum 'Deutzsch Kirchenampt' 1523.* Berlin: Merseburger, 1974. 119 pp.

Honterus, Johannes. See "Transylvania" in part 1 above.

Hubatsch, Walther. *Geschichte der evangelischen Kirche Ostpreussens.* 3 vols. Göttingen: Vandenhoeck & Ruprecht, 1968.

Hubert, Friedrich, ed. *Die Strassburger liturgischen Ordnungen im Zeitalter der Reformation nebst eine Bibliographie der Strassburger Gesangbücher.* Göttingen, 1900.

Irwin, Joyce L. *Neither Voice nor Heart Alone: German Lutheran Theology of Music in the Age of the Baroque.* American University Studies, series VII (theology and religion), vol. 132. New York: Peter Lang, 1993.

Janota, Johannes. *Studien zu Funktion und Typus des deutschen geistlichen Liedes im Mittelalter.* Münchener Texte und Untersuchungen zur deutschen Literatur des Mittelalters, vol. 23. Munich: C. H. Beck, 1968.

Jenny, Markus. "Ein Brief von Sixt Dietrich über Luther und die Kirchengemeinde in Wittenberg." *Jahrbuch für Liturgik und Hymnologie* 5 (1960): 134–35.

———. *Luthers geistliche Lieder und Kirchengesänge.* Archiv zur Weimarer Ausgabe der Werke Martin Luthers, vol. 4. Cologne: Böhlau, 1985.

Johnson, Cleveland. *Vocal Compositions in German Organ Tablatures 1550–1650.* New York: Garland, 1989.

Jonas, Justus. See "Regensburg" and "Wittenberg" in part 1 above.

Kalb, Friedrich. *Theology of worship in 17th-Century Lutheranism.* Translated by Henry P. A. Hamann. St. Louis: Concordia, 1965. A translation of *Die Lehre vom Kultus der lutherischen Kirche zur Zeit der Orthodoxie* (Berlin: Lutherisches Verlagshaus, 1959).

Kantz, Caspar. See "Nördlingen" in part 1 above.

Karant-Nunn, Susan C. *Luther's Pastors: The Reformation in the Ernestine Countryside.* Transactions of the American Philosophical Society, vol. 69, part 8 (1979). Philadelphia: American Philosophical Society, 1979.

———. *The Reformation of Ritual: An Interpretation of Early Modern Germany.* London and New York: Routledge, 1997.

Karlstadt, Andreas Bodenstein von. See "Wittenberg" in part 1 above.

Kästner, Abraham. *De icto mvsico.* Leipzig, 1740. 4 f. Lesure: 440.

Kätzel, Heinrich. *Musikpflege und Musikerziehung in Reformationsjahrhundert dargestellt am Beispiel der Stadt Hof.* Berlin: Evangelische Verlagsanstalt, 1957.

Kauffmann, Georg Friedrich. *Harmonische Seelenlust: Präludien über die bekanntesten Chorallieder für Orgel.* Edited by Pierre Pidoux. Kassel: Bärenreiter, 1980.

———. *Harmonische Seelenlust musicalischer Gönner und Freunde das ist: Kurtze, jedoch nach besondern Genie und guter Grace elaborirte Praeludia von 2. 3. und 4. Stimmen, über die bekanntesten Choral-Lieder.* Leipzig: J. Th. Boethius, 1733–36. Reprint: edited by Pierre Pidoux, Kassel, 1957. Appeared in fascicles.

———. *62 Choräle mit beziffertem Bass für Orgel.* Edited by Pierre Pidoux. Kassel: Bärenreiter, 1951.

Kayser, Karl, ed. *Die reformatorischen Kirchenvisitationen in den welfischen Landen 1542–1544: Instruktionen, Protokolle, Abschiede und Berichte der Reformatoren.* Göttingen: Vandenhoeck & Ruprecht, 1896. xii, 657 pp.

Keiser, Martin. See "Wasungen" in part 1 above.

Keuchenthal, Johannes. *KirchenGesenge Latinisch vnd Deudsch.* Wittenberg, 1573. [4], 590, [14] f. *RISM* 1573[11].

Kevorkian, Tanya. "The Reception of the Cantata during Leipzig Church Services 1700–1750." *Early Music* 30 (February 2002): 27–38.

Kirwan-Mott, Anne. *The Small-Scale Sacred Concerto in the Early Seventeenth Century.* Studies in British Musicology, no. 3. Ann Arbor: UMI, 1981. 688 pp.

Kittelson, James M. "Successes and Failures in the German Reformation: the Report from Strasbourg." *Archiv für Reformationsgeschichte* 73 (1982): 153–75.

————. "Visitations and Popular Religious Culture: Further Reports from Strasbourg." In *Pietas et Societas: New Trends in Reformation Social History: Essays in Memory of Harold J. Grimm,* edited by Kyle C. Sessions and Phillip N. Bebb, 89–101. Kirksville, Mo.: Sixteenth Century Journal Publishers, 1985.

Koch, Eduard Emil. *Geschichte des Kirchenlieds und Kirchengesangs mit besonderer Rücksicht auf Würtemberg.* 2 vols. Stuttgart, 1847.

Kolb, Christian. *Die Geschichte des Gottesdienstes in der evangelischen Kirche Württembergs.* Stuttgart, 1913.

Köpfel, Wolf. See "Strassburg" in part 1 above.

Korth, Hans-Otto. "Gemeindegesang. B. Der deutsche evangelische Gemeindegesang. I. Gemeindegesang und Kirchenlied in der Reformationszeit" and "II. Der evangelische Gemeindegesang in Straßburg." In *Die Musik in Geschichte und Gegenwart,* 2d ed., Sachteil, vol. 3 (1995), cols. 1162–1174. Kassel: Bärenreiter and Stuttgart: Metzler, 1994–.

Köster, Dr. "Die Naumburger Kirchen- und Schulordnung von D. Nicolaus Medler aus dem Jahre 1537." *Neue Mitteilungen aus dem Gebiet historisch-antiquarischer Forschungen* 19 (1898): 497–569; also appendix pp. 1–32.

Kremer, Joachim. *Das norddeutsche Kantorat im 18. Jahrhundert.* Kieler Schriften zur Musikwissenschaft, vol. 43. Kassel: Bärenreiter, 1995.

Krickeberg, Dieter. *Das protestantische Kantorat im 17. Jahrhundert: Studien zum Amt des deutschen Kantors.* Berliner Studien zur Musikwissenschaft, vol. 6. Berlin: Merseburger, 1965.

Lauterbach, Anton. See "Pirna" in part 1 above.

Lauterbach, Christoph. *M. Christian Gerbers Pfarrers zu Lockwitz bey Dresden Unerkante Sünden, aus seinen von dieser Materie bißher unterschiedlich geschriebenen Büchern in einer vornehmen . . . Zusammenkunft discurs-weise erwogen und gehandelt.* Leipzig, 1703. According to the preface to Gerber (1711), "Lauterbach" is not the author's real name. No copy has been located.

Leaver, Robin A. *'Goostly Psalmes and Spirituall Songes': English and Dutch Metrical Psalms from Coverdale to Utenhove 1535–1566.* Oxford: Clarendon Press, 1991.

————. ed. *J. S. Bach and Scripture: Glosses from the Calov Bible Commentary.* St. Louis: Concordia, 1985.

————. "Lutheran Vespers as a Context for Music." In *Church, Stage, and Studio: Music and Its Contexts in Seventeenth-Century Germany,* ed. Paul Walker, 143–61. Studies in Music, no. 107. Ann Arbor: UMI Research Press, 1990.

[Leibniz, Johann Friedrich]. *Leipziger Kirchen-Andachten, darinnen der erste Theil das Gebetbuch, oder die Ordnung des gantzen öffentlichen Gottes-Dienstes durchs gantze Jahr.* Leipzig, 1694. [24], 288, [4], 310, [10] pp. The preface is signed by "J. F. L."

Leichsenring, Hugo. *Hamburgische Kirchenmusik im Reformationszeitalter.* Dissertation, Berlin, 1922. [8], 175, xxi pp. Reprint: Hamburger Beiträge zur Musikwissenschaft, vol. 20, edited by Jeffery T. Kite-Powell (Hamburg: Karl Dieter Wagner, 1982).

Lesure, François, ed. *Écrits imprimés concernant la musique.* 2 vols. Répertoire international des sources musicales, series B, part 6, vols. 1–2. Munich: G. Henle, 1971.

The Liber usualis with Introduction and Rubrics in English. Tournai: Desclée, 1953.

Ligarius, Johannes. See "East Frisia" in part 1 above.

Liliencron, Rochus von. *Liturgisch-musikalische Geschichte der evangelischen Gottesdienste von 1523 bis 1700.* Schleswig: Julius Bergas, 1893. Reprint: Hildesheim: Olms, 1970.

Lindberg, Carter. *The European reformations.* Cambridge, Mass.: Blackwell, 1996.

Lindenberg, Horst. *Die liturgisch-musikalische Entwicklung der evangelisch-lutherischen Hauptgottesdienste in den deutschen Städten von 1700–1750.* Dissertation, Berlin, 1925.

Linke, Georg. See "Ritschenhausen" in part 1 above.

Lippert. "Kirchenvisitation anno 1586 im Fürstentum Vohenstrauss." *Beiträge zur bayerischen*

Kirchengeschichte 4 (1898): 164–85. The author's first name is unknown; the attribution in the source reads "Von Pfarrer Lippert in Amberg."

Lipphardt, Walther. "Die Anfänge des deutschen Kirchenliedes in althochdeutscher Zeit." *Musik und Altar* 13 (1961): 73–77.

———. "Die liturgische Function deutscher Kirchenlieder in den Klöstern Niedersächsischer Zisterzienserinnen des Mittelalters." *Zeitschrift für katholische Theologie* 94 (1972): 158–98.

Löner, Caspar. See "Nördlingen" in part 1 above.

Lossius, Lucas. *Psalmodia, hoc est, Cantica sacra veteris ecclesi\|ae selecta.* Wittenberg, 1561. [8], 360, [4] f. Reprint: Stuttgart: Cornetto, 1996. *RISM* 1561[20].

Luther, Martin. See also "Saxony, Albertine"; "Saxony, Ernestine"; and "Wittenberg (Luther)" in part 1 above.

———. *D. Martin Luthers Werke: kritische Gesamtausgabe.* 4 series. Weimar: Böhlau, 1883–.

———. *Luther's Works.* Edited by Jaroslav Pelikan and Helmut T. Lehmann. 55 vols. St. Louis: Concordia and Philadelphia: Fortress, 1958–86.

Lutheran Book of Worship. Prepared by the churches participating in the Inter-Lutheran Commission on Worship. Minneapolis: Augsburg and Philadelphia: Board of Publication, Lutheran Church in America, 1978.

The Lutheran Hymnal. Authorized by the synods constituting the Evangelical Lutheran Synodical Conference of North America. St. Louis: Concordia, 1941.

Lutheran Worship. Prepared by the Commission on Worship of the Lutheran Church—Missouri Synod. St. Louis: Concordia, 1982.

Lütkens, Nicolaus. *Hymnosophia sacra wie gottselige Christen dem Herrn klüglich singen und spielen müssen, bey Einweihung einer neuen Orgel, Anno 1726. am Tage S. Michaëlis, aus dem Fest-Evangelio Matth. XIIX.I.f. seiner in Christo geliebten Gemeine fürgetragen.* [Hamburg?], 1728. 47, [5] pp. Lesure: 520.

Mager, Inge. "Lied und Reformation: Beobachtungen zur reformatorischen Singbewegung in norddeutschen Städten." In *Das protestantische Kirchenlied im 16. und 17. Jahrhundert: Text-, musik- und theologiegeschichtliche Probleme,* ed. Alfred Dürr and Walther Killy, 25–38. Wiesbaden: Otto Harrassowitz, 1986.

———. "Zur vergessen Problematik des Psalmliedes im 16. und 17. Jahrhundert." *Jahrbuch für Liturgik und Hymnologie* 37 (1998):139–49.

Mahrenholz, Christhard. *Musicologica et liturgica: Gesammelte Aufsätze von Christhard Mahrenholz als Festgabe zu seinem 60. Geburtstag am 11. August 1960.* Kassel: Bärenreiter, 1960.

Marbach, Christian. *Evangelische Singe-Schule, darinnen diejenigen Dinge deutlich gelehret und wiederholet werden.* Breslau and Leipzig, 1726. [18], 216 pp. Reprint: Hildesheim: Olms, 1991. Lesure: 534.

Marcus, Kenneth H. "Hymnody and hymnals in Basel, 1526–1606." *Sixteenth Century Journal* 32/3 (Fall 2001): 723–41.

[Marpurg, Friedrich Wilhelm]. *Des critischen Musicus an der Spree erster Band.* Berlin, 1750. [8], 406 pp., 5 folded leaves. Lesure: 542. This is a 1750 reprint of issues of this weekly periodical from 1749–50. The author's name is from Adlung 1758:22, who cites Marpurg's *Abhandlung von der Fuge* (Berlin, 1753).

———. *Historisch-kritische Beyträge zur Aufnahme der Musik.* 5 vols. Berlin, 1754–78. 562, 576, 560, 564, 534 pp. Lesure: 543.

Martius, Christian Ernst. *Daß eine wohleingerichtete Kirchenmusik Gott wohlgefällig, angenehm und nützlich sey, und was zu einer guten Ausführung derselben erforderlich.* Plauen, 1762. 14 f. Lesure: 553.

Mattheson, Johann. *Der musicalische Patriot.* Hamburg, 1728. 376 pp. Reprint: Kassel: Bärenreiter, 1975. Lesure: 562.

———. *Der neue Göttingische aber viel schlechter, als die alten Lacedämonischen, urtheilende Ephorus, wegen der Kirchen-Music eines andern belehret.* Hamburg, 1727. 124 pp. Lesure: 562.

———. *Der vollkommene Capellmeister, das ist gründliche Anzeige aller derjenigen Sachen, die einer wissen, können, und vollkommen inne haben muß, der einer Capelle mit Ehren und Nutzen vorstehen will.* Hamburg, 1739. 484, [20] pp. Lesure: 564. There is an English translation by Ernest C. Harriss (Ann Arbor: UMI Research Press, 1981).

[Mayer, Johann Friedrich]. . . . *Kurtzer Bericht von Pietisten. Samt denen königlichen schwedischen Edicten wider dieselben.* Leipzig, 1706. 84 pp. The essay is dated "Stockholm, den 6. Octobr. 1694." The author is not named in the source, but is identified in the title and/or preface to Stryk (1707), Francke (1706) and Breithaupt (1707), all of which are a response to this work. Dippel (1706) is also a response.

McMullen, Dianne Marie. *The Geistreiches Gesangbuch of Johann Anastasius Freylinghausen (1670–1739): A German Pietist Hymnal.* 2 vols. in 1. Ph.D. thesis, University of Michigan, 1987.

Medler, Nicolaus. See "Naumburg (Wenzelkirche)" in part 1 above.

Melanchthon, Philipp. See "Cologne"; "Saxony, Albertine"; and "Saxony, Ernestine" in part 1 above.

Melodeyen Gesangbuch darinn D. Luthers vnd ander Christen gebreuchlichsten Gesenge, jhren gewöhnlichen Melodeyen nach . . . begriffen sindt. Hamburg, 1604. 411, [4] pp. *RISM* 1604[05].

Mertz, Georg. *Das Schulwesen der deutschen Reformation im 16. Jahrhundert.* Heidelberg, 1902.

Meyer, Hans Bernhard. *Luther und die Messe: eine liturgiewissenschaftliche Untersuchung über das Verhältnis Luthers zum Meßwesen des späten Mittelalters.* Konfessionskundliche und kontroverstheologische Studien, vol. 11. Paderborn: Bonifatius, 1965.

[Meyer, Joachim?]. *Der abgewürdigte Wagemeister, oder der fälschlich genandten gerechten Wagschale eines verkapten, aber wohlbekannten Innocentii Franckenbergs auf dem Parnaß erkandte Ungerechtigkeit und Betrug.* [N.p.], 1729. 61 pp. Lesure: 910. Lesure considers this book anonymous, possibly by Johann Mattheson; but Voigt 1742, p. 117, gives the author as Joachim Meyer. Also, according to Becker 1836, p. 132: "Gerber in seinem neuen Tonkünstler-Lexikon (B.3, Seite 414) schreibt diese Schrift dem Doktor Meyer selbst zu, was sich wohl nicht bestätigen dürfte."

Meyer, Joachim. *Der anmaßliche Hamburgische Criticus sine Crisi entgegen gesetzet dem so genannten Göttingischen Ephoro Joh. Matthesons, und dessen vermeyntlicher Belehrungs Ungrund in Verthädigung der theatralischen Kirchen-Music gewiesen.* Lemgo, 1728. [10], 180, [1] pp. Lesure: 579.

———. *Unvorgreiffliche Gedancken über die neulich eingerissene theatralische Kirchen-Music und denen darinnen bishero üblich gewordenen Cantaten mit Vergleichung der Music voriger Zeiten zur Verbesserung der Unsrigen.* [N.p.], 1726. 70 pp. Lesure: 579. Lesure gives the place of publication as [Göttingen?], where Meyer was professor.

Mithobius, Hector. *Psalmodia Christiana . . . Das ist Gründliche Gewissens-Belehrung, was von der Christen Musica, so wol Vocali als Instrumentali zu halten?* Jena, 1665. 425, [13] pp. Lesure: 588.

Mizler, Lorenz Christoph. *Musicalischer Staarstecher in welchem rechtschaffener Musikverständigen Fehler bescheiden angemerket, eingebildeter und selbst gewachsener so genannten Componisten Thorheiten aber lächerlich gemachet werden.* Leipzig, [1740]. Lesure: 589. The issues in this serial are individually dated, and the preface is dated 1740.

Monson, Craig A. "The Council of Trent Revisited." *Journal of the American Musicological Society.* 55 (Spring 2002): 1–37.

Moser, Dietz-Rüdiger. *Musikgeschichte der Stadt Quedlinburg von der Reformation bis zur Auflösung des Stiftes (1539–1802): Beiträge zu einer Musikgeschichte des Harzraumes.* Disserta Georg-August-Universität zu Göttingen, 1967. 631 pp.

Moser, Johann Jacob. *Corpus juris evangelicorum ecclesiastici, oder Sammlung evangelisch-lutherisch und reformirter Kirchen-Ordnungen.* 2 vols. Züllichau, 1737–38. [72], 1467, [11]; [8], 1364, [8] pp.

Motz, Georg. *Abgenöthigte Fortsetzung der Vertheidigten Kirchen-Music.* [N.p.], 1708. 208 pp. Lesure: 599. The preface is dated "den letzen Decembris Anno 1705."

———. *Die vertheidigte Kirchen-Music, oder klar und deutlicher Beweis, welcher gestalten Hr. M. Christian Gerber, Pastor in Lockwitz bey Dreßden, in seinem Buch, welches er Unerkandte Sünden der Welt nennet, in dem LXXXI. Cap. da er von dem Mißbrauch der Kirchen-Music geschrieben, zu Verwersung der musicalischen Harmonie und Bestraffung der Kirchen-Music zu weit gegangen.* [N.p.], 1703. 264 pp. Lesure: 599. The preface is dated "1. Mai 1702."

Müller, Heinrich. *Geistliche Seelen Musik.* Rostock, 1659. [24], 287, [1], 931, [28] pp. RISM 1659[15].

Müller, Karl Ferdinand and Walter Blankenburg, eds. *Leiturgia: Handbuch des evangelischen Gottesdienstes.* 5 vols. Kassel: Johannes Stauda-Verlag, 1954–70.

Müntzer, Thomas. See "Allstedt" in part 1 above.

Muscovius, Johannes. . . . *Gebrauch, und Mißbrauch, des lateinischen Singens, und Betens, beym öffentlichen Gottes-Dienst.* Wittenberg, [1687]. [16], 214, [8] pp. Lesure: 606. The date is from the preface to *Gründlicher Beweiß.* Lesure's date of [ca. 1695] is too late.

———. *Gestraffter Mißbrauch der Kirchen-Music, und Kirchhöfe.* [Lauben], 1694. 111, [1] pp. Lesure: 606; Lesure misspells the first word of the title as "Bestraffter."

Musculus, Wolfgang. "Itinerarium conventus Isnachii." 1536. Manuscript in the Bern Stadtbibliothek. Reprint: Theodor Kolde, ed., *Analecta Lutherana: Briefe und Actenstücke zur Geschichte Luthers* (Gotha, 1883), pp. 216ff.; Wolfgang Herbst, *Quellen zur Geschichte des evangelischen Gottesdienstes* (Göttingen: Vandenhoeck & Ruprecht, 1968), pp. 71–73 (Latin) and 74–77 (German translation).

[Neumeister, Erdmann]. *Die allerneueste Art, zur reinen und galanten Poesie zu gelangen.* Hamburg, 1722. 602 pp. Lesure: 613. The book was written under the pseudonym "Menantes." Beck (1952), p. 9 of the bibliography, attributes the work to Christian Hunold.

Niedt, Friedrich Erhardt. . . . *Handleitung, zur Variation, wie man den General-Bass, und darüber gesetzte Zahlen variiren . . . könne.* Hamburg, 1706. 83 f. Lesure: 616.

———. . . . *Musicalische Handleitung, oder Gründlicher Unterricht.* Hamburg, 1710. 32 f. Lesure: 616. Originally published in 1700.

———. . . . *Musicalische Handleitung, zur Variation des General-Basses.* Hamburg, 1721. [12], 204 pp. This volume constitutes the second part of the *Musicalische Handleitung.* The title given in Lesure, 617, actually contains the words "anderer Theil" after "Handleitung," but the copy consulted does not.

———. . . . *Musicalischer Handleitung dritter und letzter Theil, handlend vom Contra-Punct, Canon, Motteten, Choral, Recitativ-Stylo und Cavaten.* Hamburg, 1717. [4], 68, [24], 56 pp. Lesure: 617.

Niemöller, Klaus Wolfgang. *Untersuchungen zu Musikpflege und Musikunterricht an den deutschen Lateinschulen vom ausgehenden Mittelalter bis um 1600.* Kölner Beiträge zur Musikforschung, no. 54. Regensburg: Gustav Bosse, 1969.

Nischan, Bodo. "The exorcism Controversy and Baptism in the late Reformation." *Sixteenth Century Journal* 18 (1987): 31–51.

———. *Prince, People and Confession: The Second Reformation in Brandenburg.* Philadelphia: University of Pennsylvania Press, 1994.

———. *Lutherans and Calvinists in the Age of Confessionalism.* Aldershot, Hampshire: Ashgate, 1999.

Nopp, Hieronymous. See "Regensburg" in part 1 above.

Notwendige Antwort, auff die im Fürstenthumb Anhalt ohn langsten ausgesprengte hefftige Schrifft. [Wittenberg], 1597. [1], 159 f.

Oettinger, Rebecca Wagner. *Music as Propaganda in the German Reformation*. Aldershot (Hampshire): Ashgate, 2001.

Der ohnmächtige Fündling . . . das ist: eine kurtze treuhertzige und beständige Widerlegung einer zu Elbing ohne Namen ausgestreueten Schrifft, genannt, Project etlicher wolgegründeten motiven gegen die Einführung der Lobwassers Lieder in eine ungeänderter Augspurg. Confession zugethanene Gemeine Christi. [N.p.], 1655. 148 pp. The Göttingen copy ascribes this source to Reinhold Curike in manuscript, but there is no other evidence for this. His name is written at the top right corner of the title page, and the manuscript table of contents on the flyleaf of the bound volume gives his name following the title. The name is then scratched out but is reinstated with dots under the name. *Ein Reys-Gespräch* (1655) is also attributed to Curike in the Göttingen copy, and that attribution seems unlikely for reasons given under that title, so no conclusion is drawn here concerning the author of this book.

Otto, Irmgard. *Deutsche Musikanschauung im 17. Jahrhundert.* Dissertation, Berlin, 1937. Berlin, [1937?].

Ozment, Stephen. *Protestants: The Birth of a Revolution*. New York: Doubleday, 1992.

Pacik, Rudolf. "Zur Stellung der Orgel in der katholischen Liturgie des 16. Jahrhunderts." In *Orgel und Orgelspiel im 16. Jahrhundert*, 2. Aufl., edited by Walter Salmen, 120–43. Innsbrucker Beiträge zur Musikwissenschaft, vol. 2. Innsbruck: Edition Helbling, 1978.

Pallas, Karl, ed. *Die Registraturen der Kirchenvisitationen im ehemals sächsischen Kurkreise.* 2 parts in 7 vols. Halle: Otto Hendel, 1906–18. 240, 589, 368, 676, 575, 596, 268 pp.

Parrott, Andrew. *The Essential Bach Choir*. Woodbridge (Suffolk): Boydell Press, 2000.

Petzoldt, Martin. "Zur Frage nach dem Funktionen des Kantors Johann Sebastian Bach in Leipzig." *Music und Kirche* 53 (1983): 167–73.

Petzoldt, Martin and Joachim Petri. *Johann Sebastian Bach: Ehre sei dir Gott gesungen*. Berlin: Evangelische Verlagsanstalt, 1990.

Pezel, Christoph. *Auffrichtige Rechenschafft von Lehr vn[d] Ceremonien*. Bremen, 1592. [24], 172, [2] p.

Planck, Georg. See "Dingleben" in part 1 above.

Poll, G. J. van de. *Martin Bucer's Liturgical Ideas: The Strassburg Reformer and His Connection with the Liturgies of the Sixteenth Century*. Assen: Van Gorcum, 1954.

Pomeranus, Johann. See "Bugenhagen, Johann."

Praetorius, Michael. *Gesamtausgabe der musikalischen Werke von Michael Praetorius*. Friedrich Blume, general editor. 21 vols. Wolfenbüttel: Georg Kallmeyer (vols. 1–20) and Wolfenbüttel: Möseler Verlag (vol. 21), 1928–60.

———. *Syntagma musicum.* 3 vols. Wolfenbüttel, 1614–20. 459, 236, 242 p. Lesure: 666.

Prasius, Wolfgang. See "Niederlauer" in part 1 above.

Preus, Georg. *Grund-Regeln, von der Structur und den Requisitis einer untadelhaften Orgel, worinnen hauptsächlich gezeiget wird, was bey Erbauung einer neuen und Renovirung einer alten Orgel zu beobachten sey, auch wie eine Orgel bey der Ueberlieferung müsse probiret und examiniret werden.* Hamburg, 1729. [14], 104 pp. Lesure: 668.

———. *Observationes musicae, oder Musicalische Anmerckungen, welche bestehen in Eintheilung der Thonen, deren Eigenschafft und Wirckung.* Greifswald, [1706]. Preface dated "8. Julii, Anno 1706." Lesure: 668.

Pröhle, Heinrich Andreas. *Kirchliche Sitten: ein Bild aus dem Leben evangelischer Gemeinen*. Berlin, 1858. vi, 314 pp.

Psalmen vnd geistliche Lieder, welche von fromen Christen gemacht vnd zu samen gelesen sind. Leipzig: Valentin Babst, 1545. Reprint bound with *Geystliche Lieder* (q.v.).

Rau, Johann Wilhelm. "Wünsche und Vorschläge in Absicht auf liturgische Verbesserungen." In *Liturgisches Magazin,* by Georg Friedrich Seiler, vol. 2, part 2, pp. 1–86. Erlangen, 1786.

[Raupach, Christoph]. *Veritophili Deutliche Beweis-Gründe, worauf der rechte Gebrauch der Music, beydes in den Kirchen, als ausser denselben, beruhet.* Hamburg, 1717. [24], 56 pp. Lesure: 617 (*sub* Niedt). The author is identified in the preface by Johann Mattheson and in *Critica musica,* vol. 1, p. 53. According to Becker (1836), p. 107, this work was appended to the third part of F. E. Niedt's *Musicalische Handleitung* and was not published separately.

Rauschning, Hermann. *Geschichte der Musik und Musikpflege in Danzig von den Anfängen bis zur Auflösung der Kirchenkapellen.* Quellen und Darstellungen zur Geschichte Westpreußens, no. 15. Danzig, 1931.

Rautenstrauch, Johannes. *Luther und die Pflege der kirchlichen Musik in Sachsen (14.–19. Jahrhundert).* Leipzig, 1907. Reprint: Hildesheim: Olms, 1970.

Reed, Luther D. *The Lutheran Liturgy.* Revised ed. Philadelphia: Fortress Press, 1960.

Reese, Gustave. *Music in the Renaissance.* Revised ed. New York: W. W. Norton, 1959.

Reichardt, Johann Friedrich. *Briefe eines aufmerksamen Reisenden die Musik betreffend.* 2 vols. [vol. 1:] Frankfurt und Leipzig, 1774; [vol. 2:] Frankfurt und Breslau, 1776. [8], 184 pp.; 134 pp. Lesure: 690.

Repertorium der Kirchenvisitationsakten aus dem 16. und 17. Jahrhundert in Archiven der Bundesrepublik Deutschland. Stuttgart: Klett-Cotta, 1982.

Ein Reys-Gespräch: zwischen zweyen Studenten, unterwegens von Königsberg aus, bis nacher Elbingen, von einer bitteren, wider die Lobwassers Psalmen und deroselben Melodeyen, daselbst zu Elbingen, ausgesprengten Pasquillen (Project genen[n]t) gehalten. [N.p.], 1655. 72 f. Lesure: 932. Reinhold Curike's name is on the title page of the Göttingen copy, and in the table of contents at the beginning of the bound volume he is named as author. But there is no outside evidence for this attribution, and it seems unlikely in that the tone of the book is more personal in its attack than is found in the *Rejectum projectum,* which is probably by Curike. It also seems unlikely that Curike would write two separate refutations of the same book.

Richter, Aemilius Ludwig, ed. *Die evangelischen Kirchenordnungen des sechzehnten Jahrhunderts.* 2 vols. in 1. Weimar, 1846.

Riedel, Johannes. "Vocal *Leisen* Settings in the Baroque Era." In *The Musical Heritage of the Lutheran Church,* vol. 5, pp. 108–27. St. Louis: Concordia, 1959.

Rietschel, Georg. *Die Aufgabe der Orgel im Gottesdienste bis in das 18. Jahrhundert.* Leipzig: Dürr'schen Buchhandlung, 1893. Reprint: edited by Heinz Lohmann (Hildesheim: Georg Olms, 1971).

Röbbelen, Ingeborg. *Theologie und Frömmigkeit im deutschen evangelisch-lutherischen Gesangbuch des 17. und frühen 18. Jahrhunderts.* Forschungen zur Kirchen- und Dogmengeschichte, vol. 6. Göttingen: Vandenhoeck & Ruprecht, 1957.

Röhlk, Karl. *Geschichte des Hauptgottesdienstes in der evang.-luth. Kirche Hamburgs.* Göttingen, 1899. 60 pp.

Rolle, Christian Carl. *Neue Wahrnehmungen zur Aufnahme und weitern Ausbreitung der Musik.* Berlin, 1784. 106, [2] pp.

Rorarius, Thomas. See "Reinhardtshoven" in part 1 above.

Rotz, Rhiman A. "German towns." In *Dictionary of the Middle Ages,* 13 vols., edited by Joseph R. Strayer, vol. 5 (1985), pp. 457–71. New York: Charles Scribner's Sons, 1982–89.

Routley, Erik. *Christian Hymns: An Introduction to Their Story.* Audiotape, 6 cassettes. Princeton: Prestige Publications, [n.d.].

Ruetz, Caspar. *Widerlegte Vorurtheile vom Ursprunge der Kirchenmusic, und klarer Beweis, daß die gottesdienstliche Music sich auf Gottes Wort gründe, und also göttliches Ursprungs sey.* Lübeck,

1750. [22], 114, [6] pp. Lesure: 740; reviewed in Marpurg (1754–78), vol. 1 (1755), pp. 511–13.

———. *Widerlegte Vorurtheile von der Beschaffenheit der heutigen Kirchenmusic und von der Lebens-Art einiger Musicorum*. Lübeck, 1752. [14], 175, [8] pp. Lesure: 740; reviewed in Marpurg (1754–78), vol. 1 (1755), pp. 511–13.

———. *Widerlegte Vorurtheile von der Wirkung der Kirchenmusic, und von den darzu erfoderten Unkosten*. Rostock and Wismar, 1753. [46], 152, [15] pp. Lesure: 740; reviewed in Marpurg (1754–78), vol. 1 (1755), pp. 511–13.

Ruff, Anthony. "A Millennium of Congregational Song." *Pastoral Music* 21 (February–March 1997): 11–15.

———. "Unity in Song and Sacrament in Early Seventeenth-Century Catholicism." *GIA Quarterly* 8/2 (Winter 1997): 16–18, 41.

Ruhnke, Martin. *Beiträge zu einer Geschichte der deutschen Hofmusikkollegien im 16. Jahrhundert*. Habilitationsschrift, Free University of Berlin. Berlin: Merseburger, 1963.

Runtzler, Melchior. See "Nördlingen (Georgenkirche)" in part 1 above.

Salmen, Walter. *Musikleben im 16. Jahrhundert*. Musikgeschichte in Bildern, vol. 3, part 9. Leipzig: VEB Deutscher Verlag für Musik, 1976.

Samuel, Harold. *The Cantata in Nuremburg during the Seventeenth Century*. Studies in Musicology, no. 56. Ann Arbor: UMI, 1982. 536 pp.

Sannemann, Friedrich. *Die Musik als Unterrichtsgegenstand in den evangelischen Lateinschulen des 16. Jahrhunderts: ein Beitrag zur Geschichte des Schulgesanges*. Musikwissenschaftliche Studien, no. 4. Berlin and Leipzig: E. Ebering, 1904.

Schalk, Carl, ed. *Key Words in Church Music*. St. Louis: Concordia, 1978.

Scheibe, Johann Adolph. . . . *Critischer musikus. Neue, vermehrte und verbesserte Auflage*. Leipzig, 1745. 1059 [i.e., 1056] pp. Lesure: 760.

Scheibel, Gottfried Ephraim. *Die Geschichte der Kirchen-Music alter und neuer Zeiten*. Breslau, 1738. 48 pp. Lesure: 761.

———. *Zufällige Gedancken von der Kirchen-Music, wie sie heutiges Tages beschaffen ist*. Frankfurt and Leipzig, 1721. 84 pp. Lesure: 762.

Scheidt, Samuel. *Tabulatur-Buch Hundert geistlicher Lieder und Psalmen Herrn Doctoris Martini Lutheri und anderer gottseligen Männer*. Görlitz: M. Herman, 1650. Reprint: [Scheidt Gesamtausgabe], edited by G. Harms, vol. 1 (Hamburg, 1923).

———. *Tabulatura Nova*. 3 parts. Hamburg: M. Hering, 1624; 2d ed., Hamburg: T. Gundermann, [1649?]. Reprint: [Scheidt Gesamtausgabe], edited by Chr. Mahrenholz, vols. 6–7 (Hamburg, 1953; rev. ed., 1965).

———. *Werke*. ed. Gottlieb Harms and Christhard Mahrenholz, vols. 1–13, Hamburg: Ugrino, 1923–62; vols. 14–, Leipzig: VEB Deutscher Verlag für Musik, 1971–.

Schein, Johann Hermann. *Neue Ausgabe sämtlicher Werke*. Edited by Adam Adrio. Kassel: Bärenreiter, 1963–.

Schiecke, Johann. *Incluto philosophorum ordine in illustri Tilieto benevolè concedente organum musicum, historice extructum*. Leipzig, 1693. 8 f. Lesure: 764.

Schindling, Anton and Walter Ziegler, eds. *Die Territorien des Reichs im Zeitalter der Reformation und Konfessionalisierung: Land und Konfession 1500–1650*. 7 vols. Katholisches Leben und Kirchenreform im Zeitalter der Glaubensspaltung, vols. 49–53, 57–58. Münster: Aschendorff, 1989–97.

Schmidt, Eberhard. "Betstunden in Kursachsen." *Jahrbuch für Liturgik und Hymnologie* 3 (1957): 127–30.

———. *Der Gottesdienst am Kurfürstlichen Hofe zu Dresden*. Veröffentlichungen der evangelischen Gesellschaft für Liturgieforschung, no. 12. Göttingen: Vandenhoeck & Ruprecht, 1961.

Schneider, J. "Die Kirchenvisitationen in der Herrschaft Guttenberg." *Zeitschrift für die Geschichte des Oberrheins* 30 (1878): 1–52.

Schoeberlein, Ludwig. *Schatz des liturgischen Chor- und Gemeindegesangs nebst den Altarweisen in der deutschen evangelischen Kirche.* 3 vols. Göttingen: Vandenhoeck & Ruprecht, 1865–70.

Schrader, Johann. See "Magdeburg (Schrader)" in part 1 above.

Schrems, Theobald. *Geschichte des gregorianischen Gesanges in den protestantischen Gottesdiensten.* Freiburg (Switzerland), 1930.

Schröder, Laurentz. *Ein nützliches Tractätlein vom Lobe Gottes, oder der hertzerfrewenden Musica, worinn kürtzlich vnd einfältig gezeiget wird, wie die Musica sampt jhrer Commodität vnd Nutzbarkeit einig vnd allein zur Ehre Gottes sol gerichtet seyn.* Copenhagen, 1639. [38], 226 pp. Lesure: 771.

Schuler, Louis Eugene. *Lucas Osiander and his* Fünfftzig geistliche Lieder und Psalmen: *The Development and Use of the First Cantional.* Ph.D. thesis, Washington University, 1986.

Schünemann, Georg. "Matthaeus Hertel's theoetische Schriften." *Archiv für Musikwissenschaft* 4 (1922): 336–58.

Sehling, Emil, ed. *Die evangelischen Kirchenordnungen des XVI. Jahrhunderts.* Vols. 1–8, 11–15 in 15 physical volumes to date. Leipzig: O. R. Reisland, 1902–13; Tübingen: J. C. B. Mohr (Paul Siebeck), 1955–.

Seiler, Georg Friedrich. *Liturgisches Magazin.* 2 vols. in 1. Erlangen, 1784–86. [12], 196, [10], 126, [4], 190 pp.

Selneccer, Nicolaus. *Christliche Psalmen, Lieder und Kirchengesenge.* Leipzig: J. Beyer, 1587. [33], 598 p. *RISM* 1587¹⁰.

Senn, Frank C. *Christian Liturgy: Catholic and Evangelical.* Minneapolis: Fortress, 1997.

Siebensohn, Johannes. See "Frankendorf, Holstet and Kötzschau" in part 1 above.

Simon, Matthias. "Die Nürnberger Spitalmessen der Reformationszeit." *Zeitschrift für bayerische Kirchengeschichte* 28 (1959): 143–53.

Smend, Julius. *Die evangelischen deutschen Messen bis zu Luthers Deutscher Messe.* Göttingen: Vandenhoeck & Ruprecht, 1896.

Sonnenkalb, Johann Friedrich Wilhelm. *Kurtze Entscheidung der Frage: Wie sollen die Praeludia eines Organisten bey dem Gottesdienste beschaffen seyn? Oder: Welches sind die Kennzeichen eines in seinen Amts-Verrichtungen verständigen Organisten?* Torgau, 1756. 28 pp. Lesure: 791.

Spalatin, Georg. See "Wittenberg" in part 1 above.

Spangenberg, Johann. *Cantiones ecclesiasticae latinae. Kirchengesenge Deudtsch auff die Sontage vnnd furnemliche Feste durchs gantze Jar.* Magdeburg: Michael Lotther, 1545. 2 vols. in 1: [3], clx, [2] f.; [3], cxcix, [45] f. *RISM* 1545¹⁴⁻¹⁷.

Spanuth, Friedrich. "Die Generalvisitation in Grubenhagen von 1617." *Jahrbuch der Gesellschaft für niedersächsische Kirchengeschichte* 53 (1955): 49–70.

———. "Die Grubenhagensche Kirchenvisitation von 1579 durch Superintendent Schellhammer." *Jahrbuch der Gesellschaft für niedersächsische Kirchengeschichte* 52 (1954): 103–29.

Speer, Daniel. *Grundrichtiger Unterricht der musikalischen Kunst oder Vierfaches musikalisches Kleeblatt.* Ulm, 1697. [4], 289, [1], [32], 13 pp. Reprint: Leipzig: Peters, 1974.

Spener, Philipp Jakob. *Pia desideria* (1666). Translated and edited by Theodore G. Tappert. Philadelphia: Fortress Press, 1964. Reprinted in part 1n Peter C. Erb, ed., *Pietists: Selected Writings* (New York: Paulist Press, 1983), 31–49.

Stahl, Wilhelm. *Musikgeschichte Lübecks.* Vol. 2 (Geistliche Musik). Kassel, 1952.

Stattliches, außführliches vnd gar bewegliches Schreiben der löblichen Ritterschafft im Fürstenthumb Anhalt, so mit der Calvinischen Reformation nicht zu frieden, auff die vnter J. F. G. Namen, Anno 1596. außgegangene Verantwortung. Halle, 1598. [8], 26, [2] f.

[Stein, Simon]. *Calvinismus Heidelbergensis. Dialogvs oder von der Heydelbergischen Calvinisten*

Wandel, Ordnung, Ceremonien vnd Lehrpuncten, ein Gespräch. [N.p.], 1593. 101, [1] pp. The author's name is from the Wolfenbüttel library catalog.

[Steinberg, Christian Gottlieb]. *Betrachtungen über die Kirchen-Music und heiligen Gesänge derer Rechtgläubigen und ihrem Nutzen.* Breslau and Leipzig, 1766. 125 pp. Lesure, 806. The author's name is from Lesure.

Steinhäuser, Klaus. *Die Musik an den Hessen-Darmstädtischen Lateinschulen im 16. und 17. Jahrhundert und ihre Beziehungen zum kirchlichen und bürgerlichen Leben.* Dissertation, Gießen, 1933. Düsseldorf, 1936.

Stieber, Thomas. See "Wolfstein" in part 1 above.

Stiller, Günther. *Johann Sebastian Bach und das Leipziger gottesdienstliche Leben seiner Zeit.* Kassel: Bärenreiter, 1970.

———. *Johann Sebastian Bach and Liturgical Life in Leipzig.* Translated by Herbert J. A. Bouman, Daniel F. Poellot and Hilton C. Oswald. St. Louis: Concordia, 1984. A translation of Stiller 1970.

Strauss, Gerald. *Luther's House of Learning: Indoctrination of the Young in the German Reformation.* Baltimore and London: Johns Hopkins University Press, 1978.

Strom, Jonathan. *Orthodoxy and Reform: The Clergy in Seventeenth Century Rostock.* Tübingen: Mohr Siebeck, 1999.

Stryk, Johann Samuel. *Verantwortung gegen Herrn D. Johann Friedr. Mayers . . . so genannten kurtzen Bericht von Pietisten.* Halle, 1707. 58 pp.

Stübner, Johann Christoph. *Historische Beschreibung der Kirchenverfassung in den Herzogl. Braunschweig-Lüneburgischen Landen seit der Reformation.* Goslar: Ernst Wilhelm Gottlieb Kircher, 1800.

Summarische Antwort auff das newe Wittenbergische Buch, vnterm Namen der Theologischen Facultet daselbs, wider die Anhältischen, vnd Amberger, etc. Zerbst, 1600. 76 pp.

Sutel, Johann. See "Schweinfurt" in part 1 above.

Synodal-Schluß, welcher nach der in der Fürstenthumb Gotha gehaltenen General- Kirchen- und Landes-Visitation . . . ratificirt worden. Gotha, 1645. 62 pp.

Temperley, Nicholas. *The Hymn Tune Index.* Produced with the assistance of Charles G. Manns and Joseph Herl. 4 vols. Oxford: Clarendon Press, 1998.

———. *The Music of the English Parish Church.* 2 vols. Cambridge: Cambridge University Press, 1979.

Teutsch, G. D. *Urkundenbuch der Evangelischen Landeskirche A. B. in Siebenbürgen,* 1. Theil. Hermannstadt, 1862.

Tolley, Bruce. *Pastors and Parishioners in Württemberg during the Late Reformation, 1581–1621.* Stanford, Ca.: Stanford University Press, 1995.

Treutel, Pancratius. See "Belrieth and Einhausen" in part 1 above.

Truber, Primus. See "Kempten" in part 1 above.

Türk, Daniel Gottlob. *Von den wichtigsten Pflichten eines Organisten. Ein Beytrag zur Verbesserung der musikalischen Liturgie.* Halle, 1787. 240 p. Lesure: 847. English translation by Margot Ann Greenlimb Woolard as *Daniel Gottlob Türk on the Role of the Organist in Worship (1787)* (Lanham, Md: Scarecrow Press, 2000).

Uhlhorn, Gerhard. *Urbanus Rhegius: Leben und ausgewählte Schriften.* Leben und ausgewählten Schriften der Väter und Begründer der lutherischen Kirche, vol. 7. Elberfeld, 1861.

Unschuldige Nachrichten von alten und neuen theologischen Sachen. Leipzig, 1702–19. Continues: *Altes und neues aus dem Schatz theologischer Wissenschaften* (1701). Continued by: *Fortgesetzte Sammlung von alten und neuen theologischen Sachen* (1720–50).

van de Poll, G. J. See "Poll, G. J. van de."

Vehe, Michael. *Ein new Gesangbüchlin geistlicher Lieder.* Leipzig, 1537. Reprint: facsimile, edited by Walther Lipphardt as no. 11 of *Beiträge zur mittelrheinischen Musikgeschichte* (Mainz: B. Schott's Söhne, 1970). *RISM* 1537[06].

Veit, Ludwig Andreas and Ludwig Lenhart. *Kirche und Volksfrömmigkeit im Zeitalter des Barock.* Freiburg: Herder, 1956.

[Voigt, Johann Carl]. *Gespräch von der Musik, zwischen einem Organisten und Adjuvanten, darinnen nicht nur von verschiedenen Mißbräuchen, so bey der Musik eingerissen, gehandelt, sondern auch eines und das andere beym Clavier- und Orgel-Spielen angemerket wird.* Erfurt, 1742. 140 pp. Lesure: 870. The author's name is from the catalog of the Staatsbibliothek zu Berlin. The preface is by Lorenz Mizler, and his personal copy is in the Staatsbibliothek.

Vollhardt, Reinhard. *Geschichte der Cantoren und Organisten von den Städten im Königreich Sachsen.* Berlin: Wilhelm Issleib, 1899. Reprint: Leipzig: Peters, 1978.

Volprecht, Wolfgang. See "Nuremberg" in part 1 above.

"Von der Einrichtung des gemeinschaftlichen öffentlichen Gottesdienstes bey den evangelischen Gemeinden in Augspurg." In *Liturgisches Magazin,* by Georg Friedrich Seiler, vol. 2, part 2, pp. 127–82. Erlangen, 1786.

Wackernagel, Philipp. *Das deutsche Kirchenlied von der ältesten Zeit bis zu Anfang des XVII. Jahrhunderts.* 5 vols. Leipzig, 1864–77.

———. *Bibliographie zur Geschichte des deutschen Kirchenliedes im XVI. Jahrhundert.* Frankfurt/ Main, 1855. Reprint: Hildesheim: Georg Olms, 1961.

Wagner, Conrad Ludwig. *Dissertatio iuris ecclesiastici inauguralis de iure sabbathi.* Halle, [1702]. [6], 8, 162 pp. The date is the date of the disputation; the date of printing does not appear in the source. There is a 1715 copy with the title *Dissertatio iuris ecclesiastici de iure sabbathi.*

Walter, Horst. *Musikgeschichte der Stadt Lüneburg vom Ende des 16. bis zum Anfang des 18. Jahrhunderts.* Dissertation, Cologne, 1962. Tutzing: Hans Schneider, 1967.

Walter, Johann. See *Geystliche Gsangbüchlin.*

Weismann, Eberhard. "Erhalt uns, herr, bei deinem Wort." In *Handbuch zum Evangelischen Kirchengesangbuch,* vol. 3, part 1: *Liederkunde,* part 1 (hymns 1 to 175): 501–4. Göttingen: Vandenhoeck & Ruprecht, 1970.

Werckmeister, Andreas. *Der edlen Music-Kunst Würde, Gebrauch und Mißbrauch.* Frankfurt, 1691. [12], 44 pp. Lesure: 883.

———. *Musicalische Paradoxal-Discourse oder ungemeine Vorstellunge, wie die Musica einen hohen und göttlichen Uhrsprung habe, und wie hingegen dieselbe so sehr gemissbrauchet wird.* Quedlinburg, 1707. 120 pp. Reprint: Hildesheim: Olms, 1970. Lesure: 884.

Werner, Arno. *Vier Jahrhunderte im Dienste der Kirchenmusik: Geschichte des Amtes und Standes der evangelischen Kantoren, Organisten und Stadtpfeifer seit der Reformation.* Leipzig: Merseburger, 1932. 298 pp. Reprint: Hildesheim: Olms, 1979.

Widmann, Enoch. See "Hof (Michaeliskirche)" in part 1 above.

Wilisch, Christian Friedrich. . . . *Das neue Lied des andächtig singenden Freybergs bey Einweyhung einer neuen Orgel.* Freiberg, [1735]. 46 pp. Lesure: 893.

Williams, Peter. *The Organ Music of J. S. Bach.* 3 vols. Cambridge: Cambridge University Press, 1980–84.

Winger, Thomas M. *The Priesthood of the Baptized: An Exegetical and Theological Investigation.* S.T.M. thesis, Concordia Seminary, 1992.

Wisman, Oswald. See "Queienfeld" in part 1 above.

Wissemann-Garbe, Daniela. "Neue Weisen zu den alten Liedern," *Jahrbuch für Liturgik und Hymnologie* 37 (1998): 118–38. See also *"Das deutsche Kirchenlied"* and "Garbe, Daniela."

Wolters, [Ernst Georg]. "Die Kirchenvisitationen der Aufbauzeit (1570–1600) im vormaligen Herzogtum Braunschweig-Wolfenbüttel." *Zeitschrift der Gesellschaft für niedersächsi-*

sche Kirchengeschichte 43 (1938): 204–237; 44 (1939): 64–85; 45 (1940): 153–202; 46 (1941): 99–153; *Jahrbuch der Gesellschaft für niedersächsische Kirchengeschichte* 48 (1950): 62–97.

———. "Kirchliche und sittliche Zustände in den Herzogtümern Bremen und Verden 1650 bis 1725." *Zeitschrift der Gesellschaft für niedersächsische Kirchengeschichte* 19 (1914): 1–79 and 20 (1915): 136–234.

Zahn, Johannes. *Die Melodien der deutschen evangelischen Kirchenlieder, aus den Quellen geschöpft und mitgeteilt.* 6 vols. Gütersloh, 1889–93. Reprint. Hildesheim: Olms, 1963.

Zieger, Andreas. *Das religiöse und kirchliche Leben in Preussen und Kurland im Spiegel der evangelischen Kirchenordnungen des 16. Jahrhunderts.* Cologne: Böhlau, 1967.

Ziller, Ernst. *Der Erfurter Organist Johann Heinrich Buttstädt (1666–1727).* Beiträge zur Musikforschung, no. 3. Halle: Buchhandlung des Waisenhauses, 1935. 140 pp.

Zimmermann, Gerhard, ed. *Die brandenburgischen Kirchenvisitations-Abschiede und -Register des XVI. und XVII. Jahrhunderts. Zweiter Band: Das Land Ruppin.* Berlin: Walter de Gruyter, 1963.

INDEX

339